ḶAGHUKAUMUDĪ OF VARADARĀJA

LAGHUKAUMUDĪ

OF

VARADARĀJA

A Sanskrit Grammar

JAMES R. BALLANTYNE

MOTILAL BANARSIDASS PUBLISHERS
PRIVATE LIMITED • DELHI

Fourth Edition: Varanasi, 1891
Reprint: Delhi, 1967, 1976, 1981, 1995, 1997, 2001, 2005

ISBN: 81-208-0910-6 (Cloth)
ISBN: 81-208-0916-5 (Paper)

MOTILAL BANARSIDASS
41 U.A. Bungalow Road, Jawahar Nagar, Delhi 110 007
8 Mahalaxmi Chamber, 22 Bhulabhai Desai Road, Mumbai 400 026
120 Royapettah High Road, Mylapore, Chennai 600 004
236, 9th Main III Block, Jayanagar, Bangalore 560 011
Sanas Plaza, 1302 Baji Rao Road, Pune 411 002
8 Camac Street, Kolkata 700 017
Ashok Rajpath, Patna 800 004
Chowk, Varanasi 221 001

Printed in India
BY JAINENDRA PRAKASH JAIN AT SHRI JAINENDRA PRESS,
A-45 NARAINA, PHASE-I, NEW DELHI-110 028
AND PUBLISHED BY NARENDRA PRAKASH JAIN FOR
MOTILAL BANARSIDASS PUBLISHERS PRIVATE LIMITED,
BUNGALOW ROAD, DELHI 110 007

PREFACE.

THE grammatical compendium of which this is a translation is current among the pandits of the North-west provinces, and of most of the other provinces of India. The translation is one of a series of attempts to encourage and facilitate the interchange of ideas between the pandits and the senior English students of the Government Colleges. How different the arrangement of a Sanskrit treatise on Grammar is from that of an English treatise on the subject, may be inferred from the facts stated in the subjoined extract from the preface to the Hindí version of the same compendium.

The groundwork of the grammatical literature of the Sanskrit is comprised in Páṇini's eight Lectures, entitled "*The Ashtádhyáyí.*" Each of the lectures is divided into four sections, and each section into a number of *sútras,* or succinct aphorisms. On these Mr. Colebrooke remarks :—"The studied brevity of the *Páṇiníya* "*sútras* renders them in the highest degree obscure; even with "the knowledge of the key to their interpretation, the student "finds them ambiguous. In the application of them when under-"stood, he discovers many seeming contradictions; and with every "exertion of practised memory, he must experience the utmost "difficulty in combining rules dispersed in apparent confusion "through different portions of Páṇini's eight Lectures."

The same accomplished scholar adds :—The outline of Páṇini's "arrangement is simple; but numerous exceptions, and frequent "disgressions, have involved it in much seeming confusion. The "first two lectures (the first section especially, which is in a "manner the key of the whole grammar) contain definitions; in "the three next are collected affixes, by which verbs and nouns "are inflected. Those which appertain to verbs occupy the "third lecture:—the fourth and fifth contain such as are affixed "to nouns. The remaining three lectures treat of the changes "which roots and affixes undergo in special cases, or by general "rules of orthography, and which are all effected by the addition, "or by the substitution, of one or more elements. The apparent "simplicity of the design vanishes in the perplexity of the struc-"ture. The endless pursuit of exceptions and limitations so dis-"joins the general precepts, that the reader cannot keep in view "their intended connexion, and mutual relation. He wanders in "an intricate maze, and the clew of the labyrinth is continually "slipping from his hands."

Such a work as that above described being obviously unsuited for a beginner, a different arrangement of Páṇini's *sútras* was attempted by several grammarians, "for the sake of bringing into one view the rules which must be remembered in the inflections of one word, and those which must be combined even for a single variation of a single term." This arrangement, Mr. Colebrooke adds, "is certainly preferable; but the *sútras* of Páṇini, thus "detached from their context, are wholly unintelligible; without "the commentator's exposition, they are indeed, what Sir Wil-"liam Jones has somewhere termed them, 'dark as the darkest "oracle."'

Such an arrangement as that here referred to, is adopted in the *Siddhánta Kaumudí* of *Bhaṭṭojí Díkshita* and in its abridgement the *Laghu Siddhánta Kaumudí* of *Varadarája*.

One of the first objects of this edition of the Grammar is to explain each term and each process, on its first occurrence, with something of that fulness of illustration, which the pandits think it better to defer imparting until a later stage in the pupil's course. According to the established system, the juvenile pupil, who has only commenced learning the language in which the grammar is written, cannot proceed three lines in advance of the point at which his preceptor's last lecture broke off. If he can proceed half a line in advance of it, it is more than was to have been expected.

Another omission of the native grammars is supplied to a certain extent in this edition. When a word is given as an example under a rule, perhaps six or eight rules have previously had a share in bringing the radical word into the form to which the ultimate rule applies. For instance, when we wish to determine one particular pronoun, (to quote from Mr. Wollaston's preface to his practical Grammar of the Sanskrit) "six rules are to be referred to "in forming the word, and the student must be able to remember "them all before he can do it, for there is no *reference* to them "whatsoever. Yet such references are much more neccessary than "those that are annexed to the propositions in Euclid, because the "solution of these words is generally more complicated than that "of the theorems."

References are supplied in this edition, not to every rule required, yet to more than the attentive student is likely to have forgotten.

J. R. B.

Benares College, July 31*st,* 1849.

PREFACE

TO THE SECOND EDITION.

THE translation of the Laghu Kaumudí by the late Dr. Ballantyne, which, as Professor Max Müller observes, "has enabled even beginners to find their way through the labyrinth of native grammar," has been for many years out of print, and is continually inquired for by those who wish to obtain a well-grounded knowledge of a language the students of which, in Europe alone, may be counted no longer by tens but by hundreds.

For the publication of this edition, such students are indebted to the enlightened liberality of H. H. the Mahárájah of Vizianagram, K. C. S. I., who has already munificently encouraged Sanskrit and English scholarship in this country by his endowments to the Queen's College at Benares and the Universities of Calcutta and Madras.

The Sanskrit text and English translation have been carefully revised and corrected by Pandit Bechan Ráma Tiwárí, Librarian of the Sanskrit College, and Bábú Mathurá Prasáda Miśra, Second Master of the English College.

Several of the corrections and alterations which appear in this edition were either made, suggested, or approved years ago by Dr. Ballantyne himself; and it is hoped that no change has been made in which he would not have thoroughly concurred.

For the greatly improved type, paper, and general appearance of the book we are indebted to the spirited publishers, Messrs. E. J. Lazarus and Co.

R. T. H. G.

CONTENTS.

Note.—The figures refer to the numbers of the aphorisms, and not to the page.

Pratyāhāras representing different LETTER-GROUPS

AC	=	all vowels
AṬ	=	all vowels & semivowels
AṆ	=	*a*, *i*, *u*
IK	=	a *short* vowel
EC	=	diphthongs
HAŚ	=	all the soft consonants
JAŚ	=	a soft unaspirated consonant
JHAL	=	any consonant except a semivowel or a nasal
KHAY	=	all hard consonants minus the sibilants
KHAR	=	all the hard consonants
RA	=	*ra* and *la*
ŚAR	=	sibilants
ŚAL	=	sibilants and aspirates
YAṆ	=	semivowels
YAR	=	all the consonants except *ha*
VAL	=	any consonant except *ha* and *ya*

॥ लघुकौमुदीव्याकरणम् ॥

। श्रीगणेशाय नमः ।

नत्वा सरस्वतीं देवीं शुद्धां गुण्यां करोम्यहम् ।
पाणिनीयप्रवेशाय लघुसिद्धान्तकौमुदीम् ॥

SALUTATION TO GAṆEŚA !

Having made obeisance to Saraswatí, the divine, the pure, endued with good qualities, I make this abridged Siddhánta-kaumudí in order that people may enter some way into the Páṇiníya grammar.

॥ लघुकौमुदीव्याकरणम् ॥

॥ संज्ञाप्रकरणम् ॥

अ इ उण् ।१। ऋ ऌक् ।२। ए ओङ् ।३। ऐ औच् ।४। ह य व रट् ।५। लण् ।६। ञ म ङ ण नम् ।७। झ भञ् ।८। घ ढ धष् ।९। ज ब ग ड दश् ।१०। ख फ छ ठ थ च ट तव् ।११। क पय् ।१२। श ष सर् ।१३। हल् ।१४।

इति माहेश्वराणि सूत्राण्यणादिसंज्ञार्थानि ।

No. 1.—A I UṆ; ṚI LṚIK; E OŃ; AI AUCH; HA YA VA RAṬ; LAṆ; ÑA MA ŃA ṆA NAM; JHA BHAÑ; GHA ḌHA DHASH; JA BA GA ḌA DAŚ; KHA PHA CHHA THA THA CHA ṬA TAV; KA PAY; ŚA SHA SAR; HAL. THESE groups of letters ARE THE APHORISMS OF MAHEŚWARA or Śiva; DESIGNED FOR the formation of NAMES *or pratyáháras* SUCH AS AṆ AND THE LIKE, by which whole classes of letters can, severally, be designated. See No. 8.

एषामन्त्या इतः ।

No. 2.—THE FINAL letters OF THESE aphorisms are termed 'IT.' For example, in the aphorism *a i uṇ*, the letter *ṇ* is called '*it.*' See, further, No. 7.

हकारादिष्वकार उच्चारणार्थः ।

No. 3.—THE short vowel A, IN the terms HA &C., IS IN ORDER TO THE ARTICULATION of the letters h &c. For instance, by *ha, ya, va, ra, &c.*, the bare consonants h, y, v, r, &c. are intended.

लण्मध्ये त्वित्संज्ञकः ।

No. 4.—BUT, IN the body of the sixth aphorism of No. 1, viz. LAṆ, it, i. e. the short vowel *a*, IS TERMED 'IT.' The design of this exception will appear in No. 37.

हलन्त्यम् । १ । ३ । ३ ।

उपदेशेऽन्त्यं हलित् स्यात् । उपदेश आद्योच्चारणम् । सूत्रेष्वदृष्टं पदं सूत्रान्तरादनुवर्त्तनीयं सर्वत्र ।

No. 5.—Let A CONSONANT FINAL in an *upadeśa* be called *'it'* (No 7.), An *upadesa* is defined as signifying an 'original enunciation'—that is to say, an affix, (*pratyaya*, No. 139,) or an augment (*ágama* No. 102), or a verbal root (*dhátu*, No. 49), or, in short, any form of expression which occurs only in technical treatises on grammar, and which is not a word ready for use, but one of the supposed original elements of a word.

A word which is not seen in a *sútra*, but which is necessary to complete the sense, is always to be supplied from some other *sútra*. The reason of this is as follows. In the treatises of the Sanskrit grammarians, brevity is regarded as a primary requisite. According to the author of the *Mahábháshya*, or Great Commentary, 'the grammarians esteem the abbreviation of half a short vowel as equivalent to the birth of a son.' Accordingly, *Páṇini* in his *Ashṭádhyáyí* or 'Grammar in Eight Lectures,' avoids repeating in any *sútra* the words which can be supplied from a preceding one. When the original order of the *sútras* is abandoned, as in the present work, it becomes necessary to place before the student, in the shape of a commentary, the words which *Páṇini* left him to gather from the context. Thus, to complete the *sútra* before us (viz., *hal antyam)*, the words '*upadeśe*' and '*it*' are required; and these are supplied from a previous *sútra*, which, in the present arrangement, will be found at No. 36.

अदर्शनं लोपः । १ । १ । ६० ।

प्रसक्तस्यादर्शनं लोपसंज्ञं स्यात् ।

No. 6.—LOPA (elision, or the substitution of a blank) signifies

DISAPPEARANCE. Let this be the term for the disappearance of anything previously apparent.

तस्य लोपः । १ । ३ । ९ ।

तस्येतो लोपः स्यात् । णादयोऽणाद्यर्थाः ।

No. 7.—In the room OF THAT which is called '*it*,' let there be A BLANK. Thus all the final consonants in the *Śiva-sútras* are left out of view, when these are employed to designate any class of letters; the use of the *ṇ* and the rest of the fourteen being to assist in forming the brief names of these classes, as explained in the rule here following.

आदिरन्त्येन सहेता । १ । १ । ७१ ।

अन्त्येनेता सहित आदिर्मध्यगानां स्वस्य च संज्ञा स्यात् । यथाऽणिति अ इ उ वर्णानां संज्ञा । एवमच् हलित्यादयः ।

No. 8.—Let AN INITIAL LETTER, WITH AN 'IT' LETTER AS A FINAL, be the name of itself, and of the intervening letters. Thus, let '*aṇ*,' formed of '*a*' as its initial letter, and of '*ṇ*' (No. 7.) as its final, be the name of '*a*' itself and of '*i*' and '*u*' which intervene betwixt '*a*' and '*ṇ*.' So let '*ach*' be the name of '*a*,' '*i*,' '*u*,' '*ri*,' '*lṛi*,' '*e*,' '*o*,' '*ai*,' '*au*,' that is to say, of all the vowels; let '*hal*' be the name of all the consonants between '*h*' inclusive in the fifth *Śiva-sútra*, and the '*l*' which closes the list; and '*al*' the name of all the letters together, both vowels and consonants; and so of other *pratyáháras*, or names of classes of letters.

ऊकालोऽज्झ्रस्वदीर्घप्लुतः । १ । २ । २७ ।

उश्च ऊश्च ऊ३श्च वः वां काल इव कालो यस्य सोऽच् क्रमाद्ध्रस्वदीर्घप्लुतसंज्ञः स्यात् । स प्रत्येकमुदात्तादिभेदेन त्रिधा ।

No. 9.—Let A VOWEL WHOSE TIME (or prosodial length) is THAT OF short U, long ú, and prolated ú, be called accordingly SHORT, LONG, and PROLATED. These again are severally threefold, according to the division of 'acutely accented &c.,' here following.

उच्चैरुदात्तः । १ । २ । २९ ।

No. 10.—A vowel uttered WITH A HIGH TONE is said to be ACUTELY ACCENTED. (The grammarians describe this accentuation as being the result of employing, in the utterance of the vowel, what they call the *upper half* of the organ, that is to say of the palate, lips, &c., see No. 14).

नीचैरनुदात्तः । १ । २ । ३० ।

No. 11.—A vowel uttered WITH A LOW TONE is said to be GRAVELY ACCENTED.

समाहारः स्वरितः । १ । २ । ३१ ।

स नवविधोऽपि प्रत्येकमनुनासिकाननुनासिकत्वाभ्यां द्विधा ।

No. 12—When there is A COMBINATION of the acute and grave accent, the vowel HAS THE CIRCUMFLEX ACCENT. The application of the three accents to the three several prosodial lengths gives nine varieties of each vowel. This nine-fold variety is further doubled by the presence or absence of *nasality*, which is next to be defined.

मुखनासिकावचनोऽनुनासिकः । १ । १ । ८ ।

मुखसहितनासिकयोच्चार्यमाणो वर्णोऽनुनासिकसंज्ञः स्यात् । तदित्थम् । अ इ उ ऋ एषां वर्णानां प्रत्येकमष्टादश भेदाः । ऌवर्णस्य द्वादश तस्य दीर्घाभावात् । एचामपि द्वादश तेषां ह्रस्वाभावात् ।

No. 13.—Let THAT WHICH IS PRONOUNCED BY THE NOSE ALONG WITH THE MOUTH be called NASAL. Thus, of the letters *a i u ṛi*, there are severally eighteen different modifications. Of the letter *lṛi* there are only twelve, because it does not possess the long (but only the short and the prolated) prosodial time (No. 9). Of the letters *e ai o au* also there are only twelve modifications, because these have not the short prosodial time.

तुल्यास्यप्रयत्नं सवर्णम् । १ । १ । ९ ।

ताल्वादिस्थानमाभ्यन्तरप्रयत्नश्चेत्येतद्द्वयं यस्य येन तुल्यं तन्मिथः सवर्णसंज्ञं स्यात् । ऋऌवर्णयोर्मिथः सावर्ण्यं वाच्यम् ।

No. 14.—Let two letters HAVING THE SAME ORGAN (or *place* of origin) such as the palate, &c., and attended WITH THE SAME EFFORT of utterance within the mouth, be called HOMOGENEOUS one with another. *Kátyáyana* remarks on this: 'The homogeneousness of *ṛi* and *lṛi*, one with another, should be stated.' This form of expression—viz., '*should be stated*'—distinguishes the supplementary remarks (*vártika*) of *Kátyáyana*.

अकुहविसर्जनीयानां कण्ठः । इचुयशानां तालु । ऋटुरषाणां मूर्धा । लृतुलसानां दन्ताः । उपूपध्मानीयानामोष्ठौ । ञमङणनानां नासिका च । एदैतोः कण्ठतालु । ओदौतोः कण्ठोष्ठम् । वकारस्य दन्तोष्ठम् । जिह्वामूलीयस्य जिह्वामूलम् । नासिकानुस्वारस्य ।

No. 15.—The THROAT is the organ OF the gutturals A Á KA KHA GA GHA ŃA (No. 17) HA and VISARGA; the PALATE, OF the palatals I Í CHA CHHA JA JHA ÑA YA and ŚA; the HEAD, OF the cerebrals ṚI ṚÍ ṬA ṬHA ḌA ḌHA ṆA RA and SHA; the TEETH, OF the dentals LṚI LṚÍ TA THA DA DHA NA LA and SA; the LIPS, OF the labials U Ú PA PHA BA BHA MA, AND OF UPADHMÁNÍYA, as *visarga* is called when it is written in the form of two semi-circles before *pa* or *pha* (No. 117). OF the nasal letters ÑA MA ŃA ṆA AND NA, the NOSE ALSO is an organ, in addition to the organ of the class in which each respectively appears above. The organs OF E and AI are the THROAT and the PALATE; OF O and AU, the THROAT and the LIPS; OF VA, the TEETH and the LIPS. The organ OF JIHWÁMÚLÍYA, as *visarga* is called when it is written in the form of two semi-circles before *ka* or *kha*, is the ROOT OF THE TONGUE. The NOSE is the organ OF ANUSWÁRA.

यत्नो द्विधा । आभ्यन्तरो बाह्यश्च । आद्यः पञ्चधा । स्पृष्टेषत्स्पृष्टेषद्विवृतविवृतसंवृतभेदात् । तत्र स्पृष्टप्रयत्नं स्पर्शानाम् । ईषत्स्पृष्टमन्तःस्थानाम् । ईषद्विवृतमूष्मणाम् । विवृतं स्वराणाम् । ह्रस्वस्यावर्णस्य प्रयोगे संवृतम् । प्रक्रियादशायां तु विवृतमेव । बाह्यस्त्वेकादशधा । विवारः संवारः श्वासो नादो घोषोऽघोषोऽल्पप्राणो महाप्राण उदात्तोऽनुदात्तः स्वरितश्चेति । खरो विवाराः श्वासा अघोषाश्च ।

हशः संवारा नादा घोषाश्च । वर्गाणां प्रथमतृतीयपञ्चमा यणश्चाल्पप्राणाः । वर्गाणां द्वितीयचतुर्थौ शलश्च महाप्राणाः । कादयो मावसानाः स्पर्शाः । यणोऽन्तःस्थाः । शल ऊष्माणः । अचः स्वराः । ≍क ≍ख इति कखाभ्यां प्रागर्धविसर्गसदृशो जिह्वामूलीयः । ≍प ≍फ इति पफाभ्यां प्रागर्धविसर्गसदृश उपध्मानीयः । अं अः इत्यचः परावनुस्वारविसर्गौ ।

No. 16.—THE EFFORT in utterance is TWOFOLD, that which takes place WITHIN the mouth, AND that which is EXTERNAL as regards the mouth, belonging to the throat. THE FORMER IS OF FIVE KINDS—ACCORDING TO THE DIVISION OF TOUCHED, SLIGHTLY TOUCHED, SLIGHTLY OPEN, OPEN and CONTRACTED. The EFFORT when the organ is TOUCHED by the tongue, BELONGS TO the five classes of consonants SPARŚA; when it is SLIGHTLY TOUCHED TO the semi-vowels (called ANTASTHA, because, in the common arrangement of the alphabet, they stand between the five classes and the sibilants); when the organs of speech are SLIGHTLY OPEN, TO the sibilants and the aspirate ÚSHMAN; when the organs are OPEN, TO the vowels SWARA. IN ACTUAL USE, the organ in the enunciation OF THE SHORT A is CONTRACTED: but it is considered to be OPEN only, as in the case of the other vowels, when the vowel A is IN THE STATE OF TAKING PART in some operation of grammar. (The reason for this is, that if the short *a* were held to differ from the long *á* in this respect, the *homogeneousness* mentioned in No. 14 would not be found to exist between them, and the operation of the rules depending upon that homogeneousness would be debarred. In order to restore the short *a* to its natural rights, thus infringed throughout the *Ashṭádhyáyí*, *Páṇini* with oracular brevity in his closing aphorism gives the injunction 'AA,' which is interpreted to signify "Let short *a* be held to have its organ of utterance contracted, now that we have reached the end of the work in which it was necessary to regard it as being otherwise."

The effort in utterance EXTERNAL as regards the mouth is OF ELEVEN KINDS—viz., EXPANSION of the throat, producing hard articulation; CONTRACTION of the throat, producing soft articulation; SIGHING; SOUNDING; LOW PREPARATORY MURMUR; ABSENCE OF SUCH

MURMUR; SLIGHT ASPIRATION; STRONG ASPIRATION; and the effort of ACUTE, GRAVE, and CIRCUMFLEX accentuation. IN the case of the letters in the *pratyáhára* KHAR (viz., the hard consonants *kha pha chha ṭha tha cha ṭa ta ka pa śa sha sa,*) the effort is that of VIVÁRA, ŚWÁSA, and AGHOSHA. IN the case of the letters in the *pratyáhára* HAŚ, (viz., the soft consonants *ha ya va ra la ṅa ma ńa ṇa na jha bha gha ḍha dha ja ba ga ḍa da,*) it is that of SAṄVÁRA, NÁDA, and GHOSHA. (We may here remark, that, as these two classes of consonants, the hard and soft are effectually discriminated by the *vivára,* and *saṅvára* difference, the additional distinctions of *śwása, náda, ghosha,* and *aghosha* whatever may be their utility or import elsewhere, are of no consequence here. With reference to the low preparatory murmur and its absence, the soft and hard letters are sometimes termed 'sonants' and 'surds.') THE FIRST AND THIRD LETTER IN each of THE FIVE CLASSES, in the ordinary arrangement of the alphabet (viz., *ka cha ṭa ta pa* and *ga ja ḍa da ba),* AND the letters denoted by the *pratyáhára* YAṆ (viz., the semi-vowels *ya va ra la),* are UNASPIRATED. THE SECOND AND FOURTH LETTERS OF the same CLASSES (viz., *kha chha ṭha tha pha* and *gha jha ḍha dha bha,)* AND the letters denoted by the *pratyáhára* ŚAL, (viz., the sibilants and the aspirate, *śa sha sa ha,)* are ASPIRATED. The letters in the ordinary arrangement of the alphabet, BEGINNING WITH KA, AND ENDING WITH MA, are the five classes of consonants SPARŚA. Those denoted by the *pratyáhára* YAṆ are the semi-vowels ANTASTHA; those denoted by ŚAL, the sibilants and aspirate ÚSHMAN; those denoted by ACH are the vowels SWARA. A character LIKE THE HALF OF VISARGA, when standing BEFORE KA or KHA, is called JIHWÁMÚLÍYA and when standing BEFORE PA OR PHA, is called UPADHMÁNÍYA (No. 15). A character, in the shape of A DOT, FOLLOWING A VOWEL, is called ANUSWÁRA; and one in the shape of TWO DOTS, or small circles, VISARGA.

अणुदित् सवर्णस्य चाप्रत्ययः ।१।१।६९।

अविधीयमानोऽणुदिच्च सवर्णस्य संज्ञा स्यात् । अत्रैवाण् परेण णकारेण । कु चु टु तु पु एते उदितः । तदेवम् इत्यष्टादशानां संज्ञा । तद्वेकारोकारौ । ऋकारस्त्रिंशतः । एवं लृकारोऽपि । एचो

द्वादशानाम् । अनुनासिकाननुनासिकभेदेन यवला द्विधा । तेनाननुनासिकास्ते द्वयोर्द्वयोः संज्ञा ।

No. 17.—Let a letter, denoted by the *pratyáhára* AṆ, NOT propounded as AN AFFIX or operative agent, but as something to be operated upon, AND let in like manner A LETTER FOLLOWED BY AN INDICATORY U, be the name of (and so imply) its homogeneous letters also.

Here the *pratyáhára aṇ* is made by the latter *ṇ* (of the sixth of the *sútras* of *Śiva, viz. laṇ*, and not by the *ṇ* at the end of the first *sútra.* The *pratyáhára* is therefore held to denote the semi-vowels as well as the vowels.) The letters above referred to, with an indicatory *u*, are *ku chu ṭu tu pu ;* (*ku* represents the guttural class, *chu* the palatals, *ṭu* the cerebrals, *tu* the dentals, and *pu* the labials). Hence *a* is the name of (and implies) its eighteen several varieties (No. 13) : and so *i* and *u*. The vowel *ṛi* is the name of thirty (for it denotes its own eighteen varieties, and the twelve varieties of *lṛi*, No. 13). So *lṛi* also (for it denotes its own twelve varieties, and the eighteen modifications of *ṛi*). The diphthongs *e ai o au* (*ech*) are each the name of twelve. Through the distinction of nasal and non-nasal, *ya va* and *la* are twofold ; and, by this rule, the non-nasal form of each implies both.

परः संनिकर्षः संहिता । १ । १ । १०९ ।

वर्णानामतिशयितः संनिधिः संहितासंज्ञः स्यात् ।

No. 18.—Let the CLOSEST PROXIMITY of letters be called CONTACT *(saṅhitá)*.

हलोऽनन्तराः संयोगः । १ । १ । ७ ।

अज्भिरव्यवहिता हलः संयोगसंज्ञाः स्युः ।

No. 19.—Let CONSONANTS UNSEPARATED by vowels be called A CONJUNCTION of consonants.

सुप्तिङन्तं पदम् । १ । ४ । १४ ।

सुबन्तं तिङन्तं च पदसंज्ञं स्यात् । इति संज्ञाप्रकरणम् ॥

No. 20.—Let THAT WHICH ENDS IN "SUP" (No. 137) OR IN "TIŃ" (No. 408) be called a PADA (or inflected word, as distinguished from a root, or that which has undergone no such inflection).

So much for the chapter on terms. We now come to the conjunction of vowels.

अच्सन्धिः ।

इको यणचि । ६ । १ । ७७ ।

इकः स्थाने यण् स्यादचि संहितायां विषये । सुधी उपास्य इति स्थिते ।

No. 21—Instead OF a letter denoted by the *pratyáhára* IK, let there be one denoted by the *pratyáhára* YAṆ, in each instance WHERE one denoted by the *pratyáhára* ACH immediately follows.

In the case, for example, of the word *sudhí* (meaning "the intelligent") followed by the word *upásya* ("to be worshipped").

It is to be observed that the foregoing aphorism consists solely of the three *pratyáháras ik yaṇ* and *ach*, the first having the termination of the genitive or *sixth case;* the second, that of the nominative or *first case;* and the third, that of the locative or *seventh case.* The force of these terminations is to be ascertained from other aphorisms ; because, although the author of the *Kaumudí,* in his *vṛitti* or expansion of the aphorism, has collected all that is required, yet the student, not content to receive anything on a lower authority than that of *Páṇini,* must be enabled to verify the interpretation offered to him. Holding, therefore, that we have merely got three *pratyáháras,* with different terminations, we proceed to enquire (1st) which is to give way, (2nd) which is to take its place, and (3rd) which is to be regarded as the cause of the change. For the sake of brevity we may now drop the term *pratyáhára,* and speak of *yaṇ, ach,* &c. simply.

तस्मिन्निति निर्दिष्टे पूर्वस्य । १ । १ । ६६ ।

सप्तमीनिर्देशेन विधीयमानं कार्यं वर्णान्तरेणाव्यवहितस्य पूर्वस्य बोध्यम् ।

No. 22.—WHEN A TERM IS EXHIBITED IN THE SEVENTH CASE (No. 137,) the operation directed is to be understood as affecting the state OF WHAT immediately PRECEDES that which the term denotes.

In the present instance, the term exhibited in the seventh case is *ach.* In the example *sudhí upásya*, the *u* of *upásya* is the vowel which that term denotes; and that which is to be affected is the final *í* (*ik*) of *sudhí*, which immediately precedes the *u*. By the foregoing rule, *yaṇ* is to be substituted for the *ik*, but *yaṇ* is the common name of the four letters *y v r* and *l*, and the question occurs—which of these is to be the substitute? The next rule supplies the answer.

स्थानेऽन्तरतमः । १ । १ । ५० ।

प्रसङ्गे सति सदृशतम आदेशः स्यात् । सु ध् य् उपास्य इति जाते ।

No. 23.—When a common term is obtained as a substitute, let THE LIKEST of its significates, to that IN THE PLACE of which it comes, be the actual substitute.

Of the four letters denoted by *yaṇ*, *y*, being a palatal, is the likest to *í*. Thus we have got *sudhyupásya*, which furnishes an occasion for another rule to come into operation.

अनचि च । ८ । ४ । ४७ ।

अचः परस्य यरो द्वे वा स्तो न त्वचि ।

No. 24.—Of *yar*, after *ach*, the reduplication is optional; BUT NOT IF ACH FOLLOW.

In *sudhyupásya* the *dha* is *yar* (this denoting all the consonants except *ha)*, and it follows *u* (*ach*), and it is not followed by *ach*, being followed by *ya*. Therefore, if we make the optional reduplication, we get *sudhdhyupásya*. This calls another rule into operation.

झलां जश् झशि । ८ । ४ । ५३ ।

स्पष्टम् । इति धकारस्य दकारः ।

No. 25.—Instead OF the letters called JHAL there shall be JAŚ IF JHAŚ FOLLOW.

Thus, instead of the first *dha* (*jhal*) of *sudhdhyupásya*, since *dha*, (*jhaś*) follows it, there must be *jaś*; that is to say, *ja ba ga ḍa* or *da*. Of these the likest (No. 23) is *da*. So, we get *suddhyupásya*; and the process might here terminate, did not another rule start an objection.

संयोगान्तस्य लोपः । ८ । २ । २३ ।

संयोगान्तं यत् पदं तदन्तस्य लोपः स्यात् ।

No. 26.—Let there be ELISION of the final OF THAT *pada* (No. 20) WHICH ENDS IN A COMPOUND CONSONANT.

In *suddhyupásya* the *pada suddhy* ends with a compound consonant; and, according to the rule, the whole *pada* ought to disappear. The rule, however, is limited by the qualification that follows.

अलोऽन्त्यस्य । १ । १ । ५२ ।

षष्ठीनिर्दिष्टान्त्यस्यादेशः स्यात् । इति प्राप्ते ।

No. 27.—Let the substitute take the place OF only THE FINAL LETTER of that which is denoted by a term exhibited in the genitive or *sixth case*.

An instance of elision (*lopa* No. 7) is regarded by the Sanskrit grammarians as the *substitution of a blank*. So a blank is directed to be substituted for the *y*, the final letter of the word *suddhy*, which is denoted (in No. 26) by a term, in the genitive or sixth case, viz. " of that *pada* which ends in a compound consonant." But here *Kátyáyana* interferes, and remarks as follows:—

यणः प्रतिषेधो वाच्यः । सुद्ध्युपास्यः । मद्ध्वरिः । धात्त्रंशः । लाकृतिः ।

No. 28.—" The PROHIBITION of the rule (No. 26) in the case OF YAṆ SHOULD BE STATED."

So the elision does not take place, and the formation of the word *Suddhyupásya* (a name of God—" He who is to be worshipped by the intelligent") is completed.

By a like process are formed the three words *Maddhwari* (a name of *Vishṇu*—"the foe of the demon *Madhu*,") *Dhátrańśa* (a name of *Brahmá*—"a portion of *Vishṇu* the cherisher") and *lákṛiti* ("the form of the letter *lṛi*") in which the other letters denoted by *yaṇ* are successively exhibited. The student, after making himself familiar with the process in the instance of *Suddhy-upásya*, should exercise himself in applying it to these and similar instances, not referring to his book except when his memory fails him.

We now proceed to consider the changes that depend upon the diphthongs (*ech*).

एचोऽयवायावः । ६ । १ । ७८ ।

एचः क्रमादय् अव् आय् आव् एते स्युरचि ।

No. 29.—Instead OF ECH, when *ach* follows, let there be in due order, AY AV ÁY ÁV.

The due order is ascertained by the next rule.

यथासंख्यमनुदेशः समानाम् । १ । ३ । १० ।

समसम्बन्धी विधिर्यथासंख्यं स्यात् । हरये । विष्णवे । नायकः । पावकः ।

No. 30.—When a rule involves the case OF EQUAL NUMBERS of substitutes and of things for which these are to be substituted, let THEIR MUTUAL CORRESPONDENCE (or the assignment of each to each) be ACCORDING TO THE ORDER OF ENUMERATION.

Thus *ech* denotes the four diphthongs *e o ai au*, and the four substitutes enumerated in the preceding rule are distributed among them thus—*ay* is the substitute of *e*, *av* of *o*, *áy* of *ai* and *áv* of *au*. Example: *hare+e=haraye* "to Hari," *vishṇo+e=vishṇa-ve*, "to Vishṇu," *nai+aka=náyaka* "a leader," *pau+aka=pá-vaka*, "a purifier, i. e. "Fire."

A similar change, under different circumstances, is directed by the next rule.

वान्तो यि प्रत्यये । ६ । १ । ७९ ।

यकारादौ प्रत्यये परे ओदौतोरव् आव् एतौ स्तः । गव्यम् । नाव्यम् ।

No. 31.—There shall be substituted WHAT ENDS IN V (viz. the two substitutes *av* and *áv*) for the corresponding *o* and *au*, WHEN AN AFFIX (No. 139) beginning with the letter YA FOLLOWS.

Thus *go+yam=gavyam* "belonging to a cow;" *nau+yam =návyam* "belonging to a boat."

The following *vártika* provides for a solitary case.

अध्वपरिमाणे च । गव्यूतिः ।

No. 32.—"And when the compound is employed in the sense of a measure of distance," the *o* of *go*, followed by *yúti* (though this is not an affix, No. 31) becomes *av*. Thus *go+yúti=gavyúti*, when it signifies "a distance of about four miles;" but the substitution does not take place when it signifies a "yoke of oxen" (*goyúti*).

अदेङ्गुणः । १ । १ । २ ।

अत् एङ् च गुणसंज्ञः स्यात् ।

No. 33.—Let short A and EŃ (that is to say *e* and *o*) be called GUṆA.

But why is the short *a* alone understood here in seeming contradiction to what was said in No. 17? The next rule will account for this.

तपरस्तत्कालस्य । १ । १ । ७० ।

तः परो यस्मात् स च तात्परश्चोच्चार्यमाणः समकालस्यैव संज्ञा स्यात् ।

No. 34.—Let a vowel FOLLOWED BY THE LETTER T, and a vowel following the letter *t*, be the name only OF THE LETTER WHICH HAS THE SAME PROSODIAL LENGTH. (Nos. 9 and 17.)

The letter *a* is the representation of eighteen varieties (No. 17); but when it is followed by *t*, as in the preceding rule, it represents neither the long nor the prolated modifications.

आद्गुणः ६ । १ । ८७ ।

अवर्णादचि परे पूर्वपरयोरेको गुणादेशः स्यात् । उपेन्द्रः । गङ्गोदकम् ।

No. 35.—When *ach* comes AFTER A (or á), let GUṆA be the single substitute for both.

Example *upa+indra=upendra* (a name of *Kṛishṇa*—"born subsequently to *Indra*"); *gańgá+udakam=gańgodakam* ("the water of the Ganges").—In these examples the *guṇa e* is substituted for *a* and *i*, and the *guṇa o* for *á* and *u*, because the organs employed in the pronunciation of *e* (the throat and palate) are those severally employed in the pronunciation of *a* and *i* (Nos. 16 and 23); and the organs employed in the pronunciation of *o* (the throat and lips) are those severally employed in the pronunciation of *á* and *u*.

उपदेशेऽजनुनासिक इत् । १ । ३ । २ ।

उपदेशेऽनुनासिकोऽजित्संज्ञः स्यात् । प्रतिज्ञानुनासिक्याः पाणिनीयाः । लण्सूत्रस्थावर्णेन सहोच्चार्यमाणो रेफो रलयोः संज्ञा ।

No. 36.—IN AN UPADEŚA (No. 5), let A NASAL vowel be called "IT" (No. 7).

In *Páṇini's* Grammar there is no visible sign of the nasality of a vowel—hence we can know a vowel to be nasal only from *Páṇini's* explicitly asserting that it is so, or from our finding that he treats it in such a way that we must conclude he regarded it as nasal. When speaking of the *Śiva-sútras*, it was mentioned that the vowel in the *sútra laṇ* is called "*it*." According to No. 8, therefore, this vowel may be employed as the final of a *pratyáhára*, and the *ra* in the next rule (No. 37) is held to be this *pratyáhára*, the name common to the two letters *ra* and *la*.

उरण् रपरः । १ । १ । ५१ ।

ऋ इति त्रिंशतः संज्ञेत्युक्तं तत्स्थाने योऽण् स रपरः सन्नेव प्रवर्त्तते । कृष्णर्द्धिः । तवल्कारः ।

No. 37.—AṆ, substituted IN THE PLACE OF ṚI, which (No. 17) is the representative of thirty varieties, is always FOLLOWED BY the *pratyáhárá* RA (No. 36). Example: *Kṛishṇa+ṛiddhi=Kṛishṇarddhi* ("the growth of *Kṛishṇa*"), *tava+lṛikára=tavalkára* ("thy letter *lṛi*").—The *pratyáhára aṇ* denotes *a*, *i* and u. The *a* in the two preceding examples in the *guṇa* directed by rule No. 35. [As examples of *i* and *u*, directed by other rules, we may notice *kṛí*+*uti*=*kirati*, "he scatters," and *dwaimátri*+*a*=*dwaimatura*, "having both a mother and a stepmother."] The *guṇa* substitute of *ṛi* is *a*, because *a*, like *ṛi*, has only one organ of pronunciation, whereas *e* and *o*, having two each, are less like *ṛi*. (No. 16.)

लोपः शाकल्यस्य । ८ । ३ । १९ ।

अवर्णपूर्वयोः पदान्तयोर्यवयोर्वा लोपोऽशि परे ।

No. 38.—In deference to the opinion OF ŚÁKALYA, let the ELISION be optional of the letters *ya* and *va* preceded by *a* or *á*, and at the end of a *pada* followed by *aś*.

Thus *hare iha*, by No. 29, becomes *harayiha*; then the *ya* at the end of the *pada haray*, being preceded by *a*, and followed by *i* (*aś*), may be optionally elided by this rule—the optionality of which is delicately implied in the aphorism by its being rested on the authority of the ancient grammarian *Śákalya*, the propriety of whose injunction *Páṇini* does not deny, although he does not admit it to be absolutely obligatory. The form of expression *hara iha* would then appear to furnish occasion for the operation of rule No. 35—but the rule here following debars this.

पूर्वत्रासिद्धम् । ८ । २ । १ ।

सपादसप्ताध्यायीं प्रति त्रिपाद्यसिद्धा त्रिपाद्यामपि पूर्वं प्रति परं शास्त्रमसिद्धम् । हर इह । हरयिह । विष्णा इह । विष्णाविह ।

No. 39.—AS FAR AS CONCERNS WHAT PRECEDES THEM, the three last chapters of the Grammar of *Páṇini* are AS IF THE RULES CONTAINED IN THESE THREE CHAPTERS HAD NEVER TAKEN EFFECT; and further, in these three chapters, a subsequent rule is as if it had not taken effect, so far as any preceding rule is concerned.

To understand this, it must be recollected that the grammar of *Páṇini* is divided into eight Lectures (*adhyáya*), each Lecture into four chapters (*páda*), and each chapter into a number of succinct Aphorisms (*sútra*). When the correct formation of a word is to be ascertained by the rules of this grammar, each *sútra* is conceived to present itself, or to be found *(prápta,)* when an occasion for its operation occurs. Now in the case of *hara iha* (No. 38), an occasion for the operation of No. 35 occurs, because no consonant intervenes between the *a* and *i*. But the elision of the intervening consonant (*y*) was the effect of a rule (No. 38) which stands as the nineteenth aphorism in the third chapter of *Páṇini's* eighth Lecture; and therefore, so far as rule No. 35 is concerned, which is the eighty-seventh aphorism of the first chapter of the sixth Lecture, the elision is as if it had never taken effect. Thus we have optionally *hara iha* or *harayiha* "to Hari here", and so also *vishṇa iha* or *vishṇaviha* "Oh Vishṇu! here".

वृद्धिरादैच्। १। १। १।

आदैच्च वृद्धिसंज्ञः स्यात्।

No. 40—Let LONG Á (No. 34), and AI and AU, be called VṚIDDHI.

वृद्धिरेचि। ६। १। ८८।

आदेचि परे वृद्धिरेकादेशः स्यात्। गुणापवादः। कृष्णैकत्वम्। गङ्गौघः। देवैश्वर्यम्। कृष्णौत्कण्ठ्यम्।

No. 41—WHEN ECH FOLLOWS *a*, let VṚIDDHI be the single substitute for both.

This is a contradiction *(apaváda)*, of the rule No. 35, which directs *guṇa* to be substituted in such a case. This rule takes effect, to the limitation of No. 35, because the latter has still a sphere left for its operation; whereas if No 35 were always to take effect, the operation of the present rule would always be forestalled. Such a rule as the present is tantamount to an exception to a more general rule. The Sanskrit Grammar acknowledges no irregularity, or exception to a rule—holding that a word which differs from all others of its class is "sui juris", and must have a rule of its own. (No. 32).

Thus we have *kṛishṇa+ekatwam=kṛishṇaikatwam* "oneness with *Kṛishṇa*", *gańgá+ogha=gańgaugha* "the torrent of the Ganges", *deva+aiśwaryam=devaiśwaryam* "the divinity of a God", *kṛishṇa+autkaṇṭhyam=kṛishṇautkaṇṭhyam* "a longing after *Kṛishṇa*."

एत्येधत्यूठ्सु । ६ । १ । ८९ ।

अवर्णादेजाद्योरेत्येधत्योरूठि च परे वृद्धिरेकादेशः स्यात् । उपैति । उपैधते । प्रष्ठौहः । एजाद्योः किम् । उपेतः । मा भवान् प्रेदिधत् ।

No. 42.—WHEN the verbs ETI and EDHATI, in those forms which begin with *ech*, FOLLOW *a*, AND when the substitute ÚṬH (No. 282) follows it, let *vṛiddhi* be the single substitute of the concurring vowels.

This rule limits No. 51, which had previously limited No. 35.

Hence we have *upa+eti=upaiti* "he comes near", and *upa +edhate=upaidhate* "it increases." In the example *prashṭhauhah* (the accusative or second case plural of *prashṭhaváh* "a young steer training for the plough"), the elements *prashṭha váh* and *śas* are (by Nos. 137, 156, 185, 282, 281, 5, and 283) brought to the form *prashṭha úhah,* to which the present rule applies, the result being *prashṭhauhah.*

Why do we say (of the verbs *eti* and *edhati)* "in those forms which begin with *ech ?*" Because other parts of these verbs, not beginning with *ech,* are not affected by this rule. Example: *upa+ita=upeta* "approached"—(No. 35); *má bhaván predidhat =pra+ididhat,* "Let not your honour promote".

अक्षादूहिन्यामुपसंख्यानम् । अक्षौहिणी सेना ।

No. 43.—"IT MAY BE ADDED that the substitution of *vṛiddhi* takes place also (No. 42) and not that of *guṇa,* WHEN ÚHINÍ FOLLOWS AKSHA." Thus *aksha+úhiní=akshauhiṇí* "an army."

प्रादूहोढोढ्येषैष्येषु । प्रौहः । प्रौढः । प्रौढिः । प्रैषः । प्रैष्यः ।

No. 44.—"And the substitution of *vṛiddhi* takes place also (No 42) WHEN PRA is FOLLOWED BY ÚHA ÚḌHA ÚḌHI ESHA and ESHYA. Thus *pra+úha=prauha* "a good argument," *pra+úḍha=prauḍha* "proud," *pra+úḍhi=prauḍhi* "audacity," *pra+esha=praisha.* "sending," *pra+eshya=praishya* "a servant."

ऋते च तृतीयासमासे । सुखेन ऋतः सुखार्तः । तृतीयेति किम् । परमर्तः ।

No. 45.—"AND IF SHORT ṚI FOLLOW *a* IN A COMPOUND WORD the first member of WHICH HAS the sense of THE THIRD or instrumental CASE."—Example: *sukha+ṛita=sukhárta* "affected by joy." (Nos. 37 and 73.)—Why (do we say) "which has (the sense of) the third (or instrumental case)?" Because otherwise, as in the compound *parama+ṛita=paramarta* "last-gone," this rule does not apply.

प्रवत्सतरकम्बलवसनार्णदशानामृणे । प्रार्णम् । वत्सतरार्णम् । इत्यादि ।

No. 46.—"And WHEN ṚIṆA ('a debt') FOLLOWS PRA VATSATARA KAMBALA VASANA ṚIṆA and DAŚA." Thus *prárṇa* "principal debt," *vatsatarárṇa* "debt of a steer," *kambalárṇa* "debt of a blanket," *vasanárṇa* 'debt of a cloth," *ṛiṇárṇa* "debt of a debt, compound interest," *Daśárṇá* "the river Dosaron or Dosarene" (No. 1341).

उपसर्गाः क्रियायोगे । १ । ४ । ५८ ।

प्रादयः क्रियायोगे उपसर्गसंज्ञाः स्युः ।

No. 47.—Let *pra*, &c. (No. 48) WHEN PREFIXED TO A VERB be termed *upasargas.*

प्र । परा । अप । सम् । अनु । अव । निस् । निर् । दुस् । दुर् । वि । आङ् । नि । अधि । अपि । अति । सु । उद् । अभि । प्रति । परि । उप । एते प्रादयः ।

No. 48.—By "PRA &C" we mean THE FOLLOWING particles—*prá* "before," *pará* "opposite," *apa* "off," *sam* "with," *anu* "after," *ava* "down," *nis* or *nir* "out," *dus* or *dur* "ill," *vi* "apart," *áṅ* "as far as," *ni* "within," *adhi* "over," *api* "verily," *ati* "beyond," *su* "well," *ut* "up," *abhi* "opposite," *prati* "back again," *pari* "around," *upa* "next to."

भूवादयो धातवः । १ । ३ । १ ।

क्रियावाचिनो भ्वादयो धातुसंज्ञाः स्युः ।

No. 49.—Let verbal roots BHÚ "be" VÁ "blow" *and* THE LIKE be called DHÁTU.

उपसर्गादृति धातौ। ६।१।९१।

अवर्णान्तादुपसर्गादृकारादौ धातौ परे वृद्धिरेकादेशः स्यात्।

प्रार्च्छति।

No. 50—WHEN A DHÁTU (No. 49) BEGINNING WITH ṚI FOLLOWS AN UPASARGA (No. 47) ending in *a* or *á*, let *vṛiddhi* be the single substitute for both. Thus *pra+ṛichchhati=prárchchhati* "he goes on rapidly."

एङि पररूपम्। ६।१।९४।

आदुपसर्गादेङादौ धातौ पररूपमेकादेशः स्यात्। प्रेजते। उपोषति।

No. 51.—WHEN a *dhátu* BEGINNING WITH EŃ FOLLOWS an *upasarga* ending in *a* or *á*, let the single substitute for both be THE FORM OF THE SUBSEQUENT vowel. Thus *pra+ejate=prejate* "he trembles," *upa+oshati=uposhati* "he sprinkles."

अचोऽन्त्यादि टि। १।१।६४।

अचां मध्ये योऽन्त्यः स आदिर्यस्य तट्टिसंज्ञं स्यात्।

No. 52.—Let the final portion of a word, BEGINNING WITH THE LAST OF THE VOWELS in the word, be called ṬI.

शकन्ध्वादिषु पररूपं वाच्यम्। तच्च टेः। शकन्धुः। कर्कन्धुः। मनीषा। लाङ्गलीषा। आकृतिगणोऽयम्। मार्तण्डः।

No. 53.—"It SHOULD BE STATED that THE FORM OF THE SUBSEQUENT vowel takes the place of both IN ŚAKANDHU &c.

Thus *śaka+andhu=śakandhu* "a sort of potherb," *karka+andhu=karkandhu* "the jujube," *lángala+íshā=lángalíshā* "the handle of a plough," *márta+aṇḍa=mártaṇḍa* "the sun," *manas+íshá=manísha* "intellect."

This is a class of compound words, the fact of a word's belonging to which is known only from its form, *a posteriori*, and is not discoverable by any consideration of its constituent parts *a priori*.

ओमाङोश्च । ६ । १ । ९५ ।

ओमि आङि चात् पररूपमेकादेशः स्यात् । शिवायोंनमः । शिवेहि ।

No. 54.—AND WHEN the mystic syllable OM, OR the *upasarga* ÁṄ (No, 47.) follows *a* or *á*, let the single substitute be the form of the subsequent.

Example: *Śiváya+om+namah=Śiváyonnamah* "adoration to Śiva!"; *Śiva+á+ihi=Śivehi* "oh Śiva, come." (Nos. 5, 55, and 35.)

अकः सवर्णे दीर्घः । ६ । १ । १०१ ।

अकः सवर्णेऽचि परे पूर्वपरयोर्दीर्घ एकादेशः स्यात् । दैत्यारिः । श्रीशः । विष्णूदयः । होतॄकारः ।

No. 55.—WHEN A HOMOGENEOUS VOWEL FOLLOWS AK, let the corresponding LONG vowel be the substitute for both.

Example, *daitya+ari=daityári*, "a foe of the demons," (a name of *Vishṇu*), *śrí+íśa=śríśa*, "the lord of *Śrí*," *Vishṇu+udaya=Vishṇúdaya* "the rise of *Vishṇu*," *hotṛi+ḷrikára=hotṛíkára* "the letter *ḷri* of the officiating priest." (No. 16.)

एङः पदान्तादति । ६ । १ । १०९ ।

पदान्तादेङोऽति परे पूर्वरूपमेकादेशः स्यात् । हरेऽव । विष्णोऽव ।

No. 56.—AFTER EṄ FINAL IN A PADA (No. 20) IF SHORT A come, let the single substitute for both be the form of the precedent vowel.

Example: *hare+ava=hare'va* "Oh Hari!—off;" *vishṇo+ava=vishṇo'va*. "Oh Vishṇu! off—". A character termed *ardhákára*, or "half the letter *a*," is generally written in the place of the letter thus elided, as we write an apostrophe in some analogous cases.

सर्वत्र विभाषा गोः । ६ । १ । १२२ ।

लोके वेदे चैङन्तस्य गोरति वा प्रकृतिभावः पदान्ते । गो अग्रम् । गोऽग्रम् । एङन्तस्य किम् । चित्रग्वग्रम् । पदान्ते किम् । गोः ।

No. 57.—EVERYWHERE, both in secular and sacred writing, THE ORIGINAL FORM OF the word GO ("a cow"), being a *pada* ending in EŃ, may be optionally retained before *a*.

Example: *Go+agram=go agram* or *go'gram*, "a multitude of cows." Why ending in *eń?*" Because the word *go*, at the end of the compound word *chitragu* ("having a brindled cow,") where, in the neuter, it ends in *u* (Nos. 269 and 275), has not the option of remaining unchanged. So *chitragu+agram=chitragwagram* "a multitude of brindled cows," (No. 21.) Why "being a *pada* so ending?" Because, though it end in *eń*, the rule does not apply unless the word *go* be a *pada* (No. 20), so that, in forming the ablative or fifth case, (by Nos. 137, 155, 36, 124, and 111,) we have *go+ah=goh* (by No. 193).

अनेकाल् शित् सर्वस्य । १ । १ । ५५ ।

इति प्राप्ते ।

No. 58.—Let a substitute CONSISTING OF MORE THAN ONE LETTER, or CONTAINING AN INDICATORY PALATAL Ś, take the place OF THE WHOLE of the original expression.

ङिच्च । १ । १ । ५३ ।

ङिदनेकालप्यन्त्यस्यैव स्यात् ।

No. 59.—AND let THAT WHICH HAS AN INDICATORY Ń, even though it consist of more than one letter, take the place of the final letter only of the original expression.

अवङ् स्फोटायनस्य । ६ । १ । १२३ ।

पदान्ते एङन्तस्य गोरवङ् वाऽचि । गोऽग्रम् । गवाग्रम् । पदान्ते किम् । गवि ।

No. 60.—According to the opinion OF SPHOṬÁYANA, AVAŃ may be the substitute of *go* at the end of a *pada* ending in *eń* if *ach* follow.

Thus we may have *go+agram=gavágram* a multitude of cows, " (Nos. 59. 5, and 55) as well as *go'gram* (No. 57). Why "at the end of a *pada*?" Because *go+ńi=gavi* "in a cow"—(Nos. 137, 155, and 29.)

इन्द्रे च । ६ । १ । १२४ ।

गोरवङ् स्यादिन्द्रे । गवेन्द्रः ।

No. 61.—AND IF the word INDRA FOLLOW; let *avań* (No. 60) be the substitute of *go*. Thus *go+indra=gavendra* "lord of kine"—(a name of *Kṛishṇa.)*

दूराद्धूते च । ८ । २ । ८४ ।

दूरात् संबोधने वाक्यस्य टेः प्लुतो वा ।

No. 62.—AND IN CALLING to a person FROM A DISTANCE, the substitution of the prolated modification (No. 9) of the *ṭi* (No. 52) is optional.

प्लुतप्रगृह्या अचि नित्यम् । ६ । १ । १२५ ।

एतेऽचि प्रकृत्या स्युः । आगच्छ कृष्णा ३ अत्र गौश्चरति ।

No. 63.—Let PROLATED (No. 9) AND EXCEPTED (No. 64) vowels, WHEN ACH FOLLOWS, INVARIABLY remain unaltered.

Example: *ágachchha kṛishṇá atṛa gauścharatí* (Come *Kṛishṇa!* the cow is feeding here.")

ईदूदेद्द्विवचनं प्रगृह्यम् । १ । १ । ११ ।

ईदूदेदन्तं द्विवचनं प्रगृह्यं स्यात् । हरी एतौ । विष्णू इमौ । गङ्गे अमू ।

No. 64.—Let A DUAL case-affix (No. 142) ENDING in LONG Í, Ú, OR E, be PRAGṚIHYA (No. 63).

Example: *harí etau* "these two *Haris*," *vishṇú imau* "these two *Vishṇus*," *gańge amú* "those two rivers Ganges

अदसो मात् । १ । १ । १२ ।

अस्मात् परावीदूतौ प्रगृह्यौ स्तः । अमी ईशाः । रामकृष्णावमू आसाते । मात् किम् । अमुकेऽत्र ।

No. 65.—Let *í* and *ú* coming AFTER the M OF the words ADAS (No. 386) be *pragṛihya* (No. 63).

Example: *amí íśáh* "those lords," *Rámakṛishṇávamú ásáte* "*Ráma* and *Kṛishṇa*, those two are present."—Why do we say "after the *m*?" Because in the example *amuke*+*atra*=*amuke'tra* 'those here," the *e*, preceded not by *m* but by the *k* of *akach* (No 1321), is not *pragṛihya*, which it would have been, by the influence of No. 64, which includes *e* as well as *í* and *ú*, and from which the word "dual" is not supplied here, else this rule would be useless.

चादयोऽसत्त्वे । १ । ४ । ५७ ।

अद्रव्यार्थाश्चादयो निपाताः स्युः ।

No. 66.—Let CHA &c, NOT SIGNIFYING SUBSTANCES *(dravya,)* be called *nipátas*.

प्रादयः । १ । ४ । ५८ ।

एतेऽपि तथा ।

No. 67.—And so let PRA &c. (Nos 48 and 66.)

निपात एकाजनाङ् । १ । १ । १४ ।

एकोऽज् निपात आङ्वर्जः प्रगृह्यः । इ इन्द्रः । उ उमेशः । वाक्यस्मरणयोरङित् । आ एवं नु मन्यसे । आ एवं किल तत् । अन्यत्र ङित् । ईषदुष्णम् । ओष्णम् ।

No. 68.—Let ANY NIPÁTA (No. 66.) CONSISTING OF A SINGLE VOWEL WITH THE EXCEPTION OF the *nipáta* ÁṄ, be *pragṛihya* (No 64).

Example: *i indra* "oh *Indra*!," *u umeśa* "oh lord of *Umá*!" The *nipáta á*, as an interjection either making no particular difference in the sense of the sentence or else indicating reminiscence, has no indicatory *ń*, and therefore is not subject to the exception enjoined above. Example, *á evańnu manyase* "Now thou thinkest so, not having always thought so;" *á evań kila tat* "Ah!—now I recollect—it is just so." Elsewhere, that is to say when it implies diminution, the *á* has an indicatory *ń*, and is the subject of the exception above enjoined. Example, *ání*+*ushṇam*=*oshṇam* "a little warm." (Nos 5 and 35).—

ओत् । १ । १ । १५ ।

ओदन्तो निपातः प्रगृह्यः । अहो ईशाः ।

No. 69.—A *nipáta* ending in o is *pragṛihya* (No. 64.)

Example: *aho íśáh* "Ho lords!"

संबुद्धौ शाकल्यस्येतावनार्षे । १ । १ । १६ ।

संबुद्धिनिमित्तक ओकारो वा प्रगृह्योऽवैदिक इतौ परे । विष्णो इति । विष्णविति ।

No. 70.—In deference to the opinion OF ŚÁKALYA let *ó* IN THE VOCATIVE SINGULAR WHEN FOLLOWED BY the word ITI, NOT IN THE VEDA, be optionally *pragṛihya* (No. 64.) So we may have either *vishṇo iti* by this rule, or *vishṇaviti* by No. 29, or *vishṇa iti* by the further operation of the optional rule No. 38. "'Oh *Vishṇu*!' thus &c."

मय उञो वो वा । ८ । ३ । ३३ ।

मयः परस्योञो वो वाऽचि । किम्वुक्तम् । किमु उक्तम् ।

No. 71.—Instead OF the affix UÑ, (that is to say the indeclinable affix *u*,) AFTER the *pratyáhára* MAY, if *ach* follow, there is OPTIONALLY V. Example, *kim*+*u*+*uktam*=*kimvuktam* "whether said," or *kimu uktam* (No. 68).

इकोऽसवर्णे शाकल्यस्य ह्रस्वश्च । ६ । १ । १२७ ।

पदान्ता इको ह्रस्वा वा स्युरसवर्णेऽचि । ह्रस्वविधिसामर्थ्यान्न स्वरसंधिः । चक्रि अत्र । चक्र्यत्र । पदान्ता इति किम् । गौर्यौ ।

No. 72.—And, in deference to the opinion OF ŚÁKALYA, WHEN A HETEROGENEOUS vowel FOLLOWS, let there be THE SHORT instead OF IK at the end of a *pada*.

As this injunction of shortening must not be an entirely abortive rule, the vowels shall not undergo a further change (as No. 21 would otherwise cause them to do). Example, *chakrí*+*atra*=

chakri atra "the discus-armed *Vishṇu* here." On the alternative of not shortening the vowel, we have *chakrí+atra=chakryatra* (by No. 21). Why "at the end of a *pada*"? In the example *gaurí +au=gauryau* "two goddesses *Gaurí*," there is no option (No. 21) the word ending in *í* not being a *pada*. (From No. 20 we learn what constitutes a *pada*, but how to ascertain that a word is a *pada*, when the characteristic there referred to, as it sometimes happens, has no visible representative in the word itself, we must be content to learn further on. In the meantime we have to bear in mind whether any particular rule refers to a *pada* only, or also to other forms of speech.)

अचो रहाभ्यां द्वे । ८।४।४६।

अचः पराभ्यां रेफहकाराभ्यां परस्य यरो द्वे वा स्तः । गौर्य्यौ ।

No. 73.—Of *yar*, that is to say, of all the consonants except *ha*, AFTER the letters RA or HA FOLLOWING ACH, REDUPLICATION is optional. Hence we may write *gauryyau* or *gauryau* "two goddesses *Gaurí*."

न समासे । वाप्यश्वः ।

No. 74.—The option of shortening (No. 72) does NOT hold IN A COMPOUND word. Example, *vápí+aśwa=vápyaśwa* "a horse that can walk on water," where the application of No. 21 is imperative.

ऋत्यकः । ६।१।१२८।

ऋति परे पदान्त अकः प्राग्वद्वा । ब्रह्म ऋषिः । ब्रह्मर्षिः । पदान्ताः किम् । आर्च्छत् ।

No. 75.—AK (that is to say, *a* or *á* in addition to the other vowels in No. 72) final in a *pada* may optionally take the short substitute as stated above (No. 74) WHEN short ṚI FOLLOWS. Example, *brahmá+ṛishi=brahmaṛishi* or *brahmarshi* "a divine saint." (Nos. 35 and 37).—Why "final in a *pada?* Because, to the word *árchchhat* "he was going," where the *á* is not final in a *pada* (being an augment derived from No. 478) the option of this rule does not extend; so we have *á+ṛichchhat=árchchhat* by No. 218. We now proceed to

THE CONJUNCTION OF CONSONANTS.

स्तोः श्चुना श्चुः । ८ । ४ । ४० ।

सकारतवर्गयोः शकारचवर्गाभ्यां योगे शकारचवर्गौ स्तः । रामश्शेते । रामश्चिनोति । सच्चित् । शार्ङ्गिञ्जय ।

No. 76.—In the room OF SA AND TU (that is to say, these five dentals *ta tha da dha na*, No. 17) when they come in contact WITH ŚA AND CHU, (that is say, these five palatals *cha chha ja jha ṅa*), there are ŚA AND THE PALATALS." Example, *rámas+śete=rámaśśete* "*Ráma* sleeps," *rámas+chinoti=rámaśchinoti* "*Ráma* collects," *sad+chit=sachchit* "pure reason," (No. 90,) *śárṅgin+jaya=śárṅginjaya*, "Oh *Vishṇu* be thou victorious."

शात् । ८ । ४ । ४४ ।

शात् परस्योक्तं न । विश्नः । प्रश्नः ।

No. 77.—This (No. 76) is not said of a dental which comes AFTER ŚA. Example, in *viś+na=viśna* "lustre," *praś+na=praśna* "a question," no alteration takes place.

ष्टुना ष्टुः । ८ । ४ । ४१ ।

स्तोः ष्टुना योगे ष्टुः । रामष्षष्ठः । रामष्टीकते । पेष्टा । तट्टीका । चक्रिण्ढौकसे ।

No. 78.—In the room of *sa* and *tu* (No. 76) when they come IN CONTACT WITH SHA and ṬU, (that is to say, the cerebrals *ṭa ṭha ḍa ḍha ṇa)*, there are *sha* and *ṭu*, (that is to say, there is a cerebral substitute).—Example, *rámas+shashṭha=rámashshashṭha* "*Ráma* sixth," *rámas+ṭíkate=rámashṭíkate* "*Ráma* stands," *pesh+tá=peshṭá* "a grinder," *tad+ṭíká=taṭṭíká* "a comment on that" (No. 90), *chakrin+ḍhaukase=chakriṇḍhaukase* "Oh discus-armed! thou goest."

न पदान्ताट्टोरनाम् । ८ । ४ । ४२ ।

पदान्ताट्टवर्गात् परस्यानामः स्तोः ष्टुर्न स्यात् । षट् सन्तः । षट् ते । पदान्तात् किम् ईट्टे । टोः किम् । सर्पिष्टमम् ।

No. 79.—AFTER ṬU (No. 78) FINAL IN A PADA the change of a dental to a cerebral, EXCEPT in the case of the affix NÁM, shall not take place.

Example: *shaḍ+santaḥ=shaṭsantaḥ* "six good,"—(No. 90), *shaḍ+te=shaṭṭe* "they six,"—Why "final in a *pada?*" Compare *íḍ+te=íṭṭe* "he praises," where it is not so. Why only, "after *ṭu?*" Because the cerebral *sha* is not included. Example: *sarpish+tama=sarpishṭama* "most excellent clarified butter."

अनाम्नवतिनगरीणामिति वाच्यम् । षण्णाम् । षण्णवतिः षण्णगर्यः ।

No. 80.—"IT SHOULD BE STATED that NAVATI and NAGARÍ as well as NÁM are NOT prevented by No. 79 from undergoing the cerebral change.

Example, *shaḍ+nám=shaṇṇám* "of six," *shaḍ+navati=shaṇṇavati* "ninety six," *shaḍ+nagaryah=shaṇṇagaṛyah* "six cities," whose names are feminine.

तोः षि ।८।४।४३।

न ष्टुत्वम् । सन्षष्ठः ।

No. 81.—In the room OF TU (No. 76) there is not a cerebral substitute WHEN SHA FOLLOWS. Example, *san+shashṭha=sanshashṭha* "being sixth".

झलां जशोऽन्ते ।८।२।३९।

पदान्ते झलां जशः स्युः । वागीशः ।

No. 82.—In the room OF JHAL, (that is to say, of any consonant except a semi-vowel or a nasal), let there be JAŚ, (that is to say, a soft unaspirated consonant) AT THE END of a *pada.*

Example: *vák+íśa=vágíśa* "the god of speech," a name of *Vṛihaspati.*

यरोऽनुनासिकेऽनुनासिको वा ।८।४।४५।

यरः पदान्तस्यानुनासिके परेऽनुनासिको वा स्यात् । एतन्मुरारिः । एतद्मुरारिः ।

No. 83.—In the room OF YAR final in a *pada,* WHEN A NASAL FOLLOWS, there may be OPTIONALLY A NASAL.

Example: *etad+murári=etanmurári* or *etadmurári* "that *Vishṇu.*"

प्रत्यये भाषायां नित्यम् । तन्मात्रम् । चिन्मयम् ।

No. 84.—"WHEN it is A PRATYAYA (No. 139) that FOLLOWS IN SECULAR LANGUAGE, the preceding rule (No. 83) is ABSOLUTE."

Example: *tat+mátram=tanmátram* "merely that," "a primary element," *chit+mayam=chinmayam* "formed of intellect."

तोर्लि ।८।४।६०।

परसवर्णः । तल्लयः । विद्वाँल्लिँखति । नस्यानुनासिको लः ।

No. 85.—In the room OF TU (No. 76) WHEN the letter LA FOLLOWS, one homogeneous with the latter is substituted.

Example: *tat+laya=tallaya* "its destruction." The *la* substituted for *na* is a nasal *la* (No. 17). This is sometimes indicated by writing over it the mark *chandra-vindu* as in *vidwán+likhati=vidwállikhati* "the learned man writes."

उदः स्थास्तम्भोः पूर्वस्य ।८।४।६१।

उदः परयोः स्थास्तम्भोः पूर्वसवर्णः ।

No. 86.—AFTER UD, in the room OF the words STHÁ AND STAMBHA, the substitute is a letter belonging to the class OF THE PRIOR.

Thus, suppose we have to put together *ud+sthánam*:—the aphorism, without the gloss, exhibits to us the word *ud* in the ablative or *fifth* case. We must ascertain from another rule what is the special import of the fifth case here, as we did with respect to the locative or seventh case in No. 21. The maxim of interpretation *(paribháshá)* here follows.

तस्मादित्युत्तरस्य ।१।१।६७।

पञ्चमीनिर्देशेन क्रियमाणं कार्यं वर्णान्तरेणाव्यवहितस्य परस्य ज्ञेयम् ।

No. 87.—An operation caused BY the exhibition of a term in THE ablative or FIFTH CASE, shall be understood to enjoin the substitution of something in the room OF THAT WHICH immediately FOLLOWS the word denoted by the term.

Therefore the substitution of the letter *d* enjoined by No. 86 is to be in the room of the words *sthá* and *stambha.* This again is qualified (as No. 26 by No. 27) by the following maxim.

आदेः परस्य ।१।१।५४।

परस्य यद्विहितं तत् तस्यादेर्बोध्यम् । इति सस्य थः ।

No. 88.—That which is enjoined to come in the room OF WHAT FOLLOWS is to be understood as coming in the room only OF THE FIRST letter thereof.

Therefore, in the example *ud+sthánam* (No. 86) a dental letter is to be substituted for the *s ;* and the dental which, like *s*, has the characters of *vivára* and *mahápráṇa* (No. 16), that is to say which is both hard and aspirated—viz. *th*—is the proper letter of the set. (No. 23). Thus we have *ud+ththánam,* which comes within the scope of the next rule.

झरो झरि सवर्णे ।८।४।६५।

हलः परस्य झरो वा लोपः सवर्णे झरि ।

No. 89.—There is optionally elision OF JHAR, preceded by a consonant, WHEN A HOMOGENEOUS JHAR FOLLOWS.

Thus we may have *ud+thánam* as well as *ud+ththánam,* to each of which the following rule applies.

खरि च ।८।४।५५।

खरि झलां चरः स्युः । इत्युदो दस्य तः । उत्थानम् । उत्तम्भनम् ।

No. 90.—AND WHEN KHAR FOLLOWS, let there be *char* in the room of *jhal*. Therefore, in the example in No. 89, the soft *d* is changed to the hard *t*, and we have *utthánam* or *uththánam* "uprising;" and so (No. 86) by the same process, *uttambhanam* "upholding."

झयो होऽन्यतरस्याम् ।८।४।६२।

झयः परस्य हस्य वा पूर्वसवर्णः । नादस्य घोषस्य संवारस्य महाप्राणस्य तादृशो वर्गचतुर्थः । वाग्घरिः । वाग्हरिः ।

No. 91.—In the room OF the letter HA, AFTER JHAY, there is OPTIONALLY a letter homogeneous with the prior.

The fourth letter of each class (that is to say, the soft aspirate) is the suitable substitute for *ha* (No. 16). Thus *vág+hari* may be written *vágghari* "eloquent"——"a lion in discourse."

शश्छोऽटि ।८।४।६३।

झयः परस्य शस्य छो वाऽटि । तद् शिव इत्यत्र दस्य चुत्वेन जकारे कृते खरि चेति जकारस्य चकारः । तच्छिवः । तद्शिवः ।

No. 92.—In the room OF the palatal ŚA preceded by *jhay*, there is optionally the letter CHHA WHEN AT FOLLOWS.

Example: *tad+śiva*, by this rule, optionally becomes *tad+chhiva*, and then, by Nos. 76 and 90, *tachchhiva;* on the other alternative (by Nos. 76 and 90), it becomes *tachśiva* "that *Śiva*."

छत्वममीति वाच्यम् । तच्छ्लोकेन ।

No. 93.—IT SHOULD BE STATED that the foregoing rule applies not merely when *aṭ* follows but WHEN AM (a more comprehensive *pratyáhára)* FOLLOWS. Thus we have *tad+ślokena=tachchhlokena* "by that couplet," where the *ś* is followed by *l*.

मोऽनुस्वारः ।८।३।२३।

मान्तस्य पदस्यानुस्वारो हलि । हरिं वन्दे ।

No. 94.—In the room of the letter M final in a *pada* (or, as the gloss, trusting to No. 27, words it, "in the place of a *pada* which ends in *m*,") there is ANUSWÁRA, when a consonant follows.

Example: *harim + vande = harinvande* "I salute *Vishṇu*."

नश्चापदान्तस्य झलि । ८ । ३ । २४ ।

नस्य मस्य चापदान्तस्य झल्यनुस्वारः । यशांसि । आक्रंस्यते ।

No. 95.—AND also in the room OF the letter NA and *ma* NOT FINAL IN A PADA, WHEN JHAL FOLLOWS, there is *anuswára.*

Example: *yaśán + si = yaśáṅsi* "glories;" *ákram + syate = ákraṅsyate,* "he will subdue."

अनुस्वारस्य ययि परसवर्णः । ८ । ४ । ५८ ।

शान्तः ।

No. 96.—In the room OF ANUSWÁRA, WHEN YAY FOLLOWS, a letter HOMOGENEOUS WITH THE LATTER is substituted.

Example: *śáṅ + ta = śánta* "quiet."

वा पदान्तस्य । ८ । ४ । ५९ ।

त्वङ्करोषि । त्वं करोषि ।

No. 97.—In the room OF *anuswára* FINAL IN A PADA, the substitution (enjoined by No. 96) is OPTIONAL.

Example: *twaṅkaroshi* or *twaṅ karoshi* "thou doest."

मो राजि समः क्वौ । ८ । ३ । २५ ।

क्विबन्ते राजतौ परे समो मस्य म एव स्यात् । सम्राट् ।

No. 98.—Let the letter M itself be in the room OF the *m* of the particle SAM (No. 48) WHEN the word RÁJ FOLLOWS, ENDING IN the technical affix KWIP (No. 855).

Example: *sam + ráṭ = samráṭ* "a great king."

हे मपरे वा । ८ । ३ । २६ ।

मपरे हकारे परे मस्य मो वा । किम्ह्मलयति । किं ह्मलयति ।

No. 99.—WHEN the letter H FOLLOWS, being itself FOLLOWED BY M, the substitute for a preceding *m* is optionally *m* itself.

Example, *kimhmalayati* or, by No. 94, *kiṅ hmalayati* "what does he cause to shake?"

यवलपरे यवला वा । किय्ँह्यः । किं ह्यः । किव्ँह्वलयति । किं ह्वलयति । किल्ँह्लादयति । किं ह्लादयति ।

No. 100.—" WHEN the letter *h* follows, being itself FOLLOWED BY the letters Y, V, OR L, the substitute for a preceding *m* is optionally Y, V, or L." (No. 30). Example, *kiyhyah* or, by No. 94, *kiṅ hyah* "what does it matter about yesterday?" *kivhwalayati* or *kiṅ hwalayati* "what does he cause to shake?" *kilhládayati* or *kiṅ hládayati* "what gladdens?"

नपरे नः । ८ । ३ । २७ ।

नपरे हकारे मस्य नो वा । किन्ँह्नुते । किं ह्नुते ।

No. 101.—WHEN the letter *h* follows, being itself FOLLOWED BY the letter N, the substitute for a preceding *m*, is optionally N.

Example, *kinhnute,* or, substituting *anuswára,* (No. 94) *kiṅ hnute* "what withholds?"

डः सि धुट् । ८ । ३ । २९ ।

डात् परस्य सस्य धुड्वा ।

No. 102.—DHUṬ is optionally the augment *(ágama)* OF the dentalis WHEN IT FOLLOWS the cerebral Ḍ,—as in the example *shaṭ sántah* "being six." A question here arises as to where the augment is to be placed,—with reference to which we find the following direction.

आद्यन्तौ टकितौ । १ । १ । ४६ ।

टित्कितौ यस्योक्तौ तस्य क्रमादाद्यन्तौ स्तः । षट् सन्तः । षट्त्सन्तः ।

No. 103.—Of whatsoever the augments enunciated are distinguished by an INDICATORY Ṭ OR K, they PRECEDE OR FOLLOW it accordingly. The augment of *s,* enunciated in No. 102, is distinguished by an indicatory *ṭ* (No. 5); the augment is therefore to precede the *s*. The *ṭ* is elided by Nos. 5 and 7, and the vowel by Nos. 36 and 7, and, the *dh* being changed to *t* by No. 90, we get *shaṭt-santah*, or, without the augment (No. 102), *shaṭsantah* "being six."

ङ्णोः कुक् टुक् शरि । ८ । ३ । २८ ।

वा स्तः । प्राङ् षष्ठः । प्राङ्क्षष्ठः । सुगण् षष्ठः । सुगण्ट् षष्ठः ।

No. 104.—OF ṄA AND ṆA respectively, WHEN ŚAR FOLLOWS, there are optionally the augments KUK and ṬUK. The indicatory *k* shows that the augment *follows* the letter (No. 103). Example, *prāṅ shashṭha* or *prāṅkshashṭha* "sixth anterior," *sugaṇ shash-ṭha* or *sugaṇṭshashṭha* "sixth numerator."

नश्च । ८ । ३ । ३० ।

नान्तात् परस्य सस्य धुड्वा । सन् त्सः । सन् सः ।

No. 105.—AND of the dental *s*, AFTER WHAT ENDS IN N, the augment *dhuṭ* (No. 102) is optional.

Example, *san tsah* or *san sah* "he being."

शि तुक् । ८ । ३ । ३१ ।

पदान्तस्य नस्य शे परे तुग्वा । सञ्छम्भुः । सञ्छम्भुः । सञ्च्शम्भुः । सञ्शम्भुः ।

No. 106.—Of *n* final in a *pada* there is optionally the augment TUK, WHEN the palatal ś FOLLOWS. Example, *san+t+śam-bhu=sañchchhambu* (Nos. 92 and 76), which, by the optional elision of the *ch* (No. 89) may become *sañchhambu* ("the good *Śambhu*, or *Śiva*"). *Sañchśambhu* (No. 92). Without the augment, we have *sañśambhu* by No. 76.

ङमो ह्रस्वादचि ङमुण्नित्यम् । ८ । ३ । ३२ ।

ह्रस्वात् परो यो ङम् तदन्तं यत् पदं तस्मात् परस्याचो नित्यं ङमुट् स्यात् । प्रत्यङ्ङात्मा । सुगण्णीशः । सन्नच्युतः ।

No. 107.—WHEN A VOWEL comes AFTER a *pada* ending in ṄAM preceded by a short vowel, the augment ṄAMUṬ shall INVARIABLY be applied.

The name of this augment is derived from the *pratyáhára ńam,* so that (by No. 30) it is understood to imply the reduplication of the nasal.

Example, *pratyań + átmá = pratyańńátmá* "soul evidently existent", *sugaṇ + íśa = sugaṇṇíśa* "the lord of an excellent class," *san + achyuta = sannachyuta* "existing *Vishṇu.*"

समः सुटि ।८।३।५।

समो रुः सुटि ।

No. 108.—In place OF the particle SAM, WHEN SUṬ FOLLOWS, there is *ru.*

For example, having got *sam + suṭ + karttá,* this rule, after the indicatory letters (by Nos. 36 and 7) have been elided, gives *sar + s + karttá.*

अत्रानुनासिकः पूर्वस्य तु वा ।८।३।२।

अत्र रुप्रकरणे रोः पूर्वस्यानुनासिको वा ।

No. 109.—BUT HERE, in the division of the grammar where *ru* is the subject of discussion, THE NASAL FORM is OPTIONALLY the substitute OF WHAT PRECEDES *ru.*

Thus, in the example under rule No. 108, the *a* of *sar* is optionally nasal, and this may be indicated by the mark *chandravindu* (No. 85).

अनुनासिकात् परोऽनुस्वारः ।८।३।४।

अनुनासिकं विहाय रोः पूर्वस्मात् परोऽनुस्वारागमः ।

No. 110.—AFTER what precedes *ru,* if we omit to substitute THE NASAL (of which the option is afforded by No. 109) ANUSWÁRA shall be the augment.

Thus, in the example under No. 108, if we do not substitute the nasal by No. 109, we must write *anuswára* as an augment.

खरवसानयोर्विसर्जनीयः ।८।३।१५।

खर्यवसाने च पदान्तस्य रस्य विसर्गः ।

No. 111.—Instead of the letter *r* final in *a pada,* there is VISARGA, WHEN KHAR FOLLOWS OR when there is A PAUSE (No. 144).

So the *r* in the example under No. 108 is changed to silent *h ;* thus *sanh* + *s* + *karttá.*

सम्पुङ्कानां सो वक्तव्यः । सँस्स्कर्ता । संस्स्कर्ता ।

No. 112.—"Instead OF SAM (No. 108) and also of the words PUM and KÁN, the substitution of s (for *visarga* by No. 122) SHOULD BE STATED to be invariable (to the exclusion of the optional retainment of *visarga* suggested by No. 123)."

Thus the example under No. 108 becomes *sansskarttá* (" one who completes"), the *n* representing either the sign of nasality (No. 109) or *anuswára* (No. 110).

पुमः खय्यम्परे ।८।३।६।

अम्परे खयि पुमो रुः । पुँस्कोकिलः । पुंस्कोकिलः ।

No. 113.—Instead OF the word PUM, WHEN KHAY FOLLOWED BY AM FOLLOWS it, there is *ru.*

Example, *pum* + *kokila*=*punskokila* " a male cuckoo", where the *n* represents either the sign of nasality (No. 109) or *anuswára* (No. 110). See also Nos. 111 and 112.

नश्छव्यप्रशान् ।८।३।७।

अम्परे छवि नान्तस्य पदस्य रुः ।

No. 114.—Instead OF N final in a *pada,* EXCEPTING the N in the word PRAŚÁN, WHEN CHHAV FOLLOWS, followed by *am,* there shall be *ru.*

For example, *chakrin* + *tráyaswa*—here *n* is final in a *pada,* and *chhav (t)* follows, followed by *am (r)*; hence the *n* becomes *r*, which by No. 111, becomes *visarga* before a hard consonant, the preceding vowel being either nasal, according to No. 109, or followed by *anuswára*, according to No. 110.

विसर्जनीयस्य सः ।८।३।३४।

खरि । चक्रिँस्त्रायस्व । चक्रिंस्त्रायस्व । अप्रशान् किम् । प्रशान् तनोति । पदस्येति किम् । हन्ति ।

No. 115.—Instead OF VISARGA, let there be the letter S, when *khar* (a hard consonant) follows. By this rule, in addition to No. 114, *chakrin+tráyaswa* becomes *chakrinstráyaswa* "Oh discus-armed! preserve", where the *n* represents either the nasal (No. 109) or *anuswára* (No. 110). Why did we say, in No. 114, "excepting the *n* in the word *praśán?*" Because that rule does not apply to such an instance as *praśân tanoti* "the quiet man spreads." And why "final in a *pada?*" Because it does not apply to such a case as *han+ti=hanti* "he kills," where *han* is not a *pada*.

नॄन् पे । ८ । ३ । १० ।

नॄनित्यस्य रुर्वा पे ।

No. 116.—Instead OF the *n* of the word NṚÍN, WHEN the letter P FOLLOWS, there is optionally *ru*.

कुप्वोः ≍क≍पौ च । ८ । ३ । ३७ ।

कवर्गे पवर्गे च विसर्गस्य ≍क≍पौ स्तः । चाद्विसर्गः ।

नॄँ≍ पाहि । नॄं≍ पाहि । नॄँः पाहि । नॄंः पाहि । नॄन् पाहि ।

No. 117.—AND also WHEN A consonant of the GUTTURAL class OR of the LABIAL class FOLLOWS, there are, instead of *visarga*, optionally JIHWÁMÚLÍYA AND UPADHMÁNÍYA (No. 15). The optionality of *visarga* is implied in the word "and," (No. 111). Thus the words *nṛín páhi* ("preserve thou men)" may be written (as exhibited above) in five ways, either simply, or with the nasal substitute (No. 109) and *upadhmáníya* (No. 117), or with the nasal and *visarga* (Nos. 109 and 111), or with the substitution of *anuswára* (No. 110) followed by either *upadhmáníya* or *visarga*.

तस्य परमाम्रेडितम् । ८ । १ । २ ।

द्विरुक्तस्य परमाम्रेडितं स्यात् ।

No. 118.—OF THAT which is twice uttered, let THE LATTER be called A REDUPLICATION *(ámreḍita)*.

कानाम्रेडिते । ८ । ३ । १२ ।

कान्नकारस्य रुराम्रेडिते । कॉंस्कान् । कांस्कान् ।

No. 119.—Instead OF the *n* of the word KÁN, let there be *ru*, WHEN A REDUPLICATION FOLLOWS.

Example, *kán+kán=kánskán* "which of them?," where the *n* of the first syllable is either the nasal (No. 109) or *anuswára* (No. 110). For the *s*, see Nos. 111 and 112.

छे च । ६ । १ । ७३ ।

ह्रस्वस्य छे तुक् । शिवच्छाया ।

No. 120.—AND WHEN the letter CHHA FOLLOWS, the augment of a short vowel is *tuk.* (No. 103).

Example, *śiva+chháyá=śivachchháyá* "the shadow of Śiva."—(No. 76).—

पदान्ताद्वा । ६ । १ । ७६ ।

दीर्घात् पदान्ताच्छे तुग्वा । लक्ष्मीच्छाया । लक्ष्मीछाया ।

No. 121.—When *chha* comes AFTER a long vowel FINAL IN A PADA, the augment *tuk* is OPTIONAL.

Example, *lakshmí+chháyá=lakshmíchchháyá* or *lakshmíchháyá*, "the shadow of *Lakshmí.*"—(No. 76).—

So much for the combination of consonants. We now come to

THE CHANGES OF VISARGA.

विसर्जनीयस्य सः । ८ । ३ । ३४ ।

विष्णुस्त्राता ।

No. 122.—Instead OF VISARGA, there is S, when a hard consonant follows.

Example, *vishṇuh+trátá=vishṇustrátá* "*Vishṇu* the preserver."—

वा शरि । ८ । ३ । ३६ ।

शरि विसर्गस्य विसर्गो वा । हरिः शेते । हरिश्शेते ।

No. 123.—WHEN ŚAR (a sibilant) FOLLOWS, *visarga* may OPTIONALLY be instead of *visarga*—or, in other words, it may remain unchanged.

Example, *harih śete* or *hariśśete* " *Hari* sleeps."—(No. 76).

ससजुषो रुः । ८ । २ । ६६ ।

पदान्तस्य सस्य सजुषश्च रुः स्यात् ।

No. 124.—Instead OF S, final in a *pada*, AND OF the word SAJUSH, let there be RU.

अतो रोरप्लुतादप्लुते । ६ । १ । ११३ ।

अप्लुतादतः परस्य रोरुः स्यादप्लुतेऽति । शिवोऽर्च्यः ।

No. 125.—Instead OF RU, coming AFTER AN UNPROLATED AT (short *a*), let there be U, WHEN AN UNPROLATED *at* also FOLLOWS.

Example, *śivar + archyah = śiva + u + archyah = śivo'rchyah* " *Śiva* to be worshipped." (Nos. 35 and 56).

हशि च । ६ । १ । ११४ ।

तथा । शिवो वन्द्यः ।

No. 126.—AND WHEN HAŚ (a soft consonant) FOLLOWS, *ru* shall be changed to *u*, when it is preceded by short *a*.

Example, *śivar + vandyah = śivo vandyah*; " *Śiva* to be worshipped."

भोभगोअघोअपूर्वस्य योऽशि । ८ । ३ । १७ ।

एतत्पूर्वस्य रोर्यादेशोऽशि । देवा इह । देवायिह । भोस् भगोस् अघोस् इति सान्ता निपाताः । तेषां रोर्यत्वे कृते ।

No. 127.—Instead OF RU, PRECEDED BY BHO BHAGO AGHO A or Á, Y is substituted, WHEN AŚ FOLLOWS.

Example, *devár + iha = deváyiha*, or (by No. 38) *devá iha* "the deities here,"—*Bhos bhagos* and *aghos* are interjections ending in *s*. When *y* has been substituted for their *ru* (derived from No. 124), it may chance to come under the operation of the rule here following.

हलि सर्वेषाम् ।८।३।२२।

भोभगोअघोअपूर्वस्य यस्य लोपः स्याद्धलि । भो देवाः । भगो नमस्ते । अघो याहि ।

No. 128.—Let there be elision of the Y OF ALL these, viz. the words in which it is preceded by *bho bhago agho a* or *á* (No. 127), when a consonant follows.

Example, *bho deváh* "Oh deities!", *bhago namaste* "oh! adoration to thee!", *agho yáhi* "oh! come."

रोऽसुपि ।८।२।६९।

अह्नो रेफादेशो न तु सुपि । अहरहः । अहर्गणः ।

No. 129.—R is the substitute of the word *ahan*, but NOT WHEN A CASE-AFFIX (No. 137) FOLLOWS.

Example, *ahan+ahah=aharahah* (No. 211) "day by day," *ahan+gaṇa=ahargaṇa* "a class of days."

रो रि ।८।३।१४।

रेफस्य रेफे परे लोपः ।

No. 130.—There is elision OF R, WHEN R FOLLOWS.

ढ्रलोपे पूर्वस्य दीर्घोऽणः ।६।३।१११।

ढरेफयोर्लोपनिमित्तयोः पूर्वस्याणो दीर्घः । पुना रमते । हरी रम्यः । शम्भू राजते । अणः किम् । तृढः । वृढः । मनस्रथ इत्यत्र रुत्वे कृते हशि चेत्युत्वे रो रीति लोपे च प्राप्ते ।

No. 131.—WHEN ḌHA OR R, CAUSING AN ELISION, FOLLOWS, instead OF a PRECEDING AṆ, there shall be ITS LONG vowel.

Example, *punar+ramate=puná ramate* "he again sports" (No. 130), *harir+ramyah=harí ramyah* "*Vishṇu* is beautiful," *śambhur+rájate=śambhú rájate* "*Śiva* is resplendent."

Why "of *aṇ*?" Because the rule does not include any other vowel. Example, *triḍh+ḍha=triḍha* "destroyed," *vriḍh+ḍha=vriḍha* "raised."

In the case of *manas+raṭha*, the change of *s* to *ru* (No. 124) having taken place, giving *manar+ratha*, two conflicting rules present themselves—the one (No. 126) directing that the *r* shall be changed to *u*, the other (No. 130) that the *r* shall be elided. The doubt, which rule shall take effect in such a case, has given occasion for the maxim here following.

विप्रतिषेधे परं कार्यम् । १ । ४ । २ ।

तुल्यबलविरोधे परं कार्यं स्यात् । इति प्राप्ते पूर्वत्रासिद्धमिति रो रीत्यस्यासिद्धत्वादुत्वमेव । मनोरथः ।

No. 132.—WHEN RULES of equal force PROHIBIT EACH OTHER, LET THE LAST (in the order of the *Ashṭádhyáyí*) TAKE EFFECT.

According to this maxim, in the example *manar+ratha* (under No. 131), the elision of the *r* ought to take place, by rule No. 130 which occurs in the eighth Lecture. But here the maxim (No. 39) interferes, which enjoins that a rule occurring in any of the three last Chapters of the Grammar shall be either as if it did not exist, or as if it had never come into operation, so far as concerns any rule that occurs earlier; and therefore No. 126, as if No. 130 did not exist, proceeds to substitute *u*, and thus we have *mana+u +ratha=manoratha* "a wish." (No. 35).

एतत्तदोः सुलोपोऽकोरनञ्समासे हलि । ६ । १ । १३२ ।

अककारयोरेतत्तदोर्यः सुस्तस्य लोपो हलि न तु नञ्समासे । एष विष्णुः । स शम्भुः । अकोः किम् । एषको रुद्रः । अनञ्समासे किम् । असशिवः । हलि किम् । एषोऽत्र ।

No. 133.—There is ELISION OF the SU (the case-affix of the nominative singular, No. 137) OF the pronouns ETAD AND TAD, provided they are WITHOUT the augment K (No. 1321), WHEN A CONSONANT FOLLOWS: BUT NOT if they are IN A COMPOUND WITH the privative particle NAÑ (*a*).

Example, *eshas+vishṇuh=esha vishṇuh* "that *Vishṇu*" (Nos. 338 and 169), *sas+śambhuh=sa śambhuh* "that *Śiva*" (No. 338).—Why "without the augment *k?*" Witness *eshako rudrah* "that *Śiva*." Why "not if they are in a compound with the privative particle *naṅ (a)*?" Witness *asas+śivah=asaśśivah* "not that *Śiva.*" (No. 76.) Why "when a consonant follows?" Witness *eshas+atra=esho'tra* "he here." (Nos. 124 and 125.)

सोऽचि लोपे चेत् पादपूरणम् । ६ । १ । १३४ ।

स इत्यस्य सोर्लोपः स्यादचि पादश्चेल्लोपे सत्येव पूर्येत । सेमामविड्ढि प्रभृतिम् । सैष दाशरथी रामः ।

No 134.—Let there be elision OF the *su* of SAS, even WHEN A VOWEL FOLLOWS (No. 133), IF BY THE ELISION alone THE VERSE CAN BE COMPLETED.

Example, *(sa+imám=) semám aviḍḍhi prabhṛitim* "do not separate this collection," *saisha dáśarathí rámah* "that *Ráma,* the son of *Daśaratha.*"

So much for the changes of *Visarga.* We now come to the declension of

MASCULINES ENDING IN VOWELS.

॥ अजन्तपुंलिङ्गाः ॥

अर्थवदधातुरप्रत्ययः प्रातिपदिकम् । १ । २ । ४५ ।

धातुं प्रत्ययं प्रत्ययान्तं च वर्जयित्वार्थवच्छब्दस्वरूपं प्रातिपदिकसंज्ञं स्यात् ।

No. 135.—Let any SIGNIFICANT form of word, NOT being A VERBAL ROOT (No. 49), AN AFFIX (No. 139), OR WHAT ENDS WITH AN AFFIX, be called A CRUDE FORM of word *(prátipadika).*

कृत्तद्धितसमासाश्च । १ । २ । ४६ ।

कृत्तद्धितान्तौ समासश्च तथा स्युः ।

No. 136.—AND let forms of words ending in the affixes called KṚIT (No. 329) and TADDHITA (Nos. 975 and 1067) AND COMPOUNDS (*samása,* No. 961) also be called *crude forms* (No. 135).

स्वौजसमौट्छष्टाभ्याम्भिस् ङेभ्याम्भ्यस् ङसिभ्याम्भ्यस् ङसोसाम् ङ्योस्सुप् । ४ । १ । २ ।

सु औ जस् इति प्रथमा। अम् औट् शस् इति द्वितीया। टा भ्याम् भिस् इति तृतीया। ङे भ्याम् भ्यस् इति चतुर्थी। ङसि भ्याम् भ्यस् इति पञ्चमी। ङस् ओस् आम् इति षष्ठी। ङि ओस् सुप् इति सप्तमी।

No. 137.—[In this aphorism the case-affixes are enunciated.—The cases, exclusive of the Vocative which is held to be a peculiar aspect of the nominative, are seven—1st Nominative, 2nd Accusative, 3rd Instrumental, 4th Dative, 5th Ablative, 6th Genitive, 7th Locative. The case-affixes, with their significations, are as follows:—]

	Singular.	Dual.	Plural.	
1st	*su*	*au*	*jas*	—
2nd	*am*	*auṭ*	*śas*	—
3rd	*ṭá*	*bhyám*	*bhis*	"*by.*"
4th	*ńe*	*bhyám*	*bhyas*	"*to.*"
5th	*ńasi*	*bhyám*	*bhyas*	"*from.*"
6th	*ńas*	*os*	*ám*	"*of.*"
7th	*ńi*	*os*	*sup*	"*in.*"

[After the elision of the indicatory letters, these affixes appear as follows:—

1st	*s*	*au*	*as*
2nd	*am*	*aù*	*as*
3rd	*á*	*bhyám*	*bhis*
4th	*e*	*bhyám*	*bhyas*
5th	*as*	*bhyám*	*bhyas*
6th	*as*	*os*	*ám*
7th	*i*	*os*	*su*

The reader who enters upon the study of the *Laghu Kaumudí* without any previous acquaintance with Sanskrit, will find the recollection of the rules more easy, and his apprehension of their import more distinct, if he make himself familiar with the most usual signs of the 7th, 6th, and 5th cases, for information respecting which he was referred (at Nos. 22, 27, and 87,) to the present section. When the uninflected word ends in a consonant; the affix is generally attached unaltered. Thus the 7th case singular of the word *ach*, in No. 21, is *achi*; the 7th dual of *omáń*, in No. 54, is *omáńos*; and the 7th plural of *etyedhatyúṭh*, in No. 42, is *etyedhat-yúṭhsu*. So again, the 6th case singular of *ik*, in No. 21, is *ikas*, which, by Nos. 124 and 126, becomes *iko* before a soft consonant; the 6th dual of *sajush*, in No. 124, is *sajushos*, which, by Nos. 124 and 130, becomes *sajusho* when followed by *r*; and the 6th plural of *jhal*, in No. 25, is *jhalám*, which, by No. 94, becomes *jhaláń*. So again, the 5th case singular of *eń* in No. 56, is *eńas*, which, by Nos. 124 and 111, becomes *eńah*; the 5th dual of a term ending in a vowel occurs in No. 73, *viz. rahábhyám*, which, by No. 94, changes its final to *ń*.

When the uninflected term ends in a vowel, the case-affixes are liable to several variations. Among the most noticeable modifications are the following, which take the place of the final *a*:—

	Singular.	Dual.	Plural.
5th	*át*	*ábhyám*	—
6th	*asya*	—	*ánám*
7th	*e*	—	*eshu*

Examples of these terminations occur in No. 35, where *át* becomes *ád* (by No. 82); in No. 73—*rahábhyám*; in No. 26—*saṅyogántasya*; in No. 30—*samánám*; in No. 31—*pratyaye*;—and in No. 44—*úhoḍhoḍhyeshaishyeshu*.]

ङ्याप्प्रातिपदिकात् ।४।१।१।

No. 138.—AFTER what ends with the feminine terminations ṄÍ (No. 256 &c.) or ÁP (No. 1341 &c.) OR after A CRUDE FORM (No. 135 &c.).—

[This aphorism is one of those which are said to exercise an authority (*adhikára*) over other aphorisms, inasmuch as they consist of terms which other aphorisms, in order to complete their sense, are under the necessity of borrowing. (No. 5.) Some aphorisms, such as the present, consist solely of words which, taken by themselves, convey neither a definition nor a direction, and which are enunciated solely for the purpose of avoiding the necessity of repeating the same words in a number of succeeding aphorisms.

Such aphorisms are said to be *keraládhikára*, or "intended simply to regulate the sense of others." On the other hand, in No. 21, only a portion of the aphorism, viz., the word *achi*, exercises *adhikára*, which it does over the sense of No. 55 &c.]

प्रत्ययः । ३ । १ । १ ।

No. 139.—AN AFFIX.

[This, like No. 138, is an aphorism intended solely to regulate the sense of others.]

परश्च । ३ । १ । २ ।

इत्यधिकृत्य । ङ्यन्तादाबन्तात् प्रातिपदिकाच्च परे स्वादयः प्रत्ययाः स्युः ।

No. 140.—AND SUBSEQUENT.

[This, like Nos. 138 and 139, is an aphorism intended solely to regulate the sense of others. The sense of the three aphorisms combined is as follows :—]

Let the affixes *su* &c. (No. 137) come after, or be attached to words ending in *ńí* or *áp* (that is to say, words with feminine terminations,) and after crude forms (No. 135).

सुपः । १ । ४ । १०३ ।

सुपस्त्रीणि त्रीणि वचनान्येकश एकवचनद्विवचनबहुवचनसंज्ञानि स्युः ।

No. 141.—OF SUP (which is a *pratyáhára* formed of *su* the first of the case-affixes, and the final *p* of the last of them,) let the three expressions in each successive set of three be severally termed "the expression for one" (singular), "the expression for two" (dual), and "the expression for many" (plural).

द्व्येकयोर्द्विवचनैकवचने । १ । ४ । २२ ।

द्वित्वैकत्वयोरेते स्तः ।

No. 142.—The DUAL AND the SINGULAR case-affixes are to be employed severally IN the sense of DUALITY AND UNITY.

बहुषु बहुवचनम् ।१।४।२१।

बहुत्वविवक्षायां बहुवचनं स्यात् ।

No. 143.—IN expressing MULTEITY, let A PLURAL case-affix be employed.

विरामोऽवसानम् ।१।४।११०।

वर्णानामभावोऽवसानसंज्ञः स्यात् । रुत्वविसर्गौ । रामः ।

No. 144.—Let CESSATION, or the absence of succeeding letters, be called a PAUSE *(avasána)*.

We now proceed to decline the word *ráma* (the name of an incarnation of *Vishṇu*).—Attaching the case-affix of the 1st case singular, after removing the indicatory vowel (No. 36), we get *rámas:* then the *s* becomes *ru* by No. 124, and finally *visarga* by No. 111, giving *rámaḥ*.

सरूपाणामेकशेष एकविभक्तौ ।१।२।६४।

एकविभक्तौ यानि सरूपाण्येव दृष्टानि तेषामेक एव शिष्यते ।

No. 145.—IN ANY INDIVIDUAL CASE *(vibhakti)* there is but ONE RETAINED OF the WORDS, ALWAYS SIMILAR IN FORM. [That is to say, the dual, which means "two *Rámas*," implies "*Ráma* and *Ráma;*" and the plural, which means "more *Rámas* than two," implies at least "*Ráma*, and *Ráma*, and *Ráma;*" and of these words, similar in sense as well as in form, we are to retain but one, when adding the affixes of the dual and plural. It would be otherwise had we to attach a dual affix to an aggregate signifying the two opponents "*Ráma and Rávaṇa*," or the two which, in some of their inflections, differ in sound as well as in sense, *mátṛi* "a mother," and *mátṛi* "a measurer." But when the words never differ in form, though they do so in sense, this rule may apply. Thus *śrí* signifies "beauty" and also "wealth"—and "beauty and wealth" may be implied in the dual *śriyau*.]

In the 1st case dual, then, we have *ráma+au*, which might appear to furnish occasion for the operation of the rule here following to the exclusion of No. 41, which gives way in accordance with No. 132.

प्रथमयोः पूर्वसवर्णः । ६ । १ । १०२ ।

अकः प्रथमाद्वितीययोरचि पूर्वसवर्णदीर्घ एकादेशः स्यात् । इति प्राप्ते ।

No. 146.—When *ach* OF THE FIRST OR SECOND CASE follows *ak*, let THE LONG VOWEL HOMOGENEOUS WITH THE ANTECEDENT be the substitute singly for both. By this rule *ráma+au* would become *rámá*, but the rule here following interposes.

नादिचि । ६ । १ । १०४ ।

आदिचि न पूर्वसवर्णदीर्घः । वृद्धिरेचि । रामौ ।

No. 147.—WHEN ICH FOLLOWS A OR Á, the substitution of the long vowel homogeneous with the antecedent (No. 146) shall NOT take place. Then, by No. 41, thus freed from the obstruction of No. 146, we have *ráma+au=rámau* "two *Rámas*."

चुटू । १ । ३ । ७ ।

प्रत्ययाद्यौ चुटू इतौ स्तः ।

No. 148.—PALATAL *(chu)* OR CEREBRAL *(ṭu)* LETTERS initial in an affix are to be elided. Therefore, in the affix of the 1st case plural, the *j* of *jas* is to be elided, leaving *as*.

विभक्तिश्च । १ । ४ । १०४ ।

सुप्तिङौ विभक्तिसंज्ञौ स्तः ।

No. 149.—AND *sup* (the case-affixes—No. 137) and *tiń* (the verbal affixes enunciated in No. 407) are called VIBHAKTI.

न विभक्तौ तुस्माः । १ । ३ । ४ ।

विभक्तिस्थास्तवर्गसमा नेतः । इति सस्य नेत्त्वम् । रामाः ।

No. 150.—TU (the dentals *ta tha da dha na*) and S and M, standing IN A VIBHAKTI (No. 149) are NOT to be elided. Therefore the final *s* in *jas* is not to be elided, notwithstanding Nos. 5 and 7; & *rámás*, by Nos. 124 and 111, becomes *rámáh* "*Rámas*"—more than two.

एकवचनं सम्बुद्धिः ।२।३।४९।

संबोधने प्रथमाया एकवचनं सम्बुद्धिसंज्ञं स्यात् ।

No. 151.—In the sense of the vocative, let the SINGULAR of the first case be called SAMBUDDHI.

यस्मात् प्रत्ययविधिस्तदादि प्रत्ययेऽङ्गम् ।१।४।१३।

यः प्रत्ययो यस्मात् क्रियते तदादि शब्दस्वरूपं तस्मिन् प्रत्यये परेऽङ्गं स्यात् ।

No. 152.—AFTER WHATSOEVER there is AN AFFIX (*pratyaya*) ENJOINED, let WHAT BEGINS THEREWITH, in the form in which it appears WHEN THE AFFIX FOLLOWS it, be called AN INFLECTIVE BASE (*aṅga*).

For example, in the first case singular it is enjoined that the affix *su* (No. 137) shall follow the crude form of a noun—for instance *ráma*. Then this word *ráma*, if it remain unchanged when the affix follows it, is called *aṅga*.

एङ्ह्रस्वात् सम्बुद्धेः ।६।१।६९।

एङन्ताद्ध्रस्वान्ताच्चाङ्गाद्धल्लुप्यते सम्बुद्धेश्चेत् । हे राम । हे रामौ । हे रामाः ।

No. 153.—AFTER an inflective base (No. 152) ending in *eṅ* OR IN A SHORT VOWEL, a consonant is elided if it be that OF SAMBUDDHI (No. 151). Hence the *s* is elided in *he ráma* "Oh *Ráma !*" In the dual and plural the vocative is the same as the 1st case; so *he rámau* "Oh two *Rámas !*" *he rámáh* "Oh *Rámas !*" We now come to the 2nd case, and we find *Ráma+am*, where we might expect No. 55 to take effect. But this is prevented by the rule here following.

अमि पूर्वः ।६।१।१०७।

अकोऽम्यचि पूर्वरूपमेकादेशः । रामम् । रामौ ।

No. 154.—WHEN the vowel of AM (the affix of the 2nd case singular) FOLLOWS *ak*, the form of THE PRIOR is the single substitute for both. Hence *ráma+am=rámam* "*Ráma*", *ráma+au=rámau* "two *Rámas*" (No. 141). In the 2nd case plural we find *ráma+śas* and the rule here following.

लशक्वतद्धिते । १ । ३ । ८ ।

तद्धितवर्जप्रत्ययाद्या लशकवर्गा इतः स्युः ।

No. 155.—The letters L, Ś, AND KU (that is to say, *ka kha ga gha ń*) are indicatory IN AN AFFIX NOT belonging to the class TADDHITA (the class employed in forming nominal derivatives No. 1067). Thus the example under consideration becomes *ráma+as;* then No. 146 comes into operation, and the rule here following enjoins a substitution.

तस्माच्छसो नः पुंसि । ६ । १ । १०३ ।

पूर्वसवर्णदीर्घात् परो यः शसस्सस्तस्य नः स्यात् पुंसि ।

No. 156.—AFTER THAT long vowel homogeneous with the prior (No. 146), N is substituted in place OF the S of ŚAS, IN THE MASCULINE. Thus we have *rámán :* a form which might seem to give occasion for the rule next following.

अट्कुप्वाङ्नुम्व्यवायेऽपि । ८ । ४ । २ ।

अट् कवर्गः पवर्ग आङ् नुम् एतैर्व्यस्तैर्यथासंभवमिलितैश्च व्यवधानेऽपि रषाभ्यां परस्य नस्य णः समानपदे । इति प्राप्ते ।

No. 157.—EVEN WHEN a SEPARATION is caused BY the intervention of the *pratyáhára* AT, KU, PU, (the five gutturals and five labials), ÁŃ (the particle *á*), AND NUM *(anuswára),* singly or combined in any possible way, the substitution of the cerebral for the dental *n* following *r* or *sh* in the same *pada* (No. 292) shall take place.

By this rule the final *n* in *rámán* would be replaced by a cerebral, but the rule next following prohibits the substitution.

पदान्तस्य । ८ । ४ । ३७ ।

नस्य णो न । रामान् ।

No. 158.—The cerebral *ṇ* shall not be substituted in the room OF dental *n* FINAL IN A PADA. Thus finally we have *rámán* "the *Rámas.*"

In the 3rd case singular we first find *ráma* + *ṭá,* but the rule next following enjoins a substitution.

टाङसिङसामिनात्स्याः ।७।१।१२।

अदन्ताट्टादीनामिनादयः स्युः । णत्वम् । रामेण ।

No. 159.—Let INA ÁT AND SYA be substituted in the room OF ṬÁ (3rd singular) ṄASI (5th sing.) AND ṄAS (6th sing.) after what ends in short *a.*

Thus we have *ráma* + *ina,* which after the cerebral *ṇ* has been substituted by No. 157, becomes *rámeṇa* "by *Ráma.*" (No. 35.)

In the 3rd case dual we first find *ráma* + *bhyám,* which calls into operation the rule following.

सुपि च ।७।३।१०२।

यञादौ सुप्यतोऽङ्गस्य दीर्घः । रामाभ्याम् ।

No. 160.—AND WHEN A CASE-AFFIX beginning with *yañ* FOLLOWS, the long vowel shall be substituted for the final of an inflective base (No. 152) ending in short *a.* Hence *rámábhyám* "by two *Rámas.*"

In the 3rd plural we find *ráma* + *bhis,* and here also a substitution is enjoined.

अतो भिस ऐस् ।७।१।९।

अनेकाल् शित् सर्वस्य । रामैः ।

No. 161.—AFTER what ends in SHORT A, let there be AIS in the room OF BHIS. From No. 58 we learn that this substitute takes the place not of the first letter merely (No. 88), but of the whole term *(bhis).* By Nos. 124 and 111 we thus get *rámaiḥ* "by the *Rámas.*"

In the 4th singular, we find *ráma* + *ṅe,* and again a substitution is enjoined.

ङेर्यः ।७।१।१३।

अतोऽङ्गात् परस्य ङेर्यादेशः ।

No. 162.—Let YA be the substitute OF ŃE after an inflective base ending in short *a*.

Thus we have *ráma + ya*, an instance which the rule next cited takes cognizance of.

स्थानिवदादेशोऽनल्विधौ ।१।१।५६।

आदेशः स्थानिवत् स्यान्न तु स्थान्यलाश्रयविधौ । इति स्थानिवत्वात् सुपि चेति दीर्घः । रामाय । रामाभ्याम् ।

No. 163.—A SUBSTITUTE IS LIKE (or succeeds to all the titles and liabilities of) THAT WHOSE PLACE IT SUPPLIES—BUT NOT IN the case of A RULE the occasion for the operation OF which is furnished by the LETTERS of the original term.

According to this maxim, the *ya* substituted for *ńe*, by No. 162, is, like it, entitled a case-affix (*sup*—No. 137) ; but it is not held to consist of the same letters as *ńe* ; hence, as it begins with the letter *y* (of the *pratyáhára yań*), it furnishes occasion for the operation of No. 160, by which the short *a* of the inflective base is lengthened. Thus we have *rámáya* "to *Ráma*." The 4th dual *rámábhyám* "to two *Rámas*"—is formed like the 3rd.

In the 4th plural we have first *ráma + bhyas,* which calls into operation the rule next following (and not No. 160).

बहुवचने झल्येत् ।७।३।१०३।

झलादौ बहुवचने सुप्यतोऽङ्गस्यैकारः । रामेभ्यः । सुपि किम् । पचध्वम् ।

No. 164.—WHEN A PLURAL case-affix beginning with JHAL FOLLOWS, E is the substitute for the final short *a* of an inflective base.

Thus we have *rámebhyah* "to the *Rámas*." Why do we say "case-affix ?" Because the rule does not extend to the verbal affixes. Ex. *pacha + dhwam = pachadhwam* "do ye cook."

In the 5th sing. we have first *ráma* + *ńasi*, and *át* is substituted for *ńasi* by No. 159, and we get *rámát* (No. 55), a form to which the rule next cited has reference.

वावसाने । ८ । ४ । ५६ ।

अवसाने झलां चरो वा । रामात् । रामाद् । रामाभ्याम् । रामेभ्यः । रामस्य ।

No. 165.—WHEN A PAUSE (No. 144) ENSUES, *char* may OPTIONALLY be substituted for *jhal*. So we may write *rámát* or (by No. 82) *rámád* "from *Ráma*."

The dual and plural of the 5th case are like those of the 4th :—*rámábhyám* "from two *Rámas*", *rámebhyah* "from the *Rámas*."

In the 6th sing. we have first *ráma* + *ńas* ; and, on making the substitution enjoined by No. 159, we get *rámasya* "of *Ráma*." In the dual we have first *ráma* + *os*, which brings into operation the rule next following.

ओसि च । ७ । ३ । १०४ ।

अतोऽङ्गस्यैकारः । रामयोः ।

No. 166.—AND WHEN OS FOLLOWS, then *e* is substituted for the final short *a* of an inflective base. Thus we have *ráme* + *os* = *rámayoh* "of two *Rámas*"—(No. 29).

In the 6th plural we have first *ráma* + *ám*, which calls into operation the rule next following.

ह्रस्वनद्यापो नुट् । ७ । १ । ५४ ।

ह्रस्वान्तान्नद्यन्तादाबन्ताच्चाङ्गात् परस्यामो नुडागमः ।

No. 167.—NUṬ shall be the augment OF WHAT comes AFTER an inflective base ending in A SHORT vowel, OR in NADÍ (No. 215) OR in ÁP (No. 1341).

From No. 103 we learn that this augment is to be prefixed. We thus get *ráma* + *nám*, to which the rule following has reference.

नामि । ६ । ४ । ३ ।

अजन्ताङ्गस्य दीर्घः । रामाणाम् । रामे । रामयोः । एत्वे कृते ।

No. 168.—When nám follows, the long vowel shall be substituted for the final of an inflective base which ends in a vowel. Thus we get *rámáṇám* "of the *Rámas.*" (No. 157.)

In the 7th sing. we have *ráma+ńi*, which, by Nos. 156 and 35, becomes *ráme* "in *Ráma.*" The dual is like the 6th—*rámayoh* "in two *Rámas.*"

In the 7th plural we have *ráma+su*, which, by No. 164, becomes *ráme+su*, and this calls into operation the rule following.

आदेशप्रत्यययोः । ८ । ३ । ५९ ।

इण्कुभ्यां परस्यापदान्तस्यादेशः प्रत्ययावयवश्च यः सस्तस्य मूर्धन्यादेशः । ईषद्विवृतस्य सस्य तादृश एव षः । रामेषु । एवं कृष्णादयोऽप्यदन्ताः ।

No. 169.—The cerebral substitute shall take the place of the dental *s*, when the s is part of a substitute or of an affix following *iṇ* or *ku*, and is not the final letter of the *pada.*—Of the cerebrals, the *íshadvivṛita sh* (No. 16) most resembles the *s*, and is therefore the proper substitute. Thus we get *rámeshu* "in the *Rámas.*"

In the same way are declined *kṛishṇa* and other words ending in short *a*.

[Having explained this declension very fully, we shall indicate the steps of the process as they recur in the sequel more concisely.]

सर्वादीनि सर्वनामानि । १ । १ । २७ ।

सर्व विश्व उभ उभय डतर डतम अन्य अन्यतर इतर त्वत् त्व नेम सम सिम । पूर्वपरावरदक्षिणोत्तरापराधराणि व्यवस्थायामसंज्ञायाम् । स्वमज्ञातिधनाख्यायाम् । अन्तरं बहिर्योगोपसंव्यानयोः । त्यद् तद् यद् एतद् इदम् अदस् एक द्वि युष्मद् अस्मद् भवतु किम् ।

No. 170.—Sarva &c. are called pronominals (*sarvanáma*).

This class of words consists of the following:—*sarva* "all", *viśwa* "all," *ubha* "both," *ubhaya* "both," *ḍatara ḍatama* (affixes employed in the formation of such words as *katara* "which of two?" and *katama* "which of many?") *anya* "other," *anyatara* "either," *itara* "other," *twat* or *twa* "other," *nema* "half," *sama* "all," *sima* "whole." The seven following are pronominals when they imply a relation in time or place, not when they are names—viz., *púrva* "prior, east," *para* "after," *avara* "posterior, west," *dakshiṇa* "south, right," *uttara* "inferior, other, north," *apara* "other," *adhara* "inferior, west;"—so also *swa* when it signifies "own," not when it signifies "a kinsman" or "property;" *antara* when it signifies "outer" or "an under garment;" *tyad* or *tad* "he, she, it, that," *yad* "who, which, what," *etad* "this," *idam* "this,' *adas* "this, that," *eka* "one," *dwi* "two," *yushmad* "thou," *asmad* "I," *bhavatu* "your honour, your excellency," *kim* "who? what?"—

जसः शी।७।१।१७।

अदन्तात् सर्वनाम्नो जसः शी स्यात्। अनेकाल्त्वात् सर्वादेशः। सर्वे।

No. 171.—After a pronominal ending in short *a*, let śí be the substitute OF JAS (1st case plur.). As the substitute consists of more letters than one, it takes the place of the whole (No. 58). Ex. *sarva+í=sarve* ("all"—Nos. 156 and 35).

सर्वनाम्नः स्मै।७।१।१४।

अतः सर्वनाम्नो ङेः स्मै। सर्वस्मै।

No. 172.—AFTER A PRONOMINAL ending in short *a*, SMAI is the substitute of *ńe* (4th sing).

Example, *sarvasmaí* "to all."

ङसिङ्योः स्मात्स्मिनौ।७।१।१५।

अतः सर्वनाम्न एतयोरेतौ स्तः। सर्वस्मात्।

No. 173.—After a pronominal ending in short *a*, SMÁT AND SMIN are the substitutes OF ŃASI (5th sing.) and ŃI (7th sing.) Example, *sarvasmát* "from all." (No. 160.)

आमि सर्वनाम्नः सुट्। ७।१।५२।

अवर्णान्तात् परस्य सर्वनाम्नो विहितस्यामः सुडागमः। एत्वे षत्वे। सर्वेषाम्। सर्वस्मिन्। शेषं रामवत्। एवं विश्वादयोऽप्यदन्ताः। उभशब्दो नित्यं द्विवचनान्तः। उभौ २। उभाभ्याम् ३। उभयोः २। तस्येह पाठोऽकजर्थः। डतरडतमौ प्रत्ययौ। प्रत्ययग्रहणे तदन्तग्रहणमिति तदन्ता ग्राह्याः। नेम इत्यर्धे। समः सर्वपर्यायस्तुल्यपर्यायस्तु न समानामिति ज्ञापकात्।

No. 174.—SUṬ is the augment of *ám* (6th plur.), WHEN ÁM COMES AFTER A PRONOMINAL ending in *a* or *á*. Example (Nos. 164 and 169) *sarveshám* "of all." In the 7th sing. (No. 173) *sarvasmin* "in all." The rest of the declension is like that of *ráma*. In the same way are declined *viśwa* and the other pronominals (No. 170) ending in short *a*. The word *ubha* "both" takes invariably the dual affixos. Ex. *ubhau* "both," *ubhábhyám* "by, to, or from both," *ubhayoh* "of or in both." The object of its being inserted in the list of pronominals (whilst its declension does not differ from that of *ráma*) is its taking the augment *akach* (No. 1321, which it could not take if it were not a pronominal). The terms *ḍatara* and *ḍatama* are affixes. "By citing the affix we cite that which ends therewith:"—(says *Patañjali*) so the words that end with these affixes are to be reckoned pronominals. The word *nema* is a pronominal when it signifies "half." That *sama*, which is a pronominal when synonymous with *sarva* "all," is not so when synonymous with *tulya* "like" we learn from the expression *samánám* "of equals"—in No. 30—(which would have been *sameshám*, if the word, in that sense, had been a pronominal.)

पूर्वपरावरदक्षिणोत्तरापराधराणि व्यवस्थायामसंज्ञायाम्। १। १। ३४।

एतेषां व्यवस्थायामसंज्ञायां सर्वनामसंज्ञा गणसूत्रात् सर्वत्र या प्राप्ता सा जसि वा। पूर्वे। पूर्वाः। असंज्ञायां किम्। उत्तराः कुरवः। स्वाभिधेयापेक्षावधिनियमो व्यवस्था। व्यवस्थायां किम्। दक्षिणा गायकाः। कुशला इत्यर्थः।

No. 175.—The name of pronominal (No. 170) belongs to **PÚRVA** "prior," **PARA** "after," **AVARA** "posterior," **DAKSHIṆA** "south," **UTTARA** "inferior, other, north," **APARA** "other," **AND ADHARA** "inferior," **WHEN THEY DISCRIMINATE RELATIVE POSITION, NOT** when they are **NAMES**.

The designation of pronominal assigned to these in every case by the aphorism No. 170, which implies the list of words enumerated in the commentary thereon, is optional when *jas* (1st plural) follows.—Ex. *púrve* (by No. 171) or *púrváh* (No. 151).—Why do we say "not when they are names?" Witness *uttaráh* (not *uttare*) when the word is used as a name for "the *Kurus*."

That there is "a specification, (*niyama*,) or tacit implication, of a determinate point (*avadhi*), with reference to which something is to be described by the word itself" is what we mean when we say that "a relation in time or place (*avasthá*) is implied,"—[For example, we wish to describe Benares as being *southern* (*dakshiṇa*). To do this, we may specify some point——say one of the peaks of the *Himálaya*—with reference to which Benares may be described as "a place to the southward." Again, we here may thus speak of the people to the south of the *Vindhyá* mountains, as being "southern," not with reference to the inhabitants of Ceylon, but with reference (as every one here understands, by tacit implication) to us ourselves who live to the north of the *Vindhyá* range]. Why do we say, "when a relation in time or place is implied?" Witness *dakshiṇáh* (not *dakshiṇe*) *gáthakáh*, meaning "clever singers."

स्वमज्ञातिधनाख्यायाम् ।१।१।३५।

ज्ञातिधनान्यवाचिनः स्वशब्दस्य प्राप्ता संज्ञा जसि वा । स्वे । स्वाः । आत्मीया आत्मान इति वा । ज्ञातिधनवाचिनस्तु स्वाः । ज्ञातयोऽर्था वा ।

No. 176.—The designation, as a pronominal, of the word **SWA** (No. 170) **WHEN IT SIGNIFIES SOMETHING ELSE THAN A KINSMAN OR PROPERTY**, optionally obtains when *jas* (1st plural) follows. Thus we have either *swe* (No. 171) or *swáh* (No. 151) in the sense of "own" or "selves," but *swáh* alone, in the sense of "kinsmen" or "articles of property."

अन्तरं बहिर्योगोपसंव्यानयोः । १ । १ । ३६ ।

बाह्ये परिधानीये चार्थेऽन्तरशब्दस्य प्राप्ता संज्ञा जसि वा । अन्तरे अन्तरा वा गृहाः । बाह्या इत्यर्थः । अन्तरे अन्तरा वा शाटकाः । परिधानीया इत्यर्थः ।

No. 177.—The designation, as a pronominal, of the word *antara* (No. 170) WHEN IT SIGNIFIES "OUTER" OR "A LOWER GARMENT," optionally obtains when *jas* (1st plural) follows. Thus we may write *antare* or *antaráh,* when speaking of houses "external" (for instance to the walls of the city); and so also when speaking of the petticoats worn under the upper garment.

पूर्वादिभ्यो नवभ्यो वा । ७ । १ । १६ ।

एभ्यो ङसिङ्योः स्मात्स्मिनौ वा स्तः । पूर्वस्मात् । पूर्वात् । पूर्वस्मिन् । पूर्वे । एवं परादीनाम् । शेषं सर्ववत् ।

No. 178.—AFTER THE NINE BEGINNING WITH PÚRVA, (that is to say, after *púrva, para, avara, dakshiṇa, uttara, apara, adhara, swa,* and *antara*) the substitution of *smát* and *smin* for *ńasi* and *ńi* (No. 173) is OPTIONAL.

Thus we may write either *púrvasmát* or *púrvát, púrvasmin* or *púrve* :—and so of *para* &c. In other respects the declension of these words is the same as that of *sarva.*

प्रथमचरमतयाल्पार्धकतिपयनेमाश्च । १ । १ । ३३ ।

एते जस्युक्तसंज्ञा वा स्युः । प्रथमे । प्रथमाः । तयः प्रत्ययः । द्वितये । द्वितयाः । शेषं रामवत् । नेमे । नेमाः । शेषं सर्ववत् ।

No. 179.—The words PRATHAMA "first," CHARAMA "last," TAYA (which is an affix, respecting which see the maxim cited under No. 174.—), ALPA "few," ARDHA "half," KATIPAYA "some," and NEMA "half," shall be optionally termed pronominal (No. 170) when *jas* (1st pl.) follows.

Thus we may write *prathame* or *prathamáh.* Of the affix *taya* we have an example in *dwitaye* or *dwitayáh* "second." The rest of the declension is like *ráma.* The word *nema* is enumerated among the pronominals in No. 170—therefore, though by this rule the nominative plural may be like *ráma,* the rest of the declension is like *sarva.*

तीयस्य ङित्सु वा । द्वितीयस्मै । द्वितीयायेत्यादि । एवं तृतीयः । निर्जरः ।

No. 180.—WHEN CASE-AFFIXES WITH AN INDICATORY Ń FOLLOW, (such are the 4th, 5th, 6th, and 7th singular) the term pronominal (No. 170) is OPTIONALLY a name OF what ends in TÍYA.

Example, *dwitíyasmai* or *dwitíyáya* "to the second," and so on.—So also *tṛitíya* "the third."

We now come to the declension of the word *nirjara* "imperishable,"—which is derived from the feminine word *jará* "decrepitude."

जराया जरसन्यतरस्याम् । ७ । २ । १०१ ।

अजादौ विभक्तौ । पदाङ्गाधिकारे तस्य तदन्तस्य च । निर्दिश्यमानस्यादेशा भवन्ति । एकदेशविकृतमनन्यवदिति जरशब्दस्य जरस् । निर्जरसौ । निर्जरस इत्यादि । पक्षे हलादौ च रामवत् । विश्वपाः ।

No. 181.—Instead OF JARÁ there is OPTIONALLY JARAS, when a *vibhakti* (No. 170) beginning with a vowel follows.

Where a rule refers to a *pada* or an *ańga* (No. 153), the rule, if it apply to a particular word, applies also to what ends with the word. Hence this rule, which applies to the word *jará,* applies also to *nirjara,* just as, in English, the substitution, in the plural, of "geese," for "goose," applies also to the case of "wildgeese." But here a question might arise, suggested by No 58, as to whether the substitute should not take the place of the whole word—so that the plural of "wildgoose," should become "geese" simply. To guard against this, it is declared that "Substitutes take the place of that only which is exhibited (when the substitute is enjoined)."—Thus, in *nirjara,* the substitute takes the place of the *jara* only, for *jará* only was exhibited when the substitute *jaras* was enjoined. Here another objection may be raised, for *jaras* was enjoined to take the place of *jará*, with a long final, not of *jara*, the final of which is short. This objection is met by the maxim that "What is partially altered does not thereby become something quite different," (and this is illustrated in the *Mahábháshya* by the case of a dog, which, having lost his ears, does not thereby lose his personal identity,) :—so *jaras* may be the substitute of the partially altered *jara*. Thus we get *nirjarasau* "two imperishables," *nirjarasah* "imperishables," and so on.—On the other alternative, and when the affixes begin with a consonant, the word is declined like *ráma*.

We now come to the declension of *viśwapá* "the preserver of all."

दीर्घाज्जसि च । ६ । १ । १०५ ।

विश्वपौ । विश्वपाः । हे विश्वपाः । विश्वपाम् । विश्वपौ ।

No. 182.—AND WHEN JAS (1st pl.) or *ich (pratyáhára)* COMES AFTER a LONG vowel, the long vowel homogeneous with the prior is not substituted for both (by No. 146, any more than under the circumstances stated in No. 147). We have therefore the 1st dual *viśwapau* (by No. 41), and plural *viśwapáh* (by No. 55),—In the vocative singular we have *he viśwapáh*, the same as in the nominative. In the 2nd case sing. *viśwapám* (No. 155) ; in the dual, as in the 1st case, *viśwapau*.

सुडनपुंसकस्य । १ । १ । ४३ ।

स्वादिपञ्चवचनानि सर्वनामस्थानसंज्ञानि स्युरक्लीबस्य ।

No, 183—Let SUṬ (which is a *pratyáhára* formed of *su* the first case-affix, and *auṭ* the fifth, and which serves as a name common to the five), but NOT OF a NEUTER word be called *sarvanámasthána*.

स्वादिष्वसर्वनामस्थाने । १ । ४ । १७ ।

कप्रत्ययावधिषु स्वादिष्वसर्वनामस्थानेषु पूर्वं पदं स्यात् ।

No. 184—WHEN the affixes BEGINNING WITH SU and ending with *ka* (which occurs in the 70th aphorism of the 3rd Chapter of the 5th Lecture) FOLLOW, NOT being SARVANÁMASTHÁNA

(No. 183), let what precedes be called *pada*. [This is an extension of the application of the term *pada* as laid down in No. 14].

यचि भम् । १ । ४ । १८ ।

यादिष्वजादिषु च कप्रत्ययावधिषु स्वादिष्वसर्वनामस्थानेषु पूर्वं भसंज्ञं स्यात् ।

No. 185—AND WHEN affixes, with an initial Y OR initial VOWEL, beginning with *su* and ending with *ka*, follow, not being *sarvanámasthána* (No. 183), let what precedes be called BHA.

[The question here arises, whether a word which gets the name of *bha* from this rule, and of *pada* from the one preceding, is to retain both names, or, if not, which name is to be retained. The rule next cited supplies the answer].

आ कडारादेका संज्ञा । १ । ४ । १ ।

इत ऊर्ध्वं कडाराः कर्मधारय इत्यतः प्रागेकस्यैकैव संज्ञा ज्ञेया । या परानवकाशा च ।

No. 186.—From this point (that is to say, from the 1st aphorism of the 4th Chapter of the 1st Lecture), TO the aphorism "KAḌÁRÁH *karmadháraye*" (which is the 38th aphorism of the 2nd Chapter of the 2nd Lecture) only ONE NAME of each thing named is to be recognised—viz : that which comes last (where the claims are otherwise equal—(see No. 132) and that which, were its claim disallowed, would have no other opportunity of conducing to any result (see No. 41).

आतो धातोः । ६ । ४ । १४० ।

आकारान्तो यो धातुस्तदन्तस्य भस्याङ्गस्य लोपः । अलोऽन्त्यस्य । विश्वपः । विश्वपा । विश्वपाभ्यामित्यादि । एवं शङ्खध्मादयः । धातोः किम् । हाहान् । हरिः । हरी ।

No. 187.—Let there be elision OF the final letter of an inflective base, entitled to the designation of *bha* (No. 185), when it ends in A DHÁTU (No. 49) WITH LONG Á as its final letter.

The word *viśvapá* ends in a *dhátu*, viz. *pá* (in the sense of "preserving") which has long *á* as its final letter; and the word which, by No. 152, is called an inflective base (*ańga*) when an affix follows, is, by No. 185, entitled to the designation of *bha* when the case-affix (not being one of the five first) begins with a vowel. The long *á* is then elided.

Example, *viśwapá+śas=viśwapah* (2nd case plural), *viświapá+ṭá=viśwapá* (3rd sing). Before the consonantal terminations there is no change. Example, *viśwapábhyám* (3rd dual). In the same way are declined *śańkhadhmá* "the blower of a conch-shell," and the like.—Why do we say, "when it ends in a *dhátu*?" Because primitive words, like *háhá* "a *gandharba*," do not come within the scope of the rule. Example, 2nd pl. *háhán* (Nos. 146 and 156).

We now come to the declension of a noun ending in short *i*—*hari* "a name of *Vishṇu*:" 1st s. *hariḥ*, 1st du. *harí* (No. 146).

जसि च । ७ । ३ । १०९ ।

ह्रस्वान्तस्याङ्गस्य गुणः । हरयः ।

No. 188.—AND WHEN JAS FOLLOWS, *guṇa*, shall be the substitute of the short final of an inflective base. Hence 1st pl. *hari+jas=harayaḥ*.

ह्रस्वस्य गुणः । ७ । ३ । १०८ ।

सम्बुद्धौ । हे हरे । हरिम् । हरी । हरीन् ।

No. 189.—The substitute OF A SHORT final is GUṆA, when *sambuddhi* (No. 152) follows. By this and No. 153, we get the vocative sing. *he hare.* 2nd s. *harim* (No. 154), 2nd du. *harí*, 2nd pl. *harín* (No. 156).

शेषो घ्यसखि । १ । ४ । ७ ।

शेष इति स्पष्टार्थम् । ह्रस्वौ याविदुतौ तदन्तं सखिवर्जं घिसंज्ञम् ।

No. 190.—WITH THE EXCEPTION OF the word SAKHI, THE REST of the words that end in short *i* or *u* are called GHI. The words "the rest" are said to be employed here "for the sake of distinctness."

आङो नास्त्रियाम् । ७ । ३ । १२० ।

घेः परस्याङो ना स्यादस्त्रियाम् । आङिति टासंज्ञा । हरिणा । हरिभ्याम् । हरिभिः ।

No. 191.—Let NÁ be the substitute OF ÁṄ coming after *ghi* (No. 190), but NOT IN THE FEMININE. The term *áṅ* is the ancient designation of *ṭá,* the 3rd sing. case-affix.

Example, *hari+ṭá=hariṇá* (No. 157). 3rd du. *haribhyám,* 3rd pl. *haribhih.*

घेर्ङिति । ७ । ३ । १११ ।

घिसंज्ञस्य ङिति सुपि गुणः । हरये ।

No. 192.—Let *guṇa* be the substitute OF GHI (No. 190), WHEN a case-affix WHICH HAS AN INDICATORY Ṅ FOLLOWS. Thus 4th s. *hari+ṅe=haraye* (No. 29).

ङसिङसोश्च । ६ । १ । ११० ।

एङो ङसिङसोरति पूर्वरूपमेकादेशः । हरेः । हर्योः । हरीणाम् ।

No. 193.—AND when the short *a* OF ṄASI AND ṄAS, comes after *eṅ,* let the form of the prior be the single substitute for both. Thus, 5th and 6th s. *hari+ṅasi* and so also *hari+ṅas=hareh* (No. 192). 6th and 7th du. *haryoh* (Nos. 21 and 73)—6th pl. *haríṇám* (Nos. 167, 168, and 157).

अच्च घेः । ७ । ३ । ११९ ।

इदुद्भ्यामुत्तरस्य ङेरौत् घेरत् । हरौ । हरिषु । एवं कव्यादयः ।

No. 194.—Let *aut* be the substitute of *ṅi* (the case-affix of the 7th s.), when it follows short *i* or *u,* AND let short A be the substitute OF the GHI (No. 190) itself. Thus 7th s. *harau* (No. 41). 7th pl. *harishu* (No. 169). In the same way are declined *kavi* "a poet," and the like.

अनङ् सौ । ७ । १ । ९३ ।

सख्युरङ्गस्यानङादेशोऽसम्बुद्धौ सौ ।

No. 195.—ANAŃ is the substitute of the word *sakhi,* WHEN SU FOLLOWS, provided it is not the sign of the vocative (No. 152).

The substitute, though consisting of more letters than one (No. 58), is prohibited by No. 59 from taking the place of more than the last letter. Thus we have *sakhan* + *s*.

अलोऽन्त्यात् पूर्व उपधा। १। १। ६५।

अन्त्यादलः पूर्वो यो वर्णः स उपधासंज्ञः स्यात्।

No. 196.—The letter BEFORE THE LAST LETTER of a word is called THE PENULTIMATE (*upadhá*).

सर्वनामस्थाने चासम्बुद्धौ। ६। ४। ८।

नान्तस्योपधाया दीर्घोऽसम्बुद्धौ सर्वनामस्थाने।

No. 197.—AND the long form is the substitute of the penultimate letter (No. 196) of what ends in *n,* WHEN a SARVANÁMASTHÁNA (No. 183), NOT being SAMBUDDHI (No. 152), FOLLOWS. Thus we have *sakhán* + *s*.

अपृक्त एकाल् प्रत्ययः। १। २। ४१।

No. 198.—AN AFFIX consisting of A SINGLE LETTER (exclusive of indicatory letters) is called APṚIKTA.

हल्ङ्याब्भ्यो दीर्घात् सुतिस्यपृक्तं हल्। ६। १। ६८।

हलन्तात् परं दीर्घौ यौ ङ्यापौ तदन्ताच्च परं सुतिसीत्येतदपृक्तं हल्लुप्यते।

No. 199.—SU (the 1st sing. case-affix) AND TI AND SI (the terminations of two of the persons of the verb) when reduced to A SINGLE CONSONANT (No. 198), and when standing AFTER what ends in a CONSONANT OR in the LONG vowel deduced from the feminine terminations ŃÍ (No. 256) AND ÁP (No. 1341), are elided. Thus *sakhán* + *s* becomes *sakhán*.

न लोपः प्रातिपदिकान्तस्य। ८। २। ७।

प्रातिपदिकसंज्ञकं यत् पदं तदन्तस्य नस्य लोपः। सखा।

No. 200.—There is ELISION OF N FINAL IN A *pada* which is entitled to the designation of PRÁTIPADIKA (No. 135).

The word *sakhi* is a *prátipadika*; it becomes a *pada* (No. 20) when the case-affix is added; and this name of *pada* it retains (by No. 210) after the case-affix has been elided. Thus *sakhán* is a *pada*. But *sakhán* is also entitled to the designation of *prátipadika*, like *sakhi* the place of which it occupies, according to No. 163. Thus, by the present rule, the form of the word becomes finally *sakhá* "a friend."

सख्युरसम्बुद्धौ । ७ । १ । ९२ ।

सख्युरङ्गात् परं सम्बुद्धिवर्जं सर्वनामस्थानं णिद्वत् स्यात् ।

No 201.—Let a *sarvanámasthána* (No. 183) coming AFTER the word SAKHI, NOT IN THE sense of the VOCATIVE SINGULAR, be like that which contains an indicatory *ṇ*.

अचो ञ्णिति । ७ । २ । ११५ ।

अजन्ताङ्गस्य वृद्धिर्ञिति णिति च परे । सखायौ । सखायः । हे सखे । सखायम् । सखायौ । सखीन् । सख्या । सख्ये ।

No. 202.—Let *vṛiddhi* be the substitute OF an inflective base ending in A VOWEL, WHEN THAT WHICH HAS AN INDICATORY Ñ OR Ṇ FOLLOWS.

Thus *sakhi*, when the 1st dual case-affix is to be annexed, becomes *sakhai* (No. 201), and *sakhai+au=sakháyau* (No. 29), —so also 1st pl. *sakháyah*. The vocative sing. (by Nos. 189 and 153) is *he sakhe*. In the 2nd s. and du., *sakháyam* and *sakháyau*, Nos. 201 and 202 again apply: 2nd pl. *sakhín* (Nos. 146 and 156), 3rd s. *sakhyá*, 4th s. *sakhye*.

ख्यत्यात् परस्य । ६ । १ । ११२ ।

खितिशब्दाभ्यां खीतीशब्दाभ्यां कृतयणादेशाभ्यां परस्य ङसिङसोरत उः । सख्युः ।

No. 203.—Short *u* is the substitute OF the *a* of *ńasi* and *ńas* FOLLOWING the words KHI AND TI or khí and tí which have substituted *yaṇ* (No. 21) for the final vowel.

Khi and *ti* are the terminations of the words *sakhi* and *pati*, which they are here employed to designate. The long forms *khí* and *tí* indicate certain derivative forms; see No. 223.

The words "which have substituted *yaṇ*," are employed to show that rule No. 192 does not apply here; and the same object is attained in the aphorism by writing not *khi* and *ti* but *khya* and *tya*, the *a* in which is intended merely to facilitate pronunciation.

Thus we have 5th and 6th s. *sakhyuh*.

औत् । ७ । ३ । ११८ ।

इतः परस्य ङेरौत् । सख्यौ । शेषं हरिवत् ।

No. 204.—AUT is the substitute OF ṄI after short *i*. Hence 7th s. *sakhyau*. The rest is like *hari* (No. 187).

पतिः समास एव । १ । ४ । ८ ।

घिसंज्ञः । पत्ये । पत्युः २ । पत्यौ । शेषं हरिवत् । समासे तु भूपतये । कतिशब्दो नित्यं बहुवचनान्तः ।

No. 205.—The word PATI is called *ghi* (No. 190) ONLY when it is IN A COMPOUND (*samása*).

Hence in the 4th s. *patye* "to a master," No. 192 does not apply; in 5th and 6th s. *patyuh*, No. 203, not No. 193, applies; and in 7th s. *patyau*, No. 204 applies, but not 194. The rest is like *hari*. But in a compound, as in *bhúpataye* "to the lord of the earth," *pati* is treated as *ghi* (No. 191 &c.).

The word *kati* "how many?" takes the plural terminations only.

बहुगणवतुडति संख्या । १ । १ । २३ ।

No. 206.—Let the words BAHU, and GAṆA, and those which end in VATU and ḌATI be called *saṅkhyá*.

The word *kati* is one of those which end in *ḍati*, the *ḍ* in which affix is indicatory.

डति च । १ । १ । २५ ।

डत्यन्ता संख्या षट्संज्ञा स्यात् ।

No. 207.—AND let a *saṅkhyá* (No. 206) which ends in ḌATI be called *shaṭ* (No. 324).

Thus the word *kati* is called *shaṭ*.

षड्भ्यो लुक् । ७ । १ । २२ ।

जश्शसोः ।

No. 208.—Let there be ELISION (*luk*) of *jas* and *śas* AFTER words termed SHAṬ (No. 207).

प्रत्ययस्य लुक्श्लुलुपः । १ । १ । ६१ ।

लुक्श्लुलुप्शब्दैः कृतं प्रत्ययादर्शनं क्रमात् तत्तत्संज्ञं स्यात् ।

No. 209.—Let the disappearance OF AN AFFIX when it is caused by the words LUK, ŚLU, OR LUP be designated by these terms respectively (to distinguish it from the ordinary elision termed *lopa*—No. 6).—

प्रत्ययलोपे प्रत्ययलक्षणम् । १ । १ । ६२ ।

प्रत्यये लुप्तेऽपि तदाश्रितं कार्यं स्यात् । इति जसि चेति गुणे प्राप्ते ।

No. 210.—WHEN ELISION (*lopa*) OF AN AFFIX HAS TAKEN PLACE, THE AFFIX shall still exert its influence, and the operations dependent upon it shall take place as if it were present.

The word *lakshaṇa*, in the aphorism, signifies "that by which a thing is recognised." A case-affix is recognised (No. 152) by its causing that which it follows to take the name of *aṅga*. In accordance with the present rule therefore the word *kati* retains the name of *aṅga*, though the affixes *jas* and *śas* have been elided by No. 208; and, in virtue of its having the name of *aṅga*, it ought to take a *guṇa* substitute through the operation of No. 188. But the rule following debars this.

न लुमताङ्गस्य । १ । १ । ६३ ।

लुमता शब्देन लुप्ते तन्निमित्तमङ्गकार्यं न स्यात् । कति २ । कतिभिः । कतिभ्यः २ । कतीनाम् । कतिषु । युष्मदस्मद्षट्संज्ञकास्त्रिषु सरूपाः । त्रिशब्दो नित्यं बहुवचनान्तः । त्रयः । त्रीन् । त्रिभिः । त्रिभ्यः २ ।

No. 211.—When an affix is elided BY the enunciation of one of the three terms (in No. 209) CONTAINING the letters LU, the effect which it is competent to cause in respect OF AN AŃGA or inflective base shall NOT take place.

In the 1st pl. of *kati*, the affix *jas* is elided by the enunciation of *luk* (No. 208), and therefore the substitution of *guṇa* which the elided *jas* would otherwise (by Nos. 210 and 188) have been competent to cause, does not take place.

Thus we have 1st and 2nd pl. *kati* "how many?" 3rd *katibhih*, 4th and 5th *katibhyah*, 6th *katínám* (Nos. 167 and 168), 7th *katishu* (No. 169).

The words *yushmad* "thou," *asmad* "I," and the words called *shaṭ* (Nos. 324 and 207) retain the same form in all the three genders.

The word *tri* "three," is always plural.

Example, 1st pl. *trayah* (No. 188), 2nd *trín* (Nos. 146 and 156), 3rd *tribhih*, 4th and 5th *tribhyah*.

त्रेस्त्रयः । ७ । १ । ५३ ।

आमि । त्रयाणाम् । त्रिषु । गौणत्वेऽपि । प्रियत्रयाणाम् ।

No. 212.—TRAYA is the substitute OF TRI, when *ám* follows.

Example, 6th pl. *trayáṇám* (Nos. 167 and 168), 7th *trishu* (No. 169).

And this rule applies also when *tri* is final in a compound adjective.

Example, *priyatrayáṇám* "of those who have three dear friends."

त्यदादीनामः । ७ । २ । १०२ ।

एषामकारो विभक्तौ । द्विपर्यन्तानामेवेष्टिः । द्वौ २ । द्वाभ्याम् ३ । द्वयोः २ । पाति लोकमिति पपीः सूर्यः ।

No. 213.—Short A is the substitute OF TYAD &c. when a case-affix follows. "TYAD &c." (see No. 170) implies "*tyad, tad, yad, etad, idam, adas, eka,* and *dwi.*" The *Mahábháshya* directs that the list shall not extend beyond *dwi.* That this is the direction of *Patañjali* (the author of that "Great Commentary," on the aphorisms of *Páṇini*) is indicated by the form of expression "it is the wish," or "it is wished," (*ishṭih* or *ishyate.* Compare No. 14.) Thus we have 1st and 2nd du. *dwau* "two" (No. 147), 3rd 4th and 5th *dwábhyám* (No. 160), 6th and 7th *dwayoh* (No. 166).

We now come to the declension of *papí* "the sun," (the "cherisher of the world," derived from *pá,* "to cherish").

दीर्घाज्जसि च । ६ । १ । १०५ ।

दीर्घाज्जसि इचि च परे न पूर्वसवर्णदीर्घः । पप्यौ । पप्यः । हे पपीः । पपीम् । पपीन् । पप्या । पपीभ्याम् । पपीभिः । पप्ये । पपीभ्यः २ । पप्यः २ । पप्योः २ । दीर्घत्वान्न नुट् । पप्याम् । ङौ तु सवर्णदीर्घः । पपी । पपीषु । एवं वातप्रम्यादयः । बह्व्यः श्रेयस्यो यस्य स बहुश्रेयसी ।

No. 214.—AND WHEN JAS or *ich* (*pratyáhára,* No. 147) comes AFTER A LONG vowel, the long vowel homogeneous with the prior is not substituted (No. 146).

Therefore (by No. 21) 1st du. *papyau,* 1st pl. *papyah,* vocative sing. *he papíh,* 2nd s. *papím* (No. 154), 2nd pl. *papín* (No. 156), 3rd s. *papyá,* 3rd 4th and 5th du. *papíbhyám,* 3rd pl. *papíbhih,* 4th s. *papye,* 4th and 5th pl. *papíbhyah,* 5th and 6th s. *papyah,* 6th and 7th du. *papyoh.* There is not *nuṭ* (No. 167) for the vowel is long—hence 6th pl. *papyám.* When *ńi* is added, then by No. 55, 7th s. *papí,* 7th pl. *papíshu.*

In the same way are declined *vátapramí* "an antelope," and the like.

We now come to the declension of *bahuśreyasí* "a man who has many excellent qualities."

यूस्त्याख्यौ नदी । १ । ४ । ३ ।

ईदूदन्तौ नित्यस्त्रीलिङ्गौ नदीसंज्ञौ स्तः । प्रथमलिङ्गग्रहणं च । पूर्वं स्त्र्याख्यस्योपसर्जनत्वेऽपि नदीत्वं वक्तव्यमित्यर्थः ।

No. 215.—Words ending in long í and ú, always FEMININE, and having no masculine of the same form, (as the word *grámaṇí* has,) are called *nadí* (the word *nadí* "a river" being a type of the class.) "And its original gender is to be taken" into account:—that is to say, it is to be spoken of as retaining its character as a *nadí*, even when the word which was at first feminine comes to form part of a compound epithet applied to a male.

अम्बार्थनद्योर्ह्रस्वः ।७।३।१०७।

सम्बुद्धौ । हे बहुश्रेयसि ।

No. 216.—THE SHORT vowel shall be the substitute OF certain words SIGNIFYING "MOTHER," AND OF words called NADÍ (No. 215), when the affix of the vocative singular follows.

Example, *he bahuśreyasi* (No. 153)

आण्नद्याः ।७।३।११२।

नद्यन्तात् परेषां ङितामाडागमः ।

No. 217.—ÁṬ is the augment of the case-affixes with an indicatory *ṅ*, when they come AFTER a word ending with a NADÍ (No. 215).

आटश्च ।६।१।९०।

आटोऽचि परे वृद्धिरेकादेशः । बहुश्रेयस्यै । बहुश्रेयस्याः २ । बहुश्रेयसीनाम् ।

No. 218.—AND when *ach* comes AFTER ÁṬ, *vriddhi* is the single substitute for both. Thus in the 4th s. *bahuśreyasí* + *áṭ* + *ṅe* =*bahuśreyasyai*, 5th and 6th s. *bahuśreyasyáh*, 6th pl. *bahuśreyasínám* (No. 167).

ङेराम् नद्याम्नीभ्यः ।७।३।११६।

नद्यन्तादाबन्तान्नीशब्दात् परस्य ङेराम् । बहुश्रेयस्याम् । शेषं

पपीवत् । अङ्यन्तत्वान्न सुलोपः । अतिलक्ष्मीः । शेषं बहुश्रेयसीवत् । प्रधीः ।

No. 219.—ÁM is the substitute OF ŃI AFTER words ending in NADÍ (No. 215) AND in the feminine termination ÁP and the word NÍ. Hence 7th s. *bahuśreyasyám.* The rest of the declension is like *papí* (No. 213).

The word *atilakshmí* is, in the 1st s., *atilakshmíḥ* "who has surpassed *Lakshmí,*" the *su* not being elided by No. 199, because the word *lakshmí* (the name of one of the goddesses) is a primitive, and is not formed by a feminine affix *ńí.* The rest of the declension is like *bahuśreyasí* (No. 214).

We now come to *pradhí,* 1st s. *pradhíh* "a man of superior understanding."

अचि श्नुधातुभ्रुवां य्वोरियङुवङौ । ६ । ४ । ७७ ।

श्नुप्रत्ययान्तस्येवर्णोवर्णान्तस्य धातोर्भ्रू इत्यस्य चाङ्गस्येयङुवङौ स्तोऽजादौ प्रत्यये परे । इति प्राप्ते ।

No. 220.—IYAŃ AND UVAŃ are the substitutes OF what ends with the *pratyaya* ŚNU AND of what ends in A VERBAL ROOT IN I OR U (whether long or short), AND of the inflective base BHRÚ, WHEN an affix beginning with A VOWEL FOLLOWS.

This rule should include the case of *pradhí* (which is formed from the verbal root *dhyai* "to meditate"), but the rule following restricts it.

एरनेकाचोऽसंयोगपूर्वस्य । ६ । ४ । ८२ ।

धात्ववयवसंयोगपूर्वो न भवति य इवर्णस्तदन्तो यो धातुस्तदन्तस्यानेकाचोऽङ्गस्य यणजादौ प्रत्यये । प्रध्यौ २ । प्रध्यम् । प्रध्यः । प्रध्यि । शेषं पपीवत् । एवं ग्रामणीः । ङौ तु । ग्रामण्याम् । अनेकाचः किम् । नीः । नियौ । नियः । अमि शसि च परत्वादियङ् । नियम् । नियः । ङेराम् । नियाम् । असंयोगपूर्वस्य किम् । सुश्रियौ । यवक्रियौ ।

No. 221.—*Yaṇ* is the substitute OF I OR Í terminating a verbal root final in an inflective base OF MORE VOWELS THAN ONE, provided the I OR Í is NOT PRECEDED BY A COMPOUND CONSONANT forming part of the root, when an affix beginning with a vowel follows.

In *pradhí*, which is a dissyllable, the final *í* terminates an inflective base of more vowels than one, and it is not preceded by a compound consonant. The rule therefore applies, and we have 1st and 2nd du. *pradhyau*, 2nd s. *pradhyam*, 1st and 2nd pl. *pradhyah*, 7th s. *pradhyi* (No. 55 being debarred). The rest of the declension is like that of *papí* (No. 213). In the same way *grámaṇíh* "a female head of a village"; but, in the 7th s. this makes *grámaṇyám* (by No. 219, being derived from the root *ṇí* "to lead)." Why "of more vowels than one?" Witness *níh* "a leader," which makes, by No. 220, 1st and 2nd du. *niyau*, 1st pl. *niyah*, and in the 2nd s. and pl. *niyam* and *niyah* (Nos. 154 and 146 being superseded by No. 220, which occupies a later place in the *Ashṭádhyáyí*—see No. 132.). In the 7th s. *niyám* (No. 219.)—Why "provided the vowel is not preceded by a compound consonant?" Witness 1st du. *suśriyau* "two prosperous men," and *yavakriyau* "two purchasers of barley," where the final *í* is preceded by a compound consonant, and to which therefore not this rule but No. 220 applies.

[It may be worth while to review the steps which rendered necessary the enunciation of this rule with reference to the word *pradhyau*. The word might apparently have been formed at once from *pradhí+au* by No. 21, but that rule was superseded by a subsequent rule No. 146. By No. 214, however, this rule was positively forbidden to take effect, and as it therefore departs, with all its effects, No. 21 reappears, but to be again superseded by No. 220, to which the preference attaches on the principle stated under No. 41. No. 221 then supersedes No. 220, but as it does this not by positive prohibition, but by usurping a portion of its sphere of application, No. 21 is not again restored. Had it been so, the prohibitory rules would also have reappeared in an endless cycle.]

गतिश्च । १ । ४ । ६० ।

प्रादयः क्रियायोगे गतिसंज्ञाः स्युः । गतिकारकेतरपूर्वपदस्य यण् नेष्यते । । शुद्धधियौ ।

No. 222.—AND let *pra &c.* (No. 47), in combination with a verb, be called GATI (as well as *upasarga*).

It is not wished (by the author of the *Mahábháshya*) that *yaṇ* (enjoined by No. 221) should be the substitute of a word to which is prefixed any thing else than a *gati* or a *káraka* (meaning by *káraka* a case which is in grammatical relation with a verb). Therefore in the example *śuddhadhiyau* "two men of pure minds," the substitution of *yaṇ* does not take place, but No. 220 applies, because the word *śuddhadhí* means "one whose thoughts are pure," and here the word "pure," is in grammatical relation with the verb "are," in respect to which it is therefore a *káraka,* but it is not so in regard to the verb "to think," from which the word *dhí* is derived.

न भूसुधियोः । ६ । ४ । ८५ ।

एतयोरचि सुपि यण् न । सुधियौ । सुधिय इत्यादि । सुखमिच्छतीति सुखीः । सुतीः । सुख्यौ । सुत्यौ । सुख्युः २ । सुत्युः २ । शेषं प्रधीवत् । शम्भुर्हरिवत् । एवं भान्वादयः ।

No. 223.—When a case-affix beginning with a vowel comes AFTER these two viz. BHÚ and SUDHÍ, there shall NOT be *yaṇ*. (This debars Nos. 232 and 221, and gives occasion for No. 220 to come into operation). Hence, 1st. d. *sudhiyau,* "two intelligent persons," 1st. pl. *sudhiyah,* &c.

The word *sukhí* signifies "one who loves pleasure." It is declined like *sutí* "one who wishes a son:" thus—1st. s. *sukhíh, sutíh* ; 1st. d. *sukhyau, sutyau* ; 5 and 6. s. *sukhyuh, sutyuh* (No. 203). The rest is like *pradhí* (No. 220 &c.). The word *śambhu* "Śiva" is declined like *hari* "Vishṇu," and in like manner *bhánu* "the sun," &c.

तृज्वत् क्रोष्टुः । ७ । १ । ९५ ।

असम्बुद्धौ सर्वनामस्थाने । क्रोष्टुशब्दस्य क्रोष्टृ प्रयोक्तव्य इत्यर्थः ।

No. 224.—With the five first case-affixes (No. 183) excluding the case where the sense is that of the vocative singular, KROSHṬU is LIKE what ends in TṚICH. That is to say, *kroshṭṛi* is employed instead of the word *kroshṭu* "a jackal."

ऋतो ङिसर्वनामस्थानयोः । ७ । ३ । ११० ।

ऋतोऽङ्गस्य गुणो ङौ सर्वनामस्थाने च । इति प्राप्ते ।

No. 225.—WHEN ṄI (7th sing.) & THE FIVE FIRST CASE-AFFIXES COME AFTER what ends in short ṚI, *guṇa* shall be substituted for the inflective base that ends in *ṛi.* This being obtained, (another rule presents itself).

ऋदुशनस्पुरुदंसोऽनेहसां च । ७ । १ । ९४ ।

ऋदन्तानामुशनसादीनां चानङ् स्यादसम्बुद्धौ सौ ।

No. 226.—When *su*, not in the sense of the vocative, follows, let *anaṅ* be the augment of what ends in short *ṛi*, and of *uśanas* "the regent of the planet Venus," *purudaṅśas* "Indra," and *anehas* "time." [This gives *kroshṭ* + *an* + *s*.]

अप्तृन्तृच्स्वसृनप्तृनेष्टृत्वष्टृक्षत्तृहोतृपोतृप्रशास्तृणाम् । ६ । ४ । ११ ।

अबादीनामुपधाया दीर्घोऽसम्बुद्धौ सर्वनामस्थाने । क्रोष्टा । क्रोष्टारौ । क्रोष्टारः । क्रोष्टून् ।

No. 227.—When the first five case-affixes, excluding the case where the sense is that of the vocative singular, come after the word AP "water," what ends in TṚIN or TṚICH, SWASṚI "a sister," NAPTṚI "a grandson," NESHṬṚI "a priest who officiates at a sacrifice," TWASHṬṚI "a carpenter," KSHATTṚI "a charioteer," HOTṚI "a priest who recites the *Ṛig-Veda* at a sacrifice," POTṚI "a priest who officiates at a sacrifice," and PRAŚÁSTṚI "a ruler," the penultimate letter (No. 196) shall be lengthened. Thus [we get *kroshṭán* + *s*, but the *s* is elided by No. 199 and the *n* by No. 200—leaving] 1st sing. *kroshṭá*, 1st du. *kroshṭárau*, (the *ṛi* becoming *ar* by No. 225, and being lengthened to *ár* by No. 227). 1st p. *kroshṭárah.* In the 2nd p. the form *kroshṭún* is derived from *kroshṭu* by Nos. 146 and 156.

विभाषा तृतीयादिष्वचि ।७।१।९७।

अजादिषु क्रोष्टुर्वा तृज्वत् । क्रोष्ट्रा । क्रोष्ट्रे ।

No. 228.—*Kroshṭu* may OPTIONALLY be as if it ended in *ṭrich*, WHEN THE 3RD OR ANY SUBSEQUENT CASE-AFFIX THAT BEGINS WITH A VOWEL FOLLOWS. Thus, 3rd sing. *kroshṭrá*, 4th sing. *kroshṭre*.

ऋत उत् ।६।१।१११।

ऋतो ङसिङसोरत्युदेकादेशः । रपरः ।

No. 229.—When the short *a* of *ńasi* and *ńas* (5th and 6th sing.) comes AFTER SHORT ṚI, then SHORT U, followed by *r*, is the single substitute for both. [Thus we get *kroshṭur*+*s*.]

रात् सस्य ।८।२।२४।

रेफात् संयोगान्तसस्यैव लोपो नान्यस्य । रस्य विसर्गः । क्रोष्टुः । क्रोष्ट्रोः २ ।

No. 230.—There is elision OF S, but not of any other letter of the alphabet, when it comes at the end of a conjunct consonant AFTER R. *Visarga* is then substituted for the *r*, by No. 111, and we get *kroshṭuh*,—6. and 7. du. *kroshṭroh*.

नुमचिरतृज्वद्भावेभ्यो नुट् पूर्वविप्रतिषेधेन । क्रोष्टूनाम् । क्रोष्टरि । पक्षे हलादौ च शम्भुवत् । हूहूः । हूह्वौ । हूहूमित्यादि । अतिचमूशब्दे तु नदीकार्यं विशेषः । हे अतिचमु । अतिचम्वै । अतिचम्वाः २ । अतिचमूनाम् । खलपूः ।

No. 231.—"BY A PRECEDING RULE'S OPPOSITION, (contrary to *Páṇini's* direction—see No. 132,) the augment NUṬ (No. 167) takes effect IN PREFERENCE TO NUM (No. 271), the *sútra* "ACHI &c." (No. 249), and THE RESEMBLANCE TO what ends in ṬRICH (No. 224) [the enunciation of each of which is subsequent to No. 167 in the order of the *ashṭádhyáyí*.]

Hence—*kroshṭu*+*nuṭ*+*ám*=*kroshṭúnám* (No. 168). In the 7th sing. *kroshṭari*. On the alternative (of the word's not being considered as ending in *ṭrich*), and when the case-affix begins with a consonant, the word is declined like *śambhu.*

Húhúh "a celestial musician," 1st du. *húhwau*, 2nd sing. *húhúm*, &c. In the word *atichamú* "victorious over armies," the difference (from *húhú*, as regards declension), consists in its being treated as *nadí* (No. 215). Hence, voc. s. *he atichamu* (No. 216), 4th sing. *atichamwai* (Nos. 217 and 218), 5th and 6th sing. *atichamwáh*, 6th p. *atichamúnám.*

We now come to the declension of *khalapú* "a sweeper."

ओः सुपि । ६ । ४ । ८३ ।

धात्ववयवसंयोगपूर्वो न भवति य उवर्णस्तदन्तो यो धातुस्तदन्तस्यानेकाचोऽङ्गस्य यण् स्यादचि सुपि । खलप्वौ । खलप्वः । एवं सुल्वादयः । स्वभूः । स्वभुवौ । स्वभुवः । वर्षाभूः ।

No. 232.—WHEN A CASE-AFFIX, beginning with a vowel, FOLLOWS, then *yaṇ* shall be the substitute for an inflective base containing more vowels than one, if the base ends with a verbal root ending in U or Ú not preceded by a conjunct consonant forming part of the verb.

Thus we have 1st du. *khalapwau*, 1st p. *khalapwah.* In the same way *sulú* "who cuts well," &c. [But this does not apply to *swabhú* "the Self-existent," because of the prohibition by No. 223—]. 1st s. *swabhúḥ*, 1st du. *swabhuvau*, 1st p. *swabhuvah.*

We have next the declension of *varshábhú.*

वर्षाभ्वश्च । ६ । ४ । ८४ ।

अस्य यण् स्यादचि सुपि । वर्षाभ्वावित्यादि । दृन्भूः ।

No. 233.—AND the substitute OF VARSHÁBHÚ, "a frog—rainborn," shall be *yaṇ* when a vowel follows, [in spite of No. 223.] Thus we have, 1st du. *varshábhwau* and so on.

Next we have to consider the declension of *dṛinbhú* "a snake."

दृन्करपुनःपूर्वस्य भुवो यण् वक्तव्यः । दृन्भ्वौ । एवं करभूः । धाता । हे धातः । धातारौ । धातारः ।

No. 234.—"YAṆ SHOULD BE MENTIONED as the substitute OF BHÚ when PRECEDED BY DṚIN, KARA, AND PUNAR."

Thus 1st du. *dṛinbhwau.* In the same way *karabhú* "a finger-nail."

The word *dhátṛi* "the Cherisher," makes 1st sing. *dhátá,* vocative sing. *he dhátah* (Nos. 199, 225, and 111.), 1st du. *dhátárau* (Nos. 225 and 227), 1st pl. *dhátárah.*

ऋवर्णान्नस्य णत्वं वाच्यम् । धातॄणाम् । एवं नप्त्रादयः । नप्त्रादिग्रहणं व्युत्पत्तिपक्षे नियमार्थम् । तेनेह न । पिता । पितरौ । पितरः । पितरम् । शेषं धातृवत् । एवं जामात्रादयः । ना । नरौ ।

No, 235.—"IT SHOULD BE STATED THAT THE CEREBRAL Ṇ IS SUBSTITUTED FOR THE DENTAL N AFTER ṚI AND ṚÍ." Thus, 6th p. *dhátṛíṇám.* In the same way *naptṛi* &c. (No. 227). If the alternative view be taken, that these words are formed (by the affixes mentioned in No. 227), then the citing of *naptṛi* &c. (in No. 227) determines that these *alone* (of the words so ending that come under the head of *Uṇádi* No. 901) are amenable to the rule. Hence (as *pitṛi* "a father," is not cited, and is formed by an *uṇádi* affix) the rules do not apply to the example following viz. 1st sing. *pitá* (No. 221), 1st du. *pitarau,* 1st pl. *pitarah,* 2nd sing. *pitaram.* The rest is like *dhátṛi* (No. 234). In the same way *jámátṛi* "a son-in-law," &c.

The word *nṛi* "a man," makes 1st sing. *ná,* 1st du. *narau.*

नॄ च । ६ । ४ । ६ ।

अस्य नामि वा दीर्घः । नॄणाम् । नृणाम् ।

No. 236.—AND NṚI optionally substitutes the long vowel, when *nám* follows. Hence *nṛíṇám* or *nṛiṇám.*

गोतो णित् । ७ । १ । ९० ।

ओकारान्ताद्विहितं सर्वनामस्थानं णिद्वत् । गौः । गावौ । गावः ।

No. 237.—Placed AFTER a word ending in O, such as GO "a cow," each of the first five case-affixes is AS IF IT HAD AN INDICATORY cerebral Ṇ, [the effect of which—see No. 202—is to substitute *vṛiddhi* for the preceding vowel]. Thus 1. s. *go+s=gauh,* 1. d. *gávau,* 1. p. *gávah.* [The *t* in the *sútra* shows (No. 34.) that the rule speaks of the vowel *o,* not of the word *go.*]

औतोऽम्शसोः । ६ । १ । ९३ ।

ओतोऽम्शसोरच्याकार एकादेशः । गाम् । गावौ । गाः । गवा । गवे । गोः २ । इत्यादि ।

No. 238—WHEN the vowel of AM OR ŚAS comes AFTER O, the single substitute of both is long Á. Thus—2. s. *go+am=gám,* 2. du. (see No. 237) *gávau,* 2. p. *gáh.* The 3rd and 4th s. *gavá* and *gave* are formed according to the general rules for the permutation of vowels. In the 5. and 6. s. (by No. 193) *goh.* &c.

रायो हलि । ७ । २ । ८५ ।

अस्याकारादेशो हलि विभक्तौ । राः । रायौ । रायः । राभ्यामित्यादि । ग्लौः । ग्लावौ । ग्लावः । ग्लौभ्यामित्यादि ।

। इत्यजन्ताः पुंलिङ्गाः ।

No. 239.—OF RAI "wealth," WHEN a case-affix beginning with A CONSONANT FOLLOWS, long *á* shall be the substitute. Thus 1. s. *rai+s=ráh,* 1. du. *ráyau,* 1. p. *ráyah,* 3. d. *rábhyám,* &c.

Glau "the moon," is declined regularly—thus—1. s. *glauh,* 1. d. *glávau,* 1. p. *glávah,* 3. d. *glaubhyám,* &c.

So much for masculines ending in vowels.

OF FEMININE WORDS ENDING IN VOWELS.

The first example is *ramá* which, by No. 199, takes the form *ramá* in the 1st case sing.

। अजन्तस्त्रीलिङ्गाः ।

रमा ।

औङ आपः । ७ । १ । १८ ।

आबन्तादङ्गात् परस्यौङः शी स्यात् । औङित्यौकारविभक्तेः संज्ञा । रमे । रमाः ।

240.—Let *śí* be the substitute OF AUŃ AFTER an inflective base ending in ÁP. This *auń* is the name of whatever case-affix begins with *au*. Hence, 1. d. (*ramá+śí=*) *rame*, 1. p. *ramáh.*

सम्बुद्धौ च।७।३।१०६।

आप एकारः स्यात् सम्बुद्धौ। एङ्ह्रस्वादिति सम्बुद्धिलोपः। हे रमे। हे रमे। हे रमाः। रमाम्। रमे। रमाः।

241.—AND WHEN SU FOLLOWS IN THE SENSE OF THE VOCATIVE SINGULAR, let *e* be the substitute of *áp*. By No. 153 there is elision of the case-affix following *e* in the sense of the voc. sing. Thus *he rame*, voc. d. *he rame* (No. 240), voc. p. *he ramáh*, 2. s. *ramám*, 2. du. *rame*, 2. p. *ramáh.*

आङि चापः।७।३।१०५।

आङ्योसि चाप एकारः। रमया। रमाभ्याम् ३। रमाभिः।

242.—AND IF ÁŃ (No. 191) or OS FOLLOW, *e* shall be the substitute OF ÁP. Thus, 3. s. (*rame+á=*) *ramayá*, 3. 4. and 5. du. *ramábhyám*, 3. p. *ramábhih.*

याडापः।७।३।११३।

आपो ङितो याट्। वृद्धिः। रमायै। रमाभ्यः २। रमायाः २। रमयोः। रमाणाम्। रमायाम्। रमासु। एवं दुर्गाम्बिकादयः।

No. 243.—YÁṬ is the augment of whatever case-affix, FOLLOWING ÁP, has an indicatory *ń*. Thus, *vṛiddhi* being obtained from No. 61, we have 4. s. (*ramá+yáṭ+e=*) *ramáyai*, 4. and 5. p. *ramábhyah*, 5 and 6. s. *ramáyáh*, 6. d. *ramayoh* (No. 242), 6. p. *ramáṇám* (Nos. 167 and 157), 7. s. *ramáyám* (No. 219), 7. p. *ramásu.*

In the same way are declined *durgá* "the goddess *Durgá,*" *ambiká* "a mother" and the like.

सर्वनाम्नः स्याड्ढ्रस्वश्च।७।३।११४।

आबन्तात् सर्वनाम्नो ङितः स्याडापश्च ह्रस्वः। सर्वस्यै। सर्वस्याः २। सर्वासाम्। सर्वस्याम्। शेषं रमावत्। एवं विश्वादय आबन्ताः।

No. 244.—Let SYÁṬ be the augment of whatever case-affix, with an indicatory *ń*, comes AFTER A PRONOUN ending in *áp;* AND let A SHORT vowel substitute take the place of *áp*. Thus the 4. s. f. of *sarva* "all," is (*sarvá+syáṭ.+e=*) *sarvasyai*, 5. and 6. s. *sarvasyáh*, 6. p. *sarvásám* (No. 174), 7. s. *sarvasyám* (No. 219). The rest is like *ramá*. In the same way are declined *viśwá* "all," and the like, ending in *áp*.

विभाषा दिक्समासे बहुव्रीहौ । १ । १ । २८ ।

सर्वनामता वा । उत्तरपूर्वस्यै । उत्तरपूर्वायै । तीयस्येति वा संज्ञा । द्वितीयस्यै । द्वितीयायै । एवं तृतीया । अम्बार्थेति ह्रस्वः । हे अम्ब । हे अक्क । हे अल्ल । जरा । जरसौ । जरे । इत्यादि । पक्षे रमावत् । गोपा विश्वपावत् । मतिः । मतीः । मत्या ।

No. 245.—IN A COMPOUND, of the kind termed BAHUVRÍHI (No. 1034), WITH a word signifying DIRECTION (No. 175), the pronominal character is optional. Thus in the 4. s. we may have either *uttarapúrvasyai* (No. 244) or *uttarapúrváyai* (No. 243) "for what lies to the north-east."

According to No. 180, the name of pronominal is optionally given to what ends in *tíya*. Hence, 4. s. *dwitíyasyai* or *dwitíyáyai* "to the second." In the same way *tṛitíyá* "the third."

According to No. 216, a short vowel is substituted in the voc. sing. of words signifying "mother." Example, *he amba, he akka, he alla.*

In accordance with No. 181, we may have 1. s. *jará* "decrepitude," 1. d. *jarasau* or *jare* &c. On the alternative of its not being considered pronominal, the word is declined like *ramá*. *Gopá* "a cowherdess," is declined like *viśwapá* (No. 182).

Matih "sagacity," 2. p. *matíh* (No. 146), 3. s. *matyá* (No. 191).

ङिति ह्रस्वश्च । १ । ४ । ६ ।

इयङुवङ्स्थानौ स्त्रीशब्दभिन्नौ नित्यस्त्रीलिङ्गावीदूतौ ह्रस्वौ च-

वर्णावर्णौ स्त्रियां वा नदीसंज्ञौ स्तो ङिति । मत्यै । मतये । मत्याः २ । मतेः २ ।

No. 246.—Words, always feminine, ending in long *í* and *ú*, with the exception of the word *strí* "a woman," being such as admit *iyań* and *uvań* (No. 220); and also words ending in short *i* and *u* in the feminine, are optionally termed *nadí* (No. 215) when a case-affix with an indicatory *ń* follows. Hence 4. s. (by No. 218 *mati+áṭ+e*=) *matyai*, or, alternatively (No. 192) *mataye*, 5. and 6. s. *matyáh* or *mateh* (No. 193).

इदुद्भ्याम् । ७ । ३ । ११७ ।

नदीसंज्ञकाभ्यां परस्य ङेराम् । मत्याम् । मतौ । शेषं हरिवत् । एवं बुद्ध्यादयः ।

No. 247.—*Ám* is the substitute of *ńi* AFTER SHORT I OR U, when these are termed *nadí* (No. 246). Hence 7. s. *matyám* (No. 219, or, on the alternative of the name *nadí* not being taken, *matau* (Nos. 246 and 194.—The rest is like *hari* (No. 187). In the same way *buddhi* "intellect," and the like.

त्रिचतुरोः स्त्रियां तिसृ चतसृ । ७ । २ । ९९ ।

स्त्रीलिङ्गयोरेतौ स्तो विभक्तौ ।

No. 248.—TISṚI AND CHATASṚI are instead of TRI "three," AND CHATUR "four," IN THE FEMININE, when a case-affix follows.

अचि र ऋतः । ७ । २ । १०० ।

तिसृ चतसृ एतयो ऋकारस्य रेफादेशः स्यादचि । गुणदीर्घोत्वानामभावः । तिस्रः २ । तिसृभिः । तिसृभ्यः २ । आमि नुट् ।

No. 249.—WHEN A VOWEL FOLLOWS, then R shall be the substitute OF the ṚI of *tisṛi* and *chatasṛi*. Hence there is neither *guṇa* (No. 225), nor prolongation (No. 146), nor the substitution of *u* (No. 229). Thus 1. and 2. p. *tisṛah*, 3. p. *tisṛibhih*, 4. and 5. p. *tisṛibhyah*. When *ám* (6. p.) follows, *nuṭ* is obtained from No. 167; and then the preceding vowel ought to be lengthened by No. 168, but the next rule forbids this.

न तिसृचतसृ । ६ । ४ । ४ ।

एतयोर्नामि दीर्घो न । तिसृणाम् । तिसृषु । द्वे २ । द्वाभ्याम् ३ । द्वयोः २ । गौरी । गौर्यौ । गौर्यः । हे गौरि । गौर्यावित्यादि । एवं नद्यादयः । लक्ष्मीः । शेषं गौरीवत् । एवं तरीतन्त्र्यादयः । स्त्री । हे स्त्रि ।

No. 250.—TISṚI & CHATASṚI ARE NOT lengthened, when *nám* follows. Thus, 6. p. *tisṛiṇám*, 7. p. *tisrishu.*

The word *dwi* "two," becomes, in the feminine, 1. and 2. d. *dwe* (Nos. 213 and 240), 3. 4. and 5. d. *dwábhyám*, 6. and 7. d. *dwayoh* (No. 242).

Gaurí "the brilliant (goddess *Párvatí*)" is declined as follows:—1. s. *gaurí* (No. 199), 1. d. *gauryau*, 1. p. *gauryah*, voc. s. *he gauri* (No, 216), and so on. In the same way *nadí* "a river," and the like.

The word *lakshmí* "the goddess of prosperity," not being a derivative, does not fall under No. 199, and therefore makes in the 1. s. *lakshmíh.* The rest is like *gaurí.* In the same way *tarí* "a boat," *tantrí* "a guitar-string," and the like.

The word *strí* "a woman" makes 1. s. *strí* (No. 199), voc. *he stri* (No. 216).

स्त्रियाः । ६ । ४ । ७९ ।

अस्येयङ्जादौ प्रत्यये परे । स्त्रियौ । स्त्रियः ।

No. 251.—Let *iyań* be the substitute OF STRÍ, when an affix beginning with a vowel follows. Thus 1. d. *striyau*, 1. p. *striyah.*

वाम्शसोः । ६ । ४ । ८० ।

स्त्रिया इयङ् । स्त्रियम् । स्त्रीम् । स्त्रियः । स्त्रीः । स्त्रिया । स्त्रियै । स्त्रियाः २ । परत्वान्नुट् । स्त्रीणाम् । स्त्रीषु । श्रीः । श्रियौ । श्रियः ।

No. 252.—OPTIONALLY is *iyań* the substitute of ***strí***, WHEN AM OR ŚAS FOLLOWS. Thus 2. s. *striyam* or *strím* (No. 154), 2. p. *striyah* or *stríh* (No. 146), 3. s. *striyá*, 4. s. *striyai* (Nos. 217 and 218), 6. s. *striyáh*. In the 6. p. *nuṭ* is obtained, because No. 167 is a *sútra* posterior to No. 251. Hence *stríṇám*, 7. p. *stríshu*.

The word *śrí* "prosperity," makes 1. s. *śríh*, [not being formed by the feminine termination. No. 198.] 1. d. *śriyau*, 1. p. *śriyah*.

नेयङुवङ्स्थानावस्त्री । १ । ४ । ४ ।

इयङुवङोः स्थितिर्ययोस्तावीदूतौ नदीसंज्ञौ न स्तो न तु स्त्री। हे श्रीः । श्रियै । श्रिये । श्रियाः । श्रियः ।

No. 253.—The words ending in *í* or *ú* WHICH ADMIT the substitutes IYAŃ AND UVAŃ, (No. 220) are NOT called *nadí* (No. 215); but NOT SO the word STRÍ, (which is called *nadí* notwithstanding its substituting *iyań*). Hence, voc. s. *he śríh* (No. 216 not applying here), 4. s. *śriyai* (Nos. 246 and 217) or *śriye*, 6. s. *śriyáh* (Nos. 246 and 217) or *śriyah*.

वामि । १ । ४ । ५ ।

इयङुवङ्स्थानौ स्त्र्याख्यौ यू आमि वा नदीसंज्ञौ स्तो न तु स्त्री। श्रीणाम् । श्रियाम् । श्रियि । श्रियाम् । धेनुर्मतिवत् ।

No. 254.—When ÁM FOLLOWS, then feminine words ending in *í* and *ú*, which admit *iyań* and *uvań* (No. 220), are OPTIONALLY termed *nadí*; but not so the word *strí* (which is always *nadí*). Hence 6. p. *śríṇám* (No. 167) or *śriyám*, 7. s. *śriyi* or *śriyám* (No. 219).

The word *dhenu* "a milch cow" is declined like *mati* (No. 245).

स्त्रियां च । ७ । १ । ९६ ।

स्त्रीवाची क्रोष्टुस्तृजन्तवद्रूपं लभते ।

No. 255.—AND IN THE FEMININE, the word *kroshṭu* "a jackal" takes a form like what ends in *tṛich* (No. 224).

ऋन्नेभ्यो ङीप् । ४ । १ । ५ ।

ऋदन्तेभ्यो नान्तेभ्यश्च स्त्रियां ङीप्। क्रोष्ट्री गौरीवत्। भ्रूः श्रीवत्। स्वयंभूः पुंवत्।

No. 256.—AFTER WORDS ENDING IN ṚI, and after words ending in *n*, in forming the feminine, the affix is *ńíp.* Thus is formed *kroshṭrí*, which is declined like *gaurí* (No. 250).

The word *bhrú* "the eyebrow" is declined like *śrí* (No. 252), and *swayańbhú* as in the masculine (No. 232).

न षट्स्वस्रादिभ्यः। ४। १। १०।

ङीप्टापौ न।

स्वसा तिस्रश्चतस्रश्च ननान्दा दुहिता तथा।
याता मातेति सप्तैते स्वस्रादय उदाहृताः॥

स्वसा। स्वसारौ। माता पितृवत्। शसि मातॄः। द्यौर्गोवत्। राः पुंवत्। नौर्ग्लौवत्।

। इत्यजन्तस्त्रीलिङ्गाः।

No. 257.—NOT AFTER SHAṬ (No. 324), NOR AFTER SWASṚI &c, is the feminine termination *ńíp* or *ṭáp* affixed. By "*swasṛi* &c," are meant the following seven viz. *swasá* "a sister," *tisrah* "three," *chatasrah* "four," *nanándá* "a husband's sister," *duhitá* "a daughter," *yátá* "a husband's brother's wife," and *mátá* "a mother." Thus we have 1. s. *swasá* (No. 227), 1. d. *swasárau.*

The word *mátṛi* is declined like *pitṛi* (No. 235), only that in the 2 p. it makes *mátṛíh* (No. 156).

The word *dyo* "the heaven" is declined like *go* (No. 237), *rai* "wealth" as in the masculine (No. 239), and *nau* "a boat," like *glau* (No. 239).

So much for feminines ending in vowels.

OF NEUTER WORDS ENDING IN VOWELS.

। अजन्तनपुंसकलिङ्गाः ।

अतोऽम् । ७ । १ । २४ ।

अतोऽङ्गात् क्लीबात् स्वमोरम् । ज्ञानम् । एङ्ह्रस्वादिति हल्लोपः । हे ज्ञान ।

No. 258.—AFTER a neuter inflective base ending in short A, there is AM instead of *su* and *am*. Hence *jnána+su=jnánam* "knowledge." The 2nd s. is the same. In the voc. s., by No. 153, the consonant *m* is elided—thus *he jnána*.

नपुंसकाच्च । ७ । १ । १९ ।

क्लीबादौङः शी । भसंज्ञायाम् ।

No. 259.—AND AFTER A NEUTER, *śí* is instead of *au* (No. 240). As that which precedes this affix is termed *bha* (No. 185), the following rule presents itself.

यस्येति च । ६ । ४ । १४८ ।

ईकारे तद्धिते च भस्येवर्णावर्णयोर्लोपः । इत्यलोपे प्राप्ते ।

No. 260.—WHERE long í follows, AND when a *taddhita* affix follows, there is elision OF the I or *í* or A or *á* of a *bha*. The elision of the *a* having thus presented itself, *Kátyáyana* interposes.

औङः श्यां प्रतिषेधो वाच्यः । ज्ञाने ।

No. 261.—"It should be mentioned that the rule is debarred in the case where *śí* is the substitute of *au*." Hence 1. d. *jnána+śí=jnáne*.

जश्शसोः शिः । ७ । १ । २० ।

क्लीबात् ।

No. 262.—Instead OF JAS AND ŚAS, let there be *śí* after a neuter.

शि सर्वनामस्थानम् । १ । १ । ४२ ।

No. 263.—Let *śi* be termed SARVANÁMASTHÁNA.

नपुंसकस्य झलचः ।७।१।७२।

झलन्तस्याजन्तस्य च क्लीबस्य नुम् स्यात् सर्वनामस्थाने ।

No. 264.—Let *num* be the augment OF what being NEUTER ends in JHAL OR ACH, when a *sarvanámasthána* follows.

मिदचोऽन्त्यात् परः ।१।१।४७।

अचां मध्ये योऽन्त्यस्तस्मात् परस्तस्यैवान्तावयवो मित् स्यात् । उपधादीर्घः । ज्ञानानि । पुनस्तद्वत् । शेषं पुंवत् । एवं धनवनफलादयः ।

No. 265.—Let WHAT HAS AN INDICATORY M come AFTER THE LAST OF THE VOWELS, and become the final portion of that (which it augments). Thus the *n* (of *num,* No. 264) is annexed to the final *a* of *jnána,* and is regarded as a portion of the word. Then the new penultimate vowel (by No. 197) is lengthened, and we have 1. p. *jnánáni.* Again in the accusative case it is the same. The rest is like the masculine. In the same way are declined *dhana* "wealth," *vana* "a wood," *phala* "fruit," and the like.

अद्ड्डतरादिभ्यः पञ्चभ्यः ।७।१।२५।

एभ्यः क्लीबेभ्यः स्वमोरद्डादेशः स्यात् ।

No. 266.—Let ADḌ be the substitute for *su* and *am* AFTER THE FIVE, ḌATARA &C. viz., (*ḍatara, ḍatuma, anya, anyatara,* and *itara*—see No. 170) when neuter.

टेः ।६।४।१४३।

डिति भस्य टेर्लोपः । कतरत् । कतरद् । कतरे । कतराणि । हे कतरत् । शेषं पुंवत् । एवं कतमत् । इतरत् । अन्यत् । अन्यतरत् । अन्यतमस्य त्वन्यतममित्येव ।

No. 267.—When that which has an indicatory *ḍ* follows, there is elision OF the ṬI (the last vowel with anything that follows it—No. 52) of a *bha* (No. 185). Hence in the case of *katara* "which of the two?" formed by the affix *ḍatara* (No. 170), when *adḍ* is substituted for *su* or *am* by No. 266, we have 1st and 2nd s. *katara+add=katarat* (No. 165) or *katarad,* 1st and 2nd d. *katare,* 1st and 2nd p. *katarāṇi,* voc. s. *he katarat.* The rest is like the masculine. In the same way *katamat, itarat, anyat,* and *anyatarat.* But *anyatama* makes *anyatamam* (like *jnánam* No. 258), because the citation of *anyatara,* in No. 170, shows that *anyatara* and *anyatama* are not held to be formed from *anya* by the affixes *ḍatara* and *ḍatama* included in the list there given.

एकतरात् प्रतिषेधः । एकतरम् ।

No. 268.—"There should be a PROHIBITION of the substitution, directed by No. 266, for the affix that comes AFTER EKATARA." Hence 1st and 2nd s. *ekataram.*

ह्रस्वो नपुंसके प्रातिपदिकस्य ।१।२।४७।

अजन्तस्येत्येव । श्रीपं ज्ञानवत् ।

No. 269.—THE SHORT vowel shall be the substitute, IN THE NEUTER, OF A CRUDE FORM provided it end in a vowel. Hence *śrípá+su=śrípam* "having wealth," like *jnána* (No. 258).

स्वमोर्नपुंसकात् ।७।१।२३।

लुक् स्यात् । वारि ।

No. 270.—OF SU AND AM AFTER A NEUTER, let there be the elision called *luk* (Nos. 209 and 211). Hence *vári+su=vári* "water."

इकोऽचि विभक्तौ ।७।१।७३।

इगन्तस्य क्लीबस्य नुमचि विभक्तौ । वारिणी । वारीणि । न लुमतेत्यस्यानित्यत्वात् पक्षे सम्बुद्धिनिमित्तो गुणः । हे वारि । हे वारे । घेर्ङितीति गुणे प्राप्ते । वृद्ध्यौत्वतृज्वद्भावगुणेभ्यो नुम् पूर्वविप्रतिषेधेन । वारिणे । वारिणः २ । वारिणोः २ । नुमचिरेति नुट् । वारीणाम् । वारिणि । हलादौ हरिवत् ।

No. 271.—Let *num* be the augment OF a neuter ending in IK, WHEN A CASE-AFFIX beginning with ACH FOLLOWS. Hence 1. d. *vári+au=váriṇí,* 1. p. *vári+jas=váríṇi* (No. 197).

As the rule No. 211 is not invariable, we have, alternatively, the *guṇa* caused by *sambuddhi* (No. 189). Hence either *he vári* (No. 271) or *he váre.* [That the rule is not invariable, Patañjali declares in the *Mahábháshya.*]

When the affixes with an indicatory *ń* are to be added, *guṇa* is obtained from No. 192 ; but *num* takes effect to the exclusion not only of *guṇa* but of *vṛiddhi* (No. 202) and the substitution of *au* (No. 194) and the being regarded as ending in *tṛich* (No. 224) the prior rule here debarring the subsequent (contrary to the general principle laid down at No. 132). Hence 4 s. *váriṇe,* 5. and 6. s. *váriṇah,* 6. and 7. d. *váriṇoh.* In the 6. p. according to the *várti-ka* No. 231, there is *nuṭ,* and then the preceding vowel is lengthened by No. 168—thus *váríṇám.* In the 7. s. (by the same rules as the 5th and 6th) *váriṇi.* With the affixes beginning with consonants, the word is declined like *hari* (No. 187).

अस्थिदधिसक्थ्यक्ष्णामनङुदात्तः ।७।१।७५।

टादावचि ।

No. 272.—Instead OF ASTHI "a bone," DADHI "curdled milk," SAKTHI "the thigh," AND AKSHI "the eye," there shall be ANAŃ ACUTELY ACCENTED, when *ṭá* follows, or any of the subsequent terminations beginning with a vowel.

अल्लोपोऽनः ।६।४।१३४।

अङ्गावयवोऽसर्वनामस्थानयजादिस्वादिपरो योऽन् तस्याकारस्य लोपः । दध्ना । दध्ने । दध्नः २ । दध्नोः २ ।

No. 273.—There is ELISION OF the A OF AN followed by one of the affixes *su* &c. beginning with *y* or *ach,* those affixes called *sarvanámasthána* being excepted, and the *an* being a portion of the *ańga.* Hence 3. s. *dadhi+anań+ṭá=dadhná,* 4. s. *dadhne,* 5. and 6. s. *dadhnah,* 6. and 7. d. *dadhnoh.*

विभाषा ङिश्योः ।६।४।१३६।

अङ्गावयवोऽसर्वनामस्थानपरो योऽन् तस्याकारस्य लोपो वा स्यान्ङिश्योः परयोः । दध्नि । दधनि । शेषं वारिवत् । एवमस्थिसक्थ्यक्षि ।

सुधि । सुधिनी । सुधीनि । हे सुधे । हे सुधि । सुधिनेत्यादि । मधु । मधुनी । मधूनि । हे मधो । हे मधु । सुलु । सुलुनी । सुलूनि । सुलुनेत्यादि । धातृ । धातृणी । धातॄणि । धातॄणाम् । हे धातः । एवं ज्ञात्रादयः ।

No. 274.—WHEN ṄI AND ŚÍ FOLLOW, the elision is OPTIONAL of the *a* of *an*, that being a portion of the *aṅga*, and followed not by a *sarvanámasthána*.

Example, 7. s. *dadhni* or *dadhani*. The remainder is like *vári* (No. 270). In the same way *asthi*, *sakthi*, and *akshi*.

The word *sudhí* "intelligent" makes 1. s. *sudhi* (Nos. 266 and 270), 1. d. *sudhiṇí*, 1. p. *sudhíni*, voc. s. *he sudhe* (No. 189) or *he sudhi* (No. 211, see No. 271), 3. s. *sudhiná*, and so on. So 1. s. *madhu* "sweet," 1. d. *madhuní*, 1. p. *madhúni*, voc. s. *he madho* or *he madhu*, and so *sulu* "which cuts well," 1. d. *suluní*, 1. p. *sulúni*, 3. s. *suluná*, and so on. Again, 1. s. *dhátṛi* "fostering," 1. d. *dhátṛiṇí*, 1. p. *dhátṛíṇi*, 6. p. *dhátṛíṇám* (Nos. 167, 163 & 235), voc. s. *he dhátaḥ* (Nos. 186 and 110). In the same way *jṅátṛi* "intelligent," and the like.

एच इग्घ्रस्वादेशे । १ । १ । ४८ ।

प्रद्यु । प्रद्युनी । प्रद्यूनि । प्रद्युनेत्यादि । प्ररि । प्ररिणी । प्ररीणि । प्ररिणा । एकदेशविकृतमनन्यवत् । प्रराभ्याम् । प्ररीणाम् । सुनु । सुनुनी । सुनूनि । सुनुनेत्यादि ।

। इत्यजन्तनपुंसकलिङ्गाः ।

No. 275.—OF ECH IK is the substitute, WHEN SHORT A is SUBSTITUTED. Thus, 1. s. (*pra*+*dyau*+*su*=) *pradyu* "heavenly," 1. d. *pradyuní*, 1. p. *pradyúni*, 3. s. *pradyuná*, &c.; so too (*pra*+*rai* +*su*=) *prari* "possessed of great wealth", 1. d. *prariṇí*, 1. p *praríṇi*, 3. s. *prariṇá* &c. In accordance with the maxim that "what is partially altered does not become something quite different," though the *ai* has been changed to *i*, yet No. 239 applies to the 3rd d. giving *prarábhyám*, 6. p. *praríṇám*. In the same way (*su+nau+su=*) *sunu* "possessed of good boats," 1. d. *sununí*, 1. p. *sunúni*, 3. s. *sununá*, and so on.

So much for neuters ending in vowels.

MASCULINES ENDING IN CONSONANTS.

। हलन्तपुंलिङ्गाः ।

हो ढः । ८ । २ । ३१ ।

झलि पदान्ते च । लिट् । लिड् । लिहौ । लिहः । लिड्भ्याम् । लिट्सु । लिट्त्सु

No. 276—Instead OF H let there be ḌH, when *jhal* follows, or at the end of a *pada*. Thus *lih+su=liṭ* or *liḍ* (Nos. 199, 82 and 165) "who licks," 1. d. *lihau*, 1. p. *lihah*, 3. d. *liḍbhyám* (No. 184), 7. p. *liṭsu* or *liṭṭsu* (No. 102).

दादेर्धातोर्घः । ८ । २ । ३२ ।

झलि पदान्ते चोपदेशे दादेर्धातोर्हस्य घः ।

No. 277.—When *jhal* follows, or at the end of a *pada*, GH is the substitute OF the H OF WHAT verbal root, in an *upadeśa* (see No. 5, here referring to the grammatical list called *dhátupáṭha*), BEGINS WITH D.

एकाचो बशो भष् झषन्तस्य स्ध्वोः । ८ । २ । ३७ ।

धात्ववयवस्यैकाचो झषन्तस्य बशो भष् से ध्वे पदान्ते च । धुक् । धुग् । दुहौ । दुहः । धुग्भ्याम् । धुक्षु ।

No. 278.—BHASH is the substitute OF BAŚ being part OF WHAT verbal root HAS but ONE VOWEL AND ENDS IN JHASH, WHEN S OR DHW FOLLOWS, or at the end of a *pada*. Thus *duh+su=dhuk* or *dhug* "who milks" (No. 277), 1. d. *duhau*, 1. p. *duhah*, 3. d. *dhugbhyám* (No. 184), 7. p. *dhukshu* (No. 169).

वा द्रुहमुहष्णुहष्णिहाम् । ८ । २ । ३३ ।

एषां ह्रस्य वा घो झलि पदान्ते च। धुक्। धुग्। धुट्। धुड्।
द्रुहौ। द्रुहः। धुग्भ्याम्। धुड्भ्याम्। धुक्षु। धुट्सु। धुट्त्सु।
एवं मुह्।

No. 279.—When *jhal* follows, or at the end of a *pada*, *gh* shall be OPTIONALLY the substitute OF DRUH "to hate," MUH "to be foolish," SNUH "to be sick," AND SNIH "to be unctuous."

Thus *druh+su=dhruk* or *dhrug*, or, alternatively, *dhruṭ* or *dhruḍ*, "who hates," 1. d. *druhau*, 1. p. *druhah*, 3. d. *dhrug-bhyám* or, alternatively, *dhruḍbhyám*, 7. p. *dhrukshu* or *dhruṭsu*, or (No. 102) *dhruṭtsu*. In the same way *muh*.

धात्वादेः षः सः। ६। १। ६४।
स्नुट्। स्नुड्। स्नुक्। स्नुग्। एवं स्निह्।

No. 280.—S is the substitute OF SH INITIAL IN A VERBAL ROOT. Thus the root cited in No. 279, which in the grammatical list appears in the shape of *shṇuh*, becomes, when at the end of a word, in the 1. s. *snuṭ*, *snuḍ*, *snuk* or *snug*. In the same way *snih*.

इग्यणः संप्रसारणम्। १। १। ४५।

No. 281.—Let IK substituted in the place OF YAṆ be called SAṄPRASÁRAṆA.

वाह ऊठ्। ६। ४। १३२।
भस्य वाहः संप्रसारणमूठ्।

No. 282.—ŪṬH is the *saṅprasáraṇa* (No 281) OF *váh*, when this is a *bha* (No. 185). Thus we should have *ú+áh*.

संप्रसारणाच्च। ६। १। १०८।
संप्रसारणादचि पूर्वरूपमेकादेशः। वृद्धिः। विश्वौहः। इत्यादि।

No. 283.—And AFTER A SAṄPRASÁRAṆA, if *ach* follows, the form of the prior is the single substitute. Thus we have (No. 282) *ú+áh=úh*. Then (by No. 42) there is *vṛiddhi*, whence we have 2. p. *viśwa+úh+śas=viśwauhah* "the all sustaining," &c.

चतुरनडुहोरामुदात्तः ।७।१।९८।

No. 284.—OF CHATUR AND ANAḌUH ACUTELY ACCENTED ÁM is the augment, (when a *sarvanámasthána* follows). [Thus we get *anaḍwáh.* No. 265.]

सावनडुहः ।७।१।८२।

नुम् । अनड्वान् ।

No. 285.—WHEN SU FOLLOWS, *num* is the augment OF ANAḌUH. The word having been previously altered by No. 284, we have *anaḍwáh* + *num* + *su* = *anaḍwán* "an ox." [The elision of *h* by No. 26 is not perceived by No. 200—see No. 39—so that the *n* is not elided.]

अम् सम्बुद्धौ ।७।१।९९।

हे अनड्वन् । अनड्वाहौ २ । अनडुहः ।

No. 286.—WHEN SU GIVES the SENSE OF the VOCATIVE, the augment of *anaḍuh* and *chatur* is AM. Thus *he anaḍwan,* 1st and 2nd d. *anaḍwáhau,* 2nd p. *anaḍuhah.*

वसुस्रंसुध्वंस्वनडुहां दः ।८।२।७२।

सान्तस्य वस्वन्तस्य स्रंसादेश्च दः स्यात् पदान्ते । अनडुद्भ्यामित्यादि । सान्तेति किम् । विद्वान् । पदान्तेति किम् । स्रस्तम् । ध्वस्तम् ।

No. 287.—At the end of a *pada,* let D be the substitute OF that which, formed by the affix VASU, ends in *s,* and of SRAŃSU "to fall down," DHWAŃSU "to fall down," AND ANAḌUH. Thus, 3rd d. *anaḍudbhyám* &c. (No. 184). Why if it "ends in *s?*" Witness *vidwán,* the 1st s. m. of *vidwas* "learned," (where the *pada,* though formed by *vasu,* does not end in *s*). Why "at the end of a *pada?*" Witness *srastam,* and *dhwastam,* "decayed" (where the final *s* of the root is not the final of a *pada*).

सहेः साडः सः ।८।३।५६।

साड्रूपस्य सहेः सस्य मूर्द्धन्यादेशः । तुराषाट् । तुराषाड् । तुरासाहौ । तुरासाहः । तुराषाड्भ्यामित्यादि ।

No. 288.—Let there be a cerebral substitute in the room OF the S OF the root SHAHA in the shape OF SÁḌ. Hence in the 1. s. of *turásáh* "Indra," we have *turásháṭ* or *turásháḍ* (No. 276). When the *h* is not changed to *ḍh*, the present rule does not apply—thus 1st d. *turásáhau,* 1st p. *turásáhah.* In the 3rd d. again *turásháḍ-bhyám,* and so on.

दिव औत् ।७।१।८४।

दिविति प्रातिपदिकस्यौत् स्यात् सौ । सुद्यौः । सुदिवौ ।

No. 289.—Let AUT be the substitute OF the crude form DIV, when *su* follows. Thus *sudiv* becomes (*sudi+au=*) *sudyau,* and 1st s. *sudyauh* "passing pleasant days." In the 1st d. *sudivau.*

दिव उत् ।६।१।१३१।

पदान्ते । सुद्युभ्यामित्यादि । चत्वारः । चतुरः । चतुर्भिः । चतुर्भ्यः ।

No. 290.—At the end of a *pada,* let UT be the substitute OF DIV. Thus 3. d. *sudyubhyám,* and so on.

We have now to consider the declension of *chatur* "four." By No. 284 this word takes the augment *ám* in the 1st p. *chatwárah.* The declension then goes on regularly—2nd p. *chaturah,* 3rd p. *chaturbhih,* 4th p. *chaturbhyah.*

षट्चतुर्भ्यश्च ।७।१।५५।

एभ्य आमो नुडागमः ।

No. 291.—Let *nuṭ* be the augment (No. 103) of *ám* (6th p.) coming AFTER SHAṬ (No. 324) AND CHATUR.

रषाभ्यां नो णः समानपदे ।८।४।१।

No. 292.—Let Ṇ be substituted in the room OF N coming AFTER R OR SH IN THE SAME PADA.

अचो रहाभ्यां द्वे ।८।४।४६।

चतुर्णाम् ।

No. 293.—There are optionally two in the room of the *pra-*

tyáhára yar coming AFTER R OR H AFTER A VOWEL. Thus we have 6th p. *chaturṇṇám*.

रोः सुपि । ८ । ३ । १६ ।

रोरेव विसर्गः सुपि । षत्वम् । षस्य द्वित्वे प्राप्ते ।

No. 294.—Instead OF RU only (& not of the *r* which has not an indicatory *u*) there shall be *visarga*, WHEN SUP (7th p.) FOLLOWS. Hence the substitution of *visarga* does not take place in the case of *chatur*. In the 7th p. the change of *s* to *sh* is obtained from No. 169; and then the reduplication of the *sh* offering itself in No. 293, we look forward.

शरोऽचि । ८ । ४ । ४९ ।

अचि परे शरो न द्वे स्तः । चतुर्षु ।

No. 295.—There are not two in the room OF A SIBILANT, WHEN A VOWEL FOLLOWS. Hence *chaturshu*.

मो नो धातोः । ८ । २ । ६४ ।

पदान्ते । प्रशान् ।

No. 296.—At the end of a *pada*, N is the substitute OF the M OF A VERBAL ROOT. Thus 1st s. *praśám* + *su* = *praśán* "tranquil."

किमः कः । ७ । २ । १०३ ।

विभक्तौ । कः । कौ । के । इत्यादि । सर्ववत् ।

No. 297.—When a case-affix follows, KA is the substitute OF the interrogative pronoun KIM. Thus 1st s. *kah* "who?" 1st d. *kau*, 1st p. *ke* (No. 171), and so on, like *sarva* (No. 172).

इदमो मः । ७ । २ । १०८ ।

सौ । त्यदाद्यत्वापवादः ।

No. 298.—When *su* follows, let M be the substitute of the pronoun IDAM "this." This direction, to substitute *m* for *m*, debars the substitution of *a* by No. 213.

इदोऽय् पुंसि । ७ । २ । १११ ।

इदम इदोऽय् सौ पुंसि । अयम् । त्यदाद्यत्वे ।

No. 299.—When *su* follows, IN THE MASCULINE, AY is the substitute OF the ID of the pronoun *idam* (No. 298). Thus 1st s. *ayam.* In the other cases *a* is substituted for the final by No. 213.

अतो गुणे । ६ । १ । ९७ ।

अपदान्तादतो गुणे पररूपमेकादेशः ।

No. 300.—IF GUṆA come AFTER short A not final in a *pada,* the single substitute for both is the form of the subsequent.

Thus, when *a* (by No. 213) is substituted for the *m* of *idam,* we have *ida+a=ida.*

दश्च । ७ । २ । १०९ ।

इदमो दस्य मः स्याद्विभक्तौ । इमौ । इमे । त्यदादेः सम्बोधनं नास्तीत्युत्सर्गः ।

No. 301.—AND let *m* be the substitute OF the D of *idam,* when a case-affix follows. Thus 1st d. *imau* (No. 213), 1st p. *ime* (No. 171).

It is a peculiarity of the pronouns *tyad* &c. that they are not used in the vocative.

अनाप्यकः । ७ । २ । ११२ ।

अककारस्येदम इदोऽनापि विभक्तौ । आबिति प्रत्याहारः । अनेन ।

No. 302.—The substitute for the *id* OF WHAT *idam* IS WITHOUT K (No. 1321) is AN, WHEN one of the case-affixes termed ÁP FOLLOWS. This *áp* is a *pratyáhára* formed of the *á* of the 3rd case sing. and the *p* of the 7th pl. and denoting these and the intermediate cases—(Compare No. 183). Thus we have 3rd s. *anena.*

हलि लोपः । ७ । २ । ११३ ।

अककारस्येदम इदो लोप आपि हलादौ । नानर्थकेऽलोऽन्त्यविधिरनभ्यासविकारे ।

No. 303.—WHEN *áp* (No. 302) that begins with A CONSONANT

FOLLOWS, there is ELISION of the *id* of the *idam* which is without *k* (No. 1321). According to No. 27, the elision should be only of the final, and not of the whole *id*—but we are told that No. 27 does not apply to what (like *id*) has no meaning, except in the case of changes connected with the reduplication of verbs (No. 427). Thus, there remains of the word only *a*.

आद्यन्तवदेकस्मिन्।१।१।२१।

एकस्मिन् क्रियमाणं कार्यमादाविवान्त इव स्यात्। सुपि चेति दीर्घः। आभ्याम्।

No. 304.—Let an operation be performed ON A SINGLE letter AS UPON AN INITIAL OR UPON A FINAL.

For Example,—by No. 160, it is directed that a final *a* is to be lengthened before a case-affix beginning with *yań*—but a caviller might object that the solitary *a* obtained from No. 303 is *initial*, and cannot therefore be *final*. The present rule therefore declares that it is to be regarded as either the one or the other as the case may require. Hence we have 3rd du. *(a + bhyám =) ábhyám.*

नेदमदसोरकोः।७।१।११।

अककारयोरिदमदसोर्भिस ऐस् न। एभिः। अस्मै। एभ्यः। अस्मात्। अस्य। अनयोः २। एषाम्। अस्मिन्। एषु।

No. 305.—*Ais* (No. 161) is NOT substituted for *bhis* AFTER the pronouns IDAM OR ADAS WITHOUT K (No. 1321). Hence 3rd p. *ebhih* (No. 164), 4th s. *asmai* (Nos. 303 and 172), 4th p. *ebhyah*, 5th s. *asmát* (No. 173), 6th s. *asya* (No. 159), 6th and 7th du. *anayoh* (Nos. 302 and 166), 6th p. *eshám* (No. 174), 7th s. *asmin* (No. 173), 7th p. *eshu* (No. 169).

द्वितीयाटौस्स्वेनः।२।४।३४।

इदमेतदोरन्वादेशे। किंचित् कार्यं विधातुमुपात्तस्य कार्यान्तरं विधातुं पुनरुपादानमन्वादेशः। यथा। अनेन व्याकरणमधीतमेनं छन्दोऽध्यापयेति। अनयोः पवित्रं कुलमेनयोः प्रभूतं स्वमिति। एनम्। एनौ। एनान्। एनेन। एनयोः २। राजा।

No. 306.—WHEN an affix of the 2nd CASE, OR ṬÁ OR OS FOLLOWS, let ENA be the substitute of *idam* and *etad,* in the case of its re-employment *(anwádeśa)* in the subsequent members of a sentence in which the pronoun has already been used. By "re-employment" *(anwádeśa)* is meant the employment again of what has been employed to direct some operation, to direct another operation. As, for example, "The grammar has been studied by him *(anena),* now set him *(enam)* to read the *Vedas.*" Or again "Of these two *(anayoh)* the family is illustrious—and their *(enayoh)* wealth is great." The cases in this form are 2nd s. *enam,* 2nd. *enau,* 2nd p. *enán,* 3rd s. *enena,* 6th and 7th du. *enayoh.*

We now come to the declension of *rájan,* which makes 1st s. *rájá* "a king" (Nos. 197, 199, and 200).

न ङिसम्बुद्ध्योः । ८ । २ । ८ ।

नस्य लोपो न ङौ सम्बुद्धौ च । हे राजन् ।

No. 307.—There is NOT elision of *n,* WHEN ṄI or SAMBUDDHI (No. 151), FOLLOWS. Thus *he rájan* "oh king."

ङावुत्तरपदे प्रतिषेधः । ब्रह्मनिष्ठः । राजानौ । राजानः । राज्ञः ।

No. 308.—According to *Kátyáyana* there is "a PROHIBITION of No. 307, WHEN there is ṄI AND A SUBSEQUENT TERM forming a compound." Thus *brahman + nishṭha = brahmanishṭhah* "abiding in *Bráhma.*" In the 1st and 2nd d. *rájánau,* 1st p. *rájánah,* 2nd p. *rájṅah* (Nos. 185, 273, and 76).

नलोपः सुप्स्वरसंज्ञातुग्विधिषु कृति । ८ । २ । २ ।

सुब्विधौ स्वरविधौ संज्ञाविधौ कृति तुग्विधौ नलोपोऽसिद्धो नान्यत्र। राजाश्व इत्यादावित्यसिद्धत्वादात्वमेत्वमैस्त्वं च न । राजभ्याम् । यज्वा । यज्वानौ । यज्वानः ।

No. 309.—THE ELISION OF N (No. 200) shall be as if it had not taken effect (No. 39) IN SO far as regards RULES directing the application OF CASE-AFFIXES, OR relating TO ACCENTUATION OR the attribution of NAMES (as in No. 324) OR the augment TUK WHEN THERE IS A KṚIT-AFFIX (Nos. 816 and 828), but the elision shall not be so regarded elsewhere. Hence the actuality of the elision is recognised in such instances as *rája+aśwa=rájáśwa* "the king's horse," where the rule that presents itself (in this instance No. 55) is not one of those just enumerated. On the other hand, from the elision's not being regarded as having taken effect, there is neither prolongation of the vowel (No. 160) nor the change of *a* to *é* (No. 164) nor the substitution of *ais* for *bhis* (No. 161). Hence 3rd d. *rájabhyám.*

We have next to decline *yajwan* "a sacrificer," which makes 1st s. *yajwá,* 1st d. *yajwánau,* 1st p. *yajwánah.*

न संयोगाद्वमन्तात् । ६ । ४ । १३७ ।

वमान्तसंयोगादनोऽकारस्य लोपो न । यज्वनः । यज्वना । यज्वभ्याम् । ब्रह्मणः । ब्रह्मणा ।

No. 310.—There is NOT elision of the *a* of *an* (No. 273), when it comes AFTER a CONJUNCT CONSONANT ENDING IN V OR M. Thus 2nd p. *yajwanah,* 3rd s. *yajwaná,* 3rd d. *yajwabhyám.* In the same way, from *brahman* "*Brahma,*" we have 2nd p. *brahmaṇah,* 3rd s. *brahmaṇá.*

इन्हन्पूषार्यम्णां शौ । ६ । ४ । १२ ।

एषां शावेवोपधाया दीर्घो नान्यत्र । इति निषेधे प्राप्ते ।

No. 311.—The penult letter is lengthened (No. 197) of the affix IN (indicating a possessor), HAN "to strike," PÚSHAN "the sun," AND ARYAMAN "the sun," only WHEN ŚI FOLLOWS (No. 262 and 263). A prohibition thus presenting itself (to the lengthening of the penult vowel in the 1st s. of the word *vṛitrahan* "*Indra*—the destroyer of the demon *Vṛitra,*" we look forward).

सौ च । ६ । ४ । १३ ।

इन्नादीनामुपधाया दीर्घोऽसम्बुद्धौ सौ । वृत्रहा । हे वृत्रहन् ।

No. 312.—AND WHEN SU FOLLOWS, not in the sense of the vocative singular, the long vowel is the substitute of the penult of *in* &c. (No. 311). Thus 1st s. *vṛitrahá,* voc. s. *he vṛitrahan.*

एकाजुत्तरपदे णः । ८ । ४ । १२ ।

एकाजुत्तरपदं यस्य तस्मिन् समासे पूर्वपदस्थान्निमित्तात् परस्य प्रातिपदिकान्तनुम्विभक्तिस्थस्य नस्य णः । वृत्रहणौ ।

No. 313.—IN A COMPOUND THE LATTER TERM OF WHICH CONTAINS BUT ONE VOWEL, let there be a cerebral Ṇ in the room of the dental *n* that follows anything which, standing in the prior term, is qualified to cause (No. 292) the change, provided the dental *n* be at the end of a *prátipadika*, or be the augment *num* (No. 264), or occur in a *vibhakti* (No. 150). Thus 2nd d. *vṛitrahaṇau* (though the *n* is not in the same *pada* with the *r*).

हो हन्तेर्ञ्णिन्नेषु । ७ । ३ । ५४ ।

ञिति णिति प्रत्यये नकारे च परे हन्तेर्हकारस्य कुत्वम् । वृत्रघ्नः । इत्यादि । एवं शार्ङ्गिन् यशस्विन्नर्यमन् पूषन् ।

No. 314.—IF AN AFFIX WITH AN INDICATORY Ñ OR Ṇ FOLLOW, OR if N follow, *ku* (i. e. one of the gutturals *ka kha ga gha ṅa*) is the substitute OF the H OF the word HAN "to kill." Thus (No. 273) in the 2nd p. *vṛitraghnah* &c.

In the same way are declined *śárṅgin* "Indra," *yaśaswin* "famous," *aryaman* "the sun," and *púshan* "the sun."

मघवा बहुलम् । ६ । ४ । १२८ ।

मघवन्शब्दस्य वा तृ इत्यन्तादेशः । ऋ इत् ।

No. 315.—Of the word MAGHAVAN "Indra," *tṛi* is OPTIONALLY the substitute. In *tṛi* the *ṛi* is indicatory.

उगिदचां सर्वनामस्थानेऽधातोः । ७ । १ । ७० ।

अधातोरुगितो नलोपिनोऽञ्चतेश्च नुम् स्यात् सर्वनामस्थाने । मघवान् । मघवन्तौ । मघवन्तः । हे मघवन् । मघवद्भ्याम् । तृत्वाभावे । मघवा । सुटि राजवत् ।

No. 316.—Let *num* be the augment OF THAT WHICH, NOT BEING A VERBAL ROOT, HAS AN INDICATORY UK, and of the verbal root *añchu* "to go" with its *n* elided, WHEN A SARVANÁMASTHÁNA (No. 183) FOLLOWS. Thus 1. s. *maghaván* (Nos. 199, 26, and 197),

1. d. *maghavantau* (No. 265), 1. p. *maghavantah*, voc. s. *he maghavan*, 3. d. *maghavadbhyám*. If *tṛi* is not substituted (No. 315) we have 1. s. *maghavá*, and, with the five first affixes *(suṭ)*, the word is declined like the word *rájan*.

श्वयुवमघोनामतद्धिते । ६ । ४ । १३३ ।

अन्नन्तानां भानामेषामतद्धिते संप्रसारणम् । मघोनः । मघवभ्याम् । एवं श्वन् युवन् ।

No. 317.—Instead of ŚWAN "a dog," YUVAN "a young man," AND MAGHAVAN "Indra," WHEN they are called *bha* (No. 185) and when a TADDHITA affix (No. 1067) DOES NOT FOLLOW, there is the *sańprasáraṇa* (No. 281). Hence 5. s. *maghonah* (No. 283), 3. d. *maghavabhyám*. So far in like manner *śwan* and *yuvan* are declined.

न संप्रसारणे संप्रसारणम् । ६ । १ । ३७ ।

यूनः । यूना । युवभ्यामित्यादि । अर्वा । हे अर्वन् ।

No. 318.—Let there NOT be a SAŃPRASÁRAṆA, WHEN a SAŃPRASÁRAṆA FOLLOWS. Hence in 2. p. *yúnaḥ*, where the *v* of *yuvan* is replaced by the *sańprasáraṇa*, the preceding *y* is not to be changed to a vowel.

So again 3. s. *yúná*. In the 3. d. *yuvabhyám*, and so on.

The word *arvan* "a horse" makes 1. s. *arvá*, voc. s. *he arvan*.

अर्वणस्त्रसावनञः । ६ । ४ । १२७ ।

नञा रहितस्यार्वन्नन्तस्याङ्गस्य तृ इत्यन्तादेशो न तु सौ । अर्वन्तौ । अर्वन्तः । अर्वद्भ्यामित्यादि ।

No. 319.—Tṛi is the substitute OF the final of an inflective base ending in ARVAN WITHOUT the privative prefix NAŃ, but NOT WHEN SU FOLLOWS. Thus 1. d. *arvantau* (No. 316), 1. p. *arvantah*, 3. d. *arvadbhyám*, and so on.

पथिमथ्यृभुक्षामात् । ७ । १ । ८५ ।

सौ ।

No. 320.—OF the words PATHIN "a traveller," MATHIN "a churner," AND ṚIBHUKSHIN "Indra," long Á is the substitute, when *su* follows. [In the *sútra* the finals of these three words do not appear by reason of No. 200.]

इतोऽत् सर्वनामस्थाने । ७ । १ । ८६ ।

पथ्यादेः ।

No. 321.—Instead OF the short I of *pathi* &c. (No. 320) there is short A, WHEN A SARVANÁMASTHÁNA (No. 183) FOLLOWS.

थो न्थः । ७ । १ । ८७ ।

पथिमथोस्थस्य न्थादेशः सर्वनामस्थाने । पन्थाः । पन्थानौ । पन्थानः ।

No. 322.—NTH is the substitute OF the TH of the words *pathin* and *mathin*, when a *sarvanámasthána* follows. Thus 1. s. *panthāh* (No. 321), 1. d. *panthánau*, 1. p. *panthánah.*

भस्य टेर्लोपः । ७ । १ । ८८ ।

भस्य पथ्यादेष्टिलोपः । पथः । पथा । पथिभ्याम् । एवं मथिन् ऋभुक्षिन् ।

No. 323.—There is ELISION OF the ṬI (No. 52) of *pathin* &c. (No. 320), WHEN the word is a BHA (No. 185). Hence 2. p. *pathah*, 3. s. *pathá*, 3. d. *pathibhyám.* In the same way *mathin* and *ṛibhukshin* (No. 320) are declined.

ष्णान्ता षट् । १ । १ । २४ ।

षान्ता नान्ता च संख्या षट्संज्ञा स्यात् । पञ्चन्शब्दो नित्यं बहुवचनान्तः । पञ्च । पञ्च । पञ्चभिः । पञ्चभ्यः २ । नुट् ।

No. 324.—Let a numeral, ENDING IN SH OR N be called SHAṬ. The word *pañchan* "five" is always plural:—1. p. *pañcha*, 2. p. *pañcha*, 3. p. *pañchabhih*, 4. and 5. p. *pañchabhyah.* In the 6th p. the augment *nuṭ* (No. 291).

नोपधायाः । ६ । ४ । ७ ।

नान्तस्योपधाया दीर्घो नामि । पञ्चानाम् । पञ्चसु ।

325.—When *nám* follows, the long vowel is the substitute OF THE PENULT LETTER OF that which ends in N. Thus 6. p. *pañchánám*, 7. p. *pañchasu*.

अष्टन आ विभक्तौ।७।२।८४।

हलादौ वा स्यात्।

No. 326.—WHEN A CASE-AFFIX beginning with a consonant FOLLOWS, let Á be optionally the substitute OF the word ASHṬAN "eight."

अष्टाभ्य औश्।७।१।२१।

कृताकारादष्टनो जश्शसोरौश्। अष्टभ्य इति वक्तव्ये कृतात्वनिर्देशो जश्शसोर्विषय आत्वं ज्ञापयति। अष्टौ २। अष्टाभ्यः २। अष्टानाम्। अष्टासु। आत्वाभावे। अष्ट पञ्चवत्।

No. 327.—AUŚ is substituted for *jas* and *śas* coming AFTER the word ASHṬAN, when (in accordance with the option allowed by No. 326) it has taken *á* as its final.

As (it might have been expected that) *ashṭabhyah* (with a short *a*) was to be enounced (in the *sútra*), the exhibition of the word with the long *á* (*ashṭábhyah*) informs us that the substitution of long *á* (No. 326) takes place in the case of *jas* and *śas* (although these affixes do not begin with consonants).

Thus 1. and 2. p. *ashṭau*, 4. and 5. p. *ashṭábhyah*, 6. p. *ashṭánám*, 7. p. *ashṭásu*. On the alternative of the change to *á* (No. 321) not being made, *ashṭan* is declined like *pañchan* (No. 319).

ऋत्विग्दधृक्स्रग्दिगुष्णिगञ्चुयुजिक्रुञ्चां च।३।२।५९।

एभ्यः क्विन्प्रत्ययः सुप्युपपदे। युजिक्रुञ्चोः केवलयोः। क्रुञ्चेर्नलोपाभावश्च निपात्यते। कनावितौ।

No. 328.—AFTER ṚITWIK "a domestic chaplain," DADHṚIK "impudent," SRAK "a garland," DIK "a direction," USHṆIK "a quatrain," AÑCHU "to worship," YUJIR "to join," AND KRUÑCH "to approach," there shall be the affix *kwin*.

This affix comes after *anchu* only when a word ending with a case-affix precedes it in composition. It comes after *yujir* and *kruncha* when these are uncombined. The non-elision of the *n* (by 363) of *kruncha* is an irregularity.

The letters *k* and *n* are indicatory in the affix *kwin*.

कृदतिङ् । ३ । १ । ९३ ।

अत्र धात्वधिकारे तिङ्भिन्नः प्रत्ययः कृत्संज्ञः स्यात् ।

329.—In this portion of the *sútras* in which there is a reference (No. 138) to verbal roots, let any affix EXCEPT TIŃ (No. 407) be called KṚIT.

वेरपृक्तस्य । ६ । १ । ६७ ।

लोपः ।

No. 330.—OF VI when REDUCED TO A SINGLE LETTER (Nos. 198 and 36) there is elision.

क्विन्प्रत्ययस्य कुः । ८ । २ । ६२ ।

क्विन् प्रत्ययो यस्मात् तस्य कवर्गोऽन्तादेशः पदान्ते । इत्यस्यासिद्धत्वाच्चोः कुरिति कुत्वम् । ऋत्विग् । ऋत्विक् । ऋत्विजौ । ऋत्विग्भ्याम् ।

No. 331.—At the end of a *pada*, A letter of the GUTTURAL class is the substitute for the final OF that after which THE AFFIX KWIN comes.

As this *sútra* is non-existent in the sight of No. 333, the *j* of *ṛitwij* is (by No. 333, though the *Siddhánta Kaumudí* traces the change through Nos. 334 and 32, back to No. 331) changed to a guttural, and we have 1. s. *ṛitwig* or *ṛitwik*, 1. d. *ṛitwijau*, 3. d. *ṛitwigbhyám*.

युजेरसमासे । ७ । १ । ७१ ।

युजेः सर्वनामस्थाने नुम् स्यादसमासे । सुलोपः । संयोगान्तलोपः । कुत्वेन नस्य ङः । युङ् । युञ्जौ । युञ्जः । युग्भ्याम् ।

No. 332.—When a *sarvanámasthána* (No. 183) follows, let *num* be the augment OF YUJ NOT IN A COMPOUND. In the 1. s. when we have *yuj+su*, the *su* is elided by No. 199; then the *j* is elided by No26; and then the dental *n* is changed to the guttural *ń* by No. 331, giving *yuń* "who joins," 1st d. *yuñjau*, 1st p. *yuñjah*, 3rd d. *yugbhyám* (No. 333).

चोः कुः । ८ । २ । ३० ।

चवर्गस्य कवर्गः स्याज्झलि पदान्ते च । सुयुक् । सुयुजौ । सुयुग्भ्याम् । खन् । खञ्जौ । खन्भ्याम् ।

No. 333.—When *jhal* follows, or at the end of a *pada*, instead OF the PALATAL class of letters, let there be A GUTTURAL.

Thus in the compound formed of *su* "well," and *yuj* "to join," we have 1st s. *suyuk* "who applies himself well," 1st d. *suyujau*, 3rd d. *suyugbhyám*.

The word *khan* "who limps" (from the root *khaji* No. 497) makes 1st d. *khañjau*, 3rd d. *khanbhyám*.

व्रश्चभ्रस्जसृजमृजयजराजभ्राजच्छशां षः । ८ । २ । ३६ ।

झलि पदान्ते च । जश्त्वचर्त्वे । राट् । राड् । राजौ । राजः । राड्भ्याम् । एवं विभ्राट् देवेट् विश्वसृट् ।

No. 334.—When *jhal* follows, or at the end of a *pada*, let SH be the substitute OF VRAŚCHA "to cut," BHRASJA "to fry," SṚIJA "to create," MṚIJA "to rub," YAJA "to worship," RÁJA "to shine," BHRÁJA "to shine," AND of what ends in the letter CHH OR Ś.

Then, by Nos. 82 and 165, we have 1st s. *ráṭ* or *ráḍ* "a ruler, 1st d. *rájau*, 1st p. *rájah*, 3rd d. *ráḍbhyám*. In the same way *vibhráṭ* "who shines much," *deveṭ* "a worshipper of the gods," and *viśwasṛiṭ* "the creator of the universe.

परौ व्रजेः षः पदान्ते । परावुपपदे व्रजेः क्विप् स्याद्दीर्घश्च पदान्ते षत्वमपि । परिव्राट् । परिव्राजौ ।

No. 335.—"WHEN PARI (No. 48) is the first member in the compound, the affix *kwip* shall come AFTER VRAJ, the vowel shall be lengthened, and SH shall be substituted AT THE END OF A PADA." Thus 1st s. *parivráṭ* "a wandering mendicant," 1st d. *parivrájau.*

विश्वस्य वसुराटोः ।६।३।१२८।

दीर्घः । विश्वाराट् । विश्वाराड् । विश्वराजौ । विश्वाराड्भ्याम् ।

No. 336.—OF VIŚWA, WHEN VASU "wealth" OR RÁṬ (No. 334) FOLLOWS, the vowel is lengthened. Thus 1st s. *viśwáráṭ* or *viśwáráḍ* "a universal ruler. In the 1st d. the vowel is not lengthened, because the word is not in the form of *ráṭ* :—thus *viśwarájau.* In the 3rd d. again we have *viśwáráḍbhyám.*

स्कोः संयोगाद्योरन्ते च ।८।२।२९।

पदान्ते झलि च यः संयोगस्तदाद्योः स्कोर्लोपः । भृट् । सस्य श्चुत्वेन शः । झलां जश् झशीति शस्य जः । भृज्जौ । भृड्भ्याम् । त्यदाद्यत्वं पररूपत्वम् ।

No. 337.—AT THE END of a *pada*, or when *jhal* follows, there is elision OF S OR A GUTTURAL, INITIAL IN A COMPOUND CONSONANT.

Thus *bhrasj* (by a special rule) is changed to *bhṛisj*, which by the present rule becomes *bhṛij ;* it then becomes *bhṛish* by No. 334, *bhṛiḍ* by No. 82, and optionally *bhṛiṭ* by No. 165. In the 1st d. as the word is not at the end of a *pada*, the *s* does not drop, but it changes to a palatal by No. 76. Then, by No. 25, the *ś* becomes *j*, giving *bhṛijjau.* In the 3rd d. *bhṛiḍbhyám.*

Now as regards the pronouns *tyad* &c., there is the substitution of *a* (No. 213), and the substitution of the form of the subsequent (No. 300).

तदोः सः सावनन्त्ययोः ।७।२।१०६।

त्यदादीनां तदयोरनन्त्ययोः सः स्यात् सौ । स्यः । त्यौ । त्ये । सः । तौ । ते । यः । यौ । ये । एषः । एतौ । एते ।

No. 338.—WHEN SU FOLLOWS, let S be substituted in the room OF the T OR D, NOT being FINAL, of *tyad* &c.

Thus *tyad* "that" makes in the 1st s. *syah* (No. 213) :—1st d. *tyau*, 1st p. *tye* (No. 71). *Tad* "that" makes 1st s. *sah*, 1st d. *tau*, 1st p. *te*. The relative *yad* does not change its *d*, because it is final. It makes 1st s. *yah*, 1st d. *yau*, 1st p. *ye:*—*etad* "this" makes 1st s. *eshah* (Nos. 338 and 169), 1st d. *etau*, 1st p. *ete*.

ङे प्रथमयोरम् । ७ । १ । २८ ।

युष्मदस्मद्भ्यां परस्य ङे इत्येतस्य प्रथमाद्वितीययोश्चामादेशः ।

No. 339.—AM is the substitute OF ŃE (4. s.) AND OF the affixes of THE FIRST AND SECOND CASES coming after the pronouns *yushmad* "thou," and *asmad* "I."

त्वाहौ सौ । ७ । २ । ९४ ।

अनयोर्मपर्यन्तस्य त्वाहावादेशौ स्तः ।

No. 340.—TWA AND AHA are the substitutes of the portion as far as the *m* of these two (*yushmad* and *asmad*), WHEN SU FOLLOWS. That is to say, *twa* is substituted for *yushm*, and *aha* for *asm*.

शेषे लोपः । ७ । २ । ९० ।

एतयोष्टिलोपः । त्वम् । अहम् ।

No. 341.—IN THE REMAINING cases (i. e. where *á* is not substituted as by No. 343, nor *y* as by No. 348) there is ELISION of the last vowel and what follows it (No. 52) of these two (*yushmad* and *asmad*). Thus the *ad* of *yushmad* being elided, and *twa* substituted for the other portion by No. 340, and *am* substituted for *su* by No. 339, we have 1st s. *twam* "thou" (No. 300). In like manner *aham* "I."

युवावौ द्विवचने । ७ । २ । ९२ ।

द्वयोरुक्तावनयोर्मपर्यन्तस्य युवावौ स्तो विभक्तौ ।

No. 342.—When a case-affix follows IN THE DUAL, YUVA AND ÁVA are the substitutes of these two (*yushmad* and *asmad*) as far as the *m*.

प्रथमायाश्च द्विवचने भाषायाम् । ७ । २ । ८८ ।

श्रोड्येतयोरात्वं लोके । युवाम् । श्रावाम् ।

No. 343.—AND there is the substitution of long *á* IN THE FIRST CASE DUAL of these two IN SECULAR LANGUAGE (but not in the *Vedas*). Thus 1st d. *yuvám* and *ávám*. [The 2nd d. being the same as the 1st, the author employs *auṅ* which (see No. 240) denotes both. But, according to *Páṇini's* view, the 2nd d. would be formed by No. 346.]

यूयवयौ जसि । ७ । २ । ९३ ।

अनयोर्मपर्यन्तस्य । यूयम् । वयम् ।

No. 344.—WHEN JAS FOLLOWS, YÚYA AND VAYA are substituted for these two *(yushmad* and *asmad)* as far as the *m*. Thus 1st p. *yúyam* (Nos. 339, 341, and 300) and *vayam*,

त्वमावेकवचने । ७ । २ । ९७ ।

एकस्योक्तावनयोर्मपर्यन्तस्य त्वमौ स्तो विभक्तौ ।

No. 345.—When a case-affix follows IN THE SINGULAR, TWA AND MA are the substitutes of these two *(yushmad* and *asmad)* as far as the *m*.

द्वितीयायां च । ७ । २ । ८७ ।

अनयोरात् स्यात् । त्वाम् । माम् ।

No. 346—AND IN THE SECOND CASE the substitute of these two *(yushmad* and *asmad)* shall be long *á*. Thus 2nd s. *twám* and *mám*.

शसो न । ७ । १ । २९ ।

आभ्यां शसो नः स्यादमोऽपवादः । आदेः परस्य । संयोगान्तलोपः । युष्मान् । अस्मान् ।

No. 347.—The letter N is the substitute OF ŚAS coming after these two *(yushmad* and *asmad)*.

This debars No. 339. Then, as the change is directed by a term in the 5th case (No. 87), and the substitute takes the place (by No. 88) of the first letter only of what follows the term in the 5th case, the word would end in *ns*, but the *s* is elided by No. 26, and then the substitution of long *á* being obtained from No. 346, we have 2nd p. *yushmán* and *asmán*.

योऽचि। ७। २। ८९।

अनयोर्यकारादेशः स्यादनादेशेऽजादौ परतः। त्वया। मया।

No. 348.—Let the letter Y be the substitute of these two *(yushmad* and *asmad)*, WHEN an affix beginning with A VOWEL, and not having a substitute, FOLLOWS.

Thus 3rd s. *twayá* and *mayá*.

युष्मदस्मदोरनादेशे। ७। २। ८६।

अनयोरात् स्यादनादेशे हलादौ। युवाभ्याम्। आवाभ्याम्। युष्माभिः। अस्माभिः।

No. 349.—Let long *á* be the substitute OF these two, YUSHMAD AND ASMAD, WHEN AN AFFIX FOLLOWS, beginning with a consonant and NOT HAVING A SUBSTITUTE. Thus 3rd d. *yuvábyhám* (No. 342) and *ávábhyám*, 3rd p. *yushmábhih* and *asmábhih*.

तुभ्यमह्यौ ङयि। ७। २। ९५।

अनयोर्मपर्यन्तस्य। टिलोपः। तुभ्यम्। मह्यम्।

No. 350.—TUBHYA AND MAHYA are the substitutes of these two *(yushmad* and *asmad)* as far as the *m*, WHEN ŃE FOLLOWS. The last of the vowels with what follows it is elided by No. 341, and then, by No. 339, we get 4th s. *tubhyam* and *mahyam*.

भ्यसोऽभ्यम्। ७। १। ३०।

आभ्यां परस्य। युष्मभ्यम्। अस्मभ्यम्।

No. 351— ABHYAM is the substitute OF BHYAS coming after these two *(yushmad* and *asmad)*. Thus 4th p. *yushmabhyam* and *asmabhyam*. [The affix being a substitute, the long *á* of No. 349 does not appear here.]

एकवचनस्य च। ७। १। ३२।

आभ्यां ङसेरत्। त्वत्। मत्।

No. 352.—AND also of *ńasi*, the affix OF THE SINGULAR in the fifth case, coming after these two *(yushmad* and *asmad),* the substitute is *at.* Thus 5th s. *twat* and *mat* (Nos. 345 and 300).

पञ्चम्या अत् । ७ । १ । ३१ ।

आभ्यां पञ्चम्या भ्यसोऽत् स्यात् । युष्मत् । अस्मत् ।

No. 353.—Let AT be the substitute of *bhyas* OF THE FIFTH CASE, when it comes after these two *(yushmad* and *asmad).* Thus 5th p. *yushmat* and *asmat* (No. 341).

तवममौ ङसि । ७ । २ । ९६ ।

अनयोर्मपर्यन्तस्य ।

No. 354.—WHEN ŃAS FOLLOWS, TAVA AND MAMA are the substitutes of these two *(yushmad* and *asmad)* as far as the *m.*

युष्मदस्मद्भ्यां ङसोऽश् । ७ । १ । २७ ।

तव । मम । युवयोः । आवयोः ।

No. 355.—AFTER YUSHMAD AND ASMAD, AŚ is the substitute OF ŃAS. Thus 6th s. *tava* and *mama* (No. 354), 6th d. *yuvayoh* and *ávayoh* (Nos. 342 and 348).

साम आकम् । ७ । १ । ३३ ।

आभ्यां साम आकम् । युष्माकम् । अस्माकम् । त्वयि । मयि । युवयोः । आवयोः । युष्मासु । अस्मासु ।

No. 356.—ÁKAM is the substitute OF SÁM (the affix of the 6th p. of most pronominals, see No. 174) coming after these two *(yushmad* and *asmad).* Thus 6th p. *yushmákam* and *asmákam,* 7. s. *twayi* and *mayi* (No. 348), 7th d. *yuvayoh* and *ávayoh,* 7th p. *yushmásu* and *asmásu* (No. 349).

युष्मदस्मदोः षष्ठीचतुर्थीद्वितीयास्थयोर्वांनावौ । ८ । १ । २० ।

पदात् परयोरपादादौ स्थितयोः षष्ठ्यादिविशिष्टयोर्वांनावावित्यादेशौ स्तः ।

No. 357.—VÁM AND NAU are the substitutes of YUSHMAD AND ASMAD ATTENDED BY THE AFFIXES OF THE SIXTH, FOURTH, OR SECOND CASE, provided they stand after a *pada*, and not at the beginning of a hemistich. [This form is restricted to the dual by the three rules following.]

बहुवचनस्य वस्नसौ।८।१।२१।

उक्तविधयोरनयोः षष्ठ्यादिबहुवचनान्तयोर्वस्नसौ स्तः।

No. 358.—VAS AND NAS are the substitutes of those two falling under the descriptions above given (in No. 357) when in the 6th case &c. OF THE PLURAL.

तेमयावेकवचनस्य।८।१।२२।

उक्तविधयोरनयोः षष्ठीचतुर्थ्येकवचनान्तयोस्ते मे एतौ स्तः।

No. 359.—TE AND ME are the substitutes of those two falling under the descriptions above given (in No. 357) in the 6th and 4th cases OF THE SINGULAR.

त्वामौ द्वितीयायाः।८।१।२३।

द्वितीयैकवचनान्तयोस्त्वा मा इत्यादेशौ स्तः।

श्रीशस्त्वावतु मापीह दत्तात् ते मेऽपि शर्म सः।
स्वामी ते मेऽपि स हरिः पातु वामपि नौ विभुः॥
सुखं वां नौ ददात्वीशः पतिर्वामपि नौ हरिः।
सोऽव्याद्वो नः शिवं वो नो दद्यात् सेव्योऽत्र वः स नः॥

No. 360.—TWÁ AND MÁ are the substitutes OF these *(yushmad* and *asmad)* in THE SECOND CASE singular. Examples,—"May the Lord preserve thee *(twá)* and me *(má)* also here—may he give to thee *(te)*, and to me *(me)* also, felicity! That *Hari* is thy *(te)* lord and mine *(me)* also. May the Omnipresent preserve you two *(vám)* and also us two *(nau)*. May God give felicity to you two *(vám)* and to us two *(nau)*. *Hari* is the lord of you two *(vám)* and also of us two *(nau)*. May he preserve you *(vah)* and us *(nah)* may he give prosperity to you *(vah)* and to us *(nah)*. He is the object of worship here of you *(vah)* and of us *(nah)*."

एकवाक्ये युष्मदस्मदादेशा एकतिङ् वाक्यम् । तेनेह न । ओदनं पच तव भविष्यति । एते वांनावादय आदेशा अनन्वादेशे वा वक्तव्याः । अन्वादेशे तु नित्यं स्युः । धाता ते भक्तोऽस्ति धाता तव भक्तोऽस्ति । तस्मै ते नम इत्येव । सुपात् । सुपाद् । सुपादौ ।

No. 361.—"IN A SIMPLE SENTENCE THESE SUBSTITUTES (see Nos. 357 &c.) OF YUSHMAD AND ASMAD MAY BE (optionally) USED, BUT IN A SUBSEQUENT REFERENCE THEY MUST BE INVARIABLY EMPLOYED." For example—we may say "Brahmá is Thy *(te* or *tava)* worshipper," but, in the sequel "to Thee *(te)* that art such, our reverence is due," the form "te" alone is admissible.

We now come to the declension of the word *supát* or *supád* "having handsome feet,"—1st d. *supádau.*

पादः पत् । ६ । ४ । १३० ।

पाच्छब्दान्तं यदङ्गं भं तदवयवस्य पाच्छब्दस्य पदादेशः । सुपदः । सुपदा । सुपाद्भ्याम् । अग्निमत् । अग्निमथौ । अग्निमथम् ।

No. 362.—PAT is the substitute OF the word PÁD when part of an inflective base ending in the word *pád* and entitled to the name of *bha* (No. 185). Hence 2nd p. *supadah,* 3rd s. *supadá,* but 3rd d. *supádbhyám.*

The word *agnimath* "who kindles fire" makes 1st s. *agnimat* (Nos. 199, 82, and 165), 1st d. *agnimathau,* 2nd s. *agnimatham.*

अनिदितां हल उपधायाः क्ङिति । ६ । ४ । २४ ।

हलन्तानामनिदितामङ्गानामुपधाया नस्य लोपः किति ङिति । नुम् । संयोगान्तस्य लोपः । नस्य कुत्वेन ङः । प्राङ् । प्राञ्चौ । प्राञ्चः ।

No. 363.—WHEN THAT WHICH HAS an INDICATORY K OR Ń FOLLOWS, there is elision OF the *n* which is THE PENULTIMATE letter (No. 196) OF inflective bases ending in CONSONANTS and NOT HAVING an INDICATORY SHORT I. For example, the word *práńch* "eastern" is formed from the root *ańchu* "to go" (the indicatory vowel in which is not *i* but *u*) by the affix *kwin* (No. 328) which has an indicatory *k.* Thus in forming the 1. s. after eliding the affix (by No. 199) we have, by this rule, *prách.* Then by No. 316 *num* is directed, which, by No. 265, makes *pránch,* then there is elision of the final consonant (No. 26), and finally, the *n* having been changed to a guttural by No. 331, we have *práṅ.* In the 1. d. *práṅchau,* 1. p. *práṅchah.*

अचः । ६ । ४ । १३८ ।

लुप्तनकारस्याञ्चतेर्भस्याकारस्य लोपः ।

No. 364.—There is elision of the letter *a* OF ACH (i. e. of the root *aṅchu*) of which the *n* has been elided, when it is entitled to the name of *bha* (No. 185).

चौ । ६ । ३ । १३८ ।

लुप्ताकारनकाराञ्चतौ परे पूर्वस्याणो दीर्घः । प्राचः । प्राग्भ्याम् । प्रत्यङ् । प्रत्यञ्चौ । प्रतीचः । प्रत्यग्भ्याम् । उदङ् । उदञ्चौ ।

No. 365.—WHEN *aṅchu,* having its *a* elided (by No. 364) and its *n* (by No. 365)—and thus reduced to CHI, *i. e. ch,*—FOLLOWS, a long vowel is substituted for the *aṇ* (or short vowel) that precedes. Thus in the 2. p. the vowel of the prefix *pra* (No. 47) being lengthened, we have *práchah,* 3. d. *prágbhyám* (Nos. 184 and 331).

The word *pratyaṅch* "western" (in which the prefix is *prati*) in like manner (No. 363) makes 1st s. *pratyaṅ,* 1st d. *pratyaṅchau,* 2nd p. *pratíchah* (No. 365), 3rd d. *pratyagbhyám.*

The word *udaṅch* "northern" makes 1. s. *udaṅ,* 1. d. *udaṅchau.*

उद ईत् । ६ । ४ । १३९ ।

उच्छब्दात् परस्य लुप्तनकाराञ्चतेर्भस्याकारस्य ईत् । उदीचः । उदग्भ्याम् ।

No. 366.—LONG í is the substitute of the letter *a* of the root *aṅchu,* deprived of its *n* and called *bha* (No. 185), when it comes AFTER the word UT (No. 48). Thus 2nd p. *udíchah,* 3rd d. *udagbhyám.*

समः समि । ६ । ३ । ९३ ।

अप्रत्ययान्तेऽञ्चतौ । सम्यङ् । सम्यञ्चौ । समीचः । सम्यग्भ्याम् ।

No. 367.—Instead OF the prefix SAM (No. 48) there is SAMI, when *añchu* follows not ending with a *pratyaya* (as, for example, when the affix *kwin* is elided by Nos. 330 &c.). Hence 1st s. *samyań* "moving equally, right," 1st d. *samyañchau*, 2nd p. *samíchah* (No. 365), 3rd d. *samyagbhyám*.

सहस्य सध्रिः । ६ । ३ । ९५ ।

तथा । सध्र्यङ् ।

No. 368.—Under the same circumstances (No. 367), there is SADHRI instead OF SAHA. Thus 1. s. *sadhryań* "moving with."

तिरसस्तिर्यलोपे । ६ । ३ । ९४ ।

अलुप्ताकारेऽञ्चतावप्रत्ययान्ते तिरसस्तिर्यादेशः । तिर्यङ् । तिर्यञ्चौ । तिरश्चः । तिर्यग्भ्याम् ।

No. 369—TIRI is the substitute OF TIRAS, WHEN *añchu*, whose *a* is NOT ELIDED (No. 364) and which does not end in a visible affix (see No. 367), follows. Thus 1. s. *tiryań* "moving crookedly," 1. d. *tiryañchau*, 2. p. *tiraśchah* (the *a* of *añchu* being here elided by No. 364), 3. d. *tiryagbhyám*.

नाञ्चेः पूजायाम् । ६ । ४ । ३० ।

पूजार्थस्याञ्चतेरुपधाया नस्य लोपो न । प्राङ् । प्राञ्चौ । नलोपाभावादलोपो न । प्राञ्चः । प्राङ्भ्याम् । प्राङ्क्षु । एवं पूजार्थे प्रत्यङ्ङादयः । क्रुङ् । क्रुञ्चौ । क्रुङ्भ्याम् । पयोमुक् । पयोमुग् । पयोमुचौ । पयोमुग्भ्याम् । उगित्वान्नुम् ।

No. 370.—There is NOT elision (see No. 363) of the penultimate *n* OF the root AÑCHU, WHEN IT SIGNIFIES "TO WORSHIP." Thus the word *práñch* "a worshipper" makes 1. s. *práń* (Nos. 199, 26, and 331), 1. d. *práñchau*. As the *n* is not elided, the elision of the *a* (No. 364) does not take place, and we have 2. p. *práñchah*, 3. d. *práńbhyám* (Nos. 26 and 331), 7. p. *práńkshu* (Nos. 26, 331, 104, and 169). In like manner are *pratyań* &c. declined when the signification relates to "worship."

The word *kruñch* "a curlew" makes, in like manner, 1. s. *kruñ*, 1. d. *kruñchau*, 3. d. *kruñbhyám*.

The word *payomuch* "a cloud" makes 1. s. *payomuk* or *payomug* (Nos. 333 and 165), 1. d. *payomuchau*, 3. d. *payomugbhyám* (No. 333).

In consequence of its being formed by an affix with an indicatory *u*, the word *mahat* "great" takes *num* by No. 316.

सान्तमहतः संयोगस्य । ६ । ४ । १० ।

सान्तसंयोगस्य महतश्च यो नकारस्तस्योपधाया दीर्घोऽसम्बुद्धौ सर्वनामस्थाने । महान् । महान्तौ । महान्तः । हे महन् । महद्भ्याम् ।

No. 371.—When a *sarvanámasthána*, the affix implying the vocative singular excepted, follows, the long vowel becomes the substitute of that which immediately precedes the letter *n* OF A COMPOUND CONSONANT ENDING IN S OR THAT OF the word MAHAT. Thus 1. s. *mahán* (Nos. 316, 371, 199, and 26), 1. d. *mahántau*, 1. p. *mahántah*, voc. s. *he mahan*, 3. d. *mahadbhyám*.

अत्वसन्तस्य चाधातोः । ६ । ४ । १४ ।

अत्वन्तस्योपधाया दीर्घो धातुभिन्नासन्तस्य चासम्बुद्धौ । धीमान् । धीमन्तौ । धीमन्तः । हे धीमन् । शसादौ महद्वत् । भातेर्डवतुः । डित्त्वसामर्थ्यादभस्यापि टेर्लोपः । भवान् । भवन्तौ । शत्रन्तस्य तु भवन् ।

No. 372.—The long vowel is the substitute of the penultimate letter OF what ends in ATU, AND OF WHAT, NOT BEING A VERBAL ROOT, ENDS IN AS, when the 1st singular case-affix, not with the force of the vocative, follows. Thus in the case of the word *dhímat* "intelligent," formed of *dhí* "intellect" and the affix *matup*, we find 1. s. *dhímán* (Nos. 316, 199, and 26), 1. d. *dhímantau*, 1. p. *dhímantah*, voc. s. *he dhíman*. When *śas* (2. p.) and the remaining affixes follow, it is like *mahat* (No. 371).

The honorific pronoun *bhavat* "Your Honour," is formed of *bhá* "to shine" and the affix *ḍavatu*. From rule No. 267 we learn that an affix having an indicatory *ḍ* causes the elision of *ṭi*, i. e. of the final vowel and what may follow it, in whatever is called *bha* (No. 185), and the elision of *ṭi* (here the final vowel of the root) takes place in order that the possession of an indicatory *ḍ* by *ḍavatu* may not be nugatory. Hence 1. s. *bhaván* (Nos. 372, 316, 199, and 26), 2. d. *bhavantau*. Of the word *bhavat*, when it ends with the participial affix *śatṛi* and signifies "being," the 1. s. is *bhavan*.

उभे अभ्यस्तम् । ६ । १ । ५ ।

षाष्ठद्वित्वप्रकरणे ये द्वे विहिते ते उभे समुदिते अभ्यस्तसंज्ञे स्तः ।

No. 373.—Where reduplication is treated of in the Sixth Lecture, the two which are directed, BOTH taken together (not either separately) are called ABHYASTA—"a reduplicate."

नाभ्यस्ताच्छतुः । ७ । १ । ७८ ।

अभ्यस्ताच्छतुर्नुम् न । ददत् । ददतौ ।

No. 374.—OF ŚATṚI AFTER A REDUPLICATED TERM there shall NOT be the augment *num* (No. 316). Hence *dadat*, the present participle of *dá* "to give," as it is a reduplicate, makes 1. s. *dadat*, 1. d. *dadatau*.

जक्षित्यादयः षट् । ६ । १ । ६ ।

षड्धातवोऽन्ये जक्षितिश्च सप्तम एते अभ्यस्तसंज्ञाः स्युः । जक्षत् । जक्षतौ । जक्षतः । एवम् । जाग्रत् । दरिद्रत् । शासत् । चकासत् । गुप् । गुपौ । गुपः । गुब्भ्याम् ।

No. 375.—Let JAKSHITI &c., SIX verbs, with *jakshiti* itself as the seventh, be termed "reduplicate." Their being so termed brings them under No. 374, and we have 1. s. *jakshat* "eating,' 1. d. *jakshatau*, 1. p. *jakshatah*. In the same way *jágrat* "waking," *daridrat* "poor," *śásat* "ruling," *chakásat* "shining."

The word *gup* "concealing" makes 1. s. *gup*, 1. d. *gupau*, 1. p. *gupah*, 3. d. *gubbhyám* (No. 82).

त्यदादिषु दृशोऽनालोचने कञ् च । ३ । २ । ६० ।

त्यदादिषूपपदेष्वज्ञानार्थदृशेः कञ् । चात् क्विन् ।

No. 376.—AND KAṄ shall be the affix AFTER DṚIŚ, NOT SIGNIFYING "PERCEPTION," WHEN TYAD &c. (No. 170) precede it in combination. By the word "and" in the *sútra*. we are reminded that the affix *kwin* may be employed; and it is this latter that will be employed in the present instance.

आ सर्वनाम्नः । ६ । ३ । ९१ ।

दृग्दृशवतुषु । तादृक् । तादृशौ । तादृशः । तादृग्भ्याम् । व्रश्चेति षः । जश्त्वचर्त्वे । विड् । विट् । विशौ । विशः । विड्भ्याम् ।

No. 377.—When the word *dṛig* or *dṛiś*, or the affix *vatu*, follows, LONG Á is the substitute OF A PRONOUN. Thus *tad+dṛiś* (Nos. 27 and 55) becomes *tádṛiś* "such," and 1. s. *tádṛik* (Nos. 199, 334, 82, 331, and 165), 1. d. *tádṛiśau*, 1. p. *tádṛiśah*, 3. d. *tádṛigbhyám* (Nos. 334 &c.).

In the example *viś* "who enters," the final is changed to *sh* by No. 334, and then, by Nos. 82 and 165, we have 1. s. *viḍ* or *viṭ*. Again 1. d. *viśau*, 1. p. *viśah*, 3. d. *viḍbhyám*.

नशेर्वा । ८ । २ । ६३ ।

नशेः कवर्गोऽन्तादेशो वा पदान्ते । नक् । नट् । नशौ । नशः । नग्भ्याम् । नड्भ्याम् ।

No. 378.—A guttural letter is OPTIONALLY the substitute OF the final of NAŚ at the end of a *pada*. Thus 1. s. *nak* or, alternatively, *naṭ* (Nos. 334, 82, and 165) "who destroys," 1. d. *naśau*, 1. p. *naśah*, 3. d. *nagbhyám* (No. 378) or *naḍbhyám* (Nos. 334 &c.).

स्पृशोऽनुदके क्विन् । ३ । २ । ५८ ।

अनुदके सुप्युपपदे स्पृशेः क्विन् । घृतस्पृक् । घृतस्पृशौ । घृतस्पृशः । दधृक् । दधृषौ । दधृग्भ्याम् । रत्नमुट् । रत्नमुषौ । रत्नमुड्भ्याम् । षट् । षड्भिः । षड्भ्यः २ । षण्णाम् । षट्सु । रुत्वं प्रति षत्वस्यासिद्धत्वात् ससजुषोरिति रुत्वम् ।

No. 379.—The affix KWIN shall come AFTER the root SPṚIŚ,

WHEN the preceding member of the compound is an inflected word OTHER THAN UDAKA. Thus the word *ghṛitaspriś* "who touches clarified butter" makes 1. s. *ghṛitaspṛik* (Nos. 199, 334, 82, and 331), 1. d. *ghṛitaspṛiśau*, 1. p. *ghṛitaspṛiśah*.

The word *dadhṛish* "arrogant" makes 1. s. *dadhṛik* (Nos. 199, 82, and 331), 1. d. *dadhṛishau*, 3 d. *dadhṛigbhyám*..

The word *ratnamush* "a stealer of gems" makes 1. s. *ratnamuṭ* (Nos. 199, 82, and 165), 1. d. *ratnamushau*, 3. d. *ratnamuḍbhyám*.

The numeral *shash* "six" makes 1. p. *shaṭ* (Nos. 324, 208, 82, and 165), 3. p. *shaḍbhih*, 4. and 5. p. *shaḍbhyah*, 6. p. *shaṇṇám* (Nos. 82, 78, and 84), 7. p. *shaṭsu* (Nos. 82 and 90).

In the case of *pipaṭhish* "one who wishes to read," the fact that this crude word ends in *sh* (caused by No. 169) is disregarded by No. 124 (an earlier rule in the *tripádí*—see No. 39) which directs *ru* to be substituted—making (after the elision of *su* by No. 199) *pipaṭhir*.

र्वोरुपधाया दीर्घ इकः । ८ । २ । ७६ ।

रेफवान्तयेारुपधाया इको दीर्घः पदान्ते । पिपठीः । पिपठिषौ । पिपठीर्भ्याम् ।

No. 380.—THE LONG vowel is the substitute OF IK being the PENULTIMATE letter OF what ends in R OR V, at the end of a *pada*. Thus 1. s. *pipaṭhíh* (Nos. 199, 123, and 111), 1. d. *pipaṭhishau*, 3. d. *pipaṭhírbhyám*.

नुम्विसर्जनीयशर्व्यवायेऽपि । ८ । ३ । ५८ ।

एतैः प्रत्येकं व्यवधानेऽपि इण्कुभ्यां परस्य मूर्धन्यादेशः । ष्टुत्वेन पूर्वस्य षः । पिपठीष्षु । पिपठीःषु । चिकीः । चिकीर्षौ । चिकीर्भ्याम् । चिकीर्षु । विद्वान् । विद्वांसौ । हे विद्वन् ।

No. 381.—And EVEN WHEN there is A SEPARATION caused BY NUM, and VISARGA, AND A SIBILANT, severally, the cerebral substitute takes the place of the dental *s* coming after *iṇ* or *ku*.

Thus, when *su* (7. p.) is to be attached, then the word *pipaṭhish*, by Nos. 123, 380, and 110, becomes *pipaṭhíh*;—the *su* is then changed to *shu* by No. 169; and finally, by the optional rule No. 78, we have either *pipaṭhíshshu* or *pipaṭhíhshu*.

The word *chikírsh* "who wishes to do" makes 1. s. *chikíh*. Here the affix is first elided by No. 199; then the final *sh* (regarded as *s*) is elided by No. 230, this rule (according to No. 39) regarding as inoperative the rule No. 169, which had changed the *s* to *sh*, and finally the *r* becomes *visarga* by No. 111. Then 1. d. *chikírshau*, 3. d. *chikírbhyám*, 7. p. *chikírshu*. In the 7. p. the *s* is elided by No. 230, but the *r* is not changed to *visarga* by No. 110, that rule being debarred in this case by No. 294.

The word *vidwas* "wise" (formed by the affix *vasu*) makes 1. s. *vidwán* (Nos. 316, 371, 199, and 26), 1. d. *vidwáṅsau*, voc. s. *he vidwan*.

वसोः संप्रसारणम् । ६ । ४ । १३१ ।

वस्वन्तस्य भस्य संप्रसारणं स्यात् । विदुषः । वसुस्रंस्विति दः । विद्वद्भ्याम् ।

No. 382.—Let the SAṄPRASÁRAṆA (No. 281) be the substitute OF a *bha* (No. 185) which ends in VASU. Thus in the 2nd. p. the *v*, i. e. *w*, of *vidwas* becomes *u* (No. 283), and finally (by No. 169) we have *vidushah*. According to No. 287, the *s* final in a *pada* is changed to *d*, and we have 3rd d. *vidwadbhyám*.

पुंसोऽसुङ् । ७ । १ । ८९ ।

सर्वनामस्थाने । पुमान् । हे पुमन् । पुमांसौ । पुंसः । पुम्भ्याम् । पुंसु । ऋदुशनेत्यनङ् । उशना । उशनसौ ।

No. 383.—OF the word PUṄS "a male," ASUṄ is the substitute, when a *sarvanámasthána* (No. 183) follows. Thus (regarding the *anuswára* as equal to *m*) we get *pumas* (Nos. 5, 36, and 59) from which come 1. s. *pumán* (Nos. 316 and 371), voc. s. *he puman*, 1. d. *pumáṅsau*. Again 2. p. *puṅsah*, 3. d. *pumbhyám* (No. 26), 7. p. *puṅsu*.

The word *uśanas* "the regent of the planet Venus," by No. 226, substitutes *anań*, when *su* follows, not in the sense of the vocative. Thus we have 1. s. *uśaná* (Nos. 197, 199, and 200), 1. d. *uśanasau*.

अस्य सम्बुद्धौ वाऽनङ् नलोपश्च वा वाच्यः । हे उशन । हे उशनन् । हे उशनः । हे उशनसौ । उशनोभ्याम् । उशनस्सु । अनेहा । अनेहसौ । हे अनेहः । वेधाः । वेधसौ । हे वेधः । वेधोभ्याम् ।

No. 384.—"OF THIS word *(uśanas)*, WHEN SU IN THE SENSE OF THE VOCATIVE FOLLOWS, it SHOULD BE STATED that ANAŃ is OPTIONALLY the substitute, AND OPTIONALLY there is ELISION OF the N."

Thus we have either *he uśana*, or *he uśanan*, or *he uśanah* (Nos. 199, 123, and 110), voc. d. *he uśanasau*, 3. d. *uśánobhyám* (Nos. 123 and 125), 7. p. *uśanassu*.

The word *anehas* "time" makes. 1. s. *aneհá* (Nos. 226 &c.), 1. d. *anehasau*, voc. s. *he anehah*.

The word *vedhas* "Brahmá" makes 1. s. *vedháh* (Nos. 372 and 110), 1. d. *vedhasau*, voc. s. *he vedhah*, 3. d. *vedhobhyám*.

अदस औ सुलोपश्च ।७।२।१०७।

अदस औत् स्यात् सौ सुलोपश्च । तदोरिति सः । असौ । त्यदाद्यत्वम् । पररूपत्वम् । वृद्धिः ।

No. 385.—AU is the substitute OF ADAS, when *su* follows, AND there is ELISION OF SU. In accordance with rule No. 338, the *d* is changed to *s*. Thus 1. s. *asau* "that." In the 1. d., by No. 213, there is substitution of *a* for the final of *adas*; then, by No. 300, the preceding *a* merges in the following—giving *ada*; then, when the affix is attached, *vriddhi* is substituted by No. 41; but then the next rule interposes.

अदसोऽसेर्दादु दो मः ।८।२।८०।

अदसोऽसान्तस्य दात् परस्य उदूतौ दस्य मश्च । आन्तरतम्याद्ध्रस्वस्य उः दीर्घस्य ऊः । अमू । जसः शी । गुणः ।

No. 386.—Short U and long *ú* are the substitutes of what comes AFTER the D OF ÁDAS NOT ENDING IN S, and in the room OF D there is M. The short *u* is substituted for a short vowel, the long *ú* for a long vowel, on the principle (No. 23) that, of the substitutes that offer themselves, the one employed shall be the most similar to that of which it takes the place. Thus we have, instead of *adau, amú.* In the 1st. p. long *í* is directed to be substituted for the affix by No. 171, and the substitution of *guṇa* (which would give *ada*+ *í*=*ade*) being directed, we look forward.

एत ईद्बहुवचने । ८ । २ । ८१ ।

अदसो दात् परस्यैत ईद्दस्य मो बह्वर्थोक्तौ । अमी । पूर्वत्रासिद्ध-मिति विभक्तिकार्यं प्राक् पश्चादुत्वमत्वे । अमुम् । अमू । अमून् । मुत्वे कृते घिसंज्ञायां नाभावः ।

No. 387.—IN THE PLURAL, LONG Í is the substitute OF the E (No. 386) that follows the *d* of *adas;* and instead of the *d* there is *m.* Thus 1. p. *amí.* In the 2. s. in accordance with No. 39, the several rules regarding the application of the case-affix first take place, and then we have the substitution of *u* and *m* (by No. 389). Thus 2. s. *amam* (by No. 386) becomes *amum,* 2. d. *amú,* 2. p. *amún* (instead of *adán*).

In the 3. s. *mu* having been made (by No. 386), and consequently the name *ghi* (No. 190) being applicable to the term, the substitute *ná* offers itself from No. 191. Thus we should have *amu*+*ná;* but here the question might occur, seeing that the *mu* was derived from a rule (No. 386) in the *tripádí* (No. 39), whether No. 191 does not regard the *mu* as non-existent.

The following rule refers to this point.

न मु ने । ८ । २ । ३ ।

नाभावे कर्तव्ये कृते च मुभावो नासिद्धः । अमुना । अमूभ्याम् । अमीभिः । अमुष्मै । अमीभ्यः । अमुष्मात् । अमुष्य । अमुयोः । अमीषाम् । अमुष्मिन् । अमीषु ।

इति हलन्ताः पुंलिङ्गाः ।

No. 388.—WHEN the production of NÁ IS TO TAKE PLACE OR HAS TAKEN PLACE, the existence of MU IS NOT to be regarded AS IF IT HAD NOT BEEN EFFECTED. Thus we have 3. s. *amuná.* Then 3. p. *amúbhyám* (for *adábhyám*, see No. 386), 3. p. *amíbhih* (No. 387), 4 s. *amushmai* (Nos. 172 and 169), 4. p. *amíbhyah*, 5. s. *amushmát*, 6. s. *amushya*, 6. d. *amuyoh*, 6. p. *amíshám* (No. 174), 7. s. *amushmin*, 7. p. *amíshu.*

So much for masculines ending in consonants.

FEMININES ENDING IN CONSONANTS.

। हलन्ताः स्त्रीलिङ्गाः ।

नहो धः । ८ । २ । ३४ ।

झलि पदान्ते च ।

No. 389.—The letter DH is the substitute for the final OF the verb NAHA, when *jhal* follows, or at the end of a *pada.*

नहिवृतिवृषिव्यधिरुचिसहितनिषु क्वौ । ६ । ३ । ११६ ।

क्विबन्तेषु पूर्वपदस्य दीर्घः । उपानत् । उपानहौ । उपानत्सु । क्विन्नन्तत्वात् कुत्वेन घः । उष्णिक् । उष्णिहौ । उष्णिग्भ्याम् । द्यौः । दिवौ । दिवः । द्युभ्याम् । गीः । गिरौ । गिरः । एवं पूः । चतस्रः । चतसृणाम् । का । के । काः । सर्वावत् ।

No. 390.—WHEN the verbs NAHA "to bind," VRITA "to be," VṚISH "to rain," VYADH "to pierce," RUCH "to shine," SHAHA "to bear," AND TAN "to stretch," ENDING WITH KWIP, FOLLOW, a long vowel is the substitute of the *pada* which precedes in the compound.

The word *upánah* "a slipper" (thus formed from *upa* + *nah* + *kwip*) makes 1. s. *upánat* (Nos. 330, 199, and 389), 1. d. *upánahau*, 7. p. *upánatsu.*

In the case of the word *ushṇik* "a metre of the Vedas," as it takes *gh* (No. 331) in consequence of its ending in *kwin* (No 328), we find 1. s. *ushṇik.* Again 1. d. *ushṇihau*, 3. d. *ushṇigbhyám.*

The word *div* " the sky" makes 1. s. *dyauh* (No. 289), 1. d. *divau*, 1. p. *divah*, 3. d. *dyubhyám* (No. 290).

The word *gir* " speech" makes 1 s. *gíh* (Nos. 199, 380, and 111), 1. d. *girau*, 1. p. *girah*. In the same way *pur* " a city" makes 1. s. *púh*.

The word *chatur* " four" substitutes *chatasṛi* (No. 248) in the feminine ; and, by No. 249, the letter *r* is substituted for *ṛi*, when a vowel follows. Thus we have 1. p. *chatasrah*. In the 6. p. *chatasṛiṇám*, the vowel is not lengthened—see No. 250.

The feminine of *kim* " who" is like *sarvá* (No. 244).—1. s. *ká* (Nos. 297 &c.), 1. d. *ke*, 1. p. *káh*.

यः सौ । ७ । २ । ११० ।

इदमो दस्य यः । इयम् । त्यदाद्यत्वम् । पररूपत्वम् । टाप् । दश्चेति मः । इमे । इमाः । इमाम् । अनया । हलि लोपः । आभ्याम् । आभिः । अस्यै । अस्याः २ । अनयोः । आसाम् । अस्याम् । आसु । स्रक् । स्रजः । स्रग्भ्याम् । त्यदाद्यत्वम् । टाप् । स्या । त्ये । त्याः । एवम् । तद् । एतद् । वाक् । वाचौ । वाग्भ्याम् । वाक्षु । अप् शब्दो नित्यं बहुवचनान्तः । अप्तृन्निति दीर्घः । आपः ।

No. 391.—Instead of the *d* of *idam* " this," there is Y, WHEN SU FOLLOWS. Thus 1. s. *iyam* (No. 298). In the other cases No. 213 directs the substitution of short *a* for the final, and the preceding vowel merges in this by No. 300. The word being feminine, long *á (ṭáp)* is added by No. 1341 ; the *d* is changed to *m* by No. 301 ; and, the base having thus become *imá*, we have 1. d. *ime* (No. 240), 1. p. *imáh*, 2. s. *imám*. In the 3. d. and subsequent cases the *id* is changed to *an* by No. 302 ; and, in the 3. s., *e* is substituted for the final by No. 242, giving *anayá*. By No. 303 there is elision of the *id*, when the case-affix begins with a consonant, so that we have 3. d. *ábhyám*, 3. p. *ábhih*. In the 4. s., by No. 244, *asyai*, 5. and 6. s. *asyáh*, 6. d. *anayoh* (No. 242), 6. p. *ásám* (Nos. 174 and 303), 7. s. *asyám* (Nos. 244 and 219), 7. p. *ásu*.

The word *śraj* "a garland" makes 1. s. *srak* (Nos. 328, 199, 334, 82, and 331), 1. p. *srajah*, 3. d. *sragbhyám*.

The pronoun *tyad* "that" substitutes *a* for the final (Nos. 213 and 300), and, taking the feminine termination *ṭáp*, gives 1. s. *syá* (No. 338), 1. d. *tye*, 1. p. *tyáh*. In the same way *tad* "that," and *etad* "this."

The word *vách* "speech" makes 1. s. *vák* (No. 333), 1. d. *váchau*, 3. d. *vágbhyám*, 7. p. *vákshu* (No. 169).

The word *ap* "water" always takes the terminations of the plural. By No. 227 this word lengthens the vowel in the 1. p. *ápah*.

अपो भि । ७ । ४ । ४८ ।

अपस्तकारो भादौ प्रत्यये । अद्भिः । अद्भ्यः । अपाम् । अप्सु । दिक् । दिग् । दिशः । दिग्भ्याम् । त्यदादिष्विति दृशेः क्विन्विधानादन्यत्रापि कुत्वम् । दृक् । दृग् । दृशौ । दृग्भ्याम् । त्विट् । त्विषौ । त्विड्भ्याम् । ससजुषोरिति रुत्वम् । सजूः । सजुषौ । सजूर्भ्याम् । आशीः । आशिषौ । आशीर्भ्याम् । असौ । उत्वमत्वे । अमू । अमूः । अमुया । अमूभ्याम् । अमूभिः । अमुष्यै । अमूभ्यः । अमुष्याः २ । अमुयोः २ । अमूषाम् । अमुष्याम् । अमूषु ।

इति हलन्ताः स्त्रीलिङ्गाः ।

No. 392.—The letter *t* is the substitute OF the word AP "water," WHEN a *pratyaya* beginning with BH FOLLOWS. Thus 3. p. *adbhih* (No. 82), 4. p. *adbhyah*. Again 6. p. *apám*, 7. p. *apsu*.

The word *diś* "space" makes 1. s. *dig* or *dik* (Nos. 328 and 331), 1. p. *diśah*, 3. d. *digbhyám*.

Since it is directed (No. 376) that *dṛiś* shall take the affix *kwin* when attached to the pronouns *tyad* &c, the word *dṛiś* (thus falling under rule No. 331) elsewhere also substitutes a guttural in the place of its final. Thus 1. s. *dṛik* or *dṛig* "sight," 1. d. *dṛiśau*, 3. d. *dṛigbhyám*.

The word *twish* "light" makes 1. s. *twiṭ* (No. 82), 1. d. *twishau*, 3. d. *twiḍbhyám*.

The word *sajush* "a friend," by No. 124, substitutes *r* for its final at the end of a *pada*, which the word is when, by No. 26, the *su* of the 1. s. has been rejected. The vowel is then lengthened by No. 380, and the *r* becomes *visarga* by No. 111, giving *sajúh*, 1. d. *sajushau*, 3. d. *sajúrbhyám*. In the same way *áśish* (for *áśis*) "a benediction" makes 1. s. *áśíh*, 1. d. *áśishau*, 3. d. *áśírbhyám*.

The pronoun *adas* makes 1. s. *asau* (No. 385). In the other cases, the substitution of *u* and *m* (by No. 386) having taken place, we have 1. d. *amú*, 1. p. *amúh*, 3. s. *amuyá*, 3. d. *amúbhyám*, 3. p. *amúbhih*, 4. s. *amushyai* (Nos. 244 and 169), 4. p. *amúbhyah*, 5 and 6. s. *amushyáh* (Nos. 244 and 169), 6. and 7. d. *amuyoh*, 6. p. *amúshám* (No. 174), 7. s. *amushyám* (No. 169), 7. p. *amúshu*.

So much for feminines ending in consonants.

। हलन्ता नपुंसकलिङ्गाः ।

स्वमोर्लुक् । दत्वम् । स्वनडुत् । स्वनडुही । चतुरनडुहोरित्याम् । स्वनड्वांहि । पुनस्तद्वत् । शेषं पुंवत् । वाः । वारी । वारि । वारा । वार्भ्याम् । चत्वारि । किम् । के । कानि । इदम् । इमे । इमानि ।

NEUTERS ENDING IN CONSONANTS.

No. 393.—"In the case of neuters we have ELISION *(luk)* OF SU AND AM (No. 270)." In the case of *anaḍuh* (No. 287), there is the substitution of *d*. Thus we have 1. s. *swanaḍud or swanaḍut* "having good cattle," 1. d. *swanaḍuhí* (No. 259). In the 1. p., by No. 284, there is the augment *ám*, and thus, by No. 264, we have *swanaḍwáṅhi*. Again the same in the 2. p. The rest is like the masculine (Nos. 285 &c.).

The word *vár* "water" makes 1. s. *váh* (No. 111), 1. d. *várí* (No. 259), 1. p. *vári* (No. 262), 3. s. *várá*, 3. d. *várbhyám*.

The word *chatur* "four" (by Nos. 262 and 284) makes *chatwári*.

The interrogative *kim* "who, which, what?" makes 1. s. *kim* (No. 270), 1. d. *ke* (Nos. 297 and 259), 1. p. *káni.*

The pronoun *idam* "this" makes 1. s. *idam* (No. 270), 1. d. *ime* (Nos. 301 and 259), 1. p. *imáni.*

अन्वादेशे नपुंसके एनद्वक्तव्यः। एनत्। एने। एनानि। एनेन। एनयोः। ब्रह्म। विभाषा ङिश्योः। अह्नी। अहनी। अहानि।

No. 394.—"It SHOULD BE MENTIONED (see No. 306) that IN A SUBSEQUENT PROPOSITION, ENAT is the substitute for *idam* or *etad,* IN THE NEUTER." Thus 1. s. *enat* (No. 270), 1. d. *ene* (Nos. 213 and 259), 1. p. *enáni,* 3. s. *enena,* 6. d. *enayoh.*

The word *brahman* "the Supreme" makes 1. s. *brahma* (Nos. 270 and 200).

According to No. 274, the word *ahan* "a day" makes 1. d. *ahní* or *ahaní* :—1. p. *aháni* (Nos. 263 and 197).

अहन्। ८। २। ६८।

अहन्नित्यस्य रुः पदान्ते। अहोभ्याम्। दण्डि। दण्डिनी। दण्डीनि। दण्डिना। दण्डिभ्याम्। सुपथि। टिलोपः। सुपथी। सुपन्थानि। ऊर्क्। ऊर्जी। ऊर्न्जि। नरजानां संयोगः। तत्। ते। तानि। यत्। ये। यानि। एतत्। एते। एतानि। गवाक्। गोची। गवाञ्ची। पुनस्तद्वत्। गोचा। गवाग्भ्याम्। शकृत्। शकृती। शकृन्ति। ददत्।

No. 395.—The word AHAN substitutes *ru* at the end of a *pada.* Thus 3. d. *ahobhyám* (No. 126).

The word *dandin* "having a staff" makes 1. s. *dandi* (Nos. 270 and 200), 1. d. *dandiní* (No. 259), 1. p. *dandíni* (Nos. 262 and 197), 3. s. *dandiná,* 3. d. *dandibhyám* (Nos. 184 and 200).

The word *supathin* "having a good road" makes 1. s. *supathi.* By the elision of *i* directed in No. 323, and then, by No. 259, we have 2. d. *supathí.* In the 1. p. (Nos. 263, 321, and 322) *supantháni.*

The word *úrj* "strong" makes 1. s. *úrk* (No. 333), 1. d. *úrjí*, 1. p. *únrji*, the conjunction of the consonants being in the order of *n*, *r*, and *j*.

The pronoun *tad* "that" makes 1. s. *tat* (Nos. 270 and 165), 1. d. *te*, 1. p. *táni*. So *yad* "who, which," makes 1. s. *yat*, 1. d. *ye*, 1. p. *yáni*, and *etad* "this" makes 1. s. *etat*, 1. d. *ete*, 1. p. *etáni*.

The word formed of *go* "a cow," and *añchu* "to worship," and signifying "a worshipper of cows," makes 1. s. *gavák* (Nos. 363, 59, and 333), 1. d. *gochí* (No. 56), 1. p. *gavánchi* (No. 264). Again there is the same form in the 2nd case. In the 3. s. *gochá*, 3. d. *gavágbhyám*. [N. B. This word takes a great variety of shapes, being in fact a mere grammatical fiction.]

The word *śakṛit* "ordure" makes 1. s. *śakṛit*, 1. d. *śakṛití*, 1. p. *sakṛinti* (No. 264).

The participle *dadat* "giving" makes 1. s. *dadat*.

वा नपुंसकस्य । ७ । १ । ७९ ।

अभ्यस्तात् परस्य वा नुम् सर्वनामस्थाने । ददन्ति । ददति । तुदत् ।

No. 396.—*Num* (No. 374) shall OPTIONALLY be the augment OF the affix *śatṛi* coming after a NEUTER reduplicate, when a *sarvanámasthána* (No. 263) follows. Thus 1. p. *dadanti* or *dadati*.

The participle *tudat* "paining" is next declined.

आच्छीनद्योर्नुम् । ७ । १ । ८० ।

अवर्णान्तात् परो यः शतुरवयवस्तदन्तस्य नुम् वा शीनद्योः । तुदन्ती । तुदती । तुदन्ति । भात् । भान्ती । भाती । भान्ति । पचत् ।

No. 397.—NUM shall optionally be the augment of that which ends with a portion *(a)* of the affix *śatṛi* coming AFTER what ends in A OR Á, WHEN ŚÍ (No. 259) OR a NADÍ (No. 215) FOLLOWS.

For example, the verbal root *tud* (No. 693) taking the affix *śatṛi* becomes *tuda ;* and then, with the participial affix, it becomes *tudat* (No. 300), which, by this rule, makes 1. d. *tudantí* or *tudatí.* By No. 264, I. p. *tudanti.* And so *bhát* "shining" (root *bhá*), 1. d. *bhántí* or *bhátí,* 1. p. *bhánti.*

By the *nadí,* in this aphorism, the feminine affix *ńíp (í)* is intended.

The root *pach* takes the affix *śap* (No. 419), and its participle *pachat* "cooking" falls under the next rule.

शप्श्यनोर्नित्यम् ।७।१।८१।

शप्श्यनोरात् परो यः शतुरवयवस्तादन्तस्य नुम् शीनद्योः । पचन्ती । पचन्ति । दीव्यत् । दीव्यन्ती । दीव्यन्ति । धनुः । धनुषी । सान्तेति दीर्घः । नुम्विसर्जनीयेति षः । धनूंषि । धनुषा । धनुर्भ्याम् । एवं चक्षुर्हविरादयः । पयः । पयसी । पयांसि । पयसा । पयोभ्याम् । सुपुम् । सुपुंसी । सुपुमांसि । अदः । विभक्तिकार्यम् । उत्वमत्वे । अमू । अमूनि । शेषं पुंवत् ।

इति हलन्ता नपुंसकलिङ्गाः ।

No. 398.—*Num* shall INVARIABLY be the augment OF that which ends with a portion of the affix *śatṛi* which comes after the *a* derived from ŚAP (No. 419) OR ŚYAN (No. 670), when *śí* or a *nadí* follows.

Hence *pachat* (No. 397) makes 1. d. *pachantí.* In the 1. p. *pachanti.* In like manner *dívyat* "sporting" (No. 669) makes 1. d. *dívyantí,* 1. p. *dívyanti.*

The word *dhanus* "a bow" makes 1. s. *dhanuh* (Nos. 270, 123, and 110), 1. d. *dhanushí* (No. 169). In the 1. p., as the word ends in *s* (No. 371), the vowel is lengthened, and the *s* is changed to *sh* notwithstanding the intervention of *num* (No. 381), giving *dhanúńshi.* In the 3. s. *dhanushá,* 3. d. *dhanurbhyám* (No. 123). In like manner *chakshus* "an eye," *havis* "clarified butter," &c. The word *payas* "water" makes 1. s. *payah* (Nos. 270 &c.),

1. d. *payasí*, 1. p. *payáńsi* (No. 371), 3. s. *payasá*, 3. d. *payobhyám* (Nos. 123 and 126). The word *supuńs* "of which the men are good" makes 1. s. *supum* (Nos. 270 and 26), 1. d. *supuńsí*, 1. p. *supumáńsi* (Nos. 383, 316, and 371). In the neuter of the pronoun *adas* "that," 1. s. *adah*, the various alterations of the case-affixes (directed in Nos. 259, 262, 172 &c.) first take place; and then the substitution of *ú* and *m* (No. 386) having been made, we get 1. d. *amú*, 1. p. *amúni*. The rest is like the masculine.

So much for neuters ending in consonants.

॥ अव्ययानि ॥

स्वरादिनिपातमव्ययम् ।१।१।३७।

स्वर् । अन्तर् । प्रातर् । पुनर् । सनुतर् । उच्चैस् । नीचैस् । शनैस् । ऋधक् । ऋते । युगपत् । आरात् । पृथक् । ह्यस् । श्वस् । दिवा । रात्रौ । सायम् । चिरम् । मनाक् । ईषत् । जोषम् । तूष्णीम् । बहिस् । अवस् । समया । निकषा । स्वयम् । वृथा । नक्तम् । नञ् । हेतौ । इद्धा । अद्धा । सामि । वत् । ब्राह्मणवत् । क्षत्रियवत् । सना । उपधा । तिरस् । सनत् । सनात् । अन्तरा । अन्तरेण । ज्योक् । कम् । शम् । सहसा । विना । नाना । स्वस्ति । स्वधा । अलम् । वषट् । श्रौषट् । वौषट् । अन्यत् । अस्ति । उपांशु । क्षमा । विहायसा । दोषा । मृषा । मिथ्या । मुधा । पुरा । मिथो । मिथस् । प्रायस् । मुहुस् । प्रवाहुकम् । प्रवाहिका । आर्यहलम् । अभीक्ष्णम् । साकम् । सार्धम् । नमस् । हिरुक् । धिक् । अथ । अम् । आम् । प्रताम् । प्रशान् । प्रतान् । मा । माङ् । आकृतिगणोऽयम् । च । वा । ह । अह । एव । एवम् । नूनम् । शश्वत् । युगपत् । भूयस् । कूपत् । सूपत् । कुवित् । नेत् । चेत् । चण् । यच । तच । कच्चित् । नह । हन्त । माकिम् । माकीम् । नकिः । आकीम् । माङ् । नञ् । यावत् । तावत् । त्वै । न्वै । द्वै । रै । श्रौषट् । वौषट् । स्वाहा । स्वधा ।

वषट् । ओम् । तुम् । तथाहि । खलु । किल । अथ । सुष्ठु । स्म । आदह । उपसर्गविभक्तिस्वरप्रतिरूपकाश्च । अवदत्तम् । अहंयुः । अस्तिक्षीरा । अ । आ । इ । ई । उ । ऊ । ए । ऐ । ओ । औ । पशु । शुकम् । यथा । कथाच । पाट् । प्याट् । अङ्ग । है । हे । भोः । अये । घ । विषु । एकपदे । पुत् । आतः । चादिरप्याकृतिगणः । तसिलादयः प्राक् पाशपः । शस्प्रभृतयः प्राक् समासान्तेभ्यः । अम् । आम् । कृत्वोऽर्थाः । तसिवती । नानाञौ । एतदन्तमव्ययम् । अत इत्यादि ।

OF INDECLINABLE WORDS.

No. 399.—SWAR &C. AND the PARTICLES *(nipáta)* are called INDECLINABLES.

These are *swar* "heaven," *antar* "midst, "*prátar* "in the morning," *punar* "again," *sanutar* "in concealment," *uchchais* "high," *níchais* "low," *śanais* "slowly," *ṛidhak* "rightly," *ṛite* "except," *yugapat* "at once," *árát* "far, near," *pṛithak* "apart," *hyas* "yesterday," *swas* "to-morrow," *divá* "by day," *rátrau* "in the night," *sáyam* "at eve," *chiram* "a long time," *manák* "a little," *íshat* "a little," *josham* "silently," *túshṇím* "silently," *vahis* "outside," *avas* "outside," *samayá* "near," *nikashá* "near," *swayam* "of one's self," *vṛithá* "in vain," *naktam* "at night," *naṅ* "not," *hetau* "by reason of," *iddhá* "truly," *addhá* "evidently," *sámi* "half," *vat* "like" (e. g. *bráhmaṇavat* "priestly," *kshatriyavat* "like a Kshatriya"), *saná* "perpetually," *upadhá* "division," *tiras* "crookedly," *sanat* or *sanát* "perpetually," *antará* or *antareṇa* "without, except," *jyok* "quickly," *kam* "water, ease," *śam* "ease," *sahasá* "hastily," *viná* "without," *nána* "various," *swasti* "greeting," *swadhá* (interjection) "oblation to manes," *alam* "enough," *vashaṭ*, *śrauhsaṭ* and *vaushaṭ*, (interjections) "oblation of butter," *anyat* "otherwise," *asti* "existence," *upáṅśu* "privately," *kshamá* "patience, pardon," *viháyasá* "aloft, in the air," *doshá* "in the evening," *mṛishá* and *mithyá* "falsely," *mudhá* "in vain," *purá* "formerly," *mitho* or *mithas* "mutually," *práyas* "frequently," *muhus* "repeatedly," *praváhukam* or *praváhiká* "at the same time," *áryahalam* "violently," *abhíkshṇam* "repeatedly," *sákam* or *sárdham* "with," *namas* "reverence," *hiruk* "without," *dhik* "fie!" *atha* "thus," *am* "quickly," *ám* "indeed, yes," *pratám* "with fatigue," *praśán* "alike," *pratán* "widely," *má* or *máṅ* "do not."

The foregoing class of words ("*swar* &c.)," is one the fact of a word's belonging to which is known only from its form, and could not have been inferred from its nature (see No. 53).

The following are particles (*nipáta*), viz. *cha* "and," *vá* "or," *ha* (an expletive), *aha* (vocative particle), *eva* "only, exactly," *evam* so, thus," *núnam* "certainly," *śaśwat* "continually," *yugapat* "at once," *bhúyas* "repeatedly," *kúpat* "excellently," *súpat* "excellently," *kuvit* "abundantly," *net* or *chet* "if," *chaṇ* "if" [the *ṇ* is indicatory], *yatra* "where," *tatra* "there," *kachchit* "what if?," "*naha* "no," *hanta* "ah!" *mákim, mákím,* or *nakih,* "do not," *ákím* "indeed!", *máṅ* "do not," *naṅ* "not," *yávat* "as much as," *távat* "so much," *twai, nwai,* or *dwai* "perhaps," *rai* (disrespectful interjection), *śraushaṭ, vaushaṭ* or *swáhá* (interj.) "oblation to the gods," *swadhá* "oblation to the manes," *vashaṭ* "oblation to the gods," *om* (mystical ejaculation typical of the three great deities of the Hindú mythology), *tum* "thouing," *tatháhi* "thus," (introducing an exposition), *khalu* "certainly," *kila* "indeed," *atha* "now" (auspicious inceptive), *sushṭu* "excellent," *sma* (attached to the present tense gives it a past signification), *ádaha* "fie!"

To the list of Indeclinables belong also what have, without the reality, the appearance of an *upasarga* (No. 47), of a word with one of the terminations of case or person, and of the vowels. In the example *avadattam* "given away," the *ava* is not really an *upasarga*, for if it were, the word (by VII. 4. 47.*) would be *avattam*. In the example *ahaṅyuh* "egotistic," the *ahaṅ* is not identical with the *aham* "I," terminating in a case-affix—because a pronoun, really regarded as being in the nominative case, could not be the first member in such a compound. In the example, *astikshírá*, a cow or the like "in which there is milk," the *asti* must be regarded as differing from the word *asti* "is," which ends

* When the aphorism does not occur in the *Laghu Kaumudí*, the reference is made to the *Ashṭádhyáyí*.

with the affix of the 3rd person singular, otherwise it could not have appeared as the first member in a compound. The vowels *a, á, i, í, u, ú, e, ai, o, au,* when, as interjections, they indicate various emotions, differ from the ordinary vowels. Other Indeclinables are *paśu* "well," *śukam* "quickly," *yathákathácha* "any how," *páṭ, pyáṭ, aṅga, hai, he, bhoh,* (vocative particles), *aye* "ah!" (indicating recollection), *gha* (vocative), *vishu* "on all sides," *ekapade* "at the same moment," *yuṭ* "blame," *átah* "hence."

This list also ("*cha* &c.") is one each of the various individuals composing which is to be recognised by its own shape (No. 53).

Words are indeclinable which have the following terminations viz. the *taddhita* affixes (No. 1067) beginning with *tasil* (No. 1286) reckoning as far as (but not including) *páśap* (V. 3. 47.) :—or the terminations *śas* &c. (No. 1330) reckoning as far as the aphorism "*samásántáh,*" (V. 4. 68.) :—or the *Vaidika* termination *am* or its equivalent *ám* (No. 1309) :— or the terminations that have the force of *kṛitwasuch* (i. e. which give the sense of such and such a number of times) :—or the terminations *tasi* (equivalent to *tasil*) and *vat* "like," and *ná* or *náṅ* (V. 2. 27). For example, *atah* "hence" (which ends in *tasil*) &c.

कृन्मेजन्तः। १।१।३९।

कृद्योमान्त एजन्तश्च तदन्तमव्ययम् । स्मारंस्मारम् । जीवसे । पिबध्यै ।

No. 400.—What ends in a KṚIT affix (No. 135) ENDING IN the letter M OR in ECH is indeclinable. Thus *smáram smáram* "having repeatedly remembered," *jívase* "to live," *pibadhyai* "to drink." (III. 4. 9.)

क्त्वातोसुन्कसुनः। १।१।४०।

एतदन्तमव्ययम् । कृत्वा । उदेतोः । विसृपः ।

No. 401.—What ends in KTWÁ (No. 935) or TOSUN OR KASUN (III. 4. 13) is indeclinable. Thus *kṛitwá* "having done," *udeto* "having risen," *visṛipah* "having spread."

अव्ययीभावश्च। १।१।४१।

अधिहरि ।

No. 402.—AND the kind of compound termed AVYAYÍBHÁVA (No 966) is indeclinable. Thus *adhihari* "upon *Hari* or *Vishṇu*."

अव्ययादाप्सुपः । २ । ४ । ८२ ।

अव्ययादापः सुपश्च लुक् । तच शालायाम् । अथ ।

सदृशं त्रिषु लिङ्गेषु सर्वासु च विभक्तिषु ।
वचनेषु च सर्वेषु यन्न व्येति तदव्ययम् ॥
वष्टि भागुरिरल्लोपमवाप्योरुपसर्गयोः ।
आपं चैव हलन्तानां यथा वाचा निशा दिशा ॥

अवगाहः । वगाहः । अपिधानम् । पिधानम् ॥

इत्यव्ययानि ॥

No. 403.—There is elision (*luk*—No. 209) OF ÁP (the feminine termination) AND OF SUP (the case-affixes) AFTER what is INDECLINABLE. For example, *tatra śáláyám* "in that hall." Here the indeclinable *tatra* "there" does not take either the feminine termination or a case-affix, although it is equivalent to *tasyám* "in that." So then "what changes not *(na vyeti)*, remaining alike in the three genders, and in all cases, and in all numbers, is what is termed an indeclinable *(avyaya)*."

The grammarian *Bháguri* wishes that there shall be elision of the initial *a* of *ava* and *api* (No· 48), and that *áp* shall be the termination of all feminine words which would otherwise end in consonants, e. g. *váchá* "speech" (instead of *vách*), *niśá* "night" (not *niś*), *diśá* "space" (not *diś*). [But the rule, thus resting on the authority of a single grammarian (see No. 38) is optional.] So we have either *avagáhah* or *vagáhah* "bathing," *apidhánam* or *pidhánam* "concealment."

So much for the Indeclinables.

॥ भ्वादयः ॥

OF THE VERBS.

लट् । लिट् । लुट् । लृट् । लेट् । लोट् । लङ् । लिङ् । लुङ् । लृङ् । एषु पञ्चमो लकारश्छन्दोमात्रगोचरः ।

No. 404.—THE terminations generally of the moods and tenses of the verbs are denoted in the grammar by the letter *l*. The affixes of each particular tense are denoted by the letter *l* accompanied by certain indicatory letters as follows :—Present LAṬ, 2nd Preterite LIṬ, 1st Future LUṬ, 2nd Future LṚIṬ, scriptural Imperative LEṬ, Imperative LOṬ, 1st Preterite LAṄ, Potential LIṄ, 3rd Preterite LUṄ, Conditional LṚIṄ. THE FIFTH AMONG THESE *(viz. leṭ)* OCCURS ONLY IN THE VEDAS.

लः कर्मणि च भावे चाकर्मकेभ्यः । ३ । ४ । ६९ ।

लकाराः सकर्मकेभ्यः कर्मणि कर्तरि च स्युरकर्मकेभ्यो भावे कर्तरि च ।

No. 405.—Let the letters L (above described) be placed after transitive verbs IN denoting THE OBJECT ALSO as well as the agent ; AND AFTER INTRANSITIVES IN marking THE CONDITION (i. e. the action itself, which the verb imports), ALSO as well as the agent.

[N. B.—The verb itself denotes the action : to be, or to do, generally; or to be, or to do, in a particular manner. In the active voice, the affix marks the agent : in the passive voice of a transitive verb, it marks the object ; but, in the passive form of an intransitive verb, the action itself.]

वर्तमाने लट् । ३ । २ । १२३ ।

वर्तमानक्रियावृत्तेर्धातोर्लट् स्यात् । अटाविती । उच्चारणसामर्थ्याल्लस्य नेत्वम् । भू सत्तायाम् । कर्तृविवक्षायां भू ल इति स्थिते ।

No. 406.—Let LAṬ (No. 404) be placed after a verbal root employed IN denoting PRESENT action. The *a* and the *ṭ* (in *laṭ*) are indicatory. According to No. 155 the *l* also ought to be indicatory—but it is not to be regarded as indicatory here, because nothing (in the grammar) is enounced without a purpose (and no purpose would be served by the elision of this *l*, which therefore remains).

The verb *bhú* "to be" is now to be conjugated. When it is wished to speak of an agent, the case (as far as we have yet seen) standing thus, viz: *bhú*+*l* (we look forward).

तिप्तस्झि सिप्थस्थ मिब्वस्मस् तातांझ थासाथांध्वमिड्वहिमहिङ् । ३ । ४ । ७८ ।

एतेऽष्टादश लादेशाः स्युः ।

No. 407.—Let these eighteen be the substitutes of *l* (No. 404) —viz.

	Parasmai-pada.			*Átmane-pada.*			
	Sing.	Dual.	Plural.	Sing.	Dual.	Plural.	
(Lowest.)	TIP	TAS	JHI	TA	ÁTÁM	JHA	(he, they &c.)
(Middle.)	SIP	THAS	THA	THÁS	ÁTHÁM	DHWAM	(thou, you &c.)
(Highest.)	MIP	VAS	MAS	IṬ	VAHI	MAHIŃ	(I, we &c.)

लः परस्मैपदम् । १ । ४ । ९९ ।

लादेशाः परस्मैपदसंज्ञाः स्युः ।

No. 408.—Let the substitutes of L (No. 407) be called PARASMAI-PADA—i. e. "words for another."

[Such are the terminations of a verb the action of which is addressed to another than the agent—i. e. of a transitive verb.]

तङानावात्मनेपदम् । १ । ४ । १०० ।

तङ् प्रत्याहारः शानच्कानचौ चैतत्संज्ञाः स्युः । पूर्वसंज्ञापवादः ।

No. 409.—Let the set comprised under the technical name TAŃ (i. e. the second set of nine, in No. 407, from *ta* to *mahiń* inclusive), and THE TWO ending in ÁNA—viz: the participial affixes *śánach* (No. 883) and *kánach* (No. 880) be called ÁTMANE-PADA—i. e. "words for one's self." This supersedes (in regard to these affixes) the previous name (derived from No. 408).

[Such are the terminations of a verb the action of which is addressed or reverts to the agent himself—as in the Middle Voice of the Greek.]

अनुदात्तङित आत्मनेपदम् । १ । ३ । १२ ।

अनुदात्तेतो ङितश्च धातोरात्मनेपदं स्यात् ।

No. 410.—Let the affixes called ÁTMANE-PADA (No. 409) be placed AFTER a verbal root distinguished (in the catalogue of roots called *Dhátu-páṭha*) by A GRAVELY ACCENTED INDICATORY vowel, OR by AN INDICATORY Ń.

स्वरितञितः कर्त्रभिप्राये क्रियाफले । १ । ३ । ७२ ।

स्वरितेतो ञितश्च धातोरात्मनेपदं स्यात् कर्तृगामिनि क्रियाफले ।

No. 411.—AFTER a verbal root distinguished by AN INDICATORY vowel CIRCUMFLEXLY ACCENTED, OR by AN INDICATORY Ǹ, WHEN THE (direct) FRUIT OF THE ACTION ACCRUES TO THE AGENT, let there be the *átmane-pada* affixes.

शेषात् कर्तरि परस्मैपदम् । १ । ३ । ७८ ।

आत्मनेपदनिमित्तहीनाद्धातोः कर्तरि परस्मैपदं स्यात् ।

No. 412.—AFTER THE REST, i. e. after whatever verbal root is devoid of any cause for the affixing of the *átmane-pada* terminations (Nos. 410 and 411), let THE PARASMAI-PADA affixes be employed IN marking THE AGENT.

तिङस्त्रीणि त्रीणि प्रथममध्यमोत्तमाः । १ । ४ । १०१ ।

तिङ उभयोः पदयोस्त्रयस्त्रिकाः क्रमादेतत्संज्ञाः स्युः ।

No. 413.—Let THE THREE TRIADS in both the sets (*parasmai-pada* and *átmane-pada*) OF CONJUGATIONAL AFFIXES (comprised under the general name of *tiń*—a *pratyáhára* formed of the first and last of them viz. *tip* and *mahiń*—No. 407—) be called, in order, the LOWEST, the MIDDLE, AND the HIGHEST (person).

[These, it must be borne in mind, correspond to the 3rd, 2nd, and 1st persons of European grammar.]

तान्येकवचनद्विवचनबहुवचनान्येकशः । १ । ४ । १०२ ।

लब्धप्रथमादिसंज्ञानि तिङस्त्रीणि त्रीणि प्रत्येकमेकवचनादिसंज्ञानि स्युः ।

No. 414.—Let THESE three triads of conjugational affixes, which (No. 413) have received the names of Lowest &c., be called, (as regards the three expressions in each triad—*tip tas jhi* &c.) SEVERALLY, "THE EXPRESSION FOR ONE" (singular), "THE EXPRESSION FOR TWO" (dual), AND "THE EXPRESSION FOR MANY" (plural).

युष्मद्युपपदे समानाधिकरणे स्थानिन्यपि मध्यमः । १ । ४ । १०५ ।

तिङ्वाच्यकारकवाचिनि युष्मद्यप्रयुज्यमाने प्रयुज्यमाने च मध्यमः ।

No. 415.—WHEN the pronoun YUSHMAD "thou" understood, and ALSO when the same EXPRESSED, IS THE ATTENDANT WORD IN AGREEMENT with the verb, and denotes the agent or object that is signified by the verbal termination, then let the verbal termination be THE MIDDLE (No. 413).

अस्मद्युत्तमः । १ । ४ । १०७ ।

तथाभूतेऽस्मद्युत्तमः ।

No. 416.—WHEN the pronoun ASMAD "I" IS in the same circumstances (as *yushmad* in No. 415), then let the verbal termination be THE HIGHEST (No. 413).

शेषे प्रथमः । १ । ४ । १०८ ।

भू ति इति जाते ।

No. 417.—IN all OTHER CASES (besides those provided for in Nos. 415 and 416), let the verbal termination be THE LOWEST (No. 413).

The expression *bhú+l* (No. 406) having thus become *bhú+ti* (by the substitution directed in No. 407, we look forward).

तिङ् शित् सार्वधातुकम् । ३ । ४ । ११३ ।

तिङः शितश्च धात्वधिकारोक्ता एतत्संज्ञाः स्युः ।

No. 418.—Let the affixes called TIṄ (No. 413) AND THOSE WITH AN INDICATORY Ś, which are enounced in the division of the grammar pertaining to verbal roots, be called SÁRVADHÁTUKA (i. e. "applicable to the whole of a radical term").

कर्तरि शप् । ३ । १ । ६८ ।

कर्त्रर्थे सार्वधातुके परे धातोः शप् ।

No. 419.—When a *sárvadhátuka* affix (No. 418) follows, SIGNIFYING AN AGENT, let ŚAP be placed after the verbal root. [The *ś* and the *p*, by Nos. 155 and 5, being indicatory, there remains *a*, giving *bhú*+*a*+*ti*.]

सार्वधातुकार्धधातुकयोः । ७ । ३ । ८४ ।

अनयोः परयोरिगन्ताङ्गस्य गुणः । अवादेशः । भवति । भवतः ।

No. 420.—WHEN A SÁRVADHÁTUKA (No. 418) OR AN ÁRDHADHÁTUKA affix (No. 436) FOLLOWS, then let *guṇa* (No. 33) be the substitute of an inflective base (No. 152) that ends in *ik*.

Thus *bhú* becomes *bho*, and, *av* being substituted by No. 29, we have *bhavati* "he becomes." In like manner *bhavataḥ* "they two become."

झोऽन्तः । ७ । १ । ३ ।

प्रत्ययावयवस्य झस्यान्तादेशः । अतो गुणे । भवन्ति । भवसि । भवथः । भवथ ।

No. 421.—ANT is the substitute OF the letter JH being part of an affix (as in the case of *jhi*—407). By No. 300 the *a* of *ant* supplies the place both of itself and of the preceding *a* of *bhava*—so that we have *bhavanti* "they become." Again—*bhavasi* "thou becomest," *bavathaḥ* "you two become," *bhavatha* "you become."

अतो दीर्घो यञि । ७ । ३ । १०१ ।

अतोऽङ्गस्य दीर्घो यञादौ सार्वधातुके । भवामि । भवावः । भवामः । स भवति । तौ भवतः । ते भवन्ति । त्वं भवसि । युवां भवथः । यूयं भवथ । अहं भवामि । आवां भवावः । वयं भवामः ।

No. 422—THE LONG vowel shall be the substitute OF an inflective base ending in SHORT A, WHEN a *sárvadhátuka* affix (No. 418) beginning with YAÑ FOLLOWS. Thus *(bhava+mi=) bhavámi* "I become," *bhavávah* "we two become," *bhavámah* "we become."

With the pronouns supplied, the present tense stands thus :—

Sing.	Dual.	Plu.
sa bhavati.	*tau bhavatah.*	*te bhavanti.*
twań bhavasi.	*yuváń bhavathah.*	*yúyań bhavatha.*
ahań bhavámi.	*áváń bhavávah.*	*vayań bhavámah.*

परोक्षे लिट् । ३ । २ । ११५ ।

भूतानद्यतनपरोक्षार्थवृत्तेर्धातोर्लिट् स्यात् । लस्य तिबादयः ।

No. 423.—Let LIṬ (No. 404) come after a verbal root employed IN signifying what took place before the current day and UNPERCEIVED (by the narrator).

Instead of the *l* (of *liṭ*, the *i* and *ṭ* of which are indicatory), let there be *tip* &c. (No. 407).

परस्मैपदानां णलतुसुस्थलथुसणल्वमाः । ३ । ४ । ८२ ।

लिटस्तिबादीनां णलादयः स्युः । भू अ इति स्थिते ।

No. 424.—Let there be, in the room OF the PARASMAI-PADA affixes, *tip* &c., substituted for *liṭ*, *ṇal* &c.—viz.

Sing.	Dual.	Plural.
ṆAL	ATUS	US
THAL	ATHUS	A
ṆAL	VA	MA.

Proceeding to subjoin these affixes, (the *ṇ* and *l* being elided by Nos. 148 and 5) the case standing thus—*bhú+a*—we look forward.

भुवो वुग्लुङ्लिटोः । ६ । ४ । ८८ ।

अचि ।

No. 425.—Let VUK (of which the *u* and *k* are indicatory) be the augment OF the root BHÚ, WHEN (a substitute for) LUŃ OR LIṬ beginning with a vowel FOLLOWS.

Thus *bhú+a* becomes *bhúv+a*.

लिटि धातोरनभ्यासस्य । ६ । १ । ८ ।

लिटि परेऽनभ्यासधात्ववयवस्यैकाचः प्रथमस्य द्वे स्त आदिभूतादचः परस्य तु द्वितीयस्य । भूव् भूव् अ इति स्थिते ।

No. 426.—WHEN LIṬ FOLLOWS, there are two in the room of the first portion, containing a single vowel, OF AN UNREDUPLICATED VERBAL ROOT; but, after an initial vowel, the reduplication is of the second portion (containing a single vowel) which follows it.

Thus *bhúv+a* having become *bhúvbhúv+a*, we look forward.

पूर्वोऽभ्यासः । ६ । १ । ४ ।

अत्र ये द्वे तयोः ।

No. 427.—Let THE FIRST of those two which are here spoken of (No. 426) be called THE REDUPLICATE *(abhyása)*.

हलादिः शेषः । ७ । ४ । ६० ।

अभ्यासस्यादिर्हल् शिष्यतेऽन्ये हलो लुप्यन्त ।

No. 428.—Of the reduplicate (No. 427) THE FIRST CONSONANT IS LEFT; the other consonants are elided.

Thus we have *bhúbhúv+a*.

ह्रस्वः । ७ । ४ । ५९ ।

अभ्यासस्याचः ।

No. 429.—In the room of the vowel of the reduplicate there is the SHORT vowel.

Thus we have *bhubhúv+a*.

भवतेरः । ७ । ४ । ७३ ।

भवतेरभ्यासस्योकारस्य अः स्याल्लिटि ।

No. 430.—When *liṭ* follows, let there be A instead of the *u* of the reduplicate syllable OF the verb BHÚ.

Thus we have *bhabhúv+a*.

अभ्यासे चर् च । ८ । ४ । ५४ ।

अभ्यासे झलां चरः स्युर्जशश्च । झशां जशः खयां चर इति विवेकः । बभूव । बभूवतुः । बभूवुः ।

No. 431.—IN A REDUPLICATE syllable, let there be ALSO CHAR and *jaś* instead of *jhal* :—that is to say—let there be *jaś* in the room of *jhaś*, and *char* in the room of *khay*—such is the distinction.

Thus *bhabhúv+a* becomes finally *babhúva* "he became." In the same way *babhúvatuh* (No. 424) "they two became," *babhúvuh* "they became."

लिट् च । ३ । ४ । ११५ ।

लिडादेशस्तिङार्धधातुकसंज्ञः ।

No. 432.—AND let a conjugational affix substituted for LIṬ be called *árdhadhátuka* (No. 436).

आर्धधातुकस्येड्वलादेः । ७ । २ । ३५ ।

बभूविथ । बभूवथुः । बभूव । बभूव । बभूविव । बभूविम ।

No. 433.—IṬ is the augment OF AN ÁRDHADHÁTUKA affix BEGINNING WITH VAL.

In accordance with No. 103, the *i* (of *iṭ*) is *prefixed* to the affix—giving *babhúvitha*, "thou becamest." Then *babhúvathuh* "you two became," *babhúva* "you became," *babhúva* "I became," and again *babhúviva* (No. 433), "we two became," *babhúvima* "we became."

अनद्यतने लुट् । ३ । ३ । १५ ।

भविष्यत्यनद्यतनेऽर्थे धातोर्लुट् ।

No. 434.—Let LUṬ (No. 404) come after a verbal root IN THE SENSE OF what will happen but NOT IN THE COURSE OF THE CURRENT DAY.

स्यतासी ऌलुटोः । ३ । १ । ३३ ।

धातोरेतौ स्तो ऌलुटोः परतः । शबाद्यपवादः । ऌ इति ऌङ्ऌटोर्ग्रहणम् ।

No. 435.—WHEN LṚI AND LUṬ FOLLOW, then these two, SYA AND TÁSI, are the affixes of a verbal root. This supersedes the affix *śap* &c. (No. 419). Both *lṛiṅ* and *lṛiṭ* are included in the expression "*lṛi.*"

आर्धधातुकं शेषः ।३।४।११४।

तिङ्शिद्भ्योऽन्यो धातोरिति विहितः प्रत्यय एतत्संज्ञः स्यात् । इट् ।

No. 436.—Let the remainder, i. e. affixes other than *tiṅ* and those with an indicatory *ś* (No. 418), subjoined to a verbal root be called *árdhadhátuka*—(i. e. "belonging to half the verb,"—or to six of the tenses).

The augment *iṭ* here presents itself from No. 433, and the word (through Nos. 420 and 435) attains the form *bhavitás.*

लुटः प्रथमस्य डारौरसः ।२।४।८५।

डित्वसामर्थ्यादभस्यापि टेर्लोपः । भविता ।

No. 437.—ḌÁ RAU AND RAS are substituted in the room OF the affixes of THE LOWEST (No. 413) person OF LUṬ.

As the presence of *ḍ* as an indicatory letter must not be unmeaning, there is elision of the final vowel with what follows it (No. 52), although the word is not one of those called *bha* (Nos. 185 and 187).

Thus *bhavitás* (from No. 436) becomes *bhavit,* and (with the *á* derived from the *ḍá* of this rule), *bhavitá* "he will become."

तासस्त्योर्लोपः ।७।४।५०।

सादौ प्रत्यये ।

No. 438.—There is ELISION OF TÁS (No. 435) AND of the verb AS, when an affix beginning with *s* follows.

रि च ।७।४।५१।

रादौ प्रत्यये तथा । भवितारौ । भवितारः । भवितासि । भवितास्थः । भवितास्थ । भवितास्मि । भवितास्वः । वितास्मः ।

No. 439.—AND so (as directed in No. 438) WHEN an affix beginning with R FOLLOWS.

Thus we have (No. 437) *bhavitárau* "they two will become," *bhavitárah* "they will become," *bhavitási* "thou wilt become," *bhavitásthah* "you two will become," *bhavitástha* "you will become," *bhavitásmi* "I will become," *bhavitáswah* "we two will become," *bhavitásmah* "we will become."

लृट् शेषे च । ३ । ३ । १३ ।

भविष्यदर्थाद्धातोर्लृट् क्रियार्थायां क्रियायां सत्यामसत्यां वा । स्यः । इट् । भविष्यति । भविष्यतः । भविष्यन्ति । भविष्यसि । भविष्यथः । भविष्यथ । भविष्यामि । भविष्यावः । भविष्यामः ।

No. 440.—AND IN THE REMAINING CASES, i. e. whether there be or be not another verb (denoting an action performed) for the sake of the (future) action (No. 903)—let LṚIṬ come after a verbal root employed in the sense of the future (indefinite or 2nd).

The augment *sya* being obtained from No. 435, and *iṭ* from No. 433, and the *s* being changed to *sh* by No. 169, we have *bhavishyati* "he will become," *bhavishyatah* "they two will become," *bhavishyanti* "they will become," *bhavishyasi* "thou wilt become," *bhavishyathah* "you two will become," *bhavishyatha* "you will become," *bhavishyámi* "I will become," *bhavishyávah* "we two will become," *bhavishyámah* "we will become."

लोट् च । ३ । ३ । १६२ ।

विध्याद्यर्थेषु धातोर्लोट् ।

No. 441.—AND let LOṬ (No. 404) come after a verbal root in the sense of command &c.

आशिषि लिङ्लोटौ । ३ । ३ । १७३ ।

No. 442.—IN the sense of BENEDICTION, LIŃ AND LOṬ are employed.

एरुः । ३ । ४ । ८६ ।

लोट इकारस्य उः । भवतु ।

No. 443.—Let there be U instead OF the I of an affix substituted for *loṭ* (No. 441). Thus *bhavatu* "let him become."

तुह्योस्तातङाशिष्यन्यतरस्याम् । ७ । १ । ३५ ।

आशिषि तुह्योस्तातङ् वा । परत्वात् सर्वादेशः । भवतात् ।

No. 444.—IN BENEDICTION TÁTAŃ is OPTIONALLY the substitute OF TU (No. 443) AND HI (No. 447).

The affix, though containing an indicatory *ń* (No. 59), takes the place of the whole of the original affix, because it is ruled that No. 58, which is subsequent to No. 59 in the order of the *Ashṭádhyáyí*, shall here take effect (by No. 132). Thus *bhavatát* "may he become."

लोटो लङ्वत् । ३ । ४ । ८५ ।

लोटस्तामादयः सलोपः ।

No. 445.—Let the treatment OF LOṬ (No. 441) be LIKE that of LAŃ (No. 456), and so let there be the substitution of *tám &c.* (No. 446) and the elision of *s* (No. 455).

तस्थस्थमिपां तान्तन्तामः । ३ । ४ । १०१ ।

ङितश्चतुर्णां तामादयः । भवताम् । भवन्तु ।

No. 446.—Let *tám &c.*, i. e. TÁM, TAM, TA, AND AM, be instead of the four substitutes, viz., TAS, THAS, THA, AND MIP,—of any *l* which has an indicatory *ń* (viz., *lań*, *liń*, *luń*, and *ḷriń*). Thus *bhavatám* (No. 445) "let the two become," *bhavantu* "let them become."

सेर्ह्यपिच्च । ३ । ४ । ८७ ।

लोटः सेर्हिः सोऽपिच्च ।

No. 447.—Instead OF the SI, substituted for *loṭ*, there is HI—AND this has NOT THE INDICATORY P (of the *sip*).

अतो हेः । ६ । ४ । १०५ ।

लुक् । भव । भवतात् । भवतम् । भवत ।

No. 448.—Let there be elision (*luk*—No. 209) OF HI (No. 447) AFTER what ends in SHORT A. Thus *bhava* or (No. 444) *bha-*

vatát "be thou," or "mayst thou become," *bhavatam* "do you two become," *bhavata* "become ye."

मेर्निः । ३ । ४ । ८६ ।

लोटः ।

No. 449.—Ni is the substitute OF MI in the room of *loṭ*.

आडुत्तमस्य पिच्च । ३ । ४ । ९२ ।

लोडुत्तमस्याट् पिच्च । हिन्योरुत्वं न । इकारोच्चारणसामर्थ्यात् । भवानि ।

No. 450.—Áṭ is the augment of the affixes OF THE HIGHEST person substituted in the room of *loṭ*, AND the termination is as if it had AN INDICATORY P.

The *hi* (No. 447) and *ni* (No. 449) do not undergo the change to *u* (by No. 443)—because in that case the enouncing of the *i* in these two substitutes would be unmeaning. Thus we have *bhavá-ni* "may I become"—(No. 103).

ते प्राग्धातोः । १ । ४ । ८० ।

ते गत्युपसर्गसंज्ञका धातोः प्रागेव प्रयोक्तव्याः ।

No. 451.—THESE particles, termed *gati* (No. 222) and *upa-sarga* (No. 47) are to be employed BEFORE THE VERBAL ROOT—(that is to say, they are prefixes).

आनि लोट् । ८ । ४ । १६ ।

उपसर्गस्थान्निमित्तात् परस्य लोडादेशस्यानीति नस्य णः स्यात् । प्रभवाणि ।

No. 452.—Let there be a cerebral *ṇ* in the room of the dental *n* of ÁNI (Nos 449 and 450), the substitute OF LOṬ, when it follows a letter competent to cause such a change (No. 157) standing in an *upasarga*. Thus, in consequence of the *r* in *pra*, we have *prabha-váṇi* "let me prevail."

दुरः षत्वणत्वयोरुपसर्गत्वप्रतिषेधो वक्तव्यः । दुःस्थितिः । दुर्भवानि ।

No. 453.—"IT SHOULD BE STATED THAT DUR (No. 48) IS FORBIDDEN TO SUPPORT THE CHARACTER OF AN UPASARGA, IN SO FAR AS REGARDS THE CHANGING (of *s* and *n*) TO SH AND Ṇ." Thus we have, without change, *duhsthiti* "ill fortune," and *durbhaváni* "may I be unhappy."

अन्तःशब्दस्याङ्किविधिणत्वेषूपसर्गत्वं वाच्यम् । अन्तर्भवाणि ।

No. 454.—"IT SHOULD BE STATED THAT THE WORD ANTAR SUPPORTS THE CHARACTER OF AN UPASARGA (No. 452), SO FAR AS REGARDS THE RULES FOR AŃ (III-3-104) AND KI (No. 917) AND THE CHANGE of *n* TO a cerebral Ṇ." Hence *antarbhaváṇi* "may I be within."

नित्यं ङितः । ३ । ४ । ९९ ।

सकारान्तस्य ङिदुत्तमस्य नित्यं लोपः । अलोऽन्त्यस्येति सलोपः । भवाव । भवाम ।

No. 455.—There is ALWAYS elision of an affix of the Chief person, substituted in the room OF THAT *l* WHICH HAS AN INDICATORY Ń, provided it end in *s*. By No. 27 the elision is only of the *s*, the final letter. By No. 445 this rule applies to the case of *loṭ* —so that we have *bhaváva* "may we two become," and *bhaváma* "may we become."

अनद्यतने लङ् । ३ । २ । १११ ।

अनद्यतनभूतार्थवृत्तेर्धातोर्लङ् ।

No. 456.—Let LAŃ (No. 404) come after a verbal root employed IN THE SENSE OF past BEFORE the commencement of THE CURRENT DAY.

लुङ्लङ्लृङ्क्ष्वडुदात्तः । ६ । ४ । ७१ ।

एष्वङ्गस्याट् ।

No. 457.—AṬ, ACUTELY ACCENTED, is the augment of the inflective base, WHEN LUŃ (No. 468), LAŃ (No. 456), AND LṚIŃ (No. 476) FOLLOW.

According to No. 103, this augment is one to be prefixed.

इतश्च । ३ । ४ । १०० ।

ङितो लस्य परस्मैपदमिकारान्तं यत् तस्य लोपः । अभवत् । अभवताम् । अभवन् । अभवः । अभवतम् । अभवत । अभवम् । अभवाव । अभवाम ।

No. 458.—AND there is elision of that *parasmaipada* affix (No. 408) ending in I (viz. *ti, anti, si,* and *mi,*) which is the substitute of an *l* distinguished by an indicatory *ń.* Thus *abhavat* "he became," *abhavatám* (No. 446) "they two became," *abhavan* (No. 26) "they became," *abhavah* (Nos. 124 and 111) "thou becamest," *abhavatam* (No. 446) "you two became," *abhavata* (No. 446) "you became," *abhavam* (No. 446) "I became," *abhaváva* (No. 455) "we two became," *abhaváma* "we became."

विधिनिमन्त्रणामन्त्रणाधीष्टसंप्रश्नप्रार्थनेषु लिङ् । ३ । ३ । १६१ ।

एष्वर्थेषु धातोर्लिङ् ।

No. 459.—Let LIŃ (No. 404) come after a verbal root IN these senses, viz. COMMANDING, DIRECTING, INVITING, EXPRESSION OF WISH, ENQUIRING, AND ASKING FOR.

यासुट् परस्मैपदेषूदात्तो ङिच्च । ३ । ४ । १०३ ।

लिङः परस्मैपदानां यासुडागमो ङिच्च ।

No. 460.—WHEN THE PARASMAIPADA SUBSTITUTES of *liń* FOLLOW, then YÁSUṬ (No. 103) ACUTELY ACCENTED is their augment, AND the termination is regarded as HAVING AN INDICATORY Ń.

लिङः स लोपोऽनन्त्यस्य । ७ । २ । ७९ ।

सार्वधातुकलिङोऽनन्त्यस्य सस्य लोपः । इति प्राप्ते ।

No. 461.—There is ELISION OF THE S, NOT being FINAL, of a *sárvadhátuka* substitute (No. 418) OF LIŃ.

This having presented itself, we look forward.

अतो येयः । ७ । २ । ८० ।

अतः परस्य सार्वधातुकावयवस्य यास् इत्यस्येय् । गुणः ।

No. 462.—Iy is substituted in the room of *yás* (No. 460) being part of a *sárvadhátuka* affix coming AFTER what ends in SHORT A.

Thus we have *bhava+iy+t* (No. 458); and, substituting *guṇa*, *bhavey+t*.

लोपो व्योर्वलि । ६ । १ । ६६ ।

भवेत् । भवेताम् ।

No. 463.—There is ELISION OF V AND Y, when VAL (i. e. any consonant except *h* or *y*) FOLLOWS. Thus we have *bhavet* "he may become," *bhavetám* (No. 446) "they two may become."

झेर्जुस् । ३ । ४ । १०८ ।

लिङः । भवेयुः । भवेः । भवेतम् । भवेत । भवेयम् । भवेव । भवेम ।

No. 464.—Instead OF JHI, in the room of *liń*, there shall be JUS (No. 149). Thus *bhaveyuh* (No. 462) "they may become," *bhaveh* (No. 458) "thou mayst become," *bhavetam* (No. 446) "you two may become," *bhaveta* "you may become," *bhaveyam* "I may become," *bhaveva* (No. 455) "we two may become," *bhavema*" we may become."

लिङाशिषि । ३ । ४ । ११६ ।

आशिषि लिङस्तिङार्धधातुकसंज्ञः स्यात् ।

No. 465.—WHEN THE SENSE IS THAT OF BENEDICTION, let a termination of the set called *tiń* (No. 413) substituted in the room OF LIŃ be termed *árdhadhátuka*.

किदाशिषि । ३ । ४ । १०४ ।

आशिषि लिङो यासुट् कित् । स्कोः संयोगाद्योरिति सलोपः ।

No. 466.—WHEN THE SENSE IS THAT OF BENEDICTION, then *yásuṭ*, the augment of *liń* (No. 460), is as if it were DISTINGUISHED BY AN INDICATORY K.

The *s* of *yás (yásuṭ)* is elided before *tip*, according to No. 337.

क्ङिति च । १ । १ । ५ ।

गित्किन्ङिन्निमित्ते इग्लक्षणे गुणवृद्धी न स्तः । भूयात् । भूयास्ताम् । भूयासुः । भूयाः । भूयास्तम् । भूयास्त । भूयासम् । भूयास्व । भूयास्म ।

No. 467.—AND there are not *guṇa* and *vriddhi*, when indicated by the term "*ik*," IF THAT which would otherwise cause the change HAS AN INDICATORY *g*, OR K, OR Ń.

According to No. 466, the augment *yásuṭ* (which otherwise, according to No. 420, would have caused the substitution of *guṇa* in the room of the *u* of *bhú* which is "*ik*,") is to be regarded as having an indicatory *k*—so that we have *bhúyát* (No. 458) "may he become," *bhúyástám* (No. 446) "may they two become," *bhúyásuh* (No. 464) "may they become," *bhúyáh* (No. 337) "mayst thou become," *bhúyástam* "may you two become," *bhúyásta* "may you become, " *bhúyásam* "may I become, " *bhúyáswa* "may we two become, " *bhúyásma* "may we become."

लुङ् । ३ । २ । ११० ।

भूतार्थे धातोर्लुङ् स्यात् ।

No. 468.—Let LUŃ (No. 404) come after a verbal root in the sense of what is past (indefinitely).

माङि लुङ् । ३ । ३ । १७५ ।

सर्वलकारापवादः ।

No. 469.—WHEN (the prohibitive particle) MÁŃ IS EMPLOYED, then let there be LUŃ. This sets aside all the other tenses.

स्मोत्तरे लङ् च । ३ । ३ । १७६ ।

स्मोत्तरे माङि लङ् स्याच्चाल्लुङ् ।

No. 470.—AND WHEN *it* (viz. *máń*—No. 469) IS FOLLOWED BY SMA, there may be LAŃ. By the word "and," it is signified that *luń* (No. 469) is equally admissible.

For examples, see No. 475.

स्मि लुङि । ३ । १ । ४३ ।

शबाद्यपवादः ।

No. 471.—WHEN LUŃ FOLLOWS, let CHLI be added to the verbal root. This sets aside *śap* (No. 419) and the like.

च्लेः सिच् । ३ । १ । ४४ ।

इचावितौ ।

No. 472.—Instead OF CHLI (No. 471), let there be SICH. The *i* and *ch* in *sich* are indicatory.

गातिस्थाघुपाभूभ्यः सिचः परस्मैपदेषु । २ । ४ । ७७ ।

लुक् । गापाविहेणादेशपिबती गृह्येते ।

No. 473.—WHEN THE PARASMAIPADA affixes COME AFTER the verbal roots GÁ, STHÁ "to stand," the six called GHU (No. 662), PÁ, & BHÚ, there is elision (*luk*—No. 209) OF SICH (No. 472). The roots *gá* and *pá* are here severally taken in the sense of the verb *iṇ* "to go," and of *pá* "to drink" (not "to praise," and "to protect").

भूसुवोस्तिङि । ७ । ३ । ८८ ।

भूसू एतयोः सार्वधातुके तिङि गुणो न । अभूत् । अभूताम् । अभूवन् । अभूः । अभूतम् । अभूत । अभूवम् । अभूव । अभूम ।

No. 474.—WHEN A *sárvadhátuka* TENSE-AFFIX comes AFTER these two, BHÚ "to become," AND SHÚ "to bring forth," *guṇa* is not substituted (by No. 420). Thus we have *abhút* (Nos. 457 and 458) "he became," *abhútám* (No. 446) "they two became," *abhúvan* (No. 425) they became," *abhúh* "thou becamest," *abhútam* "you two became," *abhúta* "you became," *abhúvam* "I became," *abhúva* "we two became," *abhúma* "we became."

न माङ्योगे । ६ । ४ । ७४ ।

अडाटौ न स्तः । मा भवान् भूत् । मा स्म भवत् । मा स्म भूत् ।

No. 475.—WHEN the verb is IN CONJUNCTION WITH the prohibitive particle MÁŃ, the augments *aṭ* (No. 457) and *áṭ* (No. 478) are NOT taken. Thus *má bhaván bhút* "may you, Sir, not become," *má sma bhavat* (No. 470) "may he not become," *má sma bhút* "may he not become."

लिङ्निमित्ते लृङ् क्रियातिपत्तौ। ३। ३। १३९।

हेतुहेतुमद्भावादि लिङ्निमित्तं तत्र भविष्यत्यर्थे लृङ् क्रियाया अनिष्पत्तौ गम्यमानायाम्। अभविष्यत्। अभविष्यताम्। अभविष्यन्। अभविष्यः। अभविष्यतम्। अभविष्यत। अभविष्यम्। अभविष्याव। अभविष्याम। सुवृष्टिश्चेदभविष्यत् तदा सुभिक्षमभविष्यत्। इत्यादि ज्ञेयम्। अत सातत्यगमने। २। अतति।

No. 476.—WHERE THERE IS A REASON, such as the relation of cause and effect, FOR affixing LIŃ (No. 459), there let LṚIŃ (No. 404) be affixed, WHEN THE NON-COMPLETION OF THE ACTION is to be understood.

This tense (the conditional) takes the following form—*abhavishyat* (Nos. 457, 420, 435, 433, 169, and 458) "he would become," *abhavishyatám* (No. 446) "they two would become," *abhavishyan* "they would become," *abhavishyah* "thou wouldst become," *adhavishyatam* "you two would become," *abhavishyata* "you would become," *abhavishyam* "I would become," *abhavishyáva* "we two would become," *abhavishyáma* "we would become."

"If there had been good rain, then there would have been plenty of food;"—or "If there were to be good rain, then there would be plenty of food;"—to apprehend the force of the conditional, let this and the like sentences be understood.

[In these renderings, let it be observed, there is an eye to the "non-completion of the action"—that is to say, it is implied that there was *not* good rain, nor consequent plenty:—or that the occurrence of good rain is dubious, and the desirable consequence equally so.]

The verb *at,* "to go on continuously," (which, in the catalogue of roots, is written *ata* —with a supernumerary or indicatory letter termed an *anubandha*) is next to be conjugated:—*atati* (No. 419) he goes."

अत आदेः। ७। ४। ७०।

अभ्यासस्यादेरतो दीर्घः स्यात्। आत। आततुः। आतुः।

आतिथ । आतथुः । आत । आत । आतिव । आतिम । अतिता । अतिष्यति । अततु ।

No. 477.—Let there be a long vowel in the room OF SHORT A INITIAL in a reduplicate (No. 427). Thus, in the 2nd pret., we have *áta* (No. 424) "he went," *átatuh* "they two went," *átuh* "they went," *átitha* (No. 433) "thou wentest," *átathuh* "you two went," *áta* "you went," *áta* "I went," *átiva* "we two went," *átima* "we went."

In the 1st fut. we have *atitá* (No. 437) "he will go," 2nd fut. *atishyati* (No. 440) "he will go," and imp. *atatu* (No. 443) "let him go."

आडजादीनाम्।६।४।७२।

अजादेरङ्गस्याड्लुङ्लङ्लृङ्क्षु । आतत् । अतेत् । अत्यात् । अत्यास्ताम् । लुङि सिचि इडागमे कृते ।

No. 478.—Let ÁṬ be the augment OF WHAT inflective bases BEGIN WITH A VOWEL, when *luń, lań*, or *ḷrïń* follows. Thus we have 1st pret. *átat* "he went," potential—*atet* (No. 463) "he may go," benedictive *atyát* (No. 467) "may he go," *atyástám* "may they two go."

When *luń* (No. 468) is affixed, and *sich* (No. 472) follows, and the augment *iṭ* (No. 433) has been attached—we look forward.

अस्तिसिचोऽपृक्ते।७।३।९६।

विद्यमानात् सिचोऽस्तेश्च परस्यापृक्तस्य हल ईडागमः ।

No. 479.—Let *íṭ* be the augment OF AN AFFIX CONSISTING OF A SINGLE (No. 199) *consonant* coming AFTER SICH actually present (unelided) OR AFTER the verb AS "to be."

इट ईटि।८।२।२८।

इटः परस्य सस्य लोपः स्यादीटि । सिज्लोप एकादेशे सिद्धो वाच्यः । आतीत् । आतिष्टाम् ।

No. 480.—WHEN ÍṬ (No. 479) FOLLOWS, let there be elision of *s* coming AFTER IṬ (No. 433).

[This elision of *s* (*sich*), being directed by a rule in one of the last three chapters of the grammar (No. 39), is not recognised by No. 479—which therefore acts as if the *sich* were positively present.] "It should be stated that the elision of *sich* is recognised as having taken place, in the case where a single substitute comes" (in the room of more than one element; as, for instance, when long *í* comes, by No. 55, in the room of *i* + *í*): so that we have *áti* + *ít* = *átít* "he went," *átishṭám* (Nos. 446, 169, and 78) "they two went."

सिजभ्यस्तविदिभ्यश्च । ३ । ४ । १०९ ।

सिचोऽभ्यस्ताद्विदेश्च परस्य ङित्संबन्धिनो झेर्जुस् । आतिषुः । आतीः । आतिष्टम् । आतिष्ट । आतिषम् । आतिष्व । आतिष्म । आतिष्यत् । षिधु गत्याम् । ३ ।

No. 481.—Let there be *jus* instead of *jhi* belonging to a tense designated by an *l* (No. 404) with an indicatory *ń*, when it comes AFTER SICH (No. 472) OR A REDUPLICATED verb, OR the root VID "to know." Thus *átishuh* "they went," *átíh* (Nos. 479 and 480) "thou wentest," *átishṭam* "you two went," *átishṭa* "you went," *átisham* "I went," *átishwa* "we two went," *átishma* "we went."

Conditional—*átishyat* (No. 476) "he would go." The verb *shidh (shidhu)* "to go" is next to be conjugated.

ह्रस्वं लघु । १ । ४ । १० ।

No. 482.—Let a SHORT vowel be termed "LIGHT" *(laghu)*.

संयोगे गुरु । १ । ४ । ११ ।

संयोगे परे ह्रस्वं गुरु ।

No. 483.—WHEN a CONJUNCT consonant FOLLOWS, let a short vowel be termed "HEAVY" *(guru)*.

दीर्घं च । १ । ४ । १२ ।

गुरु स्यात् ।

No. 484.—AND let a LONG vowel be termed "heavy" *(guru)*.

पुगन्तलघूपधस्य च । ७ । ३ । ८६ ।

पुगन्तस्य लघूपधस्य चाङ्गस्येको गुणः सार्वधातुकार्धधातुकयोः । धात्वादेरिति सः । सेधति । षत्वम् । सिषेध ।

No. 485.—AND let there be *guṇa* in the room OF the *ik* of THAT inflective base WHICH ENDS WITH the augment PUK (No. 749) OR which HAS A "LIGHT" vowel (No. 482) as its PENULTIMATE letter (No. 296), when a *sárvadhátuka* or an *árdhadhátuka* affix follows.

According to No. 280, *s* is substituted for the *sh* initial in the root—and we have *sedhati* "he goes." In the 2nd pret., the substituted *s* being again changed to *sh* (by No. 169), we have *sishedha* (No. 424) "he went."

असंयोगाल्लिट् कित् । १ । २ । ५ ।

असंयोगात् परोऽपिल्लिट् कित् स्यात् । सिषिधतुः । सिषिधुः । सिषेधिथ । सिषिधथुः । सिषिध । सिषेध । सिषिधिव । सिषिधिम । सेधिता । सेधिष्यति । सेधतु । असेधत् । सेधेत् । सिध्यात् । असेधीत् । असेधिष्यत् । एवं चिती संज्ञाने । ४ । शुच शोके । ५ । गद व्यक्तायां वाचि । ६ । गदति ।

No. 486.—Let a substitute of LIṬ, (No. 423), NOT coming AFTER A CONJUNCT consonant and not distinguished by an indicatory *p*, be held to have AN INDICATORY K (No. 467). Thus *sishidhatuh* "they two went," *sishidhuh* "they went, *sishedhitha* (No. 433) "thou wentest," *sishidhathuh* "you two went," *sishidha* "you went" *sishedha* "I went," *sishidhiva* (No. 433) "we two went," *sishidhima* "we went," 1st fut. *sedhitá* (No. 437) "he will go," 2nd fut. *sedhishyati* (No. 440) "he will go," imp. *sedhatu* (No. 443) "let him go," 1st pret. *asedhat* (No. 458) "he went," pot. *sedhet* (No. 463) "he should go," benedictive *sidhyát* (No. 467) "may he go," 3rd pret. *asedhít* (No. 480) "he went," cond. *asedhishyat* (No. 476) "he would go."

In the same way are conjugated *chit (chití)* "to think," and *śuch (śucha)* "to grieve."

The word *gad (gada)* "to speak plainly" is next to be conjugated, which makes *gadati* "he speaks."

नेर्गदनदपतपदघुमास्यतिहन्तियातिवातिद्रातिप्सा-तिवपतिवहतिशाम्यतिचिनोतिदेग्धिषु च ।८।४।१७।

उपसर्गस्थान्निमित्तात् परस्य नेर्णो गदादिषु परेषु । प्रणिगदति ।

No. 487.—Let cerebral *ṇ* be the substitute of the dental *n* OF the prefix NI, following a cause for such change (No. 157) standing in an *upasarga* (No. 47), WHEN the verbs *gad* &c. FOLLOW—these being GAD "to speak," NAD "to be happy," PAT "to fall," PAD "to go," the verbs termed GHU (No. 662), MÁ "to measure," SHO "to destroy," HAN "to kill," YÁ "to go," VÁ "to blow," DRÁ "to flee," PSÁ "to eat," VAP "to weave," VAH "to bear," ŚAM "to be tranquil," CHI "to collect," AND DIH "to anoint." Thus we have *praṇigadati* "he speaks loudly."

कुहोश्चुः ।७।४।६२।

अभ्यासकवर्गहकारयोश्चवर्गादेशः ।

No. 488.—Let a letter of THE PALATAL CLASS be the substitute OF a letter of THE GUTTURAL CLASS, OR OF H, in a reduplicate (No. 427).

अत उपधायाः ।७।२।११६।

वृद्धिः स्याञ्ञिति णिति च प्रत्यये । जगाद । जगदतुः । जगदुः । जगदिथ । जगदथुः । जगद ।

No. 489.—Let there be *vṛiddhi* in the room OF A PENULTIMATE SHORT A, when an affix, distinguished by an indicatory *ñ* or *ṇ*, follows. Thus we have, in the 2nd pret., *jagáda* (Nos. 488 and 424) "he spoke," *jagadatuh* "they two spoke," *jagaduh* "they spoke," *jagaditha* (No. 433) "thou spokest," *jagadathuh* "you two spoke," *jagada* "you spoke."

णलुत्तमो वा ।७।१।९१।

णित् स्यात् । जगाद । जगद । जगदिव । जगदिम । गदिता । गदिष्यति । गदतु । अगदत् । गदेत् । गद्यात् ।

No. 490.—Let NAL (No. 424), the termination of THE HIGHEST person (No. 416), be OPTIONALLY regarded as having an indicatory *n*. Thus we have either *jagáda* or *jagada* "I spoke," *jagadiva* "we two spoke," *jagadima* "we spoke." In the 1st fut. *gaditá* (No. 437) "he will speak," 2nd fut. *gadishyati* (No. 440) "he will speak," imp. *gadatu* (No. 443) "let him speak," 1st pret. *agadat* (No. 458) "he spoke," pot. *gadet* (No. 463) "he may speak," benedictive *gadyát* (No. 467) "may he speak."

अतो हलादेर्लघोः ।७।२।७।

हलादेर्लघोर्वृद्धिर्वेडादौ परस्मैपदे सिचि । अगादीत् । अगदीत् । अगदिष्यत् । गद अव्यक्ते शब्दे । १ ।

No. 491.—Let *vriddhi* be optionally the substitute OF a "LIGHT" A (No. 482) PRECEDED BY A CONSONANT, when *sich* follows, and a *parasmaipada* affix preceded by the augment *iṭ* (No. 433). Thus we have, 3rd pret, *agádít* or *agadít* (No. 480) "he spoke," cond. *agadishyat* (No. 476) "he would speak."

The verb *ṇad (ṇada)* "to sound inarticulately" is next to be conjugated.

णो नः ।६।१।६५।

धात्वादेर्णस्य नः । णोपदेशास्त्वनर्दनाटिनाथ्नाधनन्दनक्कनॄनृतः ।

No. 492.—Let there be dental N in the room OF cerebral Ṇ initial in a root.

With the exception of *nard* "to sound," *naṭ* to dance," *náth* "to beg," *nádh* "to beg," *nand* "to thrive," *nakk* "to destroy," *nṛí* "to lead," and *nṛit* "to dance," all the verbs that begin with *n* have a cerebral *ṇ* in the original enunciation.

उपसर्गादसमासेऽपि णोपदेशस्य ।८।४।१४।

उपसर्गस्थान्निमित्तात् परस्य णोपदेशस्य धातोर्नस्य णः । प्रणदति । प्रणिनदति । नदति । ननाद ।

No. 493.—Let cerebral *ṇ* be the substitute of the dental *n* OF WHAT root HAS cerebral Ṇ IN ITS ORIGINAL ENUNCIATION, when it comes AFTER a cause of such change standing in AN UPASARGA (No. 452), EVEN THOUGH THE COMPOUND BE NOT A SAMÁSA (No.

961). Thus we have *praṇadati* "he shouts," *praṇinadati* (No. 487) "he shouts."

The simple verb is conjugated thus:—*nadati* "he sounds," *nanáda* "he sounded."

अत एकहल्मध्येऽनादेशादेर्लिटि ।६।४।१२०।

लिण्निमित्तादेशादिकं न भवति यदङ्गं तदवयवस्यासंयुक्तहल्मध्यस्थस्यात एत्वमभ्यासलोपश्च किति लिटि ।

No. 494.—WHEN a substitute of LIṬ, regarded as having an indicatory *k* (No. 486), FOLLOWS, then there shall be the substitution of *e* in the room OF SHORT A, standing BETWEEN SIMPLE CONSONANTS, which forms a part OF WHAT inflective base DOES NOT BEGIN WITH A SUBSTITUTE (in the room of the letter of reduplication—No. 488—) caused by *liṭ;* and there shall be elision of the reduplicate.

थलि च सेटि ।६।४।१२१।

प्रागुक्तं स्यात् । नेदिथ । नेदथुः । नेद । ननाद । ननद । नेदिव । नेदिम । नदिता । नदिष्यति । नदतु । अनदत् । नदेत् । नद्यात् । अनादीत् । अनदीत् । अनदिष्यत् । टुनदि समृद्धौ । ८ ।

No. 495.—AND WHEN THAL (No. 424) FOLLOWS WITH IṬ, (No. 433), let what is mentioned above (No. 494) take place.

Thus—*neditha* "thou didst sound," *nedathuh* "you two did sound," *neda* "you did sound," *nanáda* or *nanada* (No. 490) "I did sound," *nediva* "we two did sound," *nedima* "we did sound,"—*naditá* "he will sound," *nadishyati* "he will sound," *nadatu* "let him sound," *anadat* "he sounded," *nadet* "he may sound," *nadyát* "may he sound," *anádít* or *anadít* (No. 491) "he sounded," *anadishyat* "he would sound."

The verb *nand* "to thrive" is next to be conjugated. In the original enunciation this root appears in the form of *ṭunadi.*

आदिर्ञिटुडवः ।१।३।५।

उपदेशे धातोराद्या एते इतः स्युः

No. 496.—Let ṄI AND ṬU AND ḌU, INITIAL in a root in its original enunciation (in the catalogue of roots) be indicatory.

इदितो नुम् धातोः ।७।१।५८।

नन्दति । ननन्द । नन्दिता । नन्दिष्यति । नन्दतु । अनन्दत् । नन्देत् । नन्द्यात् । अनन्दीत् । अनन्दिष्यत् । अर्च पूजायाम् । ६ । अर्चति ।

No. 497.—Let NUM be the augment OF A ROOT WHICH HAS AN INDICATORY SHORT I (as *ṭunadi* has). As the augment has an indicatory *m* (No. 265), it is subjoined to the last vowel—and thus we have *nandati* "he thrives," *nananda* "he throve," *nanditá* "he will thrive," *nandishyati* "he will thrive," *nandatu* "let him thrive," *anandat* "he throve," *nandet* "he may thrive," *nandyát* "may he thrive," *anandít* "he throve," *anandishyat* "he would thrive."

The verb *arch (archa)* "to worship" is next conjugated:—*archati* "he worships."

तस्मान्नुड्द्विहलः ।७।४।७१।

द्विहलो धातोर्दीर्घीभूतात् परस्य नुट् स्यात् । आनर्च । आनर्चतुः । अर्चिता । अर्चिष्यति । अर्चतु । आर्चत् । अर्चेत् । अर्च्यात् । आर्चीत् । आर्चिष्यत् । व्रज गतौ । १० । व्रजति । वव्राज । व्रजिता । व्रजिष्यति । व्रजतु । अव्रजत् । व्रजेत् । व्रज्यात् ।

No. 498.—Let NUṬ be the augment (of the short *a*) OF what root contains A DOUBLE CONSONANT, AFTER THAT lengthened (reduplicate derived from No. 477). Thus we have *ánarcha* (No. 103) "he worshipped," *ánarchatuh* "they two worshipped," *architá* "he will worship," *archishyati* "he will worship," *archatu* "let him worship," *árchat* (No. 478) "he worshipped," *archet* "he may worship," *archyát* "may he worship," *árchít* "he worshipped," *árchishyat* "he would worship."

The verb *vraj (vraja)* "to go" makes *vrajati* "he goes," *vavrája* (No. 428) "he went," *vrajitá* "he will go," *vrajishyati* "he will go," *vrajatu* "let him go," *avrajat* "he went," *vrajet* "he may go," *vrajyát* "may he go."

वदव्रजहलन्तस्याचः ।७।२।३।

एषामचो वृद्धिः सिचि परस्मैपदेषु । अव्राजीत् । अव्रजिष्यत् । कटे वर्षावरणयोः । ११ । कटति । चकाट । कटिता । कटिष्यति । कटतु । अकटत् । कटेत् । कट्यात् ।

No. 499.—Let *vriddhi* (without the option allowed by No. 491) be the substitute OF THE VOWEL OF these—viz, VAD "to speak," VRAJ "to go," AND OF WHAT inflective base ENDS IN A CONSONANT, when *sich* (No. 472) follows, and the *parasmaipada* affixes. Thus *avrájít* "he went," *avrajishyat* "he would go."

The verb *kaṭ (kaṭe)* "to rain or to appear" makes *kaṭati* "it rains," *chakáṭa* (No. 488) "it rained," *kaṭitá* "it will rain," *kaṭishyati* "it will rain," *kaṭatu* "let it rain," *akaṭat* "it rained," *kaṭet* "it may rain," *kaṭyát* "may it rain."

ह्म्यन्तक्षणश्वसजागृणिश्व्येदिताम् ।७।२।५।

हमयान्तस्य क्षणादेर्ण्यन्तस्य श्वयतेरेदितश्च वृद्धिर्नेडादौ सिचि । अकटीत् । अकटिष्यत् । गुपू रक्षणे । १२ ।

No. 500.—*Vṛiddhi* (No. 499) shall not be the substitute OF WHAT ENDS IN H, or M, OR Y, NOR OF the roots KSHAṆ "to kill," ŚWAS "to breathe," JÁGṚI "to wake," NOR OF those ending with the affix ṆI (No. 747), NOR OF ŚWI "to increase," NOR OF WHAT root IS DISTINGUISHED BY AN INDICATORY E, when *sich*, preceded by the augment *iṭ* (No. 433), follows. Thus *kaṭe* makes *akaṭít* "it rained," *akaṭishyat* "it would rain.

The verb *gup (gupú)* "to protect" is next to be conjugated.

गुपूधूपविच्छिपणिपनिभ्य आयः ।३।१।२८।

स्वार्थे ।

No. 501.—The affix ÁYA comes AFTER GUP "to protect," DHÚP "to heat," VICHCHH "to approach," PAṆ "to praise," AND PAN "to praise"—their sense remaining unaffected by it.

सनाद्यन्ता धातवः । ३ । १ । ३२ ।

सनादयः कमेर्णिङन्ताः प्रत्यया अन्ते येषां ते धातुसंज्ञकाः । धातुत्वाल्लडादयः । गोपायति ।

No. 502.—Let those words be called DHÁTU (i. e. verbal roots,) AT THE END OF WHICH ARE THE (twelve) AFFIXES BEGINNING WITH SAN (III. 1. 5.) and ending with *ṇiń*, which occurs in the aphorism III. 1. 30. (No. 560). Since the words so ending are considered as roots, they take the tense-affixes *laṭ* &c. The affix *áya* (No. 501) being one of the twelve, we have *gopáyati* "he protects."

आयादय आर्धधातुके वा । ३ । १ । ३१ ।

आर्धधातुकविवक्षायामायादयो वा स्युः ।

No. 503.—When it is desired to express one's self WITH AN ÁRDHADHÁTUKA affix, let ÁYA AND THOSE THAT FOLLOW IT (in the list of twelve—No. 502), viz: *íyań*, III. 1. 29., and *ṇiń* (No. 560), be OPTIONALLY affixed.

कास्यनेकाच आम् वक्तव्यः । लिटि । आस्कासोराम्विधानान्मस्य नेत्वम् ।

No. 504.—"ÁM SHOULD BE MENTIONED as the affix OF the verb KÁS 'to shine,' AND OF WHAT verb HAS MORE THAN ONE VOWEL," when *liṭ* follows.

That the *m* of this affix is not indicatory is ascertained by the direction that *ám* shall be applied to *ás* "to sit," and *kás* "to shine," (its application to which would be useless if the *m* were indicatory:—see Nos. 265 and 55).

अतो लोपः । ६ । ४ । ४८ ।

आर्धधातुकोपदेशे यददन्तं तस्यातो लोप आर्धधातुके ।

No. 505.—When an *árdhadhátuka* affix follows, there is ELISION OF the SHORT A of that which ends in short *a* at the time when the *árdhadhátuka* affix is directed to be attached.

आमः । २ । ४ । ८१ ।

आमः परस्य लुक् ।

No. 506.—Let there be a blank (*luk*—No. 209) in the room of what (tense-affix) comes AFTER ÁM (No. 504).

कृञ् चानुप्रयुज्यते लिटि । ३ । १ । ४० ।

आमन्ताल्लिट्पराः कृभ्वस्तयोऽनुप्रयुज्यन्ते । तेषां द्वित्वादि ।

No. 507.—AND after what ends with *ám* (No. 506), the verbs implied in the *pratyáhára* KṚIŃ (which is held to imply *kṛi* "to do," *bhú* "to become," and *as* "to be"), FOLLOWED BY LIṬ, ARE ANNEXED.

These auxiliaries undergo reduplication (No. 426) and the other consequences of taking the affixes denoted by *liṭ*.

उरत् । ७ । ४ । ६६ ।

अभ्यासऋवर्णस्यात् । वृद्धिः । गोपायांचकार । द्वित्वात् परत्वाद्यणि प्राप्ते ।

No. 508.—SHORT A is the substitute OF ṚI (or ṚÍ) in a reduplicate. Thus the root *kṛi*, having substituted *vṛiddhi* by No. 202, becomes *chakára* (Nos. 488 and 424); and this, subjoined to *gup* (altered by Nos. 501 and 504), gives *gopáyáńchakára* (Nos. 94 and 97) "he protected."

In forming the dual of this person (*kṛi*+*atus*) the change of *ṛi* to *yaṇ* first presenting itself, because the aphorism directing it (No. 21) is posterior (No. 132) to that (No. 426) which directs the reduplication—we look forward.

द्विर्वचनेऽचि । १ । १ । ५९ ।

द्वित्वनिमित्तेऽचि अच आदेशो न द्वित्वे कर्तव्ये । गोपायांचक्रतुः ।

No. 509.—WHEN (an affix beginning with) A VOWEL FOLLOWS, THAT IS A CAUSE OF REDUPLICATION, a substitute shall not take the place of a preceding vowel, whilst the reduplication is yet to be made. But, the reduplication having been made, the substitution may then take place, and thus we have *gopáyáńchakratuh* "they two protected."

एकाच उपदेशेऽनुदात्तात् । ७।२।१० ।

उपदेशे यो धातुरेकाजनुदात्तश्च तत आर्धधातुकस्येण्न ।

ऊदृदन्तैर्यौतिरुक्ष्णुशीङ्स्नुनुक्षुश्विडीङ्श्रिभिः ।
वृङ्वृञ्भ्यां च विनैकाचोऽजन्तेषु निहताः स्मृताः ॥

कान्तेषु शक्लेकः । चान्तेषु पच्मुच्रिच्वच्विच्सिचः षट् । छान्तेषु प्रच्छेकः । जान्तेषु त्यज्निज्भज्भञ्ज्भुज्भ्रस्ज्मस्ज्यज्युज्रुज्रञ्ज्विजिर्स्वञ्ज्सञ्ज्सृजः पञ्चदश । दान्तेषु अद् क्षुद् खिद् छिद् तुद् नुद् पद्य भिद् विद्य विनद् विन्द् शद् सद् स्विद्य स्कन्दिहदी षोडश । धान्तेषु क्रुध् क्षुध् बुध्य बन्ध् युध् रुध् राध् व्यध् शुध् साध् सिध्य एकादश । नान्तेषु मन्यहनौ द्वौ । पान्तेषु आप् क्षिप् छुप् तप् तिप् तृप्य दृप्य लिप् लुप् वप्शप्स्वप्सृपस्त्रयोदश । भान्तेषु यभ्रभ्लभस्त्रयः । मान्तेषु गम्नम्यम्रमश्चत्वारः । शान्तेषु क्रुश् दंश् दिश् दृश् मृश् रिश् रुश् लिश्विश्स्पृशो दश । षान्तेषु कृष् त्विष् तुष् द्विष् दुष् पुष्य पिष् विष् शिष् शुष् श्लिष् एकादश । सान्तेषु घस्वसती द्वौ । हान्तेषु दह् दिह् दुह् नह् मिह् रुह् लिह्वहोऽष्टौ ।

अनुदात्ता हलन्तेषु धातवस्त्र्यधिकं शतम् ।

गोपायांचकर्थ । गोपायांचक्रथुः । गोपायांचक्र । गोपायाचकार । गोपायांचकृव । गोपायांचकृम । गोपायांबभूव । गोपायाम्मास । जुगोप । जुगुपतुः । जुगुपुः ।

No. 510.—*Iṭ* (No. 433) shall not be the augment of an *árdhadhátuka* affix coming AFTER WHAT root, IN AN ORIGINAL ENUNCIATION, HAS A SINGLE VOWEL AND IS GRAVELY ACCENTED.

With the exception of roots ending in *ú* and *ṛí*, and with the exception of the roots *yu* "to mix," *ru* "to sound," *kshṇu* "to whet," *śí* "to sleep," *shṇu* "to distil," *ṇu* "to praise," *kshu* "to sneeze," *świ* "to increase," *ḍíṅ* "to fly," and *śri* "to serve," and *vṛi (vṛiṅ)* "to serve," and *vṛi (vṛiṅ)* "to choose," what roots, containing a single vowel, are among those that end in a vowel, are called "gravely accented."

(Among monosyllables terminated by consonants, that have their efficient vowels "gravely accented," there are)—of those that end in *k*, one only—viz. *śak (śakḷri)* "to be able:"—of those that end in *ch*, six—viz. *pach* "to cook," *much* "to be free," *rich* "to purge," *vach* "to speak," *vich* "to differ," and *sich* "to sprinkle:"—of those that end in *chh*, one only—viz. *prachchh* "to ask:"—of those that end in *j*, fifteen—viz. *tyaj* "to abandon," *nij* "to cleanse," *bhaj* "to serve," *bhañj* "to break," *bhuj* "to enjoy," *bhrasj* "to fry," *masj* "to merge," *yaj* "to sacrifice," *yuj* "to join," *ruj* "to be sick," *rañj* "to colour," *vijir* "to differ," *swañj* "to embrace," *sanj* "to embrace," and *sṛij* "to abandon:"—of those that end in *d*, sixteen, viz. *ad* "to eat," *kshud* "to pound," *khid* "to be distressed," *chhid* "to cut," *tud* "to torment," *nud* "to send," *pad* "to go," *bhid* "to break," *vid* "to be," *vid* "to consider," *vid* "to acquire," *śad* "to wither," *sad* "to wither," *swid* "to sweat," *skand* "to go," and *had* "to evacuate:"—of those that end in *dh*, eleven, viz. "*krudh* "to be angry," *kshudh* "to be hungry," *budh* "to know," *bandh* "to bind," *yudh* "to fight," *rudh* "to obstruct," *rádh* "to accomplish," *vyadh* "to pierce," *śudh* "to be pure," *sádh* "to accomplish," and *sidh* "to be accomplished:"—of those that end in *n*, two, viz. *man* "to think, and *han* "to kill:"—of those that end in *p*, thirteen, viz. *áp* "to obtain," *kship* "to throw," *chhup* "to touch," *tap* "to inflame," *tip* "to drop," *tṛip* "to be satisfied," *dṛip* "to be proud," *lip* "to smear," *lup* "to disturb," *vap* "to sow," *śap* "to vow," *swap* "to sleep," and *sṛip* "to creep:"—of those that end in *bh*, three, viz. *yabh* "to copulate," *rabh* "to begin," and *labh* "to acquire;"—of those that end in *m*, four, viz. *gam* "to go," *nam* "to bow," *yam* "to stop," and *ram* "to sport:"—of those that end in *ś*, ten, viz. *kruś* "to cry aloud," *dańś* "to bite," *diś* "to show," *dṛiś* "to see," *mṛiś* "to perceive," *riś* "to hurt," *ruś* "to hurt," *liś* "to lessen," *viś* "to enter," and *spṛiś* "to touch:"—of those that end in *sh*, eleven, viz. *kṛish* "to attract," *twish* "to shine," *tush* "to be satisfied," *dwish* "to hate," *dush* "to do wrong," *push* "to cherish," *pish* "to grind," *vish* "to pervade," *śish* "to hurt," *śush* "to dry," and *ślish* "to embrace:"—of those that end in *s*, two, viz. *ghas* "to eat," and *vas* "to dwell:"—of those that end in *h*, eight, viz. *dah* "to burn," *dih* "to smear," *duh* "to milk," *nah* "to tie," *mih* "to urine," *ruh* "to ascend," *lih* "to lick," and *vah* "to bear."

Thus the gravely accented roots, among those ending in consonants, are a hundred and three.

The root *kṛi*, being gravely accented, falls under this rule and does not take the augment *iṭ*—so that we have *gopáyáñchakartha* "thou didst protect," *gopáyáñchakrathuḥ* "you two protected, *gopáyáñchakra* "you protected," *gopáyáñchakára* "I protected," *gopáyáñchakṛiva* "we two protected," *gopáyáñchakṛima* "we protected." The same tense may be conjugated thus—*gopáyámbabhúva* (No. 507) "he protected," or *gopáyámása* "he protected." On the option allowed by No. 503, it may also be conjugated thus—*jugopa* (Nos. 426 and 488) "he protected," *jugupatuḥ* (No. 486) "they two protected," *jugupuḥ* "they protected."

स्वरतिसूतिसूयतिधूञूदितो वा ।७।२।४४।

स्वरत्यादेरूदितश्च परस्य वलादेरार्धधातुकस्येड्वा स्यात् । जुगोपिथ । जुगोप्थ । गोपायिता । गोपिता । गोप्ता । गोपायिष्यति । गोपिष्यति । गोप्स्यति । गोपायतु । अगोपायत् । गोपायेत् ।

No. 511.—*Iṭ* (No. 433) shall be OPTIONALLY the augment of an *árdhadhátuka* affix beginning with *val* coming AFTER the verbs *swṛi* &c.—viz. SWṚI "to sound," SHÚ—whether of the 2nd or 4th class of verbs—Nos. 589 and 669—"to bring forth," *and* DHÚ "to agitate," AND after WHAT root HAS AN INDICATORY LONG Ú. As the root *gupú* has an indicatory *ú*, it thus makes either *jugopitha* or *jugoptha* "thou didst protect," *gopáyitá* or *gopitá* (No. 503) or *goptá* "he will protect," *gopáyishyati* or *gopishyati* or *gopsyati* "he will protect," *gopáyatu* (the option of No. 503 not presenting itself here) "let him protect," *agopáyat* "he protected," *gopáyet* "he may protect."

नेटि ।७।२।४।

इडादौ सिचि हलन्तस्य वृद्धिर्न । अगोपायीत् । अगोपीत् । अगौप्सीत् ।

No 512.—WHEN *sich*, PRECEDFD BY IṬ, follows, *vṛiddhi* (No. 499) shall NOT be the substitute of a root ending in a consonant. Thus we have *agopáyít* or *agopít*, or (when the *iṭ* is omitted under the option allowed by No. 511) *agaupsít* "he protected."

झलो झलि । ८ । २ । २६ ।

झलः परस्य सस्य लोपो झलि । अगौप्ताम् । अगौप्सुः । अगौप्सीः । अगौप्तम् । अगौप्त । अगौप्सम् । अगौप्स्व । अगौप्स्म । अगोपायिष्यत् । अगोपिष्यत् । अगोप्स्यत् । क्षि क्षये । १३ । क्षयति । चिक्षाय । चिक्षियतुः । चिक्षियुः । एकाच इति निषेधे प्राप्ते ।

No. 513.—Let there be elision of what *s* comes AFTER a JHAL, WHEN a JHAL FOLLOWS. Thus *agauptám* "they two protected," *agaupsuh* "they protected," *agaupsíh* "thou didst protect," *agauptam* "you two protected," *agaupta* "you protected," *agaupsam* "I protected," *agaupswa* "we two protected," *agaupsma* "we protected," *agopáyishyat* or *agopishyat* (No. 503) or *agopsyat* (No. 511) "he would protect."

The next verb to be conjugated is *kshi* "to wane," which makes *kshayati* "he wanes," *chiksháya* "he waned," *chikshiyatuh* (No. 220) "they two waned," *chikshiyuh* "they waned."

A prohibition (of the augment *iṭ*—No. 433) having presented itself in rule No. 510, we look forward.

कृसृभृवृस्तुद्रुस्रुश्रुवो लिटि । ७ । २ । १३ ।

क्रादिभ्य एव लिट इण्न स्यादन्यस्मादनिटोऽपि स्यात् ।

No. 514.—It is only AFTER the verbs *kṛi* &c. viz.—KṚI "to make," SṚI "to go," BHṚI "to nourish," VṚI "to choose," SHṬU "to praise," DRU "to run," SRU "to drop," and ŚRU "to hear," that *iṭ* (No. 433) shall not be the augment, WHEN it is LIṬ that FOLLOWS;—after another verb, though it be one (No. 510) that has not *iṭ*, (when followed by a different *árdhadhátuka* affix,) the augment shall come, (if *liṭ*, beginning with *val*, follows).

अचस्तास्वत् थल्यनिटो नित्यम् । ७ । २ । ६१ ।

उपदेशेऽजन्तो यो धातुस्तासौ नित्यानिट् ततस्थल इण्न ।

No. 515.—AFTER a root which ends in A VOWEL in its original enunciation, and which is ALWAYS DEVOID OF the augment IṬ when *tási* (No. 435) follows,—THAL (No. 424), LIKE TÁSI, shall not have the augment *iṭ*.

उपदेशेऽत्वतः । ७ । २ । ६२ ।

उपदेशेऽकारवान् यस्तासौ नित्यानिट् ततः परस्य थल इण्न स्यात् ।

No. 516.—When a root (ending in a consonant), WITH SHORT A as its vowel IN THE ORIGINAL ENUNCIATION, is always devoid of the augment *iṭ* when followed by *tási*, then *thal*, coming after that root, shall not have the augment *iṭ*.

ऋतो भारद्वाजस्य । ७ । २ । ६३ ।

तासौ नित्यानिट ऋदन्तादेव थलो नेड्भारद्वाजस्य मते । तेनान्यस्य स्यादेव । अयमत्र संग्रहः ।

अजन्तोऽकारवान् वा यस्तास्यनिट् थलि वेडयम् ।
ऋदन्त ईदृङ्नित्यानिट् क्राद्यन्यो लिटि सेड्भवेत् ॥

चिचयिथ । चिचेथ । चिचियथुः । चिचिय । चिचाय । चिचय । चिचियिव । चिचियिम । चेता । चेष्यति । चयतु । अचयत् । चयेत् ।

No. 517.—In the opinion OF BHÁRADWÁJA, it is only AFTER a root which ends in SHORT ṚI, always devoid of the augment *iṭ* when *tási* follows, that *thal* shall not have the augment *iṭ*. Hence *iṭ* should be the augment of any other verb (in *Bháradwája's* opinion—in deference to which Nos. 515 and 516 are considered optional).

Here follows a couplet containing a synopsis of these rules relating to the augment *iṭ*. What root ends in a vowel, or (ending in a consonant) has a short *a*, if it be devoid of *iṭ* when *tási* follows, may optionally have *iṭ*, when *thal* follows. "What ends in short *ṛi* is, under the same circumstances, always devoid of *iṭ*. Any verb, except *kṛi* &c. (No. 514), should have *iṭ,* when *liṭ* follows (the foregoing option in the case of *thal* being borne in mind)."

Thus we have either *chikshayitha* or *chikshetha* "thou didst wane," *chikshiyathuh* "you two waned," *chikshiya* "you waned," *chiksháya* or *chikshaya* "I waned," *chikshiyiva* "we two waned," *chikshiyima* "we waned," *kshetá* "he will wane," *ksheshyati* "he will wane," *kshayatu* "let him wane," *akshayat* "he waned," *kshayet* "he may wane."

अकृत्सार्वधातुकयोर्दीर्घः । ७ । ४ । २५ ।

अजन्ताङ्गस्य दीर्घो यादौ प्रत्यये न तु कृत्सार्वधातुकयोः । चीयात् ।

No. 518.—Of an inflective base ending in a vowel, the LONG vowel shall be the substitute, when an affix, beginning with the letter *y*, follows; but NOT IF the affix be one of those called KṚIT (No 329) OR a SÁRVADHÁTUKA. Thus *kshíyát* "may he wane."

सिचि वृद्धिः परस्मैपदेषु । ७ । २ । १ ।

इगन्ताङ्गस्य वृद्धिः स्यात् परस्मैपदे सिचि । अक्षैषीत् । अक्षेष्यत् । तप संतापे । १४ । तपति । तताप । तेपतुः । तेपुः । तेपिथ । ततप्थ । तप्ता । तप्स्यति । तपतु । अतपत् । तपेत् । तप्यात् । अताप्सीत् । अताप्ताम् । अतप्स्यत् । क्रमु पादविक्षेपे । १५ ।

No. 519.—Let VṚIDDHI be the substitute of an inflective base ending in *ik,* WHEN SICH FOLLOWS AND THE PARASMAIPADA affixes ARE EMPLOYED. Thus *akshaishít* "he waned," *aksheshyat* "he would wane."

The next verb to be conjugated is *tap* (*tapa*) "to burn," which makes *tapati* "he burns," *tatápa* "he burned," *tepatuh* (No. 494) "they two burned," *tepuh* "they burned," *tepitha* (No. 495) or (optionally without the augment *iṭ*—No. 517—) *tataptha* "thou didst burn," *taptá* "he will burn," *tapsyati* "he will burn," *tapatu* "let him burn," *atapat* "he burned," *tapet* "he may burn," *tapyát* "may he burn," *atápsít* (No. 499) "he burned," *atáptám* (No. 513) "they two burned," *atapsyat* "he would burn."

The next verb to be conjugated is *kram (kramu)* "to walk."

वा भ्राशभ्लाशभ्रमुक्रमुक्लमुत्रसित्रुटिलषः । ३ । १ । ७० ।

एभ्यः श्यन् वा कर्त्रर्थे सार्वधातुके परे । पक्षे शप् ।

No. 520.—AFTER these verbs, in the active voice, viz. BHRÁŚ "to shine," BHLÁŚ "to shine," BHRAM "to whirl," KRAM "to walk," KLAM "to be sad," TRAS "to fear," TRUṬ "to cut," AND LASH "to desire," there is OPTIONALLY *śyan* (No. 669). On the other alternative there is *śap* (No. 419).

क्रमः परस्मैपदेषु । ७ । ३ । ७६ ।

क्रमो दीर्घः परस्मैपदे शिति । क्राम्यति । क्रामति । चक्राम । क्रमिता । क्रमिष्यति । क्राम्यतु । क्रामतु । अक्राम्यत् । अक्रामत् । क्राम्येत् । क्रामेत् । क्रम्यात् । अक्रमीत् । अक्रमिष्यत् । पा पाने । १६ ।

No 521.—Let a long vowel be the substitute OF the vowel of the root KRAM, WHEN an affix with an indicatory *ś* FOLLOWS, and A PARASMAIPADA. Thus we have optionally (No 520) *krámyati* or *krámati* "he walks," *chakráma* "he walked." *kramitá* "he will walk," *kramishyati* "he will walk," *krámyatu* or *krámatu* "let him walk," *akrámyat* or *akrámat* "he walked," *krámyet* or *krámet* "he may walk," *kramyát* "may he walk," *akramít* "he walked", *akramishyat* "he would walk."

The next verb to be conjugated is *pá* "to drink."

पाघ्राध्मास्थाम्नादाण्दृश्यर्तिसर्तिशदसदां पिबजिघ्रधमतिष्ठमनयच्छपश्यर्च्छधौशीयसीदाः । ७ । ३ । ७८ ।

पादीनां पिबादयः स्युरित्संज्ञकशादौ प्रत्यये । पिबादेशोऽदन्तस्तेन न गुणः । पिबति ।

No. 522.—OF the verbs *pá* &c. viz PÁ "to drink," GHRÁ "to smell," DHMÁ "to blow," SHṬHÁ "to stand," MNÁ "to acquire by study," DÁṆ "to give," DṚIŚ "to see," ṚI "to go," SṚI "to run," ŚAD to wither," AND SHAD "to decay," let the substitutes be *piba* &c. (viz. PIBA, JIGHRA, DHAMA, TISHṬHA, MANA, YACHCHHA, PAŚYA, ṚICHCHHA, DHAU, ŚÍYA, AND SÍDA, when an affix, beginning with an indicatory *ś* follows (—see No. 419).

The substitute *piba* ends in short *a* (not in *b*), hence there is not the substitution of *guṇa* (by No. 485), and we have *pibati* "he drinks."

आत औ णलः । ७ । १ । ३४ ।

पपौ ।

No. 523.—AFTER a root ending in LONG Á, there shall be AU instead OF ṆAL (No. 424). Hence *papau* "he drank."

आतो लोप इटि च । ६ । ४ । ६४ ।

अजाद्योरार्धधातुकयोः क्ङिदिटोः परयोरातो लोपः । पपतुः । पपुः । पपिथ । पपाथ । पपथुः । पप । पपौ । पपिव । पपिम । पाता । पास्यति । पिबतु । अपिबत् । पिबेत् ।

No. 524.—There shall be ELISION OF LONG Á, when an *árdhadhátuka* affix follows, beginning with a vowel and having an indicatory *k* or *ṅ*, AND WHEN the augment IṬ FOLLOWS. Hence *papatuh* (No. 486) "they two drank," *papuh* "they drank," *papitha* or (without the augment *iṭ*—517—) *papátha* "thou didst drink," *papathuh* "you two drank," *papa* "you drank," *papau* (No. 523) "I drank," *papiva* "we two drank," *papima* "we drank," *pátá* "he will drink," *pásyati* "he will drink," *pibatu* (No. 522) "let him drink," *apibat* "he drank," *pibet* "he may drink."

एर्लिङि । ६ । ४ । ६७ ।

घुसंज्ञकानां मास्थादीनां च एत्वं स्यादार्धधातुके किति लिङि । पेयात् । गातिस्थेति सिचो लुक् । अपात् । अपाताम् ।

No. 525.—Let there be a change to E of the vowel of the verbs called *ghu* (No. 662), and of the verbs *má* "to measure," *sthá* "to stand" &c. (No. 625), WHEN an *árdhadhátuka* substitute of LIṄ (No. 465), with an indicatory *k*, FOLLOWS.

Thus *peyát* "may he drink." As there is elision *(luk)* of *sich* by No. 473, we have *apát* "he drank," *apátám* "they two drank."

आतः । ३ । ४ । ११० ।

सिज्लुकि आदन्तादेव झेर्जुस् ।

No. 526.—When elision *(luk)* of *sich* takes place (No. 473), AFTER what ends in LONG Á only *jus* is the substitute of *jhi* (No. 481).

उस्यपदान्तात् । ६ । १ । ९६ ।

अपदान्तादकारादुसि पररूपमेकादेशः । अपुः । अपास्यत् ।

ग्लै हर्षक्षये । १७ । ग्लायति ।

No. 527.—WHEN US (No. 526) comes AFTER WHAT *a* or *á* IS NOT FINAL IN A PADA (No. 20), the form of the subsequent vowel shall be the single substitute of both. Thus we have *apá* + *us* (No. 526) = *apuh* "they drank," *apásyat* "he would drink."

The next verb to be conjugated is *glai* "to be languid," which makes *gláyati* "he is languid."

आदेच उपदेशेऽशिति । ६ । १ । ४५ ।

उपदेशे एजन्तस्य धातोरात्वं न तु शिति । जग्लौ । ग्लाता । ग्लास्यति । ग्लायतु । अग्लायत् । ग्लायेत् ।

No. 528.—There shall be a substitution of LONG Á for the final OF WHAT ROOT, IN THE ORIGINAL ENUNCIATION, ENDS IN ECH ; but NOT IF an affix with AN INDICATORY Ś (such as *śap*) FOLLOWS. Thus as *śap* (No. 419) is not affixed when *liṭ* (No. 432) follows, the *ai* of *glai* becomes *á*, and then, by Nos. 523 and 41, we have *jaglau* "he was languid," *glátá* "he will be languid," *glásyati* "he will be languid, *gláyatu* "let him be languid," *agláyat* "he was languid," *gláyet* "he may be languid."

वान्यस्य संयोगादेः । ६ । ४ । ६८ ।

घुमास्थादेरन्यस्य संयोगादेर्धातोरात एत्वं वार्धधातुके किति लिङि । ग्लेयात् । ग्लायात् ।

No. 529.—Let there be OPTIONALLY a change to *e* of the long *á* OF any OTHER root, BEGINNING WITH A CONJUNCT consonant, than the roots called *ghu*, and the roots *má*, *sthá*, &c. (No. 625), when an *árdhadhátuka* substitute of *liń*, with an indicatory *k* (No. 465), follows. Thus we have *gleyát* or *gláyát* (No. 528) "may he be languid."

यमरमनमातां सक् च । ७ । २ । ७३ ।

एषां सक् स्यादेभ्यः सिच इट् स्यात् परस्मैपदेषु । अग्लासीत् । अग्लास्यत् । ह्वृ कौटिल्ये । १८ । ह्वरति ।

No. 530.—OF these, viz. of the verbs YAM "to restrain," RAM "to sport," NAM "to bow," AND what roots end in LONG Á, let SAK be the augment; AND let *iṭ* be the augment of *sich* coming after these, when the *parasmaipada* affixes are employed. Thus *aglásít* (No. 479) "he was languid," *aglásyat* "he would be languid."

Then next verb to be conjugated is *hwṛi* "to bend," which makes *hwarati* "be bends."

ऋतश्च संयोगादेर्गुणः । ७ । ४ । १० ।

ऋदन्तस्य संयोगादेरङ्गस्य गुणो लिटि । उपधाया वृद्धिः । जह्वार । जह्वरतुः । जह्वरुः । जह्वर्थ । जह्वरथुः । जह्वर । जह्वार । जह्वर । जह्वरिव । जह्वरिम । ह्वर्ता ।

No. 531.—Let GUṆA (notwithstanding Nos. 486 and 467) be the substitute OF WHAT inflective base ENDS IN SHORT ṚI AND BEGINS WITH A CONJUNCT consonant, when *liṭ* follows.

After substituting *vṛiddhi* for the penultimate, by No. 489, we have *jahwára* "he bent," *jahwaratuh* "they two bent," *jahwaruh* "they bent," *jahwartha* "thou didst bend," *jahwarathuh* "you two bent," *jahwara* "you bent," *jahwára* or *jahwara* (No. 490) "I bent," *jahwariva* "we two bent," *jahwarima* "we bent," *hwartá* "he will bend."

ऋद्धनोः स्ये । ७ । २ । ७० ।

ऋतो हन्तेश्च स्यस्येट् । ह्वरिष्यति । ह्वरतु । अह्वरत् । ह्वरेत् ।

No. 532.—Let *iṭ* be the augment OF SYA (No. 435) AFTER what ends in SHORT ṚI, AND after the verb HAN "to kill." Thus *hwarishyati* "he will bend," *hwaratu* "let him bend," *ahwarat* "he bent," *hwaret*, "he may bend."

गुणोऽर्तिसंयोगाद्योः । ७ । ४ । २९ ।

ऋतः संयोगादेश्चर्‌दन्तस्य च गुणो यकि यादावार्धधातुके लिङि च । ह्वर्यात् । अह्वार्षीत् । अह्वरिष्यत् । श्रु श्रवणे । १६ ।

No. 533.—Let GUṆA be the substitute OF the verb ṚI "to go," AND OF WHAT BEGINS WITH A CONJUNCT consonant and ends with short *ṛi*, when *yak* (No. 801) or an *árdhadhátuka* substitute of *liń* (No. 465), beginning with *y*, follows. Thus *hwaryát* "may he bend," *ahwárshít* "he bent," *ahwarishyat* "he would bend."

The next verb to be conjugated is *śru* "to hear."

श्रुवः शृ च । ३ । १ । ७४ ।

श्रुवः शृ इत्यादेशः स्यात् । श्नुप्रत्ययश्च । शृणोति ।

No. 534.—OF ŚRU let ŚṚI be the substitute, AND let there be the affix *śnu* (No. 687). Thus we have *sṛiṇoti* (No. 235) "he hears."

सार्वधातुकमपित् । १ । २ । ४ ।

अपित् सार्वधातुकं ङिद्वत् । शृणुतः ।

No. 535.—A SÁRVADHÁTUKA affix, WITHOUT AN INDICATORY P, shall be like what has an indicatory *ń* (No. 467). Hence *śṛiṇutah* "they two hear."

हुश्नुवोः सार्वधातुके । ६ । ४ । ८७ ।

हुश्नुवोरनेकाचोऽसंयोगपूर्वस्योवर्णस्य यण् स्यादचि सार्वधातुके । शृण्वन्ति । शृणोषि । शृणुथः । शृणुथ । शृणोमि ।

No. 536.—WHEN A SÁRVADHÁTUKA affix, beginning with a vowel, FOLLOWS, let there be a semi-vowel in the room OF the *u* of the verb HU "to sacrifice," AND of what ends in ŚNU (No. 687), when a conjunct consonant does not precede, and there are more vowels than one in the word. Thus we have *śṛiṇwanti* "they hear," *śṛiṇoshi* "thou hearest," *śṛiṇuthah* "you two hear," *śṛiṇutha* "you hear," *śṛiṇomi* "I hear."

लोपश्चास्यान्यतरस्यां म्वोः । ६ । ४ । १०७ ।

असंयोगपूर्वस्य प्रत्ययोकारस्य लोपो वा म्वोः परयोः । शृण्वः ।

शृणुवः । शृण्मः । शृणुमः । शुश्राव । शुश्रुवतुः । शुश्रुवुः । शुश्रोथ । शुश्रुवथुः । शुश्रुव । शुश्राव । शुश्रुव । शुश्रुम । श्रोता । श्रोष्यति । शृणोतु । शृणुताम् । शृण्वन्तु ।

No. 537.—AND let there be OPTIONALLY ELISION OF THIS—i. e. of the *u* of an affix not preceded by a conjunct consonant —WHEN M OR V FOLLOWS. Thus we have *śrinwah* or *śrinuvah* "we two hear," *śrinmah* or *śrinumah* "we hear," *śuśráva* "he heard," *śuśruvatuh* "they two heard," *śuśruvuh* "they heard," *śuśrotha* "thou didst hear," *śuśruvathuh* "you two heard," *śuśruva* "you heard," *śuśráva* "I heard," *śuśruva* "we two heard," *śuśruma* "we heard," *śrotá* "he will hear," *śroshyati* "he will hear," *śrinotu* "let him hear," *śrinutám* "let the two hear," *śrinwantu* "let them hear."

उतश्च प्रत्ययादसंयोगपूर्वात् । ६ । ४ । १०६ ।

असंयोगपूर्वात् प्रत्ययोतो हेर्लुक् । शृणु । शृणुतात् । शृणुतम् । शृणुत । गुणावादेशौ । शृणवानि । शृणवाव । शृणवाम । अशृणोत् । अशृणुताम् । अशृण्वन् । अशृणोः । अशृणुतम् । अशृणुत । अशृणवम् । अशृण्व । अशृणुव । अशृण्म । अशृणुम । शृणुयात् । शृणुयाताम् । शृणुयुः । शृणुयाः । शृणुयातम् । शृणुयात । शृणुयाम् । शृणुयाव । शृणुयाम । श्रूयात् । अश्रौषीत् । अश्रोष्यत् । गम्लृ गतौ । २० ।

No. 538.—AND let there be elision *(luk)* of *hi* (No. 447), coming AFTER the SHORT U of AN AFFIX NOT PRECEDED BY A CONJUNCT consonant. Thus *śrinu* "hear thou," *śrinutát* (No. 444) "mayst thou hear," *śrinutam* "do you two hear," *śrinuta* "hear ye." The augment derived from No. 450 causes the substitution of *guna* by No. 420, and *av* having been substituted for this by No. 29, we have *śrinaváni* "let me hear," *śrinaváva* (Nos. 450 and 455) "let us two hear," *śrinaváma* "let us hear," *aśrinot* (No. 458) "he heard," *aśrinutám* "they two heard," *aśrinwan* (No. 536) "they heard," *aśrinoh* "thou didst hear," *aśrinutam* "you two heard," *aśrinuta* "you heard," *aśrinavam* "I heard," *aśrinwa* (No. 537) or *aśrinuva* "we two heard," *aśrinma* or *aśrinuma* "we heard," *śṛiṇuyát* (Nos. 460 and 461) "he may hear," *śṛiṇuyátám* "they two may hear," *śṛiṇuyuh* (Nos. 461 and 527) "they may hear," *śṛiṇuyáh* "thou mayst hear," *śṛiṇuyátam* "you two may hear," *śṛiṇuyáta* "you may hear," *śṛiṇuyám* "I may hear," *śṛiṇuyáva* "we two may hear," *śṛiṇuyáma* "we may hear," *śrúyát* (Nos. 466, 467, and 518) "may he hear," *aśraushít* (Nos. 479, 480, and 519) "he heard," *aśroshyat* "he would hear."

The next verb to be conjugated is *gam (gamlṛi)* "to go."

इषुगमियमां छः ।७।३।७७।

एषां छः शिति । गच्छति । जगाम ।

No. 539.—Let CHHA be the substitute of the finals OF these viz. ISH "to wish," GAM "to go," AND YAM "to restrain," when an affix, having an indicatory *ś*, follows, Thus (when *śap*—No. 419—follows) we have *gachchhati* "he goes," but the substitution does not take place (No. 432) in *jagáma* "he went."

गमहनजनखनघसां लोपः क्ङित्यनङि ।६।४।९८।

एषामुपधाया लोपोऽजादौ क्ङिति न त्वङि । जग्मतुः । जग्मुः । जगमिथ । जगन्थ । जग्मथुः । जग्म । जगाम । जगम । जग्मिव । जग्मिम । गन्ता ।

No. 540.—Let there be ELISION OF the penultimate of these, viz. GAM "to go," HAN "to kill," JAN "to produce," KHAN "to dig," AND GHAS "to eat", WHEN ANY affix, EXCEPT AŃ (No. 542), FOLLOWS, beginning with a vowel and DISTINGUISHED BY AN INDICATORY K OR Ń. Thus we have *jagmatuh* (No. 486) "they two went," *jagmuh* "they went," *jagamitha* (No. 517) or *jagantha* "thou didst go," *jagmathuh* "you two went," *jagma* "you went," *jagáma* or *jagama* (No. 490) "I went," *jagmiva* (No. 433) "we two went," *jagmima* "we went," *gantá* (No. 510) "he will go."

गमेरिट् परस्मैपदेषु ।७।२।५८।

गमेः सादेरार्धधातुकस्येट् परस्मैपदेषु । गमिष्यति । गच्छतु । अगच्छत् । गच्छेत् । गम्यात् ।

No. 541.—Let IṬ be the augment of an *árdhadháhtuka* affix beginning with *s*, coming AFTER the verb GAM "to go," WHEN THE PARASMAIPADA terminations ARE EMPLOYED. Thus *gamishyati* "he will go," *gachchhatu* (No. 539) "let him go," *agachchhat* "he went," *gachchhet* "he may go," *gamyát* "may he go."

पुषादिद्युताद्य्लृदितः परस्मैपदेषु । ३ । १ । ५५ ।

श्यन्विकरणपुषादेर्द्युतादेर्ऌदितश्च परस्य च्लेरङ् परस्मैपदेषु । अगमत् । अगमिष्यत् ।

इति परस्मैपदप्रक्रिया ॥

No. 542.—Let *aṅ* be the substitute of *chli* (No 471), coming AFTER the roots PUSH "to nourish" ETC., which have the class-affix *(vikaraṇa) śyan*, (i. e. which belong to the 4th conjugation—(No. 669), AND after the roots DYUT "to shine" &c., AND after THOSE WHICH (like *gamlṛi*) HAVE AN INDICATORY LṚI, WHEN THE PARASMAIPADA terminations ARE EMPLOYED. Thus *agamat* "he came," *agamishyat* (No. 541) "he would come."

So much for the conjugation of those verbs of the first class which take the *parasmaipada* terminations.

The next verb to be conjugated, viz. *edh* "to increase," takes the *átmanepada* terminations.

एध वृद्धौ । १ ।

टित आत्मनेपदानां टेरे । ३ । ४ । ७९ ।

टितो लस्यात्मनेपदानां टेरेत्वम् । एधते ।

No. 543.—Let there be a change to E OF the ṬI (No. 52) OF THE ÁTMANEPADA substitutes OF WHAT *l* (No. 404) HAS AN INDICATORY Ṭ. Thus *edh+ta* (Nos. 407 and 419) becomes *edhate* "he increases."

आतो ङितः । ७ । २ । ८१ ।

अतः परस्य ङितामाकारस्य इय् स्यात् । एधेते । एधन्ते ।

No. 544.—Let there be *iy* in the room OF the Á OF WHAT affix HAS AN INDICATORY Ń (No. 535) and comes after short *a*. Thus *edhete* (No. 463) "they two increase," *edhante* (No. 421) "they increase."

थासः से । ३ । ४ । ८० ।

टितो लस्य थासः से स्यात् । एधसे । एधेथे । एधध्वे । अतो गुणे । एधे । एधावहे । एधामहे ।

No. 545.—Let SE be the substitute OF THÁS, the substitute of an *l* that has an indicatory *ṭ*. Thus *edhase* "thou increasest," *edhethe* (No. 544) "you two increase," *edhadhwe* "you increase." When *guṇa* comes after short *a* (No. 300), the *guṇa* alone is the substitute—thus *edha+e* (No. 543)=*edhe* "I increase," *edhávahe* (No. 422) "we two increase," *edhámahe* "we increase."

इजादेश्च गुरुमतोऽनृच्छः । ३ । १ । ३६ ।

इजादिर्यो धातुर्गुरुमानृच्छत्यन्यस्ततः आम् स्याल्लिटि ।

No. 546.—When *liṭ* follows, let there be *ám* (No. 504) AFTER THAT root WHICH, being OTHER THAN the root ṚICHCHHA "to go," BEGINS WITH ICH AND HAS A HEAVY vowel (Nos. 483 and 484).

आम्प्रत्ययवत् कृञोऽनुप्रयोगस्य । १ । ३ । ६३ ।

आम् प्रत्ययो यस्मादित्यतद्गुणसंविज्ञानो बहुव्रीहिः । आम्प्रकृत्या तुल्यमनुप्रयुज्यमानात् कृञोऽप्यात्मनेपदम् ।

No. 547.—The word "*ám-pratyaya*," in this aphorism, meaning "that after which the affix *ám* (No. 504) comes," is a compound, of the kind termed *Bahuvríhi* (No. 1034), denoting that which does not exhibit (to one's perception) the characteristic implied in the name. LIKE the verb THAT TAKES THE AFFIX ÁM (if the verb be conjugated with the *átmanepada* terminations), so let the *átmanepada* terminations be those OF the verb KṚI when SUBJOINED thereto (as an auxiliary).

[Among *Bahuvríhi* compounds, the Sanskrit grammarians distinguish those denoting that of which the matters implied in the name are perceived along with the thing itself *(tadguṇa-saṅvijñána)* from those denoting what is otherwise *(atadguṇa-saṅvijñá-*

na). The stock illustration of the former kind is "*dírgha-karṇam ánaya*"—i. e. "bring Long-ear"—where the long ears accompany and mark the individual; and of the latter kind, "*dṛishṭa-ságaram ánaya*"—i. e. "bring him that has seen the ocean"—where the ocean does not accompany the man, nor enable you to recognise him among a group of persons who have never seen it. The term "*ám-pratyaya*" above-mentioned, i. e. "that which has the affix *ám*," is of the latter description. We are told that the auxiliary is to take the same tense-affixes as "that which has the affix *ám*;" but the verb, when we look at any part of it (such as *edhate*) with a tense-affix, has no *ám* then visible—the *ám*, when present, causing (No. 506) the elision of the tense-affixes.]

लिटस्तझयोरेशिरेच्। ३। ४। ८१।

लिडादेशयोस्तझयोरेशिरेचौ स्तः। एधांचक्रे। एधांचक्राते। एधांचक्रिरे। एधांचकृषे। एधांचक्राथे।

No. 548.—EŚ AND IRECH are the substitutes OF T AND JH, the substitutes OF LIṬ. Thus we have *edháṅchakre* "he increased," *edháṅchakráte* "they two increased," *edháṅchakrire* "they increased," *edháṅchakṛishe* "thou didst increase," *edháṅchakráthe* "you two increased."

इणः षीध्वंलुङ्लिटां धोऽङ्गात्। ८। ३। ७८।

इणन्तादङ्गात् परेषां षीध्वंलुङ्लिटां धस्य ढः। एधांचकृढ्वे। एधांचक्रे। एधांचकृवहे। एधांचकृमहे। एधांबभूव। एधामास। एधिता। एधितारौ। एधितारः। एधितासे। एधितासाथे।

No. 549—Let there be cerebral *ḍh* in the room OF the dental DH OF the termination *shídhwam* (No. 555), AND of a substitute OF LUṄ AND LIṬ, coming AFTER AN INFLECTIVE BASE THAT ENDS IN one of the letters of the *pratyáhára* IṆ. Thus *edháṅchakṛiḍhwe* "you increased," *edháṅchakre* "I increased," *edháṅchakṛivahe* "we two increased," *edháṅchakṛimahe* "we increased." This tense may be formed thus also—*edhámbabhúva* (No. 507) or *edhámása*, Then, *edhitá* "he will increase," *edhitárau* "they two will increase," *edhitárah* "they will increase," *edhitáse* (No. 545) "thou wilt increase," *edhitásáthe* "you two will increase."

धि च । ८ । २ । २५ ।

धादौ प्रत्यये सस्य लोपः । एधिताध्वे ।

No. 550.—AND WHEN an affix beginning with DH FOLLOWS, let there be elision of *s*. Thus *edhitádhwe* "you will increase."

ह एति । ७ । ४ । ५२ ।

तासस्त्योः सस्य हः स्यादेति परे । एधिताहे । एधितास्वहे । एधितास्महे । एधिष्यते । एधिष्येते । एधिष्यन्ते । एधिष्यसे । एधिष्येथे । एधिष्यध्वे । एधिष्ये । एधिष्यावहे । एधिष्यामहे ।

No. 551.—Let H be the substitute of the *s* of *tás* and of the verb *as* "to be," WHEN E FOLLOWS. Thus *edhitáhe* "I will increase," *edhitáswahe* "we two will increase," *edhitásmahe* "we will increase," *edhishyate* "he will increase," *edhishyete* (No. 544) "they two will increase," *edhishyante* "they will increase," *edhishyase* "thou wilt increase," *edhishyethe* "you two will increase," *edhishyadhwe* "you will increase," *edhishye* "I will increase," *edhishyávahe* "we two will increase," *edhishyámahe* "we will increase."

आमेतः । ३ । ४ । ९० ।

लोट एत आम् । एधताम् । एधेताम् । एधन्ताम् ।

No. 552.—Let there be ÁM in the room OF the E (No. 543) of *loṭ*. Thus *edhatám* "let him increase," *edhetám* (No. 544) "let the two increase," *edhantám* "let them increase."

सवाभ्यां वामौ । ३ । ४ । ९१ ।

सवाभ्यां परस्य लोडेतः क्रमाद्वामौ स्तः । एधस्व । एधेथाम् । एधध्वम् ।

No. 553.—In the room of the *e* of a substitute of *loṭ* coming AFTER S OR V, there are V AND AM respectively. Thus (instead of *edhase*) *edhaswa* "do thou increase," *edhethám* (No. 552) "do you two increase," *edhadhwam* (Nos. 543 and 553) "do you increase."

एत ऐ । ३ । ४ । ९३ ।

लोडुत्तमस्य । एधै । एधावहै । एधामहै । आटश्च । ऐधत । ऐधेताम् । ऐधन्त । ऐधथाः । ऐधेथाम् । ऐधध्वम् । ऐधे । ऐधावहि । ऐधामहि ।

No. 554.—Let AI be the substitute OF E forming part of the "highest" personal affix substituted for *loṭ*. Thus *edhai* "let me increase," *edhávahai* "let us two increase," *edhámahai* "let us increase," and then *át* (No. 478) is prefixed to make *(á+edhata=) aidhata* (No. 218) "he increased," *aidhetám* (No. 544) "they two increased," *aidhanta* (No. 421) "they increased," *aidhatháh* "thou didst increase," *aidhethám* "you two increased," *aidhadhwam* "you increased," *aidhe* "I increased," *aidhávahi* (No. 422) "we two increased," *aidhámahi* "we increased."

लिङः सीयुट् । ३ । ४ । १०२ ।

सलोपः । एधेत । एधेयाताम् ।

No. 555.—Let SÍYUṬ be the augment OF LIṄ. There is elision of the *s* by No. 461.—The *y* is elided by No. 463. Thus we have *edheta* "he may increase," *edheyátám* "they two may increase."

झस्य रन् । ३ । ४ । १०५ ।

लिङः । एधेरन् । एधेथाः । एधेयाथाम् । एधेध्वम् ।

No. 556.—Let RAN be the substitute OF JH in the room of *liṅ*. Thus *edheran* (No. 555) "they may increase," *edhetháh* "thou mayst increase," *edheyáthám* "you two may increase," *edhedhwam* "you may increase."

इटोऽत् । ३ । ४ । १०६ ।

लिङादेशस्य । एधेय । एधेवहि । एधेमहि ।

No. 557.—Let SHORT A be in the room OF IṬ, the substitute of *liṅ*. Thus *edheya* (No. 555) "I may increase," *edhevahi* "we two may increase," *edhemahi* "we may increase."

सुट्तिथोः । ३ । ४ । १०७ ।

लिङस्तथोः सुट् । यलोपः । आर्धधातुकत्वात् सलोपो न । एधिषीष्ट । एधिषीयास्ताम् । एधिषीरन् । एधिषीष्ठाः । एधिषीयास्थाम् । एधिषीध्वम् । एधिषीय । एधिषीवहि । एधिषीमहि । ऐधिष्ट । ऐधिषाताम् ।

No. 558.—Let SUṬ be the augment OF T AND TH, when part of a substitute of *liń.* The augment *síyuṭ* also is obtained from No. 555. The *y* (of *síyuṭ*) is elided by No. 463. As the substitutes of *liń,* in the sense of benediction, are *árdhadhátuka* (No. 465), the elision of the *s* (of *síyuṭ* and *suṭ*), directed by No. 461, does not take place. Thus we have *edh+i* (No. 433) *+sí+sta,* which, by Nos. 169 and 78, becomes *edhishíshṭa* "may he increase," *edhishíyástám* "may they two increase,"—then, as *suṭ* does not come except before *t* or *th*, *edhishíran* (No. 556) "may they increase," *edhishíshṭháh* "mayst thou increase," *edhishíyásthám* "may you two increase," *edhishídhwam* "may you increase," *edhishíya* (No. 557) "may I increase," *edhishívahi* "may we two increase," *edhishímahi* "may we increase," *aidhishṭa* (Nos. 478, 471, 472, 433, and 169) "he increased," *aidhishátám* "they two increased."

आत्मनेपदेष्वनतः । ७ । १ । ५ ।

अनकारात् परस्यात्मनेपदेषु झस्यात् स्यात् । ऐधिषत । ऐधिष्ठाः । ऐधिषाथाम् । ऐधिढ्वम् । ऐधिषि । ऐधिष्वहि । ऐधिष्महि । ऐधिष्यत । ऐधिष्येताम् । ऐधिष्यन्त । ऐधिष्यथाः । ऐधिष्येथाम् । ऐधिष्यध्वम् । ऐधिष्ये । ऐधिष्यावहि । ऐधिष्यामहि । कमु कान्तौ । २ ।

No. 559—Let there be *at* in the room of *jh*, NOT coming AFTER the vowel A, WHEN the terminations are THE ÁTMANEPADA. Thus *aidhishata* "they increased," *aidhishṭháh* "thou didst increase," *aidhishátham* "you two increased," *aidhiḍhwam* (Nos. 549 and 550) "you increased," *aidhishi* "I increased," *aidhishwahi* "we two increased," *aidhishmahi* "we increased," *aidhishyata* "he would increase," *aidhishyetám* (Nos. 544, 535, and 463) "they two would increase," *aidhishyanta* "they would increase," *aidhishya-*

tháh "thou wouldst increase," *aidhishyethám* "you two would increase," *aidhishyadhwam* "you would increase," *aidhishye* "I would increase," *aidhishyávahi* (No. 422) "we two would increase," *aidhishyámahi* "we would increase."

The next verb to be conjugated is *kam (kamu)* "to desire."

कमेर्णिङ् । ३ । १ । ३० ।

स्वार्थे । ङित्वात् तङ् । कामयते ।

No. 560.—Let the affix ṆIŃ (leaving *ṇi*) come AFTER the root KAM "to desire," without altering the meaning (No. 502). As the affix has an indicatory *ń*, the *átmanepada* terminations (*tań*—No. 409) are employed (No. 410). Thus we have *kámayate* (Nos. 489 and 420) "he desires."

अयामन्ताल्वाय्येत्न्विष्णुषु । ६ । ४ । ५५ ।

एषु णेरय् । कामयांचक्रे । आयादय इति णिङ् वा । चकमे । चकमाते । चकमिरे । चकमिषे । चकमाथे । चकमिध्वे । चकमे । चकमिवहे । चकमिमहे । कामयिता । कामयितासे । कमिता । कामयिष्यते । कमिष्यते । कामयताम् । अकामयत । कामयेत । कामयिषीष्ट । कमिषीष्ट ।

No. 561.—Let AY be the substitute of *ṇi*, WHEN these—viz. ÁM (No. 504), ANṬA, ÁLU, ÁYYA, ITNU, AND ISHṆU (—affixes, of which there is no further mention made in this grammatical compendium —)FOLLOW. Thus *kámayáńchakre* "he desired." In cases where, as in the 2nd pret., the affixes are *árdhadhátuka* (No. 432), the *ṇiń* (No. 560), by No. 503, is optional:—thus we may have *chakame* "he desired," *chakamáte* "they two desired," *chakamire* (No 548) "they desired," *chakamishe* "thou didst desire," *chakamáthe* "you two desired," *chakamiḍhwe* (No. 549) "you desired," *chakame* "I desired," *chakamivahe* "we two desired," *chakamimahe* "we desired," *kámayitá* "he will desire," *kámayitáse* "thou wilt desire," again (without *ṇiń*) *kamitá* "he will desire," *kámayishyate* or *kamishyate* "he will desire," *kámayatám* (No. 552) "let him desire," *akámayata* "he desired," *kámayetu* "he may desire," *kámayishíshṭa* or *kamishíshṭa* (No. 558) "may he desire."

णिश्रिद्रुस्रुभ्यः कर्तरि चङ् । ३ । १ । ४८ ।

णयन्तात् श्र्यादिभ्यश्च च्लेश्चङ् कर्त्रर्थे लुङि । कामि अत इति स्थिते ।

No. 562.—AFTER what ends in ṆI (No. 560), AND AFTER the verbs *śri* &c. *i. e.* ŚRI "to serve," DRU "to run," AND SRU "to drop," let CHAŃ be the substitute of *chli* (No. 471), WHEN *luń* follows SIGNIFYING AN AGENT. The case then standing thus—viz: *kámi+ata*, we look forward.

णेरनिटि । ६ । ४ । ५१ ।

अनिडादावार्धधातुके णेर्लोपः ।

No. 563.—Let there be elision OF ṆI, WHEN an *árdhadhátuka* affix, NOT beginning WITH the augment IṬ, FOLLOWS. Thus, in the 3rd pret., we find at this stage *kám+ata.*

णौ चङ्युपधाया ह्रस्वः । ७ । ४ । १ ।

चङ्परे णौ यदङ्गं तस्योपधाया ह्रस्वः ।

No. 564.—Let there be A SHORT vowel in the room OF THE PENULTIMATE letter of an inflective base, WHEN ṆI, FOLLOWED BY CHAŃ (No. 562), is affixed. Thus we get *kam+ata.*

चङि । ६ । १ । ११ ।

अनभ्यासधात्ववयवस्यैकाचः प्रथमस्य द्वे स्तोऽजादेर्द्वितीयस्य ।

No. 565.—WHEN CHAŃ FOLLOWS, there are two in the room of the first portion, containing a single vowel, of an unreduplicated root—but (the reduplication is) of the second portion of a root that begins with a vowel. Thus we get (by No. 488) *chakam+ata.*

सन्वल्लघुनि चङ्परेऽनग्लोपे । ७ । ४ । ९३ ।

चङ्परे णौ यदङ्गं तस्य योऽभ्यासो लघुपरस्तस्य सनीव कार्यं स्याण्णावग्लोपेऽसति ।

No. 566.—Let the effect be LIKE as if SAN (No. 752) had followed, on the reduplicate, if FOLLOWED BY A LIGHT vowel (No. 482), of an inflective base to which *ṇi*, FOLLOWED BY CHAŃ, is affixed—PROVIDED THERE IS NOT THE ELISION OF any letter in the *pratyáhára* AK occasioned by the affixing of *ṇi* (as, for example, under the provisions of No. 505, there is).

सन्यतः ।७।४।७९।

अभ्यासस्यात इत् सनि ।

No. 567.—Let short *i* be the substitute OF the SHORT A of a reduplicate, WHEN SAN FOLLOWS. Thus (No. 566) we get *chikam+ata.*

दीर्घो लघोः ।७।४।९४।

लघोरभ्यासस्य दीर्घः सन्वद्भावविषये । अचीकमत । णिङभावपक्षे ।

No. 568.—Let there be A LONG vowel in the room OF A LIGHT (vowel of a) reduplicate, in a case where the state of things is as if the affix were *san* (No. 566). Thus we have finally (No. 457) *achíkamata* "he desired."

On the alternative (allowed by No. 503) of there not being the affix *ṇiń*, the rule following applies.

कमेश्च्लेश्चङ् वाच्यः । अचकमत । अकामयिष्यत । अकमिष्यत । अय गतौ । ३ । अयते ।

No. 569.—"CHAŃ SHOULD BE STATED to be the substitute OF CHLI coming AFTER the verb KAM." Thus we have *achakamata* "he desired," *akámayishyata* or *akamishyata* (No. 503) "he would desire."

The next verb to be conjugated is *ay (aya)* "to go," which makes *ayate* "he goes."

उपसर्गस्यायतौ ।८।२।१९।

अयतावुपसर्गस्थरेफस्य लत्वम् । प्लायते । पलायते ।

No. 570.—There is a substitution of *l* for the *r* OF AN UPASARGA (No, 47), WHEN the verb AY FOLLOWS. Thus *pra+ayate=pláyate* "he flees," *pará+ayate=paláyate* "he flees."

दयायासश्च ।३।१।३७।

एभ्य आम् लिटि । अयांचक्रे । अयिता । अयिष्यते । अयताम् । आयत । अयेत । अयिषीष्ट ।

No. 571.—And AFTER these—i. e. DAY "to give," AY "to go," AND ÁS "to sit,"—let there be *ám*, when *liṭ* follows. Thus *ayáñ-chakre* "he went," *ayitá* "he will go," *ayishyate* "he will go," *ayatám* (No. 552) "let him go," *áyata* "he went," *ayeta* "he may go," *ayishíshṭa* (No. 558) "may he go."

विभाषेटः । ८ । ३ । ७९ ।

इणः परो य इट् ततः परेषां षीध्वंलुङ्लिटां धस्य वा ढः । अयिषीध्वम् । अयिषीढ्वम् । आयिष्ट । आयिध्वम् । आयिढ्वम् । आयिष्यत । द्युत दीप्तौ । ४ । द्योतते ।

No. 572.—Cerebral *ḍh* (see No. 549) is OPTIONALLY the substitute of the dental *dh* of *shídhwam*, or of a substitute of *luń* or *liṭ*, coming AFTER the augment IṬ that follows one of the letters of the *pratyáhára iṇ*. Thus *ayishídhwam* or *ayishíḍhwam* "may you go," *áyishṭa* (Nos. 478, 471, &c.) "he went," *áyidhwam* or *áyiḍhwam* "you went," *áyishyata* "he would go."

The next verb to be conjugated is *dyut (dyuta)* "to shine," which makes *dyotate* (Nos. 419 and 420) "he shines."

द्युतिस्वाप्योः संप्रसारणम् । ७ । ४ । ६७ ।

अनयोरभ्यासस्य संप्रसारणं स्यात् । दिद्युते ।

No. 573.—Let there be A VOWEL in the room OF the semi-vowel (No. 281) of the reduplicate of these two verbs—viz. DYUT "to shine," AND SWÁPI "to cause to sleep." Thus *didyute* "he shone."

द्युद्भ्यो लुङि । १ । ३ । ९१ ।

द्युतादिभ्यः परस्मैपदं वा लुङि । पुषादीत्यङ् । अद्युतत् । अद्योतिष्ट । अद्योतिष्यत । एवं श्विता वर्णे । ५ । ञिमिदा स्नेहने । ६ । ञिष्विदा स्नेहनमोचनयोः । ७ ।—मोहनयोरित्येके । ञिक्ष्विदा चेत्येके । रुच दीप्तावभिप्रीतौ च । ८ । घुट परिवर्तने । ९ । शुभ दीप्तौ । १० । क्षुभ संचलने । ११ । णभ तुभ हिंसायाम् । १२ । १३ । स्रंसु भ्रंसु ध्वंसु अवस्रंसने । १४ । १५ । १६ । ध्वंसु गतौ । १७ । स्रंभु विश्वासे । १८ । वृतु वर्तने । १९ । वर्तते । ववृते । वर्तिता ।

No. 574.—AFTER the verbs DYUT, &c. the *parasmaipada* terminations may optionally be the substitutes, WHEN LUŃ is affixed. Then, by No. 542, *ań* is in this case substituted for the *chli* (No. 471). Thus we have *adyutat*, or, on the alternative, *adyotishṭa* (Nos. 472, 433, and 169) "he shone," *adyotishyata* "he would shine."

In the same way are treated *świt (świtá)* "to be white," *mid (ṅimidá)* "to be unctuous," *shwid*; *(ṅishwidá)* "to be unctuous" and "to quit"—or, as some say—"to fascinate"—while others again say that it is not this verb, but *kshwid (ṅikshwidá)* "to be unctuous —to liberate" that comes under the rule, *ruch (rucha)* "to shine —to please," *ghuṭ (ghuṭa)* "to exchange," *śubh (śubha)* "to be beautiful," *kshubh (kshubha)* "to shake," *ṇabh (ṇabha)* and *tubh (tubha)* "to hurt," *srańs (srańsu)*, *bhrańs (bhrańsu)*, and *dhwańs (dhwańsu)*, "to fall down," *dhwańs (dhwańsu)* "to go," *srambh (srambhu)* "to trust in," and *vṛit (vṛitu)* "to be." This last makes *vartate* "he is," *vavṛite* (No. 548) "he was," *vartitá* "he will be."

वृद्भ्यः स्यसनोः । १ । ३ । ९२ ।

वृतादिभ्यः पञ्चभ्यो वा परस्मैपदं स्ये सनि च ।

No. 575.—AFTER the five verbs VṚIT "to be," &c., there shall optionally be the *parasmaipada* affixes, WHEN SYA (No. 435) OR SAN (No. 752) is attached.

न वृद्भ्यश्चतुर्भ्यः । ७ । २ । ५९ ।

वृतुवृधुशृधुस्यन्दूभ्यः सादेरार्धधातुकस्येण्न तङानयोरभावे । वर्त्स्यति । वर्तिष्यते । वर्तताम् । अवर्तत । वर्तेत । वर्तिषीष्ट । अवर्तिष्ट । अवर्त्स्यत् । अवर्तिष्यत । दद दाने । २० । ददते ।

No. 576.—The augment *iṭ* (No. 433) shall NOT be the augment of an *árdhadhátuka* affix beginning with the letter *s* and coming AFTER one of THE FOUR verbs VṚIT &c. viz. *vṛi* "to be," *vṛidh* "to grow," *śṛidh* "to break wind," or *syandú* "to ooze," in the absence of the *átmanepada* affixes (No. 409). Thus the augment *iṭ* does not appear in *vartsyati* (where the affix is a *parasmaipada*), but it does in *vartishyate* (where the affix is *átmanepada*)

" he will be," *vartatám* " let him be," *avartata* " he was," *varteta* " he may be," *vartishíshṭa* (No. 558) " may he be," *avartishṭa* " he was," *avartsyat* (No. 575) or *avartishyata* (No. 576) " he would be."

The next verb to be conjugated is *dad (dada)* " to give," which makes *dadate* " he gives."

न शसददवादिगुणानाम् । ६ । ४ । १२६ ।

शसेर्ददेर्वकारादीनां गुणशब्देन विहितो योऽकारस्तस्य एत्वाभ्यासलोपौ न । ददde । दददाते । दददिरे । ददिता । ददिष्यते । ददताम् । अददत । ददेत । ददिषीष्ट । अददिष्ट । अददिष्यत । त्रपूष लज्जायाम् । २१ । त्रपते ।

No. 577.— There shall NOT be a change to *e* (No. 494) in the case OF the verbs ŚAS " to bless," OR DAD " to give," OR OF WHAT verbs BEGIN WITH V, OR of the *a* which is appointed by the term GUṆA (as in No. 420), nor shall there be the elision of the reduplicate. Thus we have *dadade* " he gave," *dadadáte* " they two gave," *dadadire* " they gave," *daditá* " he will give," *dadishyate* " he will give," *dadatám* " let him give," *adadata* " he gave," *dadeta* " he may give," *dadishíshṭa* (No. 558) " may he give," *adadishṭa* " he gave," *adadishyata* " he would give."

The next verb to be conjugated is *trap (trapúsh)* " to be ashamed," which makes *trapate* " he is ashamed."

तॄफलभजत्रपश्च । ६ । ४ । १२२ ।

एषामत एत्वमभ्यासलोपश्च किति लिटि सेटि थलि च । त्रेपे । त्रपिता । त्रप्ता । त्रपिष्यते । त्रप्स्यते । त्रपताम् । अत्रपत । त्रपेत । त्रपिषीष्ट । त्रप्सीष्ट । अत्रपिष्ट । अत्रप्त । अत्रपिष्यत । अत्रप्स्यत ।

इत्यात्मनेपदप्रक्रिया ॥

No. 578.—There shall be the change to *e* of the *a* OF these, viz. TṚÍ " to cross," PHAL " to bear fruit," BHAJ " to serve," AND TRAP (TRAPÚSH) " to be ashamed," and also the elision of the reduplicate, when a substitute for *liṭ* with an indicatory *k* (No. 494), or *thal* with the augment *iṭ* (No. 495), follows. Thus *trepe* " he was ashamed," *trapitá* or *traptá* (without the augment *iṭ*—No. 511) "he will be ashamed," *trapishyate* or *trapsyate* "he will be ashamed," *trapatám* "let him be ashamed," *atrapata* "he was ashamed," *trapeta* "he may be ashamed," *trapishíshṭa* (No. 558) or, on the option allowed (by No. 511), *trapsíshṭa*, "may he be ashamed," *atrapishṭa* or (by No. 513, when the augment *iṭ*, on the option allowed by No. 511, is not attached,) *atrapta* "he was ashamed," *atrapishyata* or *atrapsyata* (No. 511) "he would be ashamed."

So much for the formation, or conjugation, of verbs with the *átmanepada* terminations.

श्रिञ् सेवायाम् । १ । श्रयति । श्रयते । शिश्राय । शिश्रिये । श्रयिता । श्रयिष्यति । श्रयिष्यते । श्रयतु । श्रयताम् । अश्रयत् । अश्रयत । श्रयेत् । श्रयेत । श्रीयात् । श्रयिषीष्ट । चङ् । अशिश्रियत् । अशिश्रियत । अश्रयिष्यत् । अश्रयिष्यत । भृञ् भरणे । २ । भरति । भरते । बभार । बभ्रतुः । बभ्रुः । बभर्थ । बभृव । बभृम । बभ्रे । बभृषे । भर्तासि । भर्तासे । भरिष्यति । भरिष्यते । भरतु । भरताम् । अभरत् । अभरत । भरेत् । भरेत ।

No. 579.—The verbs next to be considered take both the *parasmaipada* and the *átmanepada* terminations. Of these ŚRI *(śriṅ)* "TO SERVE," makes *śrayati* or *śrayate* "he serves," *śiśráya* or *śiśriye* "he served," *śrayitá* "he will serve," *śrayishyati* or *śrayishyate* "he will serve," *śrayatu* or *śrayatám* "let him serve," *aśrayat* or *aśrayata* "he served," *śrayet* or *śrayeta* "he may serve," *śríyát* (No. 518) or *śrayishíshṭa* (No. 558) "may he serve," substituting *chań*, instead of *sich*, for *chli* by No. 562, *aśiśriyat*, or, with the *átmanepada*, *aśiśriyata* "he served," *aśrayishyat* or *aśrayishyata* "he would serve."

The verb *bhṛi (bhṛiṅ)* "to nourish" makes *bharati* or *bharate* "he nourishes," *babhára* "he nourished," *babhratuh* (No. 424) "they two nourished," *babhruh* "they nourished," *babhartha* "thou didst nourish," *babhṛiva* "we two nourished," *babhṛima* "we nourished," *babhre* (No. 548) "he nourished," *babhṛishe* "thou didst nourish," *bhartási* or *bhartáse* "thou wilt nourish," *bharishyati* or *bharishyate* "he will nourish," *bharatu* or *bharatám* "let him nourish," *abharat* or *abharata* "he nourished," *bharet* or *bhareta* "he may nourish."

रिङ् शयग्लिङ्क्षु । ७ । ४ । २८ ।

शे यकि यादावार्धधातुके लिङि ऋतो रिङ् । रीङि प्रकृते रिङ्-विधानसामर्थ्याद्दीर्घो न । भ्रियात् ।

No. 580.—Let RIŃ be the substitute of the vowel *ṛi*, WHEN ŚA (No. 693) FOLLOWS, OR YAK (No. 801), OR an *árdhadhátuka* substitute of LIŃ beginning with the letter *y*. The substitute *ríń* presenting itself in this place, in the aphorism immediately preceding the present one (viz. VII. 4. 27), a long vowel is not substituted by No. 518—otherwise the direction to substitute *riń* (with a short vowel) would be unmeaning.—Thus we have *bhriyát* "may he nourish."

उश्च । १ । २ । १२ ।

ऋवर्णान्तात् परौ झलादी लिङ्सिचौ कितौ स्तस्तङि । भृषीष्ट । भृषीयास्ताम् । अभार्षीत् ।

No. 581.—AND *liń* and *sich*, coming AFTER what ends in ṚI OR ṚÍ, are regarded as having an indicatory *k*, when an *átmanepada* affix *(tań)* follows. Thus—without the substitution of *guṇa* (No. 467), we have *bhṛishíshṭa* (No. 558) "may he nourish," *bhṛishíyástám* "may they two nourish," *abhárshít* (Nos. 457, 471, 472, 479, and 519) "he nourished."

ह्रस्वादङ्गात् । ८ । २ । २७ ।

सिचो लोपो झलि । अभृत । अभरिष्यत् । अभरिष्यत । हृञ् हरणे । ३ । हरति । हरते । जहार । जह्रे । जहर्थ । जह्रिव । जह्रिम । जह्रिषे । हर्ता । हरिष्यति । हरिष्यते । हरतु । हरताम् । अहरत् । अहरत । हरेत् । हरेत । ह्रियात् । हृषीष्ट । हृषीयास्ताम् । अहार्षीत् । अहृत । अहरिष्यत् । अहरिष्यत । धृञ् धारणे । ४ । धरति । धरते । णीञ् प्रापणे । ५ । नयति । नयते । डुपचष् पाके ।

६ । पचति । पचते । पपाच । पेचिथ । पपक्थ । पेचे । पक्ता । भज सेवायाम् । ७ । भजति । भजते । बभाज । भेजे । भक्ता । भक्ष्यति । भक्ष्यते । अभाक्षीत् । अभक्त । अभक्षाताम् । यज देवपूजासंगतिकरणदानेषु । ८ । यजति । यजते ।

No. 582.—AFTER A SHORT INFLECTIVE BASE, there is elision of *sich*, if a *jhal* follows. Thus *abhrita* "he nourished," *abharishyat* or *abharishyata* "he would nourish."

The verb *hṛi (hṛiṅ)* "to take" makes *harati* or *harate* "he takes," *jahára* or *jahre* "he took," *jahartha* "thou didst take," *jahriva* "we two took," *jahrima* "we took," *jahrishe* "thou didst take," *hartá* "he will take," *harishyati* or *harishyate* "he will take," *haratu* or *haratám* "let him take," *aharat* or *aharata* "he took," *haret* or *hareta* "he may take," *hriyát* (Nos. 580, and 337) or *hṛishíshṭa* (Nos. 555 and 558) "may he take," *hṛishíyástám* "may they two take," *ahárshít* (No. 519) or *ahṛita* (No. 582) "he took," *aharishyat* or *aharishyata* "he would take."

In like manner *dhṛi (dhṛiṅ)* "to hold" makes *dharati* or *dharate* "he holds;" *ṇí (ṇíṅ)* "to lead" makes *nayati* or *nayate* "he leads;" *pach (ḍupachash)* "to cook" makes *pachati or pachate* "he cooks," *papácha* "he cooked," *pechitha* (Nos. 517 and 495) or *papaktha* (No. 516) "thou didst cook," *peche* (No. 494) "he cooked," *paktá* "he will cook;" *bhaj (bhaja)* "to serve" makes *bhajati* or *bhajate* "he serves," *babhája* or *bheje* (No. 578) "he served," *bhaktá* "he will serve," *bhakshyati* or *bhakshyate* "he will serve," *abhákshít* (No. 499) or *abhakta* (No. 513) "he served," *abhakshátám* "they two served;" *yaj (yaja)* "to worship a deity, to associate with, to endow," makes *yajati* or *yajate* "he worships."

लिट्यभ्यासस्योभयेषाम् । ६ । १ । १७ ।

वच्यादीनां ग्रह्यादीनां चाभ्यासस्य संप्रसारणं लिटि । इयाज ।

No. 583.—WHEN LIṬ FOLLOWS, there is a vowel (No. 281) in the room OF the semi-vowel of THE REDUPLICATE OF BOTH sets of verbs, viz. *vach*, &c. (No. 584) and *grah*, &c. (No. 675). Thus *iyája* "he worshipped."

वचिस्वपियजादीनां किति। ६। १। १५।

वचिस्वप्योर्यजादीनां च संप्रसारणं किति। ईजतुः। ईजुः। इयजिथ। इयष्ठ। ईजे। यष्टा।

No. 584.—There is a vowel (No. 281) in the room of the semivowel OF VACH "to speak," SWAP "to sleep," AND YAJ, &c., when an affix with an indicatory *k* (No. 486) follows. Thus we have *i+aj+atuh,* which, by No. 283, becomes *ij+atuh,* and, by reduplication, *ij+ij+atuh.* By Nos. 428 and 55, this becomes finally *íjatuh* "they two worshipped," and so *íjuh* "they worshipped," *iyajitha* (where there is an indicatory *p*) or (without the augment—No. 517) *iyashṭha* (Nos. 334 and 78) "thou didst worship," *íje* "he worshipped," *yashṭá* (Nos. 334 and 78) "he will worship."

षढोः कः सि। ८। २। ४१।

षस्य ढस्य च कः स्यात् सकारे परे। यक्ष्यति। यक्ष्यते। इज्यात्। यक्षीष्ट। अयाक्षीत्। अयष्ट। वह प्रापणे। ६। वहति। वहते। उवाह। ऊहतुः। ऊहुः। उवहिथ।

No. 585.—WHEN S FOLLOWS, there is K in the room OF SH OR ḌH. Thus (the *j*, by No. 334, having become *sh*), *yakshyati* or *yakshyate* "he will worship," *ijyát* (Nos. 584 and 337) or *yakshíshṭa* "may he worship," *ayákshít* (No. 499) or *ayashṭa* (Nos. 334 and 513) "he worshipped."

The verb *vah (vaha)* "to bear" makes *vahati* or *vahate* "he bears," *uváha* (No. 583) "he bore," *úhatuh* (No. 584) "they two bore," *úhuh* "they bore," *uvahitha* "thou didst bear."

झषस्तथोर्धोऽधः। ८। २। ४०।

झषः परयोस्तथोर्धः स्यान्न तु दधातेः।

No. 586.—Let there be DH in the room OF T OR TH coming AFTER A JHASH (a soft aspirate), but NOT if the *t* or *th* is a part OF the verb DHÁ "to hold." Thus, when we have *vah+tha* without the augment *iṭ* (No. 517). The *h* being changed to *ḍh* by No. 276, the *th* of *thal* becomes *dh* by the present rule, and then *ḍh* by No. 78.

ढो ढे लोपः । ८ । ३ । १३ ।

No. 587.—There is ELISION OF ḌH, WHEN ḌH FOLLOWS.

सहिवहोरोदवर्णस्य । ६ । ३ । ११२ ।

ढलोपः । उवोढ । ऊहे । वोढा । वक्ष्यति । अवाक्षीत् । अवोढाम् । अवाक्षुः । अवाक्षीः । अवोढम् । अवोढ । अवाक्षम् । अवाक्ष्व । अवाक्ष्म । अवोढ । अवक्षाताम् । अवक्षत । अवोढाः । अवक्षाथाम् । अवोढ्वम् । अवक्षि । अवक्ष्वहि । अवक्ष्महि ।

इति भ्वादयः ॥

No. 588.—When elision of *ḍh* (No. 587) has taken place, let O be the substitute in the room OF the A OF SHAH "to endure," AND VAH "to bear." Thus we have *uvoḍha* "thou didst bear," *úhe* "he bore," *voḍhá* (No. 586) "he will bear," *vakshyati* (No. 585) "he will bear," *avákshít* (No. 499) "he bore," *avoḍhám* (Nos. 513, 276, and 586) "they two bore," *avákshuh* "they bore," *avákshíh* "thou borest," *avoḍham* "you two bore," *avoḍha* "you bore," *aváksham* "I bore," *avákshwa* "we two bore," *avákshma* "we bore," or, with the *átmanepada* affixes, *avoḍha* (Nos. 513, 276, and 586) "he bore," *avakshátám* "they two bore," *avakshata* "they bore," *avoḍháh* "thou borest," *avakshátháṁ* "you two bore," *avoḍhwam* "you bore," *avakshi* "I bore," *avakshwahi* "we two bore," *avakshmahi* "we bore."

So much for the 1st class of verbs, consisting of "*bhú*, &c."

The 2nd class of verbs begins with the verb *ad (ada)* "to eat."

। अदादयः ।

अद भक्षणे । १ ।

अदिप्रभृतिभ्यः शपः । २ । ४ । ७२ ।

लुक् स्यात् । अत्ति । अत्तः । अदन्ति । अत्सि । अत्थः । अत्थ । अद्मि । अद्वः । अद्मः ।

No. 589.—Let there be elision *(luk)* OF ŚAP (No. 419) AFTER AD "to eat," &c. We then have *atti* (No. 90) "he eats," *attah* "they two eat," *adanti* "they eat," *atsi* "thou eatest," *atthah* "you two eat," *attha* "you eat," *admi* "I eat," *adwah* "we two eat," *admah* "we eat."

लिट्यन्यतरस्याम् । २ । ४ । ४० ।

अदो घस्लृ स्यात् । जघास । उपधालोपः । घस्य चर्त्वम् ।

No. 590.—Let *ghas (ghasḷri)* be OPTIONALLY the substitute of the root *ad*, WHEN LIṬ FOLLOWS. Thus we may have *jaghása* "he ate."

In making the next modification of this word, we have elision of the penultimate letter, from No. 540, and the substitution of a *char* for the *gh*, by No. 90, and we look forward.

शासिवसिघसीनां च । ८ । ३ । ६० ।

इण्कुभ्यामेषां सस्य षः । जक्षतुः । जक्षुः । जघसिथ । जक्षथुः । जक्ष । जघास । जक्षिव । जक्षिम । आद । आदतुः । आदुः ।

No. 591.—AND let there be *sh* in the room of the *s* OF these verbs—viz. ŚAS "to instruct," VAS "to dwell," AND GHAS "to eat," coming after *iṇ* or a guttural (see No. 169). Thus we have *jakshatuh* "they two ate," *jakshuh* "they ate," *jaghasitha* "thou didst eat," *jakshathuh* "you two ate," *jaksha* "you ate," *jaghása* "I ate," *jakshiva* "we two ate," *jakshima* "we ate." On the alternative allowed by No. 590, we have *áda* (No. 477) "he ate," *ádatuh* "they two ate," *áduh* "they ate."

इडत्त्यर्तिव्ययतीनाम् । ७ । २ । ६६ ।

अद् ऋ व्येञ् एभ्यस्थलो नित्यमिट् स्यात् । आदिथ । अत्ता । अत्स्यति । अत्तु । अत्तात् । अत्ताम् । अदन्तु ।

No. 592.—Let IṬ be always the augment OF *thal* coming after these—viz. AD "to eat," ṚI "to go," AND VYEṄ "to cover." Thus *áditha* "thou didst eat," *attá* "he will eat," *atsyati* "he will eat," *attu* "let him eat," *attát* (No. 444) "may he eat," *attám* (No. 446) "let the two eat," *adantu* "let them eat."

हुझल्भ्यो हेर्धिः । ६ । ४ । १०१ ।

अद्धि । अत्तात् । अत्तम् । अत्त । अदानि । अदाव । अदाम ।

No. 593—Let there be DHI instead OF HI (No. 447) AFTER the verb HU "to give," and what ends in JHAL. Thus *addhi* "do thou eat," *attát* (No. 444) "mayst thou eat," *attam* "do you two eat," *atta* "eat ye," *adáni* "let me eat," *adáva* (Nos. 445 and 455) "let us two eat," *adáma* "let us eat."

अदः सर्वेषाम् । ७ । ३ । १०० ।

अदोऽपृक्तसार्वधातुकस्याट् स्यात् । आदत् । आत्ताम् । आदन् । आदः । आत्तम् । आत्त । आदम् । आद्व । आद्म । अद्यात् । अद्याताम् । अद्युः । अद्यात् । अद्यास्ताम् । अद्यासुः ।

No. 594.—According to the opinion OF ALL the authorities, *aṭ* shall be the augment of a uniliteral affix coming AFTER the verb AD "to eat." Thus *ádat* (No. 478) "he ate," *áttám* "they two ate," *ádan* "they ate," *ádah* "thou atest," *áttam* "you two ate," *átta* "you ate," *ádam* "I ate," *ádwa* (No. 455) "we two ate," *ádma* "we ate," *adyát* (No. 461) "he may eat," *adyátám* "they two may eat," *adyuh* (No. 527) "they may eat," *adyát* (No. 337) may he eat," *adyástám* "may they two eat," *adyásuh* "may they eat."

लुङ्सनोर्घस्लृ । २ । ४ । ३७ ।

अदः । अङ् । अघसत् । आत्स्यत् । हन हिंसागत्योः । २ । हन्ति ।

No. 595.—WHEN LUŃ OR SAN (No. 752) FOLLOWS, let GHASLṚI be the substitute of the verb *ad*. Instead of *chli* (No. 471), there is *ań* (No. 542). Thus *aghasat* "he ate," *átsyat* "he would eat."

The verb *han (hana)* "to kill or to go" makes *hanti* "he kills."

अनुदात्तोपदेशवनतितनोत्यादीनामनुनासिकलोपो झलि क्ङिति । ६ । ४ । ३७ ।

अनुनासिकान्तानामेषां लोपः क्ङिति झलि । यमिरमिनमिगमिहनिमन्यतयोऽनुदात्तोपदेशाः । तनु क्षणु क्षिणु ऋणु तृणु घृणु वनु मनु

तनोत्यादयः । हतः । घ्नन्ति । हंसि । हथः । हथ । हन्मि । हन्वः । हन्मः । जघान । जघ्नतुः । जघ्नुः ।

No. 596.—WHEN THERE FOLLOWS an affix, beginning with a JHAL and DISTINGUISHED BY AN INDICATORY K OR Ṅ, there is ELISION OF THE NASAL OF the following that end in a nasal, viz. THOSE WHICH IN THEIR ORIGINAL ENUNCIATION ARE GRAVELY ACCENTED, AND VAN "to ask or beg," AND TAN "to stretch," &c.

Those which (ending in a nasal, see No. 510) are in their original enunciation gravely accented, are the following, viz: *yam* "to restrain," *ram* "to sport," *ṇam* "to bow," *gam* "to go," *han* "to kill," and *man* "to respect."

By "*tan* &c." (the verbs of the 8th class, which, *kṛi* excepted, end in a nasal,) are meant the following—viz. *tan* "to stretch," *kshaṇ* "to kill," *kshin* "to kill," *ṛiṇ* "to go," *tṛiṇ* "to eat grass," *ghṛiṇ* "to shine," *van* "to ask," and *man* "to understand."

By this rule we have *han+tas=hatah* (No. 535) "they two kill," *ghnanti* (Nos. 540 and 314) "they kill," *hańsi* (No. 94) "thou killest," *hathah* "you two kill," *hatha* "you kill," *hanmi* "I kill," *hanwah* "we two kill," *hanmah* "we kill," *jaghána* (Nos. 314, 488, and 489) "he killed," *jaghnatuh* (No. 540) "they two killed," *jaghnuh* "they killed."

अभ्यासाच्च । ७ । ३ । ५५ ।

हन्तेर्हस्य कुत्वम् । जघनिथ । जघन्थ । जघ्नथुः । जघ्न । जघान । जघन । जघ्निव । जघ्निम । हन्ता । हनिष्यति । हन्तु । हतात् । हताम् । घ्नन्तु ।

No. 597.—AND AFTER THE REDUPLICATE syllable, there is the substitution of a letter of the *k* class in the room of the *h* of the verb *han*. Thus we have *jaghanitha* (No. 517) or *jaghantha* "thou didst kill," *jaghnathuh* (No. 540) "you two killed," *jaghna* "you killed," *jaghána* (No. 489) or *jaghana* (No. 490) "I killed," *jaghniva* (No. 433) "we two killed," *jaghnima* "we killed," *hantá* (No. 510) "he will kill," *hanishyati* "he will kill," *hantu* "let him kill," *hatát* (Nos. 444 and 596) "may he kill," *hatám* "let the two kill," *ghnantu* (Nos. 540 and 314) "let them kill."

हन्तेर्जः । ६ । ४ । ३६ ।

हौ ।

No. 598.—Let JA be the substitute OF the verb HAN, when *hi* (No. 447) follows.

Then, by No. 448, the *hi* would be elided, were it not for the rule here following.

असिद्धवदत्राभात् । ६ । ४ । २२ ।

इत ऊर्ध्वमापादसमाप्तेराभीयम् । समानाश्रये तस्मिन् कर्तव्ये तदसिद्धम् । इति जस्यासिद्धत्वान्न हेर्लुक् । जहि । हतात् । हतम् । हत । हनानि । हनाव । हनाम । अहन् । अहताम् । अघ्नन् । अहन् । अहतम् । अहत । अहनम् । अहन्व । अहन्म । हन्यात् ।

No. 599.— The rules, reckoning FROM THIS one to the end of the chapter (viz. the 4th chap. of the VIth Lecture), are called *ábhíya*, (because the chapter ends with a series of rules dependent on the aphorism) "BHASYA." When that (viz. one of the rules called *ábhíya*) is to be brought into operation, having the same place (for coming into operation, as another *ábhíya* which has already taken effect), that one (which has taken effect) shall be regarded AS NOT HAVING TAKEN EFFECT.

Thus (*ja* having been substituted for *han*, by No. 598, it might have been expected that the *hi* would be elided by No. 448, but) since the change to *ja* is not regarded as having been accomplished, elision of *hi* does not take place. So we have *jahi* "do thou kill," *hatát* (Nos. 444 and 596) "mayst thou kill," *hatam* "do you two kill," *hata* "do you kill," *hanáni* "let me kill," *hanáva* "let us two kill," *hanáma* "let us kill," *ahan* (Nos. 458 and 199) "he killed," *ahatám* (No. 596) "they two killed," *aghnan* (Nos. 540, 314, and 26) "they killed," *ahan* (Nos. 458 and 199) "thou didst kill," *ahatam* "you two killed," *ahata* "you killed," *ahanam* "I killed," *ahanwa* "we two killed," *ahanma* "we killed," *hanyát* (No. 461) "he may kill."

आर्धधातुके । २ । ४ । ३५ ।

इत्यधिकृत्य ।

No. 600.—WHERE the affix in question is ÁRDHADHÁTUKA (No. 436—this aphorism having been placed as a regulator (among others of the rule following—we look forward).

हनो वध लिङि ।२।४।४२।

No. 601.—Let BADH be the substitute OF the verb HAN, WHEN LIŃ FOLLOWS.• (No. 600.)

लुङि च ।२।४।४३।

वध्यात् । वध्यास्ताम् । अवधीत् । अहनिष्यत् । यु मिश्रणामिश्रणयोः । ३ ।

No. 602.—AND WHEN LUŃ FOLLOWS (let *badh* be the substitute of *han*, as directed in No. 601—provided the affix, as ruled by No. 600, is *árdhadhátuka*). Thus we have *badhyát* (No. 337) "may he kill," *badhyástám* "may they two kill," *abadhít* "he killed," *ahanishyat* "he would kill."

The verb *yu* "to mix or to separate" is next conjugated.

उतो वृद्धिर्लुकि हलि ।७।३।८९।

लुग्विषय उतो वृद्धिः पिति हलादौ सार्वधातुके न त्वभ्यस्तस्य । यौति । युतः । युवन्ति । यौषि । युथः । युथ । यौमि । युवः । युमः । युयाव । यविता । यविष्यति । यौतु । युतात् । अयौत् । अयुताम् । अयुवन् । युयात् । इह वृद्धिर्न भाष्ये पिच्च ङिन्न ङिच्च पिन्नेति व्याख्यानात् । युयाताम् । युयुः । यूयात् । यूयास्ताम् । यूयासुः । अयावीत् । अयविष्यत् । या प्रापणे । ४ । याति । यातः । यान्ति । ययौ । याता । यास्यति । यातु । अयात् । अयाताम् ।

No. 603.—WHERE elision, through LUK, HAS TAKEN PLACE (as by No. 589), let VṚIDDHI be substituted in the room OF SHORT U, WHEN a *sárvadhátuka* affix, beginning with A CONSONANT and distinguished by an indicatory *p*, FOLLOWS:—but not if the verb be reduplicated. Thus we have *yu+tip=yauti* "he mixes," *yutah* "they two mix," *yuvanti* (No. 220) "they mix," *yaushi* (No. 169) "thou mixest," *yuthah* "you two mix," *yutha* "you mix," *yaumi* "I mix," *yuvah* "we two mix," *yumah* "we mix," *yuyáva* (No. 202) "he mixed," *yavitá* (Nos. 433 and 420) "he will mix," *yavishyati* "he will mix," *yautu* "let him mix," *yutát* (No. 444) "may he mix," *ayaut* "he mixed," *ayutám* "they two mixed," *ayuvan* (No. 457) "they mixed," *yuyát* (No. 461) "he may mix,"—here there is not *vṛiddhi* (from No. 603), because, according to the explanation in the *Mahábháshya*, "what has an indicatory *p* has not an indicatory *ń*, and what has an indicatory *ń* has not an indicatory *p*":—(so, when *yásuṭ* came, which, see No. 460, is regarded as having an indicatory *ń*, the *tip* ceased to be regarded as having an indicatory *p*, without which No. 603 does not apply). So *yuyátám* "they two may mix," *yuyuh* (No. 527) "they may mix," *yúyát* (Nos. 518 and 337) "may he mix," *yúyástám* "may they two mix," *yúyásuh* "may they mix," *ayávít* (No. 519) "he mixed," *ayavishyat* (Nos. 433 and 420) "he would mix."

The verb *yá* "to go" makes *yáti* "he goes," *yátah* "they two go," *yánti* "they go," *yayau* (No. 523) "he went," *yátá* "he will go," *yásyati* "he will go," *yátu* "let him go," *ayát* "he went," *ayátám* "they two went."

लङः शाकटायनस्यैव । ३ । ४ । १११ ।

आदन्ताल्लङो झेर्जुस् वा । अयुः । अयान् । यायात् । यायाताम् । यायुः । यायात् । यायास्ताम् । यायासुः । अयासीत् । अयास्यत् । एवं वा गतिगन्धनयोः । ५ । भा दीप्तौ । ६ । ष्णा शौचे । ७ । श्रा पाके । ८ । द्रा कुत्सायां गतौ । ९ । प्सा भक्षणे । १० । रा दाने । ११ । ला आदाने । १२ । दाप् लवने । १३ । ख्या प्रकथने । १४ । अयं सार्वधातुक एव प्रयोक्तव्यः । विद ज्ञाने । १५ ।

No. 604.—In the opinion OF SÁKAṬÁYANA ONLY (and hence optionally), *jus* is the substitute of *jhi* in the room OF LAŃ, after what ends in long *á*. Thus *ayuh* (No. 527) or *ayán* (No. 26) "they went," *yáyát* (No. 461) "he may go," *yáyátám* "they two may go," *yáyuh* (No. 527) "they may go," *yáyát* (No. 337) "may he go," *yáyástám* "may they two go," *yáyásuh* "may they go," *ayásít* "he went," *ayásyat* "he would go."

In the same way are conjugated *vá* "to go or smell," *bhá* "to shine," *shṇá* "to bathe," *śrá* "to cook," *drá* "to go badly," *psá* "to eat," *rá* "to give," *lá* "to take," *dá* "to cut," and *khyá* "to relate." This (viz. *khyá*) is to be employed only with the *sárvadhátuka* affixes.

The next verb to be conjugated is *vid* "to know."

विदो लटो वा । ३ । ४ । ८३ ।

वेत्तेर्लटः परस्मैपदानां णलादयो वा । वेद । विदतुः । विदुः । वेत्थ । विदथुः । विद । वेद । विद्व । विद्म । पक्षे । वेत्ति । वित्तः । विदन्ति ।

No. 605.—The affixes *ṇal*, &c. (No. 424) are OPTIONALLY used instead OF the *parasmaipada* substitutes of LAṬ coming AFTER the verb VID "to know." Thus *veda* (No. 485) "he knows," *vidatuh* "they two know," *viduh* "they know," *vettha* "thou knowest," *vidathuh* "you two know," *vida* "you know," *veda* "I know," *vidwa* "we two know," *vidma* "we know." On the other alternative, we have *vetti* (No. 485) "he knows," *vittah* (No. 467) "they two know," *vidanti* "they know."

उषविदजागृभ्योऽन्यतरस्याम् । ३ । १ । ३८ ।

एभ्यो लिट्याम् वा । विदेरदन्तत्वप्रतिज्ञानादामि न गुणः । विदांचकार । विवेद । वेदिता । वेदिष्यति ।

No. 606.—The augment *ám* is OPTIONALLY employed AFTER these—viz. USH "to burn," VID "to know," AND JÁGṚI "to wake," —when *liṭ* follows.

As there is an agreement (in the present instance) to regard the verb *vid* as ending in short *a* (*vida*), *guna* is not substituted (as it would otherwise have been by No. 485). Thus we have *vidáñchakára* or *viveda* "he knows," *veditá* "he will know," *vedishyati* "he will know."

विदांकुर्वन्त्वित्यन्यतरस्याम् । ३ । १ । ४१ ।

वेत्तेर्लोट्याम् गुणाभावो लोटो लुग्लोडन्तकरोत्यनुप्रयोगश्च निपात्यते । पुरुषवचने न विवक्ष्येते । विदांकरोतु ।

No. 607.—When *loṭ* comes after the verb *vid*, then OPTIONALLY the augment *ám* is irregularly attached; there is no substitution of *guṇa* (from No. 420—which fact is indicated by the exhibition of the form *vidáṅ* in the aphorism); there is elision (*luk*) of *loṭ*; and the verb *kṛi* "to make," with the terminations of the imperative, is appended, (giving, for example, VIDÁṄKURVANTU). One particular person and number is not alone intended to be spoken of (by the employment, in the aphorism, of the form *vidáṅkurvantu*).

Thus we may have *vidáṅkarotu* "let him know."

तनादिकृञ्भ्य उः । ३ । १ । ७९ ।

शपोऽपवादः ।

No. 608.—Let U come AFTER the verbs TAN, &c. (No. 719), AND after the verb KṚI "to make." This debars the application of *śap* (No. 419).

अत उत् सार्वधातुके । ६ । ४ । ११० ।

उप्रत्ययान्तस्य कृञोऽत उत् सार्वधातुके क्ङिति । विदांकुरुतात् । विदांकुरुताम् । विदांकुर्वन्तु । विदांकुरु । विदांकरवाणि । अवेत् । अवित्ताम् । अविदुः ।

No. 609.—Let SHORT U be the substitute OF the SHORT A of (*kar*, the modified form of) the verb *kṛi*, ending with the affix *u* (No. 608), WHEN A SÁRVADHÁTUKA termination, with an indicatory *k* or *ṅ*, FOLLOWS. Thus *vidáṅkurutát* (No. 607) "may he know," *vidáṅkurutám* "let the two know," *vidáṅkurvantu* "let them know," *vidáṅkuru* "know thou," *vidáṅkaraváṇi* (No. 420) "let me know," *avet* (Nos. 458, 485, and 199) "he knew," *avittám* "they two knew," *aviduh* (No. 481) "they knew."

दश्च । ८ । २ । ७५ ।

धातोर्दस्य पदान्तस्य सिपि रुर्वा । अवेः । अवेत् । विद्यात् । विद्यास्ताम् । अवेदीत् । अवेदिष्यत् । अस भुवि । १६ । अस्ति ।

No. 610.—AND when *sip* follows, *ru* is optionally the substitute OF the D of a verb, when the *d* is at the end of a *pada.* Thus we have *aveh* (No. 111) or *avet* "thou knewest," *vidyát* "he may know, or, may he know," *vidyástám* "may they two know," *avedít* "he knew," *avedishyat* "he would know."

The verb *as* "to be" makes *asti* "he is."

श्नसोरल्लोपः । ६ । ४ । १११ ।

श्नस्यास्तेश्चातो लोपः सार्वधातुके क्ङिति । स्तः । सन्ति । असि । स्थः । स्थ । अस्मि । स्वः । स्मः ।

No. 611.—Let there be ELISION OF the A OF the affix ŚNAM (No. 714) AND of the verb AS "to be," when a *sárvadhátuka* affix, with an indicatory *k* or *ń*, follows. Thus *stah* (No. 535) "they two are," *santi* "they are," *asi* (No. 438) "thou art," *sthah* "you two are," *stha* "you are," *asmi* "I am," *swah* "we two are," *smah* "we are."

उपसर्गप्रादुर्भ्यामस्तिर्यच्परः । ८ । ३ । ८७ ।

उपसर्गेणः प्रादुसश्चास्तेः सस्य षो यकारेऽचि च परे । निष्यात् । प्रनिषन्ति । प्रादुःषन्ति । यच्परः किम् । अभिस्तः ।

No. 612.—Let *sh* be the substitute of the *s* OF the verb AS "to be," coming AFTER a letter of the *pratyáhára in* in AN UPASARGA (No. 47) OR after the indeclinable word PRÁDUS "evidently," WHEN the letter Y OR A VOWEL FOLLOWS. Thus (after the *upasarga ni,* when *y* follows the *s,*) *nishyát* "he may go out;" (when a vowel follows the *s,*) *pranishanti* "they go out," *práduhshanti* "they are manifest."

Why do we say, "when the letter *y* or a vowel follows?" witness *abhistah* "they two surpass."

अस्तेर्भूः । २ । ४ । ५२ ।

आर्धधातुके । बभूव । भविता । भविष्यति । अस्तु । स्तात् । स्ताम् । सन्तु ।

No. 613.—Let BHÚ be the substitute OF the verb AS "to be," when an *árdhadhátuka* affix follows. Thus *babhúva* (No. 431) "he was," *bhavitá* "he will be," *bhavishyati* "he will be," *astu* "let him be," *stát* (Nos. 444 and 611) "may he be," *stám* "let the two be," *santu* "let them be."

घ्वसोरेद्धावभ्यासलोपश्च । ६ । ४ । ११९ ।

घोरस्तेश्चैत्वं स्याद्धावभ्यासलोपश्च । एधि । स्तात् । स्ताम् । स्त । असानि । असाव । असाम । आसीत् । आस्ताम् । आसन् । स्यात् । स्याताम् । स्युः । भूयात् । अभूत् । अभविष्यत् । इण् गतौ । १० । एति । इतः ।

No. 614.—Let there be a change to E OF a verb termed GHU (No. 662) AND of the verb AS, WHEN HI (No. 447) FOLLOWS, AND let there be ELISION OF A REDUPLICATE syllable. Then (the *hi* being changed to *dhi* by No. 593), we have *edhi* "be thou," *stát* (Nos. 444 and 611) "mayst thou be," *stam* "be you two," *sta* "be you," *asáni* "let me be," *asáva* "let us two be," *asáma* "let us be," *ásít* (Nos. 478 and 479) "he was," *ástám* "they two were," *ásan* "they were," *syát* "he may be, *syátám* "they two may be," *syuh* "they may be," *bhúyát* (No. 613) "may he be," *abhút* "he was," *abhavishyat* "he would be."

The verb *i (in)* "to go" makes *eti* (No. 420) "he goes," *itah* (Nos. 535 and 467) "they two go."

इणो यण् । ६ । ४ । ८१ ।

अजादौ प्रत्यये परे । यन्ति ।

No. 615.—Let YAṆ be the substitute OF the root IṆ, when an affix, beginning with a vowel, follows. Thus *yanti* "they go."

अभ्यासस्यासवर्णे । ६ । ४ । ७८ ।

इउवर्णयोरियङुवङौ स्तोऽसवर्णेऽचि । इयाय ।

No. 616.—*Iyań* and *uvań* are the substitutes of *i* and *u* OF A REDUPLICATE, WHEN A HETEROGENEOUS vowel FOLLOWS. Thus *iyáya* (Nos. 426, 202, and 29) "he went."

दीर्घ इणः किति । ७ । ४ । ६९ ।

इणोऽभ्यासस्य दीर्घः किति लिटि । ईयतुः । ईयुः । इययिथ । इयेथ । एता । एष्यति । एतु । ऐत् । ऐताम् । आयन् । इयात् । ईयात् ।

No. 617.—Let A LONG vowel be instead of the reduplicate OF the verb IṆ, WHEN WHAT substitute for *liṭ* HAS AN INDICATORY K (No. 486) FOLLOWS. Thus *íyatuh* "they two went," *íyuh* "they went," *iyayitha* (Nos. 433 and 517) or *iyetha* (Nos. 515, 420, and 616) "thou didst go," *etá* "he will go," *eshyati* "he will go," *etu* "let him go," *ait* (Nos. 478 and 218) "he went," *aitám* "they two went." *áyan* (No. 29) "they went," *iyát* "he may go," *íyát* (No. 518) "may he go."

एतेर्लिङि । ७ । ४ । २४ ।

उपसर्गात् परस्य इणोऽणो ह्रस्व आर्धधातुके किति लिङि । निरियात् । उभयत आश्रयणे नान्तादिवत् । अभीयात् । अणः किम् । समेयात् ।

No. 618.—Let there be a short vowel in the room OF the *aṇ* (*í*) of the verb IṆ coming after an *upasarga*, WHEN an *árdhadhátuka* substitute for LIŃ, with an indicatory *k* (No. 466), FOLLOWS. Thus *nir+íyát=niriyát* "may he go forth."

In the example *abhíyát* "may he go up to," the short vowel is not substituted; for the rule (VI. 1. 85.) that "a single letter substituted shall be regarded as the final of the preceding word and the initial of the following word," does not apply, when the operation directed depends upon both what precedes and what follows:—so then, as the *í*, in *abhíyát*, cannot be regarded as a part at once of the *upasarga* and of the verb, the rule No. 618 consequently does not apply.

Why do we say, "of the *aṇ?*" witness *sam+eyát=sameyát (=sam+á+íyát)* "may he come," where the rule does not apply, as the verb begins with *ech.*

इणो गा लुङि ।२।४।४५।

गातिस्थेति सिचो लुक् । अगात् । ऐष्यत् । शीङ् स्वप्ने । १८ ।

No. 619.—Let GÁ be the substitute OF the root IṆ, WHEN LUŃ FOLLOWS. By No. 473, there is elision *(luk)* of the *sich* (No. 472). Thus *agát* "he went," *aishyat* (Nos. 478 and 218) "he would go."

The next verb to be conjugated is *śí (śíń)* "to sleep."

शीङः सार्वधातुके गुणः ।७।४।२१।

शेते । शयाते ।

No. 620.—Let GUṆA be the substitute OF ŚÍŃ "to sleep," WHEN A SÁRVADHÁTUKA affix FOLLOWS. Thus *śete* No. 543) "he sleeps," *śayáte* (No. 29) "they two sleep."

शीङो रुट् ।७।१।६।

शीङो झादेशस्यातो रुट् । शेरते । शेषे । शयाथे । शेध्वे । शये । शेवहे । शेमहे । शिश्ये । शिश्याते । शिश्यिरे । शयिता । शयिष्यते । शेताम् । शयाताम् । शेरताम् । अशेत । अशयाताम् । अशेरत । शयीत । शयीयाताम् । शयीरन् । शयिषीष्ट । अशयिष्ट । अशयिष्यत । इङ् अध्ययने । १६ । इङिकावध्युपसर्गतो न व्यभिचरतः । अधीते । अधीयाते । अधीयते ।

No. 621.—Let RUṬ *(r)* be the augment of the *a* of the substitute for *jh* (No. 421) AFTER the verb ŚÍŃ "to sleep." Thus *śerate* (No. 559) "they sleep," *śeshe* "thou sleepest," *śayáthe* "you two sleep," *śedhwe* "you sleep," *śaye* "I sleep," *śevahe* "we two sleep." *śemahe* "we sleep," *śiśye* (Nos. 429 and 548) "he slept," *śiśyáte* "they two slept," *śiśyire* (No. 548) "they slept," *śayitá* (No. 433) "he will sleep," *śayishyate* "he will sleep," *śetám* (No. 552) "let him sleep," *śayátám* "let the two sleep," *śeratám* (No. 621) "let them sleep," *aśeta* "he slept," *aśayátám* "they two slept," *áśerata* (Nos. 559 and 621) "they slept," *śayíta* (Nos. 555 and 463) "he may sleep," *śayíyátám* "they two may sleep," *śayíran* (No. 556) "they may sleep," *śayishíshṭa* (No. 558) "may he sleep," *aśayishṭa* (Nos. 420, 472, and 433) "he slept," *aśayishyata* (No. 435) "he would sleep."

The next verb to be conjugated is *i (iń)* "to study." This verb and *i (ik)* "to remember" never appear apart from the preposition *adhi*. Thus *adhíte* (No. 543) "he studies," *adhíyate* (No. 220) "they two study," *adhíyate* (No. 559) "they study."

गाङ् लिटि ।२।४।४९।

इङः । अधिजगे । अध्येता । अध्येष्यते । अधीताम् । अधीयाताम् । अधीयताम् । अधीष्व । अधीयाथाम् । अधीध्वम् । अध्यये । अध्ययावहै । अध्ययामहै । अध्यैत । अध्यैयाताम् । अध्यैयत । अध्यैथाः । अध्यैयाथाम् । अध्यैध्वम् । अध्यैयि । अध्यैवहि । अध्यैमहि । अधीयीत । अधीयीयाताम् । अधीयीरन् । अध्येषीष्ट ।

No. 622.—Let GÁ be the substitute of the verb *i (iń)* "to study," WHEN LIṬ FOLLOWS. Thus *adhijage* (Nos. 548 and 524) "he studied," *adhyetá* (No. 420) "he will study," *adhyeshyate* "he will study," *adhítám* (No. 552) "let him study," *adhíyátám* "let the two study," *adhíyatám* (No. 559) "let them study," *adhíshwa* (No. 553) "do you study," *adhíyáthám* "do you two study," *adhídhwam* (No. 553) "do you study," *adhyayai* (No. 554) "let me study," *adhyayávahai* "let us two study," *adhyayámahai* "let us study," *adhyaita* (Nos. 478 and 218) "he studied" *adhyaiyátám* "they two studied," *adhyaiyata* (No. 559) "they studied," *adhyaithάh* "thou didst study," *adhyaiyáthám* "you two studied," *adhyaidhwam* "you studied," *adhyaiyi* "I studied," *adhyaivahi* "we two studied," *adhyaimahi* "we studied," *adhíyíta* (Nos. 555, 461, 463, and 220) "he may study," *adhíyíyátám* "they two may study," *adhíyíran* (No. 556) "they may study," *adhyeshíshṭa* (No. 558) "may he study."

विभाषा लुङ्लृङोः ।२।४।५०।

इडो गाङ् ।

No. 623.—The substitution of *gá* (No. 622) in the room of *i (iń)* "to study" is OPTIONALLY made, WHEN LUŃ AND LṚIŃ FOLLOW.

गाङ्कुटादिभ्योऽञ्णिन्ङित् । १ । २ । १ ।

गाङादेशात् कुटादिभ्यश्चाञ्णितः प्रत्यया ङितः स्युः ।

No. 624.—WHAT affixes HAVE NOT AN INDICATORY Ñ OR Ṇ shall be considered to HAVE AN INDICATORY Ń (No. 467), when they come AFTER GÁ (No. 622) AND the verbs KUṬ "to be crooked," &C.

घुमास्थागापाजहातिसां हलि । ६ । ४ । ६६ ।

एषामात ईत् स्याद्धलादौ क्ङित्यार्धधातुके । अध्यगीष्ट । अध्यैष्ट । अध्यगीष्यत । अध्यैष्यत । दुह प्रपूरणे । २० । दोग्धि । दुग्धः । दुहन्ति । धोक्षि । दुग्धे । दुहाते । दुहते । धुक्षे । दुहाथे । धुग्ध्वे । दुहे । दुह्वहे । दुह्महे । दुदोह । दुदुहे । दोग्धा । धोक्ष्यति । धोक्ष्यते । दोग्धु । दुग्धात् । दुग्धाम् । दुहन्तु । दुग्धि । दुग्धात् । दुग्धम् । दुग्ध । दोहानि । दुग्धाम् । दुहाताम् । दुहताम् । धुक्ष्व । दुहाथाम् । धुग्ध्वम् । दोहै । दोहावहै । दोहामहै । अधोक् । अदुग्धाम् । अदुहन् । अदोहम् । अदुग्ध । अदुहाताम् । अदुहत । अधुग्ध्वम् । दुह्यात् । दुहीत ।

No. 625.—WHEN an *árdhadhátuka* affix, beginning with A CONSONANT and distinguished by an indicatory *k* or *ń*, FOLLOWS, then let long *í* be the substitute of the long *á* OF the verbs termed GHU (No. 662), and of MÁ "to measure," SHṬHÁ "to stand," GÁ "to study," PÁ "to drink," HÁ "to abandon," AND SHO "to destroy." Thus *adhyagíshṭa* (No. 623) or, alternatively, *adhyaishṭa* (No. 218) "he studied," *adhyagíshyata* (No. 623) or *adhyaishyata* "he would study."

The verb *duh (duha)* "to milk" makes *dogdhi* (Nos. 277, 586, and 25) "he milks," *dugdhah* (No. 535) "they two milk," *duhanti* "they milk," *dhokshi* (Nos. 277, 278, 169, and 89) "thou milkest," or, with the *átmanepada* terminations, *dugdhe* (Nos. 543 and 535) "he milks," *duháte* "they two milk," *duhate* (No. 559) "they milk," *dhukshe* (Nos. 277, 278, 169, 90, and 535) "thou milkest," *duháthe* "you two milk," *dhugdhwe* (No. 277) "you milk," *duhe* "I milk," *duhwahe* "we two milk," *duhmahe* "we milk," *dudoha* (No. 485) or *duduhe* (No. 548) "he milked," *dogdhá* (No. 586) "he will milk," *dhokshyati* (Nos. 277 and 278) or *dhokshyate* "he will milk," *dogdhu* "let him milk," *dugdhát* (Nos. 444 and 467) "may he milk," *dugdhám* "let the two milk," *duhantu* "let them milk," *dugdhi* (No. 593) "do thou milk," *dugdhát* (No. 444) "mayst thou milk," *dugdham* "do you two milk," *dugdha* "milk ye," *doháni* "let me milk," *dugdhám* (No. 552) "let him milk," *duhátám* "let the two milk," *duhatám* (No. 559) "let them milk," *dhukshwa* (No 278) "do thou milk," *duháthám* "do you two milk," *dhugdhwam* (No. 278) "milk ye," *dohai* (No. 554) "let me milk," *dohávahai* "let us two milk," *dohámahai* "let us milk," *adhok* (Nos. 199 and 278) "he milked," *adugdhám* (No. 586) "they two milked," *aduhan* "they milked," *adoham* "I milked," *adugdha* "he milked," *aduhátám* "they two milked," *aduhata* (No. 559) "they milked," *adhugdhwam* (No. 277) "you milked," *duhyát* "he may milk," *duhíta* (No. 555) "he may milk."

लिङ्सिचावात्मनेपदेषु ।१।२।११।

इक्समीपाद्धलः परौ झलादी लिङ्सिचौ कितौ स्तस्तङि । धुक्षीष्ट ।

No. 626.—The substitutes of LIŃ (No. 459) AND SICH (No. 472), coming after a consonant that adjoins an *ik*, WHEN THE ÁTMANEPADA affixes ARE EMPLOYED, are regarded as having an indicatory *k* (No. 467). Thus, *guṇa* not being substituted, we have *dhukshíshṭa* (Nos. 277, 278, and 558) "may he milk."

शल इगुपधादनिटः क्सः ।३।१।४५।

इगुपधो यः शलन्तिस्तस्मादनिटश्च्लेः क्सादेशः । अधुक्षत् ।

No. 627.—AFTER that verb which ends in a ŚAL, with an IK for its PENULTIMATE letter, AND does NOT take the augment IṬ (No. 510), let KSA (i. e. *sa*—No. 155) be the substitute of *chli* (No. 471). Thus *adhukshat* (Nos. 277, 278, 90, and 169) "he milked."

लुग्वा दुहदिहलिहगुहामात्मनेपदे दन्त्ये।७।३।७३।

एषां क्सस्य लुग्वा दन्त्ये तङि । अदुग्ध । अधुक्षत ।

No. 628.—WHEN AN ÁTMANEPADA affix, beginning with A DENTAL, FOLLOWS, there is OPTIONALLY ELISION *(luk)* (of the vowel—see No. 27—) of the *ksa* (No. 627) OF these verbs viz. DUH "to milk," DIH "to accumulate," LIH "to lick," AND GUH "to cover." Thus (the *s* also being elided by No. 513) we have either *adugdha* (Nos. 277 and 586) or *adhukshata* (No. 627) "he milked."

क्सस्याचि।७।३।७२।

अजादौ तङि क्सस्य लोपः। अधुक्षाताम्। अधुक्षन्त। अदुग्धाः। अधुक्षथाः। अधुक्षाथाम्। अधुग्ध्वम्। अधुक्षध्वम्। अधुक्षि। अधुक्षावहि। अधुक्षामहि। अधोक्ष्यत। एवं दिह उपचये। २१। लिह आस्वादने। २२। लेढि। लीढः। लिहन्ति। लेक्षि। लीढे। लिहाते। लिहते। लिक्षे। लिहाथे। लीढ्वे। लिलेह। लिलिहे। लेढासि। लेढासे। लेक्ष्यति। लेक्ष्यते। लेढु। लीढात्। लीढाम्। लिहन्तु। लीढि। लेहानि। लीढाम्। अलेट्। अलेड्। अलिक्षत्। अलिक्षत। अलीढ। अलेक्ष्यत्। अलेक्ष्यत। ब्रूञ् व्यक्तायां वाचि। २३।

No. 629.—There is elision *(lopa)* OF KSA (Nos. 627 and 27), WHEN an *átmanepada* affix, beginning with AN ACH, FOLLOWS. Thus *adhukshátám* "they two milked," *adhukshanta* (No. 559) "they milked," *adugdháh* (Nos. 277 and 586) or *adhukshatháh* (No. 627) "thou didst milk," *adhuksháthám* "you two milked," *adhugdhwam* (No. 628) or *adhukshadhwam* "you milked," *adhukshi* "I milked," *adhukshávahi* (No. 422) "we two milked," *adhukshámahi* "we milked," *adhokshyata* (Nos. 435, 485, and 457) "he would milk."

In the same way the verb *dih (diha)* "to accumulate." The verb *lih (liha)* "to lick" makes *leḍhi* (Nos. 276, 586, and 587) "he licks," *líḍhah* (No. 131) "they two lick," *lihanti* "they lick," *lekshi*

(Nos. 276 and 585) "thou lickest,"—or *líḍhe* (No. 543) "he licks," *liháte* "they two lick," *lihate* (No. 559) "they lick," *likshe* "thou lickest," *liháthe* "you two lick," *líḍhwe* "you lick," *lileha* or *lilihe* "he licked," *leḍhási* or *leḍháse* "thou wilt lick," *lekshyati* or *lekshyate* "he will lick," *leḍhu* "let him lick," *líḍhát* (Nos. 444 and 467) "may he lick," *líḍhám* (No. 552) "let him lick," *lihantu* "let them lick," *líḍhi* (No. 447) "lick thou," *leháni* "let me lick," or *líḍhám* (No. 552) "let him lick," *aleṭ* (Nos. 276, 199, and 165) or *aleḍ* (No 82) "he licked," *alikshat* (Nos. 627, 276, and 585), or *alikshata*, or *alíḍha* (No. 628) "he licked," *alekshyat* or *alekshyata* "he would lick."

The next verb to be conjugated is *brú (brúṅ)* "to speak articulately."

ब्रुवः पञ्चानामादित आहो ब्रुवः । ३ । ४ । ८४ ।

ब्रुवो लडस्तिबादीनां पञ्चानां णलादयः पञ्च वा स्युर्ब्रुवश्चाहादेशः । आह । आहतुः । आहुः ।

No. 630.—Instead OF THE FIRST FIVE tense-affixes *tip*, &c. substituted for *laṭ*, coming AFTER the verb BRÚ "to speak," there may optionally be *ṇal*, &c. (No. 424); ÁH being at the same time the substitute in the room OF BRÚ. Thus *áha* "he says," *áhatuh* "they two say," *áhuh* "they say."

आहस्थः । ८ । २ । ३५ ।

झलि । चत्वम् । आत्थ । आहथुः ।

No. 631.—Instead OF (the final of) ÁH (No 630) there is TH, when a *jhal* follows. Then there is a change of the *th* to a *char* by No. 90, and we have *áttha* "thou sayest," *áhathuh* "you two say."

ब्रुव ईट् । ७ । ३ । ९३ ।

ब्रुवो हलादेः पित ईट् । ब्रवीति । ब्रूतः । ब्रुवन्ति । ब्रूते । ब्रुवाते । ब्रुवते ।

No. 632.—IṬ is the augment of an affix, beginning with a consonant and distinguished by an indicatory *p*, coming AFTER the verb BRÚ "to speak." Thus *bravíti* (No. 420) "he speaks," *brútah* "they two speak," *bruvanti* (No. 220) "they speak," *brúte* (No. 543) "he speaks," *bruváte* "they two speak," *bruvate* (No. 559) "they speak."

ब्रुवो वचिः । २ । ४ । ५३ ।

आर्धधातुके । उवाच । ऊचतुः । ऊचुः । उवचिथ । उवक्थ । ऊचे । वक्ता । वक्ष्यति । वक्ष्यते । ब्रवीतु । ब्रूतात् । ब्रूताम् । ब्रुवन्तु । ब्रूहि । ब्रवाणि । ब्रूताम् । ब्रवै । अब्रवीत् । अब्रूत । ब्रूयात् । ब्रुवीत । उच्यात् । वक्षीष्ट ।

No. 633.—The root VACH is the substitute OF BRÚ "to speak," when an *árdhadhátuka* affix follows. Thus *uvácha* (Nos. 432, 583, and 489) "he spoke," *úchatuh* (No. 584) "they two spoke," *úchuh* "they spoke," *uvachitha* (No. 517) or *uvaktha* (No. 333) "thou spokest," *úche* (No. 548) "he spoke," *vaktá* "he will speak," *vakshyati* or *vakshyate* "he will speak," *bravítu* (No. 632) "let him speak," *brútát* (No. 444) "may he speak," *brútám* "let the two speak," *bruvantu* (No. 220) "let them speak," *brúhi* "speak thou," *braváṇi* "let me speak," *brútám* (No. 552) "let him speak," *bravai* (No. 554) "let me speak," *abravít* (No. 632) "he spoke, "*abrúta* "he spoke," *brúyát* or *bruvíta* (Nos. 555, 463, and 220) "he may speak," *uchyát* (Nos. 466 and 584) or *vakshíshṭa* (No. 555) "may he speak."

अस्यतिवक्तिख्यातिभ्योऽङ् । ३ । १ । ५२ ।

च्लेः ।

No. 634.—Instead of *chli* (No. 471), there shall be AŃ AFTER the verbs AS "to throw," VACH "to speak," AND KHYÁ "to speak."

वच उम् । ७ । ४ । २० ।

अङि परे । अवोचत् । अवक्ष्यत् । अवक्ष्यत ।

No. 635.—When *aṅ* (No. 634) follows, let UM be the augment OF the verb VACH "to speak." Thus *avochat* (No. 265) "he spoke," *avakshyat* or *avakshyata* "he would speak."

चर्करीतं च । चर्करीतमिति यङ्लुगन्तं तददादौ बोध्यम् । ऊर्णुञ् आच्छादने । २४ ।

No. 636.—"AND a verb in the shape indicated by the term CHARKARÍTA," i. e. at the end of which the affix *yań* (No. 758) has been replaced by a blank *(luk)*, is to be regarded as belonging to the 2nd class of verbs, "*ad*, &c." (No. 589.)

The verb *úrṇu (úrṇuń)* "to cover" is next to be conjugated.

ऊर्णोतेर्विभाषा । ७ । ३ । ९० ।

वृद्धिर्हलादौ पिति सार्वधातुके । ऊर्णौति । ऊर्णोति । ऊर्णुतः । ऊर्णुवन्ति । ऊर्णुते । ऊर्णुवाते । ऊर्णुवते ।

No. 637.—When a *sárvadhátuka* affix follows, beginning with a consonant and distinguished by an indicatory *p*, then *vṛiddhi* is OPTIONALLY the substitute OF the verb ÚRṆU "to cover." Thus *úrṇauti* or *úrṇoti* "he covers," *úrṇutah* (No. 535) "they two cover," *úrṇuvanti* (No. 220) "they cover," *úrṇute* "he covers," *úrṇuváte* "they two cover," *úrṇuvate* (No. 559) "they cover."

ऊर्णोतेराम् नेति वाच्यम् ।

No. 638.—"IT SHOULD BE MENTIONED THAT the verb ÚRṆU DOES NOT TAKE ÁM" (No. 546).

न न्द्राः संयोगादयः । ६ । १ । ३ ।

अचः पराः संयोगादयो नदरा द्विर्न भवन्ति । नुशब्दस्य द्वित्वम् । ऊर्णुनाव । ऊर्णुनुवतुः । ऊर्णुनुवुः ।

No. 639.—The letters N, D, and R, following a vowel and INITIAL IN A CONJUNCT consonant, are NOT doubled (No. 426). There is a reduplication only of the syllable *ṇu*; and thus we have *úrṇunáva* (No. 202) "he covered," *úrṇunuvatuh* (No. 220) "they two covered," *úrṇunuvuh* "they covered."

विभाषोर्णोः । १ । २ । ३ ।

इडादिप्रत्ययो ङित् स्यात् । ऊर्णुनुविथ । ऊर्णुनविथ । ऊर्णुविता । ऊर्णविता । ऊर्णुविष्यति । ऊर्णविष्यति । ऊर्णौतु । ऊर्णोतु । ऊर्णवानि । ऊर्णवै ।

No. 640.—An affix, beginning with the augment *iṭ*, may OPTIONALLY be regarded as having an indicatory *ń* (No. 467), when it comes AFTER the verb ÚRṆU "to cover." Thus *úrṇunuvitha* (No. 220) or *úrṇunavitha* "thou didst cover," *úrṇuvitá* or *úrṇavitá* "he will cover," *úrṇuvishyati* or *úrṇavishyati* "he will cover," *úrṇautu* (No. 637) or *úrṇotu* "let him cover," *úrṇaváni* "let me cover," *úrṇavai* (No. 554) "let me cover."

गुणोऽपृक्ते । ७ । ३ । ९१ ।

ऊर्णोतेर्गुणोऽपृक्तहलादौ पिति सार्वधातुके । और्णोत् । और्णोः । ऊर्णुयात् । ऊर्णुयाः । ऊर्णुवीत । ऊर्णूयात् । ऊर्णुविषीष्ट । ऊर्णविषीष्ट ।

No. 641.—WHEN A *sárvadhátuka* AFFIX FOLLOWS, consisting OF A SINGLE LETTER, beginning with a consonant and distinguished by an indicatory *p*, then let GUṆA be the substitute of the verb *úrṇu* "to cover." Thus *aurṇot* (Nos. 458, 478, and 218) "he covered," *aurṇoh* "thou didst cover," *úrṇuyát* "he may cover," *úrṇuyáh* "thou mayst cover," or *úrṇuvíta* (Nos. 555 and 220) "he may cover," *úrṇúyát* (No. 518) or *úrṇuvishíshṭa* (No. 640) or *úrṇavishíshṭa* "may he cover."

ऊर्णोतेर्विभाषा । ७ । २ । ६ ।

इडादौ परस्मैपदे सिचि वृद्धिः । पक्षे गुणः । और्णावीत् । और्णवीत् । और्णुवीत् । और्णाविष्टाम् । और्णविष्टाम् । और्णुविष्टाम् । और्णुविष्ट । और्णविष्ट । और्णुविष्यत । और्णविष्यत ।

इत्यदादयः ॥

No. 642.—When *sich* (No. 472) follows, preceded by the augment *iṭ* (No. 433), the *parasmaipada* terminations being employed, then *vriddhi* is OPTIONALLY the substitute OF the verb ÚRNU "to cover." On the other alternative, *guṇa* is the substitute. Thus *aurṇávít* (No. 480) or *aurṇavít* or *aurṇuvít* (No. 640) "he covered," *aurṇávishṭám* or *aurṇavishṭám* or *aurṇuvishṭám* "they two covered," *aurṇuvishṭa* (Nos. 640 and 220) or *aurṇavishṭa* (No. 420) "he covered," *aurṇuvishyata* or *aurṇavishyata* "he would cover."

So much for the 2nd class of verbs, "*ad*, &c."

The first verb in the 3rd class is *hu* "to sacrifice or eat."

। जुहोत्यादयः ।

हु दानादनयोः । १ ।

जुहोत्यादिभ्यः श्लुः । २ । ४ । ७५ ।

शपः ।

No. 643.—Let ŚLU (one of the blanks enumerated in No. 209) be substituted in the room of *śap* (No. 419) AFTER the verbs HU, &c.

श्लौ । ६ । १ । १० ।

धातोर्द्वे स्तः । जुहोति । जुहुतः ।

No. 644.—WHEN THERE IS ŚLU, there are two in the room of a verbal root—(i. e. the root is doubled). Thus *juhoti* (Nos. 488 and 420) "he sacrifices," *juhutah* (No. 535) "they two sacrifice."

अदभ्यस्तात् । ७ । १ । ४ ।

झस्य । हुश्नुवोरिति यण् । जुह्वति ।

No. 645.—There is AT in the room of the *jh* (of a tense-affix) AFTER A REDUPLICATED verb. By No. 536, which debars No. 220, the semi-vowel is substituted for the final of the root, and we have *juhwati* "they sacrifice."

भीह्रीभृहुवां श्लुवच्च । ३ । १ । ३९ ।

एभ्यो लिट्याम् वा स्यादामि श्लाविव कार्यं च । जुहवांचकार । जुहाव । होता । होष्यति । जुहोतु । जुहुतात् । जुहुताम् । जुह्वतु । जुहुधि । जुहवानि । अजुहोत् । अजुहुताम् ।

No. 646.—*Ám* may optionally be affixed, when *liṭ* comes after these verbs viz. BHÍ "to fear," HRÍ "to be ashamed," BHṚI "to nourish," AND HU "to sacrifice;" AND, when *ám* is affixed, the effect is to be AS IF THERE WERE ŚLU (i. e. there is to be reduplication—No. 644). Thus *juhavánchakára* or *juháva* (Nos. 426 and 202) "he sacrificed," *hotá* (No. 435) "he will sacrifice," *hoshyati* "he will sacrifice," *juhotu* "let him sacrifice," *juhutát* (No. 444) "may he sacrifice," *juhutám* "let the two sacrifice," *juhwatu* (Nos.

645 and 536) "let them sacrifice," *juhudhi* (No. 593) "do thou sacrifice," *juhaváni* (No. 450) "let me sacrifice," *ajuhot* "he sacrificed," *ajuhutám* "they two sacrificed."

जुसि च। ७। ३। ८३।

इगन्ताङ्गस्य गुणोऽजादौ जुसि। अजुहवुः। जुहुयात्। हूयात्। अहौषीत्। अहोष्यत्। ञिभी भये। २। बिभेति।

No. 647.—AND WHEN JUS (No. 481), beginning with a vowel, FOLLOWS, then *guṇa* is the substitute of an inflective base that ends in an *ik* vowel. Thus *ajuhavuh* "they sacrificed," *juhuyát* "he may sacrifice," *húyát* (Nos. 465 and 466) "may he sacrifice," *ahaushít* (Nos. 472, 479, and 519) "he sacrificed," *ahoshyat* "he would sacrifice."

The verb *bhí (ṅibhí)* "to fear" makes *bibheti* (No. 644) "he fears."

भियोऽन्यतरस्याम्। ६। ४। ११५।

इः स्याद्धलादौ क्ङिति सार्वधातुके। बिभितः। बिभीतः। बिभ्यति। बिभयांचकार। बिभाय। भेता। भेष्यति। बिभेतु। बिभितात्। बिभीतात्। अबिभेत्। बिभियात्। बिभीयात्। भीयात्। अभैषीत्। अभेष्यत्। ह्री लज्जायाम्। ३। जिह्रेति। जिह्रीतः। जिह्रियति। जिह्रयांचकार। जिह्राय। ह्रेता। ह्रेष्यति। जिह्रेतु। अजिह्रेत्। जिह्रीयात्। ह्रीयात्। अह्रैषीत्। अह्रेष्यत्। पॄ पालनपूरणयोः। ४।

No. 648.—When a *sárvadhátuka* affix follows, beginning with a consonant and having an indicatory *k* or *ń* (No. 535), *i* may OPTIONALLY be the substitute OF the verb BHÍ "to fear." Thus *bibhitah* or *bibhítah* "they two fear," *bibhyati* (No. 645) "they fear," *bibhayáńchakára* (No. 646) or *bibháya* "he feared," *bhetá* "he will fear," *bheshyati* "he will fear," *bibhetu* "let him fear," *bibhitát* (Nos. 444 and 648) or *bibhítát* "may he fear," *abibhet* "he feared," *bibhiyát* (No. 648) or *bibhíyát* "he may fear," *bhíyát* (Nos. 465 and 466) "may he fear," *abhaishít* (Nos. 472, 479, and 519) "he feared," *abheshyat* "he would fear."

The verb *hrí* "to be ashamed" makes *jihreti* (No. 644) "he is ashamed," *jihrítah* "they two are ashamed," *jihriyati* (No. 645) "they are ashamed," *jihrayáñchakára* (No. 646) or *jihráya* "he was ashamed," *hretá* "he will be ashamed," *hreshyati* "he will be ashamed," *jihretu* "let him be ashamed," *ajihret* "he was ashamed," *jihríyát* "he may be ashamed," *hríyát* (Nos. 465 and 466) "may he be ashamed," *ahraishít* (Nos. 472, 479, and 519) "he was ashamed," *ahreshyat* "he would be ashamed."

The verb *pṛí* "to nourish or fill" is next to be conjugated.

अर्तिपिपर्त्योश्च । ७ । ४ । ७७ ।

अभ्यासस्य इः स्याच्छ्लौ । पिपर्ति ।

No. 649.—When there is *ślu* (No. 643), let *i* (see No. 508) be the substitute of the vowel of the reduplicate OF the verbs ṚI "to go," AND PṚÍ "to fill." Thus *piparti* "he fills."

उदोष्ठ्यपूर्वस्य । ७ । १ । १०२ ।

अङ्गावयवौष्ठ्यपूर्वो य ॠत् तदन्तस्याङ्गस्य उः ।

No. 650.—Let there be U in the room OF that inflective base which ends in *ṛí*, PRECEDED BY A LABIAL which is a portion of the base. [Thus, when we have *pṛí + tas*, this rule applies, and also No. 37 which makes the base end in *r*.]

हलि च । ८ । २ । ७७ ।

रेफवान्तस्य धातोरुपधाया इको दीर्घो हलि । पिपूर्तः । पिपुरति । पपार ।

No. 651.—AND WHEN A CONSONANT FOLLOWS, the long vowel is the substitute of an *ik* vowel being the penultimate letter of a verb which ends in *r* or *v*. Thus *pipúrtah* (No. 650) "they two fill," *pipurati* (No. 645) "they fill," *papára* (Nos. 426, 508, 202, and 37) "he filled."

शॄदॄप्रां ह्रस्वो वा । ७ । ४ । १२ ।

किति लिटि । पप्रतुः ।

No. 652.—When a substitute of *liṭ*, with an indicatory *k*, follows, A SHORT vowel is OPTIONALLY the substitute OF ŚṚÍ "to hurt," DṚÍ "to tear," AND PṚÍ "to fill." (This debars No. 653, and we have optionally) *papratuh* (No. 21) "they two filled."

ऋच्छत्यॄताम् । ७ । ४ । ११ ।

तौदादिक ऋच्छेर्ऋधातोॠदन्तानां च गुणो लिटि । पपरतुः । पपरुः ।

No. 653.—When *liṭ* follows, *guṇa* is the substitute OF the verb ṚICHCHH "to go," that belongs to the 6th class (*tud,* &c. No. 693), and of the verb ṚI "to go," AND of those that end in the long vowel ṚÍ. Thus (on the alternative allowed by No. 652) *paparatuh* "they two filled," *paparuh* "they filled."

वॄतो वा । ७ । २ । ३८ ।

वृङ्वृञ्भ्यामॄदन्ताच्चेटो दीर्घो वा स्यान्न तु लिटि । परीता । परिता । परीष्यति । परिष्यति । पिपर्तु । अपिपः । अपिपूर्ताम् । अपिपरुः । पिपूर्यात् । पूर्यात् । अपारीत् ।

No. 654.—There may be OPTIONALLY a long vowel in the room of the augment *iṭ* (No. 433) coming AFTER the verbs VṚIŃ "to serve," and VṚIÑ "to choose," AND those that end in long ṚÍ, but not when *liṭ* follows. Thus *parítá* or *paritá* "he will fill," *paríshyati* or *parishyati* "he will fill," *pipartu* "let him fill," *apipah* (Nos. 420, 199, and 110) "he filled," *apipúrtám* (Nos. 650 and 652) "they two filled," *apiparuh* (Nos. 481 and 647) "they filled," *pipúryát* (No. 651) "he may fill," *púryát* (No. 465) "may he fill," *apárít* (No. 519) "he filled."

सिचि च परस्मैपदेषु । ७ । २ । ४० ।

अत्रेटो न दीर्घः । अपारिष्टाम् । अपरीष्यत् । अपरिष्यत् ।

ओहाक् त्यागे । ५ । जहाति ।

No. 655—AND WHEN SICH (No. 472) FOLLOWS, AND THE PARASMAIPADA terminations—here there is not a long vowel in the room of the augment *iṭ* (—see No. 654). Thus *apárishṭám* (No. 519) "they two filled," *aparíshyat* (No. 654) or *aparishyat* "he would fill."

The verb *há (ohák)* "to quit" makes *jaháti* (No 644).

जहातेश्च । ६ । ४ । ११६ ।

इद्वा स्याद्धलादौ क्ङिति सार्वधातुके । जहितः ।

No. 656—AND short *i* shall be optionally the substitute OF the verb HÁ "to quit," when a *sárvadhátuka* affix follows, beginning with a consonant and having an indicatory *k* or *ń*. Thus *jahitah* (No. 535) "they two quit."

ई हल्यघोः । ६ । ४ । ११३ ।

श्नाभ्यस्तयोरात ईत् सार्वधातुके क्ङिति हलि । जहीतः ।

No. 657.—Let í be the substitute of the *á* of *śná* (No. 730), or OF a reduplicated verb not being one of those called GHU (No. 662), WHEN a *sárvadhátuka* affix, having an indicatory *k* or *ń* and beginning with A CONSONANT, FOLLOWS. Thus (on the alternative allowed by No. 656) *jahítah* "they two quit."

श्नाभ्यस्तयोरातः । ६ । ४ । ११२ ।

लोपः क्ङिति । जहति । जहौ । हाता । हास्यति । जहातु । जहितात् । जहीतात् ।

No. 658.—Let there be elision OF THE Á OF ŚNÁ (No. 730), AND OF A REDUPLICATED VERB, when an affix, with an indicatory *k* or *ń*, follows. Thus *jahati* (No. 645) "they quit," *jahau* (No. 523) "he quitted," *hátá* "he will quit," *hásyati* "he will quit," *jahátu* "let him quit," *jahitát* (Nos. 444 and 656) or *jahítát* (No. 657) "may he quit."

आ च हौ । ६ । ४ । ११७ ।

जहातेः । चादिदीतौ । जहाहि । जहिहि । जहीहि । अजहात् । अजहुः ।

No. 659.—AND WHEN HI (No. 447) FOLLOWS, the substitute for the *á* of the verb *há* "to quit" is Á, or *i* (No. 656), or *í* (No. 657). Thus *jaháhi*, or *jahihi*, or *jahíhi* "do thou quit," *ajahát* "he quitted," *ajahuh* (Nos. 481 and 658) "they quitted."

लोपो यि । ६ । ४ । ११८ ।

जहातेरालेापेा यादै। सार्वधातुके । जह्यात् । एर्लिङि । हेयात् । अहासीत् । अहास्यत् । माङ् माने शब्दे च । ६ ।

No. 660.—There is ELISION of the á of the verb há "to quit," WHEN a sárvadhátuka affix, beginning with Y, FOLLOWS. Thus jahyát (No. 460) "he may quit;" but when the affix is árdhadhátuka (No. 465), then e is substituted by No. 525, giving heyát "may he quit," ahásít (Nos. 479, 480, and 530) "he quitted," ahásyat "he would quit."

The verb má (máń) "to measure or sound" is next to be conjugated.

भृञामित् ।७।४।७६।

भृञ् माङ् ओहाङ् एषामभ्यासस्येत् स्याच्छ्लौ । मिमीते । मिमाते । मिमते । ममे । माता । मास्यते । मिमीताम् । अमिमीत । मिमीत । मासीष्ट । अमास्त । अमास्यत । ओहाङ् गतौ । ७ । जिहीते । जिहाते । जिहते । जहे । हाता । हास्यते । जिहीताम् । अजिहीत । जिहीत । हासीष्ट । अहास्त । अहास्यत । डुभृञ् धारणपोषणयोः । ८ । बिभर्त्ति । बिभृतः । बिभ्रति । बिभृते । बिभ्राते । बिभ्रते । बिभरांचकार । बभार । बभर्थ । बभृव । बिभरांचक्रे । बभ्रे । भर्त्ता । भरिष्यति । भरिष्यते । बिभर्तु । बिभराणि । बिभृताम् । अबिभः । अबिभृताम् । अबिभरुः । बिभृयात् । बिभ्रीत । भ्रियात् । भृषीष्ट । अभार्षीत् । अभृत । अभरिष्यत् । अभरिष्यत । डुदाञ् दाने । ६ । ददाति । दत्तः । ददति । दत्ते । ददाते । ददते । ददौ । ददे । दाता । दास्यति । दास्यते । ददातु ।

No. 661.—When there is ślu (No. 643), let I be the substitute of the vowel of the reduplicate syllable OF these verbs—viz. BHṚI "to nourish," má "to measure," and há (oháń) "to go." Thus mimíte (No. 657) "he measures," mimáte (No. 658) "they two measure," mimate (No. 645) "they measure," mame (Nos. 548 and 426) "he measured," mátá "he will measure," másyate "he will measure," mimítám (Nos 552 and 657) "let him measure," *amimíta* "he measured," *mimíta* (Nos. 555 and 658) "he may measure," *másíshṭa* (No. 558) "may he measure," *amásta* (No. 472) "he measured," *amásyata* "he would measure."

The verb *há* (*oháṅ*) "to go" makes *jihíte* (No. 657) "he goes," *jiháte* (No. 658) "they two go," *jihate* (Nos. 645 and 658) "they go," *jahe* (Nos. 548 and 426) "he went," *hátá* "he will go," *hásyate* "he will go," *jihítám* "let him go," *ajihíta* "he went," *jihíta* (Nos. 555 and 658) "he may go," *hásíshṭa* (No. 558) "may he go," *ahásta* (No. 472) "he went," *ahásyata* "he would go."

The verb *bhṛi* (*ḍubhṛiṅ*) "to hold or nourish" makes *bibharti* "he nourishes," *bibhṛitah* "they two nourish," *bibhrati* (No. 645) "they nourish," *bibhṛite* "he nourishes," *bibhráte* "they two nourish," *bibhrate* "they nourish," *bibharáṅchakára* (No. 646) or *babhára* (Nos. 508 and 202) "he nourished," *babhartha* "thou didst nourish," *babhṛiva* (No. 514) "we two nourished," *bibharáṅchakre* or *babhre* (No. 548) "he nourished," *bhartá* (No. 510) "he will nourish," *bharishyati* (No. 532) or *bharishyate* "he will nourish," *bibhartu* "let him nourish," *bibharáṇi* "let me nourish," *bibhṛitám* "let him nourish," *abibhah* (Nos. 420, 199, and 110) "he nourished," *abibhṛitám* "they two nourished," *abibharuh* (Nos. 481 and 647) "they nourished," *bibhṛiyát* or *bibhríta* (No. 555) "he may nourish," *bhriyát* (No. 465) or *bhṛishíshṭa* (No. 558) "may he nourish," *abhárshít* (No. 519) or *abhṛita* (No. 582) "he nourished," *abharishyat* or *abharishyata* "he would nourish."

The verb *dá* (*ḍudáṅ*) "to give" makes *dadáti* "he gives," *dattah* (No. 658) "they two give," *dadati* (No. 645) "they give," *datte* "he gives," *dadáte* "they two give," *dadate* (No. 645) "they give," *dadau* (No. 523) or *dade* (No. 548) "he gave," *dátá* "he will give," *dásyati* or *dásyate* "he will give," *dadátu* "let him give."

दाधा घ्वदाप् । १ । १ । २० ।

दारूपा धारूपाश्च धातवो घुसंज्ञाः स्यदाप्दैपौ विना । घ्वसोरित्येत्वम् । देहि । दत्तम् । अददात् । अदत्त । दद्यात् । ददीत । देयात् । दासीष्ट । अदात् । अदाताम् । अदुः ।

No. 662.—Let roots of the form of DÁ "to give" (meaning that root itself both in the third and first conjugations), *do* "to cut," and *de* "to protect," AND of the form of DHÁ "to hold," (viz. *dhá* itself and *dhe* "to drink)," EXCLUSIVE OF *dá* (DÁP) "to cut," and *dai (daip)* "to purify," be called GHU. By No. 614, the substitution of *e* is directed when *hi* follows a *ghu*—so we have *dehi* "give thou," *dattam* (No. 658) "do you two give," *adadát* or *adatta* (No. 658) "he gave," *dadyát* (No. 460) or *dadíta* (Nos. 555 and 658) "he may give," *deyát* (No. 525) or *dásíshṭa* (No. 558) "may he give," *adát* (No. 473) "he gave," *adátám* "they two gave," *aduh* (No. 524) "they gave."

स्थाघ्वोरिच्च । १ । २ । १७ ।

अनयोरिदन्तादेशः सिच्च किदात्मनेपदे । अदित । अदास्यत् । अदास्यत । डुधाञ् धारणपोषणयोः । १० । दधाति ।

No. 663.—AND SHORT I shall be the substitute OF the final of SHṬHÁ "to stand," AND of a verb termed GHU (No. 662), and the *sich* shall be as if it had an indicatory *k*, when the *átmanepada* terminations are employed. Thus, the root ending in a short vowel, we have *adita* (No. 582) "he gave," *adásyat* "he would give," *adásyata* "he would give."

The verb *dhá (ḍudhán̄)* "to hold or nurture" makes *dadháti* "he holds."

दधस्तथोश्च । ८ । २ । ३८ ।

द्विरुक्तस्य झषन्तस्य धाञो बशो भष् तथोः स्ध्वोश्च परतः । धत्तः । दधति । दधासि । धत्थः । धत्ते । दधाते । दधते । धत्से । धद्ध्वे । ध्वसोरेद्धावभ्यासलोपश्च । धेहि । अदधात् । अधत्त । दध्यात् । दधीत । धेयात् । धासीष्ट । अधात् । अधित । अधास्यत् । अधास्यत । णिजिर् शौचपोषणयोः । ११ ।

No. 664.—Let there be a *bhash* (i. e. an aspirated letter) in the room of the *baś* (i. e. the initial *d* No. 431) OF the reduplicated verb DHÁ "to hold," ending in a *jhash* (i. e. in *dh*), WHEN T OR TH AND when *s* or *dhw* follows. Thus we have *dhattah* (No. 658) "they two hold," *dadhati* (No. 645) "they hold," *dadhási* "thou holdest," *dhatthah* (No. 664) "you two hold," *dhatte* (No. 543) "he holds," *dadháte* "they two hold," *dadhate* (No. 645) "they hold," *dhatse* "thou holdest," *dhaddhwe* "you hold." According to No. 614, when *hi* follows, *e* is substituted for the vowel of the root, which is a *ghu* (No. 662), and the reduplication is elided :—so that we have *dhehi* "do thou hold," *adadhát* "he held," *adhatta* (Nos. 658 and 664) "he held," *dadhyát* (Nos. 460 and 658) or *dadhíta* (Nos. 555 and 658) "he may hold," *dheyát* (No. 525) or *dhásíshṭa* (No. 558) "may he hold," *adhát* (No. 473) or *adhita* (Nos. 663 and 582) "he held," *adhásyat* or *adhásyata* "he would hold."

The verb *ṇij (ṇijir)* "to purify or to nurture" is next to be conjugated.

इर इत्संज्ञा वाच्या ।

No. 665.—"In respect OF the syllable IR (e. g. in the verb *nijir*) THE DESIGNATION IT (No. 7) IS TO BE PREDICATED."

निजां त्रयाणां गुणः श्लौ । ७ । ४ । ७५ ।

निज्विज्विषामभ्यासस्य गुणः श्लौ । नेनेक्ति । नेनिक्तः । नेनिजति । नेनिक्ते । निनेज । निनिजे । नेक्ता । नेक्ष्यति । नेक्ष्यते । नेनेक्तु । नेनिग्धि ।

No. 666.—Let GUṆA be the substitute of the reduplicate OF THE THREE verbs ṆIJ "to purify," *vij* "to differ," and *vish* "to pervade," WHEN THERE IS ŚLU (No. 643). Thus *nenekti* (Nos. 485 and 333) "he purifies," *neniktah* (No. 535) "they two purify," *nenijati* (No. 645) "they purify," *nenikte* (No. 535) "he purifies," *nineja* (No. 426) or *ninije* (No. 548) "he purified," *nektá* "he will purify," *nekshyati* (No. 169) or *nekshyate* "he will purify," *nenektu* "let him purify," *nenigdhi* (Nos. 593 and 333) "do thou purify."

नाभ्यस्तस्याचि पिति सार्वधातुके । ७ । ३ । ८७ ।

लघूपधगुणो न । नेनिजानि । नेनिक्ताम् । अनेनेक् । अनेनिक्ताम् । अनेनिजुः । अनेनिजम् । अनेनिक्त । नेनिज्यात् । निज्यात् । नेनिजीत । निक्षीष्ट ।

No. 667.—*Guṇa* is NOT the substitute OF A REDUPLICATED

VERB with a light (No. 482) penultimate letter, **WHEN A SÁRVADHÁTUKA** affix, beginning with a **VOWEL** and **HAVING AN INDICATORY P, FOLLOWS.** This debars No. 485, and we have *nenijáni* (No. 666) "let me purify," *neniktám* (No. 552) "let him purify," *anenek* (No. 199) "he purified," *aneniktám* "they two purified," *anenijuh* (No. 481) "they purified," *anenijam* "I purified," *anenikta* "he purified," *nenijyát* "he may purify," *nijyát* (No. 465) "may he purify," *nenijíta* (No. 555) "he may purify," *nikshíshṭa* (No. 558) "may he purify."

इरितो वा । ३ । १ । ५७ ।

इरितो धातोश्च्लेरङ् वा परस्मैपदेषु । अनिजत् । अनैक्षीत् । अनिक्त । अनेक्ष्यत् । अनेक्ष्यत ।

इति जुहोत्यादयः ॥

No. 668.—*Aṅ* **IS OPTIONALLY** the substitute of *chli* (No. 471) **AFTER** what root has **AN INDICATORY IR** (No. 665), when the *parasmaipada* terminations are employed. Thus *anijat* or *anaikshít* (Nos. 472, 499, and 510) or *anikta* (No. 513) "he purified," *anekshyat* or *anekshyata* "he would purify."

So much for the 3rd class of verbs, "*hu*, &c." The verbs of the 4th class—"*div, &c.*"—are next to be conjugated.

The verb *div (divu)* signifies "to play, to be ambitious of surpassing, to traffic, to shine, to praise, to rejoice, to be mad, to sleep, to love, and to go."

। दिवादयः ।

दिवु क्रीडाविजिगीषाव्यवहारद्युतिस्तुतिमोदमदस्वप्नकान्तिगतिषु । १ ।

दिवादिभ्यः श्यन् । ३ । १ । ६९ ।

शपोऽपवादः । हलि चेति दीर्घः । दीव्यति । दिदेव । देविता । देविष्यति । दीव्यतु । अदीव्यत् । दीव्येत् । दीव्यात् । अदेवीत् । अदेविष्यत् । एवं षिवु तन्तुसंताने । २ । नृती गात्रविक्षेपे । ३ । नृत्यति । ननर्त । नर्तिता ।

No. 669.—AFTER the verbs DIV "to play," &c., let there be ŚYAN. This debars *śap* (No. 419). According to No. 651, the vowel is lengthened when a consonant follows the *v*, and we have *dívyati* "he plays," *dideva* (No. 485) "he played," *devitá* "he will play," *devishyati* "he will play," *dívyatu* (No. 651) "let him play," *adívyat* "he played," *dívyet* (No. 463) "he may play," *dívyát* (No. 465) "may he play," *adevít* (No. 480) "he played," *adevishyat* "he would play." In the same way is conjugated the verb *shiv (shivu)* "to sew."

The verb *nṛit (nṛití)* "to toss about one's body—i. e. to dance," makes *nṛityati* "he dances," *nanarta* (Nos. 508 and 485) "he danced," *nartitá* "he will dance."

सेऽसिचि कृतचृतच्छृदतृदनृतः । ७ । २ । ५७ ।

एभ्यः सिज्भिन्नस्य सादेरार्धधातुकस्येड्वा । नर्तिष्यति । नर्त्स्यति । नृत्यतु । अनृत्यत् । नृत्येत् । नृत्यात् । अनर्तीत् । अनर्तिष्यत् । अनर्त्स्यत् । त्रसी उद्वेगे । ४ । वा भ्राशेति श्यन् वा । त्रस्यति । त्रसति । तत्रास ।

No. 670.—*Iṭ* (No. 433) is optionally the augment of an *árdhadhátuka* affix, WHEN IT BEGINS WITH the letter S OTHER THAN the *s* of SICH (No. 472), coming AFTER these verbs—viz. KṚIT "to cut," CHṚIT "to hurt," CHHṚID "to light," TṚID "to kill," AND NṚIT "to dance." Thus *nartishyati* or *nartsyati* "he will dance," *nṛityatu*," "let him dance," *anṛityat* "he danced," *nṛityet* "he may dance," *nṛityát* "may he dance," *anartít* (No. 480) "he danced," *anartishyat* (No. 670) or *anartsyat* "he would dance."

The verb *tras (trasí)* "to fear," according to No. 520, optionally takes the affix *śyan* (No. 669). Thus we have *trasyati* or *trasati* (No. 419) "he fears," *tatrása* "he feared."

वा जॄभ्रमुत्रसाम् । ६ । ४ । १२४ ।

एषां क्किति लिटि सेटि थलि च एत्वाभ्यासलोपौ वा । त्रेसतुः । तत्रसतुः । त्रेसिथ । तत्रसिथ । त्रसिता । शो तनूकरणे । ५ ।

No. 671.—There is OPTIONALLY the substitution of *e*, and

elision of the reduplicate syllable, OF these verbs—viz. JṚÍ "to grow old," BHRAM "to whirl," AND TRAS "to fear," when *liṭ*, with an indicatory *k* (No. 486), and likewise when *thal*, with the augment *iṭ* (No. 433), follows. Thus *tresatuh* or *tatrasatuh* "they two feared," *tresitha* "or *tatrasitha* "thou didst fear," *trasitá* "he will fear."

The verb *śo* "to pare" is next to be conjugated.

ओतः श्यनि । ७ । ३ । ७१ ।

लोपः स्यात् श्यनि । श्यति । श्यतः । श्यन्ति । शशौ । शशतुः । शशुः । शाता । शास्यति ।

No. 672.—Let there be elision OF O, WHEN ŚYAN (No. 669) FOLLOWS. Thus *śyati* "he pares," *śyatah* "they two pare," *śyanti* "they pare," *śaśau* (Nos. 528 and 523) "he pared," *śaśatuh* (No. 524) "they two pared," *śaśuh* (Nos. 528 and 524) "they pared," *śátá* (No. 528) "he will pare," *śásyati* "he will pare."

विभाषा घ्राधेट्शाच्छासः । २ । ४ । ७८ ।

एभ्यः सिचो लुग्वा परस्मैपदेषु । अशात् । अशाताम् । अशुः ।

No. 673.—There is OPTIONALLY elision of *sich* (No. 472) AFTER these verbs—viz. GHRÁ "to smell," DHE "to drink," ŚO "to pare," CHHO "to cut," AND SHO "to destroy," when the *parasmaipada* terminations are employed. Thus *aśát* "he pared," *aśátám* "they two pared," *aśuh* (No. 524) "they pared."

यमरमनमातां सक् च । ७ । २ । ७३ ।

एषां सगेभ्यः सिच इट् परस्मैपदेषु । इट्सकौ । अशासीत् । अशासिष्टाम् । छो छेदने । ६ । छ्यति । षो अन्तकर्मणि । ७ । स्यति । ससौ । दो अवखण्डने । ८ । द्यति । ददौ । देयात् । अदात् । व्यध ताडने । ६ ।

No. 674.—AND SAK shall be the augment of these verbs—viz.—YAM "to restrain," RAM "to sport," ṆAM "to bow," AND those that end in LONG Á, and, at the same time, *iṭ* shall be the augment of the *sich* (No. 472) coming after them, when the *parasmaipada* terminations are employed. Applying then these two augments, *iṭ* and *sak*, we have *aśásít* "he pared," *aśásishṭám* "they two pared."

The verb *chho* "to cut" makes *chhyati* (No. 672) "he cuts."

The verb *sho* "to destroy" makes *syati* "he destroys," *sasau* (No. 528) "he destroyed." The verb *do* "to cut" makes *dyati* "he cuts," *dadau* "he cut," *deyát* (No. 525) "may he cut." *adát* (No. 473) "he cut."

The verb *vyadh (vyadha)* "to strike" is next to be conjugated.

ग्रहिज्यावयिव्यधिवष्टिविचतिवृश्चतिपृच्छतिभृज्जतीनां ङिति च । ६ । १ । १६ ।

एषां संप्रसारणं स्यात् किति ङिति च । विध्यति । विव्याध । विविधतुः । विविधुः । विव्यधिथ । विव्यद्ध । व्यद्धा । व्यत्स्यति । विध्येत् । विध्यात् । अव्यात्सीत् । पुष पुष्टौ । १० । पुष्यति । पुपोष । पुपोषिथ । पोष्टा । पोक्ष्यति । पुषादीत्यङ् । अपुषत् । शुष शोषणे । ११ । शुष्यति । शुशोष । अशुषत् । णश अदर्शने । १२ । नश्यति । ननाश । नेशतुः ।

No. 675.—AND let there be a *saṅprasárana* (No. 281) in the room (of the semi-vowel) OF these verbs—viz. GRAH "to take," JYÁ "to become old," VAY (the substitute of *ve*) "to weave," VYADH "to strike," VAŚ "to subdue," VYACH "to deceive," VRAŚCH "to cut," PRACHCHH "to ask," AND BHRASJ "to fry," WHEN WHAT affix HAS AN INDICATORY *k* or Ṅ FOLLOWS. Thus, the affix *śyan* being regarded as having an indicatory *ṅ* (No. 535), we have *vidhyati* (No. 283) "he strikes," *vivyádha* (No. 583) "he struck," *vividhatuh* "they two struck," *vividhuh* "they struck," *vivyadhitha* (No. 517) or *vivyaddha* (No. 586) "thou didst strike," *vyaddhá* (No. 586) "he will strike," *vyatsyati* "he will strike," *vidhyet* (Nos. 462 and 460) "he may strike," *vidhyát* (No. 465) "may he strike," *avyátsít* (No. 479) "he struck."

The verb *push (pusha)* "to nourish" makes *pushyati* "he nourishes," *puposha* (No. 485) "he nourished," *puposhitha* (No. 517) "thou didst nourish," *poshṭá* (No. 78) "he will nourish," *pokshyati* (No. 585) "he will nourish." In accordance with No. 542, this verb takes *aṅ* instead of *chli* (No. 471). Thus *apushat* "he nourished."

The verb *śush (śusha)* "to become dry" makes *śushyati* "he dries," *śuśosha* "he dried," *aśushat* (No. 542) "he dried."

The verb *ṇaś (ṇaśa)* "to perish" makes *naśyati* "he perishes," *nanáśa* "he perished," *neśatuh* (No. 494) "they two perished."

रधादिभ्यश्च ।७।२।४५।
वलाद्यार्धधातुकस्य वेट् । नेशिथ ।

No. 676.—AND after the verbs RADH "to hurt," &c., let *iṭ* (No. 433) be optionally the augment of an *árdhadhátuka* affix, beginning with a *val*. Thus *neśitha* (No. 495) "thou didst perish."

मस्जिनशोर्झलि ।७।१।६०।
नुम् । ननंष्ठ । नेशिव । नेशिम । नशिता । नंष्टा । नशिष्यति । नंक्ष्यति । नश्यतु । अनश्यत् । नश्येत् । नश्यात् । अनशत् । षूङ् प्राणिप्रसवे । १३ । सूयते । सुषुवे । क्रादिनियमादिट् । सुषुविषे । सुषुविवहे । सुषुविमहे । सोता । सविता । दूङ् परितापे । १४ । दूयते । दीङ् क्षये । १५ । दीयते ।

No. 677.—WHEN A JHAL comes AFTER the verbs MASJ "to be immersed," AND ṆAŚ "to perish," let there be the augment *num*. Thus, on the alternative allowed by No. 676, we have *nananshṭha* (No. 334) "thou didst perish," *neśiva* (No. 494) we two perished," *neśima* "we perished," *naśitá* (No. 676) or *nanshṭá* "he will perish," *naśishyati* or *nankshyati* (Nos. 334 and 585) "he will perish," *naśyatu* "let him perish," *anaśyat* "he perished," *naśyet* "he may perish," *naśyát* "may he perish," *anaśat* (No. 542) "he perished."

The verb *shú (shúṅ)* "to give birth to" makes *súyate* (No. 543) "she bears," *sushuve* (No. 220) "she bore." In accordance with the restrictive rule No. 514, this verb takes the augment *iṭ* :—thus *sushuvishe* "thou borest," *sushuvivahe* "we two bore," *sushuvimahe* "we bore," *sotá* or *savitá* (No. 511) "she will bear."

The verb *dú (dúṅ)* "to suffer or be consumed with pain" makes *dúyate* "he suffers;" and *dí (díṅ)* "to decay" makes *díyate* "he decays."

दीङो युडचि क्ङिति । ६ । ४ । ६३ ।

दीङः परस्याजादेः क्ङिदार्धधातुकस्य युट् ।

No. 678.—Let YUṬ be the augment, WHEN an *árdhadhátuka* affix, WITH AN INDICATORY K OR Ń and beginning with A VOWEL, COMES AFTER the verb Dí *(dín)* "to decay."

वुग्युटावुवङ्यणोः सिद्धौ वक्तव्यौ । दिदीये ।

No. 679.—"The augments VUK (No. 425) AND YUṬ (No. 678) ARE (in spite of No. 599) TO BE REGARDED AS HAVING TAKEN EFFECT, WHEN the substitute UVAŃ (No. 220) or a YAṆ (No. 221) PRESENTS ITSELF. Thus we have *didíye* "he decayed"—[the *yuṭ* being recognised as existent by No. 220, which would otherwise have taken effect here.]

मीनातिमिनोतिदीङां ल्यपि च । ६ । १ । ५० ।

एषामात्वं ल्यपि । चादशित्येज्निमित्ते । दाता । दास्यति । अदास्त । डीङ् विहायसा गतौ । १६ । डीयते । डिड्ये । डयिता । पीङ् पाने । १७ । पीयते । पेता । अपेष्ट । माङ् माने । १८ । मायते । ममे । जनी प्रादुर्भावे । १६ ।

No. 680.—AND WHEN the affix LYAP (No. 941) FOLLOWS, there is the substitution OF Á in the room OF these verbs, viz. Mí *(mín)* "to hurt or kill," MI *(ḍumin)* "to scatter," AND Dí *(dín)* "to decay." By the "*and*" it is implied that the same change will take place when there is a cause for the substitution of an *ech*, but unattended by an indicatory *ś*. Hence [the affixes *tási* and *sya* being such causes] we have *dátá* "he will decay," *dásyati* "he will decay," *adásta* "he decayed."

The verb *ḍí (ḍín)* "to move in the sky—i.e. to fly," makes *ḍíyate* "he flies," *ḍiḍye* (No. 221) "he flew," *ḍayitá* "he will fly."

The verb *pí (pín)* "to drink" makes *píyate* "he drinks," *petá* (No. 510) "he will drink," *apeshṭa* "he drank."

The verb *má (mán)* "to measure" makes *máyate* "he measures," *mame* "he measured."

The next verb is *jan (janí)* "to be produced or born."

ज्ञाजनोर्जा । ७ । ३ । ७९ ।

शिति । जायते । जज्ञे । जनिता । जनिष्यते ।

No. 681.—OF the verbs JÑYÁ "to know," AND JAN "to be produced," JÁ is the substitute, when what follows has an indicatory *ś*. Thus *jáyate* "he is produced," *jajñe* (Nos. 540 and 76) "he was produced," *janitá* "he will be produced," *janishyate* "he will be produced."

दीपजनबुधपूरितायिप्यायिभ्योऽन्यतरस्याम् । ३ । १ । ६१ ।

एभ्यश्च्लेश्चिणवा एकवचने तशब्दे परे ।

No. 682—AFTER these verbs—viz. DÍP "to shine," JAN "to be produced," BUDH "to teach," PÚR "to be full," TÁY "to extend," AND PYÁY "to swell," *chiṇ* is OPTIONALLY the substitute of *chli* (No. 471), when the termination *ta*, of the singular, follows.

चिणो लुक् । ६ । ४ । १०४ ।

चिणः परस्य लुक् ।

No. 683.—There is ELISION *(luk)* of what comes AFTER CHIṆ (No. 682).

जनिवध्योश्च । ७ । ३ । ३५ ।

अनयोर्न वृद्धिश्चिणि ञ्णिति कृति च । अजनि । अजनिष्ट । दीपी दीप्तौ । २० । दीप्यते । दिदीपे । अदीपि । अदीपिष्ट । पद गतौ । २१ । पद्यते । पेदे । पत्ता । पत्सीष्ट ।

No. 684.—In the room OF these two—viz. JAN "to be produced," AND BADH "to kill," there is not *vṛiddhi* (in spite of No. 489), when *chiṇ* (No. 682) follows, or a *kṛit* affix (No. 329) with an indicatory *ñ* or *ṇ*. Thus *ajani* or (on the alternative allowed by No 682) *ajanishṭa* "he was produced." The verb *díp (dípí)* "to shine" makes *dípyate* "he shines," *didípe* "he shone," *adípi* (No. 682) or *adípishṭa* "he shone."

The verb *pad (pada)* "to go" makes *padyate* "he goes," *pede* (No. 494) "he went," *pattá* "he will go," *patsíshṭa* "may he go."

चिण् ते पदः । ३ । १ । ६० ।

पदश्च्लेश्चिण् ते परे । अपादि । अपत्साताम् । अपत्सत । विद सत्तायाम् । २२ । विद्यते । वेत्ता । अवित्त । बुध अवगमने । २३ । बुध्यते । बोद्धा । भोत्स्यते । भुत्सीष्ट । अबोधि । अबुद्ध । अभुत्साताम् । युध संप्रहारे । २४ । युध्यते । युयुधे । योद्धा । अयुद्ध । सृज विसर्गे । २५ । सृज्यते । ससृजे । ससृजिषे ।

No. 685.—Let CHIN be substituted for *chli* AFTER the verb PAD "to go," WHEN the personal termination TA (of the singular) FOLLOWS. Thus *apádi* (No 683) "he went," *apatsátám* "they two went," *apatsata* "they went."

The verb *vid (vida)* "to be" makes *vidyate* "he is," *vettá* "he will be," *avitta* (No. 626) "he was."

The verb *budh (budha)* "to understand" makes *budhyate* "he understands," *boddhá* (No. 586) "he will understand," *bhotsyate* (No. 278) "he will understand," *bhutsíshṭa* "may he understand," *abodhi* (No. 683) or *abuddha* (Nos. 586 and 626) "he understood," *abhutsátám* (No. 278) "they two understood."

The verb *yudh (yudha)* "to fight" makes *yudhyate* "he fights," *yuyudhe* "he fought," *yoddhá* (No. 586) "he will fight," *ayuddha* "he fought."

The verb *sṛij (sṛija)* "to quit" makes *sṛijyate* "he quits," *sasṛije* (No. 508) "he quitted," *sasṛijishe* "thou didst quit."

सृजिदृशोर्झल्यमकिति । ६ । १ । ५८ ।

अनयोरम् झलादावकिति । स्रष्टा । स्रक्ष्यति । सृक्षीष्ट । असृष्ट । असृक्षाताम् । मृष तितिक्षायाम् । २६ । मृष्यति । मृष्यते । ममर्ष । ममर्षिथ । ममृषिषे । मर्षितासि । मर्षितासे । मर्षिष्यति । मर्षिष्यते । णह बन्धने । २७ । नह्यति । नह्यते । ननाह । ननद्ध । नेहिथ । नेहे । नद्धा । नत्स्यति । अनात्सीत् । अनद्ध ।

No. 686.—Let AM be the augment OF these two verbs, viz. SṚIJ "to quit," AND DṚIŚ "to see," WHEN an affix, beginning with A JHAL and NOT HAVING AN INDICATORY K, FOLLOWS. Thus *srashṭá* (Nos. 334 and 78) "he will quit," *srakshyati* (Nos. 334 and 585) "he will quit," *sṛikshíshṭa* "may he quit," *asṛishṭa* "he quitted," *asṛikshátám* "they two quitted."

The verb *mṛish (mṛisha)* "to endure patiently" makes *mṛishyati* or *mṛishyate* "he endures," *mamarsha* "he endured," *mamarshitha* or *mamṛishishe* "thou didst endure," *marshitási* or *marshitáse* "thou wilt endure," *marshishyati* or *marshishyate* "he will endure."

The verb *ṇah (ṇaha)* "to bind" makes *nahyati* or *nahyate* "he binds," *nanáha* "he bound," *nanaddha* or *nehitha* "thou didst bind," *nehe* "he bound," *naddhá* "he will bind," *natsyati* (No. 389) "he will bind," *anátsít* or *anaddha* "he bound."

So much for the 4th class of verbs, "*div, &c.*"

The 5th class of verbs consists of "*su, &c.*"

The verb *su (shuṅ)* means "to extract the Soma juice."

इति दिवादयः ॥

। स्वादयः ।

षुञ् अभिषवे । १ ।

स्वादिभ्यः श्नुः । ३ । १ । ७३ ।

शपोऽपवादः । सुनोति । सुनुतः । हुश्नुवोरिति यण् । सुन्वन्ति । सुन्वः । सुनुवः । सुनुते । सुन्वाते । सुन्वते । सुन्वहे । सुनुवहे । सुषाव । सुषुवे । सोता । सुनु । सुनवानि । सुनवै । सुनुयात् । सूयात् ।

No. 687.—Let there be ŚNU AFTER the verbs SU, &c.

This debars *śap* (No. 419). Thus we have *sunoti* (No. 420) "he presses out," *sunutah* "they two press out," *sunwanti (yaṇ* taking the place of the vowel by No. 536) "they press out," *sunwah* (No. 537) or *sunuvah* "we two press out," *sunute* "he presses out," *sunwáte* "thev two press out," *sunwate* "they press out," *sunwahe* (No. 537) or *sunuvahe* "we two press out," *sushâva* or *sushuve* "he pressed out," *sotá* "he will press out," *sunu* (No. 538) "do thou press out," *sunaváni* "let me press out," *sunavai* "let me press out," *sunuyát* "he may press out," *súyát* (No. 518) "may he press out."

स्तुसुधूञ्भ्यः परस्मैपदेषु ।७।२।७२।

एभ्यः सिच इट् । असावीत् । असोष्ट । चिञ् चयने । २ । चिनोति । चिनुते ।

No. 688.—Let *iṭ* be the augment of *sich* AFTER these—viz. STU "to praise," SU "to extract the Soma juice," AND DHÚ "to shake," WHEN THE PARASMAIPADA affixes ARE EMPLOYED. Thus *asávít* or *asoshṭa* "he pressed out."

The verb *chi (chiñ)* "to gather" makes *chinoti* or *chinute* "he gathers."

विभाषा चेः ।७।३।५८।

अभ्यासाच्चेः कुत्वं वा सनि लिटि च । चिकाय । चिचाय । चिक्ये । चिच्ये । अचैषीत् । अचेष्ट । स्तृञ् आच्छादने । ३ । स्तृणोति । स्तृणुते ।

No. 689—There is OPTIONALLY the substitution of a guttural in the room OF CHI "to gather" after a reduplicate syllable, when *san* (No. 752) or *liṭ* follows. Thus *chikáya* or *chicháya*, *chikye* or *chichye*, "he gathered," *achaishít* or *acheshṭa* "he gathered."

The verb *stṛi (stṛiñ)* "to cover" makes *stṛiṇoti* or *stṛiṇute* "he covers."

शर्पूर्वाः खयः ।७।४।६१।

अभ्यासस्य शर्पूर्वाः खयः शिष्यन्तेऽन्ये हलो लुप्यन्ते । तस्तार । तस्तरतुः । तस्तरे । गुणोऽर्तीति गुणः । स्तर्यात् ।

No. 690.—Of a reduplicate syllable the letters denoted by the *pratyáhára* KHAY, PRECEDED BY A ŚAR, remain :—the other consonants are elided. Thus *tastára* "he covered," *tastaratuh* " they two covered." *tastare* "he covered." By No. 533, there being the substitution of *guṇa*, we have *staryát* " may he cover."

ऋतश्च संयोगादेः । ७।२।४३।

ऋदन्तात् संयोगादेर्लिङ्सिचोरिड्वा । स्तरिषीष्ट । स्तृषीष्ट । अस्तरिष्ट । अस्तृत । धूञ् कम्पने । ४ । धूनोति । धूनुते । दुधाव । स्वरतीति वेट् । दुधविथ । दुधोथ ।

No. 691.—Let *iṭ* be optionally the augment of *liń* and *sich*, coming AFTER WHAT root ends in ṚI and BEGINS WITH A CONJUNCT consonant. Thus *starishíshṭa* or *stṛishíshṭa* "may he cover," *astarishṭa* or *astṛita* "he covered."

The verb *dhú (dhúń)* "to shake" makes *dhúnoti* or *dhúnute* "he shakes," *dudháva* "he shook," and optionally taking the augment *iṭ* by No. 511, *dudhavitha* or *dudhotha* " thou shookest."

श्र्युकः किति । ७।२।११।

श्रिञ एकाच उगन्ताच्च गित्किितोरिण्न । इति प्राप्ते । क्रादिनियमान्नित्यमिट् । दुधुविव । दुधुवे । अधावीत् । अधविष्ट । अधोष्ट । अधविष्यत् । अधोष्यत् । अधविष्यताम् । अधोष्यताम् । अधविष्यत । अधोष्यत ।

इति स्वादयः ॥

No. 692.—Let not *iṭ* be the augment, WHEN WHAT affix HAS AN INDICATORY *g* or K comes AFTER the verb ŚRI "to serve" OR what verb with one vowel ends in the *pratyáhára* UK. Notwithstanding this rule's having presented itself, the verb now under consideration always takes the augment *iṭ*, in accordance with the determining rule No. 514. Thus *dudhuviva* " we two shook," *dudhuve* "he shook," *adhávít* or *adhavishṭa* or *adhoshṭa* "he shook," *adhavishyat* or *adhoshyat* "he would shake," *adhavishyatám* or *adhoshyatám* "they two would shake," *adhavishyata* or *adhoshyata* "he would shake."

So much for the 5th class of verbs—"*su, &c.*"

The 6th class of verbs consists of "*tud*, &c."

The verb *tud* signifies "to torment."

। तुदादयः ।

तुद व्यथने । १ ।

तुदादिभ्यः शः । ३ । १ । ७७ ।

शपोऽपवादः । तुदति । तुदते । तुतोद । तुतोदिथ । तुतुदे । तोत्ता । अतौत्सीत् । अतुत्त । णुद प्रेरणे । २ । नुदति । नुदते । नुनोद । नोत्ता । भ्रस्ज पाके । ३ । ग्रहिज्येति संप्रसारणम् । सस्य श्चुत्वेन शः । शस्य जश्त्वेन जः । भृज्जति । भृज्जते ।

No. 693—Let there be ŚA AFTER TUD, &c. This debars *śap* (No. 419). Thus *tudati* or *tudate* "he torments," *tutoda* "he tormented," *tutoditha* "thou didst torment," *tutude* "he tormented," *tottá* "he will torment," *atautsít* or *atutta* "he tormented."

The verb *ṇud (ṇuda)* "to send" makes *nudati* or *nudate* "he sends," *nunoda* "he sent," *nottá* "he will send."

The verb *bhrasj* means "to fry."

In forming the present tense—a vowel is substituted for the semi-vowel by No. 675, then, by the substitution of a palatal for a dental (by No. 76), the *s* becomes *ś;* and, by the change of *ś* to *jaś* (by No. 25), it becomes *j*, giving *bhṛijjati* or *bhṛijjate* "he fries."

भ्रस्जो रोपधयो रमन्यतरस्याम् । ६ । ४ । ४७ ।

भ्रस्जो रेफस्योपधायाश्च स्थाने रमागमो वार्धधातुके । मित्त्वादन्त्यादचः परः । स्थानषष्ठीनिर्देशाद्रोपधयोर्निवृत्तिः । बभर्ज । बभर्जतुः । बभर्जिथ । बभर्ष्ठ । बभ्रज्ज । बभ्रज्जतुः । बभ्रज्जिथ । स्कोरिति सलोपः । व्रश्चेति षः । बभ्रष्ठ । बभर्जे । बभ्रज्जे । भर्ष्टा । भ्रष्टा । भर्क्ष्यति । भ्रक्ष्यति । क्ङिति रमागमं बाधित्वा संप्रसारणं पूर्वविप्रतिषेधेन । भृज्यात् । भृज्यास्ताम् । भृज्यासुः । भर्क्षीष्ट । भ्र-

चीष्ट । अभार्क्षीत् । अभ्राक्षीत् । अभर्ष्ट । अभ्रष्ट । कृष विलेखने । ४ । कृषति । कृषते । चकर्ष । चकृषे ।

No. 694.—In the room OF the R AND the PENULTIMATE letter OF the root BHRASJ, there shall be OPTIONALLY the augment RAM, when an *árdhadhátuka* affix follows. As it has an indicatory *m* (No. 265), the augment comes after the last vowel. [If the *ram* had been intended merely as an augment, the verb alone—not also certain letters of the verb—would have been cited in the aphorism. The citation of the letters with the 6th case-affix attached, in accordance with the aphorism I. 1 49—indicates that the augment is to act as a substitute—so that] the abolition of the *r* and of the penultimate letter takes place, in consequence of the direction implied in the 6th case-affix signifying "in the room of." Thus we have *babharja* "he fried," *babharjatuh* "they two fried," *babharjitha* or *babharshṭha* (No. 334) "thou didst fry; or, alternatively, *babhrajja* "he fried," *babhrajjatuh* "they two fried," *babhrajjitha* "thou didst fry." When a *jhal* follows, the *s* is elided by No. 337, and the final is changed to *sh* by No. 334:—thus (when the augment *iṭ* is not employed) we have *babhrashṭha* "thou didst fry," *babharje* or *babhrajje* "he fried," *bharshṭá* or *bhrashṭá* "he will fry," *bharkshyati* or *bhrakshyati* "he will fry." When an affix with an indicatory *k* or *ṅ* follows, the substitution of a vowel for the semivowel, by No. 675, takes place,—debarring the augment *ram* (No. 694) through the superior authority specially assigned to the earlier rule of the two [contrary to the general principle laid down in No. 132]—so that we have *bhṛijyát* "may he fry," *bhṛijyástám* "may they two fry," *bhṛijyásuh* "may they fry," *bharkshíshṭa* or *bhrakshíshṭa* "may he fry," *abhárkshít*, or *abhrákshít* *abharshṭa* or *abhrashṭa* "he fried."

The verb *kṛish* (*kṛisha*) "to draw or make furrows—to plough," makes *kṛishati* or *kṛishate* "he ploughs," *chakarsha* or *chakṛishe* "he ploughed."

अनुदात्तस्य चर्दुपधस्यान्यतरस्याम् । ६ । १ । ५९ ।

उपदेशेऽनुदात्तो य ऋदुपधस्तस्याम् वा झलादावकिति । क्रष्टा । कर्ष्टा । कृक्षीष्ट ।

No. 695.—When an affix follows, beginning with a *jhal* and not having an indicatory *k*, then *am* is OPTIONALLY the augment OF WHAT verb IS GRAVELY ACCENTED in its original enunciation, AND HAS the vowel ṚI AS ITS PENULT. Thus we have *krashṭá*, or, without the *am*, *karshṭá* "he will plough," *kṛikshíshṭa* "may he plough."

स्पृशमृशकृषतृपदृपेभ्यः सिज्वा वाच्यः । अक्राक्षीत् । अकार्क्षीत् । अकृक्षत् । अकृष्ट । अकृक्षाताम् । अकृक्षन्त । मिल संगमे । ५ । मिलति । मिलते । मिमेल । मेलिता । अमेलीत् । मुच्लृ मोचने । ६ ।

No. 696.—SICH SHOULD BE STATED TO BE OPTIONALLY the substitute OF CHLI AFTER the verbs SPṚIŚ "to touch," MṚIŚ "to perceive," KṚISH "to plough," TṚIP "to be satisfied," AND DṚIP "to be proud." Thus *akrákshít* (No. 695), *akárkshít* (No. 499), or *akṛikshat* (No. 627), or *akṛishṭa* "he ploughed," *akṛikshátám* "they two ploughed," *akṛikshanta* "they ploughed."

The verb *mil (mila)* "to mix" makes *milati* or *milate* "he mixes," *mimela* "he mixed," *melitá* "he will mix," *amelít* "he mixed."

The verb *much (muchlṛi)* signifies "to be free."

शे मुचादीनाम् । ७ । १ । ५९ ।

मुचलिपविदलुपसिचकृतखिदपिशां नुम् । मुञ्चति । मुञ्चते । मोक्ता । मुच्यात् । मुक्षीष्ट । अमुचत् । अमुक्त । अमुक्षाताम् । लुप्लृ छेदने । ७ । लुम्पति । लुम्पते । लोप्ता । अलुपत् । अलुप्त । विद्लृ लाभे । ८ । विन्दति । विन्दते । विवेद । विविदे । व्याघ्रभूतिमते सेट् । वेदिता । भाष्यमतेऽनिट् । परिवेत्ता । षिच क्षरणे । ९ । सिञ्चति । सिञ्चते ।

No. 697.—WHEN ŚA (No. 693) FOLLOWS, let *num* be the augment OF the verbs MUCH &C. i. e. of *much* "to be free," *lip* "to smear," *vid* "to find," *lup* "to cut," *sich* "to sprinkle," *kṛit* "to cut," *khid* "to hurt," and *piś* "to be organised." Thus *muṅchati* or *muṅchate* "he is free," *moktá* "he will be free," *muchyát* or *mukshíshṭa* "may he be free," *amuchat* or *amukta* "he was free," *amukshátám* "they two were free."

The verb *lup (luplṛi)* "to cut" makes *lumpati* or *lumpate* "he cuts," *loptá* "he will cut," *alupat* or *alupta* "he cut."

The verb *vid (vidlṛi)* "to find" makes *vindati* or *vindate* "he finds," *viveda* or *vivide* "he found." In the opinion of *Vyághrabhúti*, this verb takes the augment *iṭ*.—which would give *veditá* "he will find." According to the opinion of the *Mahábháshya*, it does not take the augment *iṭ*:—witness *parivettá* "he will become a house-holder before his elder brother."

The verb *sich (shicha)* "to sprinkle" makes *siṅchati* or *siṅchate* "he sprinkles."

लिपिसिचिह्वश्च । ३ । १ । ५३ ।

एभ्यश्च्लेरङ् । असिचत् ।

No. 698.—Let *aṅ* be the substitute for *chli* AFTER these verbs—viz. LIP "to smear," SICH "to sprinkle," AND HWE "to call." Thus *asichat* "he sprinkled."

आत्मनेपदेष्वन्यतरस्याम् । ३ । १ । ५४ ।

लिपिसिचिह्वः परस्य च्लेरङ् वा । असिचत । असिक्त । लिप उपदेहे । १० । उपदेहो वृद्धिः । लिम्पति । लिम्पते । लेप्ता । अलिपत् । अलिपत । अलिप्त ।

इत्युभयपदिनः ॥

No. 699.—Let *aṅ* be OPTIONALLY the substitute of *chli* after *lip* "to smear," *sich* "to sprinkle," and *hwe* "to call," WHEN THE ÁTMANEPADA terminations ARE EMPLOYED. Thus *asichata* or *asikta* "he sprinkled."

The verb *lip (lipa)* "to smear"—[which the author of the *Kaumudí* renders "to increase"] makes *limpati* or *limpate* "he smears," *leptá* "he will smear," *alipat*, or *alipata*, or *alipta* "he smeared."

So much for those verbs of this conjugation which take both *padas*.

। तुदादयः ।

कृती छेदने । ११ । कृन्तति । चकर्त । कर्तिता । कर्तिष्यति । कर्त्स्यति । अकर्तीत् । खिद परिघाते । १२ । खिन्दति । चिखेद । खेत्ता । पिश अवयवे । १३ । पिंशति । पेशिता । ओव्रश्चू छेदने । १४ । वृश्चति । वव्रश्च । वव्रश्चिथ । वव्रष्ठ । व्रश्चिता । व्रष्टा । व्रश्चिष्यति । व्रक्ष्यति । वृश्च्यात् । अव्रश्चीत् । व्यच व्याजीकरणे । १५ । विचति । विव्याच । विविचतुः । व्यचिता । व्यचिष्यति । विच्यात् । अव्याचीत् । अव्यचीत् । व्यचेः कुटादित्वमनसीति तु नेह प्रवर्तते । अनसीति पर्युदासेन कृन्मात्रविषयत्वात् । उछि उञ्छे । १६ । उञ्छः कणश आदानं कणिशाद्यर्जनं शिलमिति यादवः । ऋच्छ गतीन्द्रियप्रलयमूर्तिभावेषु । १७ । ऋच्छति । ऋच्छत्यृतामिति गुणः । द्विहल्ग्रहणस्यानेकहलुपलक्षणत्वान्नुट् । आनर्च्छ । आनर्च्छतुः । ऋच्छिता । उज्झ उत्सर्गे । १८ । उज्झति । लुभ विमोहने । १९ । लुभति ।

No. 700.—The verb to cut "KṚIT" *(kṛití)* makes *kṛintati* "he cuts," *chakarta* "he cut," *kartitá* "he will cut," *kartishyati* or *kartsyati* "he will cut," *akartít* "he cut."

The verb *khid (khida)* "to hurt" makes *khindati* "he hurts," *chikheda* "he hurt;" *khettá* "he will hurt."

The verb *piś (piśa)* "to be reduced to constituent parts" makes *pinśati* "he is decomposed," *peśitá* "he will be decomposed."

The verb *vraśch (ovraśchú)* "to cut" makes *vṛiśchati* (No. 675) "he cuts," *vavraścha* "he cut," *vavraśchitha* or *vavrashṭha* "thou didst cut," *vraśchitá* or *vrashṭá* "he will cut," *vraśchishyati* or *vrakshyati* "he will cut," *vriśchyát* (No. 675) "may he cut," *avraśchít* "he cut."

The verb *vyach* (*vyacha*) "to deceive" makes *vichati* (No. 675) "he deceives," *vivyácha* "he deceived," *vivichatuh* "they two deceived," *vyachitá* "he will deceive," *vyachishyati* "he will deceive," *vichyát* "may he deceive," *avyáchít* (No. 491) or *avyachít* "he deceived." Here the *vártika* (by which the substitution of *vṛiddhi* would have been prevented) viz. that "The verb *vyach* is to be regarded as one of the list '*kuṭ &c*,' (No. 624), when an affix other than the *kṛit* affix *as* (No. 329) follows, does not apply—for the prohibition "not the *kṛit* affix *as*" refers to the *kṛit* affix only [and not to the tense-affixes:—in the same way as the expression "not a *bráhman*" would be held to refer to a man, not to a horse or a tree.]

The verb *uṅchh (uchchhi)* means "to glean." Gleaning here means taking up grain by grain. To glean the whole ears &c., *Yádava* tells us, is expressed by the verb *śil*.

The verb *ṛichchh (ṛichchha)* "to go, to fail in faculties, to become stiff," makes *ṛichchhati* "he goes." By No. 653, *guṇa* is substituted when *liṭ* follows, and the augment *nuṭ* is derived from No. 498, since the mention of a word with two consonants serves to specify a word with more consonants than one. Thus *ánarchchha* "he went," *ánarchchhatuh* "they two went," *ṛichchhitá*, "he will go."

The verb *ujjh (ujjha)* "quit" makes *ujjhati* "he quits," and the verb *lubh (lubha)* "to bewilder" makes *lubhati* "he bewilders."

तीषसहलुभरुषरिषः । ७ । २ । ४८ ।

इच्छत्यादेः परस्य तादेरार्धधातुकस्येड्वा स्यात् । लोभिता । लोब्धा । लोभिष्यति । तृप तृम्फ तृप्तौ । २० । २१ । तृपति । ततर्प । तर्पिता । अतर्पीत् । तृम्फति ।

No. 701.—Let *it* be optionally the augment, WHEN an *árdhadhátuka* affix, beginning with T, COMES AFTER the verbs ISH "to wish," SHAHA "to endure," LUBH "to bewilder," RUSH "to hurt or kill," and RISH "to hurt or kill." Thus *lobhitá* or *lobdhá* "he will bewilder," *lobhishyati* "he will bewilder."

The verbs *tṛip* (*tṛipa*) and *tṛimph (tṛimpha)* mean "to be satisfied." The former makes *tṛipati* "he is satisfied," *tatarpa* "he was satisfied," *tarpitá* "he will be satisfied," *atarpít* "he was satisfied." The latter makes *tṛimphati* "he is satisfied."

शे तृम्फादीनां नुम् वाच्यः । आदिशब्दः प्रकारे तेन येऽत्र नकारानुषक्तास्ते तृम्फादयः । ततृम्फ । तृफ्यात् । मृड पृड सुखने । २२ । २३ । मृडति । पृडति । शुन गतौ । २४ । सुनति । इषु इच्छायाम् । २५ । इच्छति । एषिता । एष्टा । एषिष्यति । इष्यात् । ऐषीत् । कुट कौटिल्ये । २६ । गाङ्कुटादीति ङित्त्वम् । चुकुटिथ । चुकोट । चुकुट । कुटिता । पुट संश्लेषणे । २७ । पुटति । पुटिता । स्फुट विकसने । २८ । स्फुटति । स्फुटिता । स्फुर स्फुल संचलने । २९ । ३० । स्फुरति । स्फुलति ।

No. 702.—"The augment NUM (No. 497) SHOULD BE STATED to be that OF the verbs TṚIMPHA "to be satisfied" AND THE LIKE, when *śa* (No. 693) follows. The word *ádi* (usually rendered "&c") here means "of the same description as." So that here "*tṛimpha* and the like" are those verbs which include the letter *n*. Thus *tatṛimpha* (notwithstanding No. 362) "he was satisfied," and, when *śa* does not follow, *tṛiphyát* "may he be satisfied."

The verbs *mṛiḍ (mṛiḍa)* and *pṛiḍ (pṛiḍa)* "to delight" make *mṛiḍati* and *pṛiḍati* "he delights."

The *(Vaidika)* verb *sun* (*suna*) "to go" makes *sunati* "he goes."

The verb *ish* (*ishu*) "to wish" makes *ichchhati* (No. 539) "he wishes," *eshitá* (No. 701) or *eshṭá* "he will wish," *eshishyati* "he will wish," *ishyát* "may he wish," *aishít* "he wished."

The verb *kuṭ (kuṭa)* means "to become crooked." According to No. 624, the affixes after this verb, not having an indicatory *ṅ* or *n*, being regarded as having an indicatory *ṅ* (No. 467), we have *chukuṭitha* "thou didst become crooked," *chukoṭa* or *chukuṭa* (No 490) "I became crooked," *kuṭitá* "he will become crooked."

The verb *puṭ (puṭa)* "to embrace" makes *puṭati* "he embraces," *puṭitá* "he will embrace."

The verb *sphuṭ (sphuṭa)* "to blow, to blossom, to open as a bud or flower," makes *sphuṭati* "it blossoms," *sphuṭitá* "it will blossom."

The verbs *sphur (sphura)* and *sphul (sphula)* "to quiver" make *sphurati* and *sphulati* "he quivers."

स्फुरतिस्फुलत्योर्निर्निविभ्यः ।८।३।७६।

षत्वं वा । निष्फुरति निस्फुरति । णू स्तवने । ३१ । परिणूत-गुणोदयः । नुवति । नुनाव । नुविता । टुमस्जो शुद्धौ । ३२ । मज्जति । ममज्ज । मस्जिनशोरिति नुम् ।

No. 703.—There is optionally the substitution of *sh* for the *s* OF the verbs SPHUR and SPHUL "to quiver," AFTER the prefixes NIR, NI, AND VI (No. 48). Thus *nishphurati* or *nisphurati* "he perpetually quivers."

The verb *nú* means "to praise." [That the vowel of this root is long, not short as some contend, is proved by the quotation] "*parinúta-gunodaya.*—the dawning of whose praise-worthy qualities"—[which otherwise would not scan]. This verb makes *nuvati* "he praises," *nunáva* "he praised," *nuvitá* "he will praise."

The verb *masj (tumasjo)* "to purify by washing" makes *majjati* "he immerses," *mamajja* "he immersed." According to No. 677 this verb, when a *jhal* follows, takes the augment *num*, [the irregular application of which is specified in the following *vártika*].

मस्जेरन्त्यात् पूर्वो नुम् वाच्यः । संयोगादिलोपः । ममङ्क्थ । ममज्जिथ । मङ्क्ता । मङ्क्ष्यति । अमाङ्क्षीत् । अमाङ्क्ताम् । अमाङ्क्षुः । रुजो भङ्गे । ३३ । रुजति । रोक्ता । रोक्ष्यति । अरौक्षीत् । भुजो कौटिल्ये । ३४ । रुजिवत् । विश प्रवेशने । ३५ । विशति । मृश आमर्शने । ३६ । आमर्शनं स्पर्शः । अनुदात्तस्य चर्दुपधस्यान्यतरस्याम् । अम्राक्षीत् । अमार्क्षीत् । अमृक्षत् । षद्लृ विशरणगत्यवसादनेषु । ३७ । सीदतीत्यादि । शद्लृ शातने । ३८ ।

No. 704.—"The augment NUM SHOULD BE STATED TO PRECEDE THE LAST letter OF the root MASJ"—[not the last of the vowels as No. 265 directs]. By No. 337 there is elision of the *s*, the first member of the conjunct consonant (*sṅj*)—and thus we have *mamaṅkthu* (No. 333) or *mamajjitha* "thou didst immerse," *maṅktá* "he will immerse," *maṅkshyati* "he will immerse," *amáṅkshít* "he immersed," *amáṅktám* (No. 513) "they two immersed," *amáṅkshuh* "they immersed."

The verb *ruj (rujo)* "to break" makes *rujati* "he breaks," *roktá* "he will break," *rokshyati* "he will break," *araukshít* "he broke."

The verb *bhuj (bhujo)* "to bend" is conjugated like *ruj* "to break."

The verb *viś* (*viśa*) "to enter" makes *viśati* "he enters."

The verb *mṛiś* (*mṛiśa*) means "to touch." "Touching" means "perceiving through the sense of touch." By No. 695, which states that a root gravely accented, or having the vowel *ṛi* as its penult, optionally takes the augment *am*, we have *amrákshít* (No. 695) or *amárkshít*, or (by Nos. 696 and 627) *amṛikshat* "he touched."

The verb *sad* (*shadlṛi*) "to go to decay, to despond," makes *sídati* (No. 522) he desponds"—and so on.

The verb *śad* (*śadlṛi*) means "to decay."

शदेः शितः । १ । ३ । ६० ।

शिद्भाविनोऽस्मात् तङानौ स्तः । शीयते । शीयताम् । शीयेत । अशीयत । शशाद । शत्ता । शत्स्यति । अशदत् । अशत्स्यत् । कॄ विक्षेपे । ३६ ।

No. 705.—AFTER this verb, viz. ŚAD "to decay," WHEN it has one of the affixes with AN INDICATORY Ś [such as the conjugational affix *śa*—No. 693], there are the affixes *taṅ* and *ána* [i. e. the *átmanepada* affixes—No. 409]. Thus *śíyate* (No. 522) "it decays," *śíyatám* "let it decay," *śíyeta* "it may decay," *aśíyata* "it decayed,"—[but where the *śa* is absent] *śaśáda* "it decayed," *śattá* "it will decay," *śatsyati* "it will decay," *aśadat* "it decayed," *aśatsyat* "it would decay."

The verb *kṛí* means "to scatter."

ॠत इद्धातोः । ७ । १ । १०० ।

किरति । चकार । चकरतुः । चकरुः । करिता । करीता । कीर्यात् ।

No. 706.—Let SHORT I be the substitute OF WHAT VERBAL ROOT ENDS IN LONG ṚÍ. Thus *kirati* "he scatters," *chakára* (Nos. 653 and 489) "he scattered," *chakaratuh* (No. 653) "they two scattered," *chakaruh* "they scattered," *karitá* or *karítá* (No. 654) "he will scatter," *kíryát* (No. 651) "may he scatter."

किरतौ लवने । ६ । १ । १४० ।

उपात् किरतेः सुट् छेदने । उपस्किरति ।

No. 707.—Let *suṭ* be the augment of the verb KṚÍ SIGNIFYING "TO CUT," coming after the prefix *upa*. Thus *upaskirati* "he cuts."

अड्भ्यासव्यवायेऽपि । ६ । १ । १३६ ।

No. 708.—EVEN WHEN the augment AṬ (No. 457) OR A REDUPLICATE syllable INTERVENES—(rule No. 707 applies).

सुट् कात् पूर्व इति वक्तव्यम् । उपास्किरत् । उपचस्कार ।

No. 709.—"IT SHOULD BE STATED THAT the augment SUṬ (Nos. 707 and 708) IS placed BEFORE the K (of the verb *kṛí*). Thus *upáskirat & upachaskára* (No. 488) "he cut."

हिंसायां प्रतेश्च । ६ । १ । १४१ ।

उपात् प्रतेश्च किरतेः सुट् हिंसायाम् । उपस्किरति । प्रतिस्किरति । गॄ निगरणे । ४० ।

No. 710.—Let *suṭ* be the augment of the verb *kṛí*, coming after the prefix *upa* AND AFTER PRATI, IN THE SENSE OF INJURING. Thus *upaskirati* or *pratiskirati* "he injures."

The verb *gṛí* means "to swallow."

अचि विभाषा । ८ । २ । २१ ।

गिरते रेफस्य लोऽजादौ प्रत्यये । गिलति । गिरति । जगाल । जगार । जगलिथ । जगरिथ । गलिता । गलीता । गरिता । गरीता ।

प्रच्छ ज्ञीप्सायाम् । ४१ । ग्रहिज्येति संप्रसारणम् । पृच्छति । पप्रच्छ । पप्रच्छतुः । पप्रच्छुः । प्रष्टा । प्रक्ष्यति । अप्राक्षीत् । मृङ् प्राणत्यागे । ४२ ।

No. 711.—Let there be OPTIONALLY *l* in the room of the *r* of the verb *gṛí* "to swallow," WHEN an affix. beginningwith A VOWEL, FOLLOWS. Thus *gilati* or *girati* "he swallows," *jagála* or *jagára* "he swallowed," *galitá, galítá* (No. 654), *garitá*, or *garítá* "he will swallow."

The verb *prachchh* "to ask," substituting a vowel for the semi-vowel according to No. 675, makes *pṛichchhati* "he asks," *paprachchha* "he asked," *paprachchhatuh* "they two asked," *paprachchhuh* "they asked," *prashṭá* (No. 334) "he will ask," *prakshyati* "he will ask," *aprákshít* "he asked."

The verb *mṛi (mṛiń)* means "to die."

म्रियतेर्लुङ्लिङोश्च । १ । ३ । ६१ ।

लुङ्लिङोः शितश्च प्रकृतिभूतान्मृङस्तङानौ नान्यत्र । रिङ् । इयङ् । म्रियते । ममार । मर्ता । मरिष्यति । मृषीष्ट । अमृत । पृङ् व्यायामे । ४३ । प्रायेणायं व्याङ्पूर्वः । व्याप्रियते । व्यापप्रे । व्यापप्राते । व्यापरिष्यते । व्यापृत । व्यापृषाताम् । जुषी प्रीतिसेवनयोः । ४४ । जुषते । जुजुषे । ओविजी भयचलनयोः । ४५ । प्रायेणोत्पूर्वः । उद्विजते ।

No. 712.—The *átmanepada* affixes (No. 409) come AFTER the root MṚI "to die," WHEN it takes LUŃ, LIŃ, and an affix with an indicatory *ś*, but not elsewhere. By No 580, the substitution of *riń (ri)* is directed, and, by No. 220, that of *iyań (iy)*—so that we have *mriyate* "he dies," *mamára* "he died," *martá* "he will die," *marishyati* "he will die," *mṛishíshṭa* "may he die," *amṛita* "he died."

The verb *pṛi (pṛiń)*, in the sense of "to be active," is generally preceded by the prefixes *vi* and *áń*. Thus *vyápriyate* "he is busied," *vyápapre* (No. 548) "he was busied," *vyápapráte* "they two were busied," *vyáparishyate* "he will be busied," *vyápṛita* "he was busied," *vyápṛishátám* "they two were busied."

The verb *jush (jushí)* "to delight to serve," makes *jushate* "he serves," *jujushe* "he served."

The verb *vij (ovijí)* in the sense of "to fear, to tremble," is generally preceded by the affix *ut.* Thus *udvijate* "he fears."

विज इट्।१।२।२।

विजेः पर इडादिप्रत्ययो ङिद्वत् । उद्विजिता ।

इति तुदादयः ॥

No. 713.—An affix, PRECEDED BY the augment IṬ, and coming AFTER the verb VIJ "to fear," is as if it had an indicatory *ṅ* (No. 467). Hence *udvijitá* "he will fear."

So much for the 6th class of verbs—"*tud, &c.*"

The 7th class of verbs consists of "*rudh, &c.*"

The verb *rudh (rudhir)* means "to obstruct."

। रुधादयः ।

रुधिर् आवरणे । १ ।

रुधादिभ्यः श्नम्।३।१।७८।

शपोऽपवादः । रुणद्धि । श्नसोरल्लोपः । रुन्द्धः । रुन्धन्ति । रुणत्सि । रुन्द्धः । रुन्द्ध । रुणध्मि । रुन्ध्वः । रुन्ध्मः । रुन्द्धे । रुन्धाते । रुन्धते । रुन्त्से । रुन्धाथे । रुन्द्धे । रुन्धे । रुन्ध्वहे । रुन्ध्महे । रुरोध । रुरुधे । रोद्धा । रोत्स्यति । रोत्स्यते । रुणद्धु । रुन्द्धात् । रुन्द्धाम् । रुन्धन्तु । रुन्द्धि । रुणधानि । रुणधाव । रुणधाम । रुन्द्धाम् । रुन्धाताम् । रुन्धताम् । रुन्त्स्व । रुणधै । रुणधावहै । रुणधामहै । अरुणत् । अरुणद् । अरुन्द्धाम् । अरुन्धन् । अरुन्द्ध । अरुन्धाताम् । अरुन्धत । रुन्ध्यात् । रुन्धीत । रुध्यात् । रुत्सीष्ट । अरुधत् । अरौत्सीत् । अरोत्स्यत् । अरोत्स्यत । भिदिर् विदारणे । २ । छिदिर् द्वैधीकरणे । ३ । युजिर् योगे । ४ । रिचिर् विरेचने । ५ । रिणक्ति । रिङ्क्ते । रिरेच । रेक्ता । रेक्ष्यति । अरिणक् । अरिचत् ।

अरैक्षीत् । अरिक्त । विचिर् पृथग्भावे । ६ । विनक्ति । विङ्क्ते । क्षुदिर् संपेषणे । ७ । क्षुणत्ति । क्षुन्ते । क्षोत्ता । अक्षुदत् । अक्षौत्सीत् । अक्षुत्त । उच्छृदिर् दीप्तिदेवनयोः । ८ । छृणत्ति । छृन्ते । चच्छर्द । सेऽसिचीति वेट् । चच्छृत्से । चच्छृदिषे । छर्दिता । छर्दिष्यति । छर्त्स्यति । अच्छृदत् । अच्छर्दीत् । अच्छर्दिष्ट । उतृदिर् हिंसानादरयोः । ६ । तृणत्ति । तृन्ते । कृती वेष्टने । १० । कृणत्ति । तृह हिसि हिंसायाम् । ११ । १२ ।

No. 714.—After the verbs rudh "to obstruct," &c, there is śnam. This debars *śap* (No. 419). Thus we have *ruṇaddhi* (Nos. 157 and 586) "he obstructs," and, the *a* being elided according to No. 611, *runddhah* "they two obstruct," *rundhanti* "they obstruct," *ruṇatsi* "thou obstructest," *runddhah* (Nos. 95 and 96) "you two obstruct," *runddha* "you obstruct," *ruṇadhmi* "I obstruct," *rundhwah* "we two obstruct," *rundhmah* "we obstruct." With the *átmanepada* terminations, we have *runddhe* "he obstructs," *rundháte* "they two obstruct," *rundhate* (No. 559) "they obstruct," *runtse* "thou obstructest," *rundháthe* "you two obstruct," *runddhwe* "you obstruct," *rundhe* "I obstruct," *rundhwahe* "we two obstruct," *rundhmahe* "we obstruct." Then again *rurodha* or *rurudhe* "he obstructed," *roddhá* "he will obstruct, *rotsyati* or *rotsyate* "he will obstruct," *ruṇaddhu* "let him obstruct," *runddhát* (No. 444) may he obstruct," *runddhám* "let the two obstruct," *rundhantu* "let them obstruct," *runddhi* "do thou obstruct," *ruṇadháni* "let me obstruct," *ruṇadháva* "let us two obstruct," *ruṇadháma* "let us obstruct," or, again, *runddhám* "let him obstruct," *rundhátám* "let the two obstruct," *rundhatám* (No. 559) "let them obstruct," *runtswa* "do thou obstruct," *ruṇadhai* "let me obstruct," *ruṇadhávahai* "let us two obstruct," *ruṇadhámahai* "let us obstruct," *aruṇat* (No, 165) or *aruṇad* "he obstructed," *arunddhám* "they two obstructed," *arundhan* "they obstructed," *arunddha* "he obstructed," *arundhátám* "they two obstructed," *arundhata* "they obstructed," *rundhyát* or *rundhíta* "he may obstruct," *rudhyát* or *rutsíshṭa* "may he obstruct," *arudhat* (No. 668) or *arautsít* "he obstructed," *arotsyat* or *arotsyata* "he would obstruct."

In the same way are conjugated *bhid (bhidir)* "to break," *chhid (chhidir)* "to split," and *yuj (yujir)* "to join."

The verb *rich (richir)* "to purge" makes *riṇakti* or *riṅkte* "he purges," *rirecha* "he purged," *rektá* "he will purge," *rekshyati* "he will purge," *ariṇak* (No. 199) "he purged," *arichat* (No. 668) or *araikshít* or *arikta* "he purged."

The verb *vich (vichir)* "to differ or be separate" makes *vinakti* or *viṅkte* "he differs."

The verb *kshud (kshudir)* "to pound" makes *kshuṇatti* or *kshunte* "he pounds," *kshottá* "he will pound," *akshudat* "he pounded," *akshautsít* or *akshutta* "he pounded."

The verb *chhṛid (uchchhṛidir)* "to shine or play" makes *chhṛiṇatti* or *chhṛinte* "he shines," *chachchharda* "he shone." According to No. 670, the augment *iṭ* being optional when *s* follows, we have *chachchhṛitse* or *chachchhṛidishe* "thou didst shine," *chharditá* "he will shine," *chhardishyati* or *chhartsyate* "he will shine," *achchhṛidat* "he shone," *achchhardít* or *achchhardishṭa* "he shone."

The verb *tṛid (utṛidir)* "to injure or disregard" makes *tṛiṇatti* or *tṛinte* "he injures;" and *kṛit (kṛití)* "to surround" makes *kṛiṇatti* "he surrounds."

The verbs *tṛih (tṛiha)* and *his* (*hisi*) mean "to kill or injure in any manner."

तृणह इम् । ७ । ३ । ९२ ।

तृहः श्नमि कृते इम् हलादौ पिति । तृणेढि । तृण्ढः । ततर्ह । तर्हिता । अतृणेट् । श्नान्नलोपः । हिनस्ति । जिहिंस । हिंसिता । उन्दी क्लेदने । १३ । उनत्ति । उन्त्तः । उन्दन्ति । उन्दांचकार । औनत् । औन्ताम् । औन्दन् । औनः । औनदम् । अञ्जू व्यक्तिम्रक्षणकान्तिगतिषु । १४ । अनक्ति । अङ्क्तः । अञ्जन्ति । आनञ्ज । आनञ्जिथ । आनङ्क्थ । अञ्जिता । अङ्क्ता । अङ्ग्धि । अनजानि । आनक् ।

No. 715.—Of *tṛih* "to injure," when *śnam* (No. 714) has

been applied (and the form has thence become TṚIṆAH), let IM be the augment, when an affix, beginning with a consonant and distinguished by an indicatory *p*, follows. Thus *tṛiṇeḍhi* "he injures," *tṛiṇḍhah* "they two injure," *tatarha* "he injured," *tarhitá* "he will injure," *atṛiṇeṭ* (Nos. 199 and 276 "he injured."

The verb *his (hisi)* "to injure" having taken *num* by No. 497, and rejecting the *n* by No. 717, makes *hinasti* "he injures," *jihiṅsa* "he injured," *hiṅsitá* "he will injure."

The verb *und (undí)* "to moisten" makes *unatti* (No. 717) "he moistens," *untah* "they two moisten," *undanti* "they moisten," *undáṅchakára* (No. 546) "he moistened," *aunat* (Nos. 478 and 218) "he moistened," *auntám* "they two moistened," *aundan* "they moistened" *aunah* "thou didst moisten," *aunadam* "I moistened."

The verb *aṅj (aṅjú)* "to make clear, to anoint, to be beautiful, to go," makes *anakti* "he makes clear," *aṅktah* "they two make clear," *aṅjanti* "they make clear," *ánaṅja* "he made clear," *ánaṅjitha* or *ánaṅktha* "thou didst make clear," *aṅjitá* or *aṅktá* "he will make clear," *aṅdhi* "do thou make clear," *anajáni* "let me make clear," *ának* "he made clear."

अञ्जेः सिचि । ७ । २ । ७१ ।

अञ्जेः सिचो नित्यमिट् । आञ्जीत् । तञ्चू संकोचने । १५ । तनक्ति । तङ्क्ता । तञ्चिता । ओविजी भयचलनयोः । १६ । विनक्ति । विङ्क्तः । विज इडिति ङित्त्वम् । विविजिथ । विजिता । अविनक् । अविजीत् । शिष्लृ विशेषणे । १७ । शिनष्टि । शिंष्टः । शिंषन्ति । शिनक्षि । शिशेष । शिशेषिथ । शेष्टा । शेक्ष्यति । हेर्धिः । शिण्ढि । शिनषाणि । अशिनट् । शिंष्यात् । शिष्यात् । अशिषत् । एवं पिष्लृ संचूर्णने । १८ । भञ्जो आमर्दने । १९ ।

No. 716.—*Iṭ* is always the augment of SICH AFTER the verb AṄJ "to make clear." Thus *áṅjít* (No. 480) "he made clear."

The verb *taṅch (taṅchú)* "to shrink" makes *tanakti* "he shrinks," *taṅktá* or *taṅchitá* "he will shrink."

The verb *vij (ovijí)* "to be afraid, to tremble," makes *vinakti* "he trembles," *viṅktah* "they two tremble." According to No. 713, the augment *iṭ* being regarded as having an indicatory *ṅ* (No. 467), we have *vivijitha* "thou didst tremble," *vijitá* "he will tremble," *avinak* (No. 199) "he trembled," *avijít* "he trembled."

The verb *śish (śishlṛi)* "to distinguish or individualize" makes *śinashṭi* "it distinguishes," *śiṅshṭah* "they two distinguish," *śiṅshanti* "they distinguish," *śinakshi* "thou distinguishest," *śiśesha* "it distinguished," *śiśeshitha* "thou didst distinguish," *śeshṭá* "it will distinguish," *sekshyati* "it will distinguish. By No. 593 *dhi* being substituted for *hi*, we have *śiṇḍhi* "do thou distinguish," *śinasháṇi* "let me distinguish," *aśinaṭ* (No. 165) "it distinguished," *śiṅshyát* "it may distinguish," *śishyát* "may it distinguish," *aśishat* "it distinguished."

In like manner *pish (pishlṛi)* "to grind" is conjugated.

The verb *bhañj (bhañjo)* means "to break."

श्नान्नलोपः । ६ । ४ । २३ ।

श्नमः परस्य नस्य लोपः स्यात् । भनक्ति । बभञ्जिथ । बभङ्क्थ । भङ्क्ता । भङ्ग्धि । अभाङ्क्षीत् । भुज पालनाभ्यवहारयोः । २० । भुनक्ति । भोक्ता । भोक्ष्यति । अभुनक् ।

No. 717.—Let there be ELISION OF the letter N coming AFTER ŚNAM (No. 714). Thus we have *bhanakti* "he breaks," *babhañjitha* or *babhaṅktha* "thou didst break," *bhaṅktá* "he will break," *bhaṅgdhi* (No. 593) "do thou break," *abháṅkshít* "he broke."

The verb *bhuj (bhuja)* "to protect or eat" makes *bhunakti* "he eats," *bhoktá* "he will eat," *bhokshyati* "he will eat," *abhunak* "he ate."

भुजोऽनवने । १ । ३ । ६६ ।

तङानौ स्तः । ओदनं भुङ्क्ते । अनवने किम् । महीं भुनक्ति । ञिइन्धी दीप्तौ । २१ । इन्द्धे । इन्धाते । इन्धते । इंत्से । इन्द्ध्वे । इन्धांचक्रे । इन्धिता । इन्द्धाम् । इन्धाताम् । इनधै । ऐन्द्ध । ऐन्धाताम् । ऐन्द्धाः । विद विचारणे । २२ । विन्ते । वेत्ता ।

इति रुधादयः ॥

No. 718.—The *átmanepada* affixes (No. 409) are put AFTER the verb BHUJ, NOT IN THE SENSE OF PROTECTING. Thus we may say *odanań bhuńkte* "he eats boiled rice." Why "not in the sense of protecting"? Witness the phrase—*mahíń bhunakti* "he preserves the earth."

The verb *indh (ńi-indhí)* "to shine" makes *inddhe* "he shines," *indháte* "they two shine," *indhate* "they shine," *ińtse* "thou shinest," *inddhwe* "you shine," *indháńchakre* (No. 546) "he shone," *indhitá* "he will shine," *inddhám* "let him shine," *indhátám* "let the two shine," *inadhai* "let me shine," *ainddha* "he shone," *aindhátám* "they two shone," *ainddháh* "thou didst shine.

The verb *vid (vida)* "to consider" makes *vinte* "he considers," *vettá* "he will consider."

So much for the 7th class of verbs—"*rudh, &c.*"

The 8th class of verbs consists of "*tan, &c.*"

The verb *tan (tanu)* means "to expand."

। तनादयः ।

तनु विस्तारे । १ ।

तनादिकृञ्भ्य उः । ३ । १ । ७९ ।

शपोऽपवादः । तनोति । तनुते । ततान । तेने । तनितासि । तनितासे । तनिष्यति । तनिष्यते । तनुताम् । अतनोत् । तनुयात् । तन्वीत । तन्यात् । तनिषीष्ट । अतनीत् । अतानीत् ।

No. 719.—AFTER the verbs "TAN, &C.," AND the verb KṚI "to make," let there be U. This debars *śap* (No. 419). Thus we have *tanoti* or *tanute* "he expands," *tatána* or *tene* (No. 494) he expanded," *tanitási* or *tanitáse* "thou wilt expand," *tanishyati* or *tanishyatè* "he will expand," *tanutám* "let him expand, *atanot* "he expanded," *tanuyát* or *tanwíta* "he may expand," *tanyát* or *tanishíshṭa* "may he expand," *atanít* or *atánít* (No. 491) "he expanded."

तनादिभ्यस्तथासोः। २। ४। ७९।

तनादेः सिचो वा लुक् तथासोः। अतत। अतनिष्ट। अतथाः। अतनिष्ठाः। अतनिष्यत्। अतनिष्यत। षणु दाने। २। सनोति। सनुते।

No. 720.—There is optionally elision *(luk)* of *sich* (No. 472) AFTER "TAN, &C.," WHEN the affixes TA and THÁS FOLLOW. Thus *atata* (No. 596) or *atanishṭa* "he expanded," *atatháh* or *atanishṭháh* "thou didst expand," *atanishyat* or *atanishyata* "he would expand."

The verb *shaṇ (shaṇu)* "to give" makes *sanoti* or *sanute* "he gives."

ये विभाषा। ६। ४। ४३।

जनसनखनामात्वं वा यादौ क्ङिति। सायात्। सन्यात्।

No. 721.—There is OPTIONALLY the substitution of long *á* in the room of the verbs *jan* "to be born," *san* "to give," and *khan* "to dig," WHEN an affix, beginning with Y and distinguished by an indicatory *k* or *ń*, FOLLOWS. Thus *sáyát* or *sanyát* "may he give."

जनसनखनां सन्झलोः। ६। ४। ४२।

एषामाकारः सनि झलादौ क्ङिति। असात। असनिष्ट। असाथाः। असनिष्ठाः। क्षणु हिंसायाम्। ३। क्षणोति। क्षणुते। ह्म्यन्तेति न वृद्धिः। अक्षणीत्। अक्षत। अक्षणिष्ट। अक्षथाः। अक्षणिष्ठाः। क्षिणु च। ४। उप्रत्यये लघूपधस्य गुणो वा। क्षिणोति। क्षेणोति। क्षेणिता। अक्षेणीत्। अक्षित। अक्षेणिष्ट। तृणु अदने। ५। तृणोति। तर्णोति। तृणुते। तर्णुते। डुकृञ् करणे। ६।

No. 722.—Long *á* is the substitute OF these verbs viz. JAN "to be born," SAN "to give," AND KHAN "to dig," WHEN the affix SAN (No. 752), OR an affix, beginning with A JHAL and distinguished by an indicatory *k* or *ń*, FOLLOWS. Thus *asáta* or *asanishṭa* "he gave," *asátháh* or *asanishṭháh* "thou didst give."

The verb *kshaṇ (kshaṇu)* "to injure" makes *kshaṇoti* or *kshaṇute* "he injures," According to No. 500, there being no substitution of *vṛiddhi*, we have *akshaṇít*, *akshata* (No. 720), or *akshaṇishṭa* "he injured," *akshatháh* or *akshaṇishṭháh* "thou didst injure."

The verb *kshiṇ (kshiṇu)* "to injure" (which, as a root followed by the affix *u* No. 719, and having a light penult, substitutes *guṇa*, No. 485, only optionally) makes *kshiṇoti* or *ksheṇoti* "he injures," *ksheṇitá* "he will injure," *aksheṇít*, *akshita* (No. 720), or *aksheṇishṭa* "he injured."

The verb *tṛiṇ (tṛiṇu)* "to eat, to graze," makes *tṛiṇoti*, *tarṇoti*, *tṛiṇute*, or *tarṇute* "he grazes."

The verb *kṛi (ḍukṛiñ)* means "to make."

अत उत् सार्वधातुके । ६ । ४ । ११० ।

कुरुतः ।

No. 723.—In the room OF THE SHORT A of the verb *kṛi* "to make," (in the form of *karu*—No. 719)—let there be SHORT U, WHEN a SÁRVADHÁTUKA affix (with an indicatory *k* or *ṅ*) FOLLOWS. Thus *kurutah* "they two make."

न भकुर्छुराम् । ८ । २ । ७९ ।

भस्य कुर्छुरोरुपधाया न दीर्घः । कुर्वन्ति ।

No. 724.—There is NOT a long substitute (No. 651) in the room OF the penult of a BHA (No. 185) AND of the verbs KṚI "to make," and CHHUR "to cut." Thus *kurvanti* "they make."

नित्यं करोतेः । ६ । ४ । १०८ ।

करोतेः प्रत्ययोकारस्य नित्यं लोपो म्वोः । कुर्वः । कुर्मः । कुरुते । चकार । चक्रे । कर्ता । करिष्यति । करिष्यते । करोतु । कुरुताम् । अकरोत् । अकुरुत ।

No. 725.—There is ALWAYS elision of the *u* of an affix AFTER the verb KṚI "to make," when the letter *m* or *v* follows. Thus *kurvah* "we two make," *kurmah* "we make," *kurute* "he makes," *chakára* or *chakre* "he made," *kartá* "he will make," *karishyati* or *karishyate* "he will make," *karotu* or *kurutám* "let him make," *akarot* or *akuruta* "he made."

ये च । ६ । ४ । १०९ ।

कृञ उलोपो यादौ प्रत्यये । कुर्यात् । कुर्वीत । क्रियात् । कृषीष्ट । अकार्षीत् । अकृत । अकरिष्यत् । अकरिष्यत ।

No. 726.—AND there is elision of *u* after the verb *kṛi* "to make," WHEN an affix, beginning with Y, FOLLOWS. Thus *kuryát* or *kurvíta* (No. 723) "he may make," *kriyát* or *kṛishíshṭa*" "may he make," *akárshít* or *akṛita* (No. 582) "he made," *akarishyat* or *akarishyata* he would make."

सम्परिभ्यां करोतौ भूषणे । ६ । १ । १३७ ।

No. 727.—WHEN the verb KṚI "to make" comes AFTER SAM OR PAṚI (No. 48) IN THE SENSE OF ORNAMENTING—(then the proceeding directed in No. 728 takes place).

समवाये च । ६ । १ । १३८ ।

सुट् । संस्करोति । अलंकरोतीत्यर्थः । संस्कुर्वन्ति । संघीभवन्तीत्यर्थः । संपूर्वस्य क्वचिदभूषणेऽपि सुट् । संस्कृतं भक्षा इति ज्ञापकात् ।

No. 728.—AND (when the compound—No. 727—is) IN THE SENSE OF AGGREGATION, there is the augment *suṭ*. Thus *sańskaroti*—that is to say "he ornaments, *sańskurvanti*—that is to say "they congregate." This *suṭ* is sometimes the augment of *kṛi* preceded by *sam*, even when it does not signify "ornamenting":—as we learn by inspecting the aphorism No. 1119—viz. "*sańskṛitań bhakshá́h*"—where the expression refers to the "preparation of food."

उपात् प्रतियत्नवैकृतवाक्याध्याहारेषु च । ६ । १ । १३९ ।

कृञः सुट् । चात् प्रागुक्तयोरर्थयोः । प्रतियत्नो गुणाधानम् । विकृतमेव वैकृतं विकारः । वाक्याध्याहार आकाङ्क्षितैकदेशपूरणम् ।

उपस्कृता कन्या । उपस्कृता ब्राह्मणाः । एधो दकस्योपस्कुरुते । उपस्कृतं भुङ्क्ते ।उपस्कृतं ब्रूते । वनु याचने । ७ । वनुते । ववने । मनु अवबोधने । ८ । मनुते । मेने । मनिता । मनिष्यते । मनुताम् । अमनुत । मन्वीत । मनिषीष्ट । अमनिष्ट । अमनिष्यत ।

इति तनादयः ॥

No. 729.—AND AFTER UPA (No. 48) IN THE several SENSES OF ACQUIRING A new PROPERTY, of ALTERATION, AND of the SUPPLYING of ELLIPSES IN DISCOURSE, the verb *kṛi* takes the augment *suṭ*. By the "and" it is signified that the verb has also the two meanings mentioned before (in Nos. 727 and 728). By "acquiring a new property" is meant "the taking of a quality." By "alteration," or modification, is meant "change." By "the supplying of ellipses in discourse" is meant "the filling up of those parts which the sense requires." Examples of these five employments of the word follow, signifying "a damsel adorned;" "assembled bráhmans;" "the wood gives a new property to the water" (or "he prepares the fuel and water for an oblation"); "he eats something changed" (or different from what is proper—"as bread with rice);" "he speaks without ellipsis."

The verb *van (vanu)* "to ask or beg" makes *vanute* "he begs," *vavane* "he begged."

The verb *man (manu)* "to know, to conceive," makes *manute* "he conceives," *mene* "he conceived," *manitá* "he will conceive," *manishyate* "he will conceive," *manutám* "let him conceive," *amanuta* "he conceived," *manwíta* "he may conceive," *manishíshṭa* "may he conceive," *amanishṭa* "he conceived," *amanishyata* "he would conceive."

So much for the 8th class of verbs—"*tan, &c.*"

The 9th class of verbs consists of "*krí, &c.*"

The verb *krí (ḍukríñ)* means "to buy, or exchange goods."

। क्र्यादयः ।

डुक्रीञ् द्रव्यविनिमये । १ ।

क्र्यादिभ्यः श्ना । ३ । १ । ८१ ।

शपोऽपवादः । क्रीणाति । ईहल्यघोः । क्रीणीतः । श्नाभ्यस्तयोरातः । क्रीणन्ति । क्रीणासि । क्रीणीथः । क्रीणीथ । क्रीणामि । क्रीणीवः । क्रीणीमः । क्रीणीते । क्रीणाते । क्रीणते । क्रीणीषे । क्रीणाथे । क्रीणीध्वे । क्रीणे । क्रीणीवहे । क्रीणीमहे । चिक्राय । चिक्रियतुः । चिक्रियुः । चिक्रेथ । चिक्रयिथ । चिक्रिये । क्रेता । क्रेष्यति । क्रेष्यते । क्रीणातु । क्रीणीतात् । क्रीणीताम् । अक्रीणात् । अक्रीणीत । क्रीणीयात् । क्रीणीत । क्रीयात् । क्रेषीष्ट । अक्रैषीत् । अक्रेष्ट । अक्रेष्यत् । अक्रेष्यत । प्रीञ् तर्पणे कान्तौ च । २ । प्रीणाति । प्रीणीते । श्रीञ् पाके । ३ । श्रीणाति । श्रीणीते । मीञ् हिंसायाम् । ४ ।

No. 730.—After the verbs krí "to buy," &c., there is śná. This debars śap (No. 419). Thus kríṇáti "he buys." By No. 657, the á being changed to í, kríṇítah "they two buy." By No. 658, the á being elided, kríṇanti "they buy," kríṇási "thou buyest," kríṇíthah "you two buy," kríṇítha "you buy," kríṇámi "I buy," kríṇívah "we two buy," kríṇímah "we buy," kríṇíte (No. 657) "he buys," kríṇáte "they two buy," krínate "they buy," kríṇíshe "thou buyest," kríṇáthe "you two buy," kríṇídhwe "you buy," kríṇe "I buy," kríṇívahe "we two buy," kríṇímahe "we buy," chikráya "he bought," chikriyatuh "they two bought," chikriyuh "they bought," chikretha (No. 515) or chikrayitha (No. 517) "thou didst buy," chikriye "he bought," kretá "he will buy," kreshyati or kreshyate "he will buy," kríṇátu "let him buy," kríṇítát "may he buy," kríṇítám "let him buy," akríṇát or akríṇíta "he bought," kríṇíyát or kríṇíta "he may buy," kríyát or kreshíshṭa "may he buy," akraishít or akreshṭa "he bought," akreshyat or akreshyata "he would buy."

The verb prí (prín) "to please, to love," makes príṇáti or príṇíte "he pleases;" and śrí (śrín) "to cook" makes śríṇáti or śríṇíte "he cooks."

The verb mí (mín) means "to injure."

हिनुमीना । ८ । ४ । १५ ।

उपसर्गस्थान्निमित्तात् परस्यैतयोर्नस्य णः स्यात् । प्रमीणाति । प्रमीणीते । मीनातीत्यात्वम् । ममौ । मिम्यतुः । ममिथ । ममाथ । मिम्ये । माता । मास्यति । मीयात् । मासीष्ट । अमासीत् । अमासिष्टाम् । अमास्त । षिञ् बन्धने । ५ । सिनाति । सिनीते । सिषाय । सिष्ये । सेता । स्कुञ् आप्रवने । ६ ।

No. 731.—Let there be a cerebral *ṇ* in the room of the dental *n* of the verbs *hi* "to go," and *mí* "to hurt" (which, with the conjugational affixes, appear in the shape of HINU and MÍNÁ,) coming after a due cause of such change and ending in an *upasarga.* Thus *pramíṇáti* or *pramíṇíte* "he injures greatly." By No. 680, there being a substitution of *á*, *mamau* (No. 523) "he injured," *mimyatuh* "they two injured," *mamitha* (Nos. 517 and 524) or *mamátha* "thou didst injure," *mimye* "I injured," *mátá* "he will injure," *másyati* "he will injure," *míyát* or *másíshṭa* "may he injure," *amásít* "he injured," *amásishṭám* "they two injured," *amásta* "he injured."

The verb *shi (shiṅ)* "to bind" makes *sindruti* of *siníte* "he binds," *sisháya* or *sishye* "he bound," *setá* "he will bind."

The verb *sku* (*skuṅ*) means "to go by leaps."

स्तन्भुस्तुन्भुस्कन्भुस्कुन्भुस्कुभ्यः श्नुश्च । ३ । १ । ८२ । चात् श्ना । स्कुनोति । स्कुनुते । स्कुनाति । स्कुनीते । चुस्काव । चुस्कुवे । स्कोता । अस्कौषीत् । अस्कोष्ट । स्तन्भ्वादयश्चत्वारः सौत्राः सर्वे रोधनार्थाः परस्मैपदिनः ।

No. 732.—AND there is ŚNU (No. 687) AFTER STANBH, STUNBH, SKANBH, or SKUNBH "to hinder, to be dull or insensible," AND SKU "to go by leaps." By the "and" it is meant that they may optionally take *śná.* Thus *skunoti, skunute, skunáti,* or *skuníte* (No. 657) "he goes by leaps," *chuskáva* or *chuskuve* "he went by leaps," *skotá* "he will go by leaps," *askaushít* or *askoshṭa* "he went by leaps."

The four verbs *stanbh, &c.,* which are exhibited only in an aphorism (and not in *Páṇini's* catalogue of Roots), all have the sense of "hindering," and take the *parasmaipada* terminations.

हलः श्नः शानज्झौ । ३ । १ । ८३ ।

स्तभान ।

No. 733.—Let ŚÁNACH be substituted in the room OF ŚNÁ (No. 730) coming AFTER A CONSONANT, WHEN the affix HI (No. 447) FOLLOWS. Thus *stabhána* (Nos. 448 and 363) "do thou hinder."

जॄस्तन्भुम्रुचुम्लुचुग्रुचुग्लुचुग्लुञ्चुश्विभ्यश्च । ३ । १ । ५८ ।

च्लेरङ् वा ।

No. 734.—AND, optionally, *aṅ* is the substitute of *chli* (No. 471) AFTER the verbs JṚÍ "to grow old, STANBH "to hinder," MRUCH "to go," MLUCH "to go," GRUCH "to steal," GLUCH "to steal," GLUṄCH "to go," AND ŚWI "to go."

स्तन्भेः । ८ । ३ । ६७ ।

स्तन्भेः सौत्रस्य सस्य षः स्यात् । व्यष्टभत् । अस्तम्भीत् । युञ् बन्धने । ७ । युनाति । युनीते । योता । क्नूञ् शब्दे । ८ । क्नूनाति । क्नूनीते । क्नविता । दॄञ् हिंसायाम् । ९ । दॄणाति । दॄणीते । द्रूञ् हिंसायाम् । १० । द्रूणाति । द्रूणीते । पूञ् पवने । ११ ।

No. 735.—Let there be *sh* in the room OF the *s* of the aphoristic (No. 732) verb STANBH (if the change be required by a due cause thereof in an *upasarga*). Thus *vyashṭabhat* (No. 363) "he hindered," *astambhít* (Nos. 95 and 96) "he injured."

The verb *yu (yuṅ)* "to bind" makes *yunáti* or *yuníte* (No. 657) "he binds," *yotá* "he will bind."

The verb *knú (knúṅ)* "to sound" makes *knúnáti* or *knúníte* "it sounds," *knavitá* "it will sound."

The verb *dṛí (dṛíṅ)* "to injure" makes *dṛíṇáti* or *dṛíṇíte* "he injures;" and *drú (drúṅ)* "to injure" makes *drúṇáti* or *drúṇíte* "he injures."

The verb *pú (púṅ)* means "to purify."

प्वादीनां ह्रस्वः । ७ । ३ । ८० ।

पूञ्लूञ्स्तृञ्कॄञ्वॄञ्धूञ्शॄपॄवॄभॄमॄजॄझॄघॄनॄध्वॄकॄॠगॄज्यारीलीव्लीप्लीनां चतुर्विंशतेः शिति ह्रस्वः । पुनाति । पुनीते । पविता । लूञ् छेदने । १२ । लुनाति । लुनीते । स्तॄञ् आच्छादने । १३ । स्तृणाति । शर्पूर्वाः खयः । तस्तार । तस्तरतुः । तस्तरे । स्तरिता । स्तरीता । स्तृणीयात् । स्तृणीत । स्तीर्यात् ।

No. 736.—When an affix with an indicatory *ś* follows, let A SHORT vowel be the substitute OF the twenty-four verbs PÚ, &c., viz. *púñ* "to purify," *lúñ* "to cut," *stṛíñ* "to spread over," *kṛíñ* "to scatter," *vṛíñ* "to choose," *dhúñ* "to agitate," *śṛí* "to injure," *pṛí* "to nourish," *vṛí* "to choose," *bhṛí* "to nourish," *mṛí* "to injure," *jṛí* "to grow old," *jhṛí* "to grow old," *ghṛí* "to grow old," *nṛí* "to lead," *dhwṛí* "to be crooked," *kṛí* "to injure," *ṛí* "to go," *gṛí* "to sound," *jyá* "to decay," *rí* "to injure," *lí* "to adhere," *vlí* "to choose," AND *plí* "to go." Thus *punáti* or *puníte* "he purifies," *pavitá* "he will purify."

The verb *lú (lúñ)* "to cut" makes *lunáti* and *luníte* "he cuts."

The verb *stṛí (stṛíñ)* "to cover," makes *stṛiṇáti* "he covers." By No. 690 (which debars No. 428) we have *tastára* "he covered," *tastaratuh* "they two covered," *tastare* "he covered," *staritá* or *starítá* (No. 654) "he will cover," *stṛiṇíyat* or *stṛiṇíta* "he may cover," *stíryát* (Nos. 706 and 651) "may he cover."

लिङ्सिचोरात्मनेपदेषु । ७ । २ । ४२ ।

वृङ्वृञ्भ्यामॄदन्ताच्च परयोर्लिङ्सिचोरिड्वा स्यात् तङि ।

No. 737.—WHEN the ÁTMANEPADA affixes ARE EMPLOYED, then let *iṭ* be optionally the augment OF LIŃ AND SICH coming after the verbs *vṛi (vṛiñ)* "to serve" and *vṛi (vṛiñ)* "to choose," and after what ends in long *ṛí*.

न लिङि । ७ । २ । ३९ ।

वॄत इटो लिङि न दीर्घः । स्तरिषीष्ट । उश्च । अनेन कित्त्वम् । स्तीर्षीष्ट । सिचि च परस्मैपदेषु । अस्तारीत् । अस्तारिष्टाम् । अस्तारिषुः । अस्तरिष्ट । अस्तीर्ष्ट । कॄञ् हिंसायाम् । १४ । कृणाति । कृणीते । चकार । चकरे । वॄञ् वरणे । १५ । वृणाति । वृणीते । ववार । ववरे । वरिता । वरीता । उदोष्ठ्येत्युत्वम् । वूर्यात् । वरिषीष्ट । वूर्षीष्ट । अवारीत् । अवारिष्टाम् । अवरिष्ट । अवरीष्ट । अवूर्ष्ट । धूञ् कम्पने । १६ । धुनाति । धुनीते । धोता । धविता । अधावीत् । अधविष्ट । अधोष्ट । ग्रह उपादाने । १७ । गृह्णाति । गृह्णीते । जग्राह । जगृहे ।

No. 738.—The long vowel is NOT the substitute (No. 654) for the augment *iṭ* after the verbs *vṛiń* or *vṛiń*, or what ends in long *ṛí*, WHEN LIŃ FOLLOWS. Thus (No. 735) *starishíshṭa*, or, by No. 581, the affixes being regarded as having an indicatory *k*, *stírshishṭa* (No. 651) "may he cover," and, by No. 655, there being no prolongation of the augment *iṭ*, when *sich* and the *parasmaipada* affixes follow, *astárít* "he covered," *astárishṭám* "they two covered, *astárishuh* "they covered," *astarishṭa* or *astírshṭa* (No. 651) "he covered."

The verb *kṛí (kṛíń)* "to injure" makes *kṛiṇáti* (No. 736) or *kṛiṇíte* "he injures," *chakára* or *chakare* (No. 653) "he injured."

The verb *vṛí (vṛíń)* "to choose" makes *vṛiṇáti* or *vṛiṇíte* "he chooses," *vavára* or *vavare* "he chose," *varitá* or *varítá* (No. 645) "he will choose," and, by No 650, *vúryát* or *varishíshṭa* or *vúrshíshṭa* (No. 581) "may he choose," *avárít* "he chose," *avárishṭám* "they two chose," *avarishṭa* or *avaríshṭa* (No. 654) or *avúrshṭa* "he chose."

The verb *dhú (dhúń)* "to shake" makes *dhunáti* (No. 736) or *dhuníte* "he shakes," *dhotá* or *dhavitá* "he will shake," *adhávít* or *adhavishṭa* or *adhoshṭa* "he shook."

The verb *grah (graha)* "to take" makes *gṛihṇáti* (No. 675) or *gṛihṇíte* "he takes," *jagráha* or *jagṛihe* "he took."

ग्रहोऽलिटि दीर्घः ।७।२।३७।

एकाचो ग्रहेर्विहितस्येटो दीर्घो न तु लिटि । ग्रहीता । गृह्णातु ।

No. 739.—The LONG vowel is the substitute of the augment *iṭ* placed AFTER the verb GRAH "to take," containing only one vowel, but NOT WHEN LIṬ FOLLOWS. Thus *grahítá* "he will take," *gṛihṇátu* "let him take."

हलः श्नः शानज्झौ । ३ । १ । ८३ ।

हलः परस्य श्नः शानजादेशो हौ । गृहाण । गृह्यात् । ग्रहीषीष्ट । ह्म्यन्तेति न वृद्धिः । अग्रहीत् । अग्रहीष्टाम् । अग्रहीष्ट । अग्रहीषाताम् । कुष निष्कर्षे । १८ । कुष्णाति । कोषिता । अश भोजने । १९ । अश्नाति । आश । अशिता । अशिष्यति । अश्नातु । अशान । मुष स्तेये । २० । मोषिता । मुषाण । ज्ञा अवबोधने । २१ । जज्ञौ । वृङ् संभक्तौ । २२ । वृणीते । ववृषे । ववृढ्वे । वरिता । वरीता । अवरिष्ट । अवरीष्ट । अवृत ।

इति क्र्यादयः ॥

No. 740.—Let ŚÁNACH be the substitute OF ŚNÁ (No. 730) coming AFTER A CONSONANT, WHEN HI FOLLOWS. Thus *gṛiháṇa* "do thou take," *gṛihyát* or *grahíshíshṭa* (No. 739) "may he take," and, since the root ends in *h*, there being, by No. 500, no substitution of *vṛiddhi*, *agrahít* "he took," *agrahíshṭám* (No. 739) "they two took," *agrahíshṭa* "he took," *agrahíshátám* "they two took."

The verb *kush (kusha)* "to extract" makes *kushṇáti* "he extracts," *koshitá* "he will extract."

The verb *aś (aśa)* "to eat" makes *aśnáti* "he eats," *áśa* "he ate," *aśitá* "he will eat," *aśishyati* "he will eat," *aśnátu* "let him eat," *aśána* (No. 740) "do thou eat."

The verb *mush (musha)* "to steal" makes *moshitá* "he will steal," *musháṇa* (No. 740) "do thou steal."

The verb *jñá* "to know" makes *jajñau* (No. 523) "he knew."

The verb *vṛi (vṛiṅ)* "to serve," makes *vṛiṇíte* he serves," *vavṛishe* (No. 514) "thou didst serve," *vavṛiḍhwe* "you served," *varitá* or *varítá* (No. 654) "he will serve," *avarishṭa* or *avaríshṭa* or *avṛita* (No. 582) "he served."

So much for the 9th class of verbs,—"*krí, &c.*"

The 10th class of verbs consists of "*chur, &c.*"

The verb *chur (chura)* means "to steal."

। चुरादयः ।

चुर स्तेये । १ ।

सत्यापपाशरूपवीणातूलश्लोकसेनालोमत्वचवर्मवर्ण-चूर्णचुरादिभ्यो णिच् । ३ । १ । २५ ।

स्वार्थे । पुगन्तेति गुणः । सनाद्यन्ता इति धातुत्वम् । तिप्शबादि । गुणायादेशौ । चोरयति ।

No. 741.—The affix ṆICH is placed, without alteration of the sense, AFTER the words SATYA "truth" (which then takes the form of *satyápa* as exhibited in the aphorism), PÁŚA "a fetter," RÚPA "colour," VÍṆÁ "a lute," TÚLA "cotton," ŚLOKA "celebration," SENÁ "an army," LOMAN "the hair of the body," TWACHA "the skin," VARMAN "mail," VARṆA "celebration," and CHÚRṆA "powder," (all of which are then used as verbs) AND after the verbs CHUR "to steal," &c. By No. 485, these verbs (having a light penult) substitute *guna* for a simple vowel. By No. 502, words ending with the affix *ṇich* are held to be verbal roots:—hence they take the tense-affixes and conjugational affixes. Thus *chur*, by the addition of *ṇich* and the rule No. 485, having become *chori*, and this, by Nos. 419, 420, and 29, having become *choraya*, we have *chorayati* "he steals."

णिचश्च । १ । ३ । ७४ ।

णिजन्तादात्मनेपदं कर्तृगामिनि क्रियाफले । चोरयते । चोरयामास । चोरयिता । चोर्यात् । चोरयिषीष्ट । णिश्रीति चङ् । णौ चङीति ह्रस्वः । चङि द्वित्वम् । हलादिः शेषः । दीर्घो लघोरित्यभ्यासस्य दीर्घः । अचूचुरत् । अचूचुरत । कथ वाक्यप्रबन्धे । २ । अल्लोपः ।

No. 742.—AND let the *átmanepada* affixes be employed AFTER what ends with ṆICH (No. 741), when the fruit of the action goes to the agent. Thus *chorayate* "he steals (for his own use)," *chorayámása*, (No. 504) "he stole," *chorayitá* "he will steal," *choryát* or *chorayishíshṭa* "may he steal." When *luń* follows, then *chań* is substituted for *chli* by No. 562; a short vowel is substituted for the penult by No. 564; there is reduplication, by No. 565, since *chań* follows; and the first consonant alone of the reduplicate is left (No. 428); and, finally, the vowel of the reduplicate being lengthened by No. 568, we have *achúchurat* or *achúchurata* "he stole."

The verb *katha* "to speak" rejects the final *a* by No. 505.

अचः परस्मिन् पूर्वविधौ । १ । १ । ५७ ।

परनिमित्तोऽजादेशः स्थानिवत् स्थानिभूतादचः पूर्वत्वेन दृष्टस्य विधौ कर्तव्ये । इति स्थानिवत्त्वान्नोपधावृद्धिः । कथयति । अग्लोपित्वाद्दीर्घसन्वद्भावौ न । अचकथत् । गण संख्याने । ३ । गणयति ।

No. 743.—A substitute in the room OF A VOWEL, CAUSED BY SOMETHING THAT FOLLOWS, shall be regarded as that whose place it takes, WHEN A RULE WOULD else TAKE EFFECT ON WHAT STANDS ANTERIOR to the original vowel. So there the *blank* which, by No. 505, takes the place of the final *a* of *katha* (No. 742), being regarded as the *a* whose place it took (and the final consonant of the root hence seeming to be the penult)—the substitution of *vṛiddhi* for the penult, by No. 489, (which would have given *káth* instead of *kath*) does not take place, and we have *kathayati* "he speaks." As there is elision of a vowel (by No. 505) there is no substitution of a long vowel by No. 568, nor is the case like that when the affix *san* follows, as spoken of in No. 566—so that we have *achakathat* (No. 565) "he spoke."

The verb *gaṇ (gaṇa)* "to count" makes *gaṇayati* "he counts."

ई च गणः । ७ । ४ । ९७ ।

गणयतेरभ्यासस्य ईत् स्याच्चादत्चङ्परे णौ । अजीगणत् । अजगणत् ।

इति चुरादयः ॥

No. 744.—AND let LONG í be the substitute OF the reduplicate of the verb GAṆ "to count;"—by the "and" it is implied that the substitute may be short *a*—when *ṇi,* followed by *chań,* follows. Thus *ajíganat* or *ajaganat* "he counted."

So much for the 10th class of verbs—"*chur, &c.*"

The verbs "that end in *ṇi*" have next to be considered.

। णयन्ताः ।

स्वतन्त्रः कर्ता । १ । ४ । ५४ ।

क्रियायां स्वातन्त्र्येण विवक्षितोऽर्थः कर्ता स्यात् ।

No. 745.—In the case of any action, whatever thing the speaker ARBITRARILY chooses to speak of as such shall be the AGENT or nominative to the verb—(for example, in the case of cooking, it is equally allowable to say that "the fire cooks," or "the cook cooks," or "the fuel cooks").

तत्प्रयोजको हेतुश्च । १ । ४ । ५५ ।

कर्तुः प्रयोजको हेतुसंज्ञः कर्तृसंज्ञश्च ।

No. 746.—Let that which is THE MOVER THEREOF, i. e. of an agent (No. 745), be called A CAUSE AND ALSO an agent.

हेतुमति च । ३ । १ । २६ ।

प्रयोजकव्यापारे प्रेषणादौ वाच्ये धातोर्णिच् । भवन्तं प्रेरयति भावयति ।

No. 747.—AND WHEN THE OPERATION OF A CAUSER, such as the operation of *directing,* is to be expressed, let the affix *ṇich* (No 741) come after a root. Thus, to express "he causes to become," we have *bhávayati.*

ओः पुयण्ज्यपरे । ७ । ४ । ८० ।

सनि परे यदङ्गं तदवयवाभ्यासात इत् स्यात् पवर्गयण्जकारेष्ववर्णपरेषु परतः । अबीभवत् । ष्ठा गतिनिवृत्तौ ।

No. 748.—Let there be long *í* in the room OF the U of the reduplicate forming part of an inflective base (No. 152) followed by *san* (No, 566), WHEN a letter of THE LABIAL CLASS FOLLOWS, or A

YAṆ, or the letter J—each of these being followed by the vowel *a*. Thus (the root *bhú* being reduplicated, and not the *bhávi*—else there would be no *u* to operate upon) we have *abíbhavat* "he caused to become."

The verb *shṭhá* means "to stop."

अर्तिह्रीव्लीरीक्नूयीक्ष्माय्यातां पुङ्णौ । ७ । ३ । ३६ ।

स्थापयति ।

No. 749.—WHEN ṆI FOLLOWS, let PUK be the augment of the verbs ṚI "to go," HRÍ "to be ashamed," VLÍ "to choose,," RÍ "to roar," KNÚYÍ "to sound," KSHMÁY "to shake," AND of verbs ending in LONG Á. Thus *sthápayati* "he causes to stand."

तिष्ठतेरित् । ७ । ४ । ५ ।

उपधाया इश्चङ्परे णौ । अतिष्ठिपत् । घट चेष्टायाम् ।

No. 750.—When *ṇi*, followed by *chań*, follows, let SHORT I be the substitute OF the penult of the verb SHṬHÁ (in the form *sthâp*—No. 749). Thus *atishṭhipat* "he caused to stand."

The verb *ghaṭ* means "to put together."

मितां ह्रस्वः । ६ । ४ । ९२ ।

घटादीनां ज्ञपादीनां च ह्रस्वः । घटयति । ज्ञप ज्ञाने ज्ञापने च । ज्ञपयति । अजिज्ञपत् ।

इति ण्यन्तप्रक्रिया ॥

No. 751.—Let there be a SHORT vowel in the room OF (the vowel, lengthened by *ṇich*, of) THE verbs "*ghaṭ, &c,*" and "*jńap, &c,*" WHICH (in the list of verbs) HAVE AN INDICATORY M. Thus *ghaṭayati* "he puts together."

The verb *jńap* "to know or inform" makes, in like manner, *jńapayati* "he informs," *ajijńapat* (Nos. 566 and 567) "he informed."

So much for the formation of those that end in *ṇi*.

The verbs "that end in *san*" have next to be considered.

। सन्नन्ताः ।

धातोः कर्मणः समानकर्तृकादिच्छायां वा । ३ । १ । ७ ।

इषिकर्मणो धातोरिषिणैककर्तृकात् सन् वेच्छायाम् । पठ व्यक्तायां वाचि ।

No. 752.—The affix *san* is OPTIONALLY attached, IN THE SENSE OF WISHING, AFTER A ROOT EXPRESSING THE ACT wished and HAVING THE SAME AGENT OF THE ACTION as the wisher thereof.

As an example let *paṭh* "to read" be taken.

सन्यङोः । ६ । १ । ९ ।

सन्नन्तस्य यङन्तस्य च प्रथमस्यैकाचो द्वे स्तोऽजादेस्तु द्वितीयस्य । सन्यतः । पठितुमिच्छति पिपठिषति । कर्मणः किम् । गमनेनेच्छति । समानकर्तृकात् किम् । शिष्याः पठन्त्वितीच्छति गुरुः । वाग्रहणाद्वाक्यमपि । लुङ्सनोर्घस्लृ ।

No. 753.—OF the first portion, containing a single vowel, of what ends with SAN (No. 752) AND of what ends with YAŃ (No. 758), there are two; but, in the case of what begins with a vowel, the reduplication is of the second portion (—as in No. 426). Short *i* being substituted for the *a* in the reduplication, we have *pipaṭhishati* "he wishes to read."

Why do we (in No. 752) say "the act wished?" Witness *gamanenechchhati* "by going he wishes (to accomplish something)"—where the "going" is not the "act wished," and the affix *san* does not therefore apply.

Why do we say "having the same agent?" Witness *śishyáh paṭhantwitíchchhati guruh* "the teacher wishes that the pupils should read,"—(where the wisher, and the agent of the action wished are not the same).

By the employment of the expression "optionally" (No. 752), it is implied that the meaning may be expressed by a phrase also (in those cases in which the formation of a desiderative verb by means of the affix is allowable).

When *san* follows, *ghasḷri* (No. 595) is substituted for the verb *ad* "to eat."

सः स्यार्धधातुके । ७ । ४ । ४९ ।

सस्य तः स्यात् सादावार्धधातुके । अत्तुमिच्छति जिघत्सति । एकाच इति नेट् ।

No. 754.—Let there be *t* in the room OF S, WHEN an ÁRDHA-DHÁTUKA affix, beginning with S, FOLLOWS. Thus *jighatsati* (No. 753) "he wishes to eat." In consequence of No. 510, the augment *iṭ* is not applicable here.

अज्झनगमां सनि । ६ । ४ । १६ ।

अजन्तानां हन्तेरजादेशगमेश्च दीर्घो झलादौ सनि ।

No. 755.—WHEN SAN, beginning with a *jhal*, (i. e. not preceded by the augment *iṭ*) FOLLOWS, a long vowel shall be the substitute OF verbs ending in A VOWEL, AND OF the verb HAN "to strike," AND OF the verb GAM "to go"—the substitute of the vowel roots (viz. *i*, *iṇ*, *ik*, *iń*).

इको झल् । १ । २ । ९ ।

इगन्ताज्झलादिः सन् कित् । ऋत इद्धातोः । कर्तुमिच्छति चिकीर्षति ।

No. 756.—AFTER a verb ending in an IK, *san*, beginning with A JHAL (i. e. without the augment *iṭ*), shall be regarded as having an indicatory *k*. Then, applying No. 706, (the vowel having become long by No. 755) we may have *chikírshati* "he wishes to make."

सनि ग्रहगुहोश्च । ७ । २ । १२ ।

ग्रहेर्गुहेरुगन्ताच्च सन इण्न स्यात् । बुभूषति ।

इति सन्नन्ताः ॥

No. 757.—Let not *iṭ* be the augment of SAN AFTER the verbs GRAH "to take," GUH "to cover," AND what ends in an *uk*. Thus *bubhúshati* "he wishes to become."

So much for verbs "ending in *san.*"

Verbs "ending in the affix *yań*" are next to be considered.

। यङन्ताः ।

धातोरेकाचो हलादेः क्रियासमभिहारे यङ् । ३ । १ । २२ ।

पौनःपुन्ये भृशार्थे च द्योत्ये धातोरेकाचो हलादेर्यङ् ।

No. 758.—WHEN THE REPETITION OF THE ACT, OR ITS INTENSITY, IS to be indicated, let YAŃ come AFTER A ROOT HAVING A SINGLE VOWEL AND BEGINNING WITH A CONSONANT.

गुणो यङ्लुकोः । ७ । ४ । ८२ ।

अभ्यासस्य गुणो यङि यङ्लुकि च । ङिदन्तत्वादात्मनेपदम् । पुनः पुनरतिशयेन वा भवति । बोभूयते । बोभूयांचक्रे । अबोभूयिष्ट ।

No. 759.—Let GUṆA be the substitute of the reduplicate (No. 753), WHEN YAŃ FOLLOWS, OR even when A BLANK (*luk* No. 209) has been substituted for *yań*. From its ending with what has an indicatory *ń* (No. 410), a verb with this affix takes the *átmanepada* affixes. Thus *bobhúyate* "he is repeatedly or intensely," *bobhúyáńchakre* "he was repeatedly," *abobhúyishṭa* "he was repeatedly."

नित्यं कौटिल्ये गतौ । ३ । १ । २३ ।

गत्यर्थात् कौटिल्य एव यङ् न तु क्रियासमभिहारे ।

No. 760.—After a verb WITH THE SENSE OF MOTION, the affix *yań* gives ALWAYS THE SENSE OF CROOKEDNESS,—not of repetition of the action.

दीर्घोऽकितः । ७ । ४ । ८३ ।

अकितोऽभ्यासस्य दीर्घो यङ्लुकोः । कुटिलं व्रजति । वाव्रज्यते ।

No. 761.—When *yań*, or a blank substituted for it, follows, let there be A LONG vowel in the room of a reduplicate syllable which has NOT AN INDICATORY K. Thus *vávrajyate* "he moves crookedly."

यस्य हलः । ६ । ४ । ४९ ।

हलः परस्य यस्य लोप आर्धधातुके । आदेः परस्य । अतो लोपः । वाव्रजांचक्रे । वाव्रजिता ।

No. 762.—There is elision OF YA coming AFTER A CONSONANT, when an *árdhadhátuka* affix follows. Thus (when, for example, the *árdhadhátuka* affix *ám* follows) the first letter (of the syllable *ya*) is elided in accordance with No. 88, and then the vowel is elided by No. 505, giving *vávrajáñchakre* "he went crookedly," *vávrajitá* "he will go crookedly."

रीगृदुपधस्य च । ७ । ४ । ९० ।

ऋदुपधस्य धातोरभ्यासस्य रीगागमो यङ्लुकोः । वरीवृत्यते । वरीवृतांचक्रे । वरीवृतिता ।

No. 763.—AND when *yań*, or a blank substituted for it, follows, let RÍK be the augment OF the reduplicate syllable of WHAT root HAS ṚI FOR ITS PENULT. Thus *varívṛityate* "he remains repeatedly," *varívṛitáñchakre* "he remained repeatedly," *varívṛititá* "he will remain repeatedly."

क्षुभ्नादिषु च । ८ । ४ । ३९ ।

णत्वं न । नरीनृत्यते । जरीगृह्यते ।

इति यङन्तप्रक्रिया ॥

No. 764.—AND IN the case of KSHUBH "to tremble" (which, as a verb of the 9th class, No. 730, becomes *kshubhná*), &c. there is not the substitution of the cerebral *ṇ* (notwithstanding No. 157). Thus *narínṛityate* "he dances repeatedly." (In accordance with (No. 763.) we have *jarígṛihyate* "he takes repeatedly."

So much for the formation of "what ends in *yań*."

The verbs "that end with a blank substituted for *yań*" have next to be considered.

। यङ्लुगन्ताः ।

यङोऽचि च । २ । ४ । ७४ ।

यङोऽचि प्रत्यये लुक् स्याच्चकारात् तं विनापि क्वचित्। अनैमित्तिकोऽयम्। अन्तरङ्गत्वादादौ भवति। ततः प्रत्ययलक्षणेन यङन्तत्वाद्द्वित्वम्। अभ्यासकार्यम्। धातुत्वाल्लडादयः। शेषात् कर्तरीति परस्मैपदम्। चर्करीतं चेत्यदादौ पाठाच्छपो लुक्।

No. 765.—AND WHEN the affix ACH (No. 837) FOLLOWS, there may be elision OF YAŃ. By the "and" it is signified that this may take place sometimes even without that affix :—and this is not the result of anything assigned as the cause thereof, (whereas, in the other case, there was an assigned reason for the elision—viz. the affix *ach*). This elision takes place first, as it is independent of anything else (whereas the reduplication is dependent on the verb, the affix, &c). Then, after that, through the force of the affix (which remains, though the affix has been elided), since the verb is regarded as ending in *yań*, there is reduplication (No. 753), and the appropriate operations are to be performed on the reduplicate syllable. Since the word (through No. 502) is regarded as a root, the tense-affixes &c. are applicable to it. The *parasmaipada* affixes are employed in accordance with No. 412. As we read, in No. 636, that verbs with *yań* elided are to be regarded as belonging to the 2nd class, "*ad, &c.,*" we infer that there is to be elision of *śap* (No. 589).

यङो वा। ७। ३। ९४।

यङ्लुगन्तात् परस्य हलादेः पितः सार्वधातुकस्येड्वा स्यात्। भूसुवोरिति निषेधो यङ्लुकि भाषायां न। बोभूतु तेतिक्ते इति छन्दसि निपातनात्। बोभवीति। बोभोति। बोभूतः। अदभ्यस्तात्। बोभुवति। बोभवांचकार। बोभवामास। बोभविता। बोभविष्यति। बोभवीतु। बोभोतु। बोभूतात्। बोभूताम्। बोभुवतु। बोभूहि। बोभवानि। अबोभवीत्। अबोभोत्। अबोभूताम्। अबोभवुः। बोभूयात्। बोभूयाताम्। बोभूयुः। बोभूयात्। बोभूयास्ताम्। बोभूयासुः। गातिस्थेति सिचो लुक्। यङो वेतीट्पक्षे गुणं बाधित्वा नित्यत्वाद्वुक्। अबोभूवीत्। अबोभोत्। अबोभूताम्। अबोभूवुः। अबोभविष्यत्।

इति यङ्लुगन्ताः ॥

No. 766.—Let *iṭ* be OPTIONALLY the augment of a *sárvadhátuka* affix distinguished by an indicatory *p*, commencing with a consonant, and coming AFTER a verb with YAŃ elided. The prohibition (of *guṇa*) by No. 474 does not, in secular language, extend to the case where *yań* is elided. This is inferred from the fact that the form *bobhútu* in the *Veda* (in which *guṇa* is not substituted—) is one of those enumerated (in VII. 4. 65.—thus "*bobhútu tetikte* &c.,") among the irregularities. Thus we have *bobhavíti* or *bobhoti* "he is frequently," *bobhútah* "they two are frequently," substituting *at* for *jh*, by No. 645, as it is reduplicated, *bobhuvati* "they are frequently," *bobhavánchakára* or *bobhavámása* "he was frequently," *bobhavitá* "he will be frequently," *bobhavishyati* "he will be frequently," *bobhavítu* or *bobhotu* "let him be frequently," *bobhútát* "may he be frequently," *bobhútám* "let the two be frequently," *bobhuvatu* "let them be frequently," *bobhúhi* "be thou frequently," *bobhaváni* "let me be frequently," *abobhavít* or *abobhot* "they were frequently," *abobhútám* "they two were frequently," *abobhavuh* "they were frequently," *bobhúyát* "he may be frequently," *bobhúyátám* "they two may be frequently," *bobhúyuh* "they were frequently," *bobhúyát* "may he be frequently," *bobhúyástám* "may they two be frequently," *bobhúyásuh* "may they be frequently." According to No. 473, there is elision of *sich*. On the alternative of there being the augment *iṭ* from No. 766, there is the augment *vuk* from No. 425, this debarring *guṇa* (No. 420) because it presents itself *always* (whether *guṇa* is substituted or not —and therefore, according to one of the maxims of the Grammar, takes the precedence). Thus we have *abobhúvít* or *abobhot* "he was frequently," *abobhútám* "they two were frequently," *abobhúvuh* they were frequently," *abobhavishyat* "he would be frequently."

So much for those "that end with a blank substituted for *yań*."

The "nominal verbs" have next to be considered.

। नामधातवः ।

सुप आत्मनः क्यच् । ३ । १ । ८ ।

इषिकर्मण एषितुः संबन्धिनः सुबन्तादिच्छायामर्थे क्यज्वा ।

No. 767.—Let KYACH be optionally attached, in the sense of wishing, AFTER a word WITH A CASE-AFFIX expressing the object wished as connected with the wisher's SELF—(as, for example, a son,—when a man wishes to have a son of his own—not somebody else's son).

सुपो धातुप्रातिपदिकयोः ।२।४।७१।

एतयोरवयवस्य सुपो लुक् ।

No. 768.—Let there be elision (*luk*) OF A CASE-AFFIX when part of these two—VIZ. OF A ROOT AND OF A CRUDE FORM (No. 135).

क्यचि च ।७।४।३३।

अवर्णस्य ईः । आत्मनः पुत्रमिच्छति पुत्रीयति ।

No. 769.—AND WHEN KYACH (No. 767) FOLLOWS, let *í* be the substitute of *a* or *á*. Thus *putríyati* "he wishes for a son of his own."

नः क्ये ।१।४।१५।

क्यचि क्यङि च नान्तमेव पदं नान्यत् । नलोपः । राजीयति । नान्तमेवेति किम् । वाच्यति । हलि च । गीर्यति । पूर्यति । धातोरित्येव । नेह । दिवमिच्छति दिव्यति ।

No. 770.—WHEN KYA—i.e. *kyach* or *kyań* (No. 776)—FOLLOWS, only what ends in N is considered a *pada*, and no other word. So, the *n* of *rájan* being elided by No. 200, we have *rájíyati* "he wishes for a king." Why do we say "only what ends in *n*?" Witness *váchyati* "he wishes for words," (which would otherwise, by No. 333, have changed the *ch* to *k*). By No. 651 the vowel is lengthened in *gíryati* "he wishes for words," and *púryati* "he wishes for a city;" but, since the lengthening directed by No 651 applies only to a verbal root, it does not take place in the example *divyati* "he wishes for heaven."

क्यस्य विभाषा ।६।४।५०।

हलः परयोः क्यच्क्यङोर्लोपो वार्धधातुके। आदेः परस्य। अतो लोपः। तस्य स्थानिवत्त्वाल्लघूपधगुणो न। समिधिता। समिध्यिता।

No. 771.—When an *árdhadhátuka* affix follows, there is OPTIONALLY elision OF KYA—i. e. of *kyach* and *kyań*—coming after a consonant. According to No. 88 the elision here is that of the *y*, and a blank takes the place of the *a* by No. 505. Since the blank is regarded in the same light as that of which it took the place (No. 163), there is no substitution of *guṇa* by No. 485—and we have *samidhitá* or *samidhyitá* "he will wish for fuel."

काम्यच् च। ३। १। ९।

उक्तविषये काम्यच्। पुत्रमात्मन इच्छति। पुत्रकाम्यति। पुत्रकाम्यिता।

No. 772.—AND under the same circumstances (No. 767), KÁMYACH may be added. Thus *putrakámyati* "he wishes for a son of his own," *putrakámyitá* "he will wish for a son."

उपमानादाचारे। ३। १। १०।

उपमानात् कर्मणः सुबन्तादाचारेऽर्थे क्यच् पुत्रमिवाचरति पुत्रीयति छात्रम्। विष्णूयति द्विजम्।

No. 773.—Let *kyach*, IN THE SENSE OF TREATMENT, come AFTER a word with a case affix denoting THE object of COMPARISON. Thus *putríyati chhátram* "he treats the pupil as a son," *vishṇúyati dwijam* "he treats the Brahman as if he were Vishṇu.

सर्वप्रातिपदिकेभ्यः क्विब्वा वक्तव्यः। अतो गुणे। कृष्ण इवाचरति कृष्णति। स्व इवाचरति स्वति। सस्वौ।

No. 774.—"The affix KWIP SHOULD BE MENTIONED as coming OPTIONALLY AFTER PRONOUNS AND CRUDE NOUNS." Where the word is a crude noun and not a *pada*, No. 300 applies, and we may have *krishṇati* "he acts like Kṛishṇa," *swati* "he acts like himself," *saswau* "he acted like himself."

अनुनासिकस्य क्विझलोः क्ङिति। ६। ४। १५।

अनुनासिकान्तस्योपधाया दीर्घः स्यात् क्वौ झलादौ च क्ङिति । इदमिवाचरति इदामति । राजेव राजानति । पन्था इव पथीनति ।

No. 775.—A long vowel shall be the substitute for the penult OF what ends with A NASAL, WHEN KWIP (No. 855) FOLLOWS, OR an affix beginning with A JHAL and DISTINGUISHED BY AN INDICATORY K OR Ń. Thus *idámati* "he acts like this one," *rájánati* "he acts like a king," *pathínati* "it serves as a road."

कष्टाय क्रमणे । ३ । १ । १४ ।

चतुर्थ्यन्तात् कष्टशब्दादुत्साहे क्यङ् । कष्टाय क्रमते कष्टायते । पापं कर्तुमुत्सहत इत्यर्थः ।

No. 776.—The affix *kyań*, IN THE SENSE OF EXERTION, comes after the word KASHṬA "pain," with the 4th case-affix. Thus (the case-affix being elided by No. 768, and the final lengthened by No. 518) we have *kashṭáyate* "he is assiduous for trouble," i. e. "he is assiduous in the commission of sin."

शब्दवैरकलहाभ्रकण्वमेघेभ्यः करणे । ३ । १ । १७ ।

एभ्यः कर्मभ्यः करोत्यर्थे क्यङ् । शब्दं करोति शब्दायते ।

No. 777.—The affix *kyań,* IN THE SENSE OF MAKING, comes AFTER these words, as the objects of the action—viz. ŚABDA "sound," VAIRA "heroism," KALAHA "strife," ABHRA "a cloud," KAṆWA "sin," AND MEGHA "a cloud." Thus *śabdáyate* "he makes a noise."

तत् करोति तदाचष्ट इति णिच् ।

No. 778.—"In the sense of HE DOES THAT, or HE SAYS THAT," the affix *ṇich* may be employed.

प्रातिपदिकाद्धात्वर्थे बहुलमिष्ठवच्च । प्रातिपदिकाद्धात्वर्थे णिच् स्यात् । इष्ठे यथा प्रातिपदिकस्य पुंवद्भावरभावटिलोपविन्मतुब्लोपयणादिलोपप्रस्थस्फाद्यादेशभसंज्ञास्तद्वण्णावपि स्युः । इत्यग्लोपः । घटं करोत्याचष्टे वा घटयति ।

इति नामधातवः ॥

No. 779.—"The affix *ṇich* may come AFTER A CRUDE NOUN, WITH THE SENSE OF A VERB, IN AN INDEFINITE VARIETY OF WAYS, AND it shall be LIKE the affix ISHṬHA (No. 1306)." In like manner as, when *ishṭha* is affixed, there is the masculine form (substituted for the feminine), the substitution of *r* (for *ṛi*), the elision of the last vowel with what follows it (No. 52), the elision of the affixes *vin* (No. 1281) and *matup* (No. 1268), the elision of what begins with *yaṇ* (as the *r* of the syllable *ra* in the word *dúra* "far"), the substitution of *pra* (for *priya*) *stha* for *(sthira) spha* (for *sphira*) &c. (see VI. 4. 157), and the denomination *bha* (No. 185)—just so let there be also, when *ṇi* follows. Therefore, with the elision of *ak* (i. e. of the last vowel—No. 52—), we may optionally have *ghaṭayati* "he makes a jar," or "he calls it a jar."

So much for the "nominal verbs."

The class of words called "*kaṇḍú, &c.*" has next to be considered.

। कण्ड्वादयः ।

कण्ड्वादिभ्यो यक् । ३ । १ । २७ ।

एभ्यो धातुभ्यो नित्यं यक् स्यात् स्वार्थे । कण्डूञ् गात्रविघर्षणे । १ । कण्डूयति । कण्डूयते । इत्यादि ।

इति कण्ड्वादयः ॥

No. 780.—Let there be always YAK AFTER these roots—viz. KAṆḌÚ, &C.—without alteration of the sense.

Thus from the noun *kaṇḍú* "the itch" comes the verb *kaṇḍú (kaṇḍúñ)*, meaning "to itch or scratch." From this we have *kaṇḍúyati* or *kaṇḍúyate*—and so on.

So much for "*kaṇḍú, &c.*"

It is next to be considered under what circumstances the *átmanepada* affixes fall to be employed.

। आत्मनेपदम् ।

कर्तरि कर्मव्यतिहारे । १ । ३ । १४ ।

क्रियाविनिमये द्योत्ये कर्तर्यात्मनेपदम् । व्यतिलुनीते । अन्यस्य योग्यं लवनं करोतीत्यर्थः ।

No. 781.—An *átmanepada* affix is employed IN DENOTING THE AGENT, WHEN THE INTERCHANGE OF THE ACTION IS to be expressed. Thus *vyatiluníte* "he performs a cutting (of wood &c.) which was the appropriate office of another."

न गतिहिंसार्थेभ्यः । १ । ३ । १५ ।

व्यतिगच्छन्ति । व्यतिघ्नन्ति ।

No. 782.—An *átmanepada* affix is NOT employed (notwithstanding No. 781) AFTER WHAT verbs mean "to go" and "to injure." Hence *vyatigachchhanti* "they go against each other," *vyatighnanti* "they fight together."

नेर्विशः । १ । ३ । १७ ।

निविशते ।

No. 783.—An *átmanepada* affix is employed AFTER the verb VIŚ "to enter," coming AFTER NI. Thus *niviśate* "he enters in."

परिव्यवेभ्यः क्रियः । १ । ३ । १८ ।

परिक्रीणीते । विक्रीणीते । अवक्रीणीते ।

No. 784.—Also AFTER the verb KRÍ "to buy or sell," coming AFTER PARI, VI, OR AVA. Thus *parikríṇíte* "he buys," *vikríṇíte* "he sells," *avakríṇíte* "he buys."

विपराभ्यां जेः । १ । ३ । १९ ।

विजयते । पराजयते ।

No. 785.—Also AFTER the verb JI "to conquer," coming AFTER VI OR PARÁ. Thus *vijayate* "he conquers," *parájayate* "he conquers."

समवप्रविभ्यः स्थः । १ । ३ । २२ ।

संतिष्ठते । अवतिष्ठते । प्रतिष्ठते । वितिष्ठते ।

No. 786.—Also AFTER the verb SHTHÁ "to stand," coming AFTER SAM, AVA, PRA, OR VI. Thus *santishṭhate* "he stays with," *avatishṭhate* "he waits patiently," *pratishṭhate* "he sets forth," *vitishṭhate* "he stands apart."

अपह्नवे ज्ञः ।१।३।४४।

शतमपजानीते । अपलपतीत्यर्थः ।

No. 787.—Also AFTER the verb JŇÁ "to know" (preceded by *apa*) IN THE SENSE OF DENYING. Thus *śatamapajánîte* "he denies (the debt of) a hundred (rupees)."

अकर्मकाच्च ।१।३।४५।

सर्पिषो जानीते । सर्पिषोपायेन प्रवर्तत इत्यर्थः ।

No. 788.—AND AFTER (the verb *jňá* "to know") used (in certain senses) as AN INTRANSITIVE. Thus *sarpisho jánîte* "he engages (in sacrifice) by means of clarified butter."

समस्तृतीयायुक्तात् ।१।३।५४।

रथेन संचरते ।

No. 789.—Also AFTER (the verb *char* "to go") coming after SAM, and CONNECTED WITH a noun in THE 3RD CASE. Thus *rathena sancharate* "he rides with (in) a chariot."

दाणश्च सा चेच्चतुर्थ्यर्थे ।१।३।५५।

समो दाणस्तृतीयान्तेन युक्तादुक्तं स्यात् तृतीया चेच्चतुर्थ्यर्थे । दास्या संयच्छते कामी ।

No. 790.—Let the aforesaid (employment of the *átmanepada* affixes) take place AFTER the verb DÁ *(dán)* "to give," coming after *sam*, and connected with a noun in the 3rd case, PROVIDED THIS 3rd case HAVE THE SENSE OF THE 4TH. Thus *dásyá sanyachchhate kámí* "the lover gives to the female slave."

पूर्ववत् सनः ।१।३।६२।

सनः पूर्वो यो धातुस्तेन तुल्यं सन्नन्तादप्यात्मनेपदं स्यात् । एदिधिषते ।

No. 791.—Let an *átmanepada* affix come also AFTER a verb ending in the affix SAN (No. 752) in like manner AS it would come AFTER THAT verb itself WHICH STANDS BEFORE the affix *san*. Thus (as the verb *edh* "to increase,"—No. 543—takes the *átmanepada* affixes, so does it when *san* is added—giving) *edidhishate* "he wishes to increase."

हलन्ताच्च । १ । २ । १० ।

इक्समीपाद्धलः परो झलादिः सन् कित् । निविविक्षते ।

No. 792.—AND AFTER WHAT ENDS IN A CONSONANT immediately preceded by an *ik*, the affix *san*, beginning with a *jhal* (i. e. not having the augment *iṭ*), shall be regarded as having an indicatory *k*. Thus *nivivikshate* "he will wish to enter."

गन्धनावक्षेपणसेवनसाहसिक्यप्रतियत्नप्रकथनोपयोगेषु कृञः । १ । ३ । ३२ ।

गन्धनं सूचनम् । उत्कुरुते सूचयतीत्यर्थः । अवक्षेपणं भर्त्सनम् । श्येनो वर्तिकामुत्कुरुते । भर्त्सयतीत्यर्थः । हरिमुपकुरुते । सेवत इत्यर्थः । परदारान् प्रकुरुते तेषु सहसा प्रवर्तते । एधो दकस्योपस्कुरुते गुणमाधत्ते । कथाः प्रकुरुते । कथयतीत्यर्थः । शतं प्रकुरुते धर्मार्थं विनियुङ्क्ते । एषु किम् । कटं करोति । भुजो अनवने । ओदनं भुङ्क्ते । अनवने किम् । महीं भुनक्ति ।

No. 793.—Let the *átmanepada* affixes come AFTER the verb KṚI "to make," when it is used IN THESE SENSES, viz. "MANIFESTATION," "SARCASM," "SERVICE," "VIOLENCE," "CHANGE," "RECITATION," AND "ACTION TENDING TO EFFECT A DESIRED PURPOSE."

By "manifestation" is here meant "informing against,"—thus *utkurute* "he informs against." By "sarcasm" is meant "reviling,"—thus *śyeno vartikámutkurute* "the hawk reviles the quail." So, too, *harimupakurute* "he worships Hari :"—*paradárán prakurute* "he offers violence to another's wife :"—*edhodakasyopaskurute* "the wood gives a new quality to the water" (or "he prepares the wood and the water for a sacrifice):"—*katháh prakurute* "he recites stories:"—*śatan prakurute* "he distributes a hundred (pieces of money, for the sake of merit)."

Why do we say "in these senses?" Witness *kaṭan karoti* "he makes a mat,"—(in which example an *átmanepada* affix is not employed.)

According to No. 718, the verb *bhuj* takes the *átmanepada* affixes, when it does not mean "to protect." Thus *odanan bhuṅkte* "he eats boiled rice." Why do we say "when it does not mean to "protect?" Witness *mahín bhunakti* "he protects the earth."

So much for the application of the *átmanepada* affixes.

The employment of the *parasmaipada* affixes is next to be considered.

इत्यात्मनेपदप्रक्रिया ॥

। परस्मैपदम् ।

अनुपराभ्यां कृञः । १ । ३ । ७९ ।

कर्तृगे च फले गन्धनादौ च परस्मैपदं स्यात् । अनुकरोति । पराकरोति ।

No. 794.—Let the *parasmaipada* affixes come AFTER the verb KṚI "to make," coming AFTER ANU AND PARÁ, even when the fruit of the action goes to the agent, and when the sense is that of "informing against, &c" (No. 793). Thus *anukaroti* "he imitates," *parákaroti* "he does well."

अभिप्रत्यतिभ्यः क्षिपः । १ । ३ । ८० ।

क्षिप प्रेरणे । स्वरितेत् । अभिक्षिपति ।

No. 795.—And AFTER the verb KSHIP, coming AFTER ABHI, PRATI, AND ATI. The verb *kship* means "to throw." The indicatory vowel of this root is circumflexly accented (No. 411—so that, but for this rule, we should have had both *padas* in the case of) *abhikshipati* "he throws on."

प्राद्वहः । १ । ३ । ८१ ।

प्रवहति ।

No. 796.—And AFTER the verb VAHA "to bear," coming AFTER PRA. Thus *pravahati* "it (the river) flows."

परेर्मृषः । १ । ३ । ८२ ।

परिमृषति ।

No. 797.—And AFTER the verb MṚISH "to bear," coming AFTER PARI. Thus *parimṛishati* "he endures" or "he forgives."

व्याङ्परिभ्यो रमः । १ । ३ । ८३ ।

रमु क्रीडायाम् । विरमति ।

No. 798.—And AFTER the verb RAM, coming AFTER VI, ÁṄ, AND PARI. The verb *ram (ramu)* means "to sport." Thus *viramati* "he takes rest."

उपाच्च । १ । ३ । ८४ ।

यज्ञदत्तमुपरमति । उपरमयतीत्यर्थः । अन्तर्भावितण्यर्थोऽयम् ।

इति पदव्यवस्था ॥

No. 799.—AND AFTER UPA (the verb *ram* takes the *parasmaipada* affixes). Thus *yajnadattamuparamati* "he causes Yajñadatta to refrain." This is an instance of a verb involving in it the force of the affix *ṇi* (No. 747).

So much for the allotment of the *padas*.

The Impersonal and Passive forms have next to be considered.

। भावकर्मप्रक्रिया ।

भावकर्मणोः । १ । ३ । १३ ।

लस्यात्मनेपदम् ।

No. 800.—Let an *átmanepada* affix be the substitute of the affix *l* (No. 405), WHEN IT DENOTES THE ACTION of the verb OR THE OBJECT of the verb.

सार्वधातुके यक्। ३। १। ६७।

भावकर्मवाचिनि धातोर्यक् सार्वधातुके । भावः क्रिया सा च भावार्थकलकारेणानूद्यते । युष्मदस्मद्भ्यां सामानाधिकरण्याभावात् प्रथमः पुरुषः । तिङ्वाच्यक्रियाया अद्रव्यरूपत्वेन द्वित्वाद्यप्रतीतेर्न द्विवचनादि किंत्वेकवचनमेवोत्सर्गतः । त्वया मयान्यैश्च भूयते । बभूवे ।

No. 801.—Let the affix YAK come after a root, WHEN A SÁRVADHÁTUKA affix FOLLOWS, denoting the action or the object. The "action" is the force of the verb itself; and this is again marked by the affix *l* (No. 405) when it has the sense of the action—(i. e. when the verb is used impersonally). In this case there is (substituted for the *l*) an affix of the "lowest person," because the verb is not in agreement with either the pronoun "I" or "Thou".—Inasmuch as the action denoted by the tense-affix is not of the nature of a substance (to which the notions of duality or plurality might attach), since there is here no notion of duality &c., neither an affix of the dual nor of the plural is to be employed, but hence necessarily only one of the singular.

Thus *twayá mayá anyaiścha bhúyate* "it is become by thee, by me, and by others"—(i. e. "Thou becomest," "I become," and "others become,")—and, again, *babhúve* (No. 432) "it was become."

स्यसिच्सीयुट्तासिषु भावकर्मणोरुपदेशेऽज्झनग्रहदृशां वा चिण्वदिट् च। ६। ४। ६२।

उपदेशे योऽच् तदन्तानां हनादीनां च चिणीवाङ्गकार्यं वा स्यात् स्यादिषु भावकर्मणोर्गम्यमानयोः स्यादीनामिडागमश्च । चिण्वद्भावपक्षेऽयमिट् । चिण्वद्भावाद्वृद्धिः । भाविता । भविता । भाविष्यते । भविष्यते । भूयताम् । अभूयत । भाविषीष्ट । भविषीष्ट ।

No. 802.—WHEN SYA (No. 435), SICH (No. 472), SÍYUT (No. 555), OR TÁSI (No. 435) FOLLOWS, IF THE ACTION OR THE OBJECT IS TO BE UNDERSTOOD by the affix (i. e. if the verb is impersonal or passive), then, on the inflective base OF verbs which IN their

ORIGINAL ENUNCIATION end in A VOWEL and on that OF the verbs *han*, &c.—viz. HAN "to kill," GRAH "to take," AND DṚIŚ "to see,"—THERE SHALL BE OPTIONALLY THE LIKE EFFECT AS IF the affix CHIṆ HAD FOLLOWED, AND IṬ shall be the augment of these affixes *sya*, &c. The augment *iṭ*, here mentioned, is to be applied on the alternative that the case is treated as if the affix *chiṇ* had followed—(not on the other alternative allowed by the rule). The substitution of *vṛiddhi* follows from the case's being treated as if *chiṇ* (with an indicatory *ṇ*—see No. 202—) had been attached. Thus we have *bhávitá* or *bhavitá* "it will be become by some one," *bhávishyate* or *bhavishyate* "it will be become," *bhúyatám* "let it be become," *abhúyata* "it was become," *bhávishíshṭa* or *bhavishíshṭa* "may it be become."

चिण् भावकर्मणोः । ३ । १ । ६६ ।

च्लेश्चिण् स्याद्भावकर्मवाचिनि ते परे । अभावि । अभाविष्यत । अभविष्यत । अकर्मकोऽप्युपसर्गवशात् सकर्मकः । अनुभूयते आनन्दश्चैत्रेण त्वया मया च । अनुभूयेते । अनुभूयन्ते । त्वमनुभूयसे । अहमनुभूये । अन्वभावि । अन्वभाविषाताम् । अन्वभविषाताम् । णिलोपः । भाव्यते । भावयांचक्रे । भावयांबभूवे । भावयामासे । चिण्वदिट् । भाविता । आभीयत्वेनासिद्धत्वाण्णिलोपः । भावयिता । भावयिषीष्ट । अभावि । अभाविषाताम् । अभावयिषाताम् । बुभूष्यते । बुभूषांचक्रे । बुभूषिता । बुभूषिष्यते । बोभूय्यते । बोभूयिष्यते । अकृत्सार्वधातुकयोर्दीर्घः । स्तूयते विष्णुः । स्ताविता । स्तोता । स्ताविष्यते । स्तोष्यते । अस्तावि । अस्ताविषाताम् । अस्तोषाताम् । ऋ गतौ । गुणोऽर्तीति गुणः । अर्यते । स्मृ स्मरणे । स्मर्यते । सस्मरे । उपदेशग्रहणाच्चिण्वदिट् । आरिता । अर्ता । स्मारिता । स्मर्ता । अनिदितामिति नलोपः । स्रस्यते । इदितस्तु । नन्द्यते । संप्रसारणम् । इज्यते ।

No. 803.—Let CHIṆ be the substitute of *chli* (No. 471), WHEN *ta* (No. 407) follows, DENOTING THE ACTION OR THE OBJECT. Thus *abhávi* "it was become by some one," *abhávishyata* (No. 802) or *abhavishyata* "it would be become."

Even a neuter verb (—a verb "without an object,"—) may, through the force of a preposition in combination with it, become active (—or "with an object)." For example—*anubhúyate ánandaśchaitreṇa twayá mayácha* "pleasure is experienced by Chaitra, by thee, and by me:"—and then again *anubhúyete* "the two are perceived," *anubhúyante* "they are perceived," *twamanubhúyase* "thou art perceived," *ahamanubhúye* "I am perceived," *anwabhávi* "it was perceived," *anwabhávishátám* or *anwabhavishátám* "the two were perceived." The affix *ṇi* (No. 747) being elided by No. 563, we have *bhávyate* "it is caused to be," *bhávayáñchakre* or *bhávayáñbabhúve* or *bhávayámáse* "it was caused to be." When (according to No. 802) the case is regarded as if the affix *chiṇ* had followed, then the augment *iṭ* is applied—giving *bhávitá* "it will be caused to be,"—the elision of *ṇi* (No. 563) still taking place, inasmuch as No. 802, in accordance with No. 599, is regarded by No. 563 as not having taken effect. On the other alternative allowed by No. 802, *bhávayitá* "it will be caused to be," *bhávayishíshṭa* "may it be caused to be," *abhávi* "it was caused to be," *abhávishátám* or *abhávayishátám* "the two were caused to be," *bubhúshyate* "it is wished to be," *bubhúsháñchakre* "it was wished to be," *bubhúshitá* "it will be wished to be," *bubhúshishyate* "it will be wished to be," *bobhúyyate* "it is repeatedly been," *bobhúyishyate* "it will be repeatedly been."

The vowel of the root (*shṭu* "to praise") being lengthened by No. 518, we have *stúyate vishṇuh* "Vishṇu is praised:"—*stávitá* (No. 802) or *stotá* "he will be praised," *stávishyate* or *stoshyate* "he will be praised," *astávi* "he was praised," *astávishátám* or *astoshátám* "the two were praised."

The verb *ṛi* "to go," substituting *guṇa* by No. 533, makes *aryate* "it is gone."

The verb *smṛi* "to remember" makes *smaryate* "it is remembered," *sasmare* "it was remembered."

These two verbs may be treated as if *chiṇ* followed, and may take the augment *iṭ*, because, in No. 802, the expression "in the original enunciation" is included, (and hence the fact that they end in a consonant at the time when the augment *iṭ* presents itself, does not prevent their taking it). Thus *áritá* or *artá* "it will be gone," *smáritá* or *smartá* "it will be remembered."

By No. 363, the nasal of the verb *srańs* "to fall," (which has not an indicatory *i*) being elided, we have *srasyate* "it is fallen:" —but of a verb which, like *nad (nadi)* "to be happy," has an indicatory *i*, the nasal is not elided, and we have *nandyate* "it is been happy (by so and so)—i. e. so and so is happy."

In the case of the verb *yaj* "to worship," the substitution of a vowel for the semi-vowel having taken place in accordance with No. 584, (the *yak* having an indicatory *k*) we have *ijyate* "it is worshipped (by so and so)—i. e. so and so worships."

तनोतेर्यकि । ६ । ४ । ४४ ।

आदन्तादेशो वा । तायते । तन्यते ।

No. 804.—WHEN the affix YAK (No. 801) comes AFTER the verb TAN "to extend," then long *á* is optionally the substitute for the final. Thus *táyate* or *tanyate* "it is extended."

तपोऽनुतापे च । ३ । १ । ६५ ।

तपश्च्लेश्चिण् न स्यात् कर्मकर्तर्यनुतापे च । अन्वतप्त पापेन ।

घुमास्थेतीत्वम् । दीयते । धीयते । ददे ।

No. 805.—Let not *chiṇ* be the substitute of *chli* AFTER the verb TAP "to suffer," when the sense is reflective, AND WHEN THE SENSE IS THAT OF EXPERIENCING REMORSE. Thus *anwatupta pápena* "remorse was experienced by the sinner."

In the case of the verbs enumerated in No. 625, there is the substitution of long *Í*—so that we have *díyate* "it is given," *ḍhíyate* "it is held," *dade* "it was given."

आतो युक् चिण्कृतोः । ७ । ३ । ३३ ।

आदन्तानां युगागमश्चिणि ञ्णिति कृति च । दायिता । दाता । दायिषीष्ट । दासीष्ट । अदायि । अदायिषाताम् । भज्यते ।

No. 806.—Let YUK be the augment OF what ends in LONG Á, WHEN CHIṆ FOLLOWS, OR when a KṚIT affix (No. 329), with an indicatory *ṅ* or *ṇ*. Thus (it being here optional, according to No. 802, to regard *chiṇ* as following,) we have *dáyitá* or *dátá* "it will be given," *dáyishíshṭa* or *dásíshṭa* "may it be given," *adáyi* "it was given," *adáyishátám* "the two were given."

The verb *bhañj* "to break" makes *bhajyate* (No. 363) "it breaks."

भञ्जेश्च चिणि ।६४।३३॥

नलोपो वा । अभाजि । अभञ्जि । लभ्यते ।

No. 807.—AND OF the verb BHAÑJ "to break" the elision of the *n* (No. 363) is optional, WHEN CHIṆ FOLLOWS. Thus *abháji* or *abhañji* "it broke."

The verb *labh* "to gain" makes *labhyate* "it is gained."

विभाषा चिण्णमुलोः ।७।१।६९।

लभेर्नुम् । अलम्भि । अलाभि ।

इति भावकर्मप्रक्रिया ॥

No. 808.—The verb *labh* "to gain" OPTIONALLY takes the augment *num*, WHEN CHIṆ AND ṆAMUL (No. 942) FOLLOW. Thus *alambhi* or *alábhi* "it was gained."

So much on the subject of Impersonals and Passives (—or of the "action" and the "object").

The Reflective verb is next to be considered, where the object becomes the agent.

। कर्मकर्तृप्रक्रिया ।

यदा कर्मैव कर्तृत्वेन विवक्षितं तदा सकर्मकाणामप्यकर्मकत्वात् कर्तरि भावे च लकारः ।

No. 809.—When the object itself is wished to be spoken of as the agent, then the affix *l*, even in the case of verbs that have an object (i. e. transitive verbs), stands for the agent or the action (and not for the object).

कर्मवत् कर्मणा तुल्यक्रियः । ३ । १ । ८७ ।

कर्मस्थया क्रियया तुल्यक्रियः कर्ता कर्मवत् स्यात् । कार्यातिदेशोऽयम् । तेन यगात्मनेपदचिण्चिण्वदिटः स्युः । पच्यते फलम् । भिद्यते काष्ठम् । अपाचि । अभेदि । भावे । भिद्यते काष्ठेन ।

इति कर्मकर्तृप्रक्रिया ॥

No. 810.—The (*l* denoting the) agent, when the action affecting the agent is SIMILAR TO THE ACTION WHICH AFFECTS THE OBJECT, is treated AS if it were (an *l*) denoting THE OBJECT.

This direction implies the substitution (for the operations incident to a tense-affix, or *l*, denoting an agent) of all the operations, (which fall to be performed when the tense-affix, or *l*, denotes the object). Hence there shall be the affixing of *yak* (No. 801), the employment of the *átmanepada* terminations (No. 800), the substitution of *chiṇ* for *chli* (No. 803), and the treatment of the word as directed in No. 802. Thus *pachyate phalam* "the fruit ripens of itself," *bhidyate káshṭham* "the wood splits of itself," *apáchi* (No. 803) "it ripened of itself," *abhedi* "it split of itself." As an example where the tense-affix denotes the action (i. e. where the verb is impersonal), take *bhidyate káshṭhena* "it is split (of itself) by the wood—i. e. the wood splits."

So much on the subject of Reflective verbs.

Some meanings of the Tenses, not previously specified, have next to be considered.

। लकारार्थः ।

अभिज्ञावचने लृट् । ३ । २ । ११२ ।

स्मृतिबोधिन्युपपदे भूतानद्यतने धातोर्लृट् । लङोऽपवादः । वस निवासे । स्मरसि कृष्ण गोकुले वत्स्यामः । एवं बुध्यसे चेतयसे इत्यादिप्रयोगेऽपि ।

No. 811.—WHEN a word IMPLYING "RECOLLECTION" is in connection with it, a verb takes the affix LṚIṬ (No. 440) with a past signification. This sets aside *laṅ* (No. 456). The verb *vas* "to dwell" is thus employed in the following example:—*smarasi kṛishṇa gokule vatsyámah* "rememberest thou, Kṛishṇa, we were dwelling (literally—we will dwell—) at Gokula?" The construction is the same when we employ *budhyase* "dost thou know?"—*chetayase* "dost thou reflect?"—and the like.

न यदि । ३ । २ । ११३ ।

यद्योगे उक्तं न । अभिजानासि यद्वने अभुञ्ज्महि ।

No. 812.—The aforesaid (No. 811) shall NOT apply IN connection with the particle YAT. Thus *abhijánási yad vane abhuñjmahi* "thou knowest how we did eat in the forest."

लट् स्मे । ३ । २ । ११८ ।

लिटोऽपवादः । यजति स्म युधिष्ठिरः ।

No. 813.—WHEN the particle SMA FOLLOWS let LAṬ (No. 406) be employed. This debars *liṭ* (No. 423). Thus *yajati sma yudhishṭhiraḥ* "Yudhishṭhira sacrificed."

वर्तमानसामीप्ये वर्तमानवद्वा । ३ । ३ । १३१ ।

वर्तमाने ये प्रत्यया उक्तास्ते वर्तमानसामीप्ये भूते भविष्यति च वा स्युः । कदागतोऽसि । अयमागच्छामि । आगमं वा । कदा गमिष्यसि । एष गच्छामि । गमिष्यामि वा ।

No. 814.—The affixes which are employed when the sense is that of PRESENT time may be OPTIONALLY IN LIKE MANNER employed, WHEN the sense is that of past or future time NOT REMOTE FROM THE PRESENT. Thus, to the question "when didst thou come?"—it may be replied either *ayam ágachchhámi* "I come now"—or *ágamam* "I have come now?"—and, to the question "when wilt thou go?"—either *esha gachchhámi* or *gamishyámi* "I go, or I shall go, now."

हेतुहेतुमतोर्लिङ् । ३ । ३ । १५६ ।

वा स्यात् । कृष्णं नमेच्चेत् सुखं यायात् । कृष्णं नंस्यति चेत् सुखं यास्यति । भविष्यत्येवेष्यते । नेह । हन्तीति पलायते । विधिनिमन्त्रणेति लिङ् । विधिः प्रेरणम् । भृत्यादेर्निकृष्टस्य प्रवर्तनम् ।

यजेत । निमन्त्रणं नियोगकरणम् । आवश्यके श्राद्धभोजनादौ दौहित्रादेः प्रवर्तनम् । इह भुञ्जीत । आमन्त्रणं कामचारानुज्ञा । इहासीत । अधीष्टः सत्कारपूर्वको व्यापारः । पुत्रमध्यापयेद् भवान् । संप्रश्नः संप्रधारणम् । किं भो वेदमधीयीय उत तर्कम् । प्रार्थनं याञ्चा । भो भोजनं लभेय । एवं लोट् ।

इति लकारार्थप्रक्रिया ॥

इति तिङन्तप्रक्रिया समाप्ता ॥

No. 815.—When condition and consequent are spoken of, LIŃ (No. 459) may optionally be the affix. Thus "if he were to reverence *(namet)* Kṛishṇa, he would attain to *(yáyát)* felicity." This does not apply to the following:—"he strikes—therefore the other flees"—for it is meant that this shall apply only to what is future. As stated in No. 459, *liń* implies "commanding, directing, &c." "Commanding" means "ordering"—one's stimulating to action some low person, such as a dependent—by saying, for example, *yajeta* "let him worship." "Directing" means enjoining a duty—the moving of a daughter's son, or the like, in regard to such a matter as the eating of the food prepared at an exequial rite—by saying, for example, *iha bhuñjíta* "let him eat in this place." "Inviting" implies an acquiescence in one's following his inclination—as when it is said (to some one inclined to sit down somewhere) *iha ásíta* "let your honour sit down here." "Expression of wish" here implies a respectful procedure —(as when one says respectfully to a teacher) *putram adhyápayed bhaván* "let your honour teach the boy." "Enquiring" here refers to the determining on the propriety or impropriety of anything—as *kiń bho! vedam adhíyíya uta tarkam* "how, then, I pray you—shall I peruse the Veda? or shall I study logic?" "Asking for" means begging—as *bho bhojanań labheya* "O may I obtain (i. e. give me) food." In like manner is *loṭ* (No. 441) employed.

So much on the subject of the meanings of the tenses.

Thus is the discussion of "what ends with a tense-affix" concluded.

। कृदन्ताः ।

OF WORDS ENDING IN THE AFFIXES CALLED *KṚIT*.

धातोः । ३ । १ । ९१ ।

आतृतीयान्तं ये प्रत्ययास्ते धातोः परे स्युः । कृदतिङिति कृत्संज्ञा ।

No. 816.—As far as the end of the 3rd Lecture [reckoning from the present aphorism], the affixes treated of are to be [understood as coming] AFTER some VERBAL ROOT. According to No. 329, the name of these affixes is *kṛit*.

वासरूपोऽस्त्रियाम् । ३ । १ । ९४ ।

अस्मिन् धात्वधिकारेऽसरूपोऽपवादप्रत्यय उत्सर्गस्य बाधको वा स्यात् स्त्र्यधिकारोक्तं विना ।

No. 817.—In this division of the grammar, where "after some verbal root" [see No. 816] is understood in every case, let an affix which is [calculated] to debar a general one, NOT BEING OF THE SAME FORM, OPTIONALLY debar it—BUT NOT IN those cases which fall under the influence of No. 918 [for, in those cases, the supersession is compulsory].

कृत्याः । ३ । १ । ९५ ।

एवुल्तृचावित्यतः प्राक् कृत्यसंज्ञाः स्युः ।

No. 818.—Let the affixes treated of as far as the aphorism at No. 835 [reckoning from the present one] be called KṚITYA.

कर्तरि कृत् । ३ । ४ । ६७ ।

इति प्राप्ते ।

No. 819.—A KṚIT affix HAS THE SENSE OF AN AGENT. This rule having presented itself [the following one modifies it].

तयोरेव कृत्यक्तखलर्थाः । ३ । ४ । ७० ।

एते भावकर्मणोरेव स्युः ।

No. 820.—The affixes called KṚITYA (No. 818), and the affix KTA (No. 866), AND THOSE THAT HAVE THE SENSE OF KHAL (No. 933), may HAVE ONLY THOSE TWO senses, viz.—act and object.

तव्यत्तव्यानीयरः । ३ । १ । ९६ ।

धातोरेते स्युः । एधितव्यम् एधनीयं त्वया । भावे औत्सर्गिकमेकवचनं क्लीबत्वं च । चेतव्यश्चयनीयो वा धर्मस्त्वया ।

No. 821.—Let these—viz. TAVYAT, TAVYA, AND ANÍYAR, come after some verbal root. Thus *edhitavyam* (Nos. 436 and 433) or *edhaníyaṅ twayá* "thou must increase." Here the sense being that of the action itself [which is but one, and neither male nor female], there is, from the nature of the case, a singular affix, and the neuter gender is employed. [The case is otherwise with the example following—viz.] *chetavyah* or *chayaníyo dharmastwayá* "thou must gather merit."

केलिमर उपसंख्यानम् । पचेलिमा माषाः । पक्तव्या इत्यर्थः । भिदेलिमाः सरलाः । भेत्तव्याः । कर्मणि प्रत्ययः ।

No. 822.—"The affix KELIMAR SHOULD BE ENUMERATED in ADDITION [to those enumerated in No. 821"]. Thus *pachelimá másháh*—that is to say, "kidney beans are to be cooked":—*bhidelimáh saraláh* "pines are to be split." This affix denotes the *object* [alone—and cannot be employed, like those enumerated in No. 821, to denote also the *action*].

कृत्यल्युटो बहुलम् । ३ । ३ । ११३ ।

क्वचित् प्रवृत्तिः क्वचिदप्रवृत्तिः
क्वचिद्विभाषा क्वचिदन्यदेव ।
विधेर्विधानं बहुधा समीक्ष्य
चातुर्विधं बाहुलकं वदन्ति । १ ।

स्नात्यनेनेति स्नानीयं चूर्णम् । दीयतेऽस्मै दानीयो विप्रः ।

No. 823.—The affixes called KṚITYA (No. 818) AND the affix LYUṬ are DIVERSELY applicable. [That is to say] sometimes they are applied [where there was no express rule for their application]; sometimes they are not applied [in spite of an express rule for their application]; sometimes they are optionally employed or not; and sometimes there is some other result [licence permitted by the rule].

[According to the following verse from the grammar called the *Sáraswata*], "Seeing that the application of certain rules is various, they specify four kinds of varieties," [viz. the four above-mentioned, —among which the last of the four includes all the cases not included in the other three]. For example—*snáníyaṁ chúrṇam* "powder for bathing," *dáníyo vipraḥ* "a Bráhman to whom a donation is to be made." [In the first of these examples the "powder" is the "instrument" (expressible by the 3rd case); and in the second the Bráhman is the "recipient" (expressible by the 4th case);—so that in both cases the affix is applied without any express rule—the express rule for its application (No. 821) having reference only to "act" and "object" (No. 820)].

अचो यत् । ३ । १ । ९७ ।

चेयम् ।

No. 824.—The affix YAT comes AFTER [a root that ends in] A VOWEL. Thus *cheya* "what is to be gathered."

ईद्यति । ६ । ४ । ६५ ।

यति परे आत ईत् स्यात् । देयम् । ग्लेयम् ।

No. 825.—Let LONG í be the substitute of long *á*, WHEN the affix YAT (No. 824) FOLLOWS. Thus (*guṇa* being substituted by No. 420) we have *deya* "what is to be given," *gleya* "to be exhausted."

पोरदुपधात् । ३ । १ । ९८ ।

पवर्गान्तादुदुपधाद्यत् । ण्यतोऽपवादः । शप्यम् । लभ्यम् ।

No. 826.—Let the affix *yat* come AFTER a root which ends in A PALATAL PRECEDED BY SHORT A. This debars the affix *ṇyat* (No. 831), so that we have *śapya* "to be sworn," *labhya* "to be acquired."

एतिस्तुशास्वृदृजुषः क्यप् । ३ । १ । १०९ ।

एभ्यः क्यप् ।

No. 827.—The affix KYAP may come AFTER these roots—viz. I "to go," SHṬU "to praise," ŚÁS "to govern," VṚI "to choose," DṚI "to respect," and JUSH "to please."

ह्रस्वस्य पिति कृति तुक् । ६ । १ । ७१ ।

इत्यः । स्तुत्यः । शासु अनुशिष्टौ ।

No. 828.—Let TUK be the augment OF A SHORT vowel, WHEN A KṚIT affix, WITH AN INDICATORY P, FOLLOWS. Thus *itya* "to be gone"—[from the root I "to go"], *stutya* "to be praised."

The verb *śás* means "to govern."

शास इदङ्हलोः । ६ । ४ । ३४ ।

शास उपधाया इत् स्यादङि हलादौ क्ङिति च । शिष्यः । वृत्यः । आदृत्यः । जुष्यः ।

No. 829.—Let SHORT I be the substitute OF the penult of the root ŚÁS "to instruct," WHEN the affix AṄ (No. 634) FOLLOWS, OR what affix begins with A CONSONANT and has an indicatory *k* or *ṅ*. Thus [from the roots mentioned in No. 827] we may have *śishya* "to be instructed," *vṛitya* "to be chosen," *ádṛitya* "to be honoured," *jushya* "to be served."

मृजेर्विभाषा । ३ । १ । ११३ ।

मृजेः क्यब्वा । मृज्यः ।

No. 830.—Let the affix *kyap* OPTIONALLY come AFTER the root MṚIJ "to cleanse." Thus *mṛijya* "to be cleansed."

ऋहलोर्ण्यत् । ३ । १ । १२४ ।

ऋवर्णान्ताद्धलन्ताच्च ण्यत् । कार्यम् । हार्यम् । धार्यम् ।

No. 831.—Let the affix ṆYAT come AFTER what ends in ṚI or *ṛí* or in A CONSONANT. Thus *kárya* "to be made," *hárya* "to be taken," *dhárya* "to be held."

चजोः कु घिण्ण्यतोः । ७ । ३ । ५२ ।

चजोः कुत्वं स्याद्घिति ण्यति च ।

No. 832.—Let there be the substitution of A GUTTURAL in the room OF CH AND of J, WHEN an affix with an indicatory GH follows, AND WHEN the affix ṆYAT (No. 831) FOLLOWS.

मृजेर्वृद्धिः । ७ । २ । ११४ ।

मृजेरिको वृद्धिः सार्वधातुकार्धधातुकयोः । मार्ग्यः ।

No. 833.—Let VṚIDDHI be the substitute OF the *ik* (No. 1) of MṚIJ "to cleanse," when a *sárvadhátuka* or an *árdhadhátuka* affix follows:—(No. 420). Thus (on the option allowed by No. 830) *márgya* (No. 832) "to be cleansed."

भोज्यं भक्ष्ये । ७ । ३ । ६९ ।

भोग्यमन्यत् ।

इति कृत्यप्रक्रिया ॥

No. 834.—The verb *bhuj* makes BHOJYA, WHEN THE SENSE IS "TO BE EATEN," but BHOGYA otherwise—[as when the sense is "to be enjoyed"].

So much for the management of the *prakriya* affixes.

ण्वुल्तृचौ । ३ । १ । १३३ ।

धातोरेतौ स्तः । कर्तरि कृदिति कर्त्रर्थे ।

No. 835.—These two affixes, ṆWUL AND TṚICH, are placed after verbal roots. According to No. 819, they have the sense of of an "agent."

युवोरनाकौ । ७ । १ । १ ।

यु वु एतयोरनाकौ स्तः । कारकः । कर्ता ।

No. 836.—In the room OF YU AND VU, there are ANA AND AKA. Thus (*ṇwul* having been added to the root *kṛi* "to make," by No. 835; and the *ṇ* and *l* having been elided by Nos. 148, 5, and 7; and *vṛiddhi* being substituted according to Nos. 163 and 202, we have) *káraka*, and (with *tṛich*—No. 835—) *kartṛi* "a maker."

नन्दिग्रहिपचादिभ्यो ल्युणिन्यचः । ३ । १ । १३४ ।

नन्द्यादेर्ल्युर्ग्रह्यादेर्णिनिः पचादेरच् । नन्दयतीति नन्दनः । जनार्दनः । लवणः । ग्राही । स्थायी । मन्त्री । पचादिराकृतिगणोऽयम् ।

No. 837.—AFTER the verbs NAD (*nadi*) "to be happy" &c., there is the affix LYU; AFTER the verbs GRAH "to take" &c., there is ṆINI; AND AFTER the verbs PACH "to cook" &c., there is ACH.

Thus *nand+lyu* [Nos. 497, 155, and 836,] *nandana* "one who delights," *janárdana* [from *jana* "mankind" and *ardana* derived in like manner from *ard* "to pain"] "Vishṇu—the subduer of mankind," *lavaṇa* "salt" [from *lú* "to cut"—where the substitution of a cerebral *ṇ* is an irregularity]. Then again *grah+ṇini* (No. 36)=*gráhin* "who takes," *stháyin* (No. 806) "who stays," and *mantṛin* "who advises." The class of verbs "*pach* &c." is one not defined by rule—[compare No. 53].

इगुपधज्ञाप्रीकिरः कः ।३।१।१३५।

एभ्यः कः । बुधः । कृशः । ज्ञः । प्रियः । किरः ।

No. 838.—There is the affix KA AFTER THOSE verbs WHICH HAVE AN IK AS their PENULT, AND after JŃÁ "to know," PRÍ "to please," AND KṚÍ "to throw." Thus *budha* (No. 155) "who knows," *kṛiśa* "who is thin," *jńa* (No. 524) "who knows," *priya* "what pleases," *kira* (No. 706) "who throws."

आतश्चोपसर्गे ।३।१।१३६।

प्रज्ञः । सुग्लः ।

No. 839.—AND [*ka*—No. 838—shall come—] AFTER a verb ending in LONG Á, WHEN THERE IS AN UPASARGA (No. 47). Thus *prajńa* "very wise," *sugla* "very weary"—[*á* having been substituted for the *ai* of *glai* by No. 528].

गेहे कः ।३।१।१४४।

गेहे कर्त्तरि ग्रहेः कः स्यात् । गृहम् ।

No. 840.—Let the affix KA come after the verb *grah* "to take," WHEN the agent so expressed denotes A HOUSE. Thus *gṛiha* (No. 675) "a house."

कर्मण्यण् ।३।२।१।

कर्मण्युपपदे धातोरण् । कुम्भं करोति कुम्भकारः ।

No. 841.—The affix AṆ comes after a verbal root, WHEN THE OBJECT is in composition with it. Thus *kumbha-kára* "one who makes pots"—i. e. "a potter."

आतोऽनुपसर्गे कः । ३ । २ । ३ ।

अणोऽपवादः । गोदः । धनदः । कम्बलदः । अनुपसर्गे किम् । गोसंप्रदायः ।

No. 842.—The affix KA comes AFTER a verb that ends in LONG Á, WHEN there is NO UPASARGA (No. 47). This debars the *aṇ* (No. 841)—and we have *goda* "who gives a cow," *dhanada* "who gives wealth," and *kambalada* "who gives a blanket." Why "when there is no *upasarga?*" Witness *gosaṅpradáya* (No. 806) "who ceremoniously gives a cow."

मूलविभुजादिभ्यः कः । मूलानि विभुजति मूलविभुजो रथः । आकृतिगणोऽयम् । महीध्रः । कुध्रः ।

No. 843.—The affix KA comes AFTER MÚLAVIBHUJ &C. Thus *múlavibhuja* "a car (which cuts the roots—*e. g.*, of the grass, &c. in its course)." This is a class of words [not enumerated under any rule, but] to be recognised by the form [see No. 53]. Thus *mahídhra* or *kudhra* "a mountain"—"what holds the earth"—(from *dhṛi* "to hold").

चरेष्टः । ३ । २ । १६ ।

अधिकरणे उपपदे । कुरुचरः ।

No. 844.—OF the verb CHAR "to go," the affix is ṬA, when a word in composition with it is in the locative case. Thus *kuru-chara* "who goes among the Kurus."

भिक्षासेनादायेषु च । ३ । २ । १७ ।

भिक्षाचरः । सेनाचरः । आदायेति ल्यबन्तम् । आदायचरः ।

No. 845.—AND WHEN the word in composition with it is BHIKSHÁ "alms," SENÁ "an army," AND ÁDÁYA "having taken," (then *ṭa* is the affix after *char* "to go"). Thus *bhiksháchara* "a beggar"—"who goes for alms,"—*senáchara* "one who goes with the army." The word *ádáya* ends in *lyap* (No. 941):—from it we may have *ádáyachara* "who goes after having taken."

कृञो हेतुताच्छील्यानुलोम्येषु । ३ । २ । २० ।

एषु द्योत्येषु करोतेष्टः ।

No. 846.—The affix *ṭa* comes after the verb KṚI "to make," WHEN these senses are to be indicated—viz. CAUSE, HABIT, AND GOING WITH THE GRAIN.

अतः कृकमिकंसकुम्भपात्रकुशाकर्णीष्वनव्ययस्य । ८ । ३ । ४६ ।

अदुत्तरस्यानव्ययस्य विसर्गस्य समासे नित्यं सादेशः करोत्यादिषु परेषु । यशस्करी विद्या । श्राद्धकरः । वचनकरः ।

No. 847.—In a compound (No. 961), let *s* always be the substitute of *visarga* coming AFTER A, and NOT being part OF AN INDECLINABLE word (No. 399), WHEN KṚI "to make" FOLLOWS, OR KAMI "to desire," OR KAṄSA "a goblet," OR KUMBHA "a jar," OR PÁTRA "a vessel," OR KUŚÁ "a counter (in the shape of a piece of stick, used at sacrifices to keep count of the prayers)," OR KARṆÍ "the ear." Thus (as examples of the three cases under No. 846) *yaśaskarí vidyá* "honourable science," *śráddhakara* "who performs obsequies," *vachanakara* "who does what he is bid."

एजेः खश् । ३ । २ । २८ ।

ण्यन्तादेजेः खश् ।

No. 848.—The affix KHAŚ comes AFTER the verb EJ "to tremble," when it ends in *ṇi* (No. 747).

अरुर्द्विषदजन्तस्य मुम् । ६ । ३ । ६७ ।

अरुषो द्विषतोऽजन्तस्य च मुमागमः खिदन्ते परे न त्वव्ययस्य । शित्वाच्छबादिः । जनमेजयतीति जनमेजयः ।

No. 849.—When that which ends with an affix having an indicatory *kh* follows, let MUM be the augment OF the words ARUS "a vital part," DWISHAT "an enemy," AND WHAT ENDS WITH A VOWEL, provided it be not an indeclinable. Since the affix *khaś* (No. 848) has an indicatory *ś* (No. 418), the affixes *śap* (No. 419) &c. are here applicable. *Janamejaya* "who awes mankind"—[the name of a prince].

प्रियवशे वदः खच् । ३ । २ । ३८ ।

प्रियंवदः । वशंवद : ।

No. 850.—The affix KHACH comes AFTER the verb VAD "to speak," WHEN PRIYA OR VAŚA is the word in composition with it. Thus *priyaṅvada* (No. 849) "who speaks kindly," *vaśaṅvada* "who professes submission."

आत्ममाने खश् च । ३ । २ । ८३ ।

स्वकर्मके मनने वर्तमानान्मन्यतेः सुपि खश् स्यात् । चाण्णिनिः । पण्डितमात्मानं मन्यते पण्डितंमन्यः । पण्डितमानी ।

No. 851.—AND let KHAŚ come after the verb *man* "to think," when the word in composition with it is a word with a case-affix, and WHEN it is EMPLOYED TO SIGNIFY THOUGHT WHEREOF THE OBJECT is SELF. By the "and" it is meant that the affix *ṇini* (No. 856) may be employed in the same sense. Thus *paṇḍitaṅmanya* or *paṇḍitamání* "who thinks himself learned."

अन्येभ्योऽपि दृश्यन्ते । ३ । २ । ७५ ।

मनिन् क्वनिप् वनिप् विच् एते प्रत्यया धातोः स्युः ।

No. 852.—These affixes—viz. *manin*, *kwanip*, *vanip*, and *vich* ARE SEEN AFTER OTHER verbs ALSO [besides those ending in *a* :,—see Páṇini III. 2. 74].

नेड्वशि कृति । ७ । २ । ८ ।

वशादेः कृत इण्न । शॄ हिंसायाम् । सुशर्मा । प्रातरित्वा ।

No. 853.—The augment IṬ (No. 433) is NOT that of a *kṛit* affix, WHEN IT BEGINS WITH A VAŚ. The verb *śṝí* means "to injure." [Adding to this the affix *manin*—No. 852—we have] *suśarman* "who destroys well" [e. g. destroys sin or ignorance]. [From the verb *i* "to go," by adding *kwanip*, we have] *prátaritwan* (No. 828) "who goes early."

विड्वनोरनुनासिकस्यात् । ६ । ४ । ४१ ।

अनुनासिकस्यात् स्यात् । विजायत इति विजावा । ओणृ अपनयने । अवावा । विच् । रुष रिष हिंसायाम् । रोट् । रेट् । सुगण् ।

No. 854.—WHEN the affixes VIṬ (III. 2. 67) AND VAN (No. 852) FOLLOW, let LONG Á be substituted in the room OF A NASAL. Thus (from the verb *jan* "to bring forth," *vijávan* "who brings forth," and so, from the verb *oṇ (oṇṛi)* "to send away," *avávan* "who removes" (i. e. removes sin &c.). The affix *vich* (No. 852), with the verbs *rush* and *rish* "to injure," (*guṇa* being substituted by No. 485—and the *v* elided by 330,) gives *rosh* and *resh* "who injures." In the same way, from *gan* "to reckon," *sugaṇ* "who reckons well."

क्विप् च। ३। २। ७६।

अयमपि दृश्यते। उखास्रत्। पर्णध्वत्। वाहभ्रट्।

No. 855.—AND this also—viz. KWIP—is seen [after a verb—see No. 816]. Thus [the whole affix disappearing through Nos. 155, 36, and 330,] we have *ukhásrat* (Nos. 363 and 287) "falling from the pot," *parṇadhwat* "falling from the leaves," *váhabhraṭ* "falling from a car."

सुप्यजातौ णिनिस्ताच्छील्ये। ३। २। ७८।

अजात्यर्थे सुपि धातोर्णिनिस्ताच्छील्ये द्योत्ये। उष्णभोजी।

No. 856.—WHEN HABIT IS TO BE EXPRESSED, the affix ṆINI comes after a verb, PROVIDED THE WORD WITH A CASE AFFIX in composition with it DOES NOT MEAN A GENUS. Thus *ushṇabhojin* "who eats his meal hot."

मनः। ३। २। ८२।

सुपि मन्यतेर्णिनिः स्यात्। दर्शनीयमानी।

No. 857.—Let the affix *ṇini* come AFTER the verb MAN "to think," when there is a word with a case-affix in composition with it. Thus *darśaníyamánin* "who thinks himself handsome."

खित्यनव्ययस्य। ६। ३। ६६।

पूर्वपदस्य ह्रस्वः। कालिंमन्या।

No. 858.—WHEN an AFFIX WITH AN INDICATORY KH FOLLOWS, (the short vowel, by VI. 3. 61, is the substitute of the word in composition with the verb) PROVIDED IT IS NOT AN INDECLIN-

ABLE. Thus *kálinmanyá* (No. 849) "who fancies herself the goddess Kálí."

करणे यजः । ३ । २ । ८५ ।

करणे उपपदे भूतार्थयजेर्णिनिः कर्तरि । सोमेनेष्टवान् सोमयाजी । अग्निष्टोमयाजी ।

No. 859.—The affix *ṇini* in the sense of *agent* comes AFTER the verb YAJ "to sacrifice" with the sense of past time, WHEN the word in composition is IN THE INSTRUMENTAL CASE. Thus *somayájin* "who has sacrificed with the Soma juice," *agnishṭomayájin* "who has sacrificed with a five days' series of offerings."

दृशेः क्वनिप् । ३ । २ । ९४ ।

कर्मणि भूते । पारं दृष्टवान् । पारदृश्वा ।

No. 860.—The affix KWANIP, in the sense of *object*, comes AFTER the verb DṚIŚ "to see," with a past signification. Thus *páradṛiśwan* "who has seen across."

राजनि युधिकृञः । ३ । २ । ९५ ।

क्वनिप् । युधिरन्तर्भावितण्यर्थः । राजानं योधितवान् राजयुध्वा । राजकृत्वा ।

No. 861.—The affix *kwanip* comes AFTER the verbs YUDH "to fight," AND KṚI "to make," WHEN the word in composition is RÁJAN "a king." Thus *rájayudhwan* (No. 200) "who has caused the king to fight," *rájakṛitwan* (No. 828) "who has made a king."

सहे च । ३ । २ । ९६ ।

सह योधितवान् सहयुध्वा । सहकृत्वा ।

No. 862.—AND WHEN SAHA "with" is the word in composition [No. 861 applies]. Thus *sahayudhwan* "who has made to fight with," *sahakṛitwan* "who has done anything along with (another)."

सप्तम्यां जनेर्डः । ३ । २ । ९७ ।

No. 863.—WHEN the word in composition with it is IN THE LOCATIVE CASE, let the affix DA come AFTER JAN "to be produced" —[whence *jan*, by No. 267, will become *ja*].

तत्पुरुषे कृति बहुलम् । ६ । ३ । १४ ।

ङेरलुक् । सरसिजम् । सरोजम् ।

No. 864.—WHEN a word with A KṚIT affix is the last IN a compound of the kind called TATPURUSHA (No. 982), then the elision of *ńi* [the 7th case-affix of the singular—see No. 768—] need not take place—it being treated DIVERSELY [—see No. 823—] Thus *sarasija* (No. 863) or *saroja* (No. 126) "what is produced in the lake,"—(i. e. a lotus).

उपसर्गे च संज्ञायाम् । ३ । २ । ९९ ।

प्रजा स्यात् संततौ जने ।

No. 865.—AND (No. 863 shall apply) WHEN AN UPASARGA is in composition [with the verb *jan* "to be produced"], and WHEN THE SENSE is simpy APPELLATIVE. Thus *prajá* (No. 1341)—of which let the sense be "a son" or "people." [The term here being simply appellative and not descriptive cannot be explained by giving the signification of its component elements :—so the author says "let the sense be" &c.]

क्तक्तवतू निष्ठा । १ । १ । २६ ।

एतौ निष्ठासंज्ञौ स्तः ।

No. 866.—These two affixes,—viz. KTA AND KTAVATU are called NISHṬHÁ.

निष्ठा । ३ । २ । १०२ ।

भूतार्थवृत्तेर्धातोर्निष्ठा । तत्र तयोरेवेति भावकर्मणोः क्तः कर्तरि कृदिति कर्तरि क्तवतुः । स्नातं मया । स्तुतस्त्वया विष्णुः । विश्वं कृतवान् विष्णुः ।

No. 867.—Let NISHṬHÁ (No. 866) come after a verbal root employed with the sense of past time. Of the two [affixes called *nishṭhá*], *kta* is employed, according to No. 820, only in the sense of the *action* and of the *object;* whilst *ktavatu*, according to No. 819, has the sense of the *agent.* Thus *snátaṁ mayá* "I bathed" (—literally "it was bathed by me"—); *stutas twayá Vishṇuh* "Vishṇu was praised by thee," *viśwaṁ kṛitaván. vishṇuh* "Vishṇu created all things."

रदाभ्यां निष्ठातो नः पूर्वस्य च दः । ८ । २ । ४२ ।

रदाभ्यां परस्य निष्ठातस्य नो निष्ठापेक्षया पूर्वस्य धातोर्दस्य च । शॄ हिंसायाम् । शीर्णः । भिन्नः । छिन्नः ।

No. 868.—Let N be the substitute OF the T OF A NISHṬHÁ (No. 866) coming AFTER R AND D, AND [let *n* be also the substitute] OF the D OF the root that comes BEFORE the *nishṭhá.* Thus, from *śṝí* "to injure" [which, by Nos. 706 and 651, becomes *śṛí,*] we have *śírṇa* "injured;" and [from *bhid* and *chhid*] *bhinna* "separated," and *chhinna* "cut."

संयोगादेरातो धातोर्यण्वतः । ८ । २ । ४३ ।

निष्ठातस्य नः स्यात् । द्राणः । ग्लानः ।

No. 869.—Let *n* be the substitute of the *t* of a *nishṭhá* (No. 866) coming AFTER A ROOT IN LONG Á and BEGINNING WITH A CONJUNCT consonant CONTAINING A YAṆ. Thus [from *drai* "to sleep," which, by No. 528, becomes *drá,*] we have *dráṇa* "slept;" and [from *glai*] *glána* "sad."

ल्वादिभ्यः । ८ । २ । ४४ ।

एकविंशतेर्लूञादिभ्यः प्राग्वत् । लूनः । ज्या धातुः । ग्रहिज्येति संप्रसारणम् ।

No. 870.— AFTER the twenty-one roots "LÚ &C." (No. 736), let it be as above [i. e. as directed in No. 868]. Thus *lúna* "cut." In the case of the root *jyá* "to decay," according to No. 675, there is the substitution of a vowel for the semi-vowel [which, by No. 283, absorbs the final].

हलः । ६ । ४ । २ ।

अङ्गावयवाद्धलः परं यत् संप्रसारणं तदन्तस्य दीर्घः । जीनः ।

No. 871.—Let the long vowel be the substitute for what ends with a vowel-substitute (No. 281) coming AFTER A CONSONANT which is part of the base. Thus *jína* (No. 870) "decayed."

ओदितश्च । ८ । २ । ४५ ।

भुजो भुग्नः । टुओश्वि उच्छूनः ।

No. 872.—AND AFTER A ROOT THAT HAS AN INDICATORY O, [the substitute for the *t* of a *nishṭhá* is *n*]. Thus, from *bhujo* "to be crooked," *bhugna* "crooked" and from *ṭuoświ* "to increase" [with the prefix *ut*] *uchchhúna* "increased."

शुषः कः । ८ । २ । ५१ ।

निष्ठातस्य । शुष्कः ।

No. 873.—Let K be [the substitute for the *t* of a *nishṭhá*] AFTER the verb ŚUSH "to be dry." Thus *śushka* "dry."

पचो वः । ८ । २ । ५२ ।

पक्वः । क्षै हर्षक्षये ।

No. 874.—Let V be [the substitute for the *t* of a *nishṭhá*] AFTER the verb PACH "to cook." Thus *pakwa* "cooked."

The verb *kshai* means "to wane."

क्षायो मः । ८ । २ । ५३ ।

क्षामः ।

No. 875.—Let M be [the substitute of the *t* of a *nishṭhá*] AFTER the verb KSHAI "to waste away." Thus *kshàma* (No. 528) "emaciated."

निष्ठायां सेटि । ६ । ४ । ५२ ।

णेर्लोपः । भावितः । भावितवान् । दृह हिंसायाम् ।

No. 876.—WHEN A NISHṬHÁ WITH the augment IṬ FOLLOWS, there is elision of *ṇi* (No. 747). Thus *bhávita* "caused to be," *bhávitaván* "who caused to be."

The verb *ḍṛih* means "to injure."

दृढः स्थूलबलयोः । ७ । २ । २० ।

स्थूले बलवति च निपात्यते ।

No. 877.—The verb *dṛih* "to injure" takes the anomalous form DṚIḌHA, IN THE SENSE OF THICK AND OF STRONG.

दधातेर्हिः । ७ । ४ । ४२ ।

तादौ किति । हितम् ।

No. 878.—OF the verb DHÁ "to hold," the substitute is HI, when an affix, beginning with the letter *t* and having an inaicatory *k*, follows. Thus *hita* "held."

दो दद्घोः । ७ । ४ । ४६ ।

घुसंज्ञकस्य दा इत्यस्य दथ् तादौ किति । चर्त्वम् । दत्तः ।

No. 879.—Let DATH be the substitute OF the DÁ called A GHU (No. 662), when an affix, beginning with the letter *t* and having an indicatory *k*, follows. A *char* being substituted [for the *th* by No. 90], we have *datta* "given."

लिटः कानज्वा । ३ । २ । १०६ ।

No. 880.—The affix KÁNACH is OPTIONALLY the substitute OF LIṬ (No. 423).

क्वसुश्च । ३ । २ । १०७ ।

लिटः कानच्क्वसू वा स्तः । तङानावात्मनेपदम् । चक्राणः ।

No. 881.—The affix *kánach* AND KWASU are optionally the substitutes of *liṭ*—[see No. 372—]. According to No. 409, the affix *kánach* is *átmanepada* [and can therefore be attached to those roots only which take the *átmanepada* affixes—see No. 410]. Thus *chakráṇa* (No. 426) "did make."

म्वोश्च । ८ । २ । ६५ ।

मान्तस्य धातोर्नत्वं म्वोः परतः । जगन्वान् ।

No. 882.—AND there is the substitution of *n* in the room of a root that ends in *m*, WHEN M AND V FOLLOW. Thus [from the root *gam* "to go"] *jaganwas* "did go."

लटः शतृशानचावप्रथमासमानाधिकरणे । ३ । २ । १२४ ।

अप्रथमान्तेन समानाधिकरणे लट एतौ वा स्तः । शबादिः । पचन्तं चैत्रं पश्य ।

No. 883.—These two affixes ŚATṚI AND ŚÁNACH are optionally the substitutes OF LAṬ (No. 406), WHEN AGREEING WITH WHAT ENDS NOT WITH THE FIRST case-affix. [As these affixes have an indicatory *ś*] the affixes *śap* &c., (Nos. 418 and 419) are applicable. Thus *pachantaṅ chaitraṅ paśya* "behold Chaitra who is cooking (for another)."

आने मुक् । ७ । २ । ८२ ।

अदन्ताङ्गस्य । पचमानं चैत्रं पश्य । लडित्यनुवर्तमाने पुनर्लड्ग्रहणात् प्रथमासामानाधिकरण्येऽपि क्वचित् । सन् द्विजः ।

No. 884.—Let MUK be the augment of a base ending in *a*, WHEN ÁNA (Nos. 883 and 409) FOLLOWS. Thus *pachamánaṅ chaitraṅ paśya* "behold Chaitra who is cooking (for himself)."

Since the term "*laṭ*" [in No. 883] might have been supplied (No. 5) from No. 406 [which is the aphorism immediately preceding No. 883 in the order of the *Ashṭádhyáyí*—it is clear that something is intended by the double citation—and this can be nothing else except that No. 883 may apply] sometimes even when the word is in concord with a nominative. Thus *saṅ dwijah* "who is a twice-born man."

विदेः शतुर्वसुः । ७ । १ । ३६ ।

वेत्तेः परस्य शतुर्वसुरादेशो वा । विदन् । विद्वान् ।

No. 885.—The affix VASU is optionally the substitute OF ŚATṚI (No. 883) coming AFTER the root VID "to know." Thus *vidat* or *vidwas* "who knows."

तौ सत् । ३ । २ । १२७ ।

तौ शतृशानचौ सत्संज्ञौ स्तः ।

No. 886.—THOSE TWO, viz. the affixes *śatṛi* and *śánach* (No. 883) are called SAT.

ल्टः सद्वा । ३ । ३ । १४ ।

करिष्यन्तं करिष्यमाणं पश्य ।

No. 887.—An affix called SAT (No. 886) is OPTIONALLY the substitute OF LṚIṬ (No. 440). Thus *karishyantaṅ* or *karishyamáṇaṅ paśya* "behold him about to make."

आ क्वेस्तच्छीलतद्धर्मतत्साधुकारिषु । ३ । २ । १३४ ।

क्विपमभिव्याप्य वक्ष्यमाणास्तच्छीलादिषु कर्तृषु बोध्याः ।

No. 888.—The affixes to be enunciated, reckoning from this point AS FAR AS KWIP (No. 893) inclusive, are to be understood IN THE SENSE OF AGENTS "HAVING SUCH A HABIT," "HAVING SUCH AND SUCH A NATURE," AND "HAVING SKILL IN SUCH AND SUCH AN ACTION."

तृन् । ३ । २ । १३५ ।

कर्ता कटान् ।

No. 889.—The affix TṚIN (—see No. 888). Thus *kartá kaṭán* "who makes mats."

जल्पभिक्षकुट्टलुण्टवृङः षाकन् । ३ । २ । १५५ ।

No. 890.—The affix SHÁKAN comes AFTER JALP "to talk idly," BHIKSH "to seek alms," KUṬṬ "to cut," LUṆṬH "to steal," AND VṚIŃ "to serve."

षः प्रत्ययस्य । १ । ३ । ६ ।

प्रत्ययस्यादिः ष इत्संज्ञः स्यात् । जल्पाकः । वराकः ।

No. 891.—Let the letter SH being the initial OF AN AFFIX be indicatory. Thus *jalpáka* (No. 890) "a babbler," *varáka* "pitiable."

सनाशंसभिक्ष उः । ३ । २ । १६८ ।

चिकीर्षुः । आशंसुः । भिक्षुः ।

No. 892.—The affix U comes AFTER [roots that have taken] the affix SAN (No. 752), AND ÁŚASI "to wish," AND BHIKSH "to beg." Thus *chikírshu* (No. 753) "desirous of doing" *áśansu* "desirous," *bhikshu* "a beggar."

भ्राजभासधुर्विद्युतोर्जिपॄजुग्रावस्तुवः क्विप् ।३।२।१७७।

विभ्राट् । भाः ।

No. 893.—The affix KWIP (see No. 888) comes AFTER the verbs BHRÁJ "to shine," BHÁS "to shine," DHURV "to injure," DYUT "to shine," ÚRJ "to be strong," PṚÍ "to fill," JU "to move rapidly," AND SHṬU "to praise" when it is PRECEDED BY the word GRÁVAN "a stone." Thus *vibhráj* "splendid," *bhás* "light."

राल्लोपः ।६।४।२१।

रेफाच्छ्वोर्लोपः क्वौ झलादौ क्ङिति च । धूः । विद्युत् । ऊर्क् । पूः । दृशिग्रहणस्यापकर्षाज्जवतेर्दीर्घः । जूः । ग्रावस्तुत् ।

No. 894.—AFTER the letter R, let there be ELISION of the letters *chh* and *v,* when *kwi* (i. e. *kwip*—No. 893) follows, or an affix beginning with a *jhal* and having an indicatory *k* or *ń.* Thus [from *dhurv* we have] *dhur* "who injures," and so *vidyut* "lightning," *úrk* "strength," and *púr* "what fills."

In the case of *jú* "swift," (according to the opinion of the *Mahábháshya*) a long vowel is the substitute of *ju* "to move rapidly," in consequence of the "attraction" of the expression "being seen" in No. 852 (which, *Patanjali* holds, is wide enough to provide for all that the supplementary rule of *Kátyáyana,* No. 895, refers to). [In the word] *grávastut* "a stone-worshipper" (the *t* comes from No. 828).

क्विब्वचिप्रच्छ्यायतस्तुकटप्रुजुश्रीणां दीर्घोऽसंप्रसारणं च । वक्तीति वाक् ।

No. 895.—"WHEN KWIP follows, THE LONG vowel is the substitute OF VACH "to speak," PRACHCHH "to ask," ÁYATA-STU "to praise long," KAṬA-PRU "to move through a mat," JU "to move rapidly," AND ŚRÍ "to serve," AND there is NO SUBSTITUTION OF A

VOWEL for the semi-vowel (by No. 675)." Thus *vák* "the voice" (the organ which speaks).

च्छ्वोः शूडनुनासिके च । ६ । ४ । १९ ।

सतुक्कस्य छस्य वस्य च क्रमात् श् ऊठ् एतावादेशौ स्तः क्वौ अनुनासिकादौ झलादौ क्ङिति च । पृच्छतीति प्राट् । आयतं स्तौति । आयतस्तूः । कटं प्रवते कटप्रूः । जूरुक्तः । श्रयति हरिं श्रीः ।

No. 896.—AND OF CHH with *tuk* (No. 120) AND OF V, respectively, Ś AND ÚṬH are the substitutes, WHEN *kwi* follows, or A NASAL, or what, beginning with a *jhal*, has an indicatory *k* or *ń*. Thus, from *prichchhati* "he asks," *práṭ* (Nos. 165 and 334) "who asks," *áyatastú* "who praises long," *kaṭaprú* "a worm" (which gets through mats); the word *jú* has been mentioned (under No. 894); *śrí* "the goddess Lakshmí" (who serves Hari).

दाम्नीशसयुयुजस्तुतुदसिसिचमिहपतदशनहः करणे। ३ । २ । १८२ ।

दाबादेः ष्ट्रन् स्यात् करणेऽर्थे । दात्यनेन दात्रम् ।

No. 897.—Let the affix *shṭran*, WITH THE SENSE OF INSTRUMENT, come AFTER the verbs DÁP "to cut," ṆÍ "to lead," ŚAS "to hurt," YU "to join," YUJ "to join," SHṬU "to praise," TUD "to inflict pain," SHI "to bind," SHICH "to sprinkle," MIH "to urine," PAT "to fall," DAŚ "to bite," AND ṆAH "to bind." Thus *dátra* "that with which one cuts" (e. g. a sickle).

तितुत्रतथसिसुसरकसेषु च । ७ । २ । ९ ।

एषां दशानामिण्न । शस्त्रम् । योत्रम् । योक्त्रम् । स्तोत्रम् । तोत्त्रम् । सेत्रम् । सेक्त्रम् । मेढ्रम् । पत्त्रम् । दंष्ट्रा । नद्ध्री ।

No. 898.—AND the augment *iṭ* (No. 433) is not that of these ten affixes viz. TI (i. e. *ktin* or *ktich*), TUN, SHṬRAN, TAN, KTHAN, KSI, SUCH, SARAN, KAN, AND SA. Thus *śastra* (No. 897) "a weapon," *yotra* "the tie that fastens the yoke," *yoktra* "the tie of the yoke," *stotra* "a panegyric," *tottra* "a goad," *setra* "a ligament," *sektra* "a sprinkling vessel," *meḍhra* "the penis," *pattra* "a vehicle," *dańshṭrá* (No. 334) "a large tooth," *naddhrí* (Nos. 389 and 586) "a thong."

अर्त्तिलूधूसूखनसहचर इत्रः । ३ । २ । १८४ ।

अरित्रम् । लवित्रम् । धवित्रम् । सवित्रम् । खनित्रम् । सहित्रम् । चरित्रम् ।

No. 899.—Let the affix ITRA come AFTER the verbs ṚI "to go," LÚ "to cut," DHÚ "to shake," SHÚ "to bring forth," KHAN "to dig," SHAH "to bear," AND CHAR "to go." Thus *aritra* "a rudder," *lavitra* "a sickle," *dhavitra* "a fan" *savitra* "cause of production," *khanitra* "a spade," *sahitra* "patience," *charitra* "instituted observance," or "a narrative."

पुवः संज्ञायाम् । ३ । २ । १८५ ।

पवित्रम् ।

No. 900.—[The affix *itra* comes] AFTER the verb PÚ "to purify," WHEN THE SENSE IS simply APPELLATIVE [and not descriptive]. Thus *pavitra* "the sacrificial thread."

। अथोणादयः ।

Now of the affixes "*uṇ*, &c."

कृवापाजिमिस्वदिसाध्यशूभ्य उण् । करोतीति कारुः । वायुः । पायुर्गुदम् । जायुरौषधम् । मायुः पित्तम् । स्वादुः । साध्नोति परकार्यमिति साधुः । आशु शीघ्रम् ।

No. 901.—Let the affix UṆ come AFTER the verbs KṚI "to make," VÁ "to blow," PÁ "to drink," JI "to overcome," MI "to scatter," SHWAD "to be pleasant to the taste," SÁDH "to accomplish," AND AŚ "to pervade." Thus *káru* "an artisan," *váyu* "the wind," *páyu* "the organ of excretion," *jáyu* "a drug" (which "overcomes disease"), *máyu* "the bile," *swádu* "sweet," *sádhu* "who accomplishes the object of another"—hence "virtuous," *áśu* "quickly."

उणादयो बहुलम् । ३ । ३ । १ ।

एते वर्तमाने संज्ञायां च बहुलं स्युः। केचिदविहिता अप्यूह्याः।

संज्ञासु धातुरूपाणि प्रत्ययाश्च ततः परे।

कार्याद्विद्यादनूबन्धमेतच्छास्त्रमुणादिषु॥

No. 902.—Let these affixes—viz. UṆ, &c., with the force of the present [i. e. implying neither past time nor future], and with a sense simply appellative [and not descriptive], be attached DIVERSELY [—see No. 823—]. Some affixes, though there be no express injunction regarding them, are to be inferred to belong to this class. The maxim in regard to the affixes "*uṇ, &c.*" is this—that "when, in appellatives, we find the forms of verbal roots and affixes coming after them,—then one may know, from the result [as presented in the word], what are the indicatory letters [which the affix must have possessed in order to produce the result]."

तुमुन्ण्वुलौ क्रियायां क्रियार्थायाम्।३।३।१०।

क्रियार्थायां क्रियायामुपपदे भविष्यत्यर्थे धातोरेतौ स्तः। मान्तत्वादव्ययत्वम्। कृष्णं द्रष्टुं याति। कृष्णं दर्शको याति।

No. 903.—These two affixes—viz. TUMUN AND ṆWUL are placed after a verbal root, with the force of the future, WHEN the word in construction therewith is another VERB [denoting an action performed] FOR THE SAKE OF THE [future] ACTION. What ends in *tumun*, since it ends in *m*, is indeclinable, according to No. 400. Thus *kṛishṇaṅ drashṭuṅ yáti* or *kṛishṇaṅ darśako yáti*, "he goes to see [—i. e. goes for the sake of seeing—] Kṛishṇa."

कालसमयवेलासु तुमुन्।३।३।१६७।

कालः समयो वेला वा भोक्तुम्।

No. 904.—The affix TUMUN may be applied, WHEN the word in construction is [not a verb—see No. 903—but] KÁLA, SAMAYA, OR VELÁ, "time." Thus *kálo bhoktum,* or *samayo bhoktum,* or *velá bhoktum,* "time to eat"—or "time for eating."

भावे।३।३।१८।

सिद्धावस्थापन्ने धात्वर्थे वाच्ये धातोर्घञ्। पाकः।

No. 905.—The affix *ghañ* comes after a root, WHEN THE SENSE OF THE ROOT is denoted as having attained to the completed state. Thus *páka* (Nos. 489 and 832) "maturity."

अकर्तरि च कारके संज्ञायाम् । ३ । ३ । १९ ।

कर्तृभिन्ने कारके घञ् ।

No. 906.—AND the affix *ghañ* [comes after a root], WHEN THE SENSE IS that of an APPELLATIVE—THE WORD being RELATED [to the verb from which its name is deduced—see No. 945—] but NOT as AGENT.

घञि च भावकरणयोः । ६ । ४ । २७ ।

रञ्जेर्नलोपः स्यात् । रागः । अनयोः किम् । रज्यत्यस्मिन्निति रङ्गः ।

No. 907—AND WHEN GHAÑ (No. 906) FOLLOWS, IN THE SENSE OF STATE OR INSTRUMENT, there is elision of the *n* of the root *rañj* "to colour." Thus *rága* "passion" (—the instrument *by* which objects are coloured). Why in these two senses? Witness *ranga* "a theatre"—the place *in* which the passions [are addressed].

निवासचितिशरीरोपसमाधानेष्वादेश्च कः । ३ । ३ । ४१ ।

एषु चिनोतेर्घञ् आदेश्च कः । उपसमाधानं राशीकरणम् । निकायः । कायः । गोमयनिकायः ।

No. 908.—The affix *ghañ* comes after the root *chi* "to gather," AND K IS the substitute OF THE INITIAL [*ch*], IN THESE SENSES—viz.—a DWELLING, a FUNERAL PILE, THE BODY, AND COLLECTION. "Collection" means making a heap. Thus *nikáya* "a dwelling," *káya* "a funeral pile" or "the body," *gomayanikáya* "a heap of cow-dung."

एरच् । ३ । ३ । ५६ ।

इवर्णान्तात् । चयः । जयः ।

No. 909.—AFTER a root ending in I or Í, there is the affix ACH. Thus *chaya* "gathering," *jaya* "victory."

ॠदोरप् । ३ । ३ । ५७ ।

ऋवर्णान्तादुवर्णान्ताच्चाप् । करः । गरः । यवः । स्तवः । लवः । पवः ।

No. 910.—AFTER a root ending in ṚÍ, OR in U or Ú, there is the affix AP. Thus [from *kṛí* "to scatter"] *kara* "scattering," from *gṛí* "to swallow"] *gara* "poison," [from *yu* "to join"] *yava* "barley," (from *shṭu* "to praise") *stava* "praise," (from *lú* "to cut") *lava* "reaping," (from *pú* to "purify") *pava* "winnowing (corn)."

घञर्थे कविधानम् । प्रस्थः । विघ्नः ।

No. 911.—"WHEN THE SENSE IS THAT OF GHAṄ (Nos. 905, &c.) the affix KA IS DIRECTED to be employed." Thus *prastha* (No. 524) "a certain measure," *vighna* (Nos. 540 and 314) "an obstacle."

ड्वितः क्त्रिः । ३ । ३ । ८८ ।

No. 912.—The affix KTRI comes AFTER THAT verb WHICH HAS AN INDICATORY ḌU.

क्त्रेर्मम् नित्यम् । ४ । ४ । २० ।

क्त्रिप्रत्ययान्तान्मप् निर्वृत्तेऽर्थे । पाकेन निर्वृत्तं पक्त्रिमम् । डुवप् । उप्त्रिमम् ।

No. 913.—OF the affix KTRI (No. 912), MAP is ALWAYS the augment, when the sense is that of completion. Thus *paktrima* "what is ripe," [and, from the root *ḍuvap*] *uptrima* (No. 584) "sown—(as a field)."

ट्वितोऽथुच् । ३ । ३ । ८९ ।

टुवेपृ कम्पने । वेपथुः ।

No. 914.—AFTER THAT verb WHICH HAS AN INDICATORY ṬU, the affix ATHUCH comes. Thus, from *ṭuvepṛi* "to tremble," *vepathu* "a trembling."

यजयाचयतविच्छप्रच्छरक्षो नङ् । ३ । ३ । ९० ।

यज्ञः । याच्ञा । यत्नः । विश्नः । प्रश्नः । रक्ष्णः ।

No. 915.—The affix NAŃ comes AFTER the verbs YAJ "to worship," YÁCH "to ask for," YAT "to strive," VICHCHH "to shine," PRACHCHH "to ask," AND RAKSH "to preserve." Thus *yajňa* "sacrifice," *yáchňá* "solicitation," *yatna* "effort," *viśna* (VI. 4. 19.), "lustre," *praśna* "a question," *rakshṇa* "protection."

स्वपो नन् । ३ । ३ । ९१ ।

स्वप्नः ।

No. 916.—The affix NAN comes AFTER the verb SHWAP "to sleep." Thus *swapna* "a dream."

उपसर्गे घोः किः । ३ । ३ । ९२ ।

प्रधिः । उपधिः ।

No. 917.—Let the affix KI come AFTER A GHU (No. 662), WHEN AN UPASARGA [precedes it]. Thus [from *dhá* "to have"] *pradhi* "the periphery of a wheel," and *upadhi* "fraud."

स्त्रियां क्तिन् । ३ । ३ । ९४ ।

स्त्रीलिङ्गे भावे क्तिन् । घञोऽपवादः । कृतिः । स्तुतिः ।

No. 918.—To express the action by a word IN THE FEMININE, the affix KTIN is added. This supersedes *ghaǹ* (No. 905). Thus *kṛiti* "action," *stuti* "praise."

ॠल्वादिभ्यः क्तिन् निष्ठावद्वाच्यः । तेन नत्वम् । कीर्णिः । लूनिः । धूनिः । पूनिः ।

No. 919.—"AFTER verbs ending in ṚÍ, AND after the verbs LÚ "to cut," &c., the affix KTIN SHOULD BE DECLARED to be LIKE a NISHṬHÁ (No. 866)." Hence (No. 868) there is the substitution of *n* for the *t* in the examples *kírṇṇi* "scattering," *lúni* "reaping," *dhúni* "agitation," *púni* "destruction."

संपदादिभ्यः क्विप् । संपत् । विपत् । आपत् । क्तिन्नपीष्यते । संपत्तिः । विपत्तिः । आपत्तिः ।

No. 920.—"The affix KWIP comes AFTER SAŃPAT [i. e. after the verb *pad* "to go" with the prefix *sam*] &c." Thus *saňpat* "prosperity," *vipat* "calamity," *ápat* "calamity." The affix *ktin* also is wished in this case, by *Patanjali*. Thus *sanpatti, vipatti, ápatti.*

ऊतियूतिजूतिसातिहेतिकीर्तयश्च । ३ । ३ । ९७ ।

एते निपात्यन्ते ।

No. 921.—AND these words—viz. ÚTI "preserving, sport," YÚTI "joining," JÚTI "velocity," SÁTI "destruction," HETI "a weapon," AND KÍRTI "fame," are anomalous forms.

ज्वरत्वरस्रिव्यविमवामुपधायाश्च । ६ । ४ । २० ।

एषामुपधावकारयोरूठ् अनुनासिके क्वौ झलादौ क्ङिति च ।

ऊतिः । क्विप् । जूः । तूः । स्रूः । ऊः । मूः ।

No. 922.—When an affix beginning with a nasal, or *kwi* (i. e. *kwip*), or one beginning with a *jhal* and having an indicatory *k* or *ń*, follows, then *úṭh* is substituted in the room OF THE PENULTIMATE letter AND of the *v* of these words—viz. JWAR "to have fever," TWAR "to hasten," SRIV "to go," AV "to protect," AND MAV "to blind." Thus *úti* "preserving," and, with the affix *kwip, júr* "one who has fever," *túr* "one who is quick," *srú* "a sacrificial ladle," *ú* "a protector," *mú* "one who binds."

इच्छा । ३ । ३ । १०१ ।

इषेर्निपातोऽयम् ।

No. 923.—The form ICHCHHÁ "desire," from *ish* "to wish," is irregular.

अ प्रत्ययात् । ३ । ३ । १०२ ।

प्रत्ययान्तेभ्यः स्त्रियामकारः प्रत्ययः स्यात् । चिकीर्षा । पुत्रकाम्या ।

No. 924.—AFTER verbs that end in AN AFFIX, let there be the affix A, the word being feminine.

Thus [after *kṛi*, by No. 756, has become *chikírsha* "to wish to do," the affix *a* is added by this rule, and elided by No. 505, and then the feminine termination *ṭáp* (No. 1341) presents itself, so that we have] *chikírshá* "the desire to do," *putrakámyá* (No. 772) "desire of a son."

गुरोश्च हलः । ३ । ३ । १०३ ।

गुरुमतो हलन्तात् स्त्रियामः प्रत्ययः । ईहा ।

No. 925.—AND let the affix *a* come AFTER THAT verb WHICH HAS A HEAVY vowel (No. 484) AND ends in A CONSONANT, when the word [to be formed] is feminine. Thus (—see No. 924—) *íhá* "effort."

ण्यासश्रन्थो युच् । ३ । ३ । १०७ ।

अकारस्यापवादः । कारणा । हारणा ।

No. 926.—AFTER verbs ending in ṆI (No. 747) AND AFTER ÁS "to sit," AND ŚRANTH "to loose," there is the affix YUCH—to the exclusion of *a* (Nos. 924 and 925). Thus *káraṇá* (No. 836) "the causing to do," *háraṇá* "the causing to take."

नपुंसके भावे क्तः । ३ । ३ । ११४ ।

No. 927—The affix KTA is added, WHEN THE ACTION is expressed—the word being IN THE NEUTER.

ल्युट् च । ३ । ३ । ११५ ।

हसितम् । हसनम् ।

No. 928.—AND the affix LYUṬ [is added under the circumstances stated in No. 927]. Thus *hasitam* or *hasanam* (No. 836) "laughter."

पुंसि संज्ञायां घः प्रायेण । ३ । ३ । ११८ ।

No. 929.—The affix GHA is added, WHEN the word is [to be] AN APPELLATIVE, [the word being] GENERALLY IN THE MASCULINE.

छादेर्घेऽद्व्युपसर्गस्य । ६ । ४ । ९६ ।

द्विप्रभृत्युपसर्गहीनस्य छादेर्ह्रस्वो घे । दन्तच्छदः । आकुर्वन्त्यस्मिन्नित्याकरः ।

No. 930.—WHEN the affix GHA FOLLOWS, a short vowel is substituted in the room OF *chhad* "to cover" [in its form—No. 741—CHHÁDI] when DESTITUTE OF TWO OR MORE UPASARGAS. Thus *dantachchhada* "the lip" [—that by which the teeth are covered]. The word *ákara* "a mine" [is derived from *kṛi* "to do"—No. 929]. A mine is so named because men "work *(ákurvanti)* in it."

अवे तॄस्त्रोर्घञ् । ३ । ३ । १२० ।

अवतारः । अवस्तारो जवनिका ।

No. 931—WHEN there is the *upasarga* AVA, the affix GHAÑ comes AFTER the verbs TṜÍ "to cross" AND STṜÍ "to spread." Thus *avatára* "the descent (or incarnation) of a deity," *avastára* "a screen round a tent."

हलश्च । ३ । ३ । १२१ ।

हलन्ताद्घञ् । घापवादः । रमन्ते योगिनोऽस्मिन्निति रामः । अपमृज्यतेऽनेन व्याध्यादिरित्यपामार्गः ।

No. 932.—AND AFTER a verb ending in A CONSONANT, there is *ghañ* to the exclusion of *gha* (No. 929). Thus [from *ram* "to sport"] *ráma* "Ráma"—i. e. in whom the devout delight; *apámárga* "that [plant] by which disease or the like is cleared away."

ईषद्दुःसुषु कृच्छ्राकृच्छ्रार्थेषु खल् । ३ । ३ । १२६ ।

एषु दुःखसुखार्थेषूपपदेषु खल् । तयोरेवेति भावे कर्मणि च । कृच्छ्रे । दुष्करः कटो भवता । अकृच्छ्रे । ईषत्करः । सुकरः ।

No. 933.—The affix KHAL is added to a verb, when ÍSHAD AND DUR AND SU are combined with it IN THE SENSE OF UNPLEASANTLY OR PLEASANTLY. According to No. 820, this affix appears only when the sense is that of the *action* or the *object*. Thus—in the sense of unpleasantly—*dushkarah* (VIII. 3. 41.) *kaṭo bhavatá* "a mat is difficult for your honour to make;" and in the sense of pleasantly—*íshatkara* "that which is made by little at a time," *sukara* "what is made with ease."

आतो युच् । ३ । ३ । १२८ ।

खलोऽपवादः । ईषत्पानः सोमो भवता । दुष्पानः । सुपानः ।

No. 934.—AFTER a verb ending in LONG Á, there is the affix YUCH, to the exclusion of *khal* (No. 933). Thus *íshatpánah* (No. 836) *somo bhavatá* "the Soma-juice is to be drunk by you, Sir, by little at a time," *dushpána* "difficult to be drunk," *supána* "easy to be drunk."

अलंखल्वोः प्रतिषेधयोः प्राचां क्त्वा । ३ । ४ । १८ ।

प्रतिषेधार्थयोरलंखल्वोरुपपदयोः क्त्वा । दो दद्धोः । अलं दत्वा । घुमास्थेतीत्वम् । पीत्वा खलु । अलंखल्वोः किम् । मा कार्षीत् । प्रतिषेधयोः किम् । अलंकारः ।

No. 935.—According to the practice OF THE ANCIENTS, the affix KTWÁ comes after a verb, WHEN there are in combination with it ALAṄ AND KHALU IN THE SENSE OF PROHIBITION. Thus, from *dá* "to give," which, by No. 879. substitutes *dath*, we have *alaṅdatwá* "do not give" and, from *pá* "to drink," which, by No. 625, substitutes long *í*, we have *pítwá khalu* "do not drink." Why do we say "when there are *alaṅ* and *khalu*?" Witness *má kárshít* (Nos. 469 and 475) "let him not do." Why do we say "in the sense of *prohibition*?" Witness *alaṅkára* "decoration."

समानकर्तृकयोः पूर्वकाले । ३ । ४ । २१ ।

समानकर्तृकयोर्धात्वर्थयोः पूर्वकाले विद्यमानाद्धातोः क्त्वा । स्नात्वा व्रजति । द्वित्वमतन्त्रम् । भुक्त्वा पीत्वा व्रजति ।

No. 936.—WHEN THE actions signified by TWO verbs HAVE THE SAME AGENT, the affix *ktwá* comes after that verb which is concerned ABOUT A TIME ANTERIOR to that of the other. Thus *snátwá vrajati* "having bathed, he goes"—[i. e. he first bathes, and afterwards goes]. The rule is not confined to the case of *two* verbs—thus *bhuktwá pítwá vrajati* "having eaten and having drunk, he goes."

न क्त्वा सेट् । १ । २ । १८ ।

सेट् क्त्वा किन्न स्यात् । शयित्वा । सेट् किम् । कृत्वा ।

No. 937.—Let the affix KTWÁ, when WITH the augment IṬ, be as if it had NOT an indicatory *k*—[i. e. there shall be the substitution of *guṇa* in spite of No. 467]. Thus [from *śí* "to sleep"] *śayitwá* "having slept." Why do we say "when with the augment *iṭ?*" Witness *kṛitwá* "having done"—[where the augment *iṭ*—see No. 510—does not appear, and there is no substitution of *guṇa.*]

रलो व्युपधाद्धलादेः संश्च । १ । २ । २६ ।

इवर्णोवर्णोपधाद्धलादे रलन्तात् परौ क्त्वासनौ सेटौ वा कितौ स्तः । द्युतित्वा । द्योतित्वा । लिखित्वा । लेखित्वा । व्युपधात् किम् । वर्तित्वा । रलः किम् । सेवित्वा । हलादेः किम् । एषित्वा । सेट् किम् । भुक्त्वा ।

No. 938.—The affixes *ktwá* AND SAN, having the augment *iṭ*, are optionally regarded as possessing an indicatory *k*, when they come AFTER THAT verb WHICH HAS I, Í, U, OR Ú, AS its PENULT, WHICH BEGINS WITH A CONSONANT, AND ends with A RAL [i. e. any consonant but *y* or *v*]. Thus *dyutitwá* or *dyotitwá* "having shone," *likhitwá* or *lekhitwá* "having written." Why do we say "which has *u* or *i* as its penult?" Witness *vartitwá* "having remained" [where the substitution of *guṇa*, through No. 937, is compulsory]. Why after that which "ends with a *ral?*" Witness *sevitwá* "having served" [where the root ends with *v*, which is not a *ral*]. Why after that "which begins with a *consonant?*" Witness *eshitwá* "having gone." Why "having the augment *iṭ?*" Witness *bhuktwá* "having eaten"—[where, through the absence of the augment, the case does not come within the scope of No. 937].

उदितो वा । ७ । २ । ५६ ।

उदितः परस्य क्त्व इड्वा । शमित्वा । शान्त्वा । देवित्वा । द्यूत्वा । दधातेर्हिः । हित्वा ।

No. 939.—Of *ktwá* coming AFTER THAT root WHICH HAS AN INDICATORY U, *iṭ* is OPTIONALLY the augment. Thus [from *śamu* "to be tranquil"] *śamitwá* or *śántwá* (No. 775) "having been tranquil," [from *divu* "to play"] *devitwá* (No. 937) or *dyútwá* (VI. 4. 19.) "having played." The verb *dhá* "to hold" substitutes (by No. 878) *hi*, giving *hitwá* "having held."

जहातेश्च क्त्वि । ७ । ४ । ४३ ।

हित्वा । हाङस्तु हात्वा ।

No. 940.—AND OF the verb HÁ "to abandon," the substitute is *hi*—[see No. 878]. Thus *hitwá* "having abandoned." But [when *ktwá* comes] after *há* "to go," we have *hátwá* "having gone."

समासेऽनञ्पूर्वे क्त्वो ल्यप् । ७ । १ । ३७ ।

अव्ययपूर्वपदेऽनञ्समासे क्त्वो ल्यबादेशः । तुक् । प्रकृत्य । अनञ् किम् । अकृत्वा । अव्ययपूर्वपदे किम् । परमकृत्वा ।

No. 941.—WHEN the word is A COMPOUND, THE FIRST MEMBER OF WHICH IS an indeclinable but NOT NAṄ, then LYAP is substituted in the room OF KTWÁ. Thus [when *kṛi* "to make" is compounded with *pra*—No. 48—*lyap* is substituted for *ktwá;* and, as it succeeds—see No. 163—to the possession of the indicatory *k*, we have—from No. 828—the augment] *tuk*—and so *prakṛitya* "having commenced making." Why do we say "but not *naṅ*?" Witness *akṛitwá* "not having made." Why do we say "the first member of which is an *indeclinable*"? Witness *paramakṛitwá* "having made permanent."

आभीक्ष्ण्ये णमुल् च । ३ । ४ । २२ ।

आभीक्ष्ण्ये द्योत्ये पूर्वविषये णमुल् क्त्वा च ।

No. 942.—WHEN REITERATION is to be expressed, both *ktwá* AND ṆAMUL [are admissible] in the case of an action's being antecedent [to another action—see No. 936.]

नित्यवीप्सयोः । ८ । १ । ४ ।

आभीक्ष्ण्ये वीप्सायां च द्योत्ये पदस्य द्वित्वं स्यात् । आभीक्ष्ण्यं तिङन्तेष्वव्ययसंज्ञकेषु कृदन्तेषु च । स्मारं स्मारं नमति शिवम् । स्मृत्वा स्मृत्वा । पायं पायम् । भोजं भोजम् । श्रावं श्रावम् ।

No. 943.—WHEN CONTINUALNESS AND SUCCESSION are to be expressed, let the word be doubled. There may be reiteration in the case of words ending with tense-affixes, and of those ending with *kṛit* affixes which (—see No. 400—) are termed indeclinables. Thus *smáraṅ smáraṅ* (No. 942) *namati śivaṁ* "having repeatedly remembered Śiva, he bends," *smṛitwá smṛitwá* "having repeatedly remembered," *páyaṅ páyam* "having drunk repeatedly," *bhojaṅ bhojum* "having eaten repeatedly," *śrávaṅ śrávam* "having heard repeatedly."

अन्यथैवंकथमित्थंसु सिद्धाप्रयोगश्चेत् । ३ । ४ । २७ ।

एषु कृञो णमुल् स्यात् सिद्धोऽप्रयोगो यस्यैवंभूतश्चेत् कृञ् । व्यर्थत्वात् प्रयोगानर्ह इत्यर्थः । अन्यथाकारम् । एवंकारम् । कथंकारम् । इत्थंकारं भुङ्क्ते । सिद्धेति किम् । शिरोऽन्यथा कृत्वा भुङ्क्ते ।

इति कृदन्तप्रक्रिया ॥

No. 944.—WHEN the words ANYATHÁ "otherwise," EVAM "so," KATHAM "how?" AND ITTHAM "thus," are compounded with the verb, then let *ṇamul* come after *kṛiṅ* "to make," IF it be such that ITS OMISSION WOULD BE UNOBJECTIONABLE—that is to say, when, in consequence of the non-significance of the *kṛiṅ*, it is not worth employing. Thus *anyathákáram*, *evaṅkáram*, or *kathaṅkáram*, or *itthaṅkáraṅ bhuṅkte*—"he eats otherwise—he eats so—how does he eat?—he eats thus," Why do we say "if its omission would be unobjectionable?" Witness *śiro'nyathá kṛitwá bhuṅkte* "he eats, having turned his head aside"—[where the *kṛiṅ* could not be spared].

So much for the treatment of words ending with the *kṛit* affixes.

। कारकम् ।

OF THE CASES.

प्रातिपदिकार्थलिङ्गपरिमाणवचनमात्रे प्रथमा । २ । ३ । ४६ ।

नियतोपस्थितिकः प्रातिपदिकार्थः। मात्रशब्दस्य प्रत्येकं योगः। प्रातिपदिकार्थमात्रे लिङ्गमात्राद्याधिक्ये संख्यामात्रे च प्रथमा स्यात्। प्रातिपदिकार्थमात्रे। उच्चैः। नीचैः। कृष्णः। श्रीः। ज्ञानम्। लिङ्गमात्रे। तटः। तटी। तटम्। परिमाणमात्रे। द्रोणो व्रीहिः। वचनं संख्या। एकः। द्वौ। बहवः।

No. 945.—By "the sense or the crude-form" is meant that meaning which is constantly present [with the word]. The word "only" is to be taken in connection with each term severally [in the aphorism—the translation of which here follows—viz.]:—Let there be THE FIRST case-affix, WHERE THE SENSE IS ONLY THAT OF THE CRUDE-FORM, OR where there is the additional sense of GENDER only, OR MEASURE only, OR NUMBER only. Thus—where the sense is only that of the crude-form—*uchchaih* "aloft," *níchaih* "below," *kṛishṇah* "Kṛishṇa," *śríh* "the goddess Lakshmí," *jnánam* "knowledge;" where there is the additional sense of gender only—*taṭah* or *taṭí* or *taṭam* "the bank of a river;"—where there is the additional sense of measure only—*droṇo vríhih* "rice—a *droṇa* (in measure);"—"number," here means [grammatical] number—[and the reason for this being specified in the rule is this—that otherwise the word *eka* "one," would not take *su*, nor *dwi* take *au*, nor *bahu* take *jas*—for an affix is never applied in order to give a sense which is implied in the word—as *singularity* is in *eka*, *duality* in *dwi*, and *plurality* in *bahu*]—so we have *ekah*, "one," *dwau* "two," *bahavah* "many."

सम्बोधने च। २। ३। ४७।

प्रथमा। हे राम।

No. 946.—AND WHEN the sense is that of ADDRESSING, the first case-affix is employed. Thus *he ráma* (No. 153) "O Ráma!"

कर्तुरीप्सिततमं कर्म। १। ४। ४९।

कर्तुः क्रिययाप्तुमिष्टतमं कारकं कर्मसंज्ञं स्यात्।

No. 947.—Let THAT, related to the action, WHICH IT IS INTENDED SHOULD BE MOST AFFECTED by the act OF THE AGENT, be called the OBJECT.

कर्मणि द्वितीया । २ । ३ । २ ।

अनुक्ते कर्मणि द्वितीया । हरिं भजति । अभिहिते तु कर्मादौ प्रथमा । हरिः सेव्यते । लक्ष्म्या सेवितः ।

No. 948.—WHEN THE OBJECT is not denoted [by the termination of the verb—i. e. when the verb does not agree with it], let THE SECOND case-affix be attached to the words. Thus *hariṅ bhajati* "he worships Hari," where, not the object of worship, but the agent is specified by the tense-affix *tip*—No. 419—]. But when the object &c. is denoted by the termination of the verb, [let the *first* case-affix be attached to the word]. Thus *hariḥ sevyate* "Hari is served,"—[where the termination of the verb—see No. 801—specifies the *object:*] and so too in *lakshmyá sevitaḥ* "served by Lakshmí." [where—see Nos. 867 and 820—the termination specifies the *object*].

अकथितं च । १ । ४ । ५१ ।

अपादानादिविशेषैरविवक्षितं कारकं कर्मसंज्ञं स्यात् ।

No. 949.—AND let THAT related to the action, WHICH IS NOT "SPOKEN OF," [see No. 950—] as coming under any of the special relations of 'ablation' or the like [although it stands in such a relation to the verb, and, if so "spoken of," must be put in the ablative or the like,] be called *object*.

दुह्याच्पच्दण्ड्रुधिप्रच्छि-
चिब्रूशासुजिमन्थ्मुषाम् ।
एषाम् ।
कर्मयुक् स्यादकथितं
तथा स्यान्नीहृकृष्वहाम् ॥ १ ॥

गां दोग्धि पयः । बलिं याचते वसुधाम् । तण्डुलानोदनं पचति । गर्गान् शतं दण्डयति । व्रजमवरुणद्धि गाम् । माणवकं पन्थानं पृच्छति । वृक्षमवचिनोति फलानि । माणवकं धर्मं ब्रूते । शास्ति वा । शतं जयति देवदत्तम् । सुधां क्षीरनिधिं मथ्नाति । देवदत्तं

शतं मुष्णाति । ग्राममजान् नयति । हरति कर्षति वहति वा । अर्थनिबन्धनेयं संज्ञा । बलिं भिक्षते वसुधाम् । माणवकं धर्मं भाषते । अभिधत्ते । वक्ति । इत्यादि ।

No. 950.—Let that be "not spoken of," [as coming under the special relation of 'ablation' or the like—see No. 949—] which is connected with the object OF the verbs DUH "to milk," YÁCH "to ask for," PACH "to cook," DAṆḌ "to fine," RUDH "to obstruct," PRACHCHH "to ask," CHI "to collect." BRÚ "to speak," ŚÁS "to instruct," JI "to conquer," MANTH "to churn," and MUSH "to steal,"—and so too of ṆÍ "to lead," HṚI "to take," KṚISH "to drag," and VAH "to carry."

Thus—"he milks the cow (for) milk," "he asks the earth (of) Bali," "he cooks the raw rice (so that it becomes) boiled rice" [—cf. "he cooks oatmeal into porridge"—]; "he fines the Gargas a hundred (pieces of money)," "he shuts up the cow (in) the cow-pen," "he asks the boy (which is) the road," "he gathers fruit (from) the tree," "he expounds virtue (to) the boy," or "teaches him virtue," "he wins a hundred (from) Devadatta," "he churns out ambrosia (from) the ocean of milk," "he steals a hundred (from) Devadatta," "he leads the goats (to) the village," or "takes them," or "drags them."

This term [viz. the term *object* as appropriated by the present rule to something other than the direct object of the verb] is one the reason for taking which is the sense of the verb—[so that the rule is not confined to the verbs above enumerated, but applies to others which have the same sense—], hence we may have *baliṅ bhikshate vasudhám* "he begs (as well as *yáchati* asks) the earth (from) Bali," "he talks of *(bháshate)*, names *(abhidhatte)*, tells of *(vakti)* virtue (to) the boy"—&c.

साधकतमं करणम् । १ । ४ । ४२ ।

क्रियासिद्धौ प्रकृष्टोपकारकं करणसंज्ञं स्यात् । स्वतन्त्र इति कर्तृसंज्ञा ।

No. 951.—Let THAT WHICH IS ESPECIALLY AUXILIARY in the accomplishment of the action be called THE INSTRUMENT. The term "agent," as defined at No. 745, is applied to that which is spoken of as independent.

कर्तृकरणयोस्तृतीया । २ । ३ । १८ ।

अनभिहिते कर्तरि करणे च तृतीया स्यात् । रामेण बाणेन हतो बाली ।

No. 952.—WHEN THE AGENT AND THE INSTRUMENT are not specified by the termination of the verb [i. e. when the verb is not in agreement with them—[let THE THIRD case-affix be employed. Thus "Bálí was killed by Ráma with an arrow."

कर्मणा यमभिप्रैति स संप्रदानम् । १ । ४ । ३२ ।

दानस्य कर्मणा यमभिप्रैति स संप्रदानसंज्ञः ।

No. 953.—HE WHOM ONE WISHES TO CONNECT WITH THE OBJECT of giving—[i. e. with the gift—shall] be called THE RECIPIENT.

चतुर्थी संप्रदाने । २ । ३ । १३ ।

विप्राय गां ददाति ।

No. 954.—Let THE FOURTH case-affix be employed, WHEN THE SENSE IS THAT OF THE RECIPIENT. Thus "he gives a cow to the Bráhman."

नमःस्वस्तिस्वाहास्वधालंवषड्योगाच्च । २ । ३ । १६ ।

एभिर्योगे चतुर्थी । हरये नमः । प्रजाभ्यः स्वस्ति । अग्नये स्वाहा । पितृभ्यः स्वधा । अलमिति पर्याप्त्यर्थग्रहणम् । तेन दैत्येभ्यो हरिरलं प्रभुः समर्थः शक्त इत्यादि ।

No. 955.—AND let the *fourth* case-affix be employed IN CONNECTION WITH [the forms of reverential address or religious invocation] NAMAS, SWASTI, SWÁHÁ, SWADHÁ; and with ALAM AND VASHAṬ.

Thus—"Salutation to Hari"—"Prosperity to the people"—"An offering to Fire"—"An offering to the manes." The word *alam* is here taken in the sense of "sufficient for" or "equal to"—so that [the same construction is admissible with equivalent terms—and we may say] "Hari is enough for *(alam)*, or is the master of *(prabhu)*, or is a match for *(samartha)*, or is able to overcome *(śakta)*, the Titans."

ध्रुवमपायेऽपादानम् । १ । ४ । २४ ।

अपायो विश्लेषस्तस्मिन् साध्ये यद्ध्रुवमवधिभूतं कारकं तदपादानसंज्ञं स्यात् ।

No. 956.—WHEN there is DEPARTURE FROM A FIXED POINT, let it be called ABLATION. By "departure" is meant "separation." When this is to be expressed, let that fixed point which is the limit, denoted by a word dependent on the verb, be called (the limit of) ablation.

अपादाने पञ्चमी । २ । ३ । २८ ।

ग्रामादायाति । धावतोऽश्वात् पतति । इत्यादि ।

No. 957.—WHEN [the word denotes that from which there is] ABLATION (No. 956), let THE FIFTH case-affix be employed. Thus—"he comes from the village," "he falls from a galloping horse," &c.

षष्ठी शेषे । २ । ३ । ५० ।

कारकप्रातिपदिकार्थव्यतिरिक्तः स्वस्वामिभावादिः शेषस्तत्र षष्ठी । राज्ञः पुरुषः । कर्मादीनामपि संबन्धमात्रविवक्षायां षष्ठ्येव । सतां गतम् । सर्पिषो जानीते । मातुः स्मरति । एधो दकस्योपस्कुरुते । भजे शम्भोश्चरणयोः ।

No. 958.—Let THE SIXTH case-affix be employed IN THE REMAINING CASES—that is to say—where there is a sense, such as the relation between property and its owner, different from that of a word related to a verb, and from that of a crude word. Thus "the King's man."

[Here it may be observed that the application of the term *káraka* is not co-extensive with that of the term *case.* The *káraka* —as its etymology indicates—stands in a relation dependent on the *verb*—whereas the sixth case provides further for such a relation as that of one noun with another. With an eye to this, we have rendered *káraka* "that which is directly related to the action."]

Moreover, when it is intended to speak only of the relation in general [and not of the special relation] of object and the like, the sixth case-affix alone is employed. Thus "the conduct of the virtuous," "he knows clarified butter," "he remembers his mother," "he prepares the wood and water for an oblation," "he adores the two feet of Śiva."

आधारोऽधिकरणम् । १ । ४ । ४५ ।

कर्तृकर्मद्वारा तन्निष्ठक्रियाया आधारः कारकमधिकरणं स्यात् ।

No. 959.—Let that which is related to the action as THE SITE of the action, which action is located in this or that site by the agent or object, be called THE LOCATION.

[When we say "he cooks in the house," the site is determined by the agent:—and when we say "he cooks rice in a pot," the location is determined by the object.]

सप्तम्यधिकरणे च । २ । ३ । ३६ ।

चकाराद्दूरान्तिकार्थेभ्यः । औपश्लेषिको वैषयिकोऽभिव्यापकश्चेत्याधारस्त्रिधा । कटे आस्ते । स्थाल्यां पचति । मोक्षे इच्छास्ति । सर्वस्मिन्नात्मास्ति । वनस्य दूरे अन्तिके वा ।

इति विभक्त्यर्थाः ॥

No. 960.—AND WHEN the sense is that of LOCATION (No. 959), THE SEVENTH case-affix is employed. By the "and" it is meant that it is employed also after words meaning "far off" or "near." A site is of three kinds—actually contiguous, figuratively objective, and co-extensive. Thus (1) "he sits on (i. e. in contact with) the mat," or "he cooks rice in (i. e. which is actually contained within) the pot;" (2) "his desire is (bent) on salvation—(i.

e. is figuratively wrapt up in it as its object); (3) "Soul is in all" (i. e. is co-extensive with the universe). "Far from, or near, the wood."

So much for the sense of the case-affixes.

। समासः ।

OF COMPOUND WORDS.

समासः पञ्चधा ।

तत्र समसनं समासः । स च विशेषसंज्ञाविनिर्मुक्तः केवलसमासः प्रथमः । प्रायेण पूर्वपदार्थप्रधानोऽव्ययीभावो द्वितीयः । प्रायेणोत्तरपदार्थप्रधानस्तत्पुरुषस्तृतीयः । तत्पुरुषभेदः कर्मधारयः । कर्मधारयभेदो द्विगुः । प्रायेणान्यपदार्थप्रधानो बहुव्रीहिश्चतुर्थः । प्रायेणोभयपदार्थप्रधानो द्वन्द्वः पञ्चमः ।

No. 961.—COMPOUNDS ARE OF FIVE KINDS. Here a compound means an aggregation. That which is destitute of any peculiar name, being "merely a compound," is the 1st kind. That called *Avyayíbháva* (No. 966)—in which, for the most part, the sense of the first of its elements is the main one (or the independent one on which the other depends), is the 2nd kind. That called *Tatpurusha* (No. 982)—in which, for the most part, the sense of the last of its elements is the main one, is the 3rd kind. A subdivision of the *Tatpurusha* class is called *Karmadháraya* (No. 1002.) A subdivision of the *Karmadháraya* class is called *Dwigu* (No. 983). That called *Bahuvríhi* (No. 1034)—in respect whereof, for the most part, the sense of a different word is the main one (to which the sense of the compound epithet is subordinate) is the 4th kind. That called *Dwandwa* (No. 1054)—in which, for the most part, the sense of both the one and the other of its elements is a main one—(neither being subordinate to the other), is the 5th kind.

समर्थः पदविधिः ।२।१।१।

पदसंबन्धी यो विधिः स समर्थाश्रितो बोध्यः ।

No. 962.—A RULE WHICH RELATES TO complete WORDS [—and not to the roots and affixes out of which the words are constructed—] is to be understood to apply only TO THOSE words THE SENSES OF WHICH ARE CONNECTED. [For example—according to No. 992, one noun may combine with another which is in the genitive, so that for "a binder of books" we may substitute "a book-binder:"—but it is necessary that the two words should be in construction—for if we have the expression "ignorant of books—a binder of sheaves," we cannot make a compound of "books" and "binder"—the word "binder" being here connected in sense, not with "books," but with "sheaves."]

प्राक् कडारात् समासः । २ । १ । ३ ।

कडाराः कर्मधारय इत्यतः प्राक् समास इत्यधिक्रियते ।

No. 963.—The word "COMPOUND" is made the regulator of the sense [and is therefore to be understood in each aphorism] from this point AS FAR AS the aphorism "KAḌÁRÁH *karmadháraye*" (II. 2. 38).

सह सुपा । २ । १ । ४ ।

सुप् सुपा सह वा समस्यते । समासत्वात् प्रातिपदिकत्वेन सुपो लुक् । परार्थाभिधानं वृत्तिः । कृत्तद्धितसमासैकशेषसनाद्यन्तधातुरूपाः पञ्च वृत्तयः । वृत्त्यर्थावबोधकं वाक्यं विग्रहः । स च लौकिकोऽलौकिकश्चेति द्विधा । तच्च पूर्वं भूत इति लौकिकः । पूर्व अम् भूत सु इत्यलौकिकः । भूतपूर्वः । भूतपूर्वे चरडिति निर्देशात् पूर्वनिपातः ।

No. 964.—A word ending in a case-affix may optionally be compounded WITH a word ending in A CASE-AFFIX. Since that which is a 'compound' is, therefore, regarded as a crude word (No. 136), there is elision of case-affixes (No. 768). The conveying an additional meaning [besides the literal meaning, or besides that which resides in the separate portions of which it may be composed] is the 'function' [of an expression]. There are five 'functions' [of five different kinds of expression]—viz. those belonging to [what ends with] a *kṛit* affix (No. 329) or a *taddhita* affix (No. 1067),—to a 'compound' (No. 961), to a 'partial remainder' (No. 145), and to a verb that ends with *san* or the like (No. 502). An expression explanatory of the force of the 'function' is called its 'analysis' or 'solution,' and this is of two kinds—popular and technical. For example, the explanation "*púrvaṅ bhútah*" is the popular solution, and "*púrva+am, bhúta+su*" is the technical analysis, of the expression *bhútapúrvah* "formerly been" [which furnishes an example of the rule, No. 964, under consideration]. In this example the anomaly [—as regards placing the principal word first, instead of the secondary term—see No. 969—] of the word *púrva,* is in accordance with the example [of Páṇini] in the aphorism "*bhútapúrve charaṭ*" (V. 3. 53).

इवेन सह समासो विभक्त्यलोपश्च । वागर्थौ इव वागर्थाविव ।

इति केवलसमासः प्रथमः ॥

No. 965.—[A word enters into] COMPOSITION WITH IVA "like," AND there is NOT ELISION OF THE CASE-AFFIX. Thus *vágartháviva* "like a word and its meaning."

So much for the first kind—that which is "merely compound."

। अव्ययीभावः ।

OF THE AVYAYÍBHÁVA OR INDECLINABLE COMPOUND.

अव्ययीभावः । २ । १ । ५ ।

अधिकारोऽयम् । प्राक् तत्पुरुषात् ।

No. 966.—The term AVYAYÍBHÁVA—i. e. "the becoming an indeclinable"—is a regulating expression [to be understood in each aphorism] as far as No. 982.

अव्ययं विभक्तिसमीपसमृद्धिव्यृद्ध्यर्थाभावात्ययासंप्रतिशब्दप्रादुर्भावपश्चाद्यथानुपूर्व्ययौगपद्यसादृश्यसंपत्तिसाकल्यान्तवचनेषु । २ । १ । ६ ।

विभक्त्यर्थादिषु वर्तमानमव्ययं सुबन्तेन सह नित्यं समस्यते। प्रायेणाविग्रहो नित्यसमासः। प्रायेणास्वपदविग्रहो वा। विभक्तौ। हरि ङि अधि इति स्थिते।

No. 967.—AN INDECLINABLE (No. 399) employed WITH THE SENSE OF A CASE-AFFIX, OR of NEAR TO, or PROSPERITY, or ADVERSITY, or ABSENCE OF THE THING, or DEPARTURE, or NOT NOW, or the PRODUCTION OF SOME SOUND, or AFTER, or ACCORDING TO, or ORDER OF ARRANGEMENT, or SIMULTANEOUSNESS, or LIKENESS, or POSSESSION, or TOTALITY, or TERMINATION, is invariably compounded with a word that ends with a case-affix.

For the most part, that which is invariably compound has n corresponding expression made up of separate words:—or its analysis must, for the most part, be made in other words [than those of which the compound itself consists].

[As an example of an "indeclinable" employed] with the sense of a case-affix—suppose that the case stands thus—viz. *hari+ṅi+adhi*—[where the "indeclinable" *adhi* "upon" is to be employed with the sense of the 7th case-affix *ṅi*——we look forward].

प्रथमानिर्दिष्टं समास उपसर्जनम्। १। २। ४३।

समासशास्त्रे प्रथमानिर्दिष्टमुपसर्जनं स्यात्।

No. 968.—IN a rule enjoining COMPOSITION, let THAT WHICH IS EXHIBITED WITH THE 1ST case-affi. [i. e. let the word which is exhibited in the nominative] be called the UPASARJANA or "secondary." [Thus the *adhi*, in the example under No. 967, being an "indeclinable," is the *upasarjana*, because the term "indeclinable," in No. 967, is in the 1st case].

उपसर्जनं पूर्वम्। २। २। ३०।

समासे उपसर्जनं प्राक् प्रयोज्यम्। इत्यधेः प्राक् प्रयोगः। सुपो लुक्। एकदेशविकृतस्यानन्यत्वात् प्रातिपदिकसंज्ञायां स्वाद्युत्पत्तिः। अव्ययीभावश्चेत्यव्ययत्वात् सुपो लुक्। अधिहरि।

No. 969.—The UPASARJANA (No. 968) is to be placed FIRST in a compound. Hence [in the examp e proposed in No. 967] the *adhi* [being the 'indeclinable' which is exhibited with the first case-affix in No. 967] is to be placed first—[thus *adhi+hari+ńi*]. Then (No. 768) there is elision of the case-affix—[leaving *adhi+hari*]. Then, seeing that what is partially altered (No. 181) does not become something quite different,—since this [viz. the expression under consideration, after being partially altered by the elision of the case-affix,] is still called a "crude form,"—the case-affixes, *su* &c., again present themselves (—No. 140)—; and they are again, finally, elided (No 403) in consequence of this compound's being an 'indeclinable,' according to No. 402. Thus we have *adhihari* "upon Hari."

अव्ययीभावश्च ।२।४।१८।

अयं नपुंसकं स्यात् । गाः पातीति गोपाः । तस्मिन्नित्यधिगोपम् ।

No. 970.—AND let AN AVYAYÍBHÁVA compound be neuter. Thus, from *gopá* "one who tends cows," we have *adhigopam* (Nos. 269 and 971) "on the cowherd."

नाव्ययीभावादतोऽम् त्वपञ्चम्याः ।२।४।८३।

अदन्तादव्ययीभावात् सुपो न लुक् तस्य पञ्चमीं विना अमादेशः ।

No. 971.—There is NOT elision of the case-affix AFTER AN AVYAYÍBHÁVA compound that ends IN A. In the room of it,—BUT NOT IF it is THE 5TH case-affix,—there is the substitute AM.

तृतीयासप्तम्योर्बहुलम् ।२।४।८४।

अदन्तादव्ययीभावात् तृतीयासप्तम्योर्बहुलमम्भावः । उपकृष्णम् । उपकृष्णेन । मद्राणां समृद्धिः सुमद्रम् । यवनानां व्यृद्धिर्दुर्यवनम् । मक्षिकाणामभावो निर्मक्षिकम् । हिमस्यात्ययोऽतिहिमम् । निद्रा संप्रति न युज्यत इत्यतिनिद्रम् । हरिशब्दस्य प्रकाश इतिहरि । विष्णोः पश्चादनुविष्णु । योग्यतावीप्सापदार्थानतिवृत्तिसादृश्यानि यथार्थाः । रूपस्य योग्यमनुरूपम् । अर्थमर्थं प्रति प्रत्यर्थम् । शक्तिमनतिक्रम्य यथाशक्ति ।

No. 972.—The change to *am* (No. 971) OF THE 3RD AND 7TH case-affixes coming after an *Avyayíbháva* compound that ends in *a*, occurs DIVERSELY (—see No. 823). Thus *upakṛishṇam* or *upakṛishṇena* "near to Kṛishṇa;" [and, as further examples of No. 967,] *sumadram* "well (or prosperous) with the Madras," *duryavanam* "ill with the Yavanas," *nirmakshikam* "free from flies," *atihimam* "on the departure of the cold weather," *atinidram* "wakefully;"—i. e. sleep being *not now* engaged in—; *itihari* "the exclamation 'Hari' "—[thus *vaishṇavagṛihe itihari vartate* "in the house of the Vaishṇava there is the cry of 'Hari, Hari' "]—; *anuvishṇu* "after Vishṇu"—[i. e. following or worshipping him]. The meanings intended by the word *yathá*, [which, in the list at No. 967, has been rendered "according to,"] are 'correspondence,' 'severalty' or 'succession,' 'the not passing beyond something,' and 'likeness.' Thus *anurúpam* "in a corresponding manner," *pratyartham* "according to each several object or signification," *yathásakti* "according to one's ability"—[i. e. not going beyond one's power].

अव्ययीभावे चाकाले । ६ । ३ । ८१ ।

सहस्य सः स्यादव्ययीभावे न तु काले । हरेः सादृश्यं सहरि । ज्येष्ठस्यानुपूर्व्येणेत्यनुज्येष्ठम् । चक्रेण युगपत् सचक्रम् । सदृशः सख्या ससखि । क्षत्राणां संपत्तिः सक्षत्रम् । तृणमप्यपरित्यज्य सतृणमत्ति । अग्निग्रन्थपर्यन्तमधीते साग्नि ।

No. 973.—IN AN AVYAYÍBHÁVA compound let *sa* be the substitute of *saha*, BUT NOT WHEN the word in composition means a portion of TIME. Thus *sahari* "like Hari," then again, *anujyeshṭham* (No. 967) "in the order of seniority," *sachakram* "simultaneously with the wheel" (—on its crushing, for example, the head of the self-immolator), *sasakhi* "like a friend," *sakshatram* "as warriors ought," *satṛiṇam* "even to the grass" he eats—[i. e. the whole]—not leaving even a scrap—, *ságni* "as far as the chapter of fire [i. e. the whole Veda]"—he reads.

नदीभिश्च । २ । १ । २० ।

नदीभिः सह संख्या वा समस्यते । समाहारे चायमिष्यते । पञ्चगङ्गम् । द्वियमुनम् ।

No. 974.—AND WITH names of RIVERS a numeral may be compounded. It is wished [by *Patañjali*] that this should refer to their junction. Thus *pañchagañgam* "at the meeting of the five rivers Ganges" [viz. near the Mádhavaráw ghát at Benares], *dwiyamunam* "at the meeting of the two Yamunas."

तद्धिताः । ४ । १ । ७६ ।

आ पञ्चमसमाप्तेरधिकारोऽयम् ।

No. 975.—The expression "the affixes called TADDHITA" (i. e.—see No. 1067—"relating or belonging to that" which is primitive—) is the regulating expression [to be understood in all the aphorisms] from this point to the end of *Páṇini's* Fifth Lecture.

अव्ययीभावे शरत्प्रभृतिभ्यः । ५ । ४ । १०७ ।

शरदादिभ्यष्टच् स्यात् समासान्तोऽव्ययीभावे । शरदः समीपमुपशरदम् । प्रतिविपाशम् ।

No. 976.—WHEN the compound is AN AVYAYÍBHÁVA, let (the *taddhita*-affix—No. 975—) *ṭach* (No. 148) come AFTER the words ŚARAD &C., as the final of the compound. Thus *upaśaradam* (No. 971) "near the autumn," *prativipáśam* "along the river Vipáśa."

जराया जरस् च । उपजरसम् । इत्यादि ।

No. 977,—"AND JARAS substituted in the room OF JARÁ (No. 181)"—[shall come under the head of "*śarad &c*"]. Thus *upajarasam* (No. 976) "when decay is near"—&c.

अनश्च । ५ । ४ । १०८ ।

अन्नन्तादव्ययीभावाट्टच् ।

No. 978.—AND AFTER that *Avyayíbháva* which ends in AN, let there be *ṭach* (No. 976).

नस्तद्धिते । ६ । ४ । १४४ ।

नान्तस्य भस्य टेर्लोपस्तद्धिते । उपराजम् । अध्यात्मम् ।

No. 979.—WHEN A TADDHITA-affix (No. 975) FOLLOWS, there is elision OF the last vowel with what follows it (No. 51) of what ends in N and is called a *bha* (No. 185). Thus [there is elision of the *an* of *rájan* "a king" and *átman* "the soul," followed by the *taddhita*-affix *ṭach*—see No. 976.—in virtue of the commencing of which affix with a vowel these words then take the name of *bha*—and we have] *uparájam* "under the king," *adhyátmam* "over or in the spirit."

नपुंसकादन्यतरस्याम् । ५ । ४ । १०९ ।

अन्नन्तं यत् क्लीबं तदन्तादव्ययीभावाट्टज्वा । उपचर्मम् । उपचर्म ।

No. 980.—The *taddhita*-affix *ṭach* (No. 976) is OPTIONALLY placed AFTER an *Avyayíbháva* compound ending with A NEUTER word that ends in *an*. Thus *upacharmam* or *upacharma* "near the skin."

झयः । ५ । ४ । १११ ।

झयन्तादव्ययीभावाट्टज्वा । उपसमिधम् । उपसमित् ।

इत्यव्ययीभावः ॥

No. 981.—The *taddhita*-affix *ṭach* (No. 976) is optionally placed AFTER an *Avyayíbháva* compound that ends in A JHAY. Thus *upasamidham* or *upasamit* (No. 165) "near firewood."

So much for the *Avyayíbháva* compounds.

। तत्पुरुषः ।

OF THE TATPURUSHA, OR COMPOUND THE CONSTITUENTS OF WHICH ARE (GENERALLY) IN DIFFERENT CASES.

तत्पुरुषः । २ । १ । २२ ।

अधिकारोऽयम् । प्राग्बहुव्रीहेः ।

No. 982.—The term TATPURUSHA [i. e. "his man"—the expression itself—see No. 992—being an example of the kind of compound now to be treated of—] is a regulating expression [to be understood in each aphorism] as far as No. 1034.

द्विगुश्च । २ । १ । २३ ।

तत्पुरुषसंज्ञकः ।

No. 983.—AND the kind of compound called DWIGU (No. 1003) is also called *tatpurusha* (No. 982).

द्वितीयाश्रितातीतपतितगतात्यस्तप्राप्तापन्नैः । २ । १ । २४ ।

द्वितीयान्तं श्रितादिप्रकृतिकैः सुबन्तैः सह वा समस्यते । कृष्णं श्रितः । कृष्णश्रितः । इत्यादि ।

No. 984.—A word ending with THE 2ND case-affix is optionally compounded WITH the words ŚRITA "who has had recourse to," ATÍTA "who has surpassed," PATITA "who has fallen upon," GATA "who has gone to," ATYASTA "who has passed," PRÁPTA "who has reached," AND ÁPANNA "who has reached," when these are the governing words and end with case-affixes. Thus *kṛishṇaśrita* "who has had recourse to Kṛishṇa," &c.

तृतीया तत्कृतार्थेन गुणवचनेन । २ । १ । ३० ।

तृतीयान्तं तृतीयान्तार्थकृतगुणवचनेनार्थेन च सह वा प्राग्वत् । शङ्कुलया खण्डः । शङ्कुलाखण्डः । धान्येनार्थः । धान्यार्थः । तत्कृतेति किम् । अक्ष्णा काणः ।

No. 985.—A word ending with THE 3RD case-affix, as before [—see No. 984—is compounded] optionally WITH WHAT DENOTES THAT THE QUALITY of which is instrumentally caused by the thing signified by what ends with the 3rd case-affix, AND WITH the word ARTHA "wealth" [—the wealth being caused by that denoted by what ends with the 3rd case-affix]. Thus *śaṅkulákhaṇḍa* "a piece cut by the nippers"—[where the cause of the piece being *cut* is the nippers]—; *dhányártha* "wealth acquired by grain"—[where the grain is the cause of the wealth]. Why do we say "caused by the thing signified &c"? Witness *akshṇá káṇah* "blind of an eye"—[where the two words cannot form a compound, because the *eye* is not what makes the person blind].

कर्तृकरणे कृता बहुलम् ।२।१।३२।

कर्तरि करणे च तृतीया कृदन्तेन बहुलं प्राग्वत् । हरित्रातः । नखभिन्नः । कृद्ग्रहणे गतिकारकपूर्वस्यापि ग्रहणम् । नखनिर्भिन्नः ।

No. 986.—[That which ends with] the 3rd case-affix, WHEN it denotes THE AGENT OR THE INSTRUMENT, as before [see No. 984—is compounded] DIVERSELY (No. 823) with what ends with A KṚIT affix. Thus *haritráta* "preserved by Hari," *nakhabhinna* "divided by the nails." In the taking of *krit* [in the present rule] is implied that of the same when a preposition (No. 222) or a word directly related to the action (No. 958) precedes:—thus [the combination is not obstructed, by the preposition *nir*, in the example] *nakhanirbhinna* "quite divided by the nails."

चतुर्थी तदर्थार्थबलिहितसुखरक्षितैः ।२।१।३६।

चतुर्थ्यन्तार्थाय यत् तद्वाचिना अर्थादिभिश्च चतुर्थ्यन्तं वा प्राग्वत् । यूपाय दारु । यूपदारु । तदर्थेन प्रकृतिविकृतिभाव एवेष्टः । तेनेह न । रन्धनाय स्थाली ।

No. 987.—A word ending with THE 4TH case-affix, as before [—see No. 984,—is compounded optionally] WITH what denotes THAT WHICH IS FOR THE PURPOSE of what ends with the 4th case-affix—AND SO too WITH the words ARTHA "on account of," BALI "a sacrifice," HITA "salutary," SUKHA "pleasant," AND RAKSHITA "kept." Thus *yúpadáru* "wood for a stake." By the expression "for the purpose thereof" the special relation of a material and its modification alone is [by Patañjali] here held [to be intended]. Hence, in the case of such an expression as "a vessel for washing," composition does not take place—for the washing is not a modified form of the vessel, as a stake is a modified form of the wood which it is made of.

अर्थेन नित्यसमासो विशेष्यलिङ्गता चेति वक्तव्यम् । द्विजाया-

यम् । द्विजार्थः सूपः । द्विजार्था यवागूः । द्विजार्थं पयः । भूतबलिः । गोहितम् । गोसुखम् । गोरक्षितम् ।

No. 988.—"WITH ARTHA 'on account of,' IT SHOULD BE STATED THAT COMPOSITION takes place INVARIABLY, AND THAT THE COMPOUND TAKES THE GENDER OF THAT WHICH IT QUALIFIES." Thus *dwijárthah súpah* "broth for the Bráhman," *dwijárthá yavágúh* "gruel for the Bráhman," *dwijárthaṅ payah* "milk for the Bráhman." [Examples of composition with the other words enumerated in No. 987 are] *bhútabali* "a sacrifice for [all] beings," *gohita* "what is good for cows," *gosukha* "what is pleasant for cows," *gorakshita* "what is kept for cows"—(as grass).

पञ्चमी भयेन । २ । १ । ३७ ।

चोराद्भयम् । चोरभयम् ।

No. 989.—A word ending with THE 5TH case-affix may be compounded WITH the word BHAYA "fear." Thus *chorabhaya* "fear [by reason] of a thief."

स्तोकान्तिकदूरार्थकृच्छ्राणि क्तेन । २ । १ । ३९ ।

No. 990.—Words WITH THE SENSE OF STOKA "a little," ANTIKA "near," DÚRA "far,"—AND also the word KṚICHCHHRA "penance," [may be compounded] WITH what ends in KTA (No. 867).

पञ्चम्याः स्तोकादिभ्यः । ६ । ३ । २ ।

अलुगुत्तरपदे । स्तोकान्मुक्तः । अन्तिकादागतः । अभ्यासादागतः । दूरादागतः । कृच्छ्रादागतः ।

No. 991.—There is not elision OF THE 5TH case-affix (No. 768) AFTER words with the sense of STOKA &c. (No. 990), when a word in composition with them follows. Thus *stokánmukta* "loosed from a little distance," *antikádágata* "come from near," *abhyásádágata* "come from studying," *dúrádágata* "come from far," *kṛichchhrádágata* "come with difficulty."

षष्ठी । २ । २ । ८ ।

सुबन्तेन प्राग्वत् । राजपुरुषः ।

No. 992.—A word ending with THE 6TH case-affix, as before, [—see, No. 984—is optionally compounded] with what ends with a case-affix. Thus *rájapurusha* (No. 200) "the king's man." [This example, with the demonstrative pronoun *tat* substituted for the word *rájan*, gives the compound *tatpurusha* "his man," which is taken as the type and name of the class,—see No. 982.]

पूर्वापराधरोत्तरमेकदेशिनैकाधिकरणे ।२।२।१।

अवयविना सह पूर्वादयः समस्यन्ते एकत्वसंख्याविशिष्टश्चेदवयवी । षष्ठीसमासापवादः । पूर्वं कायस्य पूर्वकायः । अपरकायः । एकाधिकरणे किम् । पूर्वश्छात्राणाम् ।

No. 993.—The words PÚRVA "front," APARA "near," ADHARA "lower," AND UTTARA "upper," are compounded WITH WHAT [word signifies a thing that] HAS PARTS, PROVIDED that THE THING having parts IS DISTINGUISHED numerically BY UNITY. This debars No. 992 [which would have placed the words *púrva* &c. last in the compound;—whereas, being here exhibited in the nominative case—see No. 969—they take the precedence]. Thus *púrvakáya* "the front of the body," *aparakáya* "the back of the body." Why do we say "provided it is the site of unity [i. e. provided it be *one*]"? Witness *púrvaśchhátráṇám* "the foremost of the pupils"—[where composition does not take place, the pupils being more than one].

अर्धं नपुंसकम् ।२।२।२।

समांशवाच्यर्धशब्दो नित्यं क्लीबे प्राग्वत् । अर्धं पिप्पल्या अर्धपिप्पली ।

No. 994.—The word ARDHA, which, when it signifies exactly equal parts (i. e. halves) is always NEUTER, as before [i. e. as directed in No. 993—enters into composition]. Thus *ardhapippalí* "a half of the pepper."

सप्तमी शौण्डैः ।२।१।४०।

सप्तम्यन्तं शौण्डादिभिः प्राग्वत् । अक्षेषु शौण्डः । अक्षशौण्डः ।

इत्यादि । द्वितीया तृतीयेत्यादियोगविभागादन्यत्रापि द्वितीयादिविभक्तीनां प्रयोगवशात् समासो ज्ञेयः ।

No. 995.—A word ending with THE 7TH case-affix, as before [i. e. as directed in No. 984—is optionally compounded] WITH the words ŚAUṆḌA "skilled" &c. Thus *akshaśauṇḍa* "skilled in dice"—and so of others.

[It had been stated that words ending with the 2nd, 3rd, and other case-affixes—see Nos. 984, 985, &c.,—may form compounds with certain words specified in the aphorisms; but a greater latitude is found necessary—so] on the ground of usage [in the works of good authors] it is to be considered allowable to form compounds out of words ending with the 3rd and other case-affixes, elsewhere also [than where directed in the aphorisms], by disjoining the expressions 2nd, 3rd &c. [from their appropriate aphorisms], and attaching them [to others].

दिक्संख्ये संज्ञायाम् ।२।१।५०।

संज्ञायामेवेति नियमार्थं सूत्रम् । पूर्वेषुकामशमी । सप्त ऋषयः । सप्तर्षयः । तेनेह न । उत्तरा वृक्षाः । पञ्च ब्राह्मणाः ।

No. 996.—A word signifying a POINT of the compass OR a NUMBER [enters into composition] WHEN the sense is that of an APPELLATIVE.—The aphorism is intended to restrict the composition of such words to the case where the sense is that of an appellative. Thus *púrveshukámaśamí* "(the town of) Ishukámaśamí-in-the-East," *saptarshayah* "the Seven-sages," (i. e. the constellation of the Great Bear). Hence not here—viz. in *uttará vṛiksháh* "northern trees," *pañcha bráhmaṇáh* "five Bráhmans."

तद्धितार्थोत्तरपदसमाहारे च ।२।१।५१।

तद्धितार्थे विषये उत्तरपदे च परतः समाहारे च वाच्ये दिक्संख्ये प्राग्वत् । पूर्वस्यां शालायां भवः पूर्वाशाला इति समासे जाते । सर्वनाम्नो वृत्तिमात्रे पुंवद्भावः ।

No. 997.—In a case WHERE the SENSE is that OF A TADDHITA-affix (No. 975), AND WHEN AN ADDITIONAL MEMBER comes after the compound, **AND WHEN AN AGGREGATE** is to be expressed, then a word signifying a point of the compass or a number, as before [—see No. 996—becomes compounded]. Thus, when a compound is formed out of the words *púrvasyáṅ śáláyáṅ bhavah* "that which is in the eastern hall," [in which analytical exposition—see No. 964—of the compound in question, the word *bhava*—see No. 998—serves to represent the force of a *taddhita*-affix—] the compound having (—see No. 964—) reached the form of *púrvá* + *śálá*, [the feminine termination of the *púrvá* is rejected—because Patañjali declares that], "the masculine state belongs to a pronominal, when exercising any of the five functions" [specified under No. 964].

दिक्पूर्वपदादसंज्ञायां ञः । ४ । २ । १०७ ।

अस्माद्भवाद्यर्थे ञः स्यादसंज्ञायाम् ।

No. 998.—Let [the *taddhita*-affix—see No. 975—] ÑA, with the sense of "being" &c., come **AFTER A WORD PRECEDED BY** another that signifies **A POINT** of the compass—**PROVIDED** the compound is **NOT AN APPELLATIVE.** [Thus, from No. 997, we have *púrvaśálá* + *ña*.]

तद्धितेष्वचामादेः । ७ । २ । ११७ ।

ञिति णिति च तद्धितेष्वचामादेरचो वृद्धिः स्यात् । यस्येति च । पौर्वशालः । पञ्च गावो धनं यस्येति त्रिपदे बहुव्रीहौ ।

No. 999.—Let *vṛiddhi* be substituted in the room **OF THE FIRST** vowel **OF THE VOWELS, WHEN TADDHITA**-affixes **FOLLOW**, having an indicatory *ñ* (No. 998). or *ṇ*. The final vowel, moreover, being elided by No. 260, we have *paurvaśála* "who is in the eastern hall"—(No. 997).

In the case of the *Bahuvríhi* compound (No. 1034) consisting of three terms—signifying "whose wealth is five cows"—[the rule following applies].

द्वन्द्वतत्पुरुषयोरुत्तरपदे नित्यसमासवचनम् ।

No. 1000.—"**WHEN AN ADDITIONAL NUMBER** comes **AFTER** (what would else be but optionally) **A DWANDWA** compound (No.

1054) OR A TATPURUSHA (No. 982), the compounding is TO BE SPOKEN OF AS INVARIABLE"

गोरतद्धितलुकि । ५ । ४ । ९२ ।

गोऽन्तात् तत्पुरुषाट्टच् स्यात् समासान्तो न तु तद्धितलुकि । पञ्चगवधनः ।

No. 1001.—Let (the *taddhita*-affix) *ṭach* be as the final of the compound AFTER a *Tatpurusha* that ends with the word GO "a cow"—but NOT when there is ELISION OF the TADDHITA-affix. Thus *pañchagavadhana* "whose wealth consists of five cows."

तत्पुरुषः समानाधिकरणः कर्मधारयः । १ । २ । ४२ ।

No. 1002.—A TATPURUSHA compound (No. 982) THE CASE OF each member of WHICH IS THE SAME, is called KARMADHÁRAYA (—i. e. "that which comprehends the object"—but why so named does not seem to be anywhere explained).

संख्यापूर्वो द्विगुः । २ । १ । ५२ ।

तद्धितार्थेत्यत्रोक्तस्त्रिविधः संख्यापूर्वो द्विगुसंज्ञः स्यात् ।

No. 1003.—Let a compound, THE FIRST member OF WHICH IS A NUMERAL, and which is of one of the three kinds specified in No. 997, be called DWIGU—[the word *dwigu* itself—an instance of this kind of compound—signifying "of the value of two cows]."

द्विगुरेकवचनम् । २ । ४ । १ ।

द्विग्वर्थः समाहार एकवत् स्यात् ।

No. 1004—An aggregate expressed by A DWIGU shall be like *one*—i. e. shall be SINGULAR.

स नपुंसकम् । २ । ४ । १७ ।

समाहारे द्विगुर्द्वन्द्वश्च नपुंसकं स्यात् । पञ्चानां गवां समाहारः पञ्चगवम् ।

No. 1005.—When the sense is an aggregate, IT—a *Dwigu* or a *Dwandwa* compound (No. 1054—shall be A NEUTER. Thus *pañchagavam* "an aggregate of five cows."

विशेषणं विशेष्येण बहुलम् । २ । १ । ५७ ।

भेदकं भेद्येन समानाधिकरणेन बहुलं प्राग्वत् । नीलमुत्पलं नीलोत्पलम् । बहुलग्रहणात् क्वचिन्नित्यम् । कृष्णसर्पः । क्वचिन्न । रामो जामदग्न्यः ।

No. 1006—The QUALIFIER (or discriminator) [is compounded] WITH the thing thereby QUALIFIED (or discriminated) DIVERSELY (No. 823), as before [—i. e. as directed in No. 984]. Thus *nílotpala* "a blue lotus." By taking, in the rule, the expression "diversely" it is meant that in some cases it is imperative to make a compound—as in the case of *kṛishṇasarpa* "a black snake," and sometimes it is forbidden—thus *rámo jámadagnyah* "Ráma (called also) Jámadagnya" (as being the son of Jamadagni)."

उपमानानि सामान्यवचनैः । २ । १ । ५५ ।

घनश्यामः ।

No. 1007.—OBJECTS OF COMPARISON are compounded WITH WORDS DENOTING WHAT IS LIKENED to them Thus *ghanaśyáma* "cloud-black"—[i. e. something black as a cloud].

शाकपार्थिवादीनामुत्तरपदलोपो वक्तव्यः । शाकप्रियः पार्थिवः । शाकपार्थिवः । देवब्राह्मणः ।

No. 1008.—THE ELISION OF THE SECOND MEMBER IN the compounds ŚÁKAPÁRTHIVA &c. should be stated." Thus the word *priya* "beloved" is elided in the example *śákapárthiva* "the king of the era"—i. e. the king *beloved* by (the people of) his era, *devabráhmaṇa* "a Bráhman beloved by the gods."

नञ् । २ । २ । ६ ।

नञ् सुपा प्राग्वत् ।

No. 1009.—The indeclinable privative NAṄ, as before [i. e. as directed in the foregoing rules—combines] with what ends with a case affix.

नलोपो नञः । ६ । ३ । ७३ ।

नञो नस्य लोप उत्तरपदे । अब्राह्मणः ।

No. 1010.—There is ELISION OF the N OF NAǸ (No. 1009), when a word follows in composition with it. Thus *abráhmaṇa* "who is not a Bráhman"—(though a man).

तस्मान्नुडचि । ६ । ३ । ७४ ।

लुप्तनकारान्नञ उत्तरपदस्याजादेर्नुट् । अनश्वः । नैकधेत्यादौ तु नशब्देन सह सुप् सुपेति समासः ।

No. 1011.—Let NUṬ be the augment OF a word beginning with A VOWEL that comes, in composition, AFTER THAT *naǹ* (No. 1010) of which the *n* has been elided. Thus *anaśwa* "(an animal) which is not a horse." But in such an expression as *naikadhá* "not at one time," there is composition with the word *na* [i. e. *naǹ* with its indicatory final dropped] in accordance with No. 964 ['indeclinables' being regarded as if they had case-affixes, though these have been elided—see Nos. 403 and 210].

कुगतिप्रादयः । २ । २ । १८ ।

एते समर्थेन नित्यं समस्यन्ते । कुत्सितः पुरुषः । कुपुरुषः ।

No. 1012.—The word KU (No. 399), those called GATI (Nos. 222 and 1013), and PRA &c. (No. 48), are invariably compounded with that with which they are connected in sense. Thus *kupurusha* "a paltry man."

ऊर्यादिच्विडाचश्च । १ । ४ । ६१ ।

ऊर्यादयश्च्व्यन्ता डाजन्ताश्च क्रियायोगे गतिसंज्ञाः स्युः । ऊरीकृत्य । शुक्लीकृत्य । पटपटाकृत्य । सुपुरुषः ।

No. 1013.—AND let the words ÚRÍ (No. 399) "assent," AND THE LIKE, AND those that end with CHWI (No. 1332), AND those that end with ḌÁCH (No. 1338), when in composition with a verb, be called *gati* (No. 222). Thus (No. 1012) *úríkṛitya* (No. 936) "having promised," *śuklíkṛitya* "having made white," *paṭapaṭá-kṛitya* "having made a clattering," *supurusha* (Nos. 1012 and 48) "a good man."

प्रादयो गताद्यर्थे प्रथमया । प्रगत आचार्यः । प्राचार्यः ।

No. 1014.—"The words PRA &c. (No. 48), WHEN THE SENSE IS that of GONE OR THE LIKE, combine WITH what ends with THE 1ST case-affix." Thus *práchárya* "a hereditary teacher" (like Vaśishṭha in the family of Ráma).

अत्यादयः क्रान्ताद्यर्थे द्वितीयया । अतिक्रान्तो मालामिति विग्रहे ।

No. 1015.—"The words ATI &c. (No. 48), WHEN THE THING DENOTED is GONE BEYOND or the like, combine WITH what ends with THE 2ND case-affix." Thus we may have, as the analysis of a compound *atikránto málám* "which has surpassed the necklace:"—[but, in regard to the compound, some further considerations are necessary].

एकविभक्ति चापूर्वनिपाते । १ । २ । ४४ ।

विग्रहे यन्नियतविभक्तिकं तदुपसर्जनं न तु तस्य पूर्वनिपातः ।

No. 1016.—AND that which, in the analytical statement of the sense of a compound, has ONE fixed CASE [whilst the word with it is compounded may vary its case] is called *upasarjana* (No. 968), BUT DOES NOT (necessarily) STAND FIRST (No. 969) [This furnishes occasion for the next rule].

गोस्त्रियोरुपसर्जनस्य । १ । २ । ४८ ।

उपसर्जनं यो गोशब्दः स्त्रीप्रत्ययान्तं च तदन्तस्य प्रातिपदिकस्य ह्रस्वः । अतिमालः ।

No. 1017.—Let a short vowel be the substitute OF a crude word No. 135) which ends with the word GO "a cow," AND of that which ends with what has as its termination A FEMININE affix (No. 1341), WHEN regarded as AN UPASARJANA (No. 1016). Thus [the example under No. 1015 becomes] *atimála* "exceeding the necklace (in beauty).

अवादयः क्रुष्टाद्यर्थे तृतीयया । अवक्रुष्टः कोकिलया । अवकोकिलः ।

No 1018.—"The words AVA &c. (No. 48), WHEN THE THING DENOTED is CRIED OUT &c., are compounded WITH what ends with

THE 3RD case-affix." Thus *avakokila* "what is announced by the cuckoo."—(e. g. the spring).

पर्यादयो ग्लानाद्यर्थे चतुर्थ्या । परिग्लानोऽध्ययनाय पर्यध्ययनः ।

No. 1019.—"The words PARI &c. (No. 48), WHEN THAT DENOTED IS WEARY &c., are compounded WITH what ends with THE 4TH case-affix." Thus *paryadhyayana* "weary of study."

निरादयः क्रान्ताद्यर्थे पञ्चम्या । निष्क्रान्तः कौशाम्ब्या निष्कौशाम्बिः ।

No. 1020.—"The words NIR &c. (No. 48), WHEN THE THING DENOTED IS GONE BEYOND &c., are compounded WITH what ends with THE 5TH case-affix." Thus *nishkauśámbi* "who has gone beyond Kauśámbí."

तत्रोपपदं सप्तमीस्थम् । ३ । १ । ९२ ।

सप्तम्यन्ते पदे कर्मणीत्यादौ वाच्यत्वेन स्थितं यत् कुम्भादि तद्वाचकं पदमुपपदं स्यात् ।

No. 1021.— HERE [i. e. in the division of the Grammar referring to verbal roots] let the word, such as "*pot*" or the like, denoting that which, in virtue of its being a significate, is IMPLIED in a term exhibited IN THE 7TH case, such as *karmaṇi* (No. 841), be called UPAPADA (No. 1022).

उपपदमतिङ् । २ । २ । १९ ।

उपपदं समर्थेन नित्यं समस्यतेऽतिङन्तश्च समासः । कुम्भं करोतीति कुम्भकारः । अतिङ् किम् । मा भवान् भूत् । माङि लुङीति सप्तमीनिर्देशान्माङुपपदम् । गतिकारकोपपदानां कृद्भिः सह समासवचनं प्राक् सुबुत्पत्तेः । व्याघ्री । अश्वक्रीती । कच्छपी । इत्यादि ।

No. 1022.—AN UPAPADA (No. 1021) is always compounded with that with which it is in construction— and the compound does NOT end IN A TENSE-AFFIX. Thus *kumbhakára* (No. 841) "one who makes pots." Why do we say "not in a tense-affix"? Witness *má bhaván bhút* "let not your Honour become"—where *máń* as having been exhibited, in No. 469, in the 7th case, takes the name of *upapada* [but is not compounded with *bhút*].

The compounding of a *gati* (No. 222) or a *káraka* (No. 945), or an *upapada* (No. 1021) with what ends with a *kṛit*-affix is declared to be effected before the case-affixes present themselves. Thus we have *vyághrí* "a tigress," *aśwakrítí* "a female (e. g. cow or the like) bought in exchange for a horse," *kachchhapí* "a she-tortoise." [The word *vyághrí* is said to be derived from the root *ghrá* "to smell," with the *gati*-prefixes *vi* and *á*, because the animal "goes smelling about." By Nos. 839 and 524, short *a* is found in the room of the long *á*. Then, if the *vi+á+ghrá* were not held to have become a compound before the case-affixes present themselves, in forming the feminine we should have to follow No. 1341 instead of No. 1373—for we should be forming the feminine of a verbal and not of a word denoting a genus. And so of the other examples].

तत्पुरुषस्याङ्गुलेः संख्याव्ययादेः ।५।४।८६।

संख्याव्ययादेरङ्गुल्यन्तस्य तत्पुरुषस्य समासान्तोऽच् स्यात् । द्वे अङ्गुली प्रमाणमस्य द्व्यङ्गुलम् । निर्गतमङ्गुलिभ्यो निरङ्गुलम् ।

No. 1023.—Let the affix *ach* be the final OF the TATPURUSHA compound WHICH BEGINS WITH A NUMERAL OR AN INDECLINABLE AND ENDS WITH AŃGULI "an inch." Thus *dwyańgula* (No. 260) "of the measure of two inches," *nirańgula* "exceeding in measure the breadth of the fingers (of a hand)."

अहःसर्वैकदेशसंख्यातपुण्याच्च रात्रेः ।५।४।८७।

एभ्यो रात्रेरच् स्यात् । चात् संख्याव्ययादेः । अहर्ग्रहणं द्वन्द्वार्थम् ।

No. 1024.—AND let the affix *ach* come AFTER the word RÁTRI "night," when it comes AFTER AHAN "a day," SARVA "all," WHAT SIGNIFIES A PORTION, AND SAŃKHYÁTA "numbered," AND PUṆYA "holy." By the "and" is meant that this is to hold also when the compound "begins with a numeral or an indeclinable."

The word *ahan* "a day" is taken, in this aphorism, with a view to its entering into a *Dwandwa* compound—(No. 1054).

रात्राह्नाहाः पुंसि । २ । ४ । २९ ।

एतदन्तौ द्वन्द्वतत्पुरुषौ पुंस्येव । अहश्च रात्रिश्चाहोरात्रः । सर्वरात्रः । संख्यातरात्रः ।

No. 1025.—*Dwandwa* (No. 1054) and *Tatpurusha* compounds ending in RÁTRA (i. e. *rátri+ach*—see No. 1024), AND AHNA (V. 4. 88.) AND AHA (Nos. 1027 and 979), appear IN THE MASCULINE only. Thus *ahorátrah* (No. 395, in spite of No. 129, taking effect as directed by Kátyáyana) "day and night," *sarvarátrah* "the whole night," *sankhyátarátrah* "a night numbered (as the 1st, 2d, 13th, &c.)."

संख्यापूर्वं रात्रं क्लीबम् । द्विरात्रम् । त्रिरात्रम् ।

No. 1026.—"The word RÁTRA 'night,' (No. 1025) PRECEDED in composition BY A NUMERAL, is NEUTER." Thus *dwirátram* "a space of two nights," *trirátram* "a space of three nights."

राजाहःसखिभ्यष्टच् । ५ । ४ । ९१ ।

एतदन्तात् तत्पुरुषाट्टच् । परमराजः ।

No. 1027.—The *taddhita*-affix ṬACH comes AFTER a *Tatpurusha* compound (No. 982) that ends with the word RÁJAN "a king," AHAN "a day," OR SAKHI "a friend." Thus *paramarájah* "a supreme king."

आन्महतः समानाधिकरणजातीययोः । ६ । ३ । ४६ ।

महाराजः । प्रकारवचने जातीयर् । महाप्रकारो महाजातीयः ।

No. 1028.—Let LONG Á be the substitute (of the final) OF MAHAT "great," WHEN A WORD IN THE SAME CASE FOLLOWS, AND WHEN JÁTÍYAR (V. 3. 69.) FOLLOWS. Thus *mahárájah* (No 1027) "a great king." The word *játíyar* means "kind:"—thus *mahájátíyah* "like the great."

द्व्यष्टनः संख्यायामबहुव्रीह्यशीत्योः । ६ । ३ । ४७ ।

आत् स्यात् । द्वादश । अष्टाविंशतिः ।

No. 1029.—Let long *á* be the substitute OF DWI "two" AND ASHṬAN "eight," WHEN A NUMERAL FOLLOWS, but NOT WHEN the compound is A BAHUVRÍHI (No. 1034), NOR WHEN AŚÍTI "eighty" FOLLOWS. Thus *dwádaśa* "twelve" (2+10), *ṅśatiashṭávi* (No. 200) "twenty-eight."

परवल्लिङ्गं द्वन्द्वतत्पुरुषयोः ।२।४।२६।

कुक्कुटमयूर्याविमे । मयूरीकुक्कुटाविमौ । अर्धपिप्पली ।

No. 1030.—The GENDER OF A DWANDWA (No. 1054) OR TATPURUSHA compound (No. 982) IS LIKE that of the LAST word in it. Thus *kukkuṭamayúryávime* "those two (fem.) the cock and the peahen," *mayúríkukkuṭávimau* "those two (mas.) the peahen and the cock," *ardhapippalí* "the half of the pepper" (which is fem.—though *ardha* here—see No. 994—is neuter).

द्विगुप्राप्तापन्नालंपूर्वगतिसमासेषु न । पञ्चकपालः पुरोडाशः । प्राप्तो जीविकां प्राप्तजीविकः । आपन्नजीविकः । अलं कुमार्यै अलंकुमारिः । अत एव ज्ञापकात् समासः । निष्कौशाम्बिः ।

No. 1031.—"This (dependence of the gender on that of the last word—No. 1030—) does NOT hold IN A DWIGU compound (No. 1003), nor in compounds THE FIRST member of which is PRÁPTA 'obtained,' ÁPANNA 'obtained,' ALAM 'enough,' AND a GATI (No. 1012)." Thus *pañchakapálah puroḍáśah* "cakes soaked in butter (and offered at a sacrifice) in a dish with five compartments"—[though *kapála* is neuter], *práptajívikah* or *ápannajívikah* "who has obtained a livelihood"—[though *jíviká* is fem.], *alaṅkumárih* "who is a suitable match for the girl"—which, only by the present rule, could be known to be a case justifying composition; (so too, where a *gati* is the first member] *nishkauśámbih* "(a man) who has come out of Kauśámbí" [though the name of the place is feminine].

अर्धर्चाः पुंसि च ।२।४।३१।

अर्धर्चादयः पुंसि क्लीबे च स्युः । अर्धर्चः । अर्धर्चम् । एवं ध्वजतीर्थशरीरमण्डपयूषदेहाङ्कुशकलशपात्रसूत्रादयः ।

No. 1032.—The words ARDHARCHA &c. may be MASCULINE AND neuter. Thus *ardharcha* or *ardharcham* "half a verse (of Scripture)." In like manner [the following words may be either masc. or neut., viz.] *dhwaja* "a flag," *tírtha* "a place of pilgrimage," *śaríra* "the body," *maṇḍapa* "a shed," *yúsha* "pease-soup," *deha* "the body," *ańkuśa* "a goad for an elephant," *kalaśa* "a jar," *pátra* "a vessel," *sútra* "a thread," &c.

सामान्ये नपुंसकम् । मृदु पचति । प्रातः कमनीयम् ।

इति तत्पुरुषः ॥

No. 1033.—(By common consent) the NEUTER is employed WHEN the application is GENERAL [i. e. when nothing is qualified in particular by the word in question]. Thus *mridu pachati* "he cooks soft (anything in general that he does cook)," *prátah kamaníyam* "in the morning it is pleasant"—(i. e. things in general are so).

So much for the *Tatpurusha* compounds.

। बहुव्रीहिः ।

OF THE BAHUVRÍHI OR ATTRIBUTIVE COMPOUND.

शेषो बहुव्रीहिः ।२।२।२३।

अधिकारोऽयम् । प्राग्द्वन्द्वात् ।

No. 1034.—Let THE REST be called BAHUVRÍHI. This is a regulating expression [to be understood in each aphorism] as far as No. 1054.

अनेकमन्यपदार्थे ।२।२।२४।

अनेकं प्रथमान्तमन्यस्य पदस्यार्थे वर्तमानं वा समस्यते स बहुव्रीहिः ।

No. 1035.—[A collection of] MORE words THAN ONE, in the nominative, employed TO DENOTE THE SAME THING AS ANOTHER WORD, is optionally compounded:—this is a *Bahuvríhi* compound (No. 1034).

सप्तमीविशेषणे बहुव्रीहौ ।२।२।३५।

सप्तम्यन्तं विशेषणं च बहुव्रीहौ पूर्वं स्यात् । कण्ठेकालः । अत एव ज्ञापकाद्व्यधिकरणपदो बहुव्रीहिः ।

No. 1036.—A word in THE 7TH CASE, AND AN EPITHET shall stand first IN a BAHUVRÍHI compound. Thus *kanṭhekála* "who is black in the throat—(Śiva)." [Had the noun not been in the 7th case, the epithet must have come first—thus *kálakanṭha* "black-throated"]. From this we learn that a *Bahuvríhi* compound may consist of words in different cases—[though No. 1035 speaks of them as being all alike in the nominative].

हलदन्तात् सप्तम्याः संज्ञायाम् । ६ । ३ । ९ ।

हलन्ताददन्ताच्च सप्तम्या अलुक् । त्वचिसारः । प्राप्तमुदकं यं प्राप्तोदको ग्रामः । ऊढरथोऽनड्वान् । उपहृतपशू रुद्रः । उद्धृतौदना स्थाली । पीताम्बरो हरिः । वीरपुरुषको ग्रामः ।

No. 1037.—There is not elision OF THE 7TH case-affix AFTER what ends in A CONSONANT OR SHORT A, WHEN the sense is that of AN APPELLATIVE. Thus *twachisára* "a bambu" (the pith, or strength, of which is in its cuticle).

[Other examples of *Bahuvríhi* compounds are] *práptodako grámah* "a village at which the water has come," *úḍharatho. naḍwán* "an ox by which the car is borne," *upahṛitapaśú rudrah* (No. 131) "Rudra, to whom cattle are offered (by being turned loose)," *uddhṛitaudaná sthálí* "a pot from which the boiled rice has been taken out," *pítámbaro harih* "Hari, whose garments are yellow," *vírapurushako grámah* "a village the men of which are heroes."

प्रादिभ्यो धातुजस्य वाच्यो वा चोत्तरपदलोपः । प्रपतितपर्णः । प्रपर्णः ।

No. 1038.—"The OPTIONAL compounding OF WHAT ARISES FROM A VERBAL ROOT coming AFTER PRA &c. (No. 48), SHOULD BE STATED, AND THE ELISION OF THE TERM SUBSEQUENT (—here subsequent to the prefix)." Thus *praparṇah* "(a tree) of which the leaves are all fallen"—[the word *patita* being omitted in the compound].

नञोऽस्त्यर्थानां वाच्यो वा चोत्तरपदलोपः। अविद्यमानपुत्रोऽपुत्रः।

No. 1039.—"The compounding OF words SIGNIFYING 'WHAT EXISTS,' coming AFTER the negative NAṄ (No. 1010), SHOULD BE STATED, AND THE OPTIONAL ELISION OF THE SECOND OF THE TERMS." Thus *avidyamánaputra* or *aputra* "of whom there exists not a child"—(i. e. childless).

स्त्रियाः पुंवद्भाषितपुंस्कादनूङ् समानाधिकरणे स्त्रियामपूरणीप्रियादिषु। ६। ३। ३४।

उक्तपुंस्कादनूङ् ऊङोऽभावो यत्र तथाभूतस्य स्त्रीवाचकशब्दस्य पुंवाचकस्येव रूपं समानाधिकरणे न तु पूरण्यां प्रियादौ च। गोस्त्रियोरिति ह्रस्वः। चित्रगुः। रूपवद्भार्यः। अनूङ् किम्। वामोरूभार्यः।

No. 1040.—WHEN THERE IS NOT ÚṄ AFTER WHAT is employed in SPEAKING OF what is MASCULINE,—i. e. where there is the absence of the feminine affix *úń*—(see No. 1376) the form OF such a FEMININE word becomes LIKE the MASCULINE, WHEN a FEMININE word IN THE SAME CASE FOLLOWS (in the compound)—but NOT IF this (word that follows) is an ORDINAL, OR is the word PRIYA "beloved" &c.

[Thus—when we mean to speak of a man as having "a brindled cow"—the two words *chitrá gauh* being converted into an epithet], *gau* becomes short, by No. 1017, [and then, by the present rule, the *chitrá*, which is "followed by a feminine word in the same case"—viz. by *gauh*—, becomes "like the masculine"—i. e. becomes *chitra*—so that we have] *chitraguh* "(a man) who has a brindled cow." In like manner [from *rúpavatí bháryá* "a handsome wife"] *rúpavadbháryah* "who has a handsome wife." Why do we say "when there is not *úń*"? Witness *vámorúbháryah* "one who has a wife with handsome thighs"—[where the feminine affix *úń*—No. 1380—by which the final of the word *uru* "a thigh" was lengthened, remains].

अप् पूरणीप्रमाण्योः। ५। ४। ११६।

पूरणार्थप्रत्ययान्तं यत् स्त्रीलिङ्गं तदन्तात् प्रमाण्यन्ताच्च बहुव्रीहेरप् स्यात् । कल्याणी पञ्चमी यासां रात्रीणां ताः कल्याणीपञ्चमा रात्रयः । स्त्री प्रमाणी यस्य स्त्रीप्रमाणः । अप्रियादिषु किम् । कल्याणीप्रियः । इत्यादि ।

No. 1041.—WHEN a feminine word ends with an affix giving the sense of AN ORDINAL, let the affix AP be AFTER the *Bahuvríhi* compound (No. 1034) which ends therewith or with the word PRAMÁṆÍ "a witness." Thus *kalyáṇípanchamá rátrayah* "nights, the fifth of which is auspicious," *strípramáṇah* "having a woman for witness or authority"—(a suit &c). Why do we say (in No. 1040) "not if this is the word *priya* &c"? Witness *kalyáṇípriyah* "whose beloved is an honourable woman" :—and so on.

बहुव्रीहौ सक्थ्यक्ष्णोः स्वाङ्गात् षच् ।५।४।११३।

स्वाङ्गवाचिसक्थ्यक्ष्यन्ताद्बहुव्रीहेः षच् । दीर्घसक्थः । जलजाक्षी । स्वाङ्गात् किम् । दीर्घसक्थि शकटम् । स्थूलाक्षा वेणुयष्टिः । अक्ष्णोऽदर्शनादिति वक्ष्यमाणोऽच् ।

No. 1042.—Let the affix SHACH come AFTER the words SAKTHI "the thigh" AND AKSHI "the eye" final IN A BAHUVRÍHI compound and denoting A PART OF THE BODY. Thus *dírghasakthah* "whose thighs are long," *jalajákshí* (No. 1348) "lotus-eyed." Why do we say "denoting a part of the body"? Witness *dírghasakthi śakaṭam* "a cart with long shafts," *sthúlákshá veṇuyashṭih* "a bambu-staff with large eyes"—[meaning the marks at the joints left on removing the twigs that grew there]. In this last example, as will be stated in No. 1064, the affix is *ach*.

द्वित्रिभ्यां ष मूर्ध्नः ।५।४।११५।

द्विमूर्धः । त्रिमूर्धः ।

No. 1043.—Let the affix SHA be placed AFTER the word MÚRDHAN "the head" coming AFTER DWI "two" OR TRI "three." Thus *dwimúrdhah* (No. 979) "who has two heads," *trimúrdhah* "who has three heads."

अन्तर्बहिर्भ्यां च लोम्नः । ५ । ४ । ११७ ।

अप् स्यात् । अन्तर्लोमः । बहिर्लोमः ।

No. 1044.—AND let the affix *ap* be placed AFTER the word LOMAN "hair" coming AFTER the word ANTAR "within" OR VAHIS "without." Thus *antarlomah* "that (as a fur garment) of which the hair is inside," *vahirlomah* "that of which the hair is outside."

पादस्य लोपोऽहस्त्यादिभ्यः । ५ । ४ । १३८ ।

हस्त्यादिवर्जितादुपमानात् परस्य पादस्य लोपः । व्याघ्रस्येव पादावस्य व्याघ्रपात् । अहस्त्यादिभ्यः किम् । हस्तिपादः । कुशूलपादः ।

No. 1045.—There is ELISION OF (the last letter) of the word PÁDA "a foot," employed as an object of comparison, but NOT AFTER the words HASTIN "an elephant" &C. Thus *vyághrapát* "whose feet are like those of a tiger." Why do we say "not after *hastin &c.*"? Witness *hastipádah* "whose feet are like those of an elephant," *kuśúlapádah* "whose feet are like large grain jars."

संख्यासुपूर्वस्य । ५ । ४ । १४० ।

लोपः स्यात् । द्विपात् । सुपात् ।

No. 1046.—Let there be elision OF it (i. e. of the final of *páda* "a foot"—No. 1045) PRECEDED BY A NUMERAL AND by SU. Thus *dwipát* "whose feet are two"—(i. e. a biped), *supát* "whose feet are good."

उद्विभ्यां काकुदस्य । ५ । ४ । १४८ ।

लोपः स्यात् । उत्काकुत् । विकाकुत् ।

No. 1047.—Let there be elision (of the final) OF KÁKUDA "the palate" AFTER UT AND VI. Thus *utkákud* "who has a high palate," *vikákud* "who has a wrongly formed palate."

पूर्णाद्विभाषा । ५ । ४ । १४९ ।

पूर्णकाकुत् । पूर्णकाकुदः ।

No. 1048.—AFTER the word PÚRṆA (the elision of the final of *kákuda*—No. 1047 takes place) OPTIONALLY. Thus *púrṇakákud* or *púrṇakákudah* "whose palate is complete."

सुहृद्दुर्हृदौ मित्रामित्रयोः । ५ । ४ । १५० ।

सुहृन्मित्रम् । दुर्हृदमित्रः ।

No. 1049.—The forms SUHṚID AND DURHṚID, WITH THE SENSE OF FRIEND AND FOE [are the only forms admissible, whether you suppose them to be compounds of *hṛid* or of *hṛidaya* "the heart"]. Thus *suhṛid* "whose heart is well-affected," *durhṛid* "whose heart is ill-affected."

उरःप्रभृतिभ्यः कप् । ५ । ४ । १५१ ।

No. 1050.—AFTER the word URAS "the breast" &c. [when final in a compound], let there be the affix KAP.

कस्कादिषु च । ८ । ३ । ४८ ।

इण्विण उत्तरस्य विसर्गस्य षोऽन्यस्य तु सः । इति सः । व्यूढोरस्कः । प्रियसर्पिष्कः ।

No. 1051.—AND IN the words KASKA "who? who? &c." SH is the substitute of *visarga* coming after an *iṇ*—but of another (i. e. of *visarga* coming not after an *iṇ*) there is *s*. Thus *vyúḍhoraskaḥ* "whose chest is broad," *priyasarpishkaḥ* "to whom clarified butter is pleasant."

निष्ठा । २ । २ । ३६ ।

निष्ठान्तं बहुव्रीहौ पूर्वं स्यात् । युक्तयोगः ।

No. 1052.—What ends with A NISHṬHÁ (No. 866) shall stand first in a *Bahuvríhi* compound. Thus *yuktayoga* "who is devoted to devotion."

शेषाद्विभाषा । ५ । ४ । १५४ ।

अनुक्तसमासान्ताद्बहुव्रीहेः कब्वा । महायशस्कः । महायशाः ।

इति बहुव्रीहिः ॥

No. 1053.—The affix *kap* is OPTIONALLY placed AFTER THE REMAINDER—i. e. after any *Bahuvríhi* compound in respect of which no other affix is enjoined as the final of the compound. Thus *maháyaśaskah* or *maháyaśas* "whose renown is great."

So much for the *Bahuvríhi* Compounds.

। द्वन्द्वः ।

OF THE DWANDWA OR AGGREGATIVE COMPOUND

चार्थे द्वन्द्वः । २ । २ । २९ ।

अनेकं सुबन्तं चार्थे वर्तमानं वा समस्यते स द्वन्द्वः । समुच्चयान्वाचयेतरेतरयोगसमाहाराश्चार्थाः । तत्रेश्वरं गुरुं च भजस्वेति परस्परनिरपेक्षस्यानेकस्यैकस्मिन्नन्वयः समुच्चयः । भिक्षामट गां चानयेत्यन्यतरस्यानुषङ्गिकत्वेनान्वयोऽन्वाचयः । अनयोरसामर्थ्यात् समासो न । धवखदिरौ छिन्धीति मिलितानामन्वय इतरेतरयोगः । संज्ञापरिभाषमिति समूहः समाहारः ।

No. 1054.—When a set of several words ending with case-affixes stands IN A RELATION EXPRESSIBLE BY "AND," the set is optionally made into a compound :—this is called DWANDWA "doubling" or "coupling." The meanings that may be indicated by "*and*" are "community of reference," "collateralness of reference," "mutual conjunction," and "lumping." For example—*íśwaraṅ guruṅ cha bhajaswa* "reverence God and thy teacher"—here the dependence, on one (and the same verb), of the mutually unrelated set of more than one, is what we call "community of reference." In the example *bhikshámaṭa gáṅ chánaya* "go for alms and bring the cow," the relation founded on the one or the other's being concerned in a collateral action—is what we call "collateralness of reference." In these two cases composition does not take place, because the words are not directly related to one another—(No. 962). In the example *dhavakhadirau chhindhi* "cleave (alike) the Mimosa and the Grislea"—the relation of the two mixed up (in one action of which they are spoken of as the joint object) is what we call "mutual conjunction." "Lumping" is aggregation (into a neuter singular word)—as in the example *saṅjṅáparibhásham* "an appellative and a maxim of interpretation."

राजदन्तादिषु परम् । २ । २ । ३१ ।

एषु पूर्वप्रयोगार्हं परं स्यात् । दन्तानां राजा राजदन्तः ।

No. 1055.—IN the words RÁJADANTA AND THE LIKE, let that be put LAST which is (according to No. 969) proper to be placed first. Thus *rájadantah* "a chief of teeth" (i. e. an eye-tooth).

धर्मादिष्वनियमः । अर्थधर्मौ । धर्मार्थौ । इत्यादि ।

No. 1056.—"In regard to the words DHARMA AND THE LIKE, there is NO fixed RULE." Thus *arthadharmau* or *dharmárthau* "wealth and virtue" or "virtue and wealth" &c.

द्वन्द्वे घि । २ । २ । ३२ ।

पूर्वं स्यात् । हरिहरौ ।

No. 1057.—IN A DWANDWA compound, let a word called GHI (No. 190) stand first. Thus *hariharau* "Hari and Hara."

अजाद्यदन्तम् । २ । २ । ३३ ।

ईशकृष्णौ ।

No. 1058.—[And likewise—see No. 1057—] WHAT BEGINS WITH A VOWEL AND ENDS WITH SHORT A. Thus *íśakṛishṇau* "the Lord and Kṛishṇa."

अल्पाच्तरम् । २ । २ । ३४ ।

शिवकेशवौ ।

No. 1059.—[And likewise—see (No. 1057—] THAT WHICH HAS FEWER VOWELS. Thus *śivakeśavau* "S'iva and Keśava."

पिता मात्रा । १ । २ । ७० ।

मात्रा सहोक्तौ पिता वा शिष्यते । पितरौ । मातापितरौ ।

No. 1060.—The word PITṚI "father," when spoken of ALONG WITH MÁTṚI "mother," is optionally left alone. Thus *pitarau* or *mátápitarau* "one's parents."

द्वन्द्वश्च प्राणितूर्यसेनाङ्गानाम् । २ । ४ । २ ।

एषां द्वन्द्व एकवत् । पाणिपादम् । मार्दङ्गिकपाणविकम् । रथिकाश्वारोहम् ।

No. 1061.—AND A DWANDWA compound OF words signifying members of LIVING BEINGS, AND PLAYERS (or singers or dancers), AND component PARTS OF AN ARMY, shall be singular. Thus *páṇipádam* "the hand and foot," *márdańgikapáṇavikam* "players on the *mṛidańga* and *paṇava* (kinds of drums)," *rathikáśwároham* "the chariots and the cavalry."

द्वन्द्वाच्चुदषहान्तात् समाहारे । ५ । ४ । १०६ ।

चवर्गान्ताद्दषहान्ताच्च द्वन्द्वाट्टच् स्यात् समाहारे । वाक्त्वचम् । त्वक्स्रजम् । शमीदृषदम् । वाक्त्विषम् । छत्रोपानहम् । समाहारे किम् । प्रावृट्शरदौ ।

इति द्वन्द्वः ॥

No. 1062.—AND AFTER A DWANDWA compound, ENDING IN A PALATAL, or D, or SH, OR H, let there be the affix *ṭach*, WHEN the compound is a neuter AGGREGATE. Thus *váktwacham* "the organs of speech and of touch," *twaksrajam* "the skin and a chaplet," *śamídṛishadam* "Acacia-suma and a stone," *váktwisham* "eloquence and splendour," *chhatropánaham* "umbrella and shoes." Why do we say "when the compound is a neuter aggregate"? Witness *právṛiṭśaradau* "the rains and the cold weather."

So much for the *Dwandwa* Compounds.

। समासान्ताः ।

OF THE AFFIXES WHICH COME AT THE END OF COMPOUNDS.

ऋक्पूरब्धूःपथामानक्षे । ५ । ४ । ७४ ।

ऋगाद्यन्तस्य समासस्य अप्रत्ययोऽन्तावयवः । अक्षे या धूस्तदन्तस्य न । अर्धर्चः । विष्णुपुरम् । विमलापं सरः । राजधुरा । अक्षे तु । अक्षधूः । दृढधूरक्षः । सखिपथः । रम्यपथो देशः ।

No. 1063.—The affix *a* is the end-portion of a compound which ends with ṚICH "a verse (of Scripture)," PUR "a city," AP "water," DHUR "a burthen," PATHIN "a road"—but not of that which ends with *dhur* when relating to AKSHA "an axle-tree." Thus *ardharcha* "half a verse (of Scripture)," *vishṇupura* "the city of Vishṇu," *vimalápaṅ sarah* "a lake the water of which is pure," *rájadhurá* (No. 1341) "the king's load (of government),"—but, when relating to *aksha,—akshadhúh* "the shafts attached to the axle-tree," *dṛiḍhadhúrakshah* "an axle the shafts attached to which are strong." Then, again, *sakhipathah* "the road of a friend," *ramyapatho deśah* "a place the road of which is pleasant."

अक्ष्णोऽदर्शनात् ।५।४।७६।

अचक्षुःपर्यायादक्ष्णोऽच् स्यात् । गवामक्षीव गवाक्षः ।

No. 1064.—Let the affix *ach* come [in a compound] AFTER the word AKSHI, when it is NOT a synonyme of THE ORGAN OF VISION. Thus *gavákska* "a bull's eye (a small window, so called).

उपसर्गादध्वनः ।५।४।८५।

प्रगतोऽध्वानं प्राध्वो रथः ।

No. 1065.—[Let the affix *ach* come, in a compound] AFTER ADHWAN "a road," coming AFTER AN UPASARGA (No. 48). Thus *prádhwo rathah* "a carriage that has got upon the road."

न पूजनात् ।५।४।६९।

पूजनार्थात् परेभ्यः समासान्ता न स्युः । सुराजा । अतिराजा ।

इति समासान्ताः ॥

No. 1066.—[The *taddhita* affixes—see No. 1027 &c.—] which come at the end of compounds, shall NOT come after words coming AFTER what is intended for PRAISE. Thus (in spite of No. 1027) *surájan* "a good king," *atirájan* "a pre-eminent king."

So much for the affixes which come at the end of Compounds.

। तद्धिताः ।

OF WORDS ENDING WITH TADDHITA AFFIXES.

समर्थानां प्रथमाद्वा । ४ । १ । ८२ ।

इदमधिक्रियते । प्राग्दिश इति यावत् ।

No. 1067.—(The *taddhita* affixes) ON THE ALTERNATIVE (of their being employed at all), come AFTER the word that is signified by) THE FIRST OF THE WORDS IN CONSTRUCTION (in an aphorism). This applies to all the aphorisms as far as No. 1284.

[N. B.—Primitive nouns having been formed from verbs by adding the *kṛit* affixes—No. 816—, other nouns may again be derived from the primitive nouns, to imply every possible relation to the things, actions, or notions, which the primitives express. The affixes forming these derivative nouns are called *tad-dhita* because the nouns denote something 'relating or belonging to that' which is primitive.]

अश्वपत्यादिभ्यश्च । ४ । १ । ८४ ।

एभ्योऽण् स्यात् प्राग्दीव्यतीयेष्वर्थेषु ।

No. 1068.—AND let the affix *aṇ*, in the senses of the various affixes occurring antecedently (in the order of the *Ashṭádhyáyí*) to No. 1203 come AFTER these—viz., AŚWAPATI "a lord of horses," &c.

तद्धितेष्वचामादेः । ७ । २ । ११७ ।

ञिति णिति च तद्धिते परेऽचामादेरचो वृद्धिः स्यात् । अश्वपतेरपत्यादि । आश्वपतम् । गाणपतम् ।

No. 1069.—WHEN A TADDHITA affix FOLLOWS, with an indicatory *ñ* or *ṇ*, let there be *vṛiddhi* in the room OF THE FIRST vowel AMONG THE VOWELS. Thus, to denote the offspring &c. of (one of the kings styled) *Aśwapati*, we may have *áśwapata* (No. 1068). So again, *gáṇapata* "the offspring &c., of *Gaṇapati* (i. e of *Gaṇeśa*).

दित्यदित्यादित्यपत्युत्तरपदाण्ण्यः । ४ । १ । ८५ ।

प्राग्दीव्यतीयेष्वर्थेषु । दितेरपत्यं दैत्यः । अदितेरादित्यस्य वा आदित्यः । प्राजापत्यः ।

No. 1070.—Let the affix ṆYA, in the senses of the various affixes occurring antecedently to No. 1203, come AFTER the proper names DITI, ADITI, AND ÁDITYA "the sun," AND THAT WHICH HAS the word PATI AS ITS FINAL MEMBER. Thus *daitya* "a descendant of Diti," *áditya* "a descendant of Aditi," or "(a descendant) of the sun," *prájápatya* "a descendant of *Prajápati.*

देवाद्यञञौ । दैव्यम् । दैवम् ।

No. 1071.—"AFTER DEVA "a god," let there be the affixes YAṄ AND AṄ." Thus *daivya* or *daiva* "divine."

बहिषष्टिलोपो यञ् च । बाह्यः । ईकक् च ।

No. 1072.—"Let there be ELISION OF the ṬI (No. 52) OF VAHIS "out," AND let there be the affix YAṄ." Thus *váhya* "external." And the affix *íkak* may be employed (which gives occasion to the rule following).

किति च । ७ । २ । ११८ ।

अचामादेरचो वृद्धिः स्यात् । बाहीकः ।

No. 1073.—AND WHEN IT (the *taddhita* affix) HAS AN INDICATORY K, let there be *vṛiddhi* in the room of the first vowel of the vowels (in the word). Thus *váhíka* "external."

गोरजादिप्रसङ्गे यत् । गोरपत्यादि । गव्यम् ।

No. 1074.—"WHEN an affix BEGINNING WITH A VOWEL PRESENTS ITSELF AFTER the word GO "a cow," let the affix YAT (be substituted for it)." Thus "what is descended (or procured &c.) from a cow" is expressed by *gavya* (No. 31).

उत्सादिभ्योऽञ् । ४ । १ । ८६ ।

औत्सः । इत्यपत्यादिविकारान्तार्थाः प्रत्ययाः ॥

No. 1075.—Let the affix AṄ come AFTER UTSA &C. Thus *autsa* "a descendant of Utsa."

So much for the affixes that convey the senses beginning with "posterity" (No. 1077) and ending with "change" (No. 1195).

स्त्रीपुंसाभ्यां नञ्स्नञौ भवनात्। ४। १। ८७।

धान्यानां भवन इत्यतः प्रागर्थेष्वाभ्यामेतौ स्तः। स्त्रैणः। पौंस्नः।

No. 1076.—In the senses specified in the aphorisms reckoning from this one AS FAR AS No. 1249, the two NAÑ AND ŚNAÑ come AFTER these two words STRÍ "a female" AND PUṄS "a male." Thus *straiṇa* "female," *pauṅsna* "male."

तस्यापत्यम्। ४। १। ९२।

षष्ठ्यन्तात् कृतसंधेः समर्थादपत्येऽर्थे उक्ता वक्ष्यमाणाश्च प्रत्यया वा स्युः।

No. 1077.—Let the affixes already mentioned, or to be mentioned, come optionally, in the sense of THE OFFSPRING THEREOF, after what word ending with the sixth case-affix, and having completed its junction [with whatever it may require to be compounded with], is in grammatical relation thereto.

[N. B. Were the affix applied to a word standing at the end of a compound, before the word had completed its junction with the other words in the compound, then such a rule as No. 1069 would not apply to the whole term, and the alteration directed would fall upon the wrong letter.]

ओर्गुणः। ६। ४। १४६।

उवर्णान्तस्य भस्य गुणस्तद्धिते। उपगोरपत्यमौपगवः। आश्वपतः। दैत्यः। औत्सः। स्त्रैणः। पौंस्नः।

No. 1078.—Let GUNA be in the room OF a *bha* (No. 185) ending in U or Ú, when a *taddhita* affix follows. Thus *aupagava* (No. 1069) "a descendant of Upagu," [and then, as examples of No.

1077] *áśwapata* "a descendant of an Aśwapati," *daitya* "a descendant of Diti," *autsa* "a descendant of *Utsa*," *straiṇa* "produced from a woman," *pauṅsna* "produced by a man."

अपत्यं पौत्रप्रभृति गोत्रम्। ४। १। १६२।

अपत्यत्वेन विवक्षितं पौत्रादि गोत्रसंज्ञं स्यात्।

No. 1079.—Let what is spoken of as POSTERITY, BEGINNING WITH GRANDSONS, be callod GOTRA.

एको गोत्रे। ४। १। ९३।

प्रत्ययः स्यात्। उपगोर्गोत्रापत्यमौपगवः।

No. 1080.—WHEN DESCENDANTS, BEGINNING WITH THE GRANDSON (No. 1079), are spoken of, let there be but ONE affix. Thus *aupagava* "a descendant such as a grandson or still lower descendant of Upagu"—[the word being the same as that—No. 1078—which denotes "a son of Upagu"]

गर्गादिभ्यो यञ्। ४। १। १०५।

गोत्रापत्ये। गर्गस्य गोत्रापत्यं गार्ग्यः। वात्स्यः।

No. 1081.—Let YAN be the affix AFTER GARGA AND THE LIKE, when the sense is that of a descendant not nearer than a grandson (No. 1079). Thus *gárgya* "a grandson, or still lower descendant, of Garga," *vátsya* "a descendant of Vatsa."

यञञोश्च। २। ४। ६४।

गोत्रे यद्यञन्तमञन्तं च तदवयवयोरेतयोर्लुक् तत्कृते बहुत्वे न तु स्त्रियाम्। गर्गाः। वत्साः।

No. 1082.—AND there is elision OF these two, YAN (No. 1081) AND AÑ (No. 1075), being parts of what, ending with *yañ* or *añ*, has the sense of a descendant not nearer than a grandson (No. 1079), when the word [of itself, and not as part of a compound epithet dependent on another word] takes the plural,—but not in the feminine. Thus *gargáh* "the male descendants of Garga," *vatsáh* "the male descendants of Vatsa."

जीवति तु वंश्ये युवा । ४ । १ । १६३ ।

वंश्ये पित्रादौ जीवति पौत्रादेर्यदपत्यं चतुर्थादि तद्युवसंज्ञमेव स्यात् ।

1083.—BUT WHEN ONE IN A LINE of descent, beginning with a father (and reckoning upwards), IS ALIVE, let the descendant of a grandson or still lower descendant, beginning (therefore) with the fourth (in the order of descent) be called YUVAN [—and not *gotra* No. 1079].

गोत्राद्यून्यस्त्रियाम् । ४ । १ । ९४ ।

यून्यपत्ये गोत्रप्रत्ययान्तादेव प्रत्ययः स्यात् स्त्रियां तु न युवसंज्ञा ।

No. 1084.—WHEN a descendant of the description denoted by YUVAN (No. 1083) is spoken of, let the affix be attached only AFTER what already ends with an affix marking a DESCENDANT AS LOW AT LEAST AS A GRANDSON :—but, IN THE FEMININE, the word is NOT termed *yuvan*, [nor treated accordingly].

यञिञोश्च । ४ । १ । १०१ ।

गोत्रे यौ यञिञौ तदन्तात् फक् ।

No. 1085.—AND let *phak* come AFTER what ends with YAÑ AND IÑ, signifying a descendant (No. 1075) at least as low as a grandson, [when a further descendant, of the description mentioned in No. 1083, is to be denoted].

आयनेयीनीयियः फढखछघां प्रत्ययादीनाम् । ७ । १ । २ ।

प्रत्ययादेः फस्य आयन् ढस्येय् खस्य ईन् छस्य ईय् घस्य इय् एते स्युः । गर्गस्य युवापत्यं गार्ग्यायणः । दाक्षायणः ।

No. 1086.—Let there be ÁYAN in the room OF PHA, EY in the room OF ḌHA, ÍN in the room OF KHA, ÍY in the room OF CHHA, AND IY in the room OF GHA, being INITIALS OF AFFIXES. Thus *gárgyáyaṇa* (No. 1085) "a distant descendant of Garga," *dák-*

sháyana "a distant descendant of Daksha"—[Garga and Daksha being alive, or some one intermediate between them and the descendants so named being alive].

अत इञ्। ४। १। ९५।

अपत्येऽर्थे। दाक्षिः।

No. 1087.—Let IÑ, in the sense of a descendant, come AFTER what ends in SHORT A. Thus *dákshi* (No. 260) "a descendant of Daksha."

बाह्वादिभ्यश्च। ४। १। ९६।

बाहविः। औडुलोमिः। आकृतिगणोऽयम्।

No. 1088.—AND AFTER BÁHU &c. [let *iñ*, No. 1087, come]. Thus *báhavi* (No. 1078) "a descendant of Báhu," *auḍulomi* "a descendant of Uḍuloman."

This is a class of words recognizable only by the form—(see No. 53).

अनृष्यानन्तर्ये विदादिभ्योऽञ्। ४। १। १०४।

ये त्वत्रानृषयस्तेभ्योऽपत्येऽन्यत्र तु गोत्रे। विदस्य गोत्रं वैदः। वैदौ। विदाः। पुत्रस्यापत्यं पौत्रः। पौत्रौ। पौत्राः। एवं दौहित्रादयः।

No. 1089.—Let there be the affix AÑ AFTER VIDA &c., IN THE SENSE OF IMMEDIATE DESCENDANT (or son) AFTER those which are NOT names of sanctified SAGES, but otherwise in the sense of a descendant not nearer than a grandson (No. 1079). Thus *vaida* "the descendant (not nearer than a grandson) of (the sanctified sage) Vida," which in the dual becomes *vaidau*, and in the plural *vidáh* (No. 1082); then again *pautra* "a son's son (i. e. a grandson)"—dual *pautrau*, plural *pautráh*—(No. 1082 not applying to this, because the derivation is not of the kind called *gotra*—No. 1079). In the same way *dauhitra* (No. 1069) "a daughter's son," and the like.

शिवादिभ्योऽण्। ४। १। ११२।

अपत्ये । शैवः । गाङ्गः ।

No. 1090.—Let the affix AṆ come AFTER ŚIVA &c., in the sense of offspring. Thus *śaiva* "a descendant of Śiva," *gáṅga* "a descendant of Gaṅgá."

ऋष्यन्धकवृष्णिकुरुभ्यश्च । ४ । १ । ११४ ।

ऋषिभ्यः । वासिष्ठः । वैश्वामित्रः । अन्धकेभ्यः । श्वाफल्कः । वृष्णिभ्यः । वासुदेवः । कुरुभ्यः । नाकुलः । साहदेवः ।

No. 1091.—AND (the affix *aṇ* may come) AFTER names of sanctified SAGES, AND of persons belonging to the ANDHAKA, VṚISHṆI, AND KURU race. It comes after the names of sages in the examples *vásishṭha* "a descendant of (the sage) *Vasishṭha*," and *vaiśwámitra* "a descendant of Viśwámitra," after the *Andhakas* in *śwáphalka* "a descendant of Śwaphalka, after the *Vṛishṇis* in *vásudeva* "the son of Vasudeva," and after the *Kurus* in *nákula* "a descendant of Nakula," and *sáhadeva* "a descendant of Sahadeva."

मातुरुत् संख्यासंभद्रपूर्वायाः । ४ । १ । ११५ ।

संख्यादिपूर्वस्य मातृशब्दस्य उदादेशः स्यादण् प्रत्ययश्च । द्वैमातुरः । षाण्मातुरः । सांमातुरः । भाद्रमातुरः ।

No. 1092.—Let U be the substitute OF the word MÁTṚI "a mother" PRECEDED BY A NUMERAL, OR by SAM, OR BHADRA ; and let there be the affix *aṇ*. Thus *dwaimátura* (No. 37) "having a mother and a step-mother"—(meaning Gaṇeśa), *sháṇmátura* "having six mothers"—(meaning Kártikeya who was brought up by the six Krittikás), *sáṅmátura* "whose mother is good," *bhádramátura* "having an illustrious mother."

स्त्रीभ्यो ढक् । ४ । १ । १२० ।

स्त्रीप्रत्ययान्तेभ्यो ढक् । वैनतेयः ।

No. 1093.—AFTER words ending with FEMININE affixes (No. 1341), let there be the affix ḌHAK (No. 1086). Thus *vainateya*, "the son of Vinatá"—(meaning Garuḍa).

कन्यायाः कनीन च । ४ । १ । ११६ ।

चादण् । कानीनो व्यासः कर्णश्च ।

No. 1094.—AND let KANÍNA be the substitute OF KANYÁ. By the "and" the affixing of *aṇ* is indicated. Thus *kánína* "the son of an unmarried woman"—e. g. Vyása or Karṇa.

राजश्वशुराद्यत् । ४ । १ । १३७ ।

No. 1095.—AFTER RÁJAN AND ŚWAŚURA, let there be the affix YAT.

राज्ञो जातावेव ।

No. 1096.—"AFTER RÁJAN, ONLY WHEN IT MEANS THE regal CASTE," (does the affix directed by No. 1095 come).

ये चाभावकर्मणोः । ६ । ४ । १६८ ।

यादौ तद्धितेऽन् प्रकृत्या स्यान्न तु भावकर्मणोः । राजन्यः । जातावेवेति किम् ।

No. 1097.—AND WHEN a *taddhita* affix, beginning with Y, follows, let AN (if the word ends in *an*) remain in its shape unaltered, but NOT WHEN THE SENSE IS THAT OF ACTION OR STATE. Thus *rájanya* (Nos. 1095 and 1096) "a Kshatriya or man of the regal caste"——(whereas "the royal state of a king," by No. 979, would be *rájya*). Why do we say, in No. 1096, "only when it means the regal caste"? [For the reply see the example under the next rule].

अन् । ६ । ४ । १६७ ।

अन् प्रकृत्याणि परे । राजनः । श्वशुर्यः ।

No. 1098.—Let AN (at the end of a word) remain in its original form (in spite of No. 979), when the affix *aṇ* follows. Thus *rájana* "the son of a king" (who need not have had a Kshatriya mother, in which case he will not be of the Kshatriya race—see No. 1097). Then, again, by No. 1095, we have *śwaśurya* "the son of a father-in-law."

क्षत्राद्घः । ४ । १ । १३८ ।

क्षत्रियः । जातावित्येव । क्षात्रिरन्यः ।

No. 1099.—AFTER KSHATRA, let there be the affix GHA. Thus *kshatriya* (Nos. 1086 and 260) "one of the caste of the Kshatras." This is the form of the derivative only when the caste is spoken of—for otherwise the derivative is *kshátri* (No. 1087) "a descendant of a Kshatra" (not necessarily by a Kshatra mother).

रेवत्यादिभ्यष्ठक् । ४ । १ । १४६ ।

No. 1100.—AFTER REVATÍ &c., let there be ṬHAK.

ठस्येकः । ७ । ३ । ५० ।

अङ्गात् परस्य ठस्येकादेशः । रैवतिकः ।

No. 1101.—Let IKA be the substitute OF ṬHA coming (without the intervention of any letter) after an inflective base (No. 152). Thus *raivatika* "a descendant of Revatí."

जनपदशब्दात् क्षत्रियादञ् । ४ । १ । १६८ ।

जनपदक्षत्रियवाचकाच्छब्दादञपत्ये । पाञ्चालः ।

No. 1102.—Let there be AÑ, to denote progeny, AFTER A WORD WHICH, while it EXPRESSES A COUNTRY, expresses ALSO A KSHATRIYA. Thus *pánchála* "the descendant of the Kshatriya who gave his name to the country of Panchála."

क्षत्रियसमानशब्दाज्जनपदात् तस्य राजन्यपत्यवत् । पञ्चालानां राजा पाञ्चालः ।

No. 1103.—"(Let the same affix—see No. 1102—) AS WHEN the sense is that of PROGENY, WHEN the sense is that of the KINGS THEREOF, come AFTER the name of A COUNTRY OF THE SAME NAME AS A KSHATRIYA." Thus *pánchála* "the king of the Kshatriyas (or of the country) of Panchála."

पुरोरण् । पौरवः ।

No. 1104.—"Let AṆ come AFTER PURU." Thus *paurava* "a descendant of Puru."

पाण्डोर्ड्यण् । पाण्ड्यः ।

No. 1105.—"Let ḌYAṆ come AFTER PÁṆḌU." Thus *páṇḍya* "a descendant of Páṇḍu.

कुरुनादिभ्यो ण्यः । ४ । १ । १७२ ।

कौरव्यः । नैषध्यः ।

No. 1106.—Let there be ṆYA AFTER KURU AND names BEGINNING WITH N (signifying both a country and its Kshatriya inhabitants). Thus *kauravya* (No. 1078) "a descendant of Kuru," *naishadhya* "a descendant of Nishadha."

ते तद्राजाः । ४ । १ । १७४ ।

अञादयस्तद्राजसंज्ञाः स्युः ।

No. 1107.—Let THESE, viz. the affixes *añ* &c., be called TADRÁJA (No. 1027—i. e. "the king thereof").

तद्राजस्य बहुषु तेनैवास्त्रियाम् । २ । ४ । ६२ ।

बहुष्वर्थेषु तद्राजस्य लुक् तत्कृते बहुत्वे न तु स्त्रियाम् । पञ्चालाः । इत्यादि ।

No. 1108.—There shall be elision OF a TADRÁJA (No. 1107) affix, WHEN the meanings are MANY (i. e. when the word is plural) WHEN BY THE WORD ITSELF [and not by the word standing as part of a compound epithet dependent on another word] the plural is taken—but NOT IN THE FEMININE. Thus (as the plural of *páñchála*—No. 1103 we have) *pañcháláh* "the kings of Pañchála, or their descendants." And so of others.

कम्बोजाल्लुक् । ४ । १ । १७५ ।

अस्मात् तद्राजस्य लुक् । कम्बोजः । कम्बोजौ ।

No. 1109.—AFTER the word KAMBOJA, there is elision of the *tadrája* affix (No. 1107). Thus *Kamboja* "the king of Kamboja," *kambojau* "two kings of Kamboja."

कम्बोजादिभ्य इति वक्तव्यम् । चोलः । शकः । केरलः । यवनः ।

इत्यपत्याधिकारः ॥

No. 1110.—"IT SHOULD BE SAID (in No. 1109) 'AFTER KAMBOJA AND THE LIKE.'" Thus *chola* "the king of Chola," *śaka* "the king of Scythia," *kerala* "the king of Kerala," *yavana* "the king of Greece."

So much for the subject of Patronymics (or for the division of the Grammar where the words—"in the sense of progeny"—exert an influence—having to be supplied in each rule).

तेन रक्तं रागात् । ४ । २ । १ ।

अण् स्यात् । कषायेण रक्तं वस्त्रं काषायम् ।

No. 1111.—Let *aṇ* come after a word denoting A COLOUR, to signify what is COLOURED THEREBY. Thus *káshâya* "coloured of a dull red"—as cloth.

नक्षत्रेण युक्तः कालः । ४ । २ । ३ ।

अण् स्यात् ।

No. 1112.—Let *aṇ* come (after the name of an asterism) to signify a TIME CONNECTED WITH THE ASTERISM.

तिष्यपुष्ययोर्नक्षत्राणि यलोप इति वाच्यम् । पुष्येण युक्तं पौषमहः ।

No. 1113.—"IT SHOULD BE MENTIONED THAT THERE IS ELISION OF the Y, WHEN AṆ (No. 1112) COMES AFTER the ASTERISM OF TISHYA OR (as it is also called) PUSHYA." Thus *paushu* "belonging—as a day—to the asterism Pushya"—(i. e. to the month of December, in which month the moon is full in that asterism).

लुबविशेषे । ४ । २ । ४ ।

पूर्वेण विहितस्य लुप् षष्टिदण्डात्मकस्य कालस्यावान्तरविशेषश्चेन्न गम्यते । अद्य पुष्यः ।

No. 1114.—There shall be ELISION (*lup*, No. 209,) of the affix enjoined by the preceding aphorism (No. 1112), IF NO SPECIFICATION is to be understood of an included portion of the time consisting of twenty-four hours (or sixty *daṇḍas*). Thus *adya pushyah* "to-day belongs to the asterism Pushya"—(meaning by "to-day" neither the day-time in particular, nor the night-time in particular, but both alike).

दृष्टं साम । ४ । २ । ७ ।

तेनेत्येव । वसिष्ठेन दृष्टं वासिष्ठं साम ।

No. 1115.—Let *aṇ* come after what ends with the 3rd case-affix in the sense of SEEN—the thing seen by the one whose name is in the 3rd case, being the SÁMA-VEDA. Thus *vásishṭhaṅ sáma* "the (portion of the) Sáma seen by (or revealed to) Vasishṭha."

वामदेवाड्ड्यड्ड्यौ । ४ । २ । ९ ।

वामदेवेन दृष्टं साम वामदेव्यम् ।

No. 1116.—Let ḌYAT AND ḌYA come AFTER the name VÁMADEVA (under the circumstances set forth in No. 1115). Thus *vámadevya* (No. 260) "the (portion of the) Sáma seen by Vámadeva."

परिवृतो रथः । ४ । २ । १० ।

अस्मिन्नर्थेऽण् प्रत्ययो भवति । वस्त्रेण परिवृतो वास्त्रो रथः ।

No. 1117.—The affix *aṇ* comes (after a word in the 3rd case, in the sense of SURROUNDED—the thing so surrounded being a CHARIOT. Thus *vástra* "surrounded with cloth"—e. g. a chariot.

तत्रोद्धृतममत्रेभ्यः । ४ । २ । १४ ।

शरावे उद्धृतः शाराव ओदनः ।

No. 1118.—The affix *aṇ* comes AFTER words denoting VESSELS, to signify PLACED THEREON. Thus *śaráva* "placed on a shallow dish"—as boiled rice.

संस्कृतं भक्षाः । ४ । २ । १६ ।

सप्तम्यन्तादण् स्यात् संस्कृतेऽर्थे यत् संस्कृतं भक्षाश्चेत् ते स्युः ।

भ्राष्ट्रेषु संस्कृता भ्राष्ट्रा भक्षाः ।

No. 1119.—Let *aṇ* come after what ends with the 7th case-affix, to denote what is PREPARED therein—if that which is so prepared be GRANULAR FOOD. Thus *bhráshṭra* "prepared in frying-pans"—(as barley &c).

साऽस्य देवता। ४। २। २४।

इन्द्रो देवताऽस्येति ऐन्द्रं हविः। पाशुपतम्। बार्हस्पत्यम्।

No. 1120.—An affix comes after the name of ANY DEITY, when something is to be spoken of as HIS. Thus *aindra* "belonging to the deity Indra"—as butter (in an oblation), *páśupata* "belonging to Śiva," *várhaspatya* "belonging to Vṛihaspati."

शुक्राद्घन्। ४। २। २६।

शुक्रियम्।

No. 1121.—AFTER the name ŚUKRA, there is the affix GHAN. Thus *śukriya* (Nos. 1120 and 1086) "belonging to Śukra"—(as an oblation of butter).

सोमाट्ट्यण्। ४। २। ३०।

सौम्यम्।

No. 1122.—AFTER the name SOMA, there is the affix ṬYAṆ. Thus *saumya* (No. 1069) "belonging to the Moon"—(as an oblation of butter).

वाय्वृतुपित्रुषसो यत्। ४। २। ३१।

वायव्यम्। ऋतव्यम्।

No. 1123.—AFTER VÁYU, ṚITU, PITṚI, AND USHAS, there is the affix YAT. Thus *váyavya* "belonging to the god of the winds," *ṛitavya* "belonging to the seasons"—(as an oblation of butter).

रीङ् ऋतः। ७। ४। २७।

अकृद्यकारेऽसार्वधातुके यकारे च्वौ च परे ऋतो रीङादेशः। यस्येति च। पित्र्यम्। उषस्यम्।

No. 1124.—The substitute OF SHORT ṚI shall be RÍṄ, when an affix, beginning with *y* and not being a *kṛit* (No. 329) nor a *sárvadhátuka* (No. 418), follows, or if *chwi* (No. 1332) follows. Thus, by No. 260, we have *pitrya* (No. 1123) "belonging to the progenitors," *ushasya* "belonging to the dawn"—(as butter offered in oblation).

पितृव्यमातुलमातामहपितामहाः। ४। २। ३६।

एते निपात्यन्ते। पितुर्भ्राता पितृव्यः। मातुर्भ्राता मातुलः। मातुः पिता मातामहः। पितुः पिता पितामहः।

No. 1125.—The word PITṚIVYA "a father's brother," MÁTULA "a mother's brother," MÁTÁMAHA "a mother's father," AND PITÁMAHA "a father's father," are anomalously formed.

तस्य समूहः। ४। २। ३७।

काकानां समूहः काकम्।

No. 1126.—An affix is added to a word, when the sense is a COLLECTION THEREOF. Thus *káka* "a collection of crows."

भिक्षादिभ्योऽण्। ४। २। ३८।

भैक्षम्। गर्भिणीनां समूहो गार्भिणम्। इह भस्याढे तद्धित इति पुंवद्भावे कृते।

No. 1127.—The affix AṆ comes AFTER BHIKSHÁ "alms" &c. Thus *bhaiksha* (No. 1126) "what is collected in the shape of alms," *gárbhiṇa* "a collection of pregnant females." In this example the word (*garbhiṇí* "a pregnant woman") having been reduced to the form of the masculine by the supplementary rule, that "the masculine form of a *bha* (No. 185) is substituted, when a *taddhita* affix follows without an indicatory *ḍh*" (the application of No. 979 is debarred by the rule following).

इनण्यनपत्ये। ६। ४। १६४।

अनपत्यार्थेऽणि इन् प्रकृत्या। तेन नस्तद्धित इति टिलोपो न। युवतीनां समूहो यौवतम्।

No. 1128.—WHEN the affix AṆ FOLLOWS, NOT IN THE SENSE OF OFFSPRING the termination IN shall remain in its original shape. Hence (in the case of *gárbhiṇa*, No. 1127) there is not elision of the last vowel and what follows it by No. 979. Then, again, (as another example of No. 1127) we have (from *yuvatí* "a young woman") *yauvata* (No. 260) "a collection of young women."

ग्रामजनबन्धुभ्यस्तल् । ४ । २ । ४३ ।

तलन्तं स्त्रियाम् । ग्रामता । जनता । बन्धुता ।

No. 1129.—The affix TAL comes AFTER GRÁMA, JANA, AND BANDHU. What ends in *tal* is feminine. Hence *grámatá* (No. 1341) "a collection of villages," *janatá* "a collection of persons," *bandhutá* "a collection of relatives."

गजसहायाभ्यां चेति वक्तव्यम् । गजता । सहायता ।

No. 1130.—"IT SHOULD BE STATED that this (affixing of *tal*—No. 1129) takes place ALSO AFTER GAJA AND SAHÁYA." Thus *gajatá* "a collection of elephants," *saháyatá* "a collection of allies."

अह्नः खः क्रतौ । अहीनः ।

No. 1131.—"The affix KHA comes AFTER AHAN 'a day' IN THE SENSE OF A SACRIFICE." Thus *ahína* (No. 1086) "a particular sacrifice—one lasting a certain number of days."

अचित्तहस्तिधेनोष्ठक् । ४ । २ । ४७ ।

No. 1132.—AFTER things WITHOUT CONSCIOUSNESS, AND HASTI "an elephant," AND DHENU "a milch cow," there is the affix ṬHAK.

इसुसुक्तान्तात् कः । ७ । ३ । ५१ ।

इस्उस्उक्तान्तात् परस्य ठस्य कः । साक्तुकम् । हास्तिकम् । धैनुकम् ।

No. 1133.—Let K be the substitute of ṬH AFTER WHAT ENDS WITH IS, OR US, OR an UK, OR T. Thus *sáktuka* (No. 1132) "a quantity of flour," *hástika* "a collection of elephants," *dhainuka* "a collection of milch cows."

तदधीते तद्वेद । ४ । २ । ५९ ।

No. 1134.—(Let an affix come after a word denoting some subject of study) IN THE SENSE OF WHO HAS STUDIED THAT, or WHO UNDERSTANDS THAT.

न य्वाभ्यां पदान्ताभ्यां पूर्वौ तु ताभ्यामैच्। ७। ३। ३।

पदान्ताभ्यां यकारवकाराभ्यां परस्य न वृद्धिः किंतु ताभ्यां पूर्वौ क्रमादेतावागमौ स्तः। व्याकरणमधीते वेद वा वैयाकरणः।

No. 1135.—There is NOT *vṛiddhi* (by No. 1069) in the room of what stands AFTER the letters Y AND V, being the FINALS OF PADAS, BUT there are, BEFORE THE TWO, RESPECTIVELY, the two augments AI AND AU. Thus *vaiyákaraṇa* "one who has studied, or who knows, the grammar"—where the *y* of *vyákaraṇa* "grammar" is at the end of a *pada*, inasmuch as the prefix *vi* is one of the Indeclinables—(No. 399).

क्रमादिभ्यो वुन्। ४। २। ६१।

क्रमकः। पदकः। शिक्षकः। मीमांसकः।

No. 1136.—AFTER KRAMA &c., let there be the affix VUN (in the sense of "who knows the thing"). Thus *kramaka* (No. 836) "one who knows the order," *padaka* "one who knows the verses (of the Veda)," *śikshaka* "one who knows one of the six Vedáṅgas," *mímáṅsaka* "one who knows the Mímáṅsá philosophy."

तदस्मिन्नस्तीति देशे तन्नाम्नि। ४। २। ६७।

उदुम्बराः सन्त्यस्मिन् देशे औदुम्बरो देशः।

No. 1137.—(An affix is placed after a word expressive of anything) in the sense of—THAT thing IS IN THIS—THE PLACE TAKING A NAME THEREFROM. Thus *audumbara* "a country in which there are glomerous fig-trees."

तेन निर्वृत्तम्। ४। २। ६८।

कुशाम्बेन निर्वृत्ता नगरी कौशाम्बी।

No. 1138.—In the sense of what is COMPLETED BY HIM (an affix is placed after the person's name). Thus *kauśámbí* "the city completed by Kuśámba."

तस्य निवासः । ४ । २ । ६९ ।

शिवीनां निवासो देशः शैवः ।

No. 1139.—When the sense is HIS DWELLING-PLACE, (an affix is placed after the person's name). Thus *śaiva* "the country of the Śivis."

अदूरभवश्च । ४ । २ । ७० ।

विदिशाया अदूरभवं वैदिशम् ।

No. 1140.—AND when the sense is WHAT IS NOT FAR OFF therefrom (an affix is placed after the name of a place). Thus *vaidiśa* "what is not far off from the city Vidiśá."

जनपदे लुप् । १ । २ । ५१ ।

जनपदे वाच्ये चातुरर्थिकस्य लुप् ।

No. 1141.—WHEN A COUNTRY is to be expressed, there is ELISION *(lup)* of a "quadruply significant" affix—[i. e. of an affix which conveys the senses specified in Nos. 1137, 1138, 1139, and 1140].

लुपि युक्तवद्व्यक्तिवचने । १ । २ । ५१ ।

लुपि सति प्रकृतिवल्लिङ्गवचने स्तः । पञ्चालानां निवासो जनपदः पञ्चालाः । कुरवः । अङ्गाः । वङ्गाः । कलिङ्गाः ।

No. 1142.—WHEN there is elision by LUP (No. 1141), the GENDER AND NUMBER remain AS IN the ORIGINAL term. Thus *pancháláh* "the country which is the dwelling-place of the Panchálas," *kuravah* "the country of the Kurus," *angáh* "the country of the Angas," *bangáh* "the country of the Bangas," *kalingáh* "the country of the Kalingas."

वरणादिभ्यश्च । ४ । २ । ८२ ।

अजनपदार्थ आरम्भः । वरणानामदूरभवं नगरं वरणाः ।

No. 1143.—AND AFTER the words VARAṆÁ &c. (elision takes place as directed in No. 1142). The origination of this rule is for the sake of what is not a *country* [like the words referred to in No.

1142]. Thus *varanáh* "the city [—not the country—] not far from the country of the Varaṇás."

कुमुदनडवेतसेभ्यो ड्मतुप् । ४ । २ । ८७ ।

No. 1144.—The affix ḌMATUP comes AFTER the words KUMUDA "a lotus," NAḌA "a reed," AND VETASA "a ratan."

झयः । ८ । २ । १० ।

झयन्तान्मतोर्मस्य वः । कुमुद्वान् । नड्वान् ।

No. 1145.—Let there be *v* in the room of the *m* of the affix *matu* (No. 1144) AFTER what ends in A JHAY. Thus *kumudwat* (No. 267) abounding in lotuses," *naḍwat* "abounding in reeds."

मादुपधायाश्च मतोर्वोऽयवादिभ्यः । ८ । २ । ९ ।

मवर्णावर्णान्तान्मवर्णावर्णोपधाच्च यवादिवर्जितात् परस्य मतोर्मस्य वः । वेतस्वान् ।

No. 1146.—Let there be v in the room OF the *m* of the affix MATU (No. 1144) coming AFTER a word the final of which is M OR A or á, OR THE PENULTIMATE letter OF WHICH IS M OR A or á—but NOT AFTER the word YAVA "barley" &c. Thus *vetaswat* (Nos. 1144 and 267) "abounding in ratans."

नडशादाड्ड्वलच् । ४ । २ । ८८ ।

नड्वलः ।

No. 1147.—AFTER the words NAḌA "a reed" AND ŚÁDA "young grass," there is the affix ḌWALACH. Thus *naḍwala* (No. 267) "abounding with reeds."

शिखाया वलच् । ४ । २ । ८९ ।

शिखावलः ।

इति चातुरर्थिकाः ॥

No. 1148.—AFTER the word ŚIKHÁ "a crest," there is the affix VALACH. Thus *śikhávala* "crested (as a peacock)."

So much for the affixes "quadruply significant" (see No. 1141.)

शेषे । ४ । २ । ९२ ।

अपत्यादिचतुरर्थ्यन्तादन्योऽर्थः शेषस्तत्राणादयः स्युः । चक्षुषा गृह्यते चाक्षुषं रूपम् । श्रावणः शब्दः । औपनिषदः पुरुषः । दृषदि पिष्टा दार्षदाः सक्तवः । चतुर्भिरुह्यते चातुरं शकटम् । चातुर्दश्यां दृश्यते चातुर्दशं रक्षः । तस्य विकार इत्यतः प्राक् शेषाधिकारः ।

No. 1149.—Let a meaning, other than those of which "progeny" (No. 1077) was the first mentioned and the "quadruple signification" (No. 1141) the last, be called "the remainder,"—and IN that REMAINDER of senses, too, let there be the affixes *aṇ* &C. Thus *chákshusha* "visible"—viz. colour, which is apprehended by vision, *śrávaṇa* "audible"—viz. sound, *aupanishada* "treated of in scripture"—viz. soul, *dárshada* "ground on a stone"—viz. the flour of fried corn, *chátura* "ridden in by four persons"—viz. a kind of cart, *cháturdaśa* "who is seen on the fourteenth day of the month"—viz. a goblin.

The regulating influence of the expression "*in the remainder*" extends from this aphorism forward as far as that marked No. 1195.

राष्ट्रावारपाराद्घखौ । ४ । २ । ९३ ।

राष्ट्रे जातादी राष्ट्रियः । अवारपारीणः ।

No. 1150.—AFTER the words RÁSHṬRA "a country" AND AVÁRAPÁRA "both banks," there are respectively, the affixes GHA AND KHA. Thus *ráshṭriya* (No. 1086) "born &c., in a country," *avárapáríṇa* "who or what goes or extends to both banks."

अवारपाराद्विगृहीतादपि विपरीताच्चेति वक्तव्यम् । अवारीणः । पारीणः । पारावारीणः । इह प्रकृतिविशेषाद्घादयष्ट्युट्युलन्ता उच्यन्ते तेषां जातादयोऽर्थविशेषाः समर्थविभक्तयश्च वक्ष्यन्ते ।

No. 1151.—"IT SHOULD BE STATED (in addition to what is stated in No. 1150) THAT the affix may come AFTER the word AVÁRAPÁRA (not only in the form in which it is there exhibited, but) ALSO WHEN IT IS TAKEN SEPARATELY in pieces, AND when it is INVERTED." Thus *aváríṇa* "belonging to this bank of the river," *páríṇa* "belonging to the other bank," *páráváríṇa* "belonging to the other bank as well as to this."

There shall now be mentioned derivatives which end with those affixes the first whereof is *gha* (No. 1150) and the last whereof are *ṭyu* and *ṭyul* (No. 1171), with specification of the original terms (to which the application of those affixes is appropriate); and their varieties of meaning—such as "being produced therefrom," and the like—shall be mentioned; and also the declensional cases in connection with which the affixes are appropriately applicable.

ग्रामाद्यखञौ ।४।२।९४।

ग्राम्यः । ग्रामीणः ।

No. 1152.—AFTER the word GRÁMA "a village," let there be the affix Y OR KHAÑ. Thus *grámya* or *gráminạ* (No. 1086) "rustic."

नद्यादिभ्यो ढक् ।४।२।९७।

नादेयम् । माहेयम् । वाराणसेयम् ।

No. 1153.—AFTER the words NADÍ "a river" &c., let there be the affix ḌHAK." Thus *nádeya* (No. 1086) "aquatic," *máheya* "earthen," *váráṇaseya* "belonging to Benares."

दक्षिणापश्चात्पुरसस्त्यक् ।४।२।९८।

दाक्षिणात्यः । पाश्चात्यः । पौरस्त्यः ।

No. 1154.—AFTER the words DAKSHIṆÁ, PAŚCHÁT, AND PURAS, let there be the affix TYAK. Thus *dákshiṇátya* "produced in the south," *páśchátya* "produced in the west," *paurastya* "produced in the east."

द्युप्रागपागुदक्प्रतीचो यत् ।४।२।१०१।

दिव्यम् । प्राच्यम् । अपाच्यम् । उदीच्यम् । प्रतीच्यम् ।

No. 1155.—AFTER DYU "the sky," PRÁCH, APÁCH, UDACH, AND PRATÍCH, let there be the affix YAT. Thus *divya* "celestial," *práchya* "eastern," *apáchya* "southern," *udíchya* (No. 366) "northern," *pratíchya* "western."

अव्ययात् त्यप् ।४।२।१०४।

अमेहक्कतसित्रेभ्य एव । अमात्यः । इहत्यः । क्कत्यः । ततस्त्यः । तत्रत्यः ।

No. 1156.—Let there be the affix TYAP AFTER AN INDECLINABLE—that is to say, however, only after *amá* "together," *iha* "here," *kwa* "where?," and (those that end in) *tasi* (No. 1286) and *tra* (No. 1291). Thus *amátya* "a minister," *ihatya* "produced here," *kwatya* "produced where?," *tatastya* "produced thence," *tatratya* "produced there."

त्यब्नेर्ध्रुवे । नित्यः ।

No. 1157.—"Let TYAP come AFTER the indeclinable NI IN THE SENSE OF CONSTANTLY." Thus *nitya* "eternal."

वृद्धिर्यस्याचामादिस्तद्वृद्धम् । १ । १ । ७३ ।

यस्य समुदायस्याचां मध्ये आदिर्वृद्धिस्तद्वृद्धसंज्ञं स्यात् ।

No. 1158.—Let THAT whole word AMONG THE VOWELS OF WHICH THE FIRST is A VṚIDDHI be called VṚIDDHA.

त्यदादीनि च । १ । १ । ७४ ।

वृद्धसंज्ञानि स्युः ।

No. 1159.—AND let TYAD &c., (No. 170) be called *vṛiddha* (No. 1158).

वृद्धाच्छः । ४ । २ । ११४ ।

शालीयः । तदीयः ।

No. 1160.—AFTER a word called VṚIDDHA (Nos. 1158 and 1159), let there be the affix CHHA. Thus *śálíya* (Nos. 1086 and 260) "belonging to a hall," *tadíya* "belonging to that."

वा नामधेयस्य । वृद्धसंज्ञा । देवदत्तीयः । दैवदत्तः ।

No. 1161.—"The appellation *vṛiddha* (No. 1158) is OPTIONALLY that OF A PROPER NAME (whether it have a *vṛiddhi* in its first syllable or not)." Thus *devadattíya* (No. 1160) or *daivadatta* "belonging to Devadatta."

गहादिभ्यश्च । ४ । २ । १३८ ।

गहीयः ।

No. 1162.—AND AFTER the words GAHA &c., (there is the affix *chha*—No. 1160). Thus *gahíya* "belonging to a cave."

युष्मदस्मदोरन्यतरस्यां खञ् च । ४ । ३ । १ ।

चाच्छः । पक्षेऽण् । युवयोर्युष्माकं वायं युष्मदीयः । अस्मदीयः ।

No. 1163.—AND AFTER YUSHMAD AND ASMAD (No. 170), OPTIONALLY let there be the affix KHAŃ. By the "and" it is meant that the affix may be *chha* (No. 1160); and on the alternative, which is optional, the affix will be *aṇ*. Thus (when the affix *chha* is used) *yushmadíya* "what belongs to you two, or to all of you," *asmadíya* "what belongs to us."

तस्मिन्नणि च युष्माकास्माकौ । ४ । ३ । २ ।

युष्मदस्मदोरेतावादेशौ स्तः खञि अणि च । यौष्माकीणः । आस्माकीनः । यौष्माकः । आस्माकः ।

No. 1164.—WHEN THIS affix, viz. *khań* (No. 1163), is added, AND when AṆ is added, then YUSHMÁKA AND ASMÁKA are the substitutes of *yushmad* and *asmad*. Thus *yaushmákíṇa* "belonging to you," *ásmákína* "belonging to us," (and so, too, with the affix *aṇ*) *yaushmáka* and *ásmáka*.

तवकममकावेकवचने । ४ । ३ । ३ ।

एकार्थवाचिनोर्युष्मदस्मदोस्तवकममकौ स्तः खञि अणि च । तावकीनः । तावकः । मामकीनः । मामकः । छे तु ।

No. 1165.—In the room of *yushmad* and *asmad*, EXPRESSING ONE individual, there are TAVAKA AND MAMAKA, when the affix *khań* or *aṇ* follows. Thus *távakína* or *távaka* "belonging to thee," *mámakína* or *mámaka* "belonging to me." But when the affix is *chha* (then the rule following applies).

प्रत्ययोत्तरपदयोश्च । ७ । २ । ९८ ।

मपर्यन्तयोरनयोरेकार्थवाचिनोस्त्वमौ स्तः प्रत्यये उत्तरपदे च परतः । त्वदीयः । मदीयः । त्वत्पुत्रः । मत्पुत्रः ।

No. 1166.—AND WHEN AN AFFIX follows, OR A WORD IN COMPOSITION, the *twa* and *ma* are put in the room of those two (viz. *yushmad* and *asmad*) as far as the *m* (i. e. in the room of *yushm* and *asm*), when they signify a single individual. Thus *twadíya* "belonging to thee," *madíya* "belonging to me," *twatputra* "thy son," *matputra* "my son."

मध्यान्मः । ४ । ३ । ८ ।

मध्यमः ।

No. 1167.—AFTER the word MADHYA "the middle," there is the affix MA. Thus *madhyama* "middlemost."

कालाट्ठञ् । ४ । ३ । ११ ।

कालिकम् । मासिकम् । सांवत्सरिकम् ।

No. 1168.—AFTER a word expressive of TIME, there is the affix ṬHAÑ. Thus *kálika* (No. 1101) "temporal," *másika* "monthly," *sáṅvatsarika* "annual."

अव्ययानां भमात्रे टिलोपः । सायंप्रातिकः । पौनःपुनिकः ।

No. 1169.—"There is ELISION OF THE LAST VOWEL AND WHAT FOLLOWS IT OF INDECLINABLES, IF ONLY they be entitled to the name of BHA (No. 185)." Thus (from *prátar*) *sáyaṅprátika* "belonging to evening and morning," (and, from *punar*,) *paunahpunika* "happening again and again."

प्रावृष एण्यः । ४ । ३ । १७ ।

प्रावृषेण्यः ।

No. 1170.—AFTER the word PRÁVṚISH "the rainy season," there is the affix EṆYA. Thus *právṛisheṇya* "what belongs to the season of the rains."

सायंचिरंप्राह्णेप्रगेऽव्ययेभ्यष्ट्युट्युलौ तुट् च । ४ । ३ । २३ ।

सायमित्यादिभ्यश्चतुर्भ्योऽव्ययेभ्यश्च कालवाचिभ्यष्ट्युट्युलौ स्तस्तयोस्तुट् च । सायंतनम् । चिरंतनम् । प्राह्णे प्रगे अनयोरेदन्तत्वं निपात्यते । प्राह्णेतनम् । प्रगेतनम् । दोषातनम् ।

No. 1171.—AFTER the four, *sáyam* &c.—i. e. after SÁYAM "at eve," CHIRAM "for a long time," PRÁHNE "in the forenoon," PRAGE "at dawn," AND after INDECLINABLES expressing time, there are the affixes ṬYU AND ṬYUL, AND their augment TUṬ. Thus, *sáyantana* (No. 836) "what is of the evening," *chirantana* "lasting" or "delayed long." In the case of *práhṇe* and *prage* the termination in *e* (in spite of No. 768) is anomalous; and we have *práhṇetana* "what is of the forenoon," and *pragetana* "what is of the early morn." (As an example of the rule applied to an indeclinable expressing time, take) *doshátana* "belonging to the night."

तत्र जातः । ४ । ३ । २५ ।

सप्तमीसमर्थाज्जात इत्यर्थेऽणादयो घादयश्च स्युः । स्रुघ्ने जातः । स्रौघ्नः । उत्से जातः । औत्सः । राष्ट्रे जातः । राष्ट्रियः । अवारपारे जातः । अवारपारीणः । इत्यादि ।

No. 1172.—Let there be the affixes *aṇ* &c., and *gha* &c., in the sense of PRODUCED THEREIN, after what in the 7th case is in grammatical relation (as the locality). Thus *sraughna* "born in Srughna," *autsa* "born in Utsa," *ráshṭriya* "born in a country," *avárapáríṇa* (No. 1150) "born on this or the opposite bank:"—and so of others.

प्रावृषष्ठप् । ४ । ३ । २६ ।

एण्यापवादः । प्रावृषिकः ।

No. 1173.—AFTER PRÁVṚISH "the rainy season" let there be the affix ṬHAP (when the sense is that of "produced in"). This debars *eṇya* (No. 1170).—Thus *právṛishika* (No. 1101) "produced in the rainy season."

प्रायभवः । ४ । ३ । ३९ ।

तत्रेत्येव । स्रुघ्ने प्रायेण बाहुल्येन भवति । स्रौघ्नः ।

No. 1174.—[The affixes *aṇ* &c. may come] when the sense is BEING MUCH—but only after that denoting "where." Thus *sraughna* "what is much—i. e. what is abundant—in Srughna."

सं भूते । ४ । ३ । ४१ ।

स्रुघ्ने संभवति । स्रौघ्नः ।

No. 1175.—[The affixes *aṇ* &c. may come] when the sense is ADAPTED. Thus *sraughna* "what is suited to the country of Srughna."

कोशाड्ढञ् । ४ । ३ । ४२ ।

कौशेयं वस्त्रम् ।

No. 1176.—AFTER the word KOŚA "cocoon of the silkworm," let there be the affix ḌHAÑ. Thus *kauśeya* "silken"—clothes.

तत्र भवः । ४ । ३ । ५३ ।

स्रौघ्नः । औत्सः । राष्ट्रियः ।

No. 1177.—[The affixes *aṇ* &c. may come] when the sense is WHO STAYS THERE. Thus *sraughna* "who stays in Srughna," *autsa* "who stays in Utsa," *ráshṭriya* "who stays in a kingdom."

दिगादिभ्यो यत् । ४ । ३ । ५४ ।

दिश्यम् । वर्ग्यम् ।

No. 1178.—AFTER the word DIŚ &c., let there be the affix YAT. Thus *diśya* "lying in a particular tract or quarter," *vargya* "belonging to a class."

शरीरावयवाच्च । ४ । ३ । ५५ ।

दन्त्यम् । कण्ठ्यम् । अध्यात्मादेष्ठञिष्यते । अध्यात्मे भवमा-ध्यात्मिकम् ।

No. 1179.—AND AFTER what denotes A PART OF THE BODY (let there be the affix *yat*). Thus *dantya* "dental," *kaṇṭhya* "guttural."

It is wished (by Patañjali) that after the words *adhyátman* "a minister of soul" &c., there should be the affix *ṭhañ*. Thus *ádhyátmika* "relating to one of the ministers of soul" [as spoken of in the Sáṅkhya philosophy].

अनुशतिकादीनां च ।७।३।२०।

एषामुभयपदवृद्धिर्ञिति णिति किति च । आधिदैविकम् । आधिभौतिकम् । ऐहलौकिकम् । आकृतिगणोऽयम् ।

No. 1180.—AND, AFTER the words ANUŚATIKA "about a hundred" &C., when an affix with an indicatory *ñ* or *ṇ* or *k* comes, let a *vṛiddhi* be the substitute of the vowel in both members of the compound. Thus—in those terms of the Sáṅkhya—(from *adhideva* "a presiding deity") *ádhidaivika* "dependent on a presiding deity," (from *adhibhúta* the province of an organ" *ádhibhautika* "having reference to the province of an organ," (from *ihaloka* "the world here") *aihalaukika* "relating to this world." This is a class of words (see No. 53) the fact of a word's belonging to which is known only from its form.

जिह्वामूलाङ्गुलेश्छः ।४।३।६२।

जिह्वामूलीयम् । अङ्गुलीयम् ।

No. 1181.—AFTER the words JIHWÁMÚLA AND AŃGULI, let there be the affix CHHA. Thus *jihwámúlíya* (No. 1086) "residing in the root of the tongue," *aṅgulíya* "residing in the fingers."

वर्गान्ताच्च ।४।३।६३।

कवर्गीयम् ।

No. 1182.—AND AFTER WHAT ENDS WITH VARGA (let there be the affix *chha*). Thus *kavargíya* (No. 1086) "belonging to the class of *k*"—(i. e. a guttural letter—see No. 17).

तत आगतः ।४।३।७४।

स्रुघ्नादागतः । स्रौघ्नः ।

No. 1183.—[Let there be the affix *aṇ* &c.] when the sense is WHAT HAS COME THENCE. Thus *sraughna* "what has come from Srughna."

ठगायस्थानेभ्यः । ४ । ३ । ७५ ।

शुल्कशालाया आगतः शौल्कशालिकः ।

No. 1184.—AFTER words denoting SOURCES OF REVENUE, let there be the affix ṬHAK. Thus *śaulkaśálika* (No. 1101) "what is derived from the custom-house."

विद्यायोनिसंबन्धेभ्यो वुञ् । ४ । ३ । ७७ ।

औपाध्यायकः । पैतामहकः ।

No. 1185.—AFTER words relating to LEARNING AND family ORIGIN, let there be the affix VUṄ. Thus *aupádhyáyaka* (No. 836) "derived from a spiritual teacher," *paitámahaka* "derived from a grandfather."

हेतुमनुष्येभ्योऽन्यतरस्यां रूप्यः । ४ । ३ । ८१ ।

समादागतं समरूप्यम् । पक्षे गहादित्वाच्छः । समीयम् । देवदत्तरूप्यम् । दैवदत्तम् ।

No. 1186.—AFTER words denoting CAUSES AND MEN (viewed as causes), there may be OPTIONALLY the affix RÚPYA. Thus *samarúpya* "what proceeds from a like cause." On the other alternative, there is after this word the affix *chha*, from No. 1162. Thus *samíya* (No. 1086). So, again, *devadattarúpya* or *daivadatta* "what originates with Devadatta."

मयट् च । ४ । ३ । ८२ ।

सममयम् । देवदत्तमयम् ।

No. 1187.—AND (under the circumstances specified in No. 1186) there may be the affix MAYAṬ. Thus *samamaya* "consisting of the same," *devadattamaya* "in the form of Devadatta."

प्रभवति । ४ । ३ । ८३ ।

हिमवतः प्रभवति हैमवती गङ्गा ।

No. 1188.—The affixes *aṇ* &c., may come when the sense is what TAKES ITS RISE. Thus *haimavatí* "which takes its rise in the snowy range"—meaning the river Ganges.

तद्गच्छति पथिदूतयोः । ४ । ३ । ८५ ।

स्रुघ्नं संगच्छति स्रौघ्नः । पन्था दूतो वा ।

No. 1189.—[The affixes *aṇ* &c., may come] when the meaning is WHAT GOES THERETO—PROVIDED THIS BE A ROAD OR a MESSENGER. Thus *sraughna* "that goes to Srughna"—i. e. the road to Srughna or a messenger to Srughna.

अभिनिष्क्रामति द्वारम् । ४ । ३ । ८६ ।

स्रुघ्नमभिनिष्क्रामति स्रौघ्नं कान्यकुब्जद्वारम् ।

No. 1190.—[The affixes *aṇ* &c., may come] when the meaning is THE GATE THAT FACES. Thus *sraughna* "which looks towards Srughna"—as one of the gates of Kányakubja does.

अधिकृत्य कृते ग्रन्थे । ४ । ३ । ८७ ।

शारीरकमधिकृत्य कृतो ग्रन्थः शारीरकीयः ।

No. 1191.—When the meaning is A BOOK MADE IN SUBSERVIENCE [to any subject, then the affixes *aṇ* &c., may come after what denotes that subject]. Thus *śárírakíya* "psychological"—meaning a book made with reference to the incorporate soul.

सोऽस्य निवासः । ४ । ३ । ८९ ।

स्रुघ्नो निवासोऽस्य स्रौघ्नः ।

No. 1192.—[The affixes *aṇ* &c., may come] when the meaning is that THIS is HIS DWELLING-PLACE. Thus *sraughna* "an inhabitant of Srughna."

तेन प्रोक्तम् । ४ । ३ । १०१ ।

पाणिनिना प्रोक्तं पाणिनीयम् ।

No. 1193.—[The affixes *aṇ* &c., may come] when the meaning is what was enounced by him. Thus *páṇiníya* "(the system of grammar) enounced by Páṇini."

तस्येदम् । ४ । ३ । १२० ।

उपगोरिदमौपगवम् ।

इति शैषिकाः ॥

No. 1194.—[The affixes *aṇ* &c., may come] when the meaning is that THIS is HIS. Thus *aupagava* "which belongs to Upagu."

So much for those affixes that convey the meanings referred to under No. 1149.

तस्य विकारः । ४ । ३ । १३४ ।

No. 1195.—[The affix *aṇ* may come] when the meaning is A MODIFICATION or product THEREOF.

अश्मनो विकारे टिलोपः । अश्मनो विकार आश्मः । भास्मनः । मार्त्तिकः ।

No. 1196.—"There is ELISION OF THE LAST VOWEL WITH WHAT FOLLOWS IT OF the word AŚMAN "a stone," WHEN the meaning is A PRODUCT thereof"—(No. 1195). Thus *áśma* "made of stone," [and then by No. 1195] *bhásmana* "made of ashes," *márttika* "made of earth."

अवयवे च प्राण्योषधिवृक्षेभ्यः । ४ । ३ । १३५ ।

चाद्विकारे । मयूरस्यावयवो विकारो वा मायूरः । मौर्वम् । काण्डं भस्म वा । पैप्पलम् ।

No. 1197.—AND [the affix *aṇ* &c., may come] AFTER a word denoting AN ANIMAL, AND a deciduous PLANT, AND a TREE, WHEN the meaning is A PART. By the "and" it is meant that the sense may be also a product—(No. 1195). Thus *máyúra* "being part of a peacock" or "made of a peacock" [—as a fan made of its feathers], *maurva* "of the Sanseviera zeylanica"—the stalk or the ashes,—*paippala* "of the Pípal-tree."

मयड्वैतयोर्भाषायामभक्ष्याच्छादनयोः । ४ । ३ । १४३ ।

प्रकृतिमात्रान्मयड्वा स्याद्विकारावयवयोः । अश्ममयम् । आश्मनम् । अभक्ष्येत्यादि किम् । मौद्गः सूपः । कार्पासमाच्छादनम् ।

No. 1198.—IN SECULAR LANGUAGE let the affix MAYAṬ come OPTIONALLY after any primitive IN THOSE TWO meanings—viz. product (No. 1195) and part (No. 1197), WHEN NEITHER FOOD NOR CLOTHING is spoken of. Thus *aśmamaya* or (by No. 1098) *áśma-*

na "made of stone." Why do we say "when neither food nor clothing is spoken of"? Witness *maudga* "made of kidney-beans"—as soup—[where the affix is *aṇ*—not *mayaṭ*]; and *kárpása* "made of cotton"—as clothing.

नित्यं वृद्धशरादिभ्यः ।४।३।१४४।

आम्रमयम् ।

No. 1199.—[The affixing of *mayaṭ*, which is optional in the case of the words specified in No. 1198, takes place] INVARIABLY AFTER WORDS THAT HAVE VṚIDDHI IN THE FIRST SYLLABLE (No. 1158), AND after the words ŚARA "a reed" &c. Thus *ámramaya* "consisting of mango-trees."

गोश्च पुरीषे ।४।३।१४५।

गोमयम् ।

No. 1200.—AND [there is the affix *mayaṭ*] AFTER the word GO "a cow," IN THE SENSE OF its DUNG. Thus *gomaya* "cow-dung."

गोपयसोर्यत् ।४।३।१६०।

गव्यम् । पयस्यम् ।

इति प्राग्दीव्यतीयाः ॥

No. 1201.—AFTER the words GO "a cow" AND PAYAS "milk," let there be the affix YAT. Thus *gavya* (No. 31) "being part of a cow," *payasya* "made of milk."

So much for the affixes that convey the meanings referred to under No. 1068.

प्राग्वहतेष्ठक् ।४।४।१।

तद्वहतीत्यतः प्राक् ठगधिक्रियते ।

No. 1202.—[In each aphorism] from this one FORWARD TO No. 1218, the affix ṬHAK bears rule.

तेन दीव्यति खनति जयति जितम् ।४।४।२।

अक्षैर्दीव्यति खनति जयति जितं वा आक्षिकम् ।

No. 1203.—[Let there be the affix *ṭhak*, No. 1202] when the sense is WHO PLAYS, DIGS, CONQUERS, or IS CONQUERED THEREWITH.

Thus *ákshika* (No. 1101) "a dicer"—i. e. who plays, conquers, or is conquered, with dice—[and so, from a word signifying an instrument for digging, may be formed what will signify "who digs therewith"].

संस्कृतम् । ४ । ४ । ३ ।

दध्ना संस्कृतं दाधिकम् । मारिचिकम् ।

No. 1204.—[So, too—No. 1202—when the sense is what is COMPOSED thereof. Thus *dádhika* "made of curds," *márichika* "made of pepper."

तरति । ४ । ४ । ५ ।

उडुपेन तरति । औडुपिकः ।

No. 1205.—[So, too—No. 1202—] when the sense is WHO CROSSES therewith. Thus *auḍupika* "who crosses by means of a raft."

चरति । ४ । ४ । ८ ।

हस्तिना चरति हास्तिकः । दध्ना चरति दाधिकः ।

No. 1206.—[So, too—No. 1202—when the sense is WHO GOES ON by means thereof. Thus *hástika* "who travels by an elephant," *dádhika* "who gets on with [—being fed on—] curds."

संसृष्टे । ४ । ४ । २२ ।

दध्ना संसृष्टं दाधिकम् ।

No. 1207.—[So, too—No. 1202—] when the sense is SMEARED therewith. Thus *dádhika* "smeared with curds."

उञ्छति । ४ । ४ । ३२ ।

बदराण्युञ्छति बादरिकः ।

No. 1208.—[So, too—No. 1202—] when we speak of him WHO GLEANS. Thus *bádarika* "who picks up jujubes."

रक्षति । ४ । ४ । ३३ ।

समाजं रक्षति सामाजिकः ।

No. 1209.—[So, too—No. 1202—] when we speak of him WHO AIDS. Thus *sámájika* "who aids an assembly"—as a spectator—[—as the French say—" qui assiste à"].

शब्ददर्दुरं करोति । ४ । ४ । ३४ ।

शब्दं करोति शाब्दिकः । दर्दुरं करोति दार्दुरिकः ।

No. 1210.—[So, too—there is the affix *ṭhak* as directed in No. 1202, after the words *śabda* "sound" and *dardura* "croaking,"] when we speak of WHAT MAKES A SOUND OR A CROAKING. Thus *śábdika* "what makes a sound," *dárdurika* "what makes a croaking."

धर्मं चरति । ४ । ४ । ४१ ।

धार्मिकः ।

No. 1211.—[So, too, there is the affix *ṭhak* after the word *dharma* "duty"] when we speak of him WHO PRACTISES duty. Thus *dhármika* "dutiful."

अधर्माच्चेति वक्तव्यम् । आधर्मिकः ।

No. 1212.—" IT SHOULD BE STATED THAT the affix (No. 1211) comes ALSO AFTER the word ADHARMA." Thus *ádharmika* " undutiful."

शिल्पम् । ४ । ४ । ५५ ।

मृदङ्गवादनं शिल्पमस्य मार्दङ्गिकः ।

No. 1213.—[So, too—No. 1202—] when we speak of one whose ART is related thereto. Thus *márdańgika* " a drummer"—whose calling is to sound the drum.

प्रहरणम् । ४ । ४ । ५७ ।

असिः प्रहरणमस्य आसिकः । धानुष्कः ।

No. 1214.—[So, too—No. 1202—] when we speak of one whose WEAPON it is. Thus *ásika* "a swordsman," *dhánushka* "a bowman."

शीलम् । ४ । ४ । ६१ ।

अपूपभक्षणं शीलमस्य आपूपिकः ।

No. 1215.—[So, too—No. 1202—] when we speek of one whose HABIT is related thereto. Thus *ápúpika* "one whose habit is to eat cakes."

निकटे वसति । ४ । ४ । ७३ ।

नैकटिको भिक्षुकः ।

इति ठगधिकारः ॥

No. 1216.—[So, too—No. 1202—*ṭhak* comes after the word *nikaṭa* "neighbouring"] when we speak of one WHO DWELLS NEAR. Thus *naikaṭika* "living near"—for example, a beggar.

So much for the rules in which the affix *ṭhak* is understood.

प्राग्घिताद्यत् । ४ । ४ । ७५ ।

तस्मै हितमित्यतः प्राग्यदधिक्रियते ।

No. 1217.—[In each aphorism] from this one FORWARD TO No. 1226, the affix YAT bears rule.

तद्वहति रथयुगप्रासङ्गम् । ४ । ४ । ७६ ।

रथं वहति रथ्यः । युग्यः । प्रासङ्ग्यः ।

No. 1218.—[Let there be the affix *yat*—No. 1217—] when we speak of WHAT BEARS IT—the thing borne being A CAR, a YOKE, OR a BREAK. Thus *rathya* "a carriage-horse," *yugya* "bearing the yoke," *prásangya* "being trained in a break."

धुरो यड्ढकौ । ४ । ४ । ७७ ।

धुर्यः । धौरेयः ।

No. 1219.—AFTER DHUR "a load," let there be YAT OR ḌHAK. Thus *dhurya* or *dhaureya* (No. 1086) "a beast of burden."

नौवयोधर्मविषमूलमूलसीतातुलाभ्यस्तार्यतुल्यप्राप्य-वध्यानाम्यसमसमितसंमितेषु । ४ । ४ । ९१ ।

नावा तार्यं नाव्यं जलम् । वयसा तुल्यो वयस्यः । धर्मेण प्राप्यं धर्म्यम् । विषेण वध्यः विष्यः । मूलेन आनाम्यं मूल्यम् । मूलेन समो मूल्यः । सीतया समितं सीत्यं क्षेत्रम् । तुलया संमितं तुल्यम् ।

No. 1220.—[Let *yat* come] AFTER the words NAU "a boat," VAYAS "age," DHARMA "merit," VISHA "poison," MÚLA "a root" MÚLA "something bought," SÍTÁ "a furrow," AND TULÁ "a balance," when the senses of the derivatives, respectively, are "TO BE CROSSED," "LIKE," "ATTAINABLE," "TO BE PUT TO DEATH," "TO BE BENT DOWN," "EQUIVALENT TO," "MEASURED OUT," AND "EQUALLY MEASURED." Thus *návya* "that can be crossed by a boat—water," *vayasya* "one of like age," *dharmya* (No. 260) "attainable through merit," *vishya* "to be put to death by poison," *múlya* "to be bent down from the root," *múlya* "the price equivalent to something bought," *sítya* (No 260) "measured out by furrows"—a field (ploughed), *tulya* "meted by a balance so as to be equal (to something else)."

तत्र साधुः । ४ । ४ । ९८ ।

सामसु साधुः सामन्यः । कर्मण्यः । शरण्यः ।

No. 1221.—[Let there be *yat*] when the sense is who is EXCELLENT IN REGARD THERETO. Thus *sámanya* "conversant with the Sáma-Veda," *karmaṇya* "fit for any act," *śaraṇya* "good for refuge."

सभाया यः । ४ । ४ । १०५ ।

सभ्यः ।

इति यतोऽवधिः ॥

No. 1222.—AFTER the word SABHÁ "an assembly," let there be the affix YAT. Thus *sabhya* (No. 260) "an assessor."

So much for the application of the affix *yat* (No. 1217).

प्राक्क्रीताच्छः । ५ । १ । १ ।

तेन क्रीतमित्यतः प्राक् छोऽधिक्रियते ।

No. 1223.—[In each aphorism] from this one FORWARD TO No. 1231, the affix CHHA bears rule.

उगवादिभ्यो यत् । ५ । १ । २ ।

उवर्णान्ताद्गवादिभ्यश्च यत् । छस्यापवादः । शङ्कव्यं दारु । गव्यम् ।

No. 1224.—AFTER what ends in U or *ú*, AND after the words GO &C., let there be the affix YAT. This debars *chha* (No. 1223). Thus *śaṅkavya* (No. 1078) "fit for a stake"—wood, *gavya* "suitable for cows."

नाभि नभं च । नभ्योऽक्षः । नभ्यमञ्जनम् ।

No. 1225.—"AND NABHA substituted FOR NÁBHI "the nave of a wheel" (should be mentioned under No. 1224). Thus *nabhya* "suitable for the nave of a wheel"—as the axle, or the grease for greasing it.

तस्मै हितम् । ५ । १ । ५ ।

वत्सेभ्यो हितो वत्सीयो गोधुक् ।

No. 1226.—[Let there be *chha*] when we speak of what is SUITABLE FOR THAT. Thus *vatsíya* "who is fit for (having the charge of) calves"—as a cow-milker.

शरीरावयवाद्यत् । ५ । १ । ६ ।

दन्त्यम् । कण्ठ्यम् । नस्यम् ।

No. 1227.—AFTER a word denoting A PART OF THE BODY, let there be the affix YAT. Thus *dantya* "suitable for the teeth," *kaṇṭhya* "suitable for the throat," NASYA "suitable for the nose."

आत्मन्विश्वजनभोगोत्तरपदात् खः । ५ । १ । ९ ।

No. 1228.—AFTER the words ÁTMAN, VIŚWAJANA, AND after BHOGA as the FINAL TERM in a compound, let there be the affix KHA.

आत्माध्वानौ खे । ६ । ४ । १६९ ।

एतौ खे प्रकृत्या स्तः । आत्मने हितमात्मनीनम् । विश्वजनीनम् । मातृभोगीणः ।

इति छयतोः पूर्णोऽवधिः ॥

No. 1229.—These two words ÁTMAN "soul" AND ADHWAN "a road," WHEN the affix KHA FOLLOWS, remain in their primitive form. Thus *átmanína* (Nos. 1228 and 1086) "suitable for one's self," *viśwajanína* "suitable for all men," *mátṛibhogíṇa* "fit to be possessed by the mother."

Here the extent of the [application of the] affixes *chha* (No. 1223) and *yat* (No. 1217) is completed.

प्राग्वतेष्ठञ्।५।१।१८।

तेन तुल्यमित्यतः प्राक् ठञधिक्रियते ।

No. 1230.—[In each aphorism] from this one FORWARD TO No. 1237, the affix ṬHAǸ bears rule.

तेन क्रीतम्।५।१।३७।

सप्तत्या क्रीतं साप्ततिकम् । प्रास्थिकम् ।

No. 1231.—[Let there be the affix *ṭhaǹ*—No. 1230—] when we speak of what is BOUGHT THEREWITH. Thus *sáptatika* (Nos. 260 and 1101) "bought with seventy," *prásthika* "bought for a *prastha* "[—i. e. for that measure of grain or the like].

तस्येश्वरः।५।१।४२।

सर्वभूमिपृथिवीभ्यामणञौ स्तः । अनुशतिकादीनां च । सर्वभूमेरीश्वरः सार्वभौमः । पार्थिवः ।

No. 1232.—When we speak of THE LORD THEREOF, the affixes *aṇ* and *aǹ*, respectively, come after the words *sarvabhúmi* "the whole earth," and *prithiví* "the earth." In accordance with No. 1180 [a *vṛiddhi* being the substitute of the vowel in both members of the compound] we have *sárvabhauma* (No. 1232) "the lord of the whole earth," *párthiva* "a lord of the earth."

पङ्क्तिविंशतित्रिंशच्चत्वारिंशत्पञ्चाशत्षष्टिसप्तत्यशीतिनवतिशतम्।५।१।५९।

एते रूढशब्दा निपात्यन्ते ।

No. 1233.—The following words, the sense of which has no relation to their etymology, are anomalous—viz. PAŃKTI "a line,"

VIṄŚATI "twenty," TRIṄŚAT "thirty," CHATWÁRIṄŚAT "forty," PAṄCHÁŚAT "fifty," SHASHṬI "sixty," SAPTATI "seventy," AŚÍṬI "eighty," NAVATI "ninety," AND ŚATA "a hundred."

तदर्हति ।५।१।६३।

श्वेतच्छत्रमर्हति श्वेतच्छत्रिकः ।

No. 1234.—[There may be *ṭhaṅ*—as in No. 1231] when we speak of one who DESERVES THAT. Thus *śwaitachchhatrika* "who deserves a white umbrella."

दण्डादिभ्यो यः ।५।१।६६।

एभ्यो यः । दण्डमर्हति दण्ड्यः । अर्घ्यः । वध्यः ।

No. 1235.—AFTER the word DAṆḌA "a fine" &c. let there be the affix YA. Thus *daṇḍya* "deserving to be fined," *arghya* "deserving worship," *vadhya* "deserving to be killed."

तेन निर्वृत्तम् ।५।१।७९।

अह्ना निर्वृत्तमाह्निकम् ।

इति ठञोऽवधिः ॥

No. 1236.—[There may be *ṭhaṅ*—as in No. 1231—] when we speak of what is ACCOMPLISHED BY MEANS THEREOF. Thus *ahnika* "to be accomplished in a day"—(a certain portion of reading).

Thus far is the extent of the affix *ṭhaṅ* (No. 1230).

तेन तुल्यं क्रिया चेद्वतिः ।५।१।११५।

ब्राह्मणेन तुल्यं ब्राह्मणवदधीते । क्रिया चेत् किम् । गुणतुल्ये मा भूत् । पुत्रेण तुल्यः स्थूलः ।

No. 1237.—Let the affix VATI be added, when we speak of what is LIKE THERETO—PROVIDED [the likeness have reference to] an ACTION. Thus *bráhmaṇavad* (No. 399) *adhíte* "he studies like a Bráhman." Why do we say "provided the likeness have reference to an action?" Because this does not apply when the likeness has reference to a quality:—thus *putreṇa tulyah sthúlah* "large like (i. e. as large as) the son."

तत्र तस्येव। ५। १। ११६।

मथुरायामिव मथुरावत् स्रुघ्ने प्राकारः। चैत्रस्येव चैत्रवन्मैत्रस्य गावः।

No. 1238.—[The affix *vati* may be employed—as in No. 1237 when we speak of something as being] LIKE what is THEREIN OR THEREOF. Thus *mathurávat* "like that in Mathurá"—speaking of the rampart of Srughna; *chaitravat* "like those of Chaitra"—speaking of Maitra's cows.

तस्य भावस्त्वतलौ। ५। १। ११९।

प्रकृतिजन्यबोधे प्रकारो भावः। गोर्भावो गोत्वम्। त्वान्तं क्लीबम्।

No. 1239.—Let the affixes TWA AND TAL come [after a word denoting anything] when we speak of THE NATURE (or genus) THEREOF. By "nature" we mean that which differences [from knowledge in general] the knowledge produced by [what is denoted by] the primitive. Thus *gotwa* "the nature of a cow" [—this being that which renders special the knowledge produced by the consideration of a cow, or which renders the knowledge different from the knowledge produced by the consideration of anything else than a cow]. What ends in *twa* is neuter.

आ च त्वात्। ५। १। १२०।

ब्रह्मणस्त्व इत्यतः प्राक् त्वतलावधिक्रियेते। अपवादैः सह समावेशार्थमिदम्। चकारो नञ्स्नञ्भ्यामपि समावेशार्थः। स्त्रिया भावः स्त्रैणम्। स्त्रीत्वम्। स्त्रीता। पौंस्नम्। पुंस्त्वम्। पुंस्ता।

No. 1240.—AND [in each aphorism] from this one forward AS FAR AS the aphorism V. 1. 136, the affixes TWA and *tal* bear rule. This rule is intended to secure admission [for these two affixes] notwithstanding bars [in the shape of subsequent aphorisms directing the employment of other affixes]. The word "and" [in the aphorism] is intended to secure their admission notwithstanding the affixes *nań* and *snań* [see No. 1079]. Thus "the nature of a female" may be expressed by either *straiṇa* (No. 1076 or *strítwa*, or *strítá*, and "the nature of a male" by *pauńsna*, or *puństwa*, or *puństá*.

पृथ्वादिभ्य इमनिज्वा। ५। १। १२२।

वावचनमणादिसमावेशार्थम्।

No. 1241.—AFTER the words PṚITHU "large" &c., there is OPTIONALLY the affix IMANICH. The expression "optionally" is employed with the intention of securing admission for the affixes *aṇ* &c.

र ऋतो हलादेर्लघोः। ६। ४। १६१।

इष्ठेमेयस्सु।

No. 1242.—Let RA be the substitute OF ṚI, PRECEDED BY a CONSONANT and NOT LONG BY POSITION (No. 483).

टेः। ६। ४। १५५।

टेर्लोप इष्ठेमेयस्सु। पृथुमृदुभृशकृशदृढपरिवृढानामेव रत्वम्। पृथोर्भावः प्रथिमा। पार्थवम्। म्रदिमा। मार्दवम्।

No. 1243.—Let there be elision OF THE LAST VOWEL WITH WHAT FOLLOWS IT, when the affixes *ishṭhan* (No. 1306), *iman* (No. 1241) and *íyasun* (No. 1310) follow. The change to *ra* (directed by No. 1242) belongs only to the words *pṛithu* "large," *mṛidu* "soft," *bhṛiśa* "much," *kṛiśa* "thin," *dṛiḍha* "strong," and *parivṛiḍha* "a superior." Thus *prathiman* (Nos. 1241 and 1243) or *párthava* "greatness," *mradiman* or *márdava* "softness."

वर्णदृढादिभ्यः ष्यञ् च। ५। १। १२३।

चादिमनिच्। शौक्ल्यम्। शुक्लिमा। दार्ढ्यम्। द्रढिमा।

No. 1244.—AND the affix SHYAÑ may come AFTER words denoting COLOURS, AND after the words DṚIḌHA "strong" &c. By the "and" it is meant that the affix *imanich* (No. 1241) may be employed. Thus *śauklya* or *śukliman* "whiteness," *dárḍhya* or *draḍhiman* (No. 1242) "firmness."

गुणवचनब्राह्मणादिभ्यः कर्मणि च। ५। १। १२४।

चाद्भावे। जडस्य भावः कर्म वा जाड्यम्। मौढ्यम्। ब्राह्मण्यम्। आकृतिगणोऽयम्।

No. 1245.—AND WHEN ACTIONS ARE SPOKEN OF [*shyañ* may come] AFTER words EXPRESSIVE OF QUALITIES, AND after the words BRÁHMAṆA &C. By the "and" it is meant that this affix may be employed when the *nature* (No. 1239) is spoken of. Thus *jáḍya* or *mauḍhya* "the nature or the conduct of an idiot," *bráhmaṇya* "the nature or the conduct of a Bráhman." This class of words ("*bráhmaṇa* &c.") is one the fact of a word's belonging to which is known only from the forms [met with in writers of authority—see No. 53].

सख्युर्यः ।५।१।१२६।

सख्यम् ।

No. 1246.—AFTER the word SAKHI "a friend" there may be the affix Y. Thus *sakhya* "friendship."

कपिज्ञात्योर्ढक् ।५।१।१२७।

कापेयम् । ज्ञातेयम् ।

No. 1247.—AFTER the words KAPI "a monkey" AND JÑÁTI "a kinsman" there may be the affix ḌHAK. Thus *kápeya* (Nos. 1086 and 1073) "the nature or conduct of a monkey," *jñáteya* "affinity."

पत्यन्तपुरोहितादिभ्यो यक् ।५।१।१२८।

सैनापत्यम् । पौरोहित्यम् ।

इति नञ्स्नञोरधिकारः ॥

No. 1248.—AFTER words ENDING IN PATI, AND after the word PUROHITA "a priest" &c., there may be the affix YAK. Thus *sainápatya* "the duty of a general," *paurohitya* "the office of a priest."

So much for the province of the affixes *nañ* and *snañ* (No. 1077).

धान्यानां भवने क्षेत्रे खञ् ।५।२।१।

मुद्गानां भवनं क्षेत्रं मौद्गीनम् ।

No. 1249.—WHEN we speak of a PLACE FOR GRAIN, OR a FIELD of it, there may be the affix KHAÑ. Thus *maudgína* (No. 1086) "fit for kidney-beans"—meaning a place for storing them or field for growing them.

व्रीहिशाल्योर्ढक्।५।२।२।

व्रैहेयम्। शालेयम्।

No. 1250.—(In the senses specified in No. 1249) the affix DHAK may c. me after the words VRÍHI AND ŚÁLI "rice." Thus *vraiheya* or *śáleya* "fit for rice"—a field.

हैयंगवीनं संज्ञायाम्।५।२।२३।

नवनीते निपातितोऽयम्।

No. 1251.—The word HAIYAŃGAVÍNA—an APPELLATIVE signifying "fresh butter"—is anomalous.

तदस्य संजातं तारकादिभ्य इतच्।५।२।३६।

तारकाः संजाता अस्य तारकितं नभः। पण्डितः। आकृतिगणोऽयम्।

No. 1252.—The affix ITACH may come AFTER the words TÁRAKA "a star" &c., when we speak of THAT WHEREOF THIS IS OBSERVED. Thus *tárakita* "starry"—[speaking of the sky, the stars of which are observed], *paṇḍita* "learned"—[in whom *paṇḍá* learning" is observed].

This class of words ("*táraka* &c.") is one the fact of a word's belonging to which is known only from the forms [met with in writers of authority—see No. 53].

प्रमाणे द्वयसज्दघ्नञ्मात्रचः।५।२।३७।

ऊरू प्रमाणमस्य ऊरुद्वयसम्। ऊरुदघ्नम्। ऊरुमात्रम्।

No. 1253.—WHEN we speak of something as being of a certain MEASURE, the affixes DWAYASACH, DAGHNACH AND MÁTRACH [may come after that to which we remark its equality]. Thus *úrudwayasa*, or *úrudaghna*, or *úrumátra*, "as high as the thigh.

यत्तदेतेभ्यः परिमाणे वतुप्।५।२।३९।

यत् परिमाणमस्य यावान् । तावान् । एतावान् ।

No. 1254.—WHEN we speak of MEASURE, let the affix VATUP come AFTER the pronouns YAD, TAD, AND ETAD. Thus *yávat* (No. 377) "as much as"—(i. e. "the measure thereof being that which"—), *távat* "so much," *etávat* "thus much."

संख्याया अवयवे तयप् । ५ । २ । ४२ ।

पञ्चावयवा अस्य पञ्चतयम् ।

No. 1255.—The affix TAYAP may come AFTER a NUMERAL WHEN [we speak of something as having that number of] PARTS. Thus *pañchataya* "having five parts."

द्वित्रिभ्यां तयस्यायज्वा । ५ । २ । ४३ ।

द्वयम् । द्वितयम् । त्रयम् । त्रितयम् ।

No. 1256.—The affix AYACH is OPTIONALLY the substitute OF TAYA (No. 1255) AFTER DWI "two" and TRI "three." Thus *dwaya* or *dwitaya* "a couple," *traya* or *tritaya* "a triad."

उभादुदात्तो नित्यम् । ५ । २ । ४४ ।

उभयम् ।

No. 1257.—AFTER the word UBHA "both," the affix *ayach*, ACUTELY ACCENTED, shall ALWAYS be employed (and never *tayap*—No. 1256). Thus *ubhaya* "the set of both."

तस्य पूरणे डट् । ५ । २ । ४८ ।

एकादशानां पूरण एकादशः ।

No. 1258.—Let ḌAṬ be the affix WHEN we speak of the COMPLETER THEREOF. Thus *ekádaśa* "the eleventh"—(i. e. the one which, added to ten, completes the eleven).

नान्तादसंख्यादेर्मट् । ५ । २ । ४९ ।

मडागमः । पञ्चानां पूरणः पञ्चमः । नान्तात् किम् । विंशः ।

No. 1259.—Let MAṬ be the augment [of the affix *ḍaṭ*—No. 1258–] AFTER WHAT numeral ENDS WITH the letter N AND IS NOT PRECEDED BY another NUMERAL [i. e. not being at the end of a compound numeral such as *trayodaśan* "thirteen"]. Thus *pañchama* "the fifth" [the completer of the five]. Why do we say "ends with the letter *ṇ*?" Witness *vinśa* (No. 1260) "the twentieth."

ति विंशतेर्डिति । ६ । ४ । १४२ ।

विंशतेर्भस्य तिशब्दस्य लोपो डिति परे । विंशः । असंख्यादेः किम् । एकादशः ।

No. 1260.—Let there be elision of the syllable TI of the word VIŃŚATI "twenty," being a *bha* (No. 185), WHEN an affix WITH an INDICATORY Ḍ FOLLOWS. Thus *vinśa* (No. 1258) "the twentieth." Why do we say (in No. 1259) "not preceded by another numeral?" Witness *ekádaśa* "the eleventh"—[from *ekádaśan* "eleven"].

षट्कतिकतिपयचतुरां थुक् । ५ । २ । ५१ ।

डटि । षण्णां पूरणः षष्ठः । कतिथः । कतिपयशब्दस्यात एव डट् । कतिपयथः । चतुर्थः ।

No. 1261.—When *ḍaṭ* (No. 1258) follows, let THUK be the augment OF the words SHASH "six," KATI "how many?," KATIPAYA "several," AND CHATUR "four." Thus *shashṭha* "the sixth" [the completer of the six—]; *katitha* "the which in order?" i. e. the first, second, or what?] The word *katipaya* [though not a numeral and hence not falling under No. 1258] takes the affix *ḍaṭ* in consequence of this rule [which directs that this affix following that word shall receive an augment]. Thus *katipayatha* "the one in order after several"—[i. e. the one in order after the second, third, or the like indefinitely—]; *chaturtha* "the fourth."

द्वेस्तीयः । ५ । २ । ५४ ।

डटोऽपवादः । द्वयोः पूरणो द्वितीयः ।

No. 1262.—AFTER the word DWI "two" let the affix be TÍYA. This debars *ḍaṭ* (No. 1258). Thus *dwitíya* "the second"—that which completes the two.

त्रेः संप्रसारणं च । ५ । २ । ५५ ।

तृतीयः ।

No. 1263.—AND AFTER the word TRI "three" [let there be *tíya*—No. 1254—] AND let a VOWEL be substituted for the semi-vowel—[i. e. let there be the vowel *ṛi* in the room of the *r*]. Thus *tṛitíya* (No. 283) "the third."

श्रोत्रियंश्छन्दोऽधीते । ५ । २ । ८४ ।

श्रोत्रियः । वेत्यनुवृत्तेश्छान्दसः ।

No. 1264.—The word ŚROTRIYAN is anomalously employed to denote one WHO HAS STUDIED THE CHHANDAS—i. e. the Scriptures. Thus (the final *n* being indicatory) *śrotriya* "a Bráhman learned in the Vedas." As the word "optionally" is supplied [from V. 2. 77.] we may also have *chhándasa* in the same sense.

पूर्वादिनिः । ५ । २ । ८६ ।

पूर्वं ज्ञातमनेन पूर्वी ।

No. 1265.—The affix INI may come AFTER the word PÚRVA "former," when we speak of one by whom something was formerly known (or the like). Thus *púrvin* "by whom something was formerly known (or the like)."

सपूर्वाच्च । ५ । २ । ८७ ।

कृतपूर्वी ।

No. 1266.—AND [the affix *ini*—No. 1265—] may come AFTER the word PÚRVA WITH some [related word prefixed] Thus *kṛitapúrvin* "who formerly made."

इष्टादिभ्यश्च । ५ । २ । ८८ ।

इष्टमनेन इष्टी । अधीती ।

No. 1267.—AND [the affix *ini*—No. 1265—] may come AFTER the words ISHṬA "wished" &c. Thus *ishṭin* "who wished," *adhítin* "who studied."

तदस्यास्त्यस्मिन्निति मतुप् । ५ । २ । ९४ ।

गावोऽस्यास्मिन् वा सन्ति गोमान् ।

No. 1268.—The affix MATUP may come after a word denoting anything, when we speak of one WHOSE IT IS, or IN WHOM IT IS. Thus *gomat* "who has cows" [as a man], or "in which there are cows" [as a pasture].

तसौ मत्वर्थे। १।४।१९।

तान्तसान्तौ भसंज्ञौ स्तो मत्वर्थे प्रत्यये । संप्रसारणम् । विदुष्मान्।

No. 1269.—Words ENDING IN T AND words ending in S are called *bha,* WHEN an affix WITH FORCE OF MATUP (No. 1268) FOLLOWS. [Thus, in the example following, by No. 382, which applies, in virtue of the word's being a *bha*], a vowel is substituted for the semi-vowel [of the word *vidwas* "a sage"] and we have *vidushmat* "where there are sages."

गुणवचनेभ्यो मतुपो लुगिष्टः । शुक्लो गुणोऽस्यास्तीति शुक्लः पटः । कृष्णः ।

No. 1270.—"The ELISION *(luk)* OF MATUP IS WISHED [by Patañjali] AFTER WORDS DENOTING QUALITIES [when we speak of one who possesses the quality]." Thus *śukla* "in which there is the quality of white"—as (white) cloth, *kṛishṇa* "in which there is the quality of black."

प्राणिस्थादातो लजन्यतरस्याम् । ५ । २ । ९६ ।

चूडालः । चूडावान् । प्राणिस्थात् किम् । शिखावान् दीपः । प्राण्यङ्गादेव । नेह । मेधावान् ।

No. 1271—The affix LACH [with the force of *matup*—No. 1268—] may OPTIONALLY come AFTER a word ENDING IN long Á and denoting something THAT EXISTS (as a member thereof) IN a LIVING BEING. Thus *chúḍála* or *chúḍávat* (No. 1245) "crested." Why do we say "that exists in a living being"? Witness *śikhávat* "crested"—when it means "a lamp" [with its crest of flame]. As the affix *lach* can be employed only after what denotes "a member or limb" of a living being, it cannot be employed in the following case—viz.—*medhávat* "possessing intelligence."

लोमादिपामादिपिच्छादिभ्यः शनेलचः । ५ । २ । १०० ।

लोमादिभ्यः शः । लोमशः । लोमवान् । पामादिभ्यो नः । पामनः ।

No. 1272.—AFTER the words LOMAN "hair of the body" &c., PÁMAN "cutaneous eruption" &c., AND PICHCHHÁ "rice-water" &c., there may be the affixes ŚA, NA, AND ILACH. Thus—the affix *śa* being placed after *loman &c.*, we may have *lomaśa* (No. 200) or (by No. 1268) *lomavat* "hairy;" and the affix *na* being placed after *páman &c.*, we may have *pámana* "scabby."

अङ्गात् कल्याणे । अङ्गना ।

No. 1273—"[And the affix *na*—No. 1272—may come] AFTER the word AṄGA 'the body,'—WHEN we speak of those whose persons are BEAUTIFUL." Thus *aṅganá* (No. 1341) "a woman."

लक्ष्म्या अच्च । लक्ष्मणः । पिच्छादिभ्य इलच् । पिच्छिलः । पिच्छवान् ।

No. 1274.—"Short A may be the substitute of the word LAKSHMÍ 'prosperity,' AND [there is the affix *na*]." Thus *lakshmaṇa* "prosperous."

The affix *ilach* [as stated in No. 1272] being optional after *pichchhá &c.*, we may have *pichchhila* or *pichchhavat* "broth of rice-water."

दन्त उन्नत उरच् । ५ । २ । १०६ ।

उन्नता दन्ता अस्य दन्तुरः ।

No. 1275.—The affix URACH may come AFTER the word DANTA "a tooth," WHEN PROMINENT teeth are connoted. Thus *dantura* "who possesses prominent teeth."

केशाद्वोऽन्यतरस्याम् । ५ । २ । १०९ ।

केशवः । केशवान् ।

No. 1276.—AFTER the word KEŚA "hair" the affix VA may OPTIONALLY come. Thus *keśava* or *keśavat* "possessing [a fine head of] hair."

अन्येभ्योऽपि दृश्यते । मणिवः ।

No. 1277.—"[This affix—*va*—No. 1276]—IS SEEN AFTER OTHER WORDS ALSO." Thus *maṇiva* "possessing a gem"—[one of the serpents of Pátála].

अर्णसो लोपश्च । अर्णवः ।

No. 1278.—"[The affix *va*—No. 1276—may come] AFTER the word ARNAS 'water,' AND then there is ELISION of the final *s*." Thus *arṇava* "the ocean."

अत इनिठनौ । ५ । २ । ११५ ।

दण्डी । दण्डिकः ।

No. 1279.—AFTER words ending in short A there may be the affixes INI AND ṬHAN [with the force of *matup*—No. 1268—]. Thus *ḍaṇḍin* or *ḍaṇḍika* (No. 1101) "having a staff."

व्रीह्यादिभ्यश्च । ५ । २ । ११६ ।

व्रीही । व्रीहिकः ।

No. 1280.—AND [the affixes mentioned in No. 1279 may come] AFTER the words VRÍHI "rice" &c. Thus *vríhin* or *vríhika* "having or bearing rice."

अस्मायामेधास्रजो विनिः । ५ । २ । १२१ ।

यशस्वी । यशस्वान् । मायावी । मेधावी । स्रग्वी ।

No. 1281.—AFTER words ending in AS, AND after MÁYÁ "illusion," AND MEDHÁ "intelligence," AND SRAJ "a garland," there may be the affix VINI. Thus *yaśaswin* or *yaśaswat* (No. 1268) "famous," *máyávin* "illusive," *medhávin* "intelligent," *sragwin* "wearing a garland."

वाचो ग्मिनिः । ५ । २ । १२४ ।

वाग्मी ।

No. 1282.—AFTER the word VÁCH "speech" there may be the affix GMINI. Thus *vágmin* (No. 333) "eloquent."

अर्श आदिभ्योऽच् । ५ । २ । १२७ ।

अर्शसः । आकृतिगणोऽयम् ।

इति मत्वर्थीयाः ॥

No. 1283.—AFTER the words ARŚAS "piles" &c., there may be the affix ACH. Thus *arśasa* "afflicted with piles." This is a class of words, the words belonging to which are known only by their forms—(No. 53).

So much for the affixes which have the same force as *matup*—(No. 1268).

प्राग्दिशो विभक्तिः । ५ । ३ । १ ।

दिक्शब्देभ्य इत्यतः प्राग्वक्ष्यमाणाः प्रत्यया विभक्तिसंज्ञाः स्युः ।

। अथ स्वार्थिकाः ।

No. 1284.—Let the affixes that are spoken of from this aphorism FORWARD as FAR AS V. 3. 27. be called VIBHAKTI.

The affixes spoken of henceforward leave to the words their own denotation [—see No. 1287.—The rule No. 1067, the affixes superintended by which produce epithets connoting the sense of the primitive and denoting something else, extends no further than this].

किंसर्वनामबहुभ्योऽद्व्यादिभ्यः । ५ । ३ । २ ।

किमः सर्वनाम्नो बहुशब्दाच्चेति प्राग्दिशोऽधिक्रियते ।

No. 1285.—[The affixes mentioned under No. 1284 are to come] AFTER the word KIM "what?" AND after a PRONOMINAL, AND BAHU "much," but NOT AFTER THOSE [of the pronominals—No. 170—] OF WHICH THE FIRST IS DWI "two" [*kim*—which is among these—having been already specified]. This set of provisions exercises an influence on each rule as far as V. 3. 27.

पञ्चम्यास्तसिल् । ५ । ३ । ७ ।

पञ्चम्यन्तेभ्यः किमादिभ्यस्तसिल् वा स्यात् ।

No. 1286.—AFTER the words *kim &c.* (No. 1285) in THE FIFTH CASE let there be optionally the affix TASIL.

कु तिहोः । ७ । २ । १०४ ।

किमः कुस्तादौ हादौ च विभक्तौ । कुतः । कस्मात् ।

No. 1287.—The substitute of *kim* "what?" is KU, WHEN a *vibhakti* (No. 1284) beginning with the letter T [called *ti*, in the aphorism, for the sake of pronunciation] OR H FOLLOWS. Thus *kutah* (No. 1286) "from what?" or "whence?"

इदम इश् । ५ । ३ । ३ ।

प्राग्दिशीये । इतः ।

No. 1288.—The substitute OF IDAM "this" is IŚ, when one of the affixes specified under No. 1284 follows. Thus *itah* (No. 1286) "from this" or "hence."

एतदोऽन् । ५ । ३ । ५ ।

प्राग्दिशीये । अनेकाल्त्वात् सर्वादेशः । अतः । अमुतः । यतः । ततः । बहुतः । द्व्यादेस्तु । द्वाभ्याम् ।

No. 1289.—The substitute OF ETAD "this," when one of the affixes specified under No. 1284 follows, is AN. As it consists of more than one letter, this substitute takes the place of the whole term (No. 58). Thus *atah* (Nos. 1286 and 200) "from this" or "hence," [and, as further applications of No. 1286, we have] *amutah* (No. 386) "hence," *yatah* "whence," *tatah* "thence," *bahutah* "from many,"—but as, after *dwi &c.* (No. 1285), the affix is not allowable, we can express "from the two, only by *dwábhyám.*

पर्यभिभ्यां च । ५ । ३ । ९ ।

तसिल् । परितः । सर्वत इत्यर्थः । अभितः । उभयत इत्यर्थः ।

No. 1290.—AND the affix *tasil* may come AFTER THE TWO words PARI "around" AND ABHI "against." Thus *paritah*—meaning "all round," and *abhitah*—meaning "on both sides."

सप्तम्यास्त्रल् । ५ । ३ । १० ।

कुत्र । यत्र । बहुत्र ।

No. 1291.—AFTER (the words *kim &c.*,—No. 1285—in) THE SEVENTH CASE let there be optionally the affix TRAL. Thus *kutra* (No. 1287) "in what?" or "where?"; *yatra* (Nos. 213 and 300) "where," *bahutra* "in many places."

इदमो हः । ५ । ३ । ११ ।

त्रलोऽपवादः । इह ।

No. 1292.—AFTER IDAM "this" (in the 7th case) let there be the affix HA. This debars *tral* (No. 1290). Thus *iha* (No. 1288) "here."

किमोऽत् । ५ । ३ । १२ ।

वा स्यात् ।

No. 1293.—AFTER KIM "what?" [in the 7th case] let there be *optionally* UT.

क्वाति । ७ । २ । १०५ ।

किमः । क्व । कुत्र ।

No. 1294.—The substitute of *kim* "what?" WHEN the affix AT (No. 1292) FOLLOWS, is KWA. Thus *kwa*, in the same sense as *kutra* (No. 1291), "where?"

इतराभ्योऽपि दृश्यन्ते । ५ । ३ । १४ ।

पञ्चमीसप्तमीतरविभक्त्यन्तादपि तसिलादयो दृश्यन्ते । दृशिग्रहणाद्भवदादियोग एव । स भवान् । ततो भवान् । तत्र भवान् । ततो भवन्तम् । तत्र भवन्तम् । एवं दीर्घायुः । देवानां प्रियः । आयुष्मान् ।

No. 1295.—THESE affixes *tasil* (No. 1286) &c., ARE SEEN coming AFTER *kim &c.* (No. 1285) ending with OTHER case-affixes ALSO besides the 5th (No. 1286) and 7th (No. 1291). By the employment of the expression "are seen" it is hinted that this may take place [not on every occasion, but] only when in juxtaposition with such a word as *bhavat* "your Honour." Thus, employed in the same sense as *sa bhaván* "your Honour," we see *tato bhaván* and *tatra bhaván*; and, in the 2d case, *tato bhavantam* and *tatra bhavantam*. So too [when the word in juxtaposition is] *dírgháyus* "long-lived," *devánám priya* "dear to the gods," or *áyushmat* "long-lived."

सर्वैकान्यकिंयत्तदः काले दा । ५ । ३ । १५ ।

सप्तम्यन्तेभ्यः कालार्थे दा स्यात् ।

No. 1296.—Let DÁ come AFTER SARVA "all," EKA "one," ANYA "other," KIM "what?" YAD "which," AND TAD "that," in the 7th case, when we speak of TIME.

सर्वस्य सोऽन्यतरस्यां दि । ५ । ३ । ६ ।

दादौ प्राग्दिशीये सर्वस्य सो वा । सर्वस्मिन् काले सदा । सर्वदा । अन्यदा । कदा । यदा । तदा । काले किम् । सर्वत्र देशे ।

No. 1297.—The substitute, OPTIONALLY, OF SARVA "all," is SA, WHEN an affix, of those specified under No. 1284, beginning with the letter D, FOLLOWS. Thus *sadá* (No. 1296) or *sarvadá* "at every time" or "always," *anyadá* "at another time," *kadá* "when?" *yadá* "when," *tadá* "then." Why "when we speak of *time*" (No. 1296)? Witness *sarvatra* [where, although the case is the 7th, the affix is not *dá*, because the sense is] "in every *place*" or "everywhere."

इदमो र्हिल् । ५ । ३ । १६ ।

सप्तम्यन्तात् ।

No. 1298.—AFTER IDAM "this," in the 7th case, let there be the affix RHIL.

एतेतौ रथोः । ५ । ३ । ४ ।

इदम एत इत् एतौ स्तो रेफादौ थकारादौ च प्राग्दिशीये परे । अस्मिन् काले एतर्हि । काले किम् । इह देशे ।

No. 1299.—Of *idam* "this" [when we speak of *time*] the substitutes are the two ETA AND IT, WHEN an affix, of those specified under No. 1284, beginning with the letter R OR beginning with the letter TH, respectively, FOLLOWS. Thus *etarhi* "at this time." Why "when we speak of time?" Witness *iha* [formed by No. 1292 when we mean] "in this *place*" or "here."

अनद्यतने र्हिलन्यतरस्याम् । ५ । ३ । २१ ।

कर्हि । कदा । यर्हि । यदा । तर्हि । तदा ।

No. 1300.—WHEN we speak of time NOT OF THE CURRENT DAY, the affix RHIL may be employed OPTIONALLY. Thus *karhi* (Nos. 297 and 260) or *kadá* (No. 1296) "when?" *yarhi* or *yadá* "when," *tarhi* or *tadá* "then."

एतदः । ५ । ३ । ५ ।

एत इत् एतौ स्तो रेफादौ थादौ च प्राग्दिशीये । एतस्मिन् काले एतर्हि ।

No. 1301.—OF ETAD "this," [when we speak of time], the substitutes are the two *eta* and *it,* when an affix, of those specified under No. 1284, beginning with the letter *r* or with the letter *th,* respectively, follows. Thus *etarhi* "at this time."

प्रकारवचने थाल् । ५ । ३ । २३ ।

प्रकारवृत्तिभ्यः किमादिभ्यस्थाल् । तेन प्रकारेण तथा ।

No. 1302.—The affix THÁL may come after the words *kim &c.,* (No. 1285) WHEN WE SPEAK OF a KIND, or manner, of being Thus *tathá* "so," "in that manner."

इदमस्थमुः । ५ । ३ । २४ ।

थालोऽपवादः ।

No. 1303.—AFTER the word IDAM "this" let there be the affix THAMU. This bebars *thál* (No. 1302).

एतदोऽपि वाच्यः । अनेन एतेन प्रकारेण वा इत्थम् ।

No. 1304.—"IT [viz., *thamu*—No. 1303] SHOULD BE STATED TO COME AFTER ETAD 'this' ALSO." Thus *ittham* (Nos. 1299 and 1301) "thus," "in this manner."

किमश्च । ५ । ३ । २५ ।

केन प्रकारेण कथम् ।

इति प्राग्दिशीयाः ।

No. 1305.—AND AFTER KIM "what?" [the affix *thamu*—No. 1303—may come. Thus *katham* (No. 297) "how?" "in what manner?"

So much for the affixes specified under No. 1284.

अतिशायने तमबिष्ठनौ। ५। ३। ५५।

अतिशयविशिष्टार्थवृत्तेः स्वार्थे एतौ स्तः। अयमेषामतिशयेनाढ्य आढ्यतमः। लघुतमः। लघिष्ठः।

No. 1306.— These two affixes, THMAP AND ISHṬHAN, come after a word, the word retaining its denotation, WHEN the sense is differenced by EXCESS. Thus *áḍhyatama* "the richest"—"he who —of these—is wealthy κατ' ἐξοχήν or *par excellence*;" *laghutama* or *laghishṭha* (No. 1243) "the lightest."

तिङश्च। ५। ३। ५६।

तिङन्तादतिशये द्योत्ये तमप् स्यात्।

No. 1307.—AND AFTER what ends with a TENSE AFFIX, when excess is to be connoted, let there be the affix *tamap* (No. 1306).

तरप्तमपौ घः। १। १। २२।

No. 1308.—Let the two affixes [of the comparative and the superlative degree, viz.] TARAP AND TAMAP be called GHA.

किमेत्तिङव्ययघादाम्वद्रव्यप्रकर्षे। ५। ४। ११।

किम एदन्तात् तिङोऽव्ययाच्च यो घस्तदन्तादामुः स्यान्न तु द्रव्यप्रकर्षे। किंतमाम्। पचतितमाम्। उच्चैस्तमाम्। द्रव्यप्रकर्षे तु। उच्चैस्तमस्तरुः।

No. 1309.—AFTER KIM "what?," AND WHAT ENDS WITH THE letter E OR with a TENSE-AFFIX, AND after an INDECLINABLE, let there be ÁMU AFTER an AFFIX OF the comparative or superlative DEGREE—but NOT IF THE EXCESS BELONGS TO a SUBSTANCE. Thus *kiṅtamám* "how excessively [it rains—or the like]!" *pachatitamám* "he cooks surprisingly," *uchchaistamám* "most loftily or loudly." But when the excess belongs [not to an action &c., but] to a substance— *uchchaistamas taruh* "a most lofty tree."

द्विवचनविभज्योपपदे तरबीयसुनौ । ५ । ३ । ५७ ।

द्वयोरेकस्यातिशये विभक्तव्ये चोपपदे सुप्तिङन्तादेतौ स्तः । पूर्वयोरपवादः । अयमनयोरतिशयेन लघुर्लघुतरः । लघीयान् । उदीच्याः प्राच्येभ्यः पटुतराः । पटीयांसः ।

No. 1310.—These two affixes TARAP AND ÍYASUN come after what ends with a case-affix or a tense-affix, WHEN THE TERM IN CONSTRUCTION with it is a DUAL, and there is excess in the one out of the two, AND WHEN [to mark excess] the term in construction is CONTRASTED [by the affix of the fifth case with the sense of "than," —II. 3. 42]. This debars the two former affixes (No. 1306). Thus *laghutara* or *laghíyas* "the lighter—[the one of the two that is light *par excellence*]; and so too when we speak of the Northerns as being "more clever" *práchyebhyah* "than the Easterns."

प्रशस्यस्य श्रः । ५ । ३ । ६० ।

इष्ठेयसोः परतः ।

No. 1311.—OF the word PRAŚASYA "excellent" let ŚRA be the substitute when *ishṭhan* (No. 1306) and *íyasun* (No. 1310) follow.

प्रकृत्यैकाच् । ६ । ४ । १६३ ।

इष्ठादावेकाच् प्रकृत्या स्यात् । श्रेष्ठः । श्रेयान् ।

No. 1312.—Let a word WITH A SINGLE VOWEL remain IN its ORIGINAL FORM when the affix *ishṭhan* or the like (No. 1311) follows. Thus *śreshṭha* "most excellent," *śreyas* "more excellent."

ज्य च । ५ । ३ । ६१ ।

प्रशस्यस्य ज्यादेश इष्ठेयसोः । ज्येष्ठः ।

No. 1313.—AND JYA may be the substitute of the word *praśasya* (No. 1311) when the affixes *ishṭhan* and *íyasun* follow. Thus *jyeshṭha* "the most excellent."

ज्यादादीयसः । ६ । ४ । १६० ।

आदेः परस्य । ज्यायान् ।

No. 1314.—Let long Á be the substitute OF the affix ÍYASUN coming AFTER JYA (No. 1313). By No. 88 the substitute takes the place of the first letter only. Thus *jyáyas* "more excellent."

बहोर्लोपो भू च बहोः । ६ । ४ । १५८ ।

बहोः परयोरिमेयसोर्लोपः स्याद्बहोश्च भूरादेशः । भूमा ।

No. 1315.—Let there be elision of *ima* (No. 1241) and *íyasun* (No. 1310) coming AFTER the word BAHU "much," AND let BHÚ be the substitute OF BAHU. Thus *bhúman* "multeity."

इष्ठस्य यिट् च । ६ । ४ । १५९ ।

बहोः परस्य इष्ठस्य लोपः स्याद्यिडागमश्च । भूयिष्ठः ।

No. 1316.—Let there be elision OF (the first letter of) ISHṬHAN (No. 1306) coming after the word *bahu* "much," AND let there be the augment YIṬ. Thus *bhúyishṭha* "most."

विन्मतोर्लुक् । ५ । ३ । ६५ ।

इष्ठेयसोः । अतिशयेन स्रग्वी । स्रजिष्ठः । स्रजीयान् । अतिशयेन त्वग्वान् । त्वचिष्ठः । त्वचीयान् ।

No. 1317.—Let there be ELISION OF VIN (No. 1281) and MATU (No. 1268) when *ishṭhan* (No. 1306) and *íyasun* (No. 1310) follow. Thus [from *sragwin* "garlanded"] *srajishṭha* "most profusely decorated with garlands," *srajíyas* "more profusely decorated with garlands," *twachishṭha* "having abundant skin or bark," *twachíyas* "having more skin."

ईषदसमाप्तौ कल्पब्देश्यदेशीयरः । ५ । ३ । ६७ ।

ईषदूनो विद्वान् । विद्वत्कल्पः । विद्वद्देश्यः । विद्वद्देशीयः । पचतिकल्पम् ।

No. 1318—The three affixes, KALPA, DEŚYA, AND DEŚÍYAR, may be employed WHEN there is a SLIGHT INCOMPLETENESS Thus *vidwatkalpa* "who is somewhat less than a learned man" —"an inferior scholar,"—and, in the same sense, *vidwaddeśya* and *vidwaddeśíya*. [So too with a verb]—*pachatikalpam* "he cooks incompletely" or "he does not finish cooking."

विभाषा सुपो बहुच् पुरस्तात् तु । ५ । ३ । ६८ ।

ईषदूनः पटुः । बहुपटुः । पटुकल्पः । सुपः किम् । पचतिकल्पम् ।

No. 1319. OPTIONALLY BAHUCH [in the sense specified in No. 1318] may come AFTER what ends with a CASE-AFFIX— BUT [instead of AFTER, let it stand] BEFORE. Thus *bahupaṭu* or *paṭukalpa* "almost clever"—"clever *minus* a little." Why do we say "after what ends with a case-affix?" Because, with a verb, we can have only such a form as *pachatikalpam*—see No. 1318.

प्रागिवात् कः । ५ । ३ । ७० ।

इवे प्रतिकृताविव्यतः प्राक् काधिकारः ।

No. 1320.—[In each aphorism] from this one FORWARD AS FAR AS No. 1326, there is the influence of the affix KA.

अव्ययसर्वनाम्नामकच् प्राक् टेः । ५ । ३ । ७१ ।

कापवादः ।

No. 1321.—Let AKACH come BEFORE THE LAST VOWEL WITH WHAT FOLLOWS it OF INDECLINABLES AND PRONOMINALS. This debars *ka* (No. 1320).

अज्ञाते । ५ । ३ । ७३ ।

कस्यायमश्वोऽश्वकः । उच्चकैः । नीचकैः । सर्वकैः ।

No. 1322.—WHEN the thing is spoken of as UNKNOWN [then let there be *ka*—No. 1320—]. Thus *aśwaka* "the horse [of whom is this]?" *uchchakaiḥ* "[is it] high?" *níchakaiḥ* "[is it] low?" *sarvakaiḥ* "[was this agreed to] by all?"

कुत्सिते । ५ । ३ । ७४ ।

कुत्सितोऽश्वोऽश्वकः ।

No. 1323.—WHEN the thing is spoken of as CONTEMPTIBLE [then let there be *ka*—No. 1320—]. Thus *aśwaka* "a sorry horse."

किंयत्तदो निर्धारणे द्वयोरेकस्य डतरच् । ५ । ३ । ९२ ।

अनयोः कतरो वैष्णवः । यतरः । ततरः ।

No. 1324.—Let the affix ḌATARACH come AFTER the words KIM "what?" YAD "which," AND TAD "that," WHEN the point in question is the DETERMINING OF THE ONE out OF TWO. Thus *katara* "which of the two?"—which one is the follower of Vishṇu?;—*yatara* "of the two the one who," *tatara* "of the two—that one."

वा बहूनां जातिपरिप्रश्ने डतमच् । ५ । ३ । ९३ ।

जातिपरिप्रश्न इति प्रत्याख्यातमाकरे । कतमो भवतां कठः । यतमः । ततमः । वाग्रहणमकजर्थम् । यकः । सकः ।

इति प्रागिवीयाः ॥

No. 1325.—OPTIONALLY [after *kim* &c.,—see No. 1324—] there may be the affix ḌATAMACH [when the object is the determining of the one] out OF MANY, THE QUESTION BEING THAT OF CASTE. The restriction conveyed in the words "the question being that of caste" is objected to in "The Mine" (—i. e. in the "Great Commentary"—). Thus *katama* "which of the number?"—which of you, Sirs, is the Bráhman?—*yatama* "of the set the one who," *tatama* "of the set—that one." The employment of the term "optionally" (in the aphorism) is for the sake of indicating *akach* (No. 1321), which may be used in like manner. Thus *yaka* "of the set the one who," *saka* "of the set—that one."

So much for the affixes spoken of under No. 1320.

इवे प्रतिकृतौ । ५ । ३ । ९६ ।

कन् स्यात् । अश्व इव प्रतिकृतिः । अश्वकः ।

No. 1326.—Let there be the affix *kan*, WHEN we speak of something which is LIKE—this being an IMITATION. Thus *aśwaka* "a figure like a horse"—[in wood or clay, or sketched on paper, &c].

सर्वप्रातिपदिकेभ्यः स्वार्थे कन् । अश्वकः ।

No. 1327.—"The affix *kan* may come AFTER ALL CRUDE FORMS (No. 134)—these RETAINING THEIR OWN SENSE." Thus *aśwaka* "a horse."

तत् प्रकृतवचने मयट् । ५ । ४ । २१ ।

प्राचुर्येण प्रस्तुतं प्रकृतं तस्य वचनं प्रतिपादनम् । भावेऽधिकरणे वा ल्युट् । आद्ये प्रकृतमन्नमन्नमयम् । अपूपमयम् । द्वितीये तु । अन्नमयो यज्ञः । अपूपमयं पर्व ।

No. 1328.—The affix MAYAṬ may be employed [after a word denoting some substance] WHEN we require an EXPRESSION FOR IT AS ABUNDANT. By "abundant" we mean "happening to be in abundance," and by its "expression" we mean "a declaring." [This word *vachana*—which has been rendered "an expression" in the aphorism—has two senses, for the affix with which it is formed—viz.] the affix *lyuṭ* conveys the force both of the *nature* (see Nos. 928 and 1239) and the *site.* In the former case [—i. e. taking *tatprakṛitavachana* to mean "the mention of that as abundant" —] we have *annamaya* "abundance of grain;" *apúpamaya* "abundance of flour;"—but in the second case [—i. e. taking it to mean "that in which something is spoken of as abundant"—] we have *annamayo yajñah* "a sacrifice at which food is abundant," *apúpamayam parva* "a festival at which there is abundance of flour."

प्रज्ञादिभ्यश्च । ५ । ४ । ३८ ।

अण् स्यात् । प्रज्ञ एव प्राज्ञः । दैवतः ।

No. 1329.—AND AFTER the words PRAJÑA "wise," &c., [retaining their denotation] there may be the affix AṆ. Thus *prájña* "wise"—simply; *daivata* [synonymous with *devatá*] "a deity."

बह्वल्पार्थाच्छस् कारकादन्यतरस्याम् । ५ । ४ । ४२ ।

बहूनि ददाति बहुशः । अल्पशः ।

No. 1330.—OPTIONALLY AFTER a word signifying MUCH OR LITTLE, IN a CASE DEPENDENT ON a VERB (see No. 945) there may be the affix ŚAS. Thus *bahuśah* "abundantly"—as where one "gives many"—and so *alpaśah* "scantily"—[giving few—or to a few only—&c].

आद्यादिभ्यस्तसेरुपसंख्यानम् । आदौ आदितः । मध्यतः । अन्ततः । पृष्ठतः । पार्श्वतः । आकृतिगणोऽयम् । स्वरेण स्वरतः । वर्णतः ।

No 1331.—"THE ADDITIONAL ASSERTION should be made OF the affix TASI as coming AFTER the words ÁDI 'first' &c." [as well as after words that are in the 5th case—see No. 1286—]. Thus *áditah* "at the first," *madhyatah* "in the middle," *antatah* "finally," *prishthatah* "behind," *párśwatah* "by the side of." This is a class of words those belonging to which are to be known only from the forms met with in writings of authority—(see No. 53). Thus we meet with *swaratah* "in respect of a vowel," and *varṇatah* "in respect of a letter"—[when speaking, for example, of some error in orthography].

कृभ्वस्तियोगे संपद्यकर्तरि च्विः । ५ । ४ । ५० ।

अभूततद्भाव इति वक्तव्यम् । विकारात्मतां प्राप्नुवत्यां प्रकृतौ वर्तमानाद्विकारशब्दात् स्वार्थे च्विर्वा स्यात् करोत्यादिभिर्योगे ।

No. 1332.—It should be stated that the "attainment" [spoken of in this aphorism] is the attainment of becoming what the thing previously was not. When something out of which something else originates arrives at the state of being that very thing so produced, the affix CHWI, without altering the sense, may optionally come,—when the word denoting the modified thing as then existing—THE AGENT THAT HAS ATTAINED to the new state—is CONJOINED WITH the verbs KṚI "to make," BHÚ "to become, AND AS "to be."

अस्य च्वौ । ७ । ४ । ३२ ।

अवर्णस्य ईत् स्याच्च्वौ । अकृष्णः कृष्णः संपद्यते तं करोति कृष्णीकरोति । ब्रह्मीभवति । गङ्गीस्यात् ।

No. 1333.—Let there be long Í in the room OF A or Á WHEN the affix CHWI (No. 1330) FOLLOWS. Suppose that one who is not black becomes black,—some one makes him so,—then we may express it thus, *kṛishṇíkaroti* "he blackens." So too *brahmíbhavati* "he becomes Brahma [as a saint when liberated from the trammels of ignorance];" *gańgísyát* "may it become the Ganges—[this tributary stream flowing on to mingle therewith."

अव्ययस्य च्वावीत्वं नेति वाच्यम् । दोषाभूतमहः । दिवाभूता रात्रिः ।

No. 1334.—"IT SHOULD BE STATED THAT there IS NOT THE CHANGE TO long í (—see No. 1333—) in the case OF an INDECLINABLE WHEN the affix CHWI FOLLOWS." Thus *doshábhútam ahah* "the day become evening," *divábhútá rátrih* "the night become day."

विभाषा साति कार्त्स्न्ये । ५ । ४ । ५२ ।

च्विविषये सातिर्वा स्यात् साकल्ये ।

No. 1335.—In a case where the affix *chwi* (No. 1332) might be employed, the affix SÁTI may OPTIONALLY be used WHEN THE TOTALITY of the change is to be suggested.

सात्पदाद्योः । ८ । ३ । १११ ।

सस्य षत्वं न । दधि सिञ्चति । कृत्स्नं शस्त्रमग्निः संपद्यतेऽग्निसाद्भवति ।

No. 1336.—There is not the change to the cerebral *sh* (see No. 169) of the dental *s* OF the affix SÁTI (No. 1335) NOR of the *s* which is INITIAL IN a PADA. Thus there is no change to *sh* in the example *dadhi sinchati* "he sprinkles curd;" nor in the example [illustrative of No. 1335] *agnisádbhavati* "the whole [weapon] is in a blaze."

च्वौ च । ७ । ४ । २६ ।

दीर्घः स्यात् । अग्नीभवति ।

No. 1337.—AND WHEN the affix CHWI (No. 1332) FOLLOWS let there be a long vowel. Thus [from *agni* "fire"] *agníbhavati* "it becomes fire."

अव्यक्तानुकरणाद्द्व्यजवरार्धादनितौ डाच् । ५ । ४ । ५७ ।

ह्यजवरं न्यूनं न तु ततो न्यूनम् । अनेकाजिति यावत् । तादृशमर्धं यस्य तस्माड्डाच् स्यात् कृभ्वस्तिभिर्योगे ।

No. 1338.—[The expression in the aphorism—viz.—] "that of which two vowels are the least"—the smallest number [of vowels]—but not less than that—means polysyllabic. AFTER that which is THE HALF OF such a POLYSYLLABIC word, being THE IMITATIVE NAME OF an INARTICULATE SOUND, let there be optionally the affix ḌÁCH—though NOT WHEN the word ITI FOLLOWS]—provided the word be combined with the verbs *kṛi, bhú,* or *as* (No. 1332).

डाचि बहुलं द्वे भवत इति डाचि विवक्षिते द्वित्वम् ।

No. 1339.—" WHEN the affix *ḍách* (No. 1338) is to be directed to be employed, then THERE ARE TWO, or there is reduplication of the word, VARIOUSLY" (see No. 823).

नित्यमाम्रेडिते डाचीति वक्तव्यम् । डाच्परं यदाम्रेडितं तस्मिन् परे पूर्वपरयोर्वर्णयोः पररूपं स्यात् । इति तकारपकारयोः पकारः । पटपटा करोति । अव्यक्तानुकरणात् किम् । दृषत् करोति । ह्यजवरार्धात् किम् । श्रत् करोति । अवरेति किम् । खरटखरटा करोति । अनितौ किम् । पटिति करोति ।

इति तद्धिताः ॥

No. 1340.—" IT SHOULD BE STATED THAT WHEN the affix ḌÁCH (No. 1338) COMES AFTER a REDUPLICATION (No. 118) which occurs when *ḍách* follows (No. 1337), then the form of the subsequent shall INVARIABLY be in the room both of the prior and of the subsequent letters." Hence [when we have *paṭat+paṭat+ḍách+karoti*] the letter *p* is substituted in the room of the *t* [of the first *paṭat*] and of the *p* [of the reduplication], giving *paṭapaṭákaroti* "he makes a noise like *paṭat, paṭat*" [—the final *t* being elided by VI. 1. 98, as in the words under No. 53]. Why do we say "after the imitative name of an inarticulate sound" (No. 1338)? Witness *dṛishat karoti* "it makes (or turns to) stone." Why do we say "after the half of that of which two vowels are the least." Witness *śrat karoti* "he utters [the exclamation implying belief or reverence] *śrat.*" Why do we say "at least"? [Because the rule does apply if there be more, as well as when there are two]—thus *kharaṭakharaṭákaroti* "he makes a sound like *kharaṭat.*" Why do we say "not if the word *iti* 'thus' follows"? Witness *paṭiti karoti* "he makes the sound called *paṭat*" (VI. I. 98).

So much for the *Taddhita* affixes.

। अथ स्त्रीप्रत्ययाः ।

NOW THE AFFIXES OF THE FEMININE.

अजाद्यतष्टाप् । ४ । १ । ४ ।

अजादीनामकारान्तस्य च वाच्यं यत् स्त्रीत्वं तत्र द्योत्ये टाप् स्यात् । अजा । एडका । अश्वा । चटका । मूषिका । बाला । वत्सा । होडा । मन्दा । विलाता । मेधा । इत्यादि । गङ्गा । सर्वा ।

No. 1341.—When that feminine nature is to be indicated which may be predicated OF [the things denoted by] the words AJA "a goat" &C., AND WHAT ENDS IN short A, let there be the affix ṬÁP. Thus [as an example of "*aja* &c.," we have] *ajá* "a she-goat," *eḍaká* "a ewe," *aśwá* "a mare," *chaṭaká* "a hen-sparrow," *múshiká* (No. 1358) "a she-mouse," *bálá* "a girl," *vatsá* "a she-calf," *hoḍá* or *mandá* or *vilátá* "a young girl" (in the language of the Vedas); *medhá* "understanding"; &c. Then [as examples of what ends in *a,* without being included in the class "*aja* &c.," we may have] *gangá* "the Ganges," *sarvá* "all."

उगितश्च । ४ । १ । ६ ।

उगिदन्तात् प्रातिपदिकान्ङीप् । भवन्ती । पचन्ती ।

No. 1342.—AND AFTER WHAT, as a crude word, HAS an INDICATORY UK, let the feminine affix be *ńíp.* Thus [from *bhavatṛi*—No. 883—in which the indicatory *ṛi* is an *uk,*] *bhavatí* (No. 398) "[a female] becoming," *pachantí* "cooking."

टिड्ढाणञ्द्वयसज्दघ्नञ्मात्रच्तयप्ठक्ठञ्कञ्क्वरपः ४।१।१५।

अनुपसर्जनं यट्टिदादि तदन्तं यददन्तं ततः स्त्रियां ङीप्। कुरुचरी। नदट्। नदी। देवट्। देवी। सौपर्णेयी। ऐन्द्री। औत्सी। ऊरुद्वयसी। ऊरुदघ्नी। ऊरुमात्री। पञ्चतयी। आक्षिकी। प्रास्थिकी। लावणिकी। यादृशी। इत्वरी।

No. 1343.—In the feminine there shall be the affix *ńíp* after what ends in short *a,* if it is not a subordinate term (No. 968) in a compound, and if the affix with which it ends has an indicatory Ṭ or if the affix be ḌHA (No. 1093), or AṆ (No. 1077) or AÑ (No. 1075), or DWAYASACH (No. 1253), or DAGHNACH (No. 1253), or MÁTRACH (No. 1253), or TAYAP (No. 1255), or ṬHAK (No. 1202), or ṬHAÑ (No. 1230), or KAÑ (No. 376), OR KWARAP (III. 2. 163) Thus [to give an example of each in order] *kuruchari* (No. 844) "who goes to the Kurus:" and [as the words *nada* "a river" and *deva* "a god" are written, in the list "*pach &c.*"—see No. 837—with an indicatory *ṭ*—thus] *nadaṭ* and *devaṭ* [we have] *nadí* "a river" and *deví* "a goddess." Then again—*sauparṇeyí* "a female descendant of Suparṇa," *aindrí* "a female descendant of Indra," *autsí* "a female descendant of Utsa," *úrudwayasí, úrudaghní,* and *úrumátrí* "reaching to the thigh," *pañchatayí* "of which the parts are five," *ákshikí* "a female dicer," *prásthikí* "containing the measure of a prastha," *lávaṇikí* "elegant," *yádriśí* "such like as," *itwari* "swift."

नञ्स्नञीकक्ख्युंस्तरुणतलुनानामुपसंख्यानम्। स्त्रैणी। पौंस्नी। शाक्तीकी। आढ्यं करणी। तरुणी। तलुनी।

No. 1344.—"IN ADDITION to the foregoing [enumerated in No. 1343] there should have been THE ENUMERATION OF the affixes NAÑ AND SNAÑ (No. 1076) AND ÍKAK (No. 1072) AND KHYUN (III. 2. 56), AND OF the words TARUṆA AND TALUNA 'a youth'." Thus *straiṇí* "female," *pauṅsní* "male," *śáktíkí* "a female spear-bearer," *áḍhyankaraṇí* "enriching," *taruṇí* or *taluní* "a young woman."

यञश्च। ४ । १ । १६ ।

यञन्तान्ङीप् । अकारलोपे कृते ।

No. 1345.—AND AFTER what ends with the affix YAṄ (No. 1072) the feminine affix is *ńíp*—elision of the *a* having been made (by No. 260).

हलस्तद्धितस्य । ६ । ४ । १५० ।

हल: परस्य तद्धितयकारस्य लोप ईति परे । गार्गी ।

No. 1346.—There is elision OF the Y of a TADDHITA affix coming AFTER a CONSONANT, when long í follows. Thus (from *gárgya gárgí* No. 1345) "a female descendant of Garga."

प्राचां ष्फस्तद्धित: । ४ । १ । १७ ।

यञन्तात् ष्फो वा स्यात् स च तद्धित: ।

No. 1347.—In the opinion OF THE ANCIENTS [and hence only optionally] there may be the affix SHPHA after what ends with the affix *yań* (No. 1072), and it is to be regarded as a TADDHITA affix —[so that the *ph* —see No.1086.—becomes *áyan*].

षिद्गौरादिभ्यश्च। ४ । १ । ४१ ।

ङीष् स्यात् । गार्ग्यायणी । नर्तकी । गौरी । अनडुही । अनड्वाही । आकृतिगणोऽयम् ।

No. 1348.—AND AFTER words ending with affixes WHICH HAVE an INDICATORY SH, AND after the words GAURA "brilliant," &c., let the feminine affix be *ńísha*. Thus *gárgyáyaní* [—with the affix *shpha*—No. 1347 "a female descendant of Garga;" *nartakí* [with *shwun*—III. I. 145] "an actress;" *gaurí* "the brilliant [goddess or Párvatí] ;" *anaḍuhí anaḍwáhí* "a cow." This is a class of words constituted by usage—see No. 53.

वयसि प्रथमे । ४ । १ । २० ।

प्रथमवयोवाचिनोऽदन्तान्ङीप् । कुमारी ।

No. 1349.—After a word ending in short *a* and expressive of EARLY AGE let the feminine affix be *ńíp*. Thus *kumárí* "a girl."

द्विगोः । ४ । १ । २१ ।

अदन्ताद्द्विगोर्ङीप् । त्रिलोकी । अजादित्वात् त्रिफला । त्र्यनीका ।

No. 1350.—AFTER a DWIGU compound (No. 983) ending in short *a* let the feminine affix be *ńíp*. Thus *trilokí* "the aggregate of the three worlds." But we find *triphalá* "the three myrobalans," because this is one of the words spoken of as "*aja &c.*" (No. 1341).—

वर्णादनुदात्तात् तोपधात् तो नः । ४ । १ । ३९ ।

वर्णवाची योऽनुदात्तान्तस्तोपधस्तदन्तादनुपसर्जनाद्वा ङीप् तकारस्य नः । एता । एनी । रोहिता । रोहिणी ।

No. 1351.—AFTER a word expressive of COLOUR, ending in a GRAVELY ACCENTED vowel, and HAVING the letter T as its PENULTIMATE letter, the word not being a subordinate in a compound, the feminine affix is optionally *ńíp*, and the letter N is substituted in the room OF the T. Thus [from *eta* "variegated"] *etá* or *ení*, [from *rohita* "red"] *rohitá* or *rohiṇí*.

वोतो गुणवचनात् । ४ । १ । ४४ ।

उदन्ताद्गुणवाचिनो वा ङीष् । मृद्वी । मृदुः ।

No. 1352.—OPTIONALLY AFTER what ends in SHORT U, being EXPRESSIVE OF a QUALITY, the feminine affix is *ńísh*. Thus [from *mṛidu* "soft"] *mṛidwí* or [without a feminine affix] *mṛiduh*.

बह्वादिभ्यश्च । ४ । १ । ४५ ।

वा ङीष् । बह्वी । बहुः ।

No. 1353.—AND AFTER the words BAHU "much" &c., the feminine affix is optionally *ńísh*. Thus *bahwí* or [without a feminine affix] *bahu*.

कृदिकारादक्तिनः । रात्री । रात्रिः ।

No. 1354.—"AFTER THE vowel I OF a KṚIT affix, NOT KTIN (No. 918)," [the feminine affix is optionally *ńísh*]. Thus *rátrí* or *rátri* "night."

सर्वतोऽक्तिन्नर्थादित्येके । शकटी । शकटिः ।

No. 1355.—"SOME SAY that the feminine affix *ńísh* may come AFTER ANY WORD ending in *i* (No. 1354) IF it have NOT THE FORCE OF the affix KTIN." Thus *śakaṭi* or *śakaṭí* "a cart."

पुंयोगादाख्यायाम् । ४ । १ । ४८ ।

या पुमाख्या पुंयोगात् स्त्रियां वर्त्तते ततो ङीष् । गोपस्य स्त्री गोपी ।

No. 1356.—WHEN THE NAME of a male is employed to denote the female IN VIRTUE OF HER [matrimonial] UNION WITH THAT MALE, the feminine affix *ńísh* comes after it. Thus *gopí* "the wife of a *gopa* or cowherd."

पालकान्तान्न । गोपालिका । अश्वपालिका ।

No. 1357.—"But NOT AFTER the word PÁLAKA 'a keeper' [does *ńísh* come by No. 1356]." Thus *gopáliká* (No. 1358) "the wife of a cow-keeper," *aśwapáliká* "the wife of a horse-keeper."

प्रत्ययस्थात् कात् पूर्वस्यात इदाप्यसुपः । ७ । ३ । ४४ ।

प्रत्ययस्थात् कात् पूर्वस्याकारस्येकारः स्यादापि स आप् सुपः परो न चेत् । सर्विका । कारिका । अतः किम् । नौका । प्रत्ययस्थात् किम् । शक्नोतीति शका । असुपः किम् । बहुपरिव्राजका नगरी ।

No. 1358.—Let there be the vowel I in the room OF the vowel A coming BEFORE the letter K STANDING IN an AFFIX, WHEN the feminine affix ÁP FOLLOWS—PROVIDED that the feminine affix ÁP does NOT come AFTER a CASE-AFFIX. Thus [from *sarvaka* "every"] *sarviká*, [from *káraka* "a maker"] *káriká*. Why do we say "of the vowel *a*"? Witness *nauká* "a boat." Why do we say "standing in an affix"? Witness *śaká* [from *śaka*] "who is able—[where the *k* belongs to the verbal root]. Why do we say "not after a case-affix"? Witness *bahuparivrájaká nagarí* "a city with many religious mendicants"—[where the feminine affix is attached after the case-affix had been elided, as explained under No. 964, in forming the compound].

सूर्याद्देवतायां चाप् । सूर्यस्य स्त्री देवता सूर्या । देवतायां किम् ।

No. 1359.—"AFTER the word SÚRYA 'the Sun,' the feminine affix is CHÁP, WHEN the GODDESS [his wife] is meant." Thus *súryá* "the goddess who is the wife of the Sun." Why "when the goddess is meant"? [See No. 1360.]

सूर्यागस्त्ययोश्छे च ङ्यां च यलोपः । सूरी कुन्ती ।

No. 1360.—"There is ELISION OF the YA OF the words SÚRYA "the sun" AND AGASTYA "the saint Agastya," WHEN the affix CHHA (No. 1160) follows, AND when the feminine affix ŃÍ follows." Thus *súrí*—meaning "Kuntí—the mortal bride of the Sun"—(see No. 1359).

इन्द्रवरुणभवशर्वरुद्रमृडहिमारण्ययवयवनमातुलाचार्याणामानुक् । ४ । १ । ४९ ।

ङीष् च । इन्द्रस्य स्त्री इन्द्राणी । वरुणानी । भवानी । शर्वाणी । रुद्राणी । मृडानी ।

No. 1361.—Let ÁNUK be the augment of the proper names INDRA, VARUṆA, BHAVA, ŚARVA, RUDRA, AND MṚIḌA, AND of the words HIMA "snow," ARAṆYA "a forest," YAVA "barley," YAVANA "Greek," MÁTULA "a maternal uncle," AND ÁCHÁRYA "a spiritual preceptor;" and, at the same time, let the feminine affix be *ńísh*. Thus *indráṇí* "the wife of Indra," and so *varuṇáni*, *bhaváni*, *śarváṇí*, *mṛiḍáni*.

हिमारण्ययोर्महत्त्वे । महद्धिमं हिमानी । महदरण्यमरण्यानी ।

No. 1362.—"OF the words HIMA 'snow' AND ARAṆYA 'a forest' [there is the augment *ánuk*, as directed in No. 1361], in the sense of GREATNESS." Thus *himáni* "much snow," *araṇyáni* "a great forest."

यवाद्दोषे । दुष्टो यवो यवानी ।

No. 1363.—"AFTER the word YAVA 'barley' [the feminine affix, as directed in No. 1361, comes] IN the sense of FAULT." Thus *yaváni* "bad barley."

यवनाल्लिप्याम् । यवनानां लिपिर्यवनानी ।

No. 1364.—"AFTER the word YAVANA 'Greek' [the feminine affix, as directed in No. 1361, comes] IN the sense of HAND-WRITING." Thus *yavanání* "the written character of the Greeks."

मातुलोपाध्याययोरानुग्वा । मातुलानी । मातुली । उपाध्यायानी । उपाध्यायी ।

No. 1365.—"OF the words MÁTULA 'a maternal uncle' AND UPÁDHYÁYA 'a spiritual preceptor' [when the feminine affix comes —to express the wife thereof—] the augment ÁNUK (No. 1361) is OPTIONAL." Thus *mátulání* or *mátulí* (No. 1356) "the wife of a maternal uncle,"—*upádhyáyání* or *upádhyáyí* "the wife of a spiritual preceptor"

आचार्यादणत्वं च । आचार्यानी ।

No. 1366.—"AND there is NOT the CHANGE TO the cerebral Ṇ [—No. 157—of the dental *n* of the augment *ánuk*—No. 1361—] AFTER the word ÁCHÁRYA 'a spiritual preceptor'." Thus *ácháryání* "the wife of a spiritual preceptor."

अर्यक्षत्रियाभ्यां वा स्वार्थे । अर्याणी । अर्या । क्षत्रियाणी । क्षत्रिया ।

No. 1367.—"AFTER the words ARYA 'a man of the Vaiśya class' AND KSHATRIYA 'a man of the military class' [the feminine affix, with the augment directed in No. 1361 comes] OPTIONALLY, WHEN the word retains ITS OWN SENSE [viz. that of a person belonging to the class]. Thus *aryáṇí* or *aryá* "a female of the Vaiśya class," *kshatriyáṇí* or *kshatriyá* "a female of the military class."

क्रीतात् करणपूर्वात् । ४ । १ । ५० ।

ङीष् । वस्त्रक्रीती । क्वचिन्न । धनक्रीता ।

No. 1368.—AFTTER the word KRÍTA "bought," PRECEDED BY the name of THE MEANS wherewith, the feminine affix is *ńísh.* Thus *vastrakrítí* "a female bought in exchange for cloth." Sometimes it is not so. Thus *dhanakrítá* "a female purchased with wealth."

स्वाङ्गाच्चोपसर्जनादसंयोगोपधात् । ४ । १ । ५४ ।

असंयोगोपधमुपसर्जनं यत् स्वाङ्गं तदन्तान्ङीष् वा । केशानतिक्रान्ता अतिकेशी । अतिकेशा । चन्द्रमुखी । चन्द्रमुखा । असंयोगोपधात् किम् । सुगुल्फा । उपसर्जनात् किम् । सुशिखा ।

No. 1369.—AND the feminine affix *ńísh* comes optionally AFTER what ends with the name of a PART OF THE BODY, when the word is SUBORDINATE IN a COMPOUND (No. 968), moreover, NOT HAVING a CONJUNCT FOR ITS PENULTIMATE letter. Thus *atikeśí* or *atikeśá* "surpassing the hair" [in beauty &c.,—or reaching above it—as deep water—]; *chandramukhí* or *chandramukhá* "moon-faced." Why do we say "not having a conjunct for its penultimate letter"? Witness *sugulphá* "a female with handsome ancles." Why do we say "subordinate in a compound"? Witness *suśikhá* "a handsome crest"—[where the *śikhá* is not subordinate or epithetical].

न क्रोडादिबह्वचः । ४ । १ । ५६ ।

क्रोडादेर्बह्वचश्च स्वाङ्गान्न ङीष् । कल्याणक्रोडा । आकृतिगणोऽयम् । सुजघना ।

No. 1370.—The feminine affix is NOT *ńísh* (No. 1369) AFTER a word denoting a part of the body when it is of the class KROḌA "the flank" &C., NOR when the word is POLYSYLLABIC. Thus *kalyáṇakroḍá* "a female with handsome flanks." This is a class of words constituted by usage—(see No. 53). Of the case where the word is polysyllabic we have an example in *sujaghaná* "a female with handsome loins."

नखमुखात् संज्ञायाम् । ४ । १ । ५८ ।

न ङीष् ।

No. 1371.—The feminine affix is not *ńísh* (No. 1369) AFTER NAKHA "the nose" AND MUKHA "the mouth," WHEN (the word at the end of which they stand is) an APPELLATIVE [No. 1372].

पूर्वपदात् संज्ञायामगः । ८ । ४ । ३ ।

पूर्वपदस्थान्निमित्तात् परस्य नस्य णः स्यात् संज्ञायां न तु गकारव्यवधाने। शूर्पणखा। गौरमुखा। संज्ञायां किम्। ताम्रमुखी कन्या।

No. 1372.—Let there be a cerebral *ṇ* in the room of a dental *n* coming AFTER a cause of such change (No. 157) standing in the PRIOR MEMBER of a compound word, WHEN the word is an APPELLATIVE—but NOT if the letter G intervenes. Thus *śúrpaṇakhá* "[the sister of Rávaṇa—viz.] Śúrpaṇakhá [—whose nails were like winnowing baskets.]" Then [as another example of No. 1371 we may have] *gauramukhá* "Fair-face." Why [in No. 1371] do we say "when an appellative"? Witness *támramukhí kanyá* "a copper-faced damsel."

जातेरस्त्रीविषयादयोपधात्। ४।१।६३।

जातिवाचि यन्न च स्त्रियां नियतमयोपधं ततो ङीष्। तटी। वृषली। कठी। बह्वृची। जातेः किम्। मुण्डा। अस्त्रीविषयात् किम्। बलाका। अयोपधात् किम्। क्षत्रिया।

No. 1373.—Let the feminine affix be *ńish* AFTER that which is expressive of a KIND, and is NOT INVARIABLY FEMININE—moreover—NOT HAVING the letter Y FOR its PENULTIMATE letter. Thus from [*taṭa*] *taṭí* "shore," *vṛishalí* "a woman of the servile tribe;" *kaṭhí* "a woman of the class of Bráhmans who read the Kaṭha section of the Rig Veda;" *bahwṛichí* "a woman of the class of Bráhmans who read the Rig Veda." Why do we say "expressive of a kind"? Witness *muṇḍá* "shaven"—[where the word expresses not a kind but a quality—see *Sáhitya Darpaṇa* §12 *b.* and *d.*] Why do we say "not invariably feminine"? Witness *baláká* "a crane"—[supposed to breed without the male]. Why do we say "not having the letter *y* for its penultimate letter"? Witness *kshatriyá* "a female Kshatriya."

योपधप्रतिषेधे गवयहयमुकयमत्स्यमनुष्याणामप्रतिषेधः। गवयी। हयी। मुकयी। हलस्तद्धितस्येति यलोपः। मनुषी। मत्स्यस्य ङ्यां यलोपः। मत्सी।

No. 1374.—"IN THE EXCLUDING [from No. 1373] OF WORDS THAT HAVE letter Y AS the PENULTIMATE, there is NOT involved the EXCLUSION OF [the following words which have a penultimate *y*—viz.—] GAVAYA "the Bos Gavaeus," HAYA "a horse," MUKAYA "a sort of animal," MATSYA "a fish," and MANUSHYA "a man." Thus *gavayí* "the female, of the Bos Gavaeus;" *hayí* "a mare," *mukayí* "a female *mukaya.*" By No. 1346 there is elision of the *y* of *manushya:*—thus *manushí* "a woman,"—and [according to Kátáyana] there is elision of the *y* of *matsya* (though this word does not end in a *taddhita* affix) when the feminine affix *ńí* follows— so that we have *matsí* "a female fish."

इतो मनुष्यजातेः ।४।१।६५।

ङीष् । दाक्षी ।

No. 1375.—"AFTER a word ENDING IN short I, denoting a RACE OF MEN, the feminine affix is *ńísh.* Thus *dákshí* "a female Dákshi, or descendant of Daksha (No. 1087)."

ऊङुतः ।४।१।६६।

उदन्तादयोपधान्मनुष्यजातिवाचिनः स्त्रियामूङ् । कुरूः । अयोपधात् किम् । अध्वर्युर्ब्राह्मणी ।

No. 1376.—AFTER a word ENDING IN short U, not having the letter *y* as its penultimate letter, and being expressive of men, the affix in the feminine is ÚŃ. Thus *kurú* "a female Kuru." Why do we say "not having the letter *y* as its penultimate letter"? Witness *adhwaryu* "a woman of the class of Bráhmans versed in the Yajur Veda."

पङ्गोश्च । पङ्गूः ।

No. 1377.—"AND [as in No. 1376] AFTFR the word PAŃGU "lame," Thus *pańgú* "(a female) lame."

श्वशुरस्योकाराकारलोपश्च । श्वश्रूः ।

No. 1378.—"AND [in addition to the affixing of the feminine affix *úń*—No. 1376—] there is ELISION OF the U and of the A OF the word ŚWAŚURA 'a father-in-law.'" Thus *śwaśru* "a mother-in-law."

ऊरूत्तरपदादौपम्ये। ४। १। ६९।

उपमानवाचिपूर्वपदमूरूत्तरपदं यत् प्रातिपदिकं तस्मादूङ्। करभोरूः।

No. 1379.—Let *úṅ* be the feminine affix AFTER THAT compound, ending in a crude word, OF WHICH THE LATTER MEMBER IS the word ÚRU "the thigh," WHEN the prior member of the compound is a word expressing an object of COMPARISON. Thus *karabhoru* "a female with thighs like the ulnar or tapering fleshy side of the hand."

संहितशफलक्षणवामादेश्च। ४। १। ७०।

अनौपम्यार्थं सूत्रम्। संहितोरूः। शफोरूः। लक्षणोरूः। वामोरूः।

No. 1380.—And (*úṅ* shall be the feminine affix after the word *úru* "the thigh" coming, in a compound,) after the words SAṄHITA "joined," ŚAPHA "a hoof," LAKSHAṆA, "a mark," AND VÁMA "handsome," &c. This aphorism is for the sake of cases where there is no *comparison* (as there is in the cases to which No. 1379 refers). Thus *saṅhitorú* "whose thighs are joined [—e. g., from obesity]," *śaphorú* "whose thighs are [put together] like [the two] hoofs [on a cow's foot]," *lakshaṇorú* "whose thighs are marked," *vámorú* "with handsome thighs."

शार्ङ्गरवाद्यञो ङीन्। ४। १। ७३।

शार्ङ्गरवादेरञो योऽकारस्तदन्ताच्च जातिवाचिनो ङीन्। शार्ङ्गरवी। वैदी। ब्राह्मणी।

No. 1381.—Let ṄÍN be the feminine affix AFTER the word ŚÁRṄGARAVA "a Śárṅgarava" &c., and after what ends with the letter *a* of the affix AṄ (No. 1075) when the word speaks of a kind [not of a wife—No. 1356]. Thus *śárṅgaraví* "a Śárṅgarava woman," *vaidí* [from *vida*, which, besides ending with the affix *aṇ*, as it is held to do when enumerated in the list "*śárṅgarava* &c.," may end with the affix *aṅ*] "a female descendant of Vida," *bráhmaṇí* "a female of the sacerdotal tribe."

नृनरयोर्वृद्धिश्च । नारी ।

No. 1382.—"AND VṚIDDHI is the substitute OF the words NṚI AND NARA 'a man' [when the feminine affix *ṅín*—No. 1381—follows." Thus *nárí* "a woman."

यूनस्तिः ।४।१।७७।

युवन्शब्दात् स्त्रियां तिः स्यात् । युवतिः ।

इति स्त्रीप्रत्ययाः ॥

No. 1383—AFTER the word YUVAN "young," when it denotes a female, let there be the affix TI. Thus *yuvati* "a young woman."

So much for the affixes of the Feminine.

शास्त्रान्तरे प्रविष्टानां बालानां चोपकारिका ।

कृता वरदराजेन लघुसिद्धान्तकौमुदी ॥

इति श्रीवरदराजकृता लघुसिद्धान्तकौमुदी समाप्ता ॥

This abridged *Siddhánta Kaumudí,* a help for those who are engaged in other studies (and have therefore little leisure) and for those also who are quite unacquainted with science, was made by the illustrious Varadarája.

Here concludes the *Laghu-siddhánta-kaumudí* made by the illustrious Varadarája.

॥ लघुकौमुदी समाप्ता ॥

THE LAGHU KAUMUDÍ IS FINISHED.

ALPHABETICAL INDEX

OF THE

APHORISMS

IN THE LAGHU KAUMUDI.

अस्मिन् ग्रन्थे मूलरूपेण येषाम् । सूत्रादीनां संमतः संनिवेशः ।
आद्यज्ञस्यादेवाशु बोधाय तेषा- । मेषा सूची रच्यतेऽकारपूर्वा ॥ १ ॥

Note.—The figures refer to the numbers of the Aphorisms, and not to the page.

* एतदादिषु सूत्रेषु यथा पदविभागादिरवलोक्यतां तथैव मूलेऽप्यनुसंधीयतामङ्कस्थल इति तत्त्वं वेदितव्यम् ।

॥ इति सूत्रवार्तिकादिसूचीपत्रम् ॥

INDEX

OF THE

CRUDE FORMS OF WORDS (PRATIPADIKAS).

यावन्तः षट्सु लिङ्गेषु सन्ति शब्दाः समागताः ।
निर्दिश्यन्तेऽत्र तावन्तः । सौलभ्याय विवित्सताम् ॥ १ ॥

Note.—The figures refer to the numbers of the aphorisms, and not to the page.

* क्वचित् क्वचिदधरादिष्वङ्कलेखः स्थलयोग्यताप्रदर्शनमात्रफलपरः ।

॥ इति षड्लिङ्गवर्तिप्रातिपदिकसूचीपत्रम् ॥

INDEX OF VERBS.

भुविमारभ्य ये यत्र धातवः समुदाहृताः ।
विदांकुर्वन्तु तांस्तूर्णमेतदर्थोऽयमुद्यमः ॥ १ ॥

Note.—The figures refer to the numbers of the aphorisms, and not to the page.

॥ इति तिङन्तधातुसूचीपत्रम् ॥